Governance and Politics in the European Union

The European Union of today cannot be studied as it once was. This original new textbook provides a much-needed update on how the EU's policies and institutions have changed in light of the multiple crises and transformations since 2010. An international team of leading scholars offers systematic accounts of the EU's institutional regime, policies and community of people and states. Each chapter is structured to explain the relevant historical developments and institutional framework, presenting the key actors and current controversies, and discussing a paradigmatic case study. Each chapter also provides ideas for group discussions and individual research topics. Moving away from the typical neutral account of the functioning of the EU, this textbook will stimulate readers' critical thinking towards the EU as it is today. It will serve as a core text for undergraduate and graduate students of politics and European studies taking courses on the politics of the EU, and those taking courses in comparative politics and international organisations, including the EU.

Ramona Coman is Associate Professor and President of the Institute for European Studies at Université libre de Bruxelles (ULB). Her research focuses on the EU's rule-of-law promotion and judicial reforms in Central and Eastern Europe. She coordinates the Jean Monnet Module 'Rule of Law and Mutual Trust in Global and European Governance'.

Amandine Crespy is Associate Professor at Université libre de Bruxelles (ULB) and Visiting Professor at the College of Europe (Bruges). Her research about social mobilisation, marketisation and socio-economic governance in the EU has been published in numerous journals and three monographs.

Vivien A. Schmidt is Jean Monnet Professor of European Integration and Professor of International Relations and Political Science, in the Frederick S. Pardee School of Global Studies, Boston University. Her research focuses on European political economy, institutions and democracy. In 2019, she was awarded the European Union Studies Association Lifetime Achievement Award.

Governance and Politics in the Post-Crisis European Union

Edited by

Ramona Coman
Université libre de Bruxelles

Amandine Crespy
Université libre de Bruxelles

Vivien A. Schmidt
Boston University

CAMBRIDGE
UNIVERSITY PRESS

CAMBRIDGE
UNIVERSITY PRESS

University Printing House, Cambridge CB2 8BS, United Kingdom

One Liberty Plaza, 20th Floor, New York, NY 10006, USA

477 Williamstown Road, Port Melbourne, VIC 3207, Australia

314–321, 3rd Floor, Plot 3, Splendor Forum, Jasola District Centre, New Delhi – 110025, India

79 Anson Road, #06–04/06, Singapore 079906

Cambridge University Press is part of the University of Cambridge.

It furthers the University's mission by disseminating knowledge in the pursuit of education, learning and research at the highest international levels of excellence.

www.cambridge.org
Information on this title: www.cambridge.org/9781108482264
DOI: 10.1017/9781108612609

© Cambridge University Press 2020

First published 2020

Printed in the United Kingdom by TJ International Ltd, Padstow Cornwall, 2020

A catalogue record for this publication is available from the British Library.

Library of Congress Cataloging-in-Publication Data
Names: Coman, Ramona, editor. | Crespy, Amandine, editor. | Schmidt, Vivien Ann, 1949–, editor.
Title: Governance and politics in the post-crisis European Union / edited by Ramona Coman, Amandine Crespy, Vivien A. Schmidt.
Description: Cambridge, United Kingdom ; New York, NY : Cambridge University Press, 2020. | Includes bibliographical references and index.
Identifiers: LCCN 2020009266 (print) | LCCN 2020009267 (ebook) | ISBN 9781108482264 (hardback) | ISBN 9781108612609 (ebook)
Subjects: LCSH: European Union. | European Union countries – Politics and government – 21st century. | Global Financial Crisis, 2008-2009 – Political aspects – European Union countries.
Classification: LCC JN30 .G6597 2020 (print) | LCC JN30 (ebook) | DDC 341.242/2–dc23
LC record available at https://lccn.loc.gov/2020009266
LC ebook record available at https://lccn.loc.gov/2020009267

ISBN 978-1-108-48226-4 Hardback
ISBN 978-1-108-71177-7 Paperback

Contents

Figures

Tables

Contributors

GERRY ALONS
Assistant Professor of International Relations at Radboud University (The Netherlands).

LÁSZLÓ ANDOR
Professor at Corvinus University in Budapest (Hungary) and at the Université libre de Bruxelles (Institute for European Studies), and former Commissioner for Employment and Social Affairs.

JOHN BACHTLER
Professor of European Policy Studies and a Director of the European Policies Research Centre, University of Strathclyde (UK).

CORNEL BAN
Associate Professor, Copenhagen Business School (Denmark).

DOROTHEE BOHLE
Professor of Political Sciences, European University Institute (Italy).

RASMUS CORLIN CHRISTENSEN
PhD Fellow, Copenhagen Business School (Denmark).

RAMONA COMAN
Associate Professor of Political Science and President of the Institute for European Studies, Université libre de Bruxelles (Belgium).

AMANDINE CRESPY
Associate Professor in Political Science, Université libre de Bruxelles, and Visiting Professor at the College of Europe in Bruges (Belgium).

FERDI DE VILLE
Assistant Professor of Political Science, Ghent University (Belgium).

MICHELLE EGAN
Professor and Jean Monnet Chair ad personam, School of International Service, American University (USA).

SERGIO FABBRINI
Director of the Luiss School of Government and Professor of Political Science and International Relations at LUISS Guido Carli (Italy).

JACOB HASSELBALCH
Post-Doctoral Fellow, Lund University (Sweden).

JOLYON HOWORTH
Jean Monnet Professor of European Politics *ad personam* and Emeritus Professor of European Politics at the University of Bath (UK), Visiting Professor of Public Policy at Harvard Kennedy School (USA).

JULIEN JEANDESBOZ
Lecturer in International Relations and EU Studies, Université libre de Bruxelles (Belgium).

JOSEPH LACEY
Assistant Professor of Political Theory at the School of Politics and International Relations, University College Dublin (Ireland).

KRISTIN MAKSZIN
Assistant Professor of Political Economy at Leiden University (The Netherlands).

GERGŐ MEDVE-BÁLINT
Senior Researcher, Hungarian Academy of Science (Hungary).

CARLOS MENDEZ
Senior Research Fellow at the European Policies Research Centre, University of Strathclyde (UK).

KALYPSO NICOLAÏDIS
Professor of International Relations and Director of the Centre for International Studies at the University of Oxford (UK).

KIRAN KLAUS PATEL
Professor and Chair of European History, Ludwig Maximilian University Munich (Germany).

LEONARD SEABROOKE
Professor of International Political Economy, Copenhagen Business School (Denmark).

VIVIEN A. SCHMIDT
Jean Monnet Professor of European Integration, Professor of International Relations and Political Science at Boston University (USA).

ELENI TSINGOU
Associate Professor of International Political Economy, Copenhagen Business School (Denmark).

SARAH WOLFF
Lecturer and Director of the Centre for European Research, Queen Mary University of London (UK), and Senior Research Associate Fellow at the Netherlands Institute for International Relations (Netherlands).

Foreword

This book was written in times of great turmoil in the European Union. The financial crisis of 2008, which turned into a debt crisis destabilising the eurozone, the crisis of the EU migration and border policies in the face of increased inflows of migrants since 2014, recurring disputes around violations of democracy and the rule of law, and the Brexit referendum in 2017 have all profoundly tarnished the EU. While its raison d'être, forged in the second half of the twentieth century, was rooted in peace, liberal democracy and welfare capitalism in a bipolar world, the EU has been increasingly regarded as unable to secure these values in the world of the twenty-first century. The past decade, we argue, constitutes a critical juncture, with particularly profound implications for how we understand the EU. Unlike many academics belonging to earlier generations of EU scholars, we do not take for granted a teleological vision of EU integration, whereby an 'ever closer Union' is the ineluctable goal of EU politics. Contemporary politics shows us how contingent and fragile the very existence of the Union is. In the same vein, we do not necessarily consider the deepening of integration in given policy areas as a positive development per se. The question that researchers and citizens alike face today is the following: more Europe to do what? Thus, we believe that only a critical analysis of the problematic aspects of integration can help reform the EU in a meaningful way that enables it to tackle the challenges of our era, namely inefficient collective responses to global warming, the rise of social inequalities, unmanaged migrations, the rise of nativist sentiment, the securitisation of societies and militarisation and the unravelling of democracy. Let us hope that the Corona virus pandemic, which hit as we went to press, will represent a break in the pattern of the EU's problematic responses to crisis over the past decade.

We, as editors of this volume, therefore believe that the EU can no longer be taught as it once was. Our first endeavour is to provide an up-to-date account of the transformations of the EU since the 2008 financial crisis while also moving away from the typical, seemingly neutral, account of the functioning of the EU which usually characterises textbooks. The structure of this book reflects the multiple facets of these transformations. The first part demonstrates that the crises have profoundly altered the EU political regime as it was designed by the Lisbon Treaty. It has also made some of our concepts and theories (for instance the opposition between supranationalism and intergovernmentalism) less and less effective in understanding the emerging paradoxical forms of integration which involve, in different ways, both more and less Europe. The second part deals extensively with how EU policies have been reshaped in response to the crises and their limited success in tackling deficits of effectiveness and democratic accountability. The third part of this volume addresses overarching existential issues that are often absent from textbooks but are crucial to the present and future of the EU, namely socio-economic disparities, conflicting values and centrifugal tendencies towards disintegration linked to a deficit of democracy.

More importantly perhaps, this textbook aims at stimulating the readers' critical thinking towards the EU. The contributors to the volume are all leading scholars in European studies or/and cognate disciplines such as history, comparative politics, international relations or international political economy, and they reassess recent developments in the EU from a critical perspective. Our purpose is to provide undergraduate and graduate students with the necessary knowledge to understand not only how the EU works, but also what the political and social implications of integration are. For this purpose, the textbook includes a number of original pedagogical features which may help instructors emphasise problematic issues, contradictions and trade-offs. Every chapter can thus be used separately to focus on a given issue. While the boxes (including key dates, key actors, legal basis and key concepts) provide some systematic basic knowledge about the various topics, the chapters are framed as thought-provoking questions providing a thread for explaining a particular aspect of EU integration. Paradigmatic case studies at the end of each chapter are there to deepen a more specific aspect and illustrate an especially salient dimension of the past decade's multiple crises. Moreover, every chapter ends not only with references for further readings, but also with two types of questions to be used by instructors for in-class debates (questions for group discussion) and/or written assignments (topics for individual research). Understanding the complex workings of the EU (e.g. legal and institutional aspects, policy reforms) and how it relates to broader political developments at the national and global levels is challenging for students. In other words, they often find it difficult to connect the 'EU from the textbooks' and the 'EU from the news'. The perspectives provided by the authors, combined with the pedagogical features described above, aim to help students bridge this gap and strengthen their knowledge and opinions both as students and as citizens.

Ramona Coman, Amandine Crespy and Vivien A. Schmidt

Acknowledgements

Various chapters in this volume were written with support from the European Commission Research and Innovation Action 'European Legitimacy in Governing through Hard Times' (#649456-ENLIGHTEN) under the Horizon 2020 programme.

Chronology

Historical Milestones of EU Integration

1951   The European Coal and Steel Community (ECSC) is set up by the six countries (Belgium, Italy, Luxembourg, the Netherlands Germany and France).

1957   The six founding members sign the Treaties of Rome, which create the European Economic Community (EEC) and the European Atomic Energy Community (Euratom).

1973   The Communities expand to the north with three new members (Denmark, Ireland and the UK).

1979   The first direct elections to the European Parliament take place.

1981   Greece accedes to the Communities.

1986   The Communities enlarge further to the south (Spain and Portugal).

1992   The Treaty of Maastricht is signed. It introduces European citizenship, foresees the creation of a monetary union, establishes the European Parliament as a co-legislator and transforms the European Communities into the European Union.

1998   The European Central Bank is created. The French–British summit of Saint-Malo launches the European Security and Defence Policy.

2001   The Laeken Declaration sets up a Convention on the Future of Europe (composed of members from national governments and parliaments and from the EU institutions), entrusted with the task of drafting a constitution for the EU.

2002   The euro becomes the currency of twelve EU countries.

2004   The EU expands to ten new member states in Central and Eastern Europe (Cyprus, the Czech Republic, Estonia, Hungary, Latvia, Lithuania, Malta, Poland, Slovakia and Slovenia).

2005   The European Constitutional Treaty is rejected by referendum in France and the Netherlands.

2007   The eastern enlargement is completed with the accession of two new members (Bulgaria and Romania).

2007   The Treaty of Lisbon is signed. The Treaty establishing the European Community is renamed the 'Treaty on the Functioning of the European Union'. Essentially based on the innovations proposed in the European Constitutional Treaty, it rationalises the functioning of the EU institutions, gives the EU full legal personality and grants the Charter of Fundamental Rights binding character.

2010   Due to skyrocketing debt levels in the aftermath of the global financial crisis, bailout packages are adopted for Greece and Ireland. Memorandums of Understanding between the EU, the International Monetary Fund and national governments impose conditionality, making loans dependent on drastic fiscal and social reforms. Portugal and Spain soon follow.

2012   The European Stability Fund is created as an international institution to grant financial assistance through loans to indebted eurozone member countries.

2013   Croatia becomes a member of the EU.

2016   A majority of British citizens vote in favour of an exit of the UK from the EU (Brexit).

2020   The United Kingdom leaves the European Union. The withdrawal agreement entered into force upon the UK's exit from the EU on 31 January 2020. The UK is no longer an EU member state and is considered a third country.

Glossary

Absolute majority (in the European Parliament) An absolute majority is the majority of all members of the European Parliament (including those absent or not voting). In its present configuration with 705 MEPs, the threshold for an absolute majority is 354 votes.

Citizens' initiative The citizens' initiative allows one million citizens from at least a quarter of EU member states to ask the European Commission to come up with proposals for new laws in fields in which it has competence.

Co-decision Term previously used for what is now the ordinary legislative procedure. Still widely used unofficially.

College of Commissioners The College is composed of twenty-seven European commissioners.

Commissioner The European Commission is made up of commissioners, each of whom is assigned responsibility for a specific policy field by the president of the Commission. Currently, there are twenty-seven, one from each member state.

Committee in the European Parliament The Europeans Parliament's (EP) twenty permanent committees draw up, amend and adopt legislative proposals, which are then voted on by the EP as a whole during plenary sessions. The political make-up of the committees reflects that of the EP. The EP can set up sub-committees, special temporary committees and formal committees of inquiry.

Conciliation Conciliation is the third and final phase of the ordinary legislative procedure. It takes place when the EP and Council can't reach agreement on a legislative proposal during the first two readings. Delegations from the Council and the EP look for a compromise acceptable to both.

Conciliation Committee The Conciliation Committee sits during the conciliation phase of the ordinary legislative procedure. It is composed of the same number of member state representatives and MEPs. The committee is responsible for drawing up a joint text, which is put to the Council and EP for approval at third reading. The European Commission takes part in its proceedings with a view to reconciling the differing positions.

Conference of Committee Chairs The EP's Conference of Committee Chairs is composed of the chairs of all standing and temporary committees. Its task is to improve cooperation between EP committees.

COREPER A Council committee made up of the permanent representatives of the member states, which prepares the work of the Council. COREPER I includes deputy ambassadors and COREPER II is made up of ambassadors.

Decision A 'decision' is binding on those to whom it is addressed (e.g. an EU country or an individual company) and is directly applicable.

Directive A 'directive' is a legislative act setting a goal to be achieved by all EU countries, but leaving the method to each member state.

EU law EU law is divided into 'primary' and 'secondary' legislation. The treaties (primary legislation) are the basis for all EU action. Secondary legislation,which includes regulations, directives and decisions, are derived from the principles and objectives set out in the treaties.

Member of the European Parliament Members of the European Parliament (MEPs) are directly elected for a five-year period. The 705 MEPs represent EU citizens.

Official Journal The *Official Journal of the European Union* (OJ) contains EU legislation, information, notices and preliminary legislative work. It is published each working day in all EU official languages. Only legal acts published in the OJ are binding.

Official language There are twenty-four official EU languages: Bulgarian, Croatian, Czech, Danish, Dutch, English, Estonian, Finnish, French, German, Greek, Hungarian, Irish, Italian, Latvian, Lithuanian, Maltese, Polish, Portuguese, Romanian, Slovak, Slovene, Spanish and Swedish. All EU law is published in all official languages.

Ordinary legislative procedure Under the ordinary legislative procedure (formerly co-decision) the European Parliament and the Council of the European Union decide jointly on Commission proposals on a wide range of areas (for example, economic governance, immigration, energy, transport, the environment and consumer protection). Most EU law is now adopted in this way.

Plenary Parliament's plenary sessions take place twelve times a year in Strasbourg, with shorter plenaries in Brussels. Plenary brings together all MEPs to debate and vote on EU legislation and adopt a position on political issues.

Political group MEPs are organised not by nationality, but by political affiliation. There are currently seven political groups in the EP. Members may belong to only one political group. Some MEPs do not belong to a political group and are known as non-attached members.

Proportionality According to the principle of proportionality, the involvement of EU institutions must be limited to what is necessary to achieve the objectives of the Treaties.

Public consultation In public consultations the European Commission asks different stakeholders, such as public authorities, member state authorities, enterprises, (private) organisations, industry associations and citizens, to submit their views on intended legislation. It usually takes the form of a questionnaire with open and closed questions.

Qualified majority in the Council A qualified majority in the Council corresponds to at least 55 per cent of the Council members (member states), comprising a minimum of 15 out of 27, representing at least 65 per cent of the EU population. A blocking minority may be formed by at least four Council members.

Rapporteur An MEP, appointed by the parliamentary committee responsible for handling a legislative proposal, who will steer the proposal through the EP and will prepare a report on it.

Regulation A 'regulation' is a directly applicable form of EU law, which has binding legal force in all member states. National governments do not have to take action to implement EU regulations.

Right of initiative The Commission's right of initiative empowers it to make proposals either because the Treaties explicitly provide for it or because the Commission considers it necessary. The Council and EP may also ask the Commission to come up with proposals.

Secretary general of the Council The head of the General Secretariat of the Council, which assists the Council and the European Council. With the president of the Council, they sign all acts adopted jointly by Parliament and Council.

Secretary general of the European Parliament The EP's most senior official, responsible for its administration. They ensure the smooth running of parliamentary business under the leadership of the president and the Bureau. With the president, they verify and sign all acts adopted jointly by the EP and Council.

Simple majority (in the EP) A proposal adopted by simple majority is approved if the number of 'yes' is higher than number of 'no' votes.

Subsidiarity According to the subsidiarity principle, the EU should not act (except in areas that fall within its exclusive competence), unless EU action is more effective than action taken at national, regional or local level. Constant checks are made to verify that EU-level action is justified.

Treaties A treaty is a binding agreement between EU member countries. It sets out EU objectives, rules for EU institutions, how decisions are made and the relationship between the EU and its member countries.

Treaty of Amsterdam The Treaty of Amsterdam came into force 1 May 1999. Its purpose was to reform the EU institutions in preparation for the arrival of future member countries. It amended, renumbered and consolidated the EU and EEC treaties and increased the use of co-decision.

Treaty of Lisbon The Lisbon Treaty entered into force on 1 December 2009. It comprises the Treaty on European Union (TEU) and the Treaty on the Functioning of the EU (TFEU). The Lisbon Treaty gave more power to the EP, changed voting procedures in the Council, introduced the citizens' initiative, created a permanent president of the European Council, a new High Representative for Foreign Affairs and a new EU diplomatic service, and clarified which powers belong to the EU, which to EU member states and which are shared.

It changed the name of co-decision to the ordinary legislative procedure and increased the number of areas to which ordinary legislative procedure is applied.

Treaty of Maastricht The Treaty of Maastricht, or the Treaty on European Union, entered in to force on 1 November 1993. It established the EU (previously the European Communities), and introduced co-decision and cooperation between EU governments on defence and justice and home affairs. It paved the way for Economic and Monetary Union and introduced elements of a political union (citizenship, a common foreign and internal affairs policy).

Treaty of Nice The Treaty of Nice entered into force on 1 February 2003. Its purpose was to reform the institutions so that the EU could function efficiently after reaching twenty-five member countries. It introduced methods for changing the composition of the Commission and redefining the voting system in the Council.

Treaty on European Union The Maastricht Treaty, in force since 1993, was amended and renamed the Treaty on European Union by the Lisbon Treaty. It establishes the EU as legal entity, and defines its values, aims, institutions and competences. It is one of the two principal treaties on which the EU is now based.

Treaty on the Functioning of the European Union The Treaty on the Functioning of the European Union (TFEU) started life as the Treaty of Rome in 1958, but has since been much amended. It sets out the organisational and functional details of the EU. It is one of the two principal treaties on which the EU is now based.

Trilogue Informal meetings attended by the EP, Council and Commission. Their purpose is to get an agreement (on a package of amendments or on the wording of laws) acceptable to the Council and EP.

Unanimity (in the Council) Unanimity requires all member states meeting within the Council to agree on a proposal before it can be adopted. Since the Lisbon Treaty only a restricted number of policies judged to be sensitive remain subject to unanimity voting.

Abbreviations

AFSJ	Area of Freedom, Security and Justice
BGs	Battle Groups
CAP	Common Agricultural Policy
CETA	Comprehensive Economic and Trade Agreement
CF	Cohesion Fund
CFSP	Common Foreign and Security Policy
CISA	Convention of 19 June 1990 implementing the Schengen Agreement
CJEU	Court of Justice of the European Union
CSDP	Common Security and Defense Policy
CSOs	civil society organisations
CSRs	Country-Specific Recommendations
DG ECFIN	Directorate-General Economy and Finance
DG EMPL	Directorate General Employment, Social Affairs and Inclusion
EBCG	European Border and Coast Guard Agency
EBRD	European Bank of Reconstruction and Development
EC	European Communities
ECB	European Central Bank
ECSC	European Coal and Steel Community
EEAS	European External Action Service
EEC	European Economic Community
EFSF	European Financial Stability Facility
EIB	European Investment Bank
EMU	Economic and Monetary Union
EP	European Parliament
ERDF	European Regional Development Fund
ESF	European Social Fund
ESM	European Stability Mechanism
EU	European Union
FDI	foreign direct investment
GATT	General Agreement on Tariffs and Trade
IMF	International Monetary Fund
NATO	North Atlantic Treaty Organization
OECD	Organisation for Economic Co-operation and Development

SEA	Single European Act
SGP	Stability and Growth Pact
TCNs	third-country nationals
TEU	Treaty on European Union
TFEU	Treaty on the Functioning of the European Union
TTIP	Transatlantic Trade and Investment Partnership

1 Introduction: The European Union as a Political Regime, a Set of Policies and a Community after the Great Recession

RAMONA COMAN, AMANDINE CRESPY AND VIVIEN A. SCHMIDT

1.1 Introduction

Regional integration in Europe has never followed a clear path. Instead, it developed as a result of a succession of painful negotiations and compromises, followed at times by moments of political enthusiasm marking historic decisions. Over the last decades, the widening and deepening of integration has gone hand in hand, to varying degrees, with mounting popular discontent. Attempts to create unity and to make the EU more akin to a federal state have received little support or have failed. Rather than putting pressure on elites to transfer power to a higher level of governance, as predicted by neo-functionalists in the 1950s, from the 1990s onwards some political parties and citizens alike have called for 'less Europe'. Mainstream as well as peripheral political parties have increasingly amplified criticism of the EU but have failed to undertake the pledged grand reforms of the Union, thus feeding discontent and claims to disintegration. This trend came to a dramatic climax when, on 23 June 2016, a majority of British people voted in favour of the United Kingdom's exit from the EU.

And yet, these powerful centrifugal forces have not meant that EU integration has come to a complete halt. In many areas such as environmental policy, trade, monetary policy and banking, migrations and borders, the EU has proven de facto the relevant level of government, calling for more joint action. While federalist ambitions have been abandoned, the way has been paved for closer cooperation, though with limited transfer of new competences from the member states to the supranational institutions. As a result, the EU has kept deepening its scope and depth in reaction to multiple crises, thereby demonstrating its ability to constantly adapt to sudden disruptions and social and political changes. At the same time, it has become very difficult for European politicians both in Brussels and in the capitals to hide the fact that integration by stealth is continuing, albeit at slower pace. Although the technicalities of EU policy-making remain opaque for the vast majority of European citizens, citizens increasingly contest, more or less directly, the implications of collective decisions (or the absence thereof) made at EU level. Paradoxically, while the EU is seen by many as an ineffective and illegitimate political system, according to the 89 Eurobarometer in 2018 Europeans trust the EU more than their national parliaments and governments. Put in theoretical terms,[1]

---

[1] For a comprehensive overview on theories of EU integration and the EU's crises, see Brack and Gürkan (forthcoming).

the EU therefore seems trapped in the functional vs. post-functional contradiction. Global problems entail constant pressures for more integration and spillovers between various policy areas, as neo-functionalists have predicted. At the same time, though, popular resentment about the effects of such Europeanisation is increasingly voiced by national elites. Because EU integration is perceived as the source of economic and cultural insecurity by the less well-off citizens, it has crystallised as a transnational political and social cleavage governing the transformation of party systems across Europe (Hooghe and Marks, 2018). This, post-functionalist scholars have been arguing, will determine the pace and shape of EU integration and can result in policy renationalisation or, considering Brexit, even polity disintegration.

In the following pages, we come back to the manifestations of the EU 'polycrisis' which have affected the EU over the past decade (1.2). Then, we discuss the effects thereof on the three constitutive dimensions of the Union, namely the EU's political regime (1.3), policy-making (1.4) and political community (1.5).

1.2   Integration through Crises

Since the establishment of the three European Communities in the 1950s, the deepening and widening of the EU have been shaped by crises. Although several authors have pointed out that this word is not a useful analytical category to understand and explain the path of EU integration, as Seabrooke and Tsingou put it, 'crisis talk is part of the everyday life' (2018: 1), in particular in EU politics. Crises are often invoked in political and academic debates to refer to a variety of situations, ranging from forms of adversity to the integration process to its viability per se. Following dictionary definitions, a crisis is generated by hard times, by difficulty, distress, reversal, catastrophes and calamity. A crisis is a problem in need of a solution, which can mark, in turn, a critical challenge at a decisive point in time. Crises can be slow- or fast-burning, defined not only by their tempo and intensity, but also by how they are perceived by citizens and political actors (Seabrooke and Tsingou, 2018: 10). Fast-burning crises are 'instant and abrupt shocks, such as plane hijacks or "run of the mill" natural disasters communities can cope with', while slow-burning ones 'are gradual and creeping, such as protracted guerrilla warfare or environmental crises, where there is political and scientific uncertainty about how to resolve the issue' (Seabrooke and Tsingou, 2018: 3). Some crises are like a 'tornado', with causes and solutions unfolding over a short time period, while others look more like an earthquake, with causes that are slow moving, followed by a 'quick' outcome (Pierson, 2004: 178). Importantly, crises may be 'real', as in material damages in natural disasters, or they may be constructed politically.

The evolution of the EU has been punctuated by moments of political and social consensus (or social indifference), and alternatively by moments of tension and conflict. Crises or critical junctures open a window of opportunity when institutional/policy change becomes possible. Critical junctures are 'choice point[s] when a particular option is adopted among two or more alternatives [...] Once a particular option is selected [in a critical juncture], it becomes progressively more difficult to return to the initial point when multiple alternatives were still available' (Capoccia and Kelemen, 2007: 347). While some crises or junctures are triggered by cumulative/gradual causes, others are generated by shocks or abrupt factors.

Section 1.2.1 provides an overview of critical junctures as well as small and big crises that have marked the evolution of the EU since its origins. It shows that since the beginning of the integration process, failure and success have been all part of the same game (Jones, 2012: 55). However, over the last decade the EU has been facing a series of simultaneous crises, which seem to be different from the ones that traditionally shaped the integration process. Not only have they occurred concurrently, they have also put under considerable strain both the viability and legitimacy of the integration process.

1.2.1   Six Decades of Integration: Two Critical Junctures and a Series of Many Other Small and Big Crises

Two critical junctures and a series of other small crises marked the course of EU integration from 1950s to 2000s. As Fabbrini put it, at the origins of the integration process there is a critical juncture that 'started with the redefinition of power relations between nation states on the European continent' (2015: xxv). By signing the Treaty of Paris in 1951 – leading to the establishment of the European Coal and Steel Community (ECSC, entered into force on 24 July 1952 for a fifty-year validity period) – and the Treaties of Rome in 1957 (entered into force in 1958) – establishing the European Economic Community (EEC) and European Atomic Energy Community (Euratom) – the six founding member states agreed to pursue a process of sectoral integration, which would ultimately lead to a common economic market (see Chapter 2). It was expected that after the establishment of the ECSC – which placed the production of coal and steel under a common High Authority to avoid war on the European continent – the process would move to new phases of sectoral economic integration, including agriculture and transport. The Treaty of Paris put in place a supranational structure of decision-making, vesting the High Authority with significant powers to uphold the supranational principle and the Council to defend the interests of the member states. In contrast, the Treaties of Rome – because of the ambition to create a common market as an area of a free movement of persons, goods, services and capital – established an institutional framework in which the power of the European Commission to initiate legislation was counterbalanced by the power of the member states, brought together in the Council. Against this backdrop, the six signatories of the Treaties of Rome agreed to establish a set of supranational institutions (the Court of Justice of the EU, the Parliamentary Assembly and the European Investment Bank (EIB)) as well as a consultative body (the European Economic and Social Committee) to implement the customs union and the common market and to develop at the supranational level a series of policies such as agriculture, transport, competition, commercial policy, etc. In doing so, member states agreed to delegate and pool sovereignty in supranational institutions in order to secure substantive agreements in their national interests (Keohane and Hoffmann, 1991).

The integration project was an ambitious one. Resistance emerged from the onset, slowing down its path to accommodate the diversity of interests and preferences (see Chapter 2). In 1954, France voted to table the ratification of the European Defence Community (EDC). The French Assembly was opposed to the idea of a rearmed Germany, even within the EDC. After the French negative vote, several French intellectuals announced the end of the European project (quoted by Jones, 2012: 53). But 1954 was not the end. The death of European integration was announced prematurely, although with the refusal of France the hopes for an EDC fell. Even before this the ECSC had been established, and its institutions were to become those of the EEC agreed only a few years later.

Forms of social and political resistance were apparent from the early years of the integration process. While the establishment of the EEC was possible thanks to the political support expressed by the ministers of foreign affairs of the six founding member states, the three communities designed to pacify the continent were perceived with scepticism by citizens and other political actors. One day after the signature of the Treaties of Rome, on 29 March 1957, the French communist newspaper *L'Humanité* portrayed social harmonisation within the common market as a measure that would bring down the standard of living of the French working class to the lowest common level. Nonetheless, these forms of resistance did not engender 'crises' until the 1960s when the French president, Charles de Gaulle, balked at measures proposed by the Commission that entailed potential reductions to national sovereignty while further empowering the Commission. Two visions were in tension: a supranational and an intergovernmental one. On the one hand, Walter Hallstein, who served as president of the Commission from 1958 to 1967, was seeking to strengthen the supranational construction, by empowering its institution, by establishing for the EEC a system of 'own resources' instead of member states' contributions and by using qualified majority voting (QMV) in the Council on a limited number of policies. In contrast, Charles de Gaulle was eager to maintain unanimous decision-making on issues that might affect French interests or sovereignty, such as proposed revisions to the emerging Common Agricultural Policy (CAP). Hallerstein's supranational vision clashed with the intergovernmental plan favoured by Charles de Gaulle, who was against any attempt to enhance the powers of both the European Commission and the Parliamentary Assembly (as well as its election by direct universal suffrage). These incompatible visions on how to adopt decisions at the European level gave rise to the 'empty chair crisis'. France withdrew its participation in the Council for six months. It recalled its minister and permanent representative from Brussels and stopped attending the Council meetings and its subcommittees from 30 June 1965 to 30 January 1966. This 'crisis' was solved by the Luxembourg Compromise signed in 1966, which stated that in case of the vital national interests of one member state, the Council would seek to find a consensus solution, creating a de facto veto right.

Not only has deepening of European integration been shaped by crises, but also its widening. The United Kingdom – which in the 1950s was against the establishment of a supranational construction like the ECSC, although it was the main producer of coal and steel – became interested in the 1960s. However, its accession demand introduced in 1961 was refused by de Gaulle, who vetoed it in 1963 and in 1967 on the grounds of weak commitment to contribute to the development of the political and economic European integration due to UK's links with its Commonwealth and to its close cooperation with the United States. De Gaulle feared that the European Commission 'would not endure for long [but] instead would become a colossal Atlantic community under American domination and direction' (de Gaulle, 1963). This 'would obviously mean the breaking up of a Community that has been built and that functions according to rules which would not bear such a monumental exception' (de Gaulle, 1967: 34440). The first enlargement was postponed until 1973, when the UK, Denmark and Ireland joined the Communities, while Norway decided to withdraw from the final negotiation stage.

While in 1969 the political elites of the six founding member states announced their ambition to relaunch the integration process, to widen and deepen it, the 1970s were marked by the quadrupling of oil prices, unemployment and inflation. The attempts to establish the Economic and Monetary Union (EMU), outlined by Luxembourg's prime minister, Pierre Werner, in a report (known as the Report Werner) in 1970, failed. The French president Georges Pompidou was against this plan, although in favour of monetary cooperation. The economic and monetary ideas promoted by France and Germany appeared to be irreconcilable. These were not only areas of protected sovereignty; these areas were also characterised by an increased diversity among member states. As a result, in the 1970s, despite various attempts to strengthen policy coordination, 'the integration process failed to help governments to respond to the international economic crises of that decade' (Fioretos, 2012: 297).

After the accession of Spain, Greece and Portugal in the early to mid-1980s, the Single European Act (SEA) marked the first revision of the treaties, signed in Luxembourg on 17 February 1986 by nine member states. It was adopted to launch the single market programme under the leadership of Jacques Delors, president of the European Commission for two consecutive terms (1985–95). This first revision of the treaties extended the Community's powers to new areas of decision-making activity, such as economic and social cohesion, social policy, research and technological development, environment, monetary policy, as well as cooperation in the field of foreign policy. It also changed the institutional setup through the extension of the QMV to new policy areas, including the internal market, social policy, economic and social cohesion, research and technological development and environmental policy. The SEA's major aim was the implementation of the single market through the adoption of 300 pieces of legislation, intended to remove the remaining physical, technical and fiscal barriers to the free movement of people, goods, services and capital.

While the SEA accelerated the path of integration through market-related policies, by adopting the Maastricht Treaty, the Communities – hereafter the EU – entered a new stage. According to Fabbrini, after the end of the Cold War and the reunification of Germany, this moment marked the second critical juncture (2015: xxvi). To make politically possible the 'return to Europe' of the former communist countries, member states agreed to proceed to a new revision of the treaties. While Central and Eastern Europeans were celebrating the collapse of communism and the dismantlement of the Berlin Wall, which separated the continent for more than five decades, in Western Europe mobilisations against EU integration grew bigger. In the 1990s, it became clear that the era of the permissive consensus – in which treaties were negotiated behind closed doors and unquestioned by Europeans – had come to an end. While at the international level, Western political elites were foreseeing a new role for 'Europe' in the world, internally the new revision was envisaged to tackle the mounting criticism related to its democratic deficit. Thus, to democratise the Union, the Treaty of Maastricht granted new powers to the European Parliament (EP) as co-legislator with the Council, recognised the role of the European political parties at the EU level, introduced European citizenship and established the Committee of the Regions. To allow those in favour of pursuing an ever closer union to advance, it introduced a weak form of the enhanced cooperation procedure (which would allow a group of countries to deepen their integration in policy areas where agreement by all member states was not forthcoming). The treaty also allowed the extension of the decision-making competences to a wide set of policies, including various sensitive areas located at the core of the state powers such as economic governance, justice and home affairs, social and employment as well as foreign and security policies (Puetter, 2014). At Maastricht, political elites decided to establish the EMU and the introduction of the euro, a strong political symbol of their will to deepen integration.

Again, despite these political ambitions the ratification of the Maastricht Treaty faced strong opposition in Denmark, where on 2 June 1992 the Danes rejected it in a referendum, with 50.7 per cent of the record turnout of 83 per cent. The treaty was ratified only after renegotiating Denmark's participation in the EU's policies and obtaining opt-outs for some specific parts of the treaty, including the EMU, Justice and Home Affairs and Common Defence Policy. Some argued that the Treaty of Maastricht was collapsing because of its rejection in Denmark and because of the little 'oui' (50.8 per cent in a referendum held in September 1992) obtained in the French referendum. Nonetheless, it entered into force after renegotiations to accommodate specific national interests. The Maastricht moment was followed by a new wave of enlargement to include Austria, Sweden and Finland in 1995; Cyprus and Malta in addition to eight former communist countries in 2004 (the Czech Republic, Estonia, Hungary, Latvia, Lithuania, Poland, Slovakia, Slovenia); followed by Romania and Bulgaria in 2007 and Croatia in 2013.

How to accommodate the interests of an increasing number of member states became a growing problem. In 1997, in Amsterdam, political elites failed to agree on a new institutional architecture to prepare the functioning of the EU with more than fifteen member states. The composition of the European Commission (in which big member states were able to designate two commissioners) and of the EP (whose number of Members of European Parliaments (MEPs) was about to double from 434 in 1989 to 751 in 2009), as well as the weight of voting rights in the Council, were at stake and important matters were all negotiated behind closed doors. The intergovernmental method, which in the past allowed member state representatives to revise the treaties, was contested not only because of its lack of transparency, coherence and global approach, but also because of its inability to satisfy diverging and increasingly numerous interests. Taking decisions for the people, but without the people, was no longer possible.

1.3 2000s: The Decade of Crises

The Treaty of Nice did not solve the institutional issues unsolved at Amsterdam. In 2001, the Laeken Declaration of the heads of state and government emphasised the need of substantial reforms to clarify the competences of the EU, to simplify its legislative procedure and to ensure the effectiveness of the decision-making process. These issues were discussed from February 2002 to July 2003 by the European Convention, a broad consultative forum which brought together representatives of member states' heads of state and governments, candidate countries, national parliaments, national parliaments of the candidate countries, as well as representatives of the EP, the Commission, the European Economic and Social Committee, the Committee of the Regions, European social partners and the European Ombudsman.

Drawing on the work of the European Convention, on 29 October 2004 political elites signed the Treaty Establishing a Constitution for Europe (TEC) in Rome. It sought to strengthen the bonds among the people of Europe and to clarify the competencies of the EU, and in so doing to reduce the increasing gap between the EU and its citizens. It granted the EU a single legal personality; it also extended QMV in the Council, reduced the size of the Commission, established a permanent presidency for the European Council and proposed the establishment of a minister for foreign affairs.

But the TEC was difficult to sell. It gave rise to protests in several countries. France and the Netherlands rejected it by referendums in 2005, which spelled its doom. The treaty went too far in its ambitions. While in the Netherlands citizens feared new rounds of enlargement, in France citizens vetoed the emergence of a 'too liberal Europe'. Following the 'neen' of the Dutch and the 'non' of the French citizens, political actors and observers alike deplored the effects of this new 'crisis'. There was no plan B on the table. 'Saying no to the Constitution means blocking the progress of the EU, it's a no to Europe', said Jacques Delors. The end of the political union was again announced. The TEC witnessed a new renegotiation to accommodate a variety of interests, including those of the new member states from Central and Eastern Europe. While the old member states were divided on institutional issues, the new ones insisted on inserting the EU's Christian heritage in the treaty, as one of the common foundations of Europe. Hence, it took three more years to sign the Lisbon Treaty on 13 December 2007. Most of the provisions which gave rise to contestation – such as the symbols of the EU – were eliminated. Despite this, the Treaty of Lisbon was rejected by Irish citizens in 2008, to ultimately enter into force 1 December 2009.

Since then, the EU has faced a series of new crises. In 2010, the eurozone crisis opened a third critical juncture that also opened up the possibility 'to redefine the institutional and policy features of the EU' (Fabbrini, 2015: xxvii). The turmoil surrounding the 2010 eurozone crisis put the EU's legitimacy at risk and created expectations for major institutional and policy change. However, as most of the chapters in this volume will show, instead of generating radical policy and institutional change, the dramatic impact of the eurozone crisis ended up reinforcing the path-dependent logic (2015: xxvii) of institutional and policy development. Although the narrative of change was central to the political discourse at the time, with debates about what to do offering a wide range of innovative ideas for solving the crisis, innovative change was in short supply in the end. Despite the 'hot' context following the financial and macroeconomic crises (Dyson and Quaglia, 2010), as several chapters in this book will show, EU institutional actors responded with lowest-common-denominator solutions through the reinforcement of long-standing neoliberal and ordoliberal ideas (Schmidt, 2010, forthcoming; Gamble, 2013).

1.3.1   The Eurozone Crisis

The origins of the eurozone crisis can be explained in many ways. As mentioned in Section 1.3, the first attempts to establish an economic and monetary union in the 1970s failed. Only in the 1990s did EMU, as enshrined in the Treaty of Maastricht, set the stage for the move towards a common currency under the rules of the Stability and Growth Pact (SGP). On the one hand, monetary policy was centralised with decisions taken at the supranational level by the European Central Bank (ECB), while on the other, economic policy was subject to coordination among member states. EMU gave rise to two processes of coordination: one top down, due to the ECB's monetary policy, and another bottom up, occurring in structural reforms to labour markets and welfare states (Dyson, 2000: 652; Featherstone and Papadimitriou, 2008). While monetary policy was centralised and defined by the ECB, labour market, wage policy and welfare state reforms took different forms reflecting the staying power of individual traditions (Dyson, 2000: 660), embedded in different models of capitalism with different employment, market and economic structures (Schmidt, 2002). EMU placed limits on public deficits and debts, depriving governments in the eurozone of currency devaluation. As a result, from the very beginning EMU faced collective action problems in fiscal policies (notably the crisis of the SGP in November 2003) and in economic reforms (especially in labour markets), where responsibility remained at the national level (Dyson, 2008: 2). In 1993, the currency crisis showed that the majority of governments would not be able to meet the convergence criteria by the 1997 deadline. By 1997, five member states had already been 'excused' for failing to bring their budget deficits under 3 per cent of gross domestic product (GDP) or their public debt down 60 per cent of GDP. In 2002, it clearly appeared that member states were unlikely to introduce structural reforms. As many observers argued, since its entry into force, the SGP has been a pact of 'wobbly stability' (*Politico*, 25 September 2002). As Jones et al. put it, 'this sequential cycle of piecemeal reform, followed by policy failure, followed by further reform, has managed to sustain both the European project and the common currency' (2016: 1010). Neither at its beginning, nor prior to 2010, did member states ever follow its rules *à la lettre*. These slow-moving causes of policy failure in the EMU did not generate change in the eurozone's institutional framework or policy ideas prior to 2008. EU institutional actors seemed to be into a 'zone of indifference' and continued to perform their tasks until the eurozone crisis forced them to revise their practices and ways of doing (Lefkofridi and Schmitter, 2014: 13; 2015).

In 2008, the European Commission noted anomalies in the Greek fiscal accounts (Jones, 2012: 60). In December 2009, the Greek government admitted that its debt had reached €300 billion, which was the highest in modern history. Its debt amounted to 113 per cent of GDP, which was double the limit (60 per cent) established by the SGP. In 2010, the problem turned into the Greek sovereign debt crisis, which threatened the very existence of the monetary union. Some argued that the Greek crisis also revealed a crisis of solidarity because of the rising tensions between creditor and debtor countries within the EU. As the contagion spread beyond Greece, also affecting Spain, Portugal and Ireland, the International Monetary Fund (IMF) director, Christine Lagarde, urged countries to act together to keep economic recovery on track. In 2011, the president of the European Commission, José Manuel Barroso, declared that the EU was facing 'its greatest challenge' (28 September 2011). Against this backdrop, it clearly appeared that the Maastricht Treaty did not prepare for the risk that a member state could experience this kind of deep fiscal distress.

Only when the problems reached a critical level in 2010 did change in the EU's modes of governance and policy become inevitable. As the chapters in this book will show, this peak in the eurozone crisis generated a 'quick' institutional outcome in the first 'three crucial years' of the crisis that have been seen as a turning point calling for a redefinition of the EU's economic governance. A new window of opportunity opened up in which EU institutional actors sought to address the failures of EMU and its policy tools. Their reform of the eurozone area focused on strengthening the rules on fiscal discipline, by adopting new ones to prevent macroeconomic imbalances, by improving the coordination of macroeconomic policies and by putting in place mechanisms of financial assistance (Fabbrini, 2015; Bickerton et al., 2015). As Jones et al. argued, 'the series of incremental reforms adopted sequentially in response to the crisis – steps including the establishment of bailout funds, tightening fiscal surveillance, and moving towards banking union – has led to one of the most rapid periods of deepening of integration in EU history' (2015: 3). Austerity and structural reform appeared as the only way forward (Schmidt, 2010; Gamble, 2013; Blyth, 2013; Matthijs and Blyth, 2016; Crespy and Vanheuverzwijn, 2017). The eurozone crisis, which entered its fast-burning phase in 2010 with the beginning of the Greek crisis, ended in 2012 with Mario Draghi's declaration that the ECB will do 'whatever it takes to save the Euro' (Schmidt, 2015, 2016).

But this was not the end of this crisis. At the domestic level, the decisions taken to save the euro have had dramatic effects both for policy and politics. To reduce public spending in the countries affected by the crisis, EU institutional actors decided to decrease public investment and to increase taxation, to freeze labour benefits, to raise the retirement age and to cut pensions, and to massively reduce the number of jobs in the public sector. These decisions gave rise to massive protests and to the emergence of new populist parties that moved from the margins of the political arena to the centre, with their election to governmental positions. The eurozone crisis brought a widening gap in prosperity between the eurozone's core and periphery members. While some countries of Europe's northern core – such as Germany, Luxembourg, Belgium, the Netherlands and Austria – saw their economies recover rapidly, Greece, Ireland, Portugal, Spain and Italy were, in contrast, negatively affected by the draconian effects of the crisis, with decreasing levels of income, rising unemployment and cuts in welfare spending and wages (Matthijs, 2017).

In other words, the eurozone crisis showed what multiple compromises over multiple countries with different interests and traditions in an enlarged EU produced. As some of the chapters in this book will show, the decisions adopted in the midst of the eurozone crisis have had consequences not only for the eurozone, but also for many other policies.

1.3.2 The Crisis of the Management of Migration

Not only the euro area but also the Schengen borderland has made headlines over the last decade. The emergence of the Schengen area became a reality in the 1980s, following a series of painful negotiations between France, Germany and the Benelux countries, whose leaders only reluctantly accepted dismantling the controls at their internal borders and trusting their neighbours. By implementing the Schengen Agreement, the EU developed a unique borderland where every day 3.5 million people cross the borders of one of the twenty-two EU Schengen members and where, according to Eurostat, 1.7 million citizens work in one country and live in another. About 57 million road transports cross EU member states every day; annually more than 18 million truckers enter Germany, and 200 million trips to another EU country are registered. Big infrastructure projects (bridges, tunnels, fast trains, etc.) emerged to better connect citizens and business within member states (Coman, 2019: 685). For many, this is everyday life in the Schengen area, a specific social and political environment where EU citizens can travel without stopping at internal borders for formalities and where the territorial markers of sovereignty between member states have disappeared. While the Schengen borderland is meant to bring economic prosperity and social development, its external borders are spaces of tragedy, loss and suffering (Van Houtum and Pijpers, 2007). As Van Houtum and Boedeltje put it, 'the border of the EU discriminates unjustly and unfairly between people on the basis of their country of origin and on the basis of papers' (2009: 229).

In recent years, the Schengen area triggered existential debate for the EU. In 2011, following the decision of the Italian authorities to grant Tunisian migrants temporary residence permits, France restored controls along its border with Italy. Germany, Austria, Belgium and the Netherlands acknowledged that they would do the same if Italy continued to deliver temporary permits to Tunisian migrants (*European Voice*, 5 April 2011). In France, President Nicolas Sarkozy declared that 'Schengen as it was done [is] no longer possible' (*Politico*, 14 September 2014). Since 2011, the influx of refugees and migrants has generated tensions among member states, which in turn has had effects on Schengen governance and the functioning of the internal market. The Danish government made known its intention to introduce checks in its border area 'as a concession' by the government to the Danish People's Party. Moreover, in Hungary a new fence 175 km long was built on the country's border with Serbia, and Prime Minister Viktor Orbán decided to 'suspend the application of EU asylum rules in order to protect Hungarian interest' (*EU Observer*, 29 April 2015; *EurActiv*, 23 June 2015). The idea of a return to uniformed patrols controlling the internal borders within the Schengen area gained a strong place in the debates.

The Schengen area was in 'crisis'. In 2011 the interior ministers met several times in extraordinary meetings in Brussels because some member states demanded to be allowed to expand the conditions under which these checks could be reinstated at the internal borders. The European Council set the agenda of the Commission, inviting it to consider how to translate its political guidance into legislation. The Commission emphasised that Schengen was one of the fundamental pillars of the internal market that operated through the free movement of goods, services, people and capital. The argument of necessity was put forward by the president of the Commission, Jean-Claude Juncker, who declared that 'less Schengen means less employment, less economic growth. Without Schengen, without the free movement of workers, without freedom of European citizens to travel, the euro makes no sense' (*Politico*, 15 January 2016).

But the year 2015 was marked by episodes of human tragedy and refugees losing their lives while trying to reach Europe. In the face of a massive increase in the number of arrivals and, in particular, in response to the death of over 800 refugees in the Mediterranean Sea in a single boat tragedy in April 2015, the European Commission adopted the 'European Agenda on Migration', which was launched in May 2015 (European Commission, 2015). The Commission proposed an emergency relocation scheme for a total of 160,000 migrants from three front-line member states, namely Hungary, Greece and Italy. But reaching consensus on the relocation of 120,000 people represented fundamental challenges. Central and Eastern European governments, along with far-right parties elsewhere in Europe, depicted the relocation proposal of the Commission as an attack on the Christian and cultural foundations of Europe. The lack of agreement on a fair burden sharing of refugees among member states led many observers to argue that the so-called 'refugee crisis' has turned into a 'solidarity crisis' (Grimmel and My Giang, 2017). Governments led by right-wing and nationalist parties adopted the rhetoric of 'fear' and in most EU member states 'the exclusionary rhetoric of othering prevailed' (Krzyżanowski et al., 2018: 1), while calls for strengthening European solidarity failed.

Faced with intra-EU disagreements and the pressing need to solve the migration management crisis, the EU externalised the problem by concluding international agreements with third states, in particular the EU–Turkey Joint Action Plan – provisionally agreed in October 2015. This agreement, as well as the EU's efforts to prevent boat departures from Libya, raised serious concerns about member states' commitment to EU values, with many arguing that the EU was undermining its human rights commitments. Observers have argued that the EU's deal with Libya was sentencing refugees to death (*The Guardian*, 5 February 2019). The so-called refugee crisis revealed the limits of integration as well as the limits of solidarity among member states and between member states and third-country nationals; it also showed the dangerous effects of the normalisation of racism, Islamophobia and nativist policies.

1.3.3   The Crisis of Values

Besides dousing the flames of the eurozone crisis and dealing with the refusal of member states to find collective solutions to migration, since 2010 EU institutional actors have had to deal with what was called 'the rule of law crisis', or the crisis of the values enshrined in the treaties. Article 2 Treaty on European Union (TEU) states that:

> the Union is founded on the values of respect for human dignity, freedom, democracy, equality, the rule of law and respect for human rights, including the rights of persons belonging to minorities. These values are common to the member states in a society in which pluralism, non-discrimination, tolerance, justice, solidarity and equality between women and men prevail.[2]

As an illustration, over the last decade the attempts of the Hungarian, Polish and Romanian governments to change the rules of the democratic game by reducing the independence of domestic judicial institutions and limiting press freedoms have attracted considerable political attention and media coverage, as the transformation of their political regimes challenges the principles of EU integration and its foundations. Attempts to alter the liberal foundations of the EU represent a more serious challenge for the EU than Brexit itself and they are by no means limited to Central and Eastern Europe. They are part of a global trend. As Hooghe and Marks put it, 'the illiberal challenge to the independence of the judiciary, separation of powers, and protection of basic liberties in Hungary and Poland is perhaps the greatest contemporary challenge to the legitimacy of the European Union' (2019: 1125). 'Illiberalism is allied to a nationalist discourse of parochialism, conservativism, and anti-elitism which is mobilised against the perceived threat of foreigners, multinationals, and the European Union' (2019: 1127). The rise of this 'illiberal' turn challenges the EU as a union of liberal democracies and as a normative power at the international level (Manners, 2002).

1.4   The EU's Political Regime: *Quo Vadis?*

Two decision-making methods have traditionally shaped the integration process: the community (supranational) method and the intergovernmental method. Scholars have portrayed the community method as the method of integration, whereas the intergovernmental one was conceived as a path to increase cooperation among

---

[2] https://eur-lex.europa.eu/legal-content/EN/TXT/?uri=celex%3A12012M%2FTXT.

member states. The former – which places supranational institutions and non-state actors in the driver's seat – deepened the integration in a series of policies seen as being technical in nature, while the latter allowed member states – represented in the Council and the European Council – to cooperate on grand initiatives and to maintain control in sensitive policy areas.

Since the entry into force of the Maastricht Treaty, EU policy-making witnessed several transformations (see Chapter 3). As many contributors show, the intensity of institutional change has been fuelled by the eurozone crisis, which put the decision-making process under considerable strain and shifted the balance of power at the EU level (see Chapter 5). The chapters in this book capture incremental changes in the power relations between the European Commission, the EP, the Council, the European Council, the ECB and the Court of Justice of the EU. All together, they illustrate the 'adaptability and resilience' of the EU policy-making (Pollack et al., 2010: 482), which is the ability of EU institutions to adapt to incremental change and sudden disruptions.

However, the degree of institutional change is disputed in the literature. Scholars remain divided over whether the transformations introduced since the Maastricht Treaty and the eurozone crisis have strengthened the power of member states (the Council and the European Council) to the detriment of supranational institutions (the European Commission, the EP and the ECB) or vice versa. While Bickerton et al. (2015) emphasised the growing empowerment of member states, other argued that the Commission has been granted new roles and power (Bauer and Becker, 2014; Savage and Verdun, 2015). As Schmidt (2016) argued, in the first years of the eurozone crisis, intergovernmental actors and presidents of the EU institutions were in the driver's seat and pushed for fast-track decisions in a variety of policy areas, as illustrated in Part II. The eurozone crisis strengthened the agenda-setting powers of the European Council (Bickerton et al., 2015; Fabbrini, 2015: 64) to the detriment of the supranational actors, while the EP remained largely a 'talking shop' (Schmidt, 2015). The EP's power had been impaired by an unbalanced intergovernmentalism and by the primacy of the European Council in the management of the crisis, and found itself in confrontation with them. In the first years of the crisis, the EP remained a vocal but still isolated actor, weakened institutionally by the strong alliance between some members of the Council and some members of the Commission.

Against this backdrop, *de jure* the European Council – which brings together the heads of state or government, the president of the Commission and the high representative for foreign affairs and security policy – has become a regular institution with the entry into force of the Lisbon Treaty and de facto has overall political leadership on all EU affairs (Piris, 2010: 208). Created in the 1970s to define the grand political orientations of the integration process and to reach agreements on contentious political issues, it has become more and more involved in 'policy detail rather than on matters of strategic coordination only' (Puetter, 2012: 59), giving political instructions to both the Commission and the Council. By institutionalising the European Council, the Lisbon Treaty established a dual executive, generating tensions between the European Council and the Commission. Thus, scholars contended that the Commission lost its role as *primus inter pares* in setting the agenda of the EU. Others maintained that the relationship between the Commission and the European Council could be best described as 'competitive cooperation' (Bocquillon and Dobbles, 2014: 21). As a result, the agenda-setting role of the European Council seems to be more conspicuous than before and this limits the room for manoeuvre of the Commission and its political leadership (even in areas which fall under the supranational method).

In a nutshell, during the two first years of the eurozone crisis, Herman Van Rompuy, the president of the European Council, became the most visible European figure at the EU level; in the context of the eurozone crisis the European Council acted as the agenda-setter, a role traditionally assigned to the Commission. It also took decisions that would traditionally fall within the Council's attributions (De Schoutheete, 2012: 13). As Fabbrini put it, the intergovernmental method became a 'subsection of the political system of the EU' (2015: 127) and an alternative to the community method (2015: 129).

In addition, the Council – which consists of ministers from the member states – meets more often and in several formations covering the totality of policy areas of the EU. Hence, decision-making at the EU level relies increasingly on the domestic expertise and coordination of national policies in a mounting number of groups, committees and exchanges among national experts, civil servants and officials (see Chapter 4). Thus, the increasing number of gatherings of ministers and experts has become a routine feature of EU governance (Puetter, 2012: 56). Moreover, a wide range of executive and regulatory agencies have been established and empowered at the expense of the supranational institutions. This complex network of committees, agencies and working groups favours the policy coordination between member states and by the same token avoids transferring power to supranational institutions (Bickerton et al., 2015: 703). One revealing example is the Eurogroup, which brings together euro area finance ministers and representatives of the Commission and the ECB. The Eurogroup acts as an 'informal forum for euro area dialogue' (Puetter, 2012: 61), but its role in EU policy-making raises political and legal questions and fuels controversies because of the stark contrast between its informal character on the one hand and the power of its decisions for member states on the other. The eurozone crisis accelerated and accentuated the empowerment of member states.

Against this backdrop, the decisions taken to save the euro increased the perception that the EP and the Commission find themselves on the losing side and that they fail to shape fundamental policy choices in the new economic governance in accordance with their political views (Crum, 2015: 1). From 2010 to 2012 the role of a supranational institution such as the European Commission and the EP had been drastically reduced, most of the decisions related to the eurozone's new governance architecture being adopted through opaque negotiations in intergovernmental meetings. Thus, it has been argued that the room for manoeuvre of the Commission in the different stages of the policy process (agenda setting, formulation, decision-making, implementation and evaluation) is diminishing. However, scholars remain divided on this finding. Whereas some scholars observed a disempowerment of the Commission, others demonstrated that the Commission's power had been strengthened in the aftermath of the eurozone crisis. For example, Crum suggests that the new prerogatives conferred on the Commission, in particular the monitoring competences to analyse the performance of member states along a set of economic and fiscal indicators, are 'administrative in kind' but also subject to political instructions from member states (2015: 5). If member states empower the Commission, this is explained by Schimmelfennig as an illustration of the willingness of member states to centralise decision-making and to reduce the uncertainty about the behaviour of other governments (2015: 188). In contrast, others maintain that the Commission has emerged as the winner of the eurozone crisis as the powers granted in the aftermath of the eurozone crisis go beyond the initiation of the policy process (Bauer and Becker, 2014: 215). The academic debate on the transformation of EU's modes of governance and the shifting of institutional balance between intergovernmental and community method is ongoing and illustrated by the chapters in Parts I and II of this volume.

1.5   EU Policies: Between Integration by Stealth and Politicisation

1.5.1   A Seeming Paradox

Since the mid-1990s, the expression 'integration by stealth' has been used by political scientists to describe how national elites are pursuing policy-making in Brussels remote from public scrutiny, without submitting their decisions to a contradictory debate in democratic fora. It is typically associated with the figure of Jean Monnet and his conception of incremental integration leading gradually to the building of a federal polity. Integration by stealth has been criticised not only for being too elitist (Featherstone, 1994), somewhat of a 'Eurocrat's dream' (Chalmers et al., 2016: 21), but also for producing policies which are not fully efficient (Majone, 2005).

Looking at the development of EU policies over the past ten years, a paradoxical picture appears *prima facie*: integration by stealth has continued while, at the same time, EU matters have been increasingly politicised, bringing about resistance. On the one hand, the crises have generated new needs for Europeans to solve problems collectively (migration flows, collapse of financial institutions, debt, recession, threats to security, etc.), and on the other hand, an increasing number of citizens and elites have expressed reluctance to give more powers to EU institutions to solve these problems. In fact, more and more political actors today reclaim national sovereignty over policies decided in Brussels, Frankfurt and elsewhere. Theoretically, this can be read as a growing tension between the (neo)functionalist logic of 'spillover' (Haas, 2004; Schmitter, 1970) and the postfunctionalist effect of 'constraining dissensus' (Down and Wilson, 2008; Hooghe and Marks, 2009). Yet, as Börzel and Risse (2018) have convincingly pointed out, the paradox is only apparent if one considers the key role played by politicisation. In EU studies, politicisation is commonly understood as the concomitant increasing salience of EU matters in the public sphere, the increasing mobilisation of a larger number of political and societal actors and the increasing polarisation among those actors (Hutter et al., 2016). The EU's multiple crises, and the sense of emergency they created, generated an increased polarisation, bringing with it increasing politicisation 'at the bottom' in domestic arenas, which in turn led to politicisation 'from the bottom up' as national leaders tended to reflect the views of their national constituencies when taking a stance at EU level (for instance, the often mentioned preferences of the German voters as far as bailouts for Greece were concerned). But politicisation has also taken place 'at the top' among the main EU political actors in the form of power struggles over solutions to the crises, for instance between Jean-Claude Juncker and Viktor Orbán or within the ECB (Schmidt, 2019a).

1.5.2   Depoliticisation and Integration by Stealth

The outcomes of the Eurocrisis in 2008–2010 can be read as a case of integration by stealth since decision makers have been 'caught between the necessity to act and the political reluctance to acknowledge fully the consequences of a multilevel governance system, notably democratic legitimacy and accountability' (Mény, 2014). In the heat of the eurozone crisis, the mandate of the ECB was stretched to new tasks including providing liquidity, helping to set up new financial instruments in the form of loans to indebted countries and ending up being the Union's actual lender of last resort (see Chapter 9). Together with the European Commission and the IMF, the ECB was also part of the so-called Troika, the informal technocratic alliance in charge of supervising the implementation of reforms attached as conditions to loans in countries under bailout programmes (namely Cyprus, Ireland, Greece and Portugal). Thus, the ECB and the Commission have been 'reinterpreting the rules by stealth' for problem-solving purposes (Schmidt, 2016b, forthcoming).

In the Eurocrisis, elites have mostly sought to depoliticise decisions about reforming EMU. Member states agreed to harden the rules of economic coordination through the revision of the SGP and the toughening of fiscal discipline on the grounds that 'there is no alternative' for a stable monetary union having to gain the trust of financial markets. Through the European Semester, budget making, macroeconomic policy and social policy have all been more centralised with multilateral surveillance of the Council associated by the bureaucratic steering from the European Commission. With regard to social policy, though, no major overhaul or leap forwards could take place in order to address adequately the social consequences of the recession and the rise of inequalities. While social policy-making at EU level remains weak and patchy, the ambiguity of the 'structural reforms' advocated by the EU institutions reflects the EU's ambivalent role in welfare states' modernisation/debasing (see Chapter 10). Only occasionally has politicisation brought about more EU regulation, as in the revision of the Posted Workers Directive, in a balancing act trying to define fair free movement of workers across diverse European labour markets (see Chapter 11). This reminds us that the single market has always been differentiated across the four freedoms and generates constant political bargains 'in order to make markets work effectively, and to reconcile different ideas about the constitutive nature of markets' (see Chapter 8).

1.5.3   Contained Politicisation and Stagnation

Politicisation has not been absent from the socio-economic realm, and it mainly took the form of popular resentment against 'austeritarianism', but with little impact on EU decision-making as such. As Della Porta and Parks argue (2018), what we have witnessed since 2008 is rather a closing down of political opportunities, as decisions have been made in diplomatic summits of the European Council or more secretive technocratic bodies. Occupy, the Indignados or more recently the Yellow Vests embody an anti-establishment form of politicisation which has left the decision-making sphere relatively autonomous. In a more diffuse manner, the crisis fuelled the will of some EU policy makers to regain legitimacy. In the face of scandals such as LuxLeaks or the Panama Papers and activism from non-governmental organisations (NGOs) calling for 'tax justice', the European Commission pushed, for instance, for more transparency and harmonisation in tax policy globally; but its efforts (and credibility) were undermined by prevailing member states' interests (see Chapter 15).

Trade can be regarded as a policy area 'in crisis', where contestation has only been on the rise ever since the Seattle summit in 1999 until massive protests against the ratification of Transatlantic Trade and Investment Partnership (TTIP) and the Comprehensive Economic and Trade Agreement (CETA) in 2013–16. In spite of growing citizens' concerns that such agreements entail unsustainable societal and environmental costs (see Chapter 7), integration by stealth continues as policy makers promote the signature of new bilateral free trade agreements (e.g. with Japan or Mexico), framing free trade as a solution to slow growth and detrimental protectionism (see Chapter 14).

As far as foreign policy and defence is concerned, some observers see Brexit and Donald Trump's erratic and aggressive leadership as constitutive factors of a crisis situation for the European foreign and defence policy (Anderson, 2019) in the sense that the functional pressure for Europeans to build a more coherent and autonomous security and defence policy has been raised. We have witnessed, especially since 2016, a proliferation of initiatives intended to substantiate the repeated calls for a 'genuinely European defence' made by European leaders (especially French presidents and, to a lesser extent, Angela Merkel). But the ambition to undertake a major policy overhaul to merge the various European military cultures is still lacking. Moreover, the emergence of the EU's 'strategic autonomy' is impeded by European leaders' unwillingness to rethink the EU's relationship with North Atlantic Treaty Organization (NATO), as argued by Howorth (see Chapter 16).

1.5.4 'Bottom-up' Politicisation and Selective Integration

The 'migration crisis', or better, the crisis of the Schengen area, illustrates how politicisation 'from the bottom up' (Schmidt, 2016) has had ambivalent effects on the Europeanisation of immigration policy (see Chapter 12). In the face of the massive influx of refugees from Syria and Africa to Europe in 2015, the European Commission proposed to revise the Dublin Agreement and, notably, to relocate approximately 160,000 refugees from Italy and Greece to other EU countries. Despite the proposal being adopted by the Council, Bulgaria, Cyprus, Hungary, Slovakia, Slovenia and Poland openly refused to implement this new mechanism and many other member states did not comply with their commitments. In 2018, only about 30,000 people had been relocated. In several EU countries, racist and xenophobic political forces have come to government by exploiting the idea that immigrants are an economic as well as a cultural threat to the native population in times of permanent austerity and generalised competition for jobs and income.

In this regard, Italy is a telling example of the political consequences of non-integration and the downward spiral of politicisation. For several years, the country had a rather liberal immigration policy, epitomised by the operation *Mare Nostrum* to save refugees from drowning in the Mediterranean Sea (2013–14), but its calls for burden sharing were met by indifference and collective inaction from the side of other EU member states. At the same time, Italy had been struggling with high debt and slow growth even before the 2008 financial crisis, and then with fiscal constraints and social retrenchment ever since the 2010 eurozone crisis. This caused a political backlash that brought to power an incongruous coalition of two populist parties with little ideologically in common, namely the far-right Lega and the difficult-to-categorise Movimento Cinque Stelle in 2018. This led to a radical change in Italy's immigration policy with the interior minister and figure-head of the Lega, Matteo Salvini, fuelling anti-immigrant discourse and prohibiting new arrivals of refugee boats into Italian ports. Political instability, though, led to a new change of government in summer 2019 and it remains to be seen how, with significant parts of the Italian public opinion highly hostile not only towards migrants but also towards the EU, the new government will deal with migration issues.

The obstacles to any renewal of EU asylum policy do not suggest that there was a complete stalemate in the whole realm of migration and border management, though. Instead, we have witnessed an increased securitisation of the field (see Chapter 12). While remaining highly divided on how they receive immigrants, member states have agreed to strengthen border control. Frontex was transformed into a better-endowed European border and coastguard agency responsible for pushing back immigrants who do not match restrictive criteria for seeking political asylum. This has had a major impact on the free circulation of persons within the Schengen area (see Chapter 13). 'Crimmigration', that is, the intellectual conflation of crime and immigration, has led a significant number of EU countries (ten in 2016, six as of September 2019) to reintroduce border controls.

In sum, policy-making resulting from the contemporary crises in the EU reflects complex dynamics of integration by stealth and politicisation. This has led to more integration or stagnation in a differentiated fashion across policy areas, depending on the degree of perceived functional pressure, and the success of some elites to politically exploit some themes more than others. The increased pervasiveness of conditionality in the discussions about the EU budget (see Chapter 6) is illustrative of how Europeans try to enforce principles and control mechanisms to tackle acute conflicts of interest and values in policy-making. The impact of such conflicts on the EU as a political community have become more salient as the multiple crises of the EU have unfolded.

1.6   The EU as a Community: From Disagreements to Differentiation?

1.6.1   The Initial Debate over the Democratic Deficit of the EU

It has become a truism to claim that the EU has been long affected by a crisis of democratic legitimacy. Ever since the mid-1990s, scholars and political actors have had controversial debates about the alleged 'democratic deficit' of the EU (Weiler et al., 1995) (see Chapter 19). For a long time, these debates have opposed those who conceived of the EU as a technocratic administration (or regulatory state in the view of Majone, 2005) geared at producing Pareto-efficient policies and sufficiently legitimated by checks and balances, and those who saw it as a polity in the making in need of more citizen participation and political competition. Increasingly, concerns have been raised not only about the EU's insufficient democratic credentials, but also about how its functioning was hollowing out democracy within national polities (Mair, 2013). While an ever wider range of policies were decided in Brussels without much public debate ('policies without politics'), domestic arenas, in turn, have remained the locus of fierce political struggles yet with an increasingly constrained autonomy for elected representatives to decide on policies ('politics without policies') (Schmidt, 2006). Citizens' dissatisfaction with national parliamentary democracy became acute when national governments adopted austerity policies under the auspices of the EU, making taxpayers and vulnerable groups suffer the consequences of the financial markets' failure (Armingeon and Guthmann, 2014).

Three main strategies have been pursued by European elites to tackle the democratic deficit which reflect three conceptions of what a European democracy should look like. The first has consisted in strengthening the powers of the EP as most elites remain convinced that parliamentarism is the essence of (representative) democracy. Yet, this was not sufficient to substantially improve the quality of linkage and representation performed by members of the EP (Brack and Costa, 2013). The second strategy, promoted primarily by the European Commission, has emphasised the need for 'good governance', a managerial vision of the political process whereby partnership replaces hierarchy and in which stakeholders' participation and 'ownership' can make policy-making more transparent. Epitomised by the *White Paper on Governance* from 2000, this vision remained geared at technocratic output legitimacy. Third, under the influence of fashionable theories of democracy and the activism of civil society organisations, a number of procedures have been introduced to enhance the participatory and deliberative nature of decision-making in the EU. Most of the institutionalised procedures (online consultations, citizens' agoras and fora, deliberation experiments at the EP, etc.) have rather turned into a democratic fig leaf (Aldrin and Hubbé, 2011) with little impact on actual decision-making. The contribution of organised civil society to the democratisation of the EU has been limited (Kohler-Koch, 2012). In turn, EU policy-making has brought about the professionalisation and bureaucratisation of organised civil society (Saurugger, 2009) and only occasional, conflict-based politicisation has constrained decision makers to change their position and prove responsive to public mobilisation (Parks, 2015). The failure of the European Citizen Initiative to bring about policy responses by the EU institutions further illustrates the pitfalls of participatory democracy in the EU.

None of those three strategies, therefore, has proved successful in responding to the EU's democratic deficit. In spite of growing criticism in the face of deteriorating policy outputs (with slow growth in the 2000s and rampant social retrenchment), the EU has remained a conservative system, hard to reform and continuously anchored in a centrist consensus with opposition forces finding very few channels for expression or effective impact. Thus, as predicted by Peter Mair (2007) (building on Robert Dahl's democratic theory), the impossibility to express 'classical opposition' over policies, has fed an 'opposition of principle' against the system itself and its personnel, in the form of Euroscepticism and populism.

1.6.2   Elusive Convergence and Conflicts of Values

Against this background, the recent financial and eurozone crises have triggered an acceleration of pre-existing centrifugal trends. Undeniably, the crises have revealed persisting conflicts in socio-economic ideas and preferences. Not only had the 'catch-up' not automatically followed from market and monetary integration, as European elites had believed; financial markets exerted punitive pressure on countries with weaker socio-economic structures, thus reinforcing the existing gap between a continental and northern wealthy core, on the one hand, and peripheries at the southern, eastern and Baltic fringes of the continent. While some catch-up took place throughout the 1990s and 2000s (Ireland being the most successful example), the 2008 financial crisis revealed the fragility of models relying heavily on credit in the south and on foreign direct investment (FDI) dependence in the east (see Chapter 17). Furthermore, said imbalances accentuated divisions among Europeans. The severe recession in many countries at the EU peripheries triggered or accentuated migrations from Southern or Eastern Europeans seeking better opportunities in prosperous core countries. One consequence of those migration flows has been the decline in support for welfare state spending in host countries, thus feeding inequalities within societies (Cappelen and Peeters, 2018). The fact that the southern periphery had to bear the cost of economic adjustment in the eurozone crisis also caused a democratic disenchantment in South European countries in particular (Armingeon et al., 2016). Persisting or growing inequalities between and within EU countries therefore raise the question of whether all countries have equally profited from the single market and the euro and, if we recognise that this is not the case, what mechanisms for more solidarity and social cohesion could or should be introduced at EU level (Sangiovanni, 2013; Crespy, 2019).

Besides the socio-economic realm, centrifugal movements affecting the EU as a community of states and citizens have concerned cultural and societal values. The role of religion, especially Christianity, in the public and political sphere and its relationship with other religions was contentious before the crisis (Foret, 2015) as the controversy on the possible accession of Turkey to the EU in the early 2000s has shown. Furthermore, there has been an ongoing debate about the existence of a so-called *Leitkultur*[3] and the best way to deal with immigration and the

---

[3] The term refers to the debate in Germany over the compatibility between Christian-based cultures and other cultures.

heterogenisation of European societies. The migration wave of 2015 contributed to the almost hysterical exacerbation of these debates. In many European countries, theories such as 'the great replacement'[4] of native populations by immigrants have taken root. Xenophobic and racist theses have been voiced particularly strongly by governing parties in Scandinavia, Austria, Italy and Central and Eastern Europe, and far-right parties have emerged where they had not existed over the past decades, for instance Vox in Spain, the Golden Dawn in Greece and Alternative für Deutschland in Germany.

Finally, a more novel aspect of EU politics, perhaps, has been the rise of the critique of liberal democracy itself (see Chapter 18). In Central and Eastern Europe, the EU had promoted a process of democratisation after the demise of communism and in the run-up to the 2004 enlargement. Yet, Poland, Hungary and the Czech Republic have witnessed a democratic backlash. There, leaders have not only diffused ultra conservative and xenophobic discourse, they have also implemented specific reforms aimed at curtailing the freedom of the press and the independence of the judiciary (Coman, 2014), thus tapping into a process of dedemocratisation or autocratisation (Tomini, 2015). This development triggered lively debates in the EU as to the possibility to adopt sanctions for the violation of the EU's common values, especially the integrity of the rule of law, according to Article 7 TEU. Such politicisation of values, including democracy, has allowed Viktor Orbán to profile himself as a hero defending the 'true Europeans' against the faceless Brussels technocracy (Coman and Leconte, 2019).

1.6.3   Brexit and Differentiated Integration

The decision by a majority of British citizens, on 25 June 2016, to leave the EU constitutes a climax in an EU torn apart by the centrifugal forces discussed above. While Brexit's outcomes still remain uncertain at the time of writing, it has been a powerful reminder that the 'ever closer' Union was in no way an ineluctable end of integration and that the EU, which had only been expanding since its origins, could be territorially affected by disintegrative forces. In fact, the British exit political saga seems to be a mirror of all Europe's current ills. The campaign, first, strongly focused on migration issues and the rapid rise of newly arrived immigrants (indistinctly from inside or outside the EU), mainly described by the UK Independence Party as a burden on public services and the welfare state. A sociological analysis of the Brexit vote, then, revealed a strongly divided country, with 'chronically economically depressed areas [...] voting to leave the EU, especially when they had experienced recent sudden changes in the composition of the local

---

[4] This racist conspiracy theory claims that the native population in Europe will be replaced by immigrants from the Middle East and Africa. While having old roots, it has been revived by the French far-right writer and activist Renaud Camus who published in 2010 a book entitled *Le Grand Remplacement*.

population' (Clegg, 2017: 38). From the point of view of political economy, this can be seen as the result of the long-standing restructuring of British capitalism with a growth model combining the prominent role of the finance industry with a weakly regulated labour market thus fuelling social inequalities (Hay and Bailey, 2019). At a deeper level of understanding, the regime crisis triggered by the Brexit referendum shows that, behind the classic EU vs. national sovereignty line of conflict, EU membership has gone hand in hand with deep constitutional change by stealth, as Bickerton argues (2019). It has upset the historically entrenched balance between parliamentarism and the executive, and eventually set off a conflict between parliamentary and popular sovereignty within the UK more than anywhere else. Finally, this regime crisis has seen the rise of a populist figure, Boris Johnson, who seeks to embody the alleged will of the people summarised in a politically powerful motto: 'taking back control' from Brussels.

The aggravation of disagreements among Europeans over the appropriate socio-economic models, the societal values, the nature of democracy and the *finalité* of the EU itself eventually raises the question of a need for greater differentiation within the EU. Far from new, this debate has gained momentum over the past ten years. Interestingly, rationalist scholars as well as theorists of *demoicracy* (see Chapter 19) agree that differentiation is a legitimate answer to the heterogeneity of dependence, capacities and preferences across EU countries (Schimmelfennig, 2019) or the heterogeneity of economic, social and cultural choices (Bellamy and Kröger, 2017). In spite of tangible functional and normative grounds, differentiated integration poses a number of practical and political dilemmas yet to be solved.

The myriad concepts which have populated the public debate can be clustered around three types which already coexist in the EU today (Holzinger and Schimmelfennig, 2012: 296). The first relies on temporal differentiation, namely the idea that all member states go in the same direction but at a different pace to accommodate adaptation ('two-' or 'multi-speed Europe'). Except for the UK and Denmark, for example, EU members were only granted a temporary opt-out of the euro and are supposed to join when meeting the economic requirements. However, as Latvia and Lithuania joined in 2014 and 2015, other countries – like Sweden or Poland – are unwilling to join for political reasons. Thus, temporary differentiation can freeze as not all member states agree on the overall direction of integration regardless of pace.

The second model is grounded on spatial differentiation, whereby various countries engage with various degrees of integration ('core Europe' or the 'Europe of concentric circles'). As pointed by Holzinger and Schimmelfennig (2012), this raises the question whether such differentiation should happen within or outside the legal framework provided by the EU treaties. Furthermore, the idea of a 'core' implies a more advanced form of political integration to which not even the founding members of the EEC subscribe to today. While the euro area is often mentioned as the most obvious 'core' of the EU, it is hard to see how nineteen countries (i.e. two-thirds of the members) could agree on and effectively reach a high degree of integration required by a federal type of integration project.

Overlapping with spatial differentiation, the third model involves sectoral differentiation where not all member states participate in all EU policies. Sometimes seen as 'anything goes' or *Europe à la carte*, a better way of conceptualising such differentiation is as making for a 'soft core' Europe constituted by overlapping clusters of member states in the many different EU policy communities (Schmidt, 2019b). Again, this is already the case with the EMU or the Schengen area. But should this logic be generalised, with member states opting in rather than opting out as a matter of exception? Here, the limited success of enhanced cooperation enshrined in the treaties (Article 20 TEU) sheds light on the dilemmas involved. Enhanced cooperation on a financial transaction tax shows how the compromises necessary to reach a critical mass of participants can also affect the effectiveness of the policy solutions agreed. After lengthy negotiations started in 2010, ten countries agreed to adopt it, but the proposal was so watered down that the tax is now expected to generate ten times less revenue than initially envisaged (i.e. €3 billion per year instead of €30 billion). A better way to use sectoral differentiation, then, would be to encourage governments to opt in or out of 'blocks' of integration in large, coherent policy domains.

In a nutshell, all three forms of differentiation already exist in the EU, but their systematisation constituting a new model of integration involves tremendous dilemmas in terms of functional problem solving and political legitimacy. Decision makers and bureaucrats from the European Commission have proved well aware of the rampant conflicts which threaten to bring about a collapse of the EU. In March 2017, it contributed to the debate by putting forward a White Paper presenting five alternative scenarios ranging from less to more integration or status quo (European Commission, 2017). However, the paper failed to trigger a debate among member states' governments (let alone citizens) where political forces would consider their options to ensure the viability of the EU and secure the collective goods it should serve to generate.

While we argue that the multiple crises from the last decade represent a critical juncture in EU politics and policy-making, it should not be seen as one which brought about a paradigm change. Rather, in the overwhelming majority of policy areas, recent multiple crises acted as an accelerator of pre-crisis trends, especially the reinforcement of ordoliberal fiscal discipline, market liberalisation (including labour markets and international trade) and the securitisation of migrations and borders. The more novel aspect to EU politics therefore lies with the increased politicisation of EU policy-making and the question of how to deal with resistance from some sections within European societies to responses to problems through more integration. So far, it can be argued, post-functional politics and the anti-EU politics that brought about the rise of populist parties in many EU countries has not led to any significant 'spill-back' via the de-Europeanisation of existing policies. Yet, it has exacerbated centrifugal forces tearing apart Europeans as a community. This involves stark divergences in values about economic models and solidarity, multiculturalism and religion, and, ultimately, democracy itself.

REFERENCES

Aldrin, P. and Hubbé, N. (2011). 'Becoming Europe's Ambassadors: A Political Analysis of the First Pan-European Deliberative Poll Experiment. A Political Reading of the First Experience of European Deliberative Democracy'. *Politique européenne*, 34(2): 95–134.

Anderson, J. (2019). 'The Integration of Core State Powers and "Polycrisis": A Series of Unfortunate Events'. Paper prepared for the international workshop Furthering or Fighting Core State Power Integration? The Post-Maastricht Ambiguities of German EU Policy, Berlin, 24–5 June 2019.

Armingeon, K. and Guthmann, K. (2014). 'Democracy in Crisis? The Declining Support for National Democracy in European Countries, 2007–2011'. *European Journal of Political Research*, 53(3): 423–42.

Armingeon, K., Guthmann, K. and Weisstanner, D. (2016). 'How the Euro Divides the Union: The Effect of Economic Adjustment on Support for Democracy in Europe'. *Socio-Economic Review*, 14(1): 1–26.

Bauer, M. B. and Becker, S. (2014). 'The Unexpected Winner of the Crisis: The European Commission's Strengthened Role in Economic Governance'. *Journal of European Integration*, 36:3, 213–29.

Bellamy, R. and Kröger, S. (2017). 'A Democratic Justification of Differentiated Integration in a Heterogeneous EU'. *Journal of European Integration*, 39(5: 625–39.

Bickerton, C. (2019). '"Parliamentary", "Popular" and "Pooled": Conflicts of Sovereignty in the United Kingdom's Exit from the European Union'. *Journal of European Integration*, 41(7): 887–902.

Bickerton J. C., Hodson, D., and Puetter U. (eds) (2015). *The New Intergovernmentalism and the Study of European Integration*. Oxford: Oxford University Press.

Blyth, M. (2013). 'Paradigms and Paradox: The Politics of Economic Ideas in Two Moments of Crisis'. *Governance* 26(2): 197–215.

Bocquillon, P. and Dobbels, M. (2014). 'An Elephant on the 13th Floor of the Berlaymont? European Council and Commission Relations in Legislative Agenda Setting'. *Journal of European Public Policy*, 21(1): 20–38.

Börzel, T. and Risse, T. (2018). 'From the Euro to the Schengen Crises: European Integration Theories, Politicization, and Identity Politics'. *Journal of European Public Policy*, 25(1): 83–108.

Brack, N. and Costa, O. (2013). 'The Challenges of Territorial Representation at the Supranational Level: The Case of French Meps'. *French Politics*, 11(1): 1–23.

Brack, N. and Gürkan, S. (eds) (forthcoming). *Theorizing the Crises of the European Union*. London: Routledge.

Capoccia, G. and Kelemen, D. (2007). 'The Study of Critical Junctures: Theory, Narrative, and Counterfactuals in Historical Institutionalism'. *World Politics* 59(3): 341–69.

Cappelen, C. and Peters, Y. (2018). 'Diversity and Welfare State Legitimacy in Europe: The Challenge of Intra-EU Migration'. *Journal of European Public Policy*, 25(9): 1336–56.

Chalmers, D., Jachtenfuchs, M. and Joerges, C. (eds) (2016). 'The Retransformation of Europe'. In D. Chalmers, M. Jachtenfuchs and C. Joerges (eds), *The End of the Eurocrat's Dream*. Cambridge: Cambridge University Press.

Clegg, D. (2017). 'Brexit, the UK Labour Market and Lessons for Social Europe'. In B. Vanhercke, S. Sabato and D. Bouget (eds), *Social Policy in the European Union: State of Play 2017*. Brussels: ETUI.

Coman, R. (2014). '*Quo Vadis* Judicial Reforms? The Quest for Judicial Independence in Central and Eastern Europe'. *Europe-Asia Studies*, 66(6): 892–924.

Coman, R. (2019). 'Values and Power Conflicts in Framing Borders and Borderlands: The 2013 Reform of EU Schengen Governance'. *Journal of Borderlands Studies*, 34(5): 685–98.

Coman, R. and Leconte, C. (2019). 'Contesting EU Authority in the Name of European Identity: The New Clothes of the Sovereignty Discourse in Central Europe'. *Journal of European Integration*, 41(7): 855–870. https://doi.org/10.1080/07036337.2019.1665660.

Crespy, A. (2019). 'Solidarité et justice sociale dans l'Union européenne: Les trois défis d'une convergence par le haut'. In R. Coman, L. Fromont and A. Weyembergh (eds), *La solidarité européenne: Enjeux et perspectives*. Bruxelles: Bruylant.

Crespy, A. and Vanheuverzwijn, P. (2017). 'What "Brussels" Means by Structural Reforms: Empty Signifier or Constructive Ambiguity?' *Comparative European Politics*, **17**, 92–111. https://doi.org/10.1057/s41295-017-0111-0.

Crum, B. J. J. (2015). 'The Emergence of an EU "Multilevel Parliamentaery Field": Is There a Role for Subnational Parliaments?' In G. Abels and A. Eppler (eds), *Subnational Parliaments in the EU Multi-Level Parliamentary System: Taking Stock of the Post-Lisbon Era*, Vol. 3. Innsbruck: StudienVerlag.

De Gaulle, C. (1967). 'General's de Gaulle press conference of November 27.' In *Congressional Record: Proceedings and Debates of the 90th Congress First Session*, Vol. 113, Part 25, November 22, 1967 to December 4, 1967, 33597–4994.

De Schoutheete, P. (2012). *The European Council and the Community Method*. Notre Europe, Policy Paper 56.

Della Porta, D. and Parks L. (2018). 'Social Movements, the European Crisis, and EU Political Opportunities'. *Comparative European Politics*, 16(1): 85–102.

Down, I. and Wilson, C. J. (2008). 'From "Permissive Consensus" to "Constraining Dissensus": A Polarizing Union?' *Acta Politica*, 43(1): 26–49.

Dyson, K. (2000). 'EMU as Europeanization: Convergence, Diversity and Contingency'. *Journal of Common Market Studies*, 38(4): 645–66.

Dyson, K. (ed.) (2008). *The Euro at 10: Europeanization, Convergence and Power*. Oxford: Oxford University Press.

Dyson, K. and Quaglia, L. (2010). *European Economic Governance and Policies*, 2 vols. Oxford: Oxford University Press.

European Commission (2015). 'Communication from the Commission to the European Parliament, the Council, the European Economic and Social Committee and the Committee of the Regions: A European Agenda on Migration'. COM(2015)240 final, 1–22.

European Commission (2017). *White Paper on the Future of Europe*. COM(2017)2025, 1 March 2017.

Fabbrini, S. (2015). *Which European Union?* Cambridge: Cambridge University Press.

Featherstone, K. (1994). 'Jean Monnet and the "Democratic Deficit" in the European Union'. *Journal of Common Market Studies*, 32(2): 149–70.

Featherstone, K. and Papadimitriou, D. (2008). *The Limits of Europeanization: Reform Capacity and Policy Conflict in Greece.* Basingstoke: Palgrave Macmillan

Fioretos, O. (2012). 'Coordinated Versus Liberal Market Economies'. In E. Jones et al. (eds), *The Oxford Handbook of the European Union.* Oxford: Oxford University Press.

Foret, F. (2015). *Religion and Politics in the European Union: The Secular Canopy.* Cambridge: Cambridge University Press.

Gamble, A. (2013). 'Neo-liberalism and Fiscal Conservatism'. In V. A. Schmidt and M. Thatcher (eds), *Resilient Liberalism in Europe's Political Economy.* Cambridge: Cambridge University Press.

Grimmel, A. and My Giang, S. (eds) (2017). *Solidarity in the EU: A Fundamental Value in Crisis.* Cham: Springer.

Haas, E. (2004). *The Unitying of Europe: Political, Social and Economic Forces 1950–1957.* Notre Dame: University of Notre Dame Press, 3rd edition.

Hay, C. and Bailey, D. (eds) (2019). *Diverging Capitalisms: Britain, the City of London and Europe.* Basingstoke: Palgrave.

Holzinger, K. and Schimmelfennig, F. (2012). 'Differentiated Integration and the European Union: Many Concepts, Sparse Theory, Few Data'. *Journal of European Public Policy*, 19(2): 292–305.

Hooghe, L. and Marks, G. (2009). 'A Postfunctionalist Theory of European Integration: From Permissive Consensus to Constraining Dissensus'. *British Journal of Political Science*, 39(1): 1–23.

Hooghe, L. and Marks, G. (2018). 'Cleavage Theory Meets Europe's Crises: Lipset, Rokkan, and the Transnational Cleavage'. *Journal of European Public Policy*, 25: 1.

Hooghe, L. and Marks, G. (2019). 'Grand Theories of European Integration in the Twenty-first Century'. *Journal of European Public Policy*, 26(8): 1113–33.

Hutter, E., Grande, S. and Kriesi, H. (eds) (2016). *Politicising Europe: Integration and Mass Politics.* Cambridge: Cambridge University Press.

Jones, E. (2012). 'The JCMS Annual Review Lecture European Crisis, European Solidarity'. *Journal of Common Market Studies*, 50, Annual Review: 53–67.

Jones, E. et al. (2016). 'Failing Forward? The Euro Crisis and the Incomplete Nature of European Integration'. *Comparative Political Studies*, 49(7): 1010–34.

Keohane, R. and Hoffmann, S. (1991). *The New European Community.* Boulder: Westview Press.

Kohler-Koch, B. (2012). 'Post-Maastricht Civil Society and Participatory Democracy'. *Journal of European Integration*, 34(7): 809–24.

Krzyżanowski, M., Triandafyllidou, A. and Wodak, R. (2018). 'The Mediatization and the Politicization of the "Refugee Crisis" in Europe'. *Journal of Immigrant & Refugee Studies*, 16:1–2, 1–14.

Lefkofridi, Z. and Schmitter, P. C. (2014). 'A Good or a Bad Crisis for the European Union?' In M. J. Rodrigues and E. Xiarchogiannopoulou (eds), *The Eurozone Crisis and the Transformation of EU Governance: Internal and External Implications.* Routledge: London.

Lefkofridi, Z. and Schmitter, P. C. (2015). 'Transcending or Descending? European Integration in Times of Crisis'. *European Political Science Review*, 7(1): 3–22.

Mair, P. (2007). 'Political Opposition and the European Union'. *Government and Opposition*, 42, (1): 1–17.

Mair, P. (2013). *Ruling the Void: The Hollowing of Western Democracy.* London: Verso.

Majone, G. (2005). *Dilemmas of European Integration: The Ambiguities and Pitfalls of Integration by Stealth.* Oxford: Oxford University Press.

Manners, I. (2002). 'Normative Power Europe: A Contradiction in Terms?' *Journal of Common Market Studies*, 40(2): 235–58.

Matthijs, M. and Blyth, M. (eds) (2016). *The Future of the Euro.* New York: Oxford University Press.

Matthijs, M. (2017). 'Integration at What Price? The Erosion of National Democracy in the Euro Periphery'. *Government and Opposition* 52(2): 266–94.

Mény, Y. (2014). 'Managing the EU Crises: Another Way of Integration by Stealth?' *West European Politics*, 37(6): 1336–53.

Parks, L. (2015). *Social Movement Campaigns on EU Policy: In the Corridors and in the Streets.* Basingstoke, Palgrave.

Pierson, P. (2004). 'Politics in Time: History, Institutions, and Social Analysis'. In J. Mahoney and D. Rueschemeyer (eds), *Comparative Historical Analysis in the Social Sciences*, Princeton: Princeton University Press.

Piris, J.-C. (2010). *The Lisbon Treaty: A Legal and Political Analysis*, Cambridge: Cambridge University Press.

Pollack, M. A., Wallace, H. and Young, A. R. (2010). 'EU Policy-making in Challenging Times: Adversity, Adaptability and Resilience'. In H. Wallace et al. (eds), *Policy-making in the European Union.* Oxford: Oxford University Press.

Puetter, U. (2014). *The European Council and the Council: New Intergovernmentalism and Institutional Change.* Oxford: Oxford University Press.

Puetter, U. (2012). 'Europe's Deliberative Intergovernmentalism: The Role of the Council and European Council in EU Economic Governance'. *Journal of European Public Policy*, 19(2): 161–78.

Sangiovanni, A. (2013). 'Solidarity in the European Union'. *Oxford Journal of Legal Studies*, 33(2): 213–41.

Saurugger, S. (2009). 'Interest Groups and Democracy in the European Union'. *West European Politics*, 31(6): 1274–91.

Savage, J. D. and Verdun, A. (2015). 'Strengthening the European Commission's Budgetary and Economic Surveillance Capacity Since Greece and the Euro Area Crisis: A Study of Five Directorates-general'. *Journal of European Public Policy*, DOI:10.1080/1350176 3.2015.1041417.

Schimmelfennig, F. (2015). 'Liberal Intergovernmentalism and the Euro Area Crisis'. *Journal of European Public Policy*, 22(2): 177–95.

Schimmelfennig, F. (2019). 'The Choice for Differentiated Europe: An Intergovernmentalist Theoretical Framework'. *Comparative European Politics*, 17(1): 176–91.

Schmidt, V. A. (2002). *The Future of European Capitalism.* Oxford: Oxford University Press.

Schmidt, V. A. (2006). *Democracy in Europe: The EU and National Polities.* Oxford and New York: Oxford University Press.

Schmidt, V. A. (2010). 'The Unfinished Architecture of Europe's Economic Union'. *Governance*, 23(4): 555–9.

Schmidt, V. A. (2015). 'Forgotten Democratic Legitimacy: "Governing by the Rules" and "Ruling by the Numbers"'. In M. Matthijs and M. Blyth (eds), *The Future of the Euro*. New York: Oxford University Press.

Schmidt, V. A. (2016). 'Reinterpreting the Rules "by Stealth" in Times of Crisis: The European Central Bank and the European Commission'. *West European Politics*, 39(5): 1032–52.

Schmidt, V. A. (2019a). 'Politicization in the EU: Between National Politics and EU Political Dynamics'. *Journal of European Public Policy*, 26(7): 1018–36.

Schmidt, V. A. (2019b). 'The Future of Differentiated Integration: A "Soft-core," Multi-clustered Europe of Overlapping Policy Communities'. *Comparative European Politics*, 17(2): 294–315.

Schmidt, V. A. (forthcoming). *Europe's Crisis of Legitimacy: Governing by Rules and Ruling by Numbers in the Eurozone*. Oxford: Oxford University Press.

Schmitter, P. (1970). 'A Revised Theory of Regional Integration'. *International Organization*, 24(4): 836–68.

Seabrooke, L. and Tsingou, E. (2018). 'Europe's Fast- and Slow-burning Crises'. *Journal of European Public Policy*, DOI:10.1080/13501763.2018.1446456.

Tomini, L. (2015). *Democratizing Central and Eastern Europe: Successes and failures of the European Union*. London: Routledge.

Van Houtum, H. and Boedeltje, F. (2009). 'Europe's Shame: Death at the Borders of the EU'. *Antipode*, 41(2): 226–30.

Van Houtum, H. and Pijpers, R. (2007). 'The European Union as a Gated Community: The Two-Faced Border and Immigration Regime of the EU'. *Antipode* 39(2): 291–309.

Weiler, J., Haltern, U. and and Mayer, F. (1995). 'European Democracy and its Critique'. *West European Politics*, 18(3): 4–39.

PART I
The EU's Political Regime

This part examines the evolution of European regional integration since World War II, with a focus on the dramatic politics of the past ten years. The turmoil surrounding the 2010 eurozone crisis put the EU's legitimacy at risk and created expectations for major policy and institutional change. Against this backdrop, it explains how recent crises have affected not only EU governance – that is, institutions and decision-making procedures – in practice but also the deeper theoretical understandings through controversies among scholars in the field.

The chapters brought together in Part I shed light on:

- How has European regional integration evolved since World War II onwards?
- How has the EU governance architecture been transformed over time?
- How have recent crises reshaped the EU's decision-making regimes?
- Which institutions are more powerful in the decision-making process?
- Which EU actors are the main drivers of European integration?
- Who is holding the steering wheel?
- What defines their decision-making procedures?
- What are the features of the new EU's political regimes?
- What is the role played by regulatory networks and policy communities in the EU's decision-making process?
- How and to what extent have recent crises also challenged traditional theories of EU integration?

To do so, Kiran Klaus Patel traces the origins and the evolution of the EU, arguing that many of the characteristics and challenges that the EU faces in our own time have deep historical roots. The chapter examines the emergence of the EU as a political regime and community. Analysing European regional integration from the twentieth to the twenty-first century in a comparative perspective, Patel shows that the first European

Communities were a 'fragile latecomer to an already densely populated field of international organisations'. The chapter shows that the evolution of the European Community has been shaped not only by crises and renegotiations between member states but also with other international organisations.

Since the beginning, the integration process stood as a difficult political dilemma on whether to allow transfer of power to supranational institutions (the Commission, the EP, the Court of Justice) or to protect national sovereignty and to resist attempts to supranationalisation by strengthening The powers of member states in the Council. Two methods of integration have driven the integration process: the community/supranational method and the intergovernmental method. As Sergio Fabbrini shows in his chapter 'Institutions and Decision-Making in the European Union', these methods developed in parallel. The former was applied for issues of low political salience regarding the single market's policies, while the latter applied to policies of high domestic political salience. The Maastricht Treaty of 1992 was the turning point for the differentiation of these two decision-making regimes. The chapter discusses the evolution of these regimes as well as the gradual empowerment of EU institutions. the chapter shows that the balance of power between institutions at the EU level has changed over the last decade but recent institutional dynamics, Fabbrini concludes, did not lead to an increase of supranationalism.

The European political regime is characterised by the participation of a wide range of actors in governance. Jacob Hasselbalch and Eleni Tsingou explain the role that regulatory networks and policy communities play in EU policy-making today. Their role in the EU decision-making process depends on what binds these groupings together along various dimensions: shared knowledge, common interests, the collective adoption of a scientific paradigm, the adherence to particular norms or visions for the future or a combination of the above. Furthermore, the role of these actors also depends on how they are positioned within regulatory frameworks. A final dimension is that the role of networks and policy communities is contingent on whether these are spaces within which dissent, controversy, and deliberation are tolerated or negotiated, and the extent to which they serve to politicise or depoliticise particular issues.

Recent crises and changes in the balance of power and decision-making procedures at the EU level have led scholars to revisit traditional theories of EU integration. As Vivien A. Schmidt explains while examining the 'old' and 'new' concepts building on intergovernmentalism, supranationalism and parliamentarism, EU scholars have long been divided on the answers. In the traditional debates, *intergovernmentalists* insisted that the member states engaged in interest-based bargaining in the Council were in charge, whereas *supranationalists* maintained that the Commission, the EP and the European Court of Justice (ECJ) drove integration via institutional dynamics of neo-functionalist *spillover*. Schmidt shows that although this divide continues today in EU studies, there are *new* arguments which distinguish the initial conceptualisations from more recent ones. As Schmidt explains in her chapter:

- The *new intergovernmentalists* insist that member state governments engaged in consensus-seeking deliberation in the (European) Council have retaken control.
- The *new supranationalists* view EU-level institutional actors as driving integration through ideational innovation and persuasion.
- The *new parliamentarists* point to new formal and informal ways in which the EP has gained increasing influence.

2 European Regional Integration from the Twentieth to the Twenty-first Century

KIRAN KLAUS PATEL

2.1 Introduction

European integration never followed a clear-cut path, and the forerunners of today's EU were never the only forums of regional integration in Europe. By the early 1950s, when the ECSC, the EU's first predecessor organisation, was established, internationalisation and globalisation had reached a point where the states of Western Europe no longer formed self-contained entities – if they ever had. Driven by the lessons of the economic and social crises of the past, and the recent experience of global war, genocide and mass displacement, hundreds of new international organisations cropped up worldwide, with a clear geographic focus on the North Atlantic region and even more on Western Europe (*Yearbook of International Organizations*, 1986: figures 2 and 3). This raises the question of why the European Communities eventually managed to turn into the primary and increasingly also the dominant forum of regional integration in (Western) Europe. This brief historical overview analyses the history of the pre-Maastricht European Communities (EC) and of the EU for the period between the Maastricht and the Lisbon Treaties in order to prepare the ground for the other chapters in this collection with their focus on current developments.

In line with the book's overall structure, the chapter first discusses the EU as a political regime, then briefly examines some of its policies and finally offers a succinct discussion of some of the key historical dimensions of the EU as political community. Overall, it demonstrates that many of the problems and challenges that the EU faces in our own time are less new than often assumed. Having said that, today's EU is a fundamentally different creature than its predecessors – most importantly because now it is the primary and increasingly also the dominant forum of regional cooperation and integration in Europe with genuine systemic relevance – a feature it did not have during the Cold War period. Even disintegration and the debate about 'less Europe' are not fundamentally new; as this chapter shows, the EU's trajectory, crises and challenges have become more critical for the fate of Europeans and non-Europeans than ever before.

2.2   The EU's Political Regime in Context

The EU was not the first and never the only forum of regional cooperation and integration in Europe. Even after 1945, as the period most relevant for this chapter, several other organisations were already moving in a similar direction before the EU's predecessors were established. These earlier and alternative efforts are ignored or marginalised in most existing textbooks and the dominant theories of European integration. Instead, the standard story tends to assume that during the postwar decades, nations basically had to choose between national sovereignty on the one hand and integration based on the EC model on the other. This underestimates two aspects: First, the EC was a fragile latecomer to an already densely populated field of international organisations; seventy years ago (and more recently too) it appeared rather unlikely that this particular organisation would one day come to be identified with Europe as a whole, or even just with Western Europe. And second, the integration process was not only shaped by the participating states and the general historical context, but also influenced by a veritable web of relationships with other Western European organisations and transnational forums (Patel, 2013b).

BOX 2.1 Key concepts

Political regime. A political regime is an arrangement of political structures and procedures with its own institutions and rules (formal and informal). Political regimes have clear substantive and geographical limits. Political regimes can refer to various spatial levels, ranging from the local to the international, and they can be studied on both empirical and normative levels.

 Political community. Political community here refers to the relationship between a political regime on the one hand and individuals and social groups on the other hand, particularly to questions regarding whether the latter support and accept a political regime and see it as legitimate.

As a latecomer to this process, the EC illustrated several lessons from the history of regional cooperation and integration during the first five years after World War II. First, it reflected the tendency to go for a rather small geographical scope, with comparably homogenous member states, instead of larger and more diverse forums. Second, it epitomised the trend to prioritise low politics instead of more contentious issues of high politics where national interests often obstructed an agreement. Third, the EC stood for a particularly intense form of integration, with more legal muscle than other and earlier efforts of regional cooperation. This in turn was only possible thanks to the homogeneity and hence the small size of this new community (Patel, 2020).

First, on size: the first significant effort of regional cooperation and integration in postwar Europe was the United Nations Economic Commission for Europe (UNECE), founded in 1947 under the auspices of the United Nations (see Table 2.1). Originally, it brought together eighteen states. The UNECE included parts of Western Europe, but also Eastern European states like Czechoslovakia and Poland, as well as the two superpowers, the United States and the Soviet Union. The UNECE understood itself as a pan-European institution with the mission of coordinating the reconstruction of Europe and keeping the spirit of the wartime alliance against Nazism and fascism alive. The latter task became obsolete just months after the UNECE had been set up (Stinsky, 2019). The escalating Cold War quickly led to the formation of three camps: East, West and neutral. By 1950, when the Schuman Declaration paved the way for the ECSC, the Iron Curtain had become a defining reality, restricting the scope of all new attempts at regional integration to one of the two main camps, and leaving comparably little room for manoeuvre for the neutrals. Since during the early Cold War, the Eastern camp prioritised a communist form of global internationalism over specifically European formats of cooperation, regional integration with an emphatic focus on Europe was soon restricted to Western Europe. Established in 1952, the ECSC reflects how the geographic scope of European regional cooperation had shrunk in the short period of five years since the UNECE had been set up: instead of the UNECE's eighteen members, it brought together a mere six Western European states (Belgium, France, West Germany, Italy, Luxembourg and the Netherlands).

Table 2.1 Founding member states of various European organisations

UNECE (1947)	Brussels Pact (1948)	OEEC (1948)	Council of Europe (1949)
Belgium, Byelorussia, Czechoslovakia, Denmark, France, Greece, Iceland, Luxembourg, Netherlands, Norway, Poland, Sweden, Turkey, United Kingdom, United States of America, Ukraine, USSR, Yugoslavia	Belgium, France, Luxembourg, Netherlands, United Kingdom	Austria, Belgium, Denmark, France, Greece, Iceland, Ireland, Italy, Luxembourg, Netherlands, Norway, Portugal, Sweden, Switzerland, Turkey, United Kingdom	Belgium, Denmark, France, Ireland, Italy, Luxembourg, Netherlands, Norway, Sweden, United Kingdom

The Federal Republic of Germany's participation as a founding member – the first time the western part of the divided country was invited to join a club of European regional integration as a founding member – also reflected the new, increasingly ineluctable contours of the Cold War (Rasch and Düwell, 2007; Gillingham, 1991).

Second, on high vs. low politics: security concerns, as the core of high politics, had defined the purpose of the Brussels Pact, established in 1948 by five Western European states. NATO, created one year later, assumed a similar role for the North Atlantic area. As the Cold War gained momentum, Western Europe's international security mostly came to be organised in a transatlantic context, with the United States as benevolent hegemon. The EU's predecessors, in contrast, were mainly preoccupied with issues of low politics, chiefly with economic questions. This held particularly true after 1954, when its attempts to build up a European Defence and a European Political Community failed. The EC's secondary role, under the radar of the most pressing concerns of international politics at a time of immense security threats, gave it the room to slowly develop and consolidate. But its low politics focus also explains why the EC was not the foremost forum of regional integration in Western Europe. This was also the case because the EC did not even monopolise questions of trade and economic governance; some twenty other regional organisations, most prominently the Organisation for Economic Co-operation and Development (OECD) (originally founded under the auspices of the Marshall Plan in 1948 under the acronym OEEC), were also busy in this field in Western Europe (Patel, 2013b; Loth, 2015: 20–74).

Third, on the precise form of integration: while the EU's predecessors had less member states and dealt with less crucial issues than other attempts at regional cooperation and integration in Europe, the EC stood out in another respect. Already the ECSC as the EU's first predecessor had greater powers in comparison to the intergovernmental setup of all other international organisations in Western Europe. Due to its supranational dimension, thanks to which member states surrendered some of their sovereignty to a High Authority, it was able to take legally binding majority decisions with immediate effect within the member states, without these first having to be implemented in national law. The two organisations that joined the ECSC on the basis of the Treaties of Rome in 1957 – the EEC and Euratom – were also partly supranational, meaning that they were able to take legally binding majority decisions with the potential of having immediate effect within the member states. All three organisations that ultimately formed the EC shared this characteristic. This supranational trait also explains why the EC originally had less member states than other international organisations in Western Europe such as the OECD or the Council of Europe, another forum set up in 1949. Many Western European states were not prvepared to accept as great a transfer of power as the EC aimed at. Next to the Cold War realities, this specificity of its legal setup and governance structures explains why the EC started out so small (De Witte and Thies, 2013; Spierenburg and Poidevin, 1994).

Having said that, it is easy to overemphasise the legal and administrative differences between the EC and other efforts of regional cooperation and integration, such as the UNECE, the Brussels Pact, the OECD or the Council of Europe, at least for the first and formative years in their existence. The characterisation of the EC as *sui generis* (of its own kind, exceptional) which already existed in the 1950s and was pushed for by its supporters is truly misleading.

In the EC, supranationalism was always highly contested, with top politicians such as Charles de Gaulle (president of the French Fifth Republic, 1959–69) and Margaret Thatcher (British prime minister, 1979–90) as strident opponents. Moreover, the transfer of powers to Brussels always remained partial and important supranational powers were not set in stone in the EC's foundational treaties (Nicola and Davies, 2017). Some of them only came into being thanks to the ECJ and its rulings since the early 1960s. With the so-called Luxembourg Compromise of January 1966, the member states made sure that vital national interests could triumph over the idea of a further shift towards supranationalism. Even if the discourse of a pursuit of an 'ever closer union' lingered and even if federalists continued to ferociously push for deeper integration, the Luxembourg Compromise had already turned the EC into a hybrid creature. Intergovernmental elements, according to which ultimate powers remain with the member states, came to play a more permanent role than originally foreseen (Ludlow, 2006: 71–124).

All in all, postwar regional cooperation and integration in Europe became a maze of partly overlapping, partly competing organisations. During the early 1960s, it was still unclear that the EC would one day outpace all others; the OECD was a particularly serious contender. Moreover, the parallel existence of multiple organisations was a permanent feature: earlier forums were not discontinued once the EC was set up; instead, conflict and cooperation between these organisations became a defining feature of Western Europe's international governance structures. It was only from the 1970s and 1980s onwards that the EC acquired the lead over normal international organisations (Patel and Kaiser, 2017; Patel, 2013b), and why it eventually developed into the 'most prominent institutional pioneer in regionalism' (Lenz and Burilkov, 2017; also see Hooghe et al., 2017).

2.3 The EC's Development into the Main Forum of (Western) European Integration

Three factors stand out when assessing why the EC developed into the primary, and increasingly the dominant, forum of integration in Western Europe. First, the focus on a customs union and a common market (originating in the ECSC and even more in the EEC) turned out to be crucial in the long run (see Chapter 8). That economic logic produced many functional connections to other areas. This was already recognised in the 1950s, in the sense of spillover effects from one policy domain to another: the creation of the common market had repercussions in other areas such as hygiene standards, consumer protection, vocational training and social policy. Research has long demonstrated that such spillovers did not come from nowhere: the integration dynamic did not always leap from one policy area to another, and where it did this certainly did not occur quasi-automatically. What mattered more was that there were groups and institutions insisting on supposed or actual inherent necessities and fighting to expand the powers of the EC – be they the Commission, the Parliament, transnational interest groups or individual member states. For example, in agriculture, once common market organisations existed for cereals, meat, dairy products and vegetables, it was only a matter of time before the vintners, the olive growers and even the flax and hemp farmers demanded similar arrangements (Knudsen, 2009; Ludlow, 2005). In each case the logic of the market raised questions that rubbed off on other policy areas, which then had to be accordingly promoted or constrained. Again, the comparison to other forums is revealing. The Council of Europe, for example, was responsible for the vital matter of human rights. But in discharging this overtly political responsibility, it found itself facing much greater resistance from member states than did the EC, with its economic focus along with its more technocratic and seemingly apolitical attire. In view of the overwhelming predominance of the nation state as the model for political order, the 'romantic' programme of European cultural and ethical unification associated with the Council of Europe offered much less spillover into other areas, or at least fewer actors successfully advocating such a course, in comparison to the economic logic of the EC (Duranti, 2017).

Second, there was European law. The piecemeal emergence of a legal culture of its own with a strong binding character, from legislation to implementation, gave the Community a great advantage over other Western European organisations. The latter were generally reliant on voluntary cooperation by their member states to implement broadly couched agreements into national law. In the EC, even ordinary citizens were able to appeal directly to the ECJ under certain conditions, which was not the case with organisations like the OECD and the Council of Europe. This lent a specific dynamic to the ECJ of the EU and the development of law in the Community. At a very general level, the role of the ECJ was frequently decisive in expanding the powers of the EC, not least by a very broad interpretation of the market-driven mandate of the treaties. The impact of European law – directly applicable and largely independent of the law of the member states – was the EU's strongest weapon (De Witte and Thies, 2013; Nicola and Davies, 2017).

Third and finally, the EC commanded larger financial resources than other Western European organisations. The OECD's budget allowed for little more than funding its secretariat, a modicum of statistical research and a few expert commissions. Matters were little different for the Council of Europe. The EEC, by contrast, possessed revenues of its own from 1970, while the ECSC had enjoyed the same since the very beginning. This made the EC comparatively independent of its member states, especially where spending decisions lay largely with the Commission and the Parliament. The arrangement was hard fought; but once in place it granted the EC a degree of freedom that its rivals could only envy. Together, these three factors propelled the EC into a position of primacy among regional organisations in Western Europe (Patel and Kaiser, 2017).

2.4   Widening, Disintegration and Venue Choice

The EC's gradual rise is also reflected in the decisions of third states. Already in the early 1960s, Turkey, Greece and Spain considered an application for membership. But the biggest success came in 1961 when the United Kingdom applied to join the EC. With this step, it chose to abandon the European Free Trade Association, yet another regional trade organisation and free trade area that the UK had set up as a competitor to the EC only one year earlier, in 1960. Even if a French veto ultimately shot down Britain's application, this plea for membership represented an almost immeasurable symbolic boost for the EC. This was even truer once new members joined, starting with the northern enlargement of 1973, when the UK, Ireland and Denmark accessed the EC, and continuing with the six further enlargement rounds that led to today's EU having more than twenty member states. This trend was further substantiated by the growing number of states negotiating association agreements and other further forms of economic and political ties with the EC (Kaiser and Elvert, 2004; Vahsen, 2010).

   This does not mean that deepening and widening were the only trends. Since its early days, the EU experienced clear counter-tendencies, even if these have been ignored in standard accounts of European integration. Disintegration commenced as early as 1962, when Algeria parted ways with the emerging EC. With its roughly eleven million inhabitants, the North African country had joined the EC as part of France's global empire. In formal terms, however, Algeria – unlike for example Tunisia or Senegal – was not a colony but a part of France itself, constituting several of its *départements*. It then left the EC in parallel to its separation from France after a bloody war of independence. Occurring in the foundational period of the EC, the event left barely a trace in the history of European integration, and the same holds true for the case of Greenland. The world's largest island with a population of just 50,000 joined the EC in 1973 as part of the Kingdom of Denmark. It left the EC in 1985 while remaining with Denmark. Admittedly, both Algeria and Greenland had not joined the EC as sovereign states, but within the context of European colonialism – a core dimension of contemporary European history that most accounts of EU history completely ignore. This colonial framework is a marked difference to today's Brexit, even if Brexit also brought up thorny questions about Europe's imperial legacy, as in the case of Gibraltar. Beyond such differences, the cases of Algeria and Greenland demonstrate that the current phase is not the first in which the status quo of European integration has been challenged and reversed. This also holds true due to dysfunctionalities which EU studies have failed to take seriously – let alone to theorise – until recently. The CAP, a central pillar of the EC during the Cold War, became dysfunctional for some time in the 1960s and 1970s because its mechanisms hinged on fixed exchange rates – and thus on questions of monetary policy which, at the time, were beyond the control of the EC (see also Chapter 7). While the CAP continued to exist, the crisis produced a temporary renationalisation of the common agricultural market. These developments were rather technical; still, they demonstrate that processes of widening and deepening were repeatedly counter-balanced by disintegration and dysfunctionalities (Patel, 2020).

Finally, the choice for the EU was never uncontested. When the economic crises of the 1970s hit Western Europe after some thirty years of immense growth, deeper integration was by no means the default mode of the respective governments in power. On questions of economic governance, which were at the core of European integration at the time, the member states often first prioritised national measures, bilateralism and other formats of international cooperation, for instance the General Agreement on Tariffs and Trade (GATT) and the OECD. Only by the mid-1980s did they opt for the EC as their key venue of economic coordination and integration (Warlouzet, 2017).

All in all, widening and deepening were never the sole directions that the integration process knew, even if this narrative dominates existing accounts. The EC was a latecomer in a densely crowded arena of regional organisations and only incrementally came to play the primary role. Crises and reorientations, such as the Luxembourg Compromise, defined its trajectory and defy simplistic and linear accounts of its history.

2.5   Policy and Polity Development by Trial and Error

No overriding logic or clear-cut division of labour defined the policy areas the EU's predecessors were active in. The ECSC was about sectoral economic integration, creating shared rules for two industries which at the time were indispensable to wage war. Their integration was meant to make a military conflict impossible – but the 1950 Schuman Declaration, the ECSC's starting point, also reflected very specific national interests on the part of the French government (Gillingham,

1991). The next two plans would have rotated the EC in a very different direction – defence and political integration – but these projects were abandoned after the French Parliament's veto in 1954. The Treaties of Rome then saw the return to a project with a sectoral, economic orientation – Euratom with its focus on nuclear power – but also the EEC with its much broader ambitions. The EEC was set up to establish a common market with free movement of goods, services, people and capital and common external trade rules (Loth, 2015: 36–74; see also Chapter 8).

The somewhat haphazard overall character of the early European Communities was also reflected in its fragmented organisational structure. While the Communities shared some institutional structures such as the Parliamentary Assembly (the predecessor of today's EP), each of them also had separate bodies. It took a whole decade until the three Communities merged further into one. Especially during this early period, EU integration was characterised by trial and error. Key actors such as Jean Monnet, one of the most influential supporters of European unity who mostly worked behind the scenes and without a major official position, tried to identify issues for which the interests of the member states overlapped sufficiently to allow for new initiatives, while also avoiding those areas in which another regional organisation was already working successfully (Schwabe, 2016).

The latter clearly mattered. It helps to explain, for instance, the divergent fate of agricultural and transport integration under the EC banner. Both fields were part of the 1957 EEC Treaty with rather vague stipulations. Ten years after the treaty, the CAP had turned into the policy domain with the largest bureaucracy, the highest costs and the biggest controversies in the whole EC. Transport, in contrast, remained marginal in EC policy-making until the 1990s – not least because more technical bodies outside the EC, such as the so-called European Conference of Ministers of Transport, took care of the international coordination needs in Western Europe. As so often, business actors and stakeholders – in this case railway companies and the transport sector more generally – mattered, and for a long time they preferred the legally less rigid and geographically broader format of the EC's contenders over integration under the banner of 'Brussels' (Patel and Schot, 2011).

Over time, however, the EU tapped into more and more policy fields, mainly thanks to its economic rationale. After the foundational period of the 1950s, which saw the creation of the three original Communities, particularly the economic and political challenges of the 1970s sparked new initiatives. This contradicts the standard narrative, according to which this decade was a 'dark age' of European integration (Keohane and Hoffmann, 1991). This misperception partly results from the fact that most of these new initiatives developed incrementally and without a firm treaty base; in fact, many of them were only later given a robust legal basis with the SEA (1986), the Maastricht Treaty (1992) and more recent treaties. Obvious examples are the efforts during the 1970s to venture into monetary policies; other than that, the decade also saw initiatives in fields as diverse as foreign and security policy, environmental protection and health. With its roots in the Treaty of Rome, regional policy slowly evolved from its roots in the CAP after the first enlargement (Hiepel, 2014; Laursen, 2014). Also from the 1970s, the EC even developed the rudiments of its own cultural policy – partly because culture was conceptualised as a sphere to be exempted from the EC's economic rationale; partly because various actors from the Commission and some of the member states felt that efforts in this field were needed to give the integration project new legitimacy (Patel, 2013a).

This expansion of the EC's policy domains implied a renegotiation of the relationship to other international organisations. The 1970s saw fierce competition between them, for instance on environmental policy as a domain that was only 'invented' as a comprehensive field of international policy-making at the decade's beginning. At the time, the OECD, the Council of Europe and even, for instance, NATO became active on this hot issue. As the most recent research shows, these forums did not just coexist and compete; time and again, they also cooperated with and emulated each other. Here and in other contexts, the EC often proved receptive to ideas, approaches and governance structures first discussed and implemented in other international organisations; repeatedly it adapted such approaches and developed them further. Its greater legal integration as well as its larger financial means helped it to eventually emerge as the key forum on environmental issues in Western Europe. And environmental policy is only one example (Kaiser and Meyer, 2016). On trade, for instance, the EC has outpaced the OECD since the 1960s and 1970s, while on regional policies and more and more also on human rights issues, it started to compete with the Council of Europe. In all these cases, the EC selectively adapted policies first developed in other forums. Also during this period, nation states did not see the EC as the only alternative to national sovereignty or to traditional diplomatic formats – instead, they shopped around for various venues. In the end, however, they more and more frequently ended up in the emporium of the EC (Patel and Kaiser, 2017).

The majority of these changes happened incrementally and remained below the radar of most citizens. During the Cold War, the EC mostly dealt with issues of comparably low political and economic salience. Admittedly, the ECSC was set up to prevent war among the member states by integrating the coal and steel sectors. However, some of its key features fell defunct only a few years after this earliest predecessor of the EU had been set up. For Western Europe's security, NATO always remained much more important than any EC policy. The common market removed trade barriers but also here, negotiations and results remained mostly technical. The CAP, finally, was a means to secure the peaceful transition of the primary sector into a post-agricultural and even a post-industrial world; in that sense, it was more a social than an economic policy. Many policy makers, experts and citizens considered its high costs a serious nuisance – still, the substantial budget earmarked for the support of farmers never threatened to wreck the stability of the member states. In that sense, the economic and systemic impact of EC policies remained secondary. Where it mattered more was at the symbolic level. Again, particularly since the 1970s, the EC came to represent all efforts of European integration, and to secure a peaceful, prosperous future for the (Western half of the) continent. This symbolic role, however, should not be confused with the actual salience and impact of its policies on the societies of its member states.

2.6   Differentiation in Integration

The EU only gained real systemic importance when the reform debates and initiatives of the 1970s and 1980s fully impacted on political practice from the 1990s onwards. The most important project in this context was the EMU, initiated on the basis of the Maastricht Treaty and achieved in three stages. The most far-reaching accomplishment was the introduction of the single currency in 1999 and actual euro notes and coins three years later. Again, the prehistory is revealing. Monetary policy, as the EMU's backbone, had remained beyond the powers of the EC in the 1950s and 1960s. That does not mean that no cooperation existed in this field. The capitalist monetary order of the time was secured by the Bretton Woods system, an international arrangement in which the US dollar was tied to gold and other Western currencies were linked to the dollar at a fixed exchange rate. But when Bretton Woods collapsed in the early 1970s, a yawning governance gap opened up which the EC sought to close through various measures. Whereas its initiatives during the 1970s and 1980s were not too successful, the EMU lifted developments to a fundamentally different level. Similar processes also characterised other fields, such as migration, where the full weight of the EU only came to be felt after the end of the Cold War (Mourlon-Druol, 2012).

The EU's complicated journey to become the foremost forum of Western European cooperation was bound up with an apparently paradoxical counter-current. At the very moment when it began to attain full-spectrum salience and primacy and deal with increasingly portentous questions, centrifugal forces accelerated. These dynamics sometimes triggered processes of disintegration and dysfunctionality, but also led to a new phenomenon within the EC: it now became clear that only certain member states were willing or able to participate in certain projects. So primacy explains why discussions about 'variable geometry', 'multi-speed Europe', 'differentiated integration' or 'Europe à la carte' increasingly gained momentum. This discussion first got serious in the mid-1970s, when the question of a common monetary policy appeared on the EC's agenda, which would involve the integration process moving into a core sphere of state sovereignty at a time when the EC's first enlargement had already made its member states more heterogeneous than in the original community of six. The same held true during the 1980s and the debate about issues such as justice and home affairs; salience helps to explain why in not all EC member states did became part of the 1985 Schengen Agreement, which largely abolished internal border checks (see Chapters 12 and 13). The more important but also diverse the EC became, the harder it was to keep all member states on board in all projects (De Witte et al., 2017).

This differentiation trend has accelerated since the early 1990s. It has played a crucial role in shaping the debate about the EU ever since, further intensifying with the Common Foreign and Security Policy and the introduction of the euro, both of which were projects from which some member states abstained (see Chapters 9 and 16). Politicians, researchers and the public for a long time tried to ignore the full implications of this development. Instead, the discussion was dominated by an understanding of differentiation that was doubly short-sighted. On the one hand teleologically, it was assumed that everyone will ultimately reach the same goal, some simply more quickly than others. Only in recent years has an awareness surfaced that permanent differentiation is the most likely outcome. On the other hand, the problem has been framed too one-sidedly in terms of progressive deepening and enlargement, making it harder to achieve homogeneity. While that is certainly correct, the EC's gradual rise to become the foremost forum for European cooperation is also relevant. One reason for the proliferation of differentiation questions within the EC and today's EU is that the power of the EC increasingly closed off established arrangements for task sharing among multiple international organisations.

The EC became the primary forum, but in the longer term this also made it more vulnerable. If everything that matters is brought under one roof, the firewalls that once separated different organisations such as the EC, the OECD and the Council of Europe are lost. Crises in one policy area can now more easily spark crises in others because they are all handled in one and the same forum. In that sense, phenomena and processes conventionally seen as emanating from crises in the EC were in fact frequently the very result of its increasing salience and primacy.

2.7   The History of the EU as Political Community

On the history of the EU as political community, only one issue can briefly be assessed here: how citizens have felt about and related to the project of European integration. (Neo-)nationalist parties, Europhobia and the crisis of EU legitimacy are often seen as recent phenomena, fully visible since the global financial and the eurozone crises of the late 2000s and with antecedents only from the early 1990s in and around the Maastricht Treaty (Hooghe and Marks, 2009). While much of this is true, the Cold War days were also no halcyon period of European integration, and the support for and the legitimacy of the EU were always more fragile than we often think.

In the 1950s, the choice for Europe was far from uncontroversial. When the EU's predecessors were established, many Western Europeans still considered their respective empires as the best form of international engagement. Among the six original member states, Belgium, France, Italy and the Netherlands were still colonial powers of sorts. Moreover, communism was especially strong in France and Italy, collecting around or even more than 30 per cent of the vote. Western European communist parties fiercely fought against all early EU treaties; French communists for instance denounced the 1957 EEC Treaty as a US-led capitalist conspiracy against the European working class and the Soviet Union. Additionally, trade unions voiced significant concerns towards European integration. They criticised the European project for not addressing social issues enough and feared that it could lead to a dismantling of the social measures introduced in the various member states since 1945 (Crespy and Verschueren, 2009).

Admittedly, the very first postwar years in particular also saw substantial support for European integration. Youth groups uprooted border markers and demolished barriers, hoping to overcome a past characterised by nationalism, xenophobia, aggression and war. Seventeen-year-old Helmut Kohl was one of many participants of this protest against the reconstruction of nation states, and decades later, as chancellor of West Germany (1982–98), he cherished these teenage memories. Meanwhile, Winston Churchill's stepson, Duncan Sandys, played a key role in establishing the British European movement. Still, all this pro-European civil society activism had a rather narrow social basis, mostly concentrated on parts of the upper (in particular the educated) middle classes (Patel, 2020).

Activism did not increase over time; quite the contrary. In the early 1950s the young were the stalwarts of pro-European engagement, leading the charge in spectacular actions like the storming of the border posts. The European Youth Campaign set up in 1951 brought together roughly 500 youth organisations from seventeen Western European states to work for closer European integration. The youth also played a central symbolic role during this phase, a fresh generation epitomising a new start for society, leaving behind the age of war and nationalism (Norwig, 2016). A good decade later, the EC was already a force to be reckoned with in Western Europe. But it had largely lost the youth. Especially for the student movement of 1968, which now saw themselves as society's avant-garde, the integration process was a relatively marginal question. Among the 68ers, there was plenty of discussion about Europe, but almost none about the EC.

This public disinterest contrasts to some extent with developments at the ideological and party-political levels where – in comparison to the first two postwar decades – the rivalry between European integration and alternative models faded from the late 1960s and especially the 1970s. As decolonisation swept across the Global South, the imperial option looked increasingly implausible. The influence of the nation-fixated far right also dwindled and Western Europe's communist parties now showed increasing openness to the EC, welcoming some of its new political initiatives and starting to regard it as an alternative to dependency on the United States. All in all, the 'EC option' became less controversial during the second half of the Cold War – which does not mean it was of any special interest to its citizens.

So why was civil society engagement not more closely meshed with the new EC institutions? Partly, this had to do with home-grown problems of the early Europe activists, for instance with the fact that the various groups pursued diverging goals. An even more important factor had to do with an essential characteristic of the European integration process: its technocratic slant, which prioritised rational planning, efficiency and a belief in progress over democratic control, balance of powers and citizen participation. Already French Foreign Minister Robert Schuman's famous 1950 speech had a strong technocratic element – it lacked any preparatory public discussion. Major decisions were never put before national parliaments. According to public surveys, a majority in France would have welcomed a British EC entry – still, its refusal by President de Gaulle sufficed to kill such plans during the 1960s. But also for men like Schuman or Monnet, efficiency and outcome counted for more than direct democratic legitimacy or civil society participation. Much as the EC claimed to represent a completely new start, it stood in fact for an elitist understanding of politics and in continuity with the manner in which economic and other questions of a technical nature had been regulated in Europe since the nineteenth century. Under this technocratic understanding of politics, decisions were best left to experts. Given the complexity and urgency of policy issues, this technocratic slant continued to impact the EC also in later decades. New initiatives in fields such as monetary and environmental policy of the 1970s did not build on new treaties between the member states and were not laid before their populations. The same holds true for the creation of new policy mechanisms such as the European Council, which gathered the heads of state and government – another innovation of the 1970s which was first established informally. Here again we see the technocratic element (Kaiser and Schot, 2014).

The technocratic tendency was never absolute. There were always strong countervailing impulses. The supposedly apolitical experts in the High Authority of the ECSC acquired a strong counterweight in the guise of the Council of Ministers (requested above all by the Benelux states) and other forums. Civil society critique was never silenced. Moreover, the EP acquired growing clout over time, especially since its direct elections in 1979. Beyond its role of making concrete proposals in specific policy domains, it also addressed the very question of the EC's democratic legitimacy in depth. Even if the EP possessed certain powers analogous to those of national parliaments, it lacked the most important dimension associated with parliamentary democracy. Also after 1979, the composition of the EP still had no influence on the composition of the executive. Direct European elections still remained first and foremost popularity tests for national governments and were treated with concomitant disinterest by voters – as the turnout figures confirm. Changes in the EP brought some more formal democratic control of the EC and its institutions but that did little to improve its image and legitimacy for citizens in the member states (Rittberger, 2005).

All this explains why the integration process left so many hearts and minds behind as it progressed. At first glance it might seem astonishing that approval ratings in opinion polls and surveys were so consistently high. However, the wording of most questionnaires was vague – it was not fully clear that 'unification' specifically meant the EC and its work. Moreover, most citizens knew shockingly little about what the EC was or did. According to a survey from 1962, many people fundamentally liked 'the idea of European unification', but as soon as discussion turned to details their opinions became very vague: the vast majority were not able to name concrete effects of the EC (Gallup International, 1962: 4). By the end of the decade, when the Commission conducted a comprehensive survey, the situation was little better: 87 per cent approved more or less strongly of the integration process (27 per cent very strongly) but only 36 per cent were able to correctly name the six member states (Commission des Communautés Européennes, 1972: 201, 55). Saying 'yes' to 'Europe' did not mean knowing even the most basic of facts about the EC.

Approval was thus often no more than lip service. People supported the integration process as long as it remained abstract and had little impact on their everyday lives. These trends continued in later years. If we consider the last decade before the Maastricht Treaty, there are two relevant findings. On the one hand, the nominal support for the integration process remained consistently high. On the other hand, it is conspicuous that there were striking gaps in this phase between general approval of European unification, approval of the interviewees' own country's membership and personal affinity to the EC. The discrepancy was especially large between abstract support for integration and concrete support for the EC, as revealed by the crucial question of regret over its possible failure. Citizens everywhere identified considerably less with the EC than with the abstract objective of European unification (Eurobarometer, 1993: 13).

Altogether, postwar European integration was primarily a project of the elites. Even if some of the few parliamentary votes and referendums held over EC matters during the Cold War achieved fantastic results, attitudes towards the integration process – even before the Maastricht Treaty – were much less robust than had long been believed. European cooperation EC-style was based more on toleration than on genuine approval. At the same time, it would be false to place the blame for the EC's technocratic tendencies on 'power-mad Eurocrats' in the European Commission. Frequently it was the member states that blocked greater accessibility, whether in the form of more direct participation or more democratic control. For example, if Charles de Gaulle criticised Brussels as a technocratic behemoth that did not mean he had any interest in further curtailing national sovereignty by enabling more direct participation, civil society engagement and democratic control. In general terms many national politicians preferred to keep the EC at arm's length; to claim the credit for successes in the integration processes while blaming Europe for any problems. Brussels was painted black in order to allow the nation state to shine.

The post-Maastricht period saw a significant rise in anti-EU feelings. Although Euroscepticism was not a new phenomenon, it has become more established during the last three decades. The Maastricht Treaty impacted national sovereignty more than earlier treaties, and these changes gave leeway to Eurosceptic parties to argue that the EU was becoming too powerful and that the nation state was, as a result, under threat. The eurozone crisis and the EU's reactions to its challenges exacerbated the sceptical feelings towards the Union. The United Kingdom's Brexit referendum and the process it triggered was a hallmark of Euroscepticism's new strength. Having said that, these forms of opposition towards the EU have also fuelled new support in other circles, thus leading to an increased polarisation over EU issues (Leruth et al., 2018).

The predecessors of today's EU were not the only forum of regional cooperation and integration that emerged in Western Europe after 1945. The Brussels Pact, NATO, OECD, UNECE and the Council of Europe are all examples of other such efforts, even if most accounts marginalise their respective contributions. It was only from the 1970s and 1980s onwards that the EC became an entity which far exceeded the roles of these other forums, thus also transcending the remit and scope of a normal international organisation. The EC's staunchest supporters – and its fiercest critics – had already seen the potential for such a development decades before. From the perspective of today, however, it is crucial to distinguish between visions and projections on the one hand and the actual role of the EC/EU on the other. From that angle, the eventual rise of the EU to become the foremost forum of cooperation and integration in Europe was not a given, nor were its capacities to impact global affairs. It arrived in such a position as the result of a decades-long process full of twists and turns. It requires rigorous historical analysis to uncover these developments, which have long been buried beneath narratives and interpretative patterns that were strongly shaped by the actors involved in the European integration process itself.

GROUP DISCUSSION

- Which three main factors explain why the EC developed into the primary and increasingly also the dominant forum of integration in (Western) Europe since the 1950s?
- How have citizens felt about and related to European integration, and why has civil society engagement not been more closely meshed with the new EC institutions since the 1950s?

TOPICS FOR INDIVIDUAL RESEARCH

- Find an example of how the EC's economic logic led to new initiatives and policy developments. Try to explain the dynamics at stake.
- Search for an example of the interrelationship between the EC's rise in importance on the one hand and tendencies to opt for differentiated integration on the other hand.

FURTHER READINGS

Dinan, D. (ed.) (2014). *Origins and Evolution of the European Union*. Oxford: Oxford University Press, 2nd edition.

Kaiser, W. and Elvert, J. (eds) (2004). *European Union Enlargement: A Comparative History*. Routledge: London.

Loth, W. (2015). *Building Europe: A History of European Unification*. Berlin: De Gruyter.

Patel, K. K. (2020). Project Europe: A History. Cambridge: Cambridge University Press.

Warlouzet, L. (2017). *Governing Europe in a Globalizing World: Neoliberalism and its Alternatives Following the 1973 Oil Crisis*. London: Routledge.

REFERENCES

Commission des Communautés Européennes. (1972). *Les Européens et l'unification de l'Europe*, Bruxelles: Commission Européenne.

Crespy, A. and Verschueren, N. (2009). 'From Euroscepticism to Resistance to European Integration: An Interdisciplinary Perspective'. *Perspectives on European Politics and Society*, 10(3): 377–93.

De Witte, B., Ott, A. and Vos, E. (eds) (2017). *Between Flexibility and Disintegration: The Trajectory of Differentiation in EU Law*. Northampton, MA: Edward Elgar, 2017.

De Witte, B. and Thies, A. (2013). 'Why Choose Europe? The Place of the European Union in the Architecture of International Legal Cooperation'. In B. Van Vooren, S. Blockmans and J. Wouters, (eds), *The EU's Role in Global Governance: The Legal Dimension*. Oxford: Oxford University Press.

Duranti, M. (2017). *The Conservative Human Rights Revolution: European Identity, Transnational Politics, and the Origins of the European Convention*. Oxford: Oxford University Press.

Eurobarometer (2013). Edited by the European Commission. Luxembourg: Office for Official Publications of the EC.

Gallup International. (1962). *L'opinion publique et l'Europe des six*. Paris: Gallup.

Gillingham, J. (1991). *Coal, Steel, and the Rebirth of Europe, 1945–1955: The Germans and French from Ruhr Conflict to Economic Community*. Cambridge: Cambridge University Press.

Hiepel, C. (ed.) (2014). *Europe in a Globalising World: Global Challenges and European Responses in the 'Long' 1970s*. Baden-Baden: Nomos.

Hooghe, L. and Marks, G. (2009). 'A Postfunctionalist Theory of European Integration: From Permissive Consensus to Constraining Dissensus'. *British Journal of Political Science*, 39: 1–23.

Hooghe, L., Marks, G., Lenz, T., Bezuijen, J., Ceka, B. and Derderyan, S. (2017). *Measuring International Authority: A Postfunctionalist Theory of Governance*, Vol. 3. Oxford: Oxford University Press.

Kaiser, W. and Elvert, J. (eds) (2004). *European Union Enlargement: A Comparative History*. Routledge: London.

Kaiser, W. and Meyer, J.-H. (eds) (2016). *International Organizations and Environmental Protection: Conservation and Globalization in the Twentieth Century*. New York: Berghahn.

Kaiser, W. and Schot, J. (2014). *Writing the Rules for Europe: Experts, Cartels, and International Organizations*. Houndmills: Palgrave Macmillan.

Keohane, R. O. and Hoffmann, S. (1991). 'Institutional Change in Europe in the 1980s'. In R. O. Keohane and S. Hoffmann (eds), *The New European Community: Decision-making and Institutional Change*. Boulder, CO: Westview Press.

Knudsen, A.-C. L. (2009). *Farmers on Welfare: The Making of Europe's Common Agricultural Policy*, Ithaca, NY: Cornell University Press.

Laursen, J. (ed.) (2014). *The Institutions and Dynamics of the European Community, 1973–83*. Baden-Baden: Nomos.

Lenz, T. and Buriklov, A. (2017). 'Institutional Pioneers in World Politics: Regional Institution Building and the Influence of the European Union'. *European Journal of International Relations*, 23: 654–80.

Leruth, B., Startin, N. and Usherwood, S. (eds) (2018). *The Routledge Handbook of Euroscepticism*. Abingdon: Routledge.

Loth, W. (2015). *Building Europe: A History of European Unification*. Berlin: De Gruyter.

Ludlow, N. P. (2005). 'The Making of the CAP: Towards a Historical Analysis of the EU's First Major Policy'. *Contemporary European History*, 14: 347–71.

Ludlow, N. P. (2006). *The European Community and the Crises of the 1960s: Negotiating the Gaullist Challenge*. London: Routledge.

Mourlon-Druol, E. (2012). *A Europe Made of Money: The Emergence of the European Monetary System*. Ithaca, NY: Cornell University Press.

Nicola, F. and Davies, B. (eds) (2017). *EU Law Stories: Contextual and Critical Histories of European Jurisprudence*. Cambridge: Cambridge University Press.

Norwig, C. (2016). *Die erste europäische Generation: Europakonstruktionen in der Europäischen Jugendkampagne 1951–1958*. Göttingen: Wallstein.

Patel, K. K. (ed.) (2013a). *The Cultural Politics of Europe: European Capitals of Culture and European Union since the 1980s*. London: Routledge.

Patel, K. K. (2013b). 'Provincialising European Union: Co-operation and Integration in Europe in a Historical Perspective'. *Contemporary European History*, 22: 649–73.

Patel, K. K. (2020). *Project Europe: A History*. Cambridge: Cambridge University Press.

Patel, K. K. and Kaiser, W. (2017). 'Multiple Connections in European Cooperation: International Organizations, Policy Ideas, Practices and Transfers 1967–1992'. *European Review of History, special issue*, 24(3): 337–57.

Patel, K. K. and Schot, J. (2011). 'Twisted Paths to European Integration: Comparing Agriculture and Transport in a Transnational Perspective'. *Contemporary European History*, 20: 383–403.

Rasch, M. and Düwell, K. (eds) (2007). *Anfänge und Auswirkungen der Montanunion auf Europa: Die Stahlindustrie in Politik und Wirtschaft*. Essen: Klartext.

Rittberger, B. (2005). *Building Europe's Parliament: Democratic Representation beyond the Nation State*. Oxford: Oxford University Press.

Schwabe, K. (2016). *Jean Monnet: Frankreich, die Deutschen und die Einigung Europas*. Baden-Baden: Nomos.

Spierenburg, D. and Poidevin, R. (1994). *The History of the High Authority of the European Coal and Steel Community*. London: Weidenfeld & Nicolson.

Stinsky, D. (2019). 'Sisyphus' Palace: The UNECE, East-West Trade, and Economic Cooperation in Postwar Europe'. Unpublished PhD thesis, Maastricht University.

Vahsen, U. (2010). *Eurafrikanische Entwicklungskooperation: Die Assoziierungspolitik der EWG gegenüber dem subsaharischen Afrika in den 1960er Jahren*, Stuttgart: Steiner Verlag.

Warlouzet, L. (2017). *Governing Europe in a Globalizing World: Neoliberalism and its Alternatives Following the 1973 Oil Crisis*. London: Routledge.

Yearbook of International Organizations (1986). Edition 1986/7: 23, Vol. 2.

3 Institutions and Decision-Making in the EU

SERGIO FABBRINI

3.1 Introduction

This chapter will investigate the decision-making structure of the EU. The EU is organised around supranational political institutions (such as the Commission and the EP) and political institutions representing member state governments (such as the Council of Ministers and the European Council). Certainly, other institutions affect the decision-making process, such as the ECJ or the ECB. However, they are technical institutions, whose functioning and deliberations are determined by their intrinsic rules rather than by political considerations. There are several interpretations of the EU decision-making structure. Börzel (2016: 12) posits that 'the EU's governance has evolved over time developing different varieties of inter- and transgovernmental negotiation and regulatory competition in the shadow of supranational hierarchy'. Wallace and Reh (2015) identified five regularised policy-making patterns (Community method, regulatory method, distributional model, intense transgovernmentalism and policy coordination) used for dealing with the various policy realms of the EU. Research on interstitial policies detected additional policy micro-patterns, although temporally bounded. This variety is generally reduced to four distinct patterns of taking decisions in the EU: Community method, centralised regulation, policy coordination and intergovernmental method. This Chapter regroups the four patterns into two basic decision-making regimes as a heuristic device for identifying the fundamental decision-making differentiation institutionalised within the EU. They are defined as decision-making regimes because they constitute a stable (although flexible) combination of rules and actors. The chapter assumes that the EU, since 1992, has ended up consolidating two decision-making regimes: supranational (inclusive of the Community method and centralised regulation) and intergovernmental (inclusive of policy coordination and intergovernmental method) which are stable decision-making regimes and not only transitory forms of intergovernmental and transgovernmental governance patterns or micro-decision-making patterns changing over time.

The basic decision-making differentiation of Table 3.1 is thus policy based, as the supranational regime deals with issues of low political salience connected to the single market's regulatory policies and the intergovernmental regime deals with policies of high domestic political salience that entered the EU agenda after

Table 3.1 EU decision-making regimes

	Regimes			
	Supranational decision-making regime		Intergovernmental decision-making regime	
	Community method	*Centralised regulation*	*Policy coordination*	*Intergovernmental method*
Policy areas (examples)	*Single market policies*	*Competition policies*	*Foreign and security policies*	*Economic policy of EMU*
Role of the Institutions				
Commission	High	Very high	Limited	Important
Council	High	High	Very high	Very high
EP	High	High	Limited	Limited
European Council	Limited	Limited	Very high	Very high

the end of the Cold War. The Maastricht Treaty of 1992 was the turning point for this differentiation. It formally recognised that the EU could proceed in the integration process into new areas for its member states provided that their governments were guaranteed an exclusive or pre-eminent decision-making role thanks to the strengthening of the intergovernmental institutions. Three distinct policy pillars were introduced with that treaty, together constituting an encompassing organisation now called the EU for the first time. Through these pillars, the unitary character of the organisation which emerged from the Treaties of Rome of 1957 was thus impaired. The differentiation of the decision-making regimes was further consolidated with the start of the EMU or eurozone in 1994, the economic policy side of which was put under the control of the intergovernmental institutions, whereas the monetary policy side was assigned to the full control of a supranational institution, the ECB. The 2009 Lisbon Treaty abolished the division into pillars, nonetheless it preserved the distinction between different decision-making regimes in relation to various European policies. It can be said that the Lisbon Treaty formalised a dual system constituted by both a supranational and intergovernmental decision-making regime, without preventing that different combinations of supranational and intergovernmental governance could develop regarding ad hoc micro-policy issues. The two regimes, and their different methods of taking decisions, have developed in parallel. However, with the post-2008 explosion of multiple crises (Caporaso and Rhodes, 2016) in policy fields under the intergovernmental governance, the two regimes have started to collide. The Chapter analyses the nature of the dual decision-making system and its functioning in the post-crisis EU (see Box 3.1).

> ## BOX 3.1 Decision-making regimes
>
> A decision-making regime consists in the institutional organisation of the policy-making process. It is equivalent to a governance regime based on regularised patterns of interaction between actors participating into the decision-making process. The EU decision-making system has a dual character in the sense that it consists of two basic decision-making regimes (supranational and intergovernmental).

3.2   The First Decades of the Integration Process

The EU was created in 1957 in Rome as a project for the construction of an integrated market on a continental scale, even if the first seed of integration was sown by the Paris Treaty of 1952 which set up the ECSC. Right from the start, it was put forward as the most advanced experiment of economic regionalism, taking the form of an integrated system to regulate a common market (see Chapter 8). It was inevitable that the EU started from a project of economic integration, after the French Assembly of the Fourth Republic voted against the European Common Defence project in 1954. After that vote, the main leaders of (Continental and Western) Europe decided to promote political integration through economic integration. Nonetheless, there is no doubt (Judt, 2005) that these leaders interpreted the creation of the (then) EEC as a response to the need to end a long era of civil wars on the European continent. If (with the Treaty of Rome of 1957) the conditions were created for a *civil* pact among former enemies, the institution of NATO in 1949 (in its turn strengthened in 1955 with the adhesion of Federal Germany) created the conditions for a *military* pact among them, a pact guaranteed by the predominant presence of the United States in that organisation (see Chapter 16). After two wars between Europeans that became global conflicts, the European nation states (starting with the continental ones) had to acknowledge that they would have no future unless they created a new political order (see also Chapter 1). The threat represented by the Cold War and the presence of the United States on the continent were the political factors that triggered the integration process.

With the EU, Western European nation states contributed to creating a supranational order aimed at facilitating increasingly close cooperation among them, on issues of common interest through the interaction between intergovernmental and supranational (frequently called 'community') institutions. The task assigned to supranational institutions (as the Commission and the ECJ) consisted of guaranteeing that the signatories to the intergovernmental agreements (the states) complied with the rules that they had set themselves. Thus, the supranational component of the EU (the Commission and the ECJ and then, increasingly, the EP) was necessary to protect the interstate component (represented originally by the Council of Ministers) from the possible fallout of rivalries among the states. In this sense, we can say that the EU is an attempt to domesticate the external relations of the European nation states, creating a supranational regime with domestic characteristics. This supranational regime is the outcome of the gradual consolidation of a complex network of institutions, some envisaged by the 1957 Rome Treaties (such as the Council of Ministers, the Commission and the EP, originally called Parliamentary Assembly constituted by delegates of national parliaments) and others not (such as the European Council of the heads of state or government). The intergovernmental institutions (the Council of Ministers and later the informal European Council) had to recognise the considerable influence that the Commission could exercise in the policy-making process, thanks to its monopoly of power in initiating legislative proposals (see Box 3.2). In addition, they also had to recognise the growth of the decision-making role of the EP, which, starting with its direct elections in 1979, had successfully claimed power, first to co-determine and then to co-decide on an increasingly broad range of policies (a power recognised from the SEA of 1986). At the same time, the supranational institutions had to recognise the strategic role of the European Council, which became (as from its first informal meetings in 1974) the arena to define the EU's long-term choices.

BOX 3.2 The legal activity of the EU

The legal activity of the EU is based on: (a) *regulations*, which are laws binding in all their elements and directly applicable in all member states. A regulation establishes direct rights and imposes duties on private parties without interference of national law. It is immediately enforceable in all member states simultaneously; (b) *directives*, which bind each member state to achieve a given result but leave the means and methods to the individual member states' discretion – it has to be transposed into national law and may concern a subgroup of member states; (c) *decisions*, which are binding too, but they are of an individual nature; and (d) *recommendations and opinions*, which are not binding but consist of orientation documents to implement and to interpret legislation.

In those three decades, the EU was thus institutionalised through interaction between supranational and intergovernmental institutions, interaction which was then termed the Community method (Dehousse, 2011), here conceptualised as a supranational decision-making regime. The supranational side and the intergovernmental side of the latter continued to grow together. Sometimes, the Commission's initiatives were resented by the Council of Ministers (as in the so-called 1965 'empty chair crisis' when French president Charles De Gaulle boycotted European institutions in a controversy regarding the ambitions of the Commission), but generally it was possible to reach cooperative relations between the two institutions. The EU has passed through a process of institutional development that routinised the decision-making process regarding the regulatory policies of the single market. This development institutionalised a complex but sufficiently stable collection of bodies which came to share the decision-making responsibility in a growing number of public policies (for this reason, the regime is defined as supranational).

In this process, the ECJ had a crucial role (Kelemen, 2011), introducing constitutional criteria in the operation of the supranational regime and in its dealings with the states participating in the integration process. The ECJ's decisions epitomised the principle of integration through law (see Box 3.3). At the end of the 1980s, the European nation states had been fully transformed into member states of the EU (Sbragia, 1994).

BOX 3.3 The ECJ and the market

By integration through law is meant a process of integration based on the approval of legislative measures, directives and regulations, judicially supervised by the ECJ. Two 1960s decisions of the ECJ laid the bases of the supranational market: one which established, in *Van Gend en Loos* of 1962, that certain community provisions have a direct effect on individual citizens and not only on the governments of the member states; and the other which established, in *Costa vs Enel* of 1964, that in the case of conflict between community legislation and the legislation of the member states, the former has priority over the latter, even if the latter was approved subsequently.

3.3 Decision-Making Differentiation: Supranationalism and Intergovernmentalism

With the fall of the Berlin Wall in November 1989 the problem of German unification came to the fore and, with the implosion of the Soviet Union in August 1991, the Cold War finally ended. Integrated Europe was forced to change its agenda. The EU could no longer limit itself to creating a single market (see Chapters 8 and 18). Above all it could no longer think that the reunification of Germany could be deferred indefinitely. Indeed, such reunification would happen at the end of 1990, with the help of the Americans and the doubts of the main European governments, and in exchange for the Germans giving up their national currency (the Deutsche mark) and supporting the formation of the EMU or eurozone to manage a new common currency (the euro). The Treaty of Maastricht of 1992, which was drafted by the previous year's Intergovernmental Conference, was the European response to these historic changes.

In preparing the treaty, it was recognised that the integration project was of a political and not solely economic nature. The name 'European Union' was introduced to mark the distance from the previous EEC. It was decided that the integration process should involve policy sectors not strictly connected to the single market. The time frames and the means were defined to adopt a common currency which could contain the economic force of Germany. However, these acknowledgements could not cancel out the divergences between states. Indeed, at the Maastricht Intergovernmental Conference, two fundamental compromises were signed. The first was the compromise between the states in favour of political integration (led by France and Germany) and the states (led by the United Kingdom) which were only interested in participating in a single market (as formalised by the SEA of 1986). The states interested in political union were authorised to go ahead, but the others could rule themselves out (through the so-called opt-out clause) of the more integrated policies (such as that of the common currency). The second compromise was celebrated in the group of states in favour of an 'ever closer union' (as recites the preamble of all the treaties since the 1957 Rome Treaties), between those (such as Italy, Belgium and the Germany of that period) which wanted to continue on the path of also constructing a supranational union in economic policy and those (such as France and the Netherlands) which instead wanted to strengthen the control of national governments over the new policies (from foreign affairs, security and financial policy in particular) (Fabbrini, 2015a).

The result was a treaty based on three pillars: the supranational one of the EC of single market and the two intergovernmental pillars of the Common Foreign and Security Policy (CFSP) and of the Justice and Home Affairs (JHA) policy. The treaty formally recognised that the EU could proceed in the integration process in crucial areas for its member states provided that their governments were guaranteed an exclusive decision-making role thanks to the strengthening of the intergovernmental institutions. This idea of *differentiating the decision-making regimes* further consolidated with the start of the eurozone in 1994. In order to respond to the German problem (i.e. to balance a country that had become, after the 1990 unification, demographically and economically asymmetrical vis-à-vis the other EU member states, and France particularly), it was decided to create a new currency, the euro (see Chapter 8), managed by a genuinely federal institution, the ECB, designed on the basis of the institutional model of the German federal bank, the

Deutsche Bundesbank, provided that the states maintained their freedom of action in policies linked to the common currency (such as fiscal and budgetary policy and more generally economic policy). However, this freedom of action, which was requested by the French government (Tuori and Tuori, 2014), was limited by the statutory definition of restrictions regarding the levels of deficit and public debt within which the economic policy of the individual states belonging to the eurozone could be undertaken. This limitation was imposed by the German government, worried that there might be a situation of moral hazard, by which some states may impose the cost of their erroneous choices (or non-choices) on other states (i.e. spending more money than is available, assuming the other states will then take care of the difference, their debt). Thus in 1997–8, the SGP was formalised, consisting of a resolution and two regulations. With the latter, the Council of Ministers of July 1997 decided to set the parameters within which the voluntary coordination should be undertaken (see Box 3.4).

BOX 3.4 The Stability and Growth Pact

The SGP consists of two regulations and one resolution. The first regulation (which came into force on 1 July 1998) intervened upstream, since it established the procedure for the surveillance of public budgets and for the coordination of the national economic policies. The second regulation (which came into force on 1 January 1999) intervened downstream, since it established the implementation procedure to be activated in the case of excessive deficit.

The decision taken in 1994 was therefore coherent with the system established in Maastricht: centralising monetary policy and decentralising the economic (budgetary and fiscal) policies connected to it (see Chapter 9). In the latter policy, the ECB received full control of the decision-making process, whereas in the latter policy, the control of the decision-making process has been assumed by the intergovernmental institution of the Council of Economic and Financial Ministers or the ECOFIN Council (and, for matters connected to the euro, by the informal Eurogroup of the economic and financial ministers of the eurozone). The integration progressed to the point of calling into question one of the bulwarks of the modern state, monetary sovereignty, but the member states and their governments had set in place an institutional model which entrusted them with control over the decision-making process relating to the new crucial policies which the end of the Cold War had pushed on to the European agenda. After three stages of convergence, the euro thus came into circulation on 1 January 2002, becoming (in 2017) the currency of nineteen (initially eleven) of the member states of the EU.

During the 1990s, the need to accommodate within the EU the new countries of Eastern and Southern Europe had ended up keeping open the so-called institutional building site. In that decade, a sequence of treaties was approved which in their turn joined those which had given birth to the integration process. Given the prospect of a doubling of the number of member states, it was then decided to move towards a rationalisation of this complex structure of treaties (a process already started with the Amsterdam Treaty, entered into force in 1999, and the Nice Treaty, entered into force in 2003), to enable the EU to operate with greater legitimacy and effectiveness. In 2002–3 a Constitutional Convention was finally called in Brussels which drafted a new text, the Constitutional Treaty (formally the Treaty Establishing a Constitution for Europe), which replaced all the other treaties. Although signed by the heads of state or government in a solemn meeting held in Rome in October 2004, the Constitutional Treaty was then blocked by French and Dutch voters in two referendums held in May and June 2005, respectively. After some reflection, it was decided to amend the existing treaties, incorporating much of the Constitutional Treaty in a new text called the Lisbon Treaty (since it was signed in the Portuguese capital). The Irish voted against the Lisbon Treaty in June 2008, but were then convinced to support that treaty in a subsequent referendum held in October 2009. The Lisbon Treaty came into force on 1 December 2009 (see Box 3.5).

BOX 3.5 The Lisbon Treaty

The Lisbon Treaty consists of three components: the Treaty of Maastricht (the Treaty on European Union) of 1992 as amended (TEU) and the Treaty of Rome of 1957 as amended and renamed the Treaty on the Functioning of the European Union (TFEU), plus the Charter of Fundamental Rights (the existence of which was acknowledged by the Intergovernmental Conference that drafted the Treaty of Nice of 2001 but which had not then formalised it).

The sequence of treaties (see Table 3.2) bears witness to the process of institutionalisation of the EU. The Lisbon Treaty seemed to represent the conclusion of that process. However, things did not turn out as many had expected. The multiple crises of the post-Lisbon period have in fact reopened the institutional building site.

Table 3.2 Treaties of the EU

Treaties	Member states	Purposes
ECSC (Paris, 1951)	Belgium, France, Germany, Italy, Luxembourg, The Netherlands	Guarantee equal access to the member states to the coal and steel market
EURATOM (Rome, 1957)	Belgium, France, Germany, Italy, Luxembourg, The Netherlands	Promote nuclear research and technology in the member states
EEC (Rome, 1957)	Belgium, France, Germany, Italy, Luxembourg, The Netherlands	Create a common market among the member states
SEA (Luxembourg, 1986)	Denmark, Belgium, France, Germany, Ireland, Italy, Luxembourg, The Netherlands, Great Britain	Launch a single market among the member states
EU (Maastricht, 1992)	Denmark, Belgium, France, Germany, Ireland, Italy, Luxembourg, The Netherlands, United Kingdom	Organisation with three pillars Supranational pillar for the single market (EEC of Rome 1957) Intergovernmental pillar for foreign and security policy (CFSP) Intergovernmental pillar for JHA policy Decision to create an economic and monetary union (eurozone)
EC (Amsterdam, 1997)	Austria, Denmark, Belgium, Finland, Greece, Germany, Ireland, Italy, Luxembourg, The Netherlands, Great Britain, Sweden	Reorganise the EEC (1957) in a new treaty (EC)
Nice (2001)	Austria, Denmark, Belgium, Finland, Greece, Germany, Ireland, Italy, Luxembourg, The Netherlands, Great Britain, Sweden	Acknowledgement of the Charter of Fundamental Rights Rationalisation of the institutional system
Lisbon (2009)	Austria, Belgium, Bulgaria, Czech Republic, Denmark, Cyprus, Estonia, Finland, France, Germany, Greece, Ireland, Italy, Latvia, Lithuania, Luxembourg, Malta, The Netherlands, Poland, Portugal, Great Britain, Romania, Slovakia, Slovenia, Spain, Sweden, Hungary Croatia (2013)	Abolition of the pillars but dual decision-making regime: supranational and intergovernmental Formal recognition of the Charter of Fundamental Rights Attribution of legal personality to the EU

3.4   The Supranational Decision-Making Regime

If the Lisbon Treaty abolished the division into pillars formalised at Maastricht, nonetheless it preserved the distinction between different decision-making regimes in relation to various European policies (Fabbrini, 2015a). It confirmed the supranational regime for regulating issues connected to the single market (see Chapter

8). And, at the same time, it institutionalised the intergovernmental regime for regulating matters which are politically sensitive for member states. In the former case, an institutional quadrilateral is operating, based on a bicameral legislature (the Council of Ministers since it is the chamber which represents governments in the form of sectoral ministers, and the EP, since it is the chamber representing citizens) and a dual executive (the European Council consisting of the heads of state or government of member states, and the Commission, with one commissioner for each member state). This quadrilateral has the features of a quasi-separation of powers system of government (see Box 3.6). It is a formal quadrilateral although the decision-making process (defined by the Lisbon Treaty as ordinary legislative procedure) involves mainly the Commission and the two legislative branches (a triangulation known as 'Community method'). It is important to notice that, within the supranational decision-making regime, there are few crucial policy areas for making the single market function (competition policy and, to a limited extent, trade policy) where the Commission enjoys high decision-making autonomy, unparalleled in other single market's areas, to the point of configuring a specific species of supranationalism definable as centralised regulation.

BOX 3.6 Separation of powers system

The separation of powers system implies that no institution can claim the ultimate decision-making power. The legislature is organised in two separate chambers and both are separate from the executive. The reciprocal separation between the various institutions is guaranteed not only by the constitution, but also by the fact that none of them require the (direct or indirect) confidence of the others for performing its functions. In the two cases of separation of powers systems in established democracies (the United States and Switzerland), sovereignty is fragmented vertically and horizontally. Specific institutional devices (generally called checks and balances) incentivise each separate institution to take into consideration the preferences of the other institutions. The government is not an institution but a process through which those institutions reach an agreed decision.

In single market policies, the Commission and its president (due both to the prerogatives and the technical competences which they have available) are more important than the European Council and its president. Although the European Council has been recognised to have an executive role, this concerns the definition of the EU's long-term strategies. The European Council is no longer (as it was before the Lisbon Treaty) the highest form of the Council of Ministers, but, in this constitution, it does not have a strictly decision-making role. It is a kind of colle-gial 'head of state' of the EU, the last resort umpire for unsolvable disputes which may emerge within the EU. The legislative co-decision-making of the Council of Ministers and of the EP is established as the ordinary procedure to approve European laws (regulations and directives), while the Commission maintains the power to start the legislative process and the European Council sees its role recog-nised as the strategic head of the EU. It is a quasi-separate system of government since, although no institution formally depends on the backing of the others to function as such, efforts have been made for connecting the election of the EP with the formation of the Commission.

BOX 3.7 The *Spitzenkandidat*

The *Spitzenkandidat* is an electoral practice imported from German political par-ties. In the elections for the EP of May 2014 and 2019, the main European political parties identified a 'top candidate' as the possible president of the Commission, should one or other of them win the relative majority (plurality) of the votes for the election of the European parliamentarians.

According to the treaty, it is the European Council that has the power to select the Commission's president, but then the vote of the EP is necessary to con-firm the choice of the European Council. With the so-called *Spitzenkandidat* strategy (see Box 3.7), the parties of the EP sought to free themselves from the control of the European Council in selecting the president of the Commission (Christiansen, 2016). In 2014, the European People's Party, which had indicated the Luxembourg politician Jean-Claude Juncker as its *Spitzenkandidat*, in obtain-ing the greatest number of seats in the EP's elections, therefore proposed Junker as president of the Commission. This proposal was accompanied by the warning to the European Council, from the main parties in the EP, that the EP would not vote for any other candidate as president of the Commission. The warning had the desired effect. The European Council indicated Juncker as candidate to the presidency of the Commission (with the contrary vote of the prime ministers of United Kingdom and Hungary), then putting that name to the EP. However, that of the European Council was only a partial surrender. Indeed, the choice of the other twenty-seven members of the Commission did not follow the electoral logic used for the president of the Commission. The commissioners were indicated by the European Council (albeit consulting the newly elected president of the Commission), for voting by the EP, on the basis of not strictly partisan consider-ations. Finally, the principle of the *Spitzenkandidat* was called into question after the 2019 elections of the EP. The *spitzenkandidat* of the plurality party (Manfred Weber of the European People's Party) was not taken into consideration for the role of the Commission's president by the European Council, not only because he was considered unfit for the job (particularly by French President Emmanuel Macron) but mainly because his party lost more than 5 per cent of the electoral vote compared to 2014 (still remaining the plurality party). The new candidate for Commission president, Ursula von der Leyen, was thus proposed by the national government leaders of the European Council disregarding EP parliamentary groups' preferences.

Thus, although the Commission and its president (proposed by the European Council) are to be elected by the EP, they cannot be compared to a parliamentary government based on fusion of powers system (Fabbrini, 2015b). The EP can dismiss the Commission as a whole only on the grounds of not respecting governmental ethics, as in 1999 (Moury, 2007), not on the grounds of political disagreement; nor can the Commission dissolve the EP, since the latter has a five-year mandate established by the treaty (see Box 3.8).

BOX 3.8 The fusion of powers system

The fusion of powers system is characterised by a confidence relation between the (majority) of the legislature and the executive. The latter may govern as long as the legislature supports it. The parliamentary system epitomises the fusion of powers' logic. The institutional feature of the fusion of powers system is the centralisation of decision-making power in the popular chamber of the legislature (or better in the government that enjoys the legislature's support). Here the government is an institution, the one controlling the last decision.

In the EU, therefore, there is no relationship of reciprocal political confidence between the parliamentary majority and the Commission. The institutions are reciprocally independent and at the same time connected to each other through a mechanism of checks and balances. In this supranational regime, the EP has acquired equal legislative standing with the Council of Ministers, motivating wisely and doggedly its requests for institutional influence with the fact of being the only institution directly elected (since 1979) by the citizens of the individual member states of the EU. At the same time, the EP, by imposing co-decision-making as the ordinary procedure of the EU in single market policies, has given legitimacy to the legislative process. In all the policies linked to the single market, the EU continues to operate through the approval of legislative provisions (regulations and directives), an activity which is rigorously monitored by the ECJ. With the

Lisbon Treaty, the supranational regime has become relatively stable. It formalises an institutional architecture which is based on a distinction between legislative and executive institutions, as in democratic systems of government. To summarise, the supranational regime consists of the Commission that, having the monopoly of legislative initiative, submits proposals of regulation and directive to either the Council of Ministers or the EP. The proposal is accepted when it is voted by the appropriate majority in the two institutions. With the Lisbon Treaty, the Council's majority is constituted by 55 per cent of ministers representing at least 65 per cent of the total population of the EU, while the EP approves through simple majority. Under the formal triangle (Commission–Council of Ministers–EP) there operates a vast network of committees engaged in preparing and negotiating the proposals to be voted on by the legislative institutions. The Lisbon Treaty has significantly increased the number of single market policies decided through the interaction between the three institutions, interaction formally called as ordinary legislative procedure.

3.5   The Intergovernmental Decision-Making Regime

The Lisbon Treaty has an intergovernmental approach. Although it abolished the division into pillars of the 1992 Maastricht Treaty, the differentiation between different decision-making regimes remained. In policy areas representing traditional core state powers (Genschel and Jachtenfuchs, 2014), such as the CFSP, the JHA policy and the economic policy for the eurozone, *inter alia*, the Lisbon Treaty suspended the above-mentioned decision-making quadrilateral, replacing it with an institutional arrangement based mainly on the European Council and the Council of Ministers of the member states. In relation to these policies, the purpose indicated by the Lisbon Treaty is that of facilitating the voluntary coordination of the policies of member states, but not their legal integration at supranational level (Box 3.9).

BOX 3.9 Integration through voluntary coordination

With the extension of integration to politically crucial policy areas for member states, governments have placed the new policies in a normative environment different from the one of the single market's regulatory policies. Here, it is *integration through the voluntary coordination* of policies by national governments, coordination which takes place within the European Council and the Council of Ministers. In relation to these policies, the purpose indicated is that of facilitating

BOX 3.9 (Cont.)

the coordination of the policies of member states, but not their legal integration at supranational level (Fabbrini and Puetter, 2016). The method for taking decisions through coordination has been variously defined: as 'open method of coordination' (Zeitlin and Pochet, 2005), 'new mode of governance' (Héritier and Rhodes, 2010) or 'deliberative intergovernmentalism' (Puetter, 2012). To simplify the variety of methods within the intergovernmental approach, a distinction may be detected between a loose 'policy coordination' (with national governments enjoying full decision-making autonomy, as in the CFSP) and a stricter 'intergovernmental method' (with national governments coordinating within a formalised framework, as in the economic policy of the eurozone).

Let us start with the CFSP (see Figure 3.1). TEU art. 24.1 is explicit in stating that 'the adoption of legislative acts shall be excluded'. Although it introduced the important innovation of a High Representative for Foreign Affairs and Security Policy, who is the permanent president (for five years) of the Foreign Affairs Council consisting of the corresponding ministers of the member states (the only formation of the Council outside of the half-year presidency system) and is at the same time the vice president of the Commission, the Lisbon Treaty did not change the intergovernmental logic established by the Treaty of Maastricht for foreign policy (and at the time protected by a specific institutional pillar). The coordination must take place (TEU, Art. 25) through decisions consisting of 'actions and positions' which, once adopted, the member states voluntarily undertake to respect. In this decision-making regime, the Commission, through its vice president, must act as technical support to the Foreign Affairs Council, but may not exercise any political role (which is the responsibility of the European Council). At the same time, the EP must be consulted but it is not allowed to exercise any checking and balancing

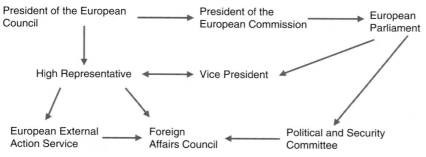

Figure 3.1 Policy coordination in the EU foreign policy

role on the intergovernmental institutions. And since the CFSP is taken through decisions, and not legislative acts, the ECJ is precluded from exercising significant judicial supervision. In sum, political initiative on specific foreign policy issues comes generally from one member state government or a small group of member state governments that, in conjunction with the High Representative, sensitise the European Council (through its president) for putting the issue on the latter's agenda. Foreign policy decisions (that have a political rather than legal character) are taken through a loose process of coordination (thus allowing one or the other national government to stand on the sides). A decision's implementation is not compulsory but voluntary, because it should be done by national actors.

The same logic is adopted in economic policy, although here the coordination between national governments takes places within a more constraining framework. The decisions are the responsibility solely of the ECOFIN Council, which may recommend the adoption of corrective measures by a member state, even if TEU, Art. 126.6 recognises that the Commission has a role in activating the procedures: for example, for excessive budget deficits on the part of a member state. In any case, the Commission may make a *proposal* but it is again the responsibility of the ECOFIN Council to decide whether to proceed or not in conformity with the Commission's proposal. This is even more true for the measures which concern member states of the eurozone (see Chapter 4), where the decision-making role of the Eurogroup (see Box 3.10) is institutionalised (Puetter, 2006). The economic policy enshrined in the Lisbon Treaty is based mainly on measures of voluntary coordination among the member states.

BOX 3.10 The Eurogroup

The Eurogroup is an informal institution constituted by the finance ministers from the eurozone, led by a permanent president for five years (elected by the other ministers and accountable to them).

The Lisbon Treaty has thus centralised, with the euro, the management of the common currency (through the supranational role of the ECB) and at the same time has decentralised to the member states of the eurozone all the (fiscal and budget) policies connected to the common currency. Both the SGP (which covers all the member states) and the measures relating to the euro are decided by the ECOFIN Council (and therefore by the Eurogroup), with a technical support role for the Commission, a very marginal controlling role for the EP and limited judicial supervision by the ECJ (see Figure 3.2). In sum, if it is true that economic policy

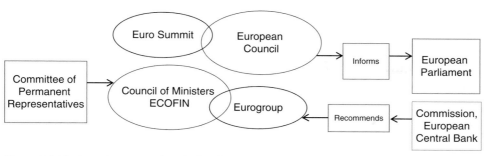

Figure 3.2 The intergovernmental method in the EU economic policy

is decided through coordination between national governments, it is also true that its policy-making process takes place within a formalised framework of rules (the SGP). This is particularly true in the eurozone where the rules are strict and their disrespect implies the opening (by the Commission unless its decision is reversed by a qualified majority of the Eurogroup) of an infringement procedure. It is thus appropriate to distinguish between a loose policy coordination and a stricter inter-governmental method, although both represent species of the same genus (the intergovernmental decision-making regime).

With the deepening of the integration process there has been constant growth in the role of national governmental leaders (through the European Council). The European Council has gradually distanced itself from the Council of Ministers, taking on a purely executive function (that of establishing the broad brushstrokes of EU policy), leaving to the Council of Ministers the role of the chamber of the states as in a federal legislative system (in single market policies). The growth of the role of the European Council has led to a downsizing of the role of the Council of Ministers as the intergovernmental institution par excellence. Moreover, the election (with the Lisbon Treaty) of a permanent president of the European Council, who is elected for two and a half years with a renewable mandate for a second term of similar length, has institutionalised its decision-making power, providing continuity to its executive action. If the Lisbon Treaty envisages that it 'meets twice every six months' (TEU, Art. 15.3), with the multiple crises which have taken place in the post-Lisbon period and with the growth in importance on the European agenda of the new strategic policies, the European Council has intensified its meet-ings. During the financial crisis or the migration crisis or the security crisis, the Commission was not the driving force of the integration process, even if it was clear that its technical skills were essential in order to translate the decisions taken by the European Council into operational measures (Puetter, 2014). In policies tra-ditionally at the heart of the national sovereignty of member states (and electorally sensitive for the fates of their incumbent governments), the intergovernmental institutions matter much more than the supranational ones (Bickerton et al., 2015).

While the supranational regime supports and justifies a decision-making system marked by an (albeit contradictory) separation of powers among the four institutions which participate in the policy-making process (a dual executive consisting of the European Council and the Commission and a bicameral legislative body consisting of the EP and the Council of Ministers), the same cannot be said for the intergovernmental regime. Here the centralisation of decision-making in the two institutions (the European Council and the Council of Ministers) which represent the governments of the member states has generated a confusion of powers (as is the case, for example, of the Foreign Affairs Council or the ECOFIN Council, at the same time both legislative and executive institutions). Legitimacy has been forgotten (Schmidt, 2015). Indeed, if we use the analytical criteria with which empirical democracies are assessed (Lijphart, 1999), it seems inappropriate to consider as legitimate a decision taken by the European Council or by the Council of Ministers in the name of the whole EU and its citizens, when the members of those institutions benefit from exclusively national legitimisation – a decision, moreover, that would be bereft of checks and balances at the EU level by the EP. The 2009 Lisbon Treaty represents the outcome of a process of institutionalisation that has created a stable, although differentiated, decision-making system. EU decision-making is much more structured than assumed by mainstream theories. Already with the 1992 Treaty of Maastricht, integration involved areas of public policies that were considered the basis of national sovereignty. After Maastricht, the deepening of the single market has continued, with an increase of policies decided through the ordinary legislative procedure. At the same time, policy areas that are politically sensitive for individual national governments (such as foreign and security policy, JHA and then economic policy) moved to Brussels where they are decided through various forms of voluntary coordination between national leaders and ministers. The regional integration process was becoming so deep (as well as so extended, with the subsequent enlargements) that it required a greater definition of its institutional arrangements and its decision-making processes.

In conclusion, the Lisbon Treaty, abolishing the division into pillars but keeping the difference in the decision-making regimes, institutionalised the decision-making differentiation started with the Treaty of Maastricht. It institutionalises a supranational regime to regulate issues connected to the single market regulatory policies and, at the same time, an intergovernmental regime to manage policies which are strategic for the member states and electorally sensitive for their governmental leaders. In the first case, the regime is based on a system of quasi-separation of powers since no institution depends on the political confidence of the others to function as such, even if, with the *Spitzenkandidat* strategy, efforts have been made to increase the political affinity between the majority in the EP and the Commission. In any case, the role and functions of the institutions are distinct and specified. In the second case, the regime is based on a system of confusion of powers since the decisions are taken by the national governmental leaders (through the European Council which coordinates them) or by their ministers (in crucial Councils of Ministers), which behave as both executive and legislative institutions. Moreover, those institutions operate largely unchecked by the supranational institutions. In strategic policies, not only is the Commission no longer the driving force of the integration process, although its technical competences continue to be indispensable to translate the decisions taken by the European Council into operational measures, but above all the EP is playing a subordinate role. Thus, while the supranational regime has led to a strengthening of the EP, which has imposed co-decision-making as the ordinary procedure of the EU, the intergovernmental regime has led to the strengthening of the European Council, which has imposed its political, not just strategic, centrality. Even if the Lisbon Treaty ended the division into pillars established by the Treaty of Maastricht of 1992, it institutionalised normative frameworks and decision-making regimes which were different for single market policies and for core state power policies. This dual approach to integration makes clear why the multiple crises of the post-Lisbon era, since they fell to the intergovernmental regime, did not lead to an increase of supranationalism, as expected by many and conceptualised by Jean Monnet some time ago.

GROUP DISCUSSION

- Why did the EU institutionalise an intergovernmental regime?
- Which are the institutional differences between supranational and intergovernmental regimes?
- Is the Commission the executive power of the EU?

TOPICS FOR INDIVIDUAL RESEARCH

- Executive power in the EU: how can the interinstitutional relations between the Commission and the European Council be qualified?
- The Commission and the *Spitzenkandidat* strategy: towards parliamentarism?

FURTHER READINGS

Bickerton, C. J., Hodson, D. and Puetter W. (eds.) (2015). *The New Intergovernmentalism: States and Supranational Actors in the Post-Maastricht Era.* Oxford: Oxford University Press.

Dehousse, R. (2011). *The 'Community Method': Obstinate or Obsolete?* New York: Palgrave Macmillan.

Fabbrini, S. (2015a). *Which European Union? Europe After the Euro Crisis.* Cambridge: Cambridge University Press.

Genschel, P. and Jachtenfuchs, M. (eds) (2014). *Beyond the Regulatory Polity? The European Integration of Core State Powers.* Oxford: Oxford University Press.

Héritier, A. and Rhodes, M. (eds) (2010). *New Modes of Governance in Europe.* New York: Palgrave Macmillan.

REFERENCES

Bickerton, C. J., Hodson, D. and Puetter, W. (eds) (2015). *The New Intergovernmentalism: States and Supranational Actors in the Post-Maastricht Era.* Oxford: Oxford University Press.

Börzel, T. A. (2016). 'From EU Governance of Crisis to Crisis of EU Governance: Regulatory Failure, Redistributive Conflict and Eurosceptic Public'. *Journal of Common Market Studies*, 54: 8–31.

Caporaso, J. A. and Rhodes, M. (eds) (2016). *The Political and Economic Dynamics of the Eurozone Crisis.* Oxford: Oxford University Press.

Christiansen, T. (2016). 'After the Spitzenkandidaten: Fundamental Change in the EU's Political System?' *West European Politics*, 39(5): 992–1010.

Dehousse, R. (2011). *The 'Community Method': Obstinate or Obsolete?* New York: Palgrave Macmillan.

Fabbrini, S. (2015a). *Which European Union? Europe After the Euro Crisis.* Cambridge: Cambridge University Press.

Fabbrini, S. (2015b). 'The European Union and the Puzzle of Parliamentary Government'. *Journal of European Integration*, 37(5): 571–86.

Fabbrini, S. and Puetter, U. (ed.) (2016). 'Integration without Supranationalisation: The Central Role of the European Council in Post-Lisbon EU Politics'. *Journal of European Integration*, Special Issue, 38(5).

Genschel, P. and Jachtenfuchs, M. (eds) (2014). *Beyond the Regulatory Polity? The European Integration of Core State Powers.* Oxford: Oxford University Press.

Héritier, A. and Rhodes, M. (eds) (2010). *New Modes of Governance in Europe.* New York: Palgrave Macmillan.

Judt, T. (2005). *Postwar: A History of Europe Since 1945.* London, Penguin Books.

Kelemen, D. (2011). *Eurolegalism: The Transformation of Law and Regulation in the European Union.* Cambridge, MA: Harvard University Press.

Lijphart, A. (1999). *Patterns of Democracy.* New Haven, CT: Yale University Press.

Moury, C. (2007). 'Explaining the European Parliament's Right to Appoint and Invest the Commission'. *West European Politics*, 30(2): 367–91.

Puetter, U. (2014). *The European Council and The Council: New Intergovernmentalism and Institutional Change.* Oxford: Oxford University Press.

Puetter, U. (2012). 'Europe's Deliberative Intergovernmentalism: The Role of the Council and European Council in EU Economic Governance'. *Journal of European Public Policy*, 19(2): 161–78.

Puetter, U. (2006). *The Eurogroup: How a Secretive Circle of Finance Ministers Shape European Economic Governance.* Manchester: Manchester University Press.

Sbragia, A. M. (1994). 'From Nation-State to Member State: The Evolution of the European Community'. In P. M. Lutzeler (ed.), *Europe after Maastricht: American and European Perspectives.* Oxford: Berghahn Books.

Schmidt, V. (2015). 'The Forgotten Problem of Legitimacy: "Governing by the Rules" and "Ruling by the Numbers"'. In M. Matthijs and M. Blyth (eds), *The Future of the Euro*. Oxford: Oxford University Press.

Tuori, K. and Tuori, K. (2014). *The Eurozone Crisis: A Constitutional Analysis*. Cambridge: Cambridge University Press.

Wallace, H. and Reh, C. (2015). 'An Institutional Anatomy and Five Policy Modes'. In H. Wallace, M. A. Pollack and A. R. Young (eds), *Policy-Making in the European Union*. Oxford: Oxford University Press, 7th Edition.

Zeitlin, J. and Pochet, P. (eds) (2005). *The Open Method of Coordination in Action: The European Employment and Social Inclusion Strategies*. Brussels: Peter Lang.

4 Regulatory Networks and Policy Communities

JACOB HASSELBALCH AND ELENI TSINGOU

4.1 Introduction

This chapter is concerned with explaining what role regulatory networks and policy communities play in EU policy-making today. Specifically, it seeks to provide working definitions for the concepts of 'regulatory networks' and 'policy communities'. These concepts developed to reflect how networked governance has become a key aspect of today's politics alongside hierarchical government structures. Thus, networks and communities serve to highlight how hybrid and flexible policy actors are operating along formal/informal and public/private dimensions, as well as across different levels of governance. While valuable as analytical devices to describe the plethora of atypical governance arrangements, how useful are they when we endeavour to explain and understand governance and politics today? The concepts are used extensively (and often interchangeably) in both the scholarly and policy literatures. By providing some more content to the terms, we can make them do more of the analytical work in understanding the range of relevant actors and their modes of interaction.

The chapter develops in three steps. Section 4.2 provides a brief overview of the development of the concepts of policy communities and regulatory networks, highlighting that the concepts are most powerful when linked to specific issue areas and policy domains. It also zooms in on the use of the concepts in the EU literature, picking up the ways in which they have been useful in navigating not only the increased hybridity of governance arrangements, but also the unique characteristics of EU decision-making processes along different institutional spaces and levels of analysis. Building on insights from existing scholarship, the chapter proceeds to outline the dimensions to consider in specifying how 'regulatory networks' and 'policy communities' can be most useful for analytical work: a grouping's identifying characteristics and commonalities, its place in a regulatory or policy process and whether it is a space for discussion. Finally, the chapter illustrates these points by providing empirical vignettes from the very diverse policy areas of electronic cigarettes, unconventional fossil fuels and demographic change.

4.2 Tracing the Origins of Regulatory Networks and Policy Communities

4.2.1 Regulation

To understand the provenance of the concepts of 'regulatory networks' and 'policy communities', we take as our point of departure Majone's (1994, 1997) work on the regulatory state (see Box 4.1). Majone argued that privatisation and deregulation spurred the rise of the regulatory state, replacing the dirigiste state of the past. The dirigiste state, from French *diriger* (meaning to direct), designates a strong state role in directing investment and intervening in the economy through state-owned enterprises and economic planning. Some have argued that the wave of privatisations experienced by European economies since the 1990s indicates a decreased role or a 'retreat of the state' from the economic sphere (Strange, 1996). In contrast, Majone views this development as a redefinition of the function of the state, not a retreat. Neither deregulation nor privatisation meant a return to laissez-faire policies. Instead, states redrew the boundaries of the public sphere by excluding some fields better left to private activity while strengthening the capacity of the state to regulate and control those activities. Where the state used to be 'rowing' the economy through intervention and direct participation in market activity, it is now more appropriate to think of it as 'steering' the economy (Osborne and Gaebler, 1992). This redefinition was of paramount importance to the European project: regulation is 'at the core of the compromise between the European Community and its member states that made the Internal Market possible' (Majone, 1994: 77).

BOX 4.1 Key concepts

Regulation. Intentional activity that seeks to control, direct or influence behaviour and the flow of events (Black, 2001). In the context of government, it implies the sustained and focused control over socially valued activities (Selznick, 1985), generally consisting of three core components: goals, monitoring and realignment (Hood et al., 2001).

Deregulation. The repeal of governmental regulation of activities in a given sphere of (typically) economic activity. Frequently associated with privatising state monopolies and opening sectors of the economy previously under the direct control of the state to market competition.

Reregulation. Following the privatisation of state monopolies and/or the liberalisation of markets, this term emphasises the growing need for regulation, especially competition regulation, to avoid the formation of private monopolies.

BOX 4.1 (Cont.)

Governance. The dispersal of the capacities and resources needed to govern (Rosenau, 2007; Scott, 2004), resulting in overlapping and complimentary arenas of authority, and multiple actors operating on the basis of formal functions, technical expertise or implementation capabilities (Avant et al., 2010). Governance also frequently takes place across multiple scales (national, international, transnational) and domains (public, private, civil society).

Regulatory state. Describes the trend of states moving from a dirigiste role (a strong role for the state in directing investment and intervening in the economy through state-owned enterprises and economic planning) towards an emphasis on the regulation and steering of private economic activity (Majone, 1994, 1997).

Post-regulatory state. A reaction to the idea of the regulatory state that goes beyond a rebalancing of the responsibilities of government to emphasise the growing role of non-state actors, non-state laws and non-state forms of rule making, monitoring and enforcement (Black, 2001; Scott, 2004).

European regulatory state. The mutually reinforcing rise of regulatory modes of governance at both the European and member state level (Bach and Newman, 2007; Lodge, 2008).

European Administrative Space. An area in which increasingly integrated administrations jointly exercise powers delegated to the EU in a system of shared sovereignty (Hofmann, 2008).

Regulatory networks. Networked forms of governance marked by a clear authority and mandate to govern a specific area. The closest analogues in the literature are 'networks of rule' (Rose and Miller, 1992) and 'policy networks' (Marsh and Rhodes, 1992).

Policy communities. Groups built on shared understanding, knowledge and norms or common routines, dispositions, and socialisation. Communities may act within regulatory networks, but do not wield regulatory power on their own. They tend to influence the policy agenda or support policy processes with expertise. The closest analogues in the literature are 'epistemic communities' (Cross, 2013; Haas, 1992), 'communities of practice' (Wenger, 1998) or 'issue networks' (Wilkinson et al., 2010).

A growing role for regulation led some scholars to emphasise a trend of 'reregulation' (see Box 4.1) rather than deregulation, describing the emerging reality as one of 'freer markets, more rules' (Vogel, 1996) in finance, but also in telecommunications and the utilities sectors. When state monopolies were privatised, competition regulation was necessary to avoid replacing public monopolies with private ones. Regulation in the sense of sustained and focused control over socially valued activities (Selznick, 1985) in time demanded the formation of specialised agencies entrusted with fact finding, rule making and enforcement (Majone, 1994). The growing complexity and technicality of market regulation was especially caused by the unification and alignment of disparate bodies of national law in the creation of the Internal Market (see Chapter 8). Additionally, European regulatory agencies, lacking the capability to exercise their power through fiscal policy, sought to increase their influence by expanding the scope and scale of regulation and standardisation (Majone, 1994: 89–90). This necessitated the creation of specialised agencies operating at the European level and outside the line of hierarchical control of partisan politics or central administration, whose shifting political priorities should only have a limited ability to affect the stable development of well-functioning markets, increasingly seen as a matter of technical standardisation rather than political steering. At the same time, however, the bureaucracies of European member states were 'forced to develop regulatory capacities on an unprecedented scale' (Majone, 1997: 146) in order to deal with and implement in national law the rapidly growing body of European law. Taken together, the rise of regulatory modes of governance at both the European and member state level has made it commonplace to talk of a 'European regulatory state' (Bach and Newman, 2007; Lodge, 2008). This regulatory state is not necessarily uniform but allows for a certain degree of national discretion. For some scholars, the defining characteristic is one of 'experimentalist governance', that is the possibility to define common goals but adapt them in local contexts, with peer review and policy assessments and reappraisals moving things along (Zeitlin, 2016). These approaches share a technocratic understanding of the purpose of regulatory networks and are agnostic about the normative content of goals and rules.

4.2.2   Governance

As regulatory agencies grew in importance, analysts began shifting their focus from centralised government to decentralised governance (Braithwaite and Drahos, 2000). The primary characteristic defining the 'age of governance' is the dispersal of the capacities and resources needed to govern (Rosenau, 2007; Scott, 2004). The rise of the regulatory state as discussed above is the most proximate cause of this shift from government to governance, but, analytically, the regulatory state concept does not fully cover all the observed changes to the landscape of rule making, monitoring and enforcement. Specifically, the dispersal of governance went beyond mere delegation from central government to regulatory agencies – going one step further, regulatory agencies are themselves involved in multiple and overlapping networks of other actors upon whom they draw for relevant expertise and capabilities in dealing with the technicalities of market regulation (Radaelli, 1999). Charting empirically the explosion and diffusion in the number of regulatory agencies in the past decades, Jordana et al. (2011: 1362) argue that their rapid growth is primarily owed to 'the increasing importance of social networks of professionals, regulocrats, and epistemic communities that are active in international organisations or also share similar cultural identities, alongside the increasing embeddedness of the national in the global and the global in the national'. Scholars of governance concur that the demand for in-depth, technology-specific and sector-specific expertise has been critical in fostering more frequent and open interaction between staff in regulatory agencies and external networks of market actors, experts and other involved stakeholders (Mazzucato, 2013; Newman, 2008; Woll, 2008). Social relations in the conduct of governance thereby become an important target of inquiry. Not only is governance characterised by overlapping and complementary arenas of authority, and multiple actors operating on the basis of formal functions, technical expertise or implementation capabilities (Avant et al., 2010); it is also the result of interactions taking place across levels of analysis. For the EU, this includes the national and regional levels of the regulatory framework, but also the international level of engagement with states and international organisations and transnational standard-setting across the public/private divide (Büthe & Mattli, 2011).

It is only a small step further to conceive of the study of these social relations in network or community terms. Before delving into this it is important to note that the age of governance has not arrived without contestation, including from critical scholarship. From this perspective, the shift from hierarchical command and control to decentred regulation is understood as a move towards a 'post-regulatory state' (see Box 4.1), which suggests a freeing of regulation from the sovereign state and a recognition that regulation operates in ways that go beyond a mere rebalancing of responsibilities between governments, agencies and networks. The notion of a regulatory state does not go far enough in emphasising the growing role of non-state actors, non-state laws and non-state forms of rule making, monitoring and enforcement (Black, 2001; Scott, 2004). While scholars of the post-regulatory state thus agree with the general message of the age of governance that regulation is now carried out by a wider group of actors, they add that this shift has also introduced and reinforced other *forms* of regulation, including self-regulation and peer regulation, that have been analytically approached through governmentality studies (Rose et al., 2006). While recognising the authority of some central organisations in regulatory matters, this approach views regulation more as a diffused set of practices, concepts and rationalities that permeate all levels of society.

The implication of governmentality and the idea of the post-regulatory state is that external networks and communities do more than simply carry out the wishes of regulatory agencies or centralised governments – they are themselves key policy sites. Regulation does not only flow from the agency to the target, but is transmitted through network structures. According to Rose and Miller (1992), governmentality is implemented by 'centres of calculation' embedded in 'networks of rule'. Centres of calculation are those key sites where the complexity of social reality is broken down, simplified and made calculable through techniques and instruments that bracket out some aspects of a phenomenon for closer inspection and leave out others (Latour, 2005). The organisations and personnel that provide these forms of calculation wield great power in the networks of rule, as they get to define the reality of the issue and how it is regulated (Callon et al., 2009), which raises questions about the consequences of these rearrangements for democracy and legitimacy (Klijn and Skelcher, 2007).

4.2.3 Networks and Policy Communities

This insight sheds additional light on the idea of 'networked governance', a term coined in the 1990s by British public administration scholars to describe the perceived changes in the move from government to governance – a shift pioneered in some ways by the British state (e.g. Rhodes, 1996). Moran (2003: 4) was highly critical of voluntary and self-regulatory forms of governance in the British context, arguing that it often led to 'informal, oligarchic, and secretive' processes, resulting in what he called 'club government'. Scholars in this tradition also used the concept of 'policy networks' (Marsh and Rhodes, 1992), focusing on power and actors that had direct access to decision-making.

These developments in public administration are what created the conditions of emergence for the concepts of regulatory networks and policy communities. The concepts partly describe the shift, but are simultaneously directly implicated in bringing it about.

The main difference between regulatory networks and policy communities is that regulatory networks imply direct involvement in regulatory activity, while policy communities need not be directly involved. Regulatory networks are 'networks of rule' (Rose and Miller, 1992), with authority and a mandate to govern. Policy communities may be involved in regulatory networks, but they may also merely be setting the agenda for a specific policy issue or accumulating knowledge on the issue in the hope of influencing or becoming recognised as a future centre of calculation or as a norm entrepreneur. They may or may not offer explicit solutions to regulatory or policy-making puzzles. Policy networks, as understood by Marsh and Rhodes (1992), are what we call regulatory networks here. We prefer using 'regulatory' because it sets a stronger requirement than mere 'policy'.

Regulation, broadly defined, describes intentional activity that seeks to control, direct or influence behaviour and the flow of events (Black, 2001). It consists of three core components: goals, monitoring and realignment (Hood et al., 2001). The goal component is the standard against which actions can be compared; monitoring entails a mechanism for feedback and evaluation of performance; and realignment requires some form of corrective action or response that is triggered when the targets of regulation deviate too far from the standard. A regulatory network (see Box 4.1) must have precise expectations about which of these components are delegated to or carried out by which actors, and all three components must be represented within the network. In contrast to regulation, policy can describe any formal or informal law by which some expectations and directions are set – it does not connote the same meaning of organised monitoring and enforcement. An example of a regulatory network might be the European medicines regulatory network, a closely coordinated network of national competent authorities in the European member states working with the European Medicines Agency (EMA) and the European Commission. The national authorities supply thousands of experts that take part in the EMA's working groups and scientific committees. The EMA is central in the hub, while the Commission takes binding decisions based on EMA recommendations. The network ensures consistent information and authorisation of medicines in the single market.

Policy communities (see Box 4.1) more closely resemble the concepts of 'epistemic communities' (Cross, 2013; Haas, 1992) or 'communities of practice' (Wenger, 1998). They are defined by a standard of commonality. Epistemic communities are built on shared understanding, knowledge and norms. The concept has been especially effective for understanding groups of scientists addressing environmental issues. Communities of practice are built on shared routines, dispositions and socialisation, and have been prominent in analyses of security debates. Whereas networks imply transmission and delegation, communities imply commonality and identity. Shared interest in the policy issue is the main entrance ticket. The concept of 'issue network', sometimes used interchangeably with policy network, is often used to describe how a like-minded group of actors can set the agenda and bring

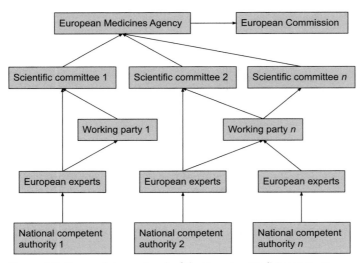

Figure 4.1 The regulatory network of the European Medicines Agency

attention to a policy issue (Wilkinson et al., 2010). We think this is also captured by our understanding of a policy community. An example of a policy community might be the Rethink Plastic Alliance, an alliance of European NGOs (including Greenpeace, Friends of the Earth Europe, the Environmental Investigation Agency, the European Environmental Bureau, Zero Waste Europe and many others) all working towards designing and delivering policy solutions for a future free from plastic pollution. They support this agenda through research publications, policy briefs, lobbying and social media. The alliance is also involved in the global Break Free From Plastic movement, showing how European policy communities may leverage global connections to increase pressure on policymakers, or vice versa, and how their European experiences may be uploaded and diffused through global communities.

Both regulatory networks and policy communities are present and important in EU affairs, internally and externally, and have remained so through the crisis into the post-crisis period. As examples of regulatory networks with global relevance, consider European standard-setting in domains such as transport fuel, health and safety of consumer products, chemicals and so on. European standards often become de facto global standards for many kinds of products and services by virtue of the technical expertise of European standard setters and the size of the single market. Standards are technical documents designed to be used as rules,

Figure 4.2 The policy community of the Rethink Plastic Alliance

guidelines or definitions. They are created through a consensus-seeking process bringing together manufacturers, consumers, regulators and national and international standard-setting bodies. In the EU, this work is carried out by the regulatory network of the European Committee for Standardization (CEN), which comprises the thirty-four standard-setting bodies of the national members and involves more than 50,000 technical experts from industry, associations, public administrations, academia and civil society. The national standard-setting bodies are responsible for operating the technical groups that draw up the standards, while the management centre of CEN coordinates the process from Brussels.

In defining the EU as a regional state, highly shaped by and shaping the shift to governance, Schmidt (2006) argues that the diffusion of political and regulatory activity through multiple authorities at different levels with different forms of governing creates a complex and compound system of governance. Regulatory networks and policy communities play important roles in these relationships, either in formal arrangements with EU agencies (Hobolth and Martinsen, 2013; Mastenbroek and Martinsen, 2018) or in informal, agenda-setting coalitions or lobbying work (Binderkrantz and Rasmussen, 2015; Junk, 2016; Klüver, 2013). Questions remain about the best way of governing over, through and in networks and communities (Carstensen and Schmidt, 2016; Klijn, 2008; Torfing and Sørensen, 2014). During times of crisis (Seabrooke and Tsingou, 2019) and in the post-crisis EU, the answers depend in particular on whether the issue area can be defined as technical, on the constellation of actors involved, as well as on the resources available.

In EU studies, scholars working on the European Administrative Space (see Box 4.1) provide another entry point into the discussion on regulatory networks and policy communities (e.g. Bach and Newman, 2007; Levi-Faur, 2011; Hobolth and Martinsen, 2013; Egeberg et al., 2014; Maggetti and Gilardi, 2014; Mastenbroek and Martinsen, 2018). The European Administrative Space denotes 'an area in which increasingly integrated administrations jointly exercise powers delegated to the EU in a system of shared sovereignty' (Hofmann, 2008). Literature on the European Administrative Space recognises that around the Commission's policy development, decision-making and implementation functions, a large administrative apparatus is required. This apparatus extends from the EU's directorate-generals, agencies, committees and national seconded experts to the national regulatory bodies of member states. Studies on European regulatory networks have done much to explain their establishment (Thatcher, 2011; Blauberger and Rittberger, 2015), functioning (Hofmann, 2008; Kelemen and Tarrant, 2011) and impact (Maggetti and Gilardi, 2011), and attention is now turning to their normative aspects and implementation of EU laws (Mastenbroek and Martinsen, 2018). But the literature on the European Administrative Space is less concerned with how regulatory networks interact with policy communities.

Similarly, while there is work on how policy communities can influence agendas and policy debates, we do not know much about how they function *within* regulatory networks. For studies on influence and agenda setting, there is a vast literature on lobbying and interest groups in the EU that tells us how different types of policy communities work together to achieve their goals, for example as 'advocacy coalitions' (Sabatier, 1998; Meijerink, 2005; Nohrstedt, 2013), or through 'lobbying styles' (Mahoney, 2008; Woll, 2012; Binderkrantz and Rasmussen, 2015), or how they make strategic use of framing to ensure coherent messages and identities (Baumgartner and Mahoney, 2008; Klüver, 2013; Klüver et al., 2015). We also know the specifics of how corporations (Bouwen, 2002; Smith et al., 2010) and NGOs build policy communities (Junk, 2016) through lobbying. Building across this divide between regulatory networks and communities can offer much in terms of understanding how European regulation works in practice and how it intervenes in or is shaped by the actions of concerned communities. It also highlights the role and reactions of involved professionals, and of citizens and civil society, as relevant. Conversely, it also tells us about the structural limits to governance and legitimacy that regulatory networks may place upon the aspirations of such communities.

4.3 Operationalising Regulatory Networks and Policy Communities

We are often driven to identify a network or community when in the process of making sense of the governance actors in a particular issue area. We look at formal functions, and the attributes that bring a particular type of actor to the policy arena. We start detecting patterns, and that is where we can distinguish commonalities: shared knowledge, similar interests, the collective adoption of a scientific paradigm, the adherence to particular norms or visions for the future or a combination of the above. A big part of this task is linked to the expertise of actors. This is about scientific knowledge and professional expertise, which carries recognised competence credentials. It is also, however, about technical expertise, about being in possession of the right tools to deal with regulatory complexity. For such traits and aspirations to be shared, the network or community relies on socialisation processes linked to education and professional backgrounds, as well as ongoing and regular interaction, whether formal or informal.

A second set of questions to consider when studying regulatory networks and policy communities is their links to power. As discussed above, a regulatory network implies a formal role in at least one part of the policy-making process, from problem identification to decision-making, implementation, evaluation and enforcement. A policy community need not have a specified role or indeed an active policy agenda. The place of the network or community in the overall governance framework thus needs to be considered. What is the group's role, what are the interaction and feedback mechanisms that it is a part of and how is it legitimated? Turning to their issue area, this may be broadly or narrowly defined, following a sector, problem, or time-frame logic. Several further questions are open to investigation: Do network or community members have a clear understanding of the boundaries of the issue? Is the issue clearly defined or are there overlaps? Does the issue lend itself to exclusive treatment by those in the network or community or are other actors to be involved? Is the issue sufficiently institutionalised or are these groups building institutional capacity in handling it? How are they resourced? How resilient is the group when under stress and what are the factors determining its longevity, from issue relevance to inertia through strategies for self-preservation.

A shared understanding and a focused definition of the issue area are generally to be expected when identifying regulatory networks and policy communities. The extent to which these are settings where disagreement is possible, however, can vary over time and across issue areas. Some groupings encourage or tolerate deliberation and dissent, different types of expertise and extensive engagement with civil society. Others are mechanisms for consensus formation, ironing out differences in a closed setting, presenting a coherent approach that promotes particular policy goals or resisting calls for greater representation in policy-making. Others still are concerned with debates about what constitutes 'good science' or 'good regulation', with little explicit interest in the world of policy and no strategy to push their issue area on policy agendas. Nevertheless, most operate in technocratic frameworks. These frameworks privilege the inclusion of certain types of ideas when policy options are outlined. They also, on the whole, dampen the political salience of issues and depoliticise the policy arena.

BOX 4.2 Analysing 'regulatory networks' and 'policy communities': key questions

1. What binds them together? Shared knowledge, common interests, collective adoption of a scientific paradigm?
2. What is the issue area and how well is it defined and delineated from others? What is the role of the network/community under study in the governance of the issue area and how is it legitimated?
3. Are there spaces where dissent is permitted and consensus is negotiated? Do these spaces serve to depoliticise the issues at hand?
4. What is the regulatory role of networks and communities? Regulatory networks are generally directly involved in regulatory activity. This not the case for policy communities.

4.4 Policy Vignettes: Examples of Community and Network Interactions

4.4.1 Vaping: A Regulatory Network Catches a Community Unawares

Electronic cigarettes, or e-cigarettes, are a recent innovation. They allow nicotine users to mimic the sensation of smoking conventional cigarettes without inhaling tar and other harmful by-products of combusting tobacco leaves. They do this by using battery power to heat up a nicotine-containing liquid solution to the point of vaporisation. E-cigarettes were developed and popularised in China and have very rapidly proliferated in Western markets – first through internet sales from China, and later through the marketing of new products from Western start-ups or big tobacco companies (all of which have now acquired or developed their own brands of e-cigarettes).

E-cigarettes initially spread through European markets relatively incognito, sustained by internet sales and a 'do-it-yourself' culture of vaping aficionados (Zhu et al., 2014). This enabled a passionate community to grow, united in their enthusiasm for what they held to be a revolutionary product that was saving the lives of those who could not or would not give up their nicotine addiction (or nicotine enjoyment). The community evolved through internet message boards and trade shows where close links were established between the vapers and the European small and medium-sized enterprises (SMEs) importing and selling e-cigarette equipment and liquids.

On the regulatory side, the EU's Tobacco Products Directive (TPD) was due for a revision around 2010 following a 2001 update. Early actions in the process included commissioned studies and impact assessments focused on e-cigarettes by external consultants and a series of stakeholder meetings. Another set of important meetings (ongoing since the implementation of the 2001 TPD) were those of the Regulatory Committee for Tobacco Control (RCTC). Established under Article 10 of that directive, the RCTC comprised representatives from the Directorate-General for Health and Consumers and from member state ministries and departments of health. The RCTC is a good example of a regulatory network – it was established through legislative action of a governing body and endowed with the tasks of sharing information, setting goals and monitoring outcomes of tobacco control in EU member states. Both the conveners and members exercised regulatory power in the issue area. These studies and meetings culminated in a 2012 draft proposal by the Commission on a revised TPD.

The 2012 draft proposal was the first time that the vaping policy community learned that e-cigarettes were being targeted for medicalisation. Essentially, this meant turning what they perceived to be recreational devices into pharmaceutical quitting tools that could only be bought in pharmacies and had to pass randomised controlled trials demonstrating their efficacy. This was an option endorsed by most of the authorities in the RCTC, but something the vaping community strongly objected to – they did not see themselves as patients in need of a 'cure', but rather as empowered adults who had taken control of their nicotine use into their own hands and away from big tobacco companies (Hasselbalch, 2016). The structure of the regulatory network of the RCTC made it impossible for them to gain access to the values and viewpoints of the vaping policy community. This vignette is therefore instructive in demonstrating that it matters for policy outcomes whether regulatory networks, including seemingly technical or neutral ones, are spaces where dissent can be voiced and engaged with, or whether they are constructed in such a way that dissent is glossed over or not even registered.

4.4.2   Fracking: A Policy Community Informs Regulatory Network Preferences

Hydraulic fracturing, or fracking, is a recent hydrocarbon production technique combining horizontal drilling and pressurised injection of sand, water and chemicals into layers of hydrocarbon-containing rock (frequently shale), which is thereby fractured, allowing oil or gas to flow freely and be collected at the wellhead. The technique was developed in the United States, quickly setting off an energy boom and access to abundant hydrocarbons. Some energy companies are hoping to replicate that success in the EU, but the scale of European production and exploration is still very low in comparison.

Fracking came to the attention of EU policymakers through the concerted efforts of a well-organised anti-fracking policy community, comprising environmental NGOs, green politicians and activists. Their opposition to fracking rested on a shared adherence to both technical and normative positions. In technical terms, they raised a number of concerns about the safety of fracking for the environment and human health. Some of the most common objections included the risks of: triggering earthquakes, polluting aquifers, overland chemical spills and air pollution (Food and Water Europe et al., 2012). Even if these risks could be mitigated by different measures taken by the oil and gas companies, the community voiced doubts that the EU or member state bureaucracies would be able to monitor and enforce the application of such measures. In normative terms, the anti-fracking policy community held that further exploration and production of hydrocarbons was irresponsible given that even existing reserves could not be fully utilised if a two-degree global warming target were to be respected. The only defensible course of action, in their view, was to accelerate the shift to a renewable and sustainable energy system free of fossil fuels.

In contrast to the e-cigarette case, fracking was very much put on the agenda by the actions of this policy community – the vaping policy community wanted the Commission to take e-cigarettes *off* the agenda. The anti-fracking policy community succeeded in building momentum behind their message in a way that took the oil and gas companies by surprise and left them in a difficult position to counter warnings. Some technical experts from the oil and gas sector found the risks greatly exaggerated and sensationalised, including by media outlets more willing to escalate the controversy than tone it down (Cotton, 2015).

Although this mobilisation and momentum behind the anti-fracking stance made it impossible for the Commission to ignore the issue, that did not mean that strong-worded or binding regulation would necessarily emerge from the regulatory process itself. In particular, oil and gas sector professionals found a much more receptive audience within the Commission than among the public, where their demonstration of technical and scientific expertise could convince a critical mass of regulatory officials that the risks were under control (Hasselbalch, 2017). This resulted in the construction of a regulatory network that was based on a set of non-binding recommendations and guidelines rather than binding regulations or directives. The Commission suggested a number of best practices and asked member states to report on implementation and monitoring progress, after which they would be graded on a scorecard. It also established a scientific network to gather more information on best available techniques and environmental risks. This network enforced a strictly scientific consideration of facts and had no tolerance of dissent or political positions, but as it was open to both NGO and industry participation, this separation of science and politics did not materialise and the network was quickly dismantled.

This vignette showcases the difficulties of involving policy communities in regulatory networks that restrict the scope for exercising dissent or challenging the network's mandate. The greater challenge lies in balancing input, output and throughput legitimacy in looser governance structures such as regulatory networks. Governance beyond the state must involve civil society participants, but doing so in a way that allows both political contestation and effective regulation is a difficult balancing act.

4.4.3   Demographic Change: A Community Building and then Losing Momentum

A policy understanding of demographic change at the EU level is derived from statistical trends (an ageing population), observable changes in European demographics (fewer babies born, a greater share of the population entering the 65+ phase, migration flows), and the impact of demographics on the European workforce (skills and human capital) and on Europe's finances (pensions). These different ways of defining issues linked to demographic change lead to different policy concerns. At the EU level, and across two directorate-generals, DG EMPL and DG ECFIN, four areas of policy activity can be identified: skill gaps and human capital; pension reform; work–life balance and policies enabling choice on family formation; and active/healthy ageing.

For both the authorities and the European public, issues relating to demographic change are important in terms of long-term planning but not urgent in terms of action and resources. They can also be controversial in that they touch upon the private lives of citizens and threaten some long-held social rights. There is concern about whether Europe will have enough skilled workers with the right type of skills where and when they are needed; about pension provision and large numbers of needy elderly falling into poverty; about the ability of people of reproductive age to reconcile work and family and afford housing; and about the logistics in place for an older society in urban and rural environments. The issues are seen as cross-cutting, and as a result they can be taken on by different types of institutional actors (those in charge of employment, health, social justice or finance) – or none. They can also fall between the cracks of the EU's multilevel governance and competence patchwork. As a result, even though the bulk of the EU's work on demographic change falls under 'employment', authority on these issues is highly diffuse, policy timelines fragmented and funding support scarce. With limited institutionalisation, it is 'policy entrepreneurs' who can take the initiative to consolidate policy knowledge on these issues and to position them in a way where they can secure longevity and resources (De la Porte and Natali, 2018).

In the past decade, DG EMPL tried to develop a focused demographic strategy, including through links with expert groups. The aspiration was to help build and consolidate a policy community through regular events and publications, tapping into growing demographic expertise, widespread agreement on the causes of the demographic change trends at play in Europe and significant academic consensus on the range of policy options. But the expertise lies within an academic group of mostly demographers which exhibits epistemic community characteristics but has not had the resources or incentives to morph into, or contribute to, a policy community. Additionally, even though demographic change is linked to many social matters of concern to advocacy groups and rights organisations, interests are too diverse and often seen as in opposition to each other (for example, young vs. old, highly skilled vs. low skilled) for there to be consistent and substantial input from civil society in a policy community. At the same time, while DG EMPL took the lead through policy entrepreneurship, DG ECFIN has been an all-powerful secondary actor following the financial and eurozone crises. This led to compromises and the gradual loss of the institutional mandate for DG EMPL, with demographic issues losing prominence and becoming appendiced to a different initiative, the Social Investment Package. In essence, the incentives of different actors, as well as internal European Commission dynamics and funding prioritisations, hampered the attempt to create and mobilise a policy community (Seabrooke et al., 2019).

This vignette is largely a story of failure. It shows that even when the issues are important and considered so by the relevant actors, a body of knowledge and the initiatives of some individuals alone are not enough to build a policy community, let alone a regulatory network. In this instance, the issue has porous boundaries but the absence of urgency and resources means that there is no fight over which type of actor gets to control it, but a vacuum instead. Lack of support from civil society also removes potential legitimation mechanisms which can enhance community building.

Fleshing out the concepts of 'regulatory networks' and 'policy communities' and applying them empirically shows how we can usefully navigate the world of networked governance. To make the most of the concepts, we need to understand how the groupings are bound together, how they are positioned within broader regulatory frameworks with respect to their issue area and the extent to which they enable dissent and deliberation. We also need to determine whether the groupings are interested in policy content or are contesting resources, which are affected by crisis and post-crisis dynamics. This will enable us to understand policy action, and inaction, in the EU.

GROUP DISCUSSION

- In what issue areas are we most likely to observe the work of policy communities feeding into regulatory networks?
- What are the legitimation challenges for EU regulatory networks?

TOPICS FOR INDIVIDUAL RESEARCH

- What is the role of regulatory networks and policy communities in dealing with controversies about applying scientific knowledge in policy-making?
- What is the role of expertise in EU policy-making?

FURTHER READINGS

Bach, D. and Newman, A. L. (2007). 'The European Regulatory State and Global Public Policy: Micro-institutions, Macro-influence'. *Journal of European Public Policy*, 14(6): 827–46.

Haas, P.M. (1992). 'Introduction: Epistemic Communities and International Policy Coordination'. *International Organization*, 46(1): 1–35.

Majone, G. (1997). 'From the Positive to the Regulatory State: Causes and Consequences of Changes in the Mode of Governance'. *Journal of Public Policy*, 17(2): 139–67.

Torfing, J., and Sørensen, E. (2014). 'The European Debate on Governance Networks: Towards a New and Viable Paradigm?'. *Policy and Society*, 33(4): 329–44.

REFERENCES

Avant, D., Finnemore, M. and Sell, S. K. (eds) (2010). *Who Governs the Globe?* Cambridge: Cambridge University Press.

Bach, D. and Newman, A. L. (2007). 'The European Regulatory State and Global Public Policy: Micro-institutions, Macro-influence'. *Journal of European Public Policy*, 14(6): 827–46.

Baumgartner, F. R. and Mahoney, C. (2008). 'Forum Section: The Two Faces of Framing: Individual-Level Framing and Collective Issue Definition in the European Union'. *European Union Politics*, 9(3): 435–49.

Binderkrantz, A. S. and Rasmussen, A. (2015). 'Comparing the Domestic and the EU Lobbying Context: Perceived Agenda-setting Influence in the Multi-level System of the European Union'. *Journal of European Public Policy*, 22(4): 552–69.

Black, J. (2001). 'Decentring Regulation: Understanding the Role of Regulation and Self-Regulation in a "Post-Regulatory" World'. *Current Legal Problems*, 54(1): 103–46.

Blauberger, M. and Rittberger, B. (2015). 'Conceptualizing and Theorizing EU Regulatory Networks'. *Regulation and Governance*, 9(4): 367–76.

Bouwen, P. (2002). 'Corporate Lobbying in the European Union: Towards a Theory of Access'. *Journal of European Public Policy*, 9(3): 365–90.

Braithwaite, J. and Drahos, P. (2000). *Global Business Regulation*. Cambridge: Cambridge University Press.

Büthe, T. and Mattli, W. (2011). *The New Global Rulers: The Privatization of Regulation in the World Economy*. Princeton: Princeton University Press.

Callon, M., Lascoumes, P. and Barthe, Y. (2009). *Acting in an Uncertain World: An Essay on Technical Democracy*. Cambridge, MA: MIT Press.

Carstensen, M. B. and Schmidt, V. A. (2016). 'Power Through, Over and in Ideas: Conceptualizing Ideational Power in Discursive Institutionalism'. *Journal of European Public Policy*, 23(3): 318–37.

Cotton, M. (2015). 'Stakeholder Perspectives on Shale Gas Fracking: A Q-method Study of Environmental Discourses'. *Environment and Planning A*, 47(9): 1944–62.

Cross, M. K. D. (2013). 'Rethinking Epistemic Communities Twenty Years Later'. *Review of International Studies*, 39(1): 137–60.

De la Porte, C. and Natali, D. (2018). 'Agents of Institutional Change in EU Policy: The Social Investment Moment'. *Journal of European Public Policy*, 25(6): 828–43.

Egeberg, M., Trondal, J. and Vestlund, N. M. (2014). 'The Quest for Order: Unravelling the Relationship Between the European Commission and European Union Agencies'. *Journal of European Public Policy*, 22(5): 609–29.

Food and Water Europe, et al. (2012). 'Position Statement on Shale Gas, Shale Oil, Coal Bed Methane and "Fracking"'. www.foeeurope.org/sites/default/files/press_releases/foee_shale_gas_joint_position_240412_3.pdf (accessed 29 April 2016).

Haas, P. M. (1992). 'Introduction: Epistemic Communities and International Policy Coordination'. *International Organization*, 46(1): 1–35.

Hasselbalch, J. A. (2016). 'Professional Disruption in Health Regulation: Electronic Cigarettes in the European Union'. *Journal of Professions and Organization*, 3(1): 62–85.

Hasselbalch, J. A. (2017). *The Contentious Politics of Disruptive Innovation: Vaping and Fracking in the European Union*. PhD thesis, University of Warwick.

Hobolth, M. and Martinsen, D. S. (2013). 'Transgovernmental Networks in the European Union: Improving Compliance Effectively?' *Journal of European Public Policy*, 20(10): 1406–24.

Hofmann, H. C. H. (2008). 'Mapping the European Administrative Space'. *West European Politics*, 31(4): 662–76.

Hood, C., Rothstein, H. and Baldwin, R. (2001). *The Government of Risk: Understanding Risk Regulation Regimes*. Oxford: Oxford University Press.

Jordana, J., Levi-Faur, D. and Fernández-i-Marín, X. (2011). 'The Global Diffusion of Regulatory Agencies: Channels of Transfer and Stages of Diffusion'. *Comparative Political Studies*, 44(10): 1343–69.

Junk, W. M. (2016). 'Two Logics of NGO Advocacy: Understanding Inside and Outside Lobbying on EU Environmental Policies'. *Journal of European Public Policy*, 23(2): 236–54.

Kelemen, R. D. and Tarrant, A. D. (2011). 'The Political Foundations of the Eurocracy'. *West European Politics*, 34(5): 922–47.

Klijn, E.-H. (2008). 'Governance and Governance Networks in Europe: An Assessment of Ten Years of Research on the Theme'. *Public Management Review*, 10(4): 505–25.

Klijn, E.-H. and Skelcher, C. (2007). 'Democracy and Governance Networks: Compatible or Not?' *Public Administration*, 85(3): 587–608.

Klüver, H. (2013). *Lobbying in the European Union: Interest Groups, Lobbying Coalitions, and Policy Change*. Oxford: Oxford University Press.

Klüver, H., Mahoney, C. and Opper, M. (2015). 'Framing in Context: How Interest Groups Employ Framing to Lobby the European Commission'. *Journal of European Public Policy*, 22(4): 481–98.

Latour, B. (2005). *Reassembling the Social: An Introduction to Actor-Network-Theory*. Oxford: Oxford University Press.

Levi-Faur, D. (2011). 'Regulatory Networks and Regulatory Agencification: Towards a Single European Regulatory Space'. *Journal of European Public Policy*, 18(6): 810–29.

Lodge, M. (2008). 'Regulation, the Regulatory State and European Politics'. *West European Politics*, 31(1–2): 280–301.

Maggetti, M. and Gilardi, F. (2011). 'The Policy-making Structure of European Regulatory Networks and the Domestic Adoption of Standards'. *Journal of European Public Policy*, 18(6): 830–47.

Mahoney, C. (2008). *Brussels Versus the Beltway. Advocacy in the United States and the European Union*. Washington, DC: Georgetown University Press.

Maggetti, M. and Gilardi, F. (2014). 'Network Governance and the Domestic Adoption of Soft Rules'. *Journal of European Public Policy*, 21(9): 1293–310.

Majone, G. (1994). 'The Rise of the Regulatory State in Europe'. *West European Politics*, 17(3): 77–101.

Majone, G. (1997). 'From the Positive to the Regulatory State: Causes and Consequences of Changes in the Mode of Governance'. *Journal of Public Policy*, 17(2): 139–67.

Marsh, D. and Rhodes, R. A. W. (1992). *Policy Networks in British Government*. Oxford: Clarendon Press.

Mastenbroek, E. and Martinsen, D. S. (2018). 'Filling the Gap in the European Administrative Space: The Role of Administrative Networks in EU Implementation and Enforcement'. *Journal of European Public Policy*, 25(3): 422–35.

Mazzucato, M. (2013). *The Entrepreneurial State: Debunking Public vs. Private Sector Myths*. London and New York: Anthem Press.

Meijerink, S. (2005). 'Understanding Policy Stability and Change: The Interplay of Advocacy Coalitions and Epistemic Communities, Windows of Opportunity, and Dutch Coastal Flooding Policy 1945–2031'. *Journal of European Public Policy*, 12(6): 1060–77.

Moran, M. (2003). *The British Regulatory State: High Modernism and Hyper-Innovation*. Oxford: Oxford University Press.

Newman, A. (2008). *Protectors of Privacy: Regulating Personal Data in the Global Economy*. Ithaca, NY: Cornell University Press.

Nohrstedt, D. (2013). 'Advocacy Coalitions in Crisis Resolution: Understanding Policy Dispute in the European Volcanic Ash Cloud Crisis'. *Public Administration*, 91(4): 964–79.

Osborne, D. and Gaebler, T. (1992). *Reinventing Government: How the Entrepreneurial Spirit Is Transforming the Public Sector*. Reading, MA: Addison-Wesley.

Radaelli, C. (1999). 'The Public Policy of the European Union: Whither Politics of Expertise?' *Journal of European Public Policy*, 6(5): 757–74.

Rhodes, R. A. W. (1996). 'The New Governance: Governing without Government'. *Political Studies*, 44: 652–67.

Rose, N. and Miller, P. (1992). 'Political Power beyond the State: Problematics of Government'. *The British Journal of Sociology*, 43(2): 173–205.

Rose, N., O'Malley, P. and Valverde, M. (2006). 'Governmentality'. *Annual Review of Law and Social Science*, 2(1): 83–104.

Rosenau, J. N. (2007). 'Governing the Ungovernable: The Challenge of a Global Disaggregation of Authority'. *Regulation & Governance*, 1(1): 88–97.

Sabatier, P. A. (1998). 'The Advocacy Coalition Framework: Revisions and Relevance for Europe'. *Journal of European Public Policy*, 5(1): 98–130.

Schmidt, V. A. (2006). *Democracy in Europe: The EU and National Polities*. Oxford: Oxford University Press.

Scott, C. (2004). 'Regulation in the Age of Governance: The Rise of the Post-regulatory State'. In J. Jordana and D. Levi-Faur (eds), *The Politics of Regulation: Institutions and Regulatory Reforms for the Age of Governance*. Cheltenham: Edward Elgar.

Seabrooke, L. and Tsingou, E. (2019). 'Europe's Fast- and Slow-burning Crises'. *Journal of European Public Policy*, 26(3): 468–81.

Seabrooke, L., Tsingou, E. and Willers, J. O. (2019). 'The Political Economy of Policy Vacuums: The European Commission on Demographic Change'. *New Political Economy*, DOI :10.1080/13563467.2019.1669549.

Selznick, P. (1985). 'Focusing Organizational Research on Regulation'. In R. G. Noll (ed.), *Regulatory Policy and the Social Sciences*. Berkeley and Los Angeles: University of California Press.

Smith, K. E. et al. (2010). 'Working the System: British American Tobacco's Influence on the European Union Treaty and its Implications for Policy: An Analysis of Internal Tobacco Industry Documents'. *PLoS Medicine*, 7(1): e1000202.

Strange, S. (1996). *The Retreat of the State: The Diffusion of Power in the World Economy*. Cambridge: Cambridge University Press.

Thatcher, M. (2011). 'The Creation of European Regulatory Agencies and its Limits: A Comparative Analysis of European Delegation'. *Journal of European Public Policy*, 18(6): 37–41.

Torfing, J. and Sørensen, E. (2014). 'The European Debate on Governance Networks: Towards a New and Viable Paradigm?'. *Policy and Society*, 33(4): 329–44.

Vogel, S. (1996). *Freer Markets, More Rules: Regulatory Reform in Advanced Industrial Countries*. Ithaca, NY: Cornell University Press.

Wenger, E. (1998). *Communities of Practice: Learning, Meaning, and Identity*. Cambridge: Cambridge University Press.

Wilkinson, K., Lowe, P. and Donaldson, A. (2010). 'Beyond Policy Networks: Policy Framing and the Politics of Expertise in the 2001 Foot and Mouth Disease Crisis'. *Public Administration*, 88(2): 331–45.

Woll, C. (2008). *Firm Interests: How Governments Shape Business Lobbying on Global Trade*. Ithaca, NY: Cornell University Press.

Woll, C. (2012). 'The Brash and the Soft-spoken: Lobbying Styles in a Transatlantic Comparison'. *Interest Groups & Advocacy*, 1(2): 193–214.

Zeitlin, J. (2016). 'EU Experimentalist Governance in Times of Crisis'. *West European Politics*, 39(5): 1073–94.

Zhu, S.-H. et al. (2014). 'Four Hundred and Sixty Brands of E-cigarettes and Counting: Implications for Product Regulation'. *Tobacco Control*, 23, supplement 3 (January): iii3–iii9.

5 Rethinking EU Governance: From 'Old' to 'New' Approaches to Who Steers Integration

VIVIEN A. SCHMIDT

5.1 Introduction

Who is in charge of the EU? Who controls what happens? What is the balance of power among EU institutional actors? Scholars have long disagreed, divided over which actors exercise what kind of power. As European integration has deepened over time, with all EU actors increasingly empowered in different ways, scholarly debates evolved, but the principal divisions remained. Some scholars contended that intergovernmental actors in the Council and later the European Council were in charge. Others insisted that supranational actors in a range of EU-level administrations and agencies exercised control. While yet others saw the EP as a growing force in EU decision-making.[1]

In the early years, the main division was represented by scholarly disagreements over whether the Council through its intergovernmental decision-making was the real driver of European integration or if instead the Commission through its supranational policy formulation and implementation was the main force behind the deepening of the EU. On the intergovernmentalist side was Stanley Hoffmann (1966), who found the member states to be in charge of integration, exercising their bargaining power in the Council to protect their national interests while building Europe. On the supranationalist side was Ernst Haas (1958), who argued that neo-functionalist processes of 'spillover' from one policy area to another produced increasing integration. In the 1990s, with the advent of the Maastricht Treaty, the debates over the drivers of integration were updated by scholars on both sides. Andrew Moravcsik (1993, 1998) challenged Hoffmann's long-accepted realist intergovernmentalist view of European integration with his theory of liberal intergovernmentalism, in which he argued that the main drivers of member states' preference formation in intergovernmental bargaining were domestic socio-economic interests rather than geopolitical interests. Countering this view from the supranationalist perspective were Wayne Sandholtz and Alex Stone Sweet and colleagues, who maintained that integration moved forward because EU officials were in control, exercising institutional power through their mastery of the EU policy process (Sandholtz and Stone Sweet, 1998).

[1] This chapter builds on an article published in a symposium issue of the *Journal of Common Market Studies* (Kleine and Pollack, 2018), and on a working paper for the *Istituto Affari Internazionali*, both of which were undertaken under the auspices of the EU Commission Horizon 2020 project: European Legitimacy in Governing through Hard Times (# 649456 – ENLIGHTEN).

These now traditional debates continue to this day, pitting the intergovernmentalists, who insist that member states in the Council pursuing the national interest and/or domestic socio-economic interests are in charge, against the supranationalists, who maintain instead that supranational actors in the Commission and elsewhere drive integration via institutional dynamics of spillover and entrepreneurialism. But while this divide continues, self-styled 'new' protagonists have joined in, by building on while challenging both sides of the traditional debates. These debates pit the 'new' intergovernmentalists, who insist that the more actively engaged, consensus-seeking member state governments in the (European) Council have retaken control (e.g. Bickerton et al., 2015; Puetter, 2012), versus the 'new' supranationalists, who continue to view EU-level supranational actors such as the Commission and the ECB as driving integration through their greater role in policy design and enforcement (e.g. Bauer and Becker, 2014; Epstein and Rhodes, 2016). The one view shared by both sides is that of the declining significance of the EP and the co-decision mode of policy-making. For another set of analysts, whom we shall call the 'new' parliamentarists, the views of old and new intergovernmentalists and supranationalists are mistaken, because they fail to recognise the new formal and informal ways in which the EP has regained influence (e.g. Hix and Høyland, 2013; Héritier et al., 2016).

The main focus of this chapter is on the 'new' ways in which scholars now explain contemporary EU governance – including 'new' intergovernmentalism, 'new' supranationalism and 'new' parliamentarism – and how these contrast with one another as well as with the older approaches. The chapter will show that whatever the substantive differences among the proponents of different aspects of the newer approaches to EU governance, they share a common framework of analysis. Almost all emphasise the importance of sentient actors' ideas and discursive interactions following a constructivist or discursive institutionalist logic, in which actors' ideational powers are constructed through discourse and deliberation. But the chapter will also demonstrate that although these approaches for the most part share a common analytic framework, the 'new' EU governance approaches differ in how they theorise the exercise of such power in EU governance. New intergovernmentalists argue that member state actors are in charge of EU governance, with outcomes a result of their powers of persuasion in intergovernmental deliberation. New supranationalists contend instead that supranational actors are in control of EU governance, with outcomes a result of their powers of ideational innovation and institutional discretion. And new parliamentarists, more modestly, insist that parliamentary actors are gaining influence, with outcomes increasingly a result of their ideas and discursive interactions with the other more institutionally powerful actors.

But whatever the differences among such 'new' approaches, they are united in their opposition to the older approaches to EU governance with regard to both their rationalist or historical institutionalist frameworks of analysis and their theorisations of the exercise of power. The traditional intergovernmentalists, theorising within a rationalist framework, argue that the outcomes of member states' rationally driven, interest-based negotiations are determined by their asymmetrical bargaining power, or what we will henceforth term, for purposes of conformity with the literature, 'coercive' power (defined as relations of control by one actor over another, where these relations allow one actor to shape directly the circumstances or actions of another (Dahl, 1957; Barnett and Duvall, 2005: 43, 49; see also Carstensen and Schmidt, 2016, 2017). The traditional supranationalists, theorising within a historical institutionalist framework, contend that the outcomes of supranational actors' rules-grounded, interest-based institution building are determined by their institutional power. And the traditional parliamentarists, theorising within either a rationalist or historical institutionalist framework, insist that the outcomes of the parliamentary actors' pursuit of greater influence are enhanced by their exercise of (very weak) coercive or institutional power.

In short, while new and old theorists of EU governance may be united by a shared focus on a preferred EU actor, whether the Council, the Commission or the EP, they are divided in their views on the nature of the power exercised by their preferred actor, whether rational institutionalist, historical institutionalist and/or discursive institutionalist and constructivist (see Table 5.1).

Table 5.1 Three approaches to EU governance, old and new

EU governance	Intergovernmentalism		Supranationalism		Parliamentarism	
	Old	New	Old	New	Old	New
Analytic framework	Rational choice institutionalism	Discursive institutionalism Constructivism	Historical institutionalism	Discursive institutionalism Constructivism	Historical institutionalism	Discursive institutionalism Historical institutionalism
Empirical object of study	Council	Council and *de novo* bodies	Commission	Commission and *de novo* bodies	EP	EP
Theoretical argument	In charge via interest-based bargaining	In charge via ideas and deliberation	In control via institutional means	In control via ideas and deliberation	Gaining influence via institutional means	Gaining influence via institutional means and/or ideas and deliberation
Bases of power	Coercive	Ideational	Institutional	Ideational	Coercive/institutional	Ideational/institutional

Although applauding the newer approaches for their innovations in EU integration theory, in particular their focus on EU actors' ideational and discursive powers, this chapter suggests that it is a mistake to largely disregard the significance of coercive or institutional power, emphasised in the older approaches. The chapter shows instead that it is more useful to leave open the question of which kind of power is being exercised by which actor in order to establish through empirical analysis which kind of power or combination of powers is in play.

But the main thrust of the chapter is a critique of all such approaches for their emphasis on one or another EU institutional actor alone. Its purpose is to demonstrate the real complexity of EU governance, which involves a 'new' political dynamics of interaction affected by the politicisation of both national and EU levels.

The benefit of these debates, old and new, is that the different sides lend major insights into the changing powers and responsibilities of 'their' EU actor vis-à-vis the other EU actors. The drawback is that they are naturally more focused on demonstrating the significance of a given EU institutional actor than in shedding light on the overall picture. What they miss by assessing the institutional powers, positions, ideas and actions of any given EU actor on its own is how all such EU actors have become more dynamically interactive in EU-level governance. Equally importantly, they miss the national-level dynamics, as elucidated by post-functionalists (e.g. Hooghe and Marks, 2009, 2019), which suggests that increasing national politicisation in response to EU encroachments on national government and democracy has not only disrupted mainstream politics, with the rise of populist challenges. It has also had significant feedback effects on EU policy-making, making for more politically charged EU governance. This means that Moravcsik's (1993) original insight about the influence of domestic interests on EU-level decision-making remains a key factor in understanding EU governance today and in the future. But that insight was too narrowly focused. It must be expanded to include not just socio-economic interests but political interests more generally, meaning how national electoral politics and citizen discontent affect EU-level decision-making (Hooghe and Marks, 2019).

Politicisation is not just bottom up, however, from the national to the EU level, affecting member state positions in the Council alone. It is intra-institutional at the top, among EU actors in their ongoing interactions. Politicisation has affected all EU actors' actions and interactions, making for a 'new' dynamics of EU governance that is more political in every way. With this in mind, Schmidt's (2006) characterisation of the EU level as consisting of 'policy without politics', based on the tendency to apolitical and/or technocratic decision-making, no longer fully describes EU governance, which has increasingly become 'policy *with* politics' in the more contentious areas. At the same time, what Schmidt (2006) identified as national-level 'politics *without* policy' has only worsened, so much so that it arguably no longer fully describes the current situation, which has increasingly become 'politics *against* policy' or even 'politics *against* polity' (Schmidt, 2019, 2020).

5.2   New Intergovernmentalism

Scholars who explain EU governance as characterised by the 'new intergovernmentalism' see the EU's member state leaders in the European Council as much more legislatively active than in the past. They find that the member states have taken on an unprecedented leadership role that they exercise through consensus-seeking deliberation rather than the exercise of coercive power through interest-based bargaining (Puetter, 2012; Bickerton et al., 2015; Fabbrini, 2016). This involves much more shared authority and joint control at the EU level than was considered possible in the older approaches to intergovernmentalism, whether in the original 'realist' view, in which member states' bargaining focused on protecting national sovereignty and interests (Hoffman, 1966), or in the revisionist 'liberal' view, in which member states' hard bargaining and brinkmanship served as a conduit for domestic socio-economic interests (Moravcsik, 1993; see also Schimmelfennig, 2015a).

Moreover, unlike some of the traditional intergovernmentalists, whether realist or liberal intergovernmentalist, who tended to theorise the Commission as delegated 'agents' which the Council 'principals' could control, the new intergovernmentalists present the Council as actively seeking to reduce Commission powers through the creation of supranational agencies. Thus, they argue that member state governments, rather than delegating new powers for the Commission in view of new tasks, instead deliberately created *de novo* EU bodies and instruments outside the main EU institutions in efforts to maintain control. Such efforts involved not only keeping the Commission out of those bodies but also putting the member states *qua* member states *in*, for instance by ensuring their representation on the governing boards. Examples of such *de novo* bodies include the ECB (Hodson, 2015); new financial entities such as the temporary European Financial Stability Facility (EFSF) and the permanent European Stability Mechanism (ESM); new administrative bodies such as the European External Action Service (EEAS); and a new president for the European Council.

In conjunction with this argument, the new intergovernmentalists at the same time contend that member states' new activism sidelines the older supranationalism, which sees bureaucratic entrepreneurialism and institutional creep as having increasingly institutionally empowered the traditional supranational actors in the European Commission and the ECJ (Sandholtz and Stone Sweet, 1998). Moreover, rather than assuming that the Commission is intent on pushing 'ever closer union', as suggested by the old supranationalists, they see it as much more circumspect in its ambitions, focused on core goals and more interested in better accomplishing its main tasks (Peterson, 2015; see also Hodson, 2015).

For the new intergovernmentalists, finally, the mistake of the older intergovernmentalists has been to assume that the process is all about the pursuit of power, whether coercive power through interest-based bargaining in the Council or institutional power through budget maximising for the bureaucracy. Instead, new intergovernmentalists maintain that the decision-making process in the Council since the Maastricht Treaty of the early 1990s needs to be understood in terms of the exercise of ideational power, with member states seeking to arrive at consensual agreements through deliberation (see discussion in Carstensen and Schmidt, 2017). In the Council in particular, they highlight the deliberative processes of negotiation that leads to agreements resulting from persuasion rather than power politics (Puetter, 2012).

Thus, for example, new intergovernmentalists would reject out of hand the analysis by liberal intergovernmentalists of the eurozone crisis response of 2010 to 2012. The liberal intergovernmentalists see that response in terms of coercive power, as a game of chicken in which the strong preference to avoid the breakdown of the euro area was combined with efforts to shift the costs to the weaker euro members most in trouble (Schimmelfennig, 2015a). Instead, new intergovernmentalists focus on ideational power, mainly in terms of the consensus-based agreements forged in the Council. After all, each and every member state bought into the story of excessive public debt and failure to follow the rules, pledged themselves to austerity and agreed repeatedly to reinforce the rules of the SGP in exchange for loan bailouts or bailout mechanisms (Fabbrini, 2013; see also Schmidt, 2015).

But if we accept the new intergovernmentalist argument that the Council acts as a consensus-seeking deliberative body because member state leaders did all first agree to the restrictive rules and after to the successive reinterpretations, we at the very least need to recognise that this was not a deliberation among equals. In any of the deliberations – or, better, contestations – going back to the beginning of the crisis, Germany held outsized power to pursue its own interests (Schimmelfennig, 2015a). That power was institutional, as German opposition to doing anything delayed any decision on Greece until the markets threatened the very existence of the euro; it was ideational, given German insistence on the reinforcement of the ordoliberal rules of the SGP; and it was coercive, resulting from Germany's political veto position in any agreement as a result of its economic weight as the strongest economy in Europe (Carstensen and Schmidt, 2017).

Although this exercise of multiple kinds of power – coercive, institutional and ideational – was not akin to a 'dictatorship' by Germany (as some Southern Europeans might insist), since deliberation continued and a consensus was achieved on reinforcing 'governing by rules and numbers' in exchange for loan bailout mechanisms, the best we can say is that the Council was a deliberative political body acting in the shadow of Germany (Schmidt, 2015: 107; 2020). Notably, Fabbrini (2016) is the only new intergovernmentalist who takes account of power and interest, arguing that Council governance has moved from consensus-seeking to hierarchical domination, first by Germany with France, then by Germany alone.

Moreover, the question remains as to how we should characterise the discursive battles waged publicly by member state leaders of Italy and France to shift the interpretation of the 'stability' rules to growth (in 2012) and then to greater flexibility (in 2014). Remember that in late 2011 Italian Prime Minister Mario Monti started calling for growth, which was then taken up by François Hollande as French presidential candidate in 2012, while Italian Prime Minister Matteo Renzi, beginning in 2014, pushed for increased flexibility in the interpretation of the stability rules, supported by President Hollande. These public communicative discourses were directed not only to the citizens but also to other EU leaders, and were accompanied by internal coordinative discourses that constituted political struggles over the rules-following agenda. The result was a change in member state leaders' discourse in 2012, by adding 'growth' to stability. As for flexibility, German Chancellor Merkel agreed to it in 2014 on condition that it remained 'within the stability rules.' But her finance minister, Wolfgang Schäuble, continued to complain that the Commission was overstepping its authority in granting derogations (as the Commission implemented Council commitments to growth and then flexibility). So would we characterise these interactions as new intergovernmentalist processes of deliberative consensus-seeking? Or could they be seen as traditional intergovernmentalist processes of bargaining, where the most powerful wins (as in Schimmelfennig's 2015b critique of new intergovernmentalism)? Or some of each? The question is not just theoretical, it is empirical, depending upon whether interactions are mostly hard processes of bargaining or softer processes of persuasion.

A major problem for the new intergovernmentalist approach in general, then, is that it has done little to theorise power in the context of constructivist deliberation. The very use of the terms deliberation and consensus-seeking seems to imply that member states do not engage in the power relations and bargaining posited by the older intergovernmentalists, whether realist or liberal intergovernmentalist. But without considering coercive power in the processes of deliberation or, better, contestation, we can't explain why Germany's preferences won out, especially initially (Schimmelfennig, 2015a, 2015b). That said, by only positing coercive power and rationalist bargaining (as per the older intergovernmentalism), we can't explain why Germany conceded, over and over again, to things it had initially resisted, including agreeing to new institutional instruments of eurozone governance such as the ESM and banking union, and new guidelines for eurozone governance such as growth and flexibility, pushed by France and Italy (Schmidt, 2015; Carstensen and Schmidt, 2017).

5.3   New Supranationalism

Other scholars take a different view of the new developments in EU governance, seeing the Commission and other supranational actors continuing to be in control of EU policy-making processes. They point to the emergence of a 'new' supranationalism in which the older supranationalism of institutional power and leadership by the technical actors in the Commission has indeed diminished, much as the new intergovernmentalists argue. But in exchange, these new supranationalists contend – against the new intergovernmentalists – that the Council enabled *all* supranational technical actors, whether the Commission, the ECB or other *de novo* bodies, to gain even greater institutional powers of enforcement than in the past, and this through the very rules passed by the more active (new) intergovernmental political leaders. Moreover, in an ironic twist, according to the new supranationalists these self-same technical actors have, through the exercise of ideational power, developed and proposed to the intergovernmental political leaders the policy initiatives they themselves then enforce.

Thus, in contrast to the older supranationalism, which emphasises the Commission's use of institutional rules and dynamics to push deeper European integration along with self-empowerment and interest (Ioannou et al., 2015), the new supranationalism focuses on the Commission's ideas and institutional entrepreneurship to make European integration work better, whether or not this serves its specific power and interests (Bauer and Becker, 2014; Dehousse, 2016; Epstein and Rhodes, 2016). Notably, even new intergovernmentalists acknowledge that the Commission has adjusted to the new realities by taking a pragmatic view of the new European agencies, in particular because they were established in areas where the Commission's own powers were previously weak and served to enhance its objectives and/or provided an additional means of rule making, information and enforcement (Peterson, 2015).

In the eurozone crisis, for example, the new supranationalists have argued that the European Commission is 'the unexpected winner of the crisis' (Bauer and Becker, 2014), and that supranational actors more generally – in particular the ECB as well as the Commission – have 'availed themselves of the discretionary powers with which they were formally or informally vested to adopt decisions that did not reflect the policy preferences of all national governments, notably those of Germany' (Dehousse, 2016). The European Semester, which was long prepared by the Commission in tandem with think tanks and expert consultants, has given the Commission unprecedented oversight authority and enforcement powers with regard to member state governments' budgets (Bauer and Becker, 2014; Schmidt, 2015). Similarly, the Banking Union, spurred by the ideas of the ECB in consultation with experts and in deliberation with the member states in the Council, has given it unprecedented supervisory authority and resolution powers over member state banks (Dehousse, 2016; Epstein and Rhodes, 2016).

Along with this greater authority and responsibility, according to the new supranationalists, has come unprecedented institutional power and autonomy of action (especially the ECB) and discretion in applying the rules (in particular the Commission). The ECB's autonomy is apparent in the eurozone crisis, as it progressively reinterpreted its mandate, going from a narrow view focused on inflation fighting and insisting that it could not be a lender of last resort (LoLR) to doing almost everything that an LoLR does. This started with 'non-standard' policies of buying member state debt (despite the prohibition in the treaties) by doing it on the secondary markets, and going all the way through to quantitative easing in 2015 (Braun, 2013; Mody, 2018: chapter 8). Similarly, in the European Semester the Commission has exercised increasing flexibility in its interpretation of the rules over time, whether through derogations of the rules for individual member states (e.g. France and Italy have repeatedly been given extended time to bring their deficits under the target numbers), recalibrating the calculations (e.g. for Spain on its structural deficit in 2013), or suspending fines (e.g. on sanctions for Spain and Portugal) (Schmidt, 2016, 2020).

But why, we might ask, have the new intergovernmentalists overlooked or underplayed the rise of the new supranationalism? This may be because the new supranational actors have often sought to dissimulate their newly enhanced powers and authority. In many cases they have exercised their new autonomy and discretionary authority 'by stealth', that is, by reinterpreting the rules while not admitting it in their communications with the public or in their coordination with political leaders (Schmidt, 2015, 2016, 2020).

For example, while the ECB has radically reinterpreted its mandate over time, it has sought to hide that reinterpretation 'in plain view' for fear of possible legal challenges and member state complaints as well as to ensure its legitimacy in the eyes of the citizenry (Schmidt, 2016, 2020). The ECB claimed over and over again that it was staying strictly within its mandate even as it moved from a narrow interpretation focused on maintaining its credibility to fight inflation and denying that it could be an LoLR to an increasingly loose interpretation, justifying this with a discourse focusing on ensuring stability in the medium term (Drudi et al., 2012). This enabled it to defend its decision to do 'whatever it takes' (in Draghi's famous words in July 2012) via Open Monetary Transactions if needed, and ultimately to become a lender of last resort in almost all but name through quantitative easing.

In contrast with the ECB, the Commission remained between 'a rock and a hard place' in the context of the euro crisis, and its discourse reflected this, as it sought to hide its increasingly flexible reinterpretation of the rules with a harsh public discourse of austerity and structural reform (Schmidt, 2016, 2020). The Commission found itself sandwiched between the leaders of countries seeking greater flexibility, non-programme as well as programme countries under Troika surveillance, and member state leaders in the Council insisting on applying the rules strictly: the Germans most prominently, but also the Finns and Dutch, who kept close tabs on the Commission and held it to task in Eurogroup meetings on the European Semester.

New supranationalists, then, like the new intergovernmentalists and unlike the old supranationalists, are also mainly focused on ideational innovation and discursive interaction in order to explain how technical actors were able to prevail even against the wishes of powerful Council political leaders. But here too, it would be useful to consider how the different kinds of power played a role in the consensus-seeking behaviour. The old supranationalists' emphasis on institutional power helps us explain why supranational actors were able to act even without approval from the alleged 'principals', who held what old (realist) intergovernmentalists at least would see as a monopoly on coercive power. Such institutional power could be seen to have enabled supranational agents to 'save the euro' in the case of the ECB, or to reinterpret the rules more flexibly, if only 'by stealth', in the case of the Commission. Ideational power, however, exercised through a persuasive discourse, is also necessary to help to explain how, despite the seemingly coercive power of Germany in the Council, the ECB was able to radically reinterpret its mandate 'in plain view' and the Commission to push through derogations to the rules for member states in trouble even while insisting that it was applying harsh austerity and structural reform (Schmidt, 2016, 2020; Carstensen and Schmidt, 2017).

5.4 New Parliamentarism

The one substantive view that the intergovernmentalists and supranationalists, old and new, have in common is that they largely ignore the role of the EP, and see the co-decision process as the great loser in the shift to the new EU governance. But rather than focusing on the question of whether co-decision is no longer the *sine qua non* of processes of deeper integration, and thus the basis of EP power, we would do better to consider what may be afoot. In addition to older approaches to parliamentarism, in which the EP is seen to seek greater influence through its role in the co-decision process, a 'new' parliamentarism theorises EP empowerment through ideas and discursive persuasion outside the traditional circuits of influence. And even if such new parliamentarism remains no match for the new intergovernmentalism or the new supranationalism, it nevertheless needs to be taken into account, in particular because it demonstrates that the EP's relative influence has increased significantly in new ways as well as old since the Maastricht Treaty (Hix and Høyland, 2013; Fasone, 2014; Dinan, 2015; Héritier et al., 2016). Although the EP continues to have little coercive power in comparison to intergovernmental or supranational actors, it has wielded increasing institutional power, if only informally, by tactically using its legislative competences, as well as ideational power, in particular by becoming the 'go-to' body for legitimacy.

There can be no doubt that the co-decision process of decision-making has been supplanted to some extent by the increase in intergovernmental and supranational policy-making in recent years, in particular in the eurozone crisis – as new (and old) intergovernmentalists have argued. They even see the tacit collaboration of the EP in undermining co-decision, for example, by abandoning it so long as they increased their own importance via a more privileged role in interinstitutional negotiation (Reh et al., 2011; Bickerton et al., 2015). But even as this speaks to the weakening of co-decision, it provides evidence for 'new' parliamentarism, through the strengthening of the EP in new ways through negotiation with intergovernmental political actors through it increasing influence in 'trilogues' (Roederer-Rynning and Greenwood, 2015).

What is more, the co-decision process has also been regaining importance in conjunction with the 'new' supranationalism. Not only has the Lisbon Treaty specified new powers of oversight for the EP in areas such as economic governance, in which it was previously absent (Fasone, 2014; Héritier et al., 2016), but even the new competences approved by intergovernmental actors for both existing and *de novo* supranational actors led them to generate new legislation requiring EP approval through the co-decision process – including in the eurozone crisis in the cases of the Six Pack and the Two Pack, as well as in Banking Union (Fasone, 2014; Crum and Curtin, 2015). Informally, moreover, the EP can influence the Commission through credible threats of veto if it is not informed of the process, as well as by blocking or delaying tactics (formulated in 'old' parliamentarist terms) – as when the EP blocked the Commission and the ECB on the Single Supervisory Mechanism until the ECB conceded rights of information to the EP (Héritier et al., 2016).

More generally, while the EP's actions may in some cases seem like a grab for more institutional power, they can equally be explained in terms of the EP's commitment to the idea that intergovernmental initiatives should be converted wherever possible into the more 'constitutional' approach represented by the co-decision process (as in new parliamentarist analysis). This helps explain why the EP was in many instances willing to trade substantive policy goals for the institutionalisation of a more co-decisional process, as in the case of EP (often failed) amendments to the Six Pack and the Two Pack as well as its (failed) efforts to influence the Fiscal Compact (Héritier et al., 2016: 69).

But even where the EP is completely left out of the decision-making process, it can still play a role, having increasingly become the 'go-to' body for other EU actors concerned about their political legitimacy (Héritier et al., 2016). In the case of the ECB, for example, although the ECB president does not have to follow the EP's advice in his mandated four yearly appearances, he gains in procedural legitimacy by speaking to the EP – plus he can use this venue as part of his communicative strategy with the public more generally. It is in this light that we can understand Draghi's (12 November 2015) introductory remarks to the EP Committee on Economic and Monetary Affairs: 'The ECB's accountability to you, the European Parliament, is a central counterpart to the ECB's independence. And transparency is a precondition for your holding us to account.'

More generally, we also need to take note of the EP's growing exercise of voice, with increasingly noisy demands for accountability from both supranational and intergovernmental actors, which mostly take the form of hearings, expert testimony and committee reports. In the eurozone crisis, these have explicitly criticised Council and Commission actions, whether for the Troika's 'lack of appropriate scrutiny and democratic accountability as a whole' or for the Eurogroup's 'failing to shoulder their share of responsibility in their capacity as final decision-taker' (*EurActiv*, 14 March 2014).

Finally, equally important has been the EP's self-empowerment through the *Spitzenkandidat* in the 2014 EP elections, as the EP effectively anointed the leader of the winning political party as Commission president (Dinan, 2015). This could be conceived as having increased the EP's own powers at the expense of European Council autonomy, but also in favour of Commission autonomy through its now double accountability to the EP and the Council. Importantly, even though the *Spitzenkandidat* procedure was abrogated in the 2019 selection of the Commission president, the political link between the EP and the Commission was, if anything, reinforced in efforts to mollify the EP. The fact that the Commission had been calling itself 'political' – although not 'politicised', in response to Council accusations of not applying the rules – suggests that the Commission was fully aware of the value of its connection to the EP, and may have been seeking to rebuild its traditional supranational powers as it continued to develop its new supranationalism along with its political legitimacy.

5.5   Politics and the 'New' Dynamics of EU Governance

Part of the problem with taking one side or the other in these debates about 'who leads European integration', meaning who is in charge or control, is not only that good arguments can be made for all sides. It is also that it is very hard to choose a side because the actors themselves are in constant interaction, whether it is supranational actors persuading intergovernmental actors to take action, intergovernmental actors threatening supranational ones in order to constrain their action or parliamentary actors pushing to play a role. It is not just that the Commission or the ECB may supply the ideas that the Council then decides upon, which may result in greater enhancement of supranational actors' ability to act autonomously or with discretionary authority. It is also that the member states – inside or outside the Council – may raise political objections or threaten legal action in order to constrain such supranational actors' autonomous or discretionary action – whether they are long-standing or *de novo* actors. And supranational actors are therefore more political in considering how intergovernmental actors might respond to their initiatives, anticipating possible objections and/or consulting prior to action in order to gain preliminary agreement. Moreover, both intergovernmental and supranational actors are increasingly aware of the EP, with its growing demands for attention on grounds of political legitimacy.

Separating out the powers and responsibilities of supranational from intergovernmental or even parliamentary actors is thus more complicated than one might think. Analytically, they can be dissected as distinct phenomena. Empirically, they are thoroughly intertwined and dynamically interactive. Moreover, in certain areas, it becomes very difficult to differentiate which is which, as in the area of Common Security and Defense Policy (CSDP), where decisions taken at the EU level through consensus-oriented deliberation are intergovernmental in the sense that they involve national representatives, but supranational as they engage the member states in ways that merge national security identity and action – thereby making for supranational intergovernmentalism – or is it intergovernmental supranationalism (Howorth, 2014; see Chapter 16)?

But if we are indeed finding it increasingly difficult to sort out who is more in charge or in control, we might do better to ask what the dynamics of interaction in EU governance are, using whichever approaches – old as much as new – help account for what it is we are seeking to explain. This would mean considering the ways in which the different actors exert power, whether as a result of their coercive or ideational dominance (Germany in particular), their institutional position or ideational and discursive influence (the Commission or ECB), or their ideational and discursive, institutional or even coercive influence (the EP). We would also need to ask what power means in terms of politics, that is, which interests, institutions and/or ideas are being empowered and to what end. And finally, we would want to ask about the political implications for democracy and legitimacy in the EU.

Politics in the EU has become increasingly multilevel. There is a politics that exists purely at the national level, as a reaction to the impact of EU integration on national democracy (among other things), which puts pressure on national party politics through the increase in citizen dissatisfaction and the rise of anti-system parties. There is a politics that moves from the bottom up, through the nationally influenced politicisation of EU relations, in particular in the Council. And there is also a politics that exists solely at the top, with the increasing politicisation of the interactions of EU institutional actors.

In the EU today, even as all EU-level institutions have been strengthened through the new dynamics of governance, national-level government has weakened in terms of democracy and legitimacy (see Chapter 19). As decision-making in policy area after policy area has moved up to the EU level, European integration has increasingly encroached on issues at the very heart of national sovereignty and identity, including money, borders and security. The problem, however, is not just that EU policies have encroached on national ones, but also that citizens have had little say over these matters, let alone become engaged in EU-wide political debates about the policies. And they are not happy about it, in particular in contested areas such as the euro and immigration policy. The result is what 'post-functionalists' – who focus mainly on national-level politicisation around EU-related issues and the new cross-cutting cleavages in the electorate – have described as the shift from the 'permissive consensus' of the early years to the 'constraining dissensus' of today (Hooghe and Marks, 2009, 2019; see also Kriesi et al., 2008).

Citizens have increasingly made their displeasure heard through protests in the street and the ballot box, leading to the rise of the populist extremes, with Eurosceptic and anti-EU messages, and the increasing turnover of sitting governments. National governments ruled by mainstream parties, moreover, have found themselves caught more and more between wanting to be responsive to citizens' electoral expectations and needing to take responsibility for the EU's collectively made rules and decisions (Mair, 2013). In consequence, national governments confront dual challenges: from populism at the national level and from technocracy at the EU level (Caramani, 2017).

As a result, the national level can no longer be described only as 'politics *without* policy', because of the increasing removal of policy decisions from the national to the EU level (Schmidt, 2006). Today, it has also come to be characterised by 'politics *against* policy' in domains that are the focus of populist anger – such as the eurozone crisis, the refugee crisis and immigration policy – or even 'politics *against* polity', where the dissatisfaction turns into anger against the EU as a whole, as in the case of Brexit.

At the same time, the EU level can no longer be described solely as 'policy *without* politics', following from the seemingly apolitical (because geopolitical or socio-economic interest-based) decisions in the Council and the technocratic processes in the Commission and other supranational bodies (Schmidt, 2006). This is not only because increasing national-level politicisation has put greater pressure on EU-level actors. It is also because of the struggles for power among EU institutional actors – whether understood as coercive, institutional or ideational – that are inherently political in nature. Taken together, this multilevel politicisation helps explain the EU's new political dynamics of interaction, which makes for EU-level 'policy *with* politics'.

Today, it is not just domestic economic interests that matter (cf. Moravcsik, 1993). Citizens' political interests also matter greatly, with a significant impact on EU actors, a point also made by some contemporary liberal intergovernmentalists (Schimmelfennig, 2015a; Tsebelis, 2016). In the eurozone crisis, for example, although German and French governments sought to satisfy domestic economic interests by transferring the full costs to countries in the periphery in order to spare their own banks haircuts, they were also very concerned about citizen attitudes. Merkel in particular played to the media feeding frenzy about 'lazy Greeks' versus 'we Germans who save' in the run-up to the Greek bailout, and delayed taking any action because of concerns over electoral repercussions in regional elections in May 2010 (Schmidt, 2015, 2020). Such delays went directly against her own 'rational' interests and those of business, which would have been better served by ensuring the member states in the Council moved quickly to 'save Greece', or allowed the ECB to act as an LoLR for the country (Matthijs, 2016).

European integration theories until recently have done little to address such issues of politicisation, and have therefore missed how this has created a new politically charged dynamics of interaction, not just among intergovernmental actors but among all EU-level actors. The politicisation of Council negotiations and deliberations now arguably depends more on member state leaders' perceptions of domestic politics than on their (realist) beliefs about geopolitical interest or their (liberal intergovernmental) responses to domestic socio-economic interests. But in addition to such interest-based electoral concerns are political differences over ideas. The eurozone crisis, for example, generated a political battle of ideas between the German and Northern European proponents of austerity, fuelled by ordoliberal ideas of stability, and the more pragmatic French and Southern Europeans, supportive of neo-Keynesian stimulus (e.g. Blyth, 2013; Brunnermeier et al., 2016).

It should be noted that not all politicisation of Council negotiations involves interest-based or ideational imposition, both of which risk delegitimising the EU in the eyes of citizens. Informal accommodation in recognition of strong national interests and identity-based ideas has been a legitimising force in the EU for a very long time. Making exceptions to the rules, or 'informal governance', as Mareike Kleine (2013) explains, has been a normal part of processes of negotiated agreement in the single market, and has actually reinforced the legitimacy of the formal governance processes in cases where the political fallout from domestic groups' objections could jeopardise consensual EU-level politics or national political stability (Kleine, 2013).

But in the eurozone crisis, the Commission's making exceptions to the rules resulted in another kind of politicisation of EU governance in its relations with the Council – in particular when the Commission president quipped, when asked about making exceptions to the rules for France in the European Semester exercise, that it is: 'Because it is France' (*Reuters*, 31 May 2016). This led to a firestorm of accusations by Northern European finance ministers in the Eurogroup that the Commission president was playing politics (*Der Spiegel* online, 17 June 2016). The Commission response was that being a 'political' Commission meant paying more attention to citizen concerns, not playing politics.

Finally, even the ECB could be seen to have become increasingly 'political' in the exercise of its mandate. ECB President Mario Draghi not only went to the EP to publicly legitimate ECB policy, as mentioned above, he also quietly cultivated his relations with political leaders in the Council, most notably Chancellor Merkel. For the Banking Union in particular, Draghi engaged over the course of a year in a 'charm offensive', seeking to persuade Merkel to agree to the Banking Union even as he sought to isolate the Bundesbank (Spiegel, 2014). But in addition to such processes of persuasion on the 'outside', the ECB president, much like the new intergovernmentalists suggest, also had to engage in a constant internal process of negotiation and consensus-seeking among the ECB board member representatives of the different member states (Matthijs, 2016).

In short, EU supranational actors are increasingly aware of the political implications of their decisions, and therefore seek political, and not just technocratic, ways to shore up their own power and legitimacy not just with other EU-level actors but also with the citizens. Finally, as illustrated earlier, intergovernmental and supranational actors are also more politically sensitive to their interactions with the EP as they seek greater legitimacy, even as the EP seeks to reinforce its own influence by putting political pressure on other EU actors while attempting to forge stronger links with national parliaments and citizens.

In the EU, no one account focused on any one institutional actor and decision-making process can explain EU governance. What we are actually seeing is a growing empowerment of all EU institutional actors through an increasingly complex set of political interactions in which the 'new' dynamics of EU governance is about consensus-seeking deliberation as well as contestation, and in which power and interests remain important factors along with ideas. The one major problem with the 'new' approaches – as much as the 'old' – is that they have failed to deal with the impact of EU governance on national democracies, as the locus of power and interest as well as the seat of consensus and deliberation has moved up to the EU level. This has resulted in a politicisation of the national level in which national-level 'politics *against* policy' or even 'politics *against* polity' has replaced the earlier 'politics *without* policy'. Such national politicisation has in turn had feedback effects on all EU actors, leading to a new political dynamics of interaction among EU actors in which EU-level 'policy *with* politics' has taken the place of the earlier 'policy *without* politics'. As a result, while 'old' and 'new' may explain a continuing 'policy *without* politics' in some of the less salient domains, they do not account for the 'policy *with* politics' that we now find in the most contested areas.

How then can we depict the consequences of the 'new' political dynamics of governance for the architecture of the EU? Not as any move to some kind of 'federal superstate' in a multilevel Europe. Rather, the EU should be seen as an increasingly complex polity with a new political dynamics of interaction in which all EU actors have developed 'new' ways of wielding power and influence on top of the 'old' ones. The challenge for EU scholars therefore is to assess the comparative usefulness of these different theoretical approaches to the explanation of EU governance, taking into account the fact that differences in underlying analytic frameworks may lead to a focus on different kinds of evidence, with different theories focusing on different EU actors. My own recommendation is for scholars to remain open to a pluralism of approaches, while 'testing' the validity of any and all such approaches against one another, by comparing and contrasting the results of their empirical analyses, to evaluate which approach or combination of approaches best serves to explain the theoretical issue and/or empirical problem in question.

And how can we envision a combination of such approaches to EU governance? The member state governments continue to sit squashed all together in the driver's seat of the double-decker bus, with one collective, consensus-bound foot on the gas pedal, regulating the speed, the other multiped foot ready to apply the brakes. But the engine itself continues to run reasonably smoothly nonetheless – even if suboptimally – as supranational EU actors pump the gas through the system even when the intergovernmental actors fail to press the pedal, and ensure that the brakes don't lock even when the intergovernmental actors apply them indiscriminately. Who is holding the steering wheel is the question. Many hands, none of which has full control – although Germany may have the heaviest hand of all.

So it is only with great effort, and agreement of all the actors, that the steering wheel can be turned in a new direction, say, onto a new highway. This is why it is easier to reinforce the rules rather than invent new ones. But there are shifts, as in the eurozone's reinterpretation of the rules 'by stealth'. However, these are generally incremental, with moves onto byways rather than any sharp left or right turns, let alone U-turns, even when the rules don't work. The main danger is that member states' citizens find themselves on the top deck of the bus, along for the ride but as far away as it is possible to be from the steering wheel, unsure who is in charge or in control and increasingly unhappy about the direction. With the rise of populism as a direct response, the question is what will happen if they come storming down the narrow stairs from the top of the double-decker, to harangue the many-headed conductor and possibly to wrest away control of the steering wheel.

GROUP DISCUSSION

- Who governs the EU? The intergovernmentalists, supranationalists or parliamentarists?
- How do EU actors exercise power? Through coercive impositions, institutional constraints or persuasive ideas?

TOPICS FOR INDIVIDUAL RESEARCH

- How do the different theories of EU governance play out in the eurozone crisis? Which EU actor(s) are key to the decision-making process? Which EU actor is most responsible for the suboptimal results?
- How do the different theories of EU governance play out in the migration crisis? Which EU actor(s) are key to the decision-making process? Which EU actor is most responsible for the suboptimal results?

FURTHER READINGS

Bauer M. and Becker S. (2014). 'The Unexpected Winner of the Crisis: The European Commission's Strengthened Role in Economic Governance'. *Journal of European Integration*, 36(3): 213–29.

Bickerton, C., Hodson, D. and Puetter, U. (eds) (2015). *The New Intergovernmentalism.* Oxford: Oxford University Press.

Dehousse, R. (2016). 'Why Has EU Macroeconomic Governance Become More Supranational?'. *Journal of European Integration*, 38(5): 617–31.

Hix, S. and Høyland, B. (2013). 'Empowerment of the European Parliament', *Annual Review of Political Science*, 16: 171–89.

REFERENCES

Barnett, M. and Duvall, R. (2005). 'Power in International Politics'. *International Organization*, 59(4): 39–75.

Bauer, M. and Becker, S. (2014). 'The Unexpected Winner of the Crisis: The European Commission's Strengthened Role in Economic Governance'. *Journal of European Integration*, 36(3): 213–29.

Bickerton, C., Hodson, D. and Puetter, U. (eds) (2015). *The New Intergovernmentalism.* Oxford: Oxford University Press.

Blyth, M. (2013). *Austerity: The History of a Dangerous Idea.* Oxford: Oxford University Press.

Braun, B. (2013). 'Preparedness, Crisis Management and Policy Change'. *British Journal of Political and International Relations* 17(3): 419–44.

Brunnermeier, M., James, H. and Landau, J.-P. (2016). *The Euro and the Battle of Ideas.* Princeton: Princeton University Press.

Caramani, D. (2017). 'Will Vs. Reason: Populist and Technocratic Challenges to Representative Democracy'. *American Political Science Review*, 111(1): 54–67.

Carstensen, M. and Schmidt, V. A. (2016). 'Power Through, Over and in Ideas: Conceptualizing Ideational Power in Discursive Institutionalism'. *Journal of European Public Policy*, 23(3): 318–37.

Carstensen, M. and Schmidt, V. (2017). 'Power and Changing EU Modes of Governance in the Eurozone Crisis'. *Governance*, DOI:10.1111/gove.12318.

Crum, B. and Curtin, D. (2015). 'The Challenge of Making European Union Executive Power Accountable'. In S. Piattoni (ed.), *The European Union: Democratic Principles and Institutional Architectures in Times of Crisis.* Oxford: Oxford University Press.

Dahl, R. (1957). 'The Concept of Power'. *Behavioral Science*, 2(3): 201–15.

Dehousse, R. (2016). 'Why Has EU Macroeconomic Governance Become more Supranational?' *Journal of European Integration*, 38(5): 617–31.

Dinan, D. (2015). 'Governance and Institutions: The Year of the Spitzenkandidaten'. *Journal of Common Market Studies*, 53(1): 93–107.

Draghi, M. (2015). Speech to the EP Committee and Economic and Monetary Affairs (12 November), www.ecb.europa.eu/press/key/date/2015/html/sp151112.en.html.

Drudi, F., Durré, A. and Mogelli, F. P. (2012). 'The Interplay of Economic Reforms and Monetary Policy: The Case of the Eurozone'. *Journal of Common Market Studies*, 50(6): 881–98.

Epstein, R. and Rhodes, M. (2016). 'The Political Dynamics Behind Europe's New Banking Union'. *West European Politics*, 39(3): 415–37.

Fabbrini, S. (2013). 'Intergovernmentalism and its Limits'. *Comparative Political Studies*, 46(9): 1003–29.

Fabbrini, S. (2016). 'From Consensus to Domination: The Intergovernmental Union in a Crisis Situation'. *Journal of European Integration*, 38(5): 587–99.

Fasone, C. (2014). 'European Economic Governance and Parliamentary Representation. What Place for the European Parliament?' *European Law Journal*, 20(2): 164–85.

Haas, E. (1958). *The Uniting of Europe*. Stanford, CA: Stanford University Press.

Héritier, A., Moury, C., Magnus, G., Schoeller, K. and Meissner, I. (2016). 'The European Parliament as a Driving Force of Constitutionalisation'. Report for the Constitutional Affairs Committee of the European Parliament. PE 536.467, www.europarl.europa.eu/committees/en/supporting-analyses-search.html.

Hix, S. and Høyland, B. (2013). 'Empowerment of the European Parliament'. *Annual Review of Political Science*, 16: 171–89.

Hodson, D. (2015). '*De Novo* Bodies and the New Intergovernmentalism: The Case of the European Central Bank'. In C. Bickerton, D. Hodson and U. Puetter (eds), *The New Intergovernmentalism*. Oxford: Oxford University Press.

Hoffmann, S. (1966). 'Obstinate or Obsolete? The Fate of the Nation State and the Case of Western Europe'. *Daedalus*, 95: 892–90.

Hooghe, L. and Marks, G. (2009). 'A Postfunctionalist Theory of European Integration: From Permissive Consensus to Constraining Dissensus'. *British Journal of Political Science*, 39(1): 1–23.

Hooghe, L. and Marks, G. (2019). 'Grand Theories of European Integration in the Twenty-first Century'. *Journal of European Public Policy*, https://doi.org/10.1080/13501763.2019.156971

Howorth, J. (2014). *Security and Defence Policy in the European Union*. London: Palgrave, 2nd edition.

Ioannou, D., Leblond, P. and Niemann, A. (2015). 'European Integration and the Crisis'. *Journal of European Public Policy*, 22(2): 155–76.

Kleine, M. (2013). *Informal Governance in the European Union*. Ithaca, NY: Cornell University Press.

Kleine, M. and Pollack, M. (eds) (2018). 'Liberal Intergovernmentalism and Its Critics'. *Journal of Common Market Studies*, 5(7): 1544–61.

Kriesi, H., Grande, E. and Lachat, R. (2008). *West European Politics in the Age of Globalization*. Cambridge: Cambridge University Press.

Mair, P. (2013). *Ruling the Void: The Hollowing of Western Democracy* London: Verso.

Matthijs, M. (2016). 'Powerful Rules Governing the Euro: The Perverse Logic of German Ideas'. *Journal of European Public Policy*, 23(3): 375–91.

Mody, A. (2018). *Eurotragedy: A Drama in Nine Acts.* Oxford: Oxford University Press.

Moravcsik, A. (1993). 'Preferences and Power in the European Community: A Liberal Intergovernmentalist Approach'. *Journal of Common Market Studies*, 31(4): 611–28.

Moravcsik, A. (1998). *The Choice for Europe.* Ithaca, NY: Cornell University Press.

Peterson, J. (2015). 'The Commission and the New Intergovernmentalism'. In C. Bickerton, D. Hodson and U. Puetter (eds), *The New Intergovernmentalism.* Oxford: Oxford University Press.

Puetter, U. (2012). 'Europe's Deliberative Intergovernmentalism'. *Journal of European Public Policy*, 19(2): 161–78.

Reh, C., Héritier, A., Bressanelli, E. and Koop, C. (2011). 'The Informal Politics of Legislation'. *Comparative Political Studies*, 46(9): 1112–42.

Roederer-Rynning, C. and Greenwood, J. (2015). 'The Culture of Trilogues'. *Journal of European Public Policy*, 22(8): 1148–65.

Sandholtz, W. and Stone Sweet, A. (eds) (1998). *European Integration and Supranational Governance.* Oxford: Oxford University Press.

Schimmelfennig, F. (2015a). 'Liberal Intergovernmentalism and the Euro Area Crisis'. *Journal of European Public Policy*, 22(2): 177–95.

Schimmelfennig, F. (2015b). 'What's the News in "New Intergovernmentalism"?' *Journal of Common Market Studies*, 53: 723–30.

Schmidt, V. A. (2006). *Democracy in Europe.* Oxford: Oxford University Press.

Schmidt, V. A. (2015). 'Forgotten Democratic Legitimacy: "Governing by the Rules" and "Ruling by the Numbers"'. In M. Matthijs and M. Blyth (eds), *The Future of the Euro.* Oxford: Oxford University Press.

Schmidt, V. A. (2016). 'Reinterpreting the Rules "by Stealth" in Times of Crisis: The European Central Bank and the European Commission'. *West European Politics*, 39(5): 1032–52.

Schmidt, V. A. (2019). 'Politicization in the EU: Between National Politics and EU Political Dynamics'. *Journal of European Public Policy*, 26(7): 1018–36.

Schmidt, V. A. (2020). *Europe's Crisis of Legitimacy: Governing by Rules and Ruling by Numbers in the Eurozone.* Oxford: Oxford University Press.

Spiegel, P. (2014). 'If the Euro Falls, Europe Falls'. *Financial Times*, 14, 15, 17 May.

Tsebelis, G. (2016). 'Lessons from the Greek Crisis'. *Journal of European Public Policy*, 23(1): 25–41.

PART II
Key Policy Areas in Flux

⋅ ⋅

This part of the book reviews the developments in nine policy areas which have been particularly in flux since the outbreak of the 2008 financial crisis. The effects of the multiple EU crises on policies have been ambivalent, ranging from furthering integration by stealth to stagnation. The degree and nature of politicisation has been a key factor explaining the extent to which decision makers could agree on new means for collective problem solving at the EU level. The policy outcomes of the EU crises therefore range from stagnation to status quo or selective integration, when new instruments and rules have been decided for one specific aspect of a policy area. The chapters all address a specific question at the centre of today's political debates in each policy area.

Thus the chapters in this part explain:

- To what degree there has been change or continuity in the various EU policy areas.
  - Which specific policy instruments or rules have been set up as a result from the EU's multiple crises.
  - How this has reinforced, or altered, the pre-crisis trends and historical paths.
- What the role has been of politicisation in driving or hindering change.
- Which political forces and actors have pushed for policy change or resisted change.
  - The role of the main institutional actors.
  - The role of party politics.
  - The main ideas and discursive frames underlying the described policy developments.
- How the crisis has altered the actorness of the EU on the global stage.
- What the remaining challenges are facing the EU with regard to its various policies.

Starting with the oldest domains of EU action, it appears that very basis of EU integration seems to be in question. In their chapter, John Bachtler and Carlos Mendez review the developments relating to the EU's budget in connection with Cohesion Policy. Emphasising that the distribution of EU funds has been increasingly submitted to surveillance and control, they ask to what extent conditionality has been undermining solidarity within the EU. The institutionalisation of conditionality since 2013 can be explained by a combination of functional needs to improve policy performance; spillover effects and budgetary politics relating to economic governance and the EU budget; and policy learning from international organisations.

Conditionality is also at the core of the policy shift promoted in the field of the CAP, the oldest area of EU intervention. In her chapter, Gerry Alons explains how the CAP has been subject to countervailing forces which ultimately produced a policy shift away from a focus on price intervention to an emphasis on direct income support – increasingly subject to environmental conditionality. According to Alons, it is questionable whether this has genuinely resulted in substantial integration of environmental concerns in the EU's agricultural policy, 'greening' the CAP. In the face of legitimacy issues and the budgetary pressure precipitated by the financial and economic crisis, the Commission and the member states succeeded in relegitimating farm income support by stressing a 'productivist' dependent agriculture discourse trumping environmental considerations.

While perhaps the most stable of all achievements of EU integration, even the single market has not remained unaltered by the latest financial crisis and resulting recession. In her chapter, Michelle Egan therefore asks: is the single market becoming increasingly differentiated? Overall, the single market has proved resistant to political demands for a more differentiated framework to deal with member states' increasing heterogeneity of interests and preferences. There are, however, three areas of increased differentiation in the single market: functional differentiation due to the differing scope and depth of integration across the four freedoms (goods, capital, service and labour); territorial differentiation related to the regulatory alignment of neighbouring states to single market rules, as well as the derogations and exemptions secured by member states in specific policy areas; and governance differentiation concerning different types of single market rules, implementation and compliance, litigation and wider liberalisation commitments, along with contested adjudication over negotiated bargains and legislative outcomes.

In contrast to the three above-mentioned areas, where change has been rather incremental, the monetary union is the area of deep integration which has witnessed profound upheavals with the financial and debt crises. Analysing those changes, Cornel Ban shows that the post-2011 crisis management relying on the joint intervention of the ECB and the newly founded ESM eventually generated the LoLR function that the eurozone lacked. But while it was effective at arresting the run on sovereign bond markets and bringing most debtors back into the market, this intervention has been ineffective at generating growth rates that could put a serious dent into the high unemployment rates of much of the eurozone (especially in Southern Europe). The additional measures adopted to boost investment have also been insufficient and have had the same modest effect as those of the ECB.

While several European leaders have called for enhancing the social dimension of the EMU, their calls have had little effect. In her chapter, Amandine Crespy argues that little has been done to help tackle social inequalities due to persisting weak and fragmented governance applying to social policy at EU level. The combined recession and austerity policies have exacerbated social inequalities both within and between the member states, especially within the euro area. From 2015 on, the European Commission headed by Jean-Claude Juncker sought to go beyond 'austeritarianism'. Yet, the promotion of social regulation and the European social dialogue have decelerated over the past ten years. Furthermore, a truly pan-European agenda promoting social investment remains elusive, with many citizens suffering from socially regressive policy-making at national level. Today, the EU runs the risk of seeming too intrusive by prescribing welfare state reforms that, more often than not, lead to retrenchment, without providing instruments or resources for boosting progressive modernisation.

Labour mobility in the single market is one key issue directly related to the dilemmas and tensions aggravated by the euro crisis. European labour markets during the crisis have been characterised by deepening imbalances and divergence. László Andor explains why and how the EU should take further action to reconcile competitiveness and social justice. Mobility, he contends, should not be assumed to be the main adjustment mechanism to intra-European imbalances. The debates triggered by the crisis have fed the understanding that mobility of workers in the EU should not only be free but also fair. The sense of fairness can only be restored if the EU is seen as protecting the rights of citizens, including their right to free movement, while at the same time paying attention to the associated risks and generating policies to tackle them. This requires legislative activity but also appropriate budgetary decisions and institution building that address the problems effectively.

In addition to intra-EU mobility, migrations from outside the EU have destabilised the EU as the inflow of migrants has degenerated into divisive politics. Sarah Wolff's chapter considers the so-called 'refugee crisis' of 2015 and its impact from a policy and institutional perspective. While being normatively committed to the Geneva Convention and to protect migrants and refugees' rights, the EU has opted for the status quo, with restrictive policies favouring more security. And it has done little to reconcile the conflicting trends of liberalisation, politicisation, de-politicisation and securitisation in the construction of the Area of Freedom, Security and Justice since the mid-2000s. The EU as well as most member states at supranational level has prioritised Europe's own internal security and the economic well-being of its citizenry over collective problem solving, burden sharing and human rights.

Deepening the examination of policy change in this realm, Julien Jeandesboz explains that the Schengen area is experiencing a combination of migration and security crises affecting the political, institutional and policy dynamics in the areas of border control, visa and police cooperation in the EU. A central claim of his chapter is that 'crisis' is not only an analytical category but also a category of practice. Labelling an issue as a crisis enables specific political and policy actors to justify and legitimise previously contentious or contested courses of action. He therefore shows how the context of 'crisis' has served to accelerate the reliance on large-scale information systems collecting and analysing individuals' personal data (for instance the European Travel Information and Authorisation System) potentially infringing on fundamental rights and freedoms. Moreover, for outsiders of the Schengen area, the EU or 'the West' are not subject to extensive scrutiny and suspicion in the name of security and migration control.

Besides migration, other policy areas also show how the EU is struggling with how to regulate its mechanisms of openness and closure to the outside, with how to defend global principles that are consistent with its internal policies or with how to maintain unity while stepping up its presence as a unified actor on the international stage. In his chapter, Ferdi De Ville looks into how trade has taken on a more normative meaning over the past decade. In the face of the financial crisis, trade policy was presented as the indispensable instrument both for economic recovery and for maintaining the EU's leading role in the world. This has led to the unprecedented levels of contestation in recent years, as for example in the campaign against the TTIP. While the European Commission has tried to respond to this contestation through institutional and substantial reforms, it remains to be seen if these incremental changes will succeed in boosting legitimacy while maintaining the effectiveness of the policy domain.

In addition to the policy areas where it has long been influential, the financial crisis has led the EU to take action in new policy areas where it has sought to assert itself as a normative global player, but has faced contentious politicisation as well as a lack of unity. In their chapter about global tax governance, Rasmus Corlin Christensen and Leonard Seabrooke discuss the extent to which the EU has succeeded in promoting global tax justice. In recent years, the EU and its agencies have developed policies to reform the European and international tax regimes, including harmonising corporate tax policy and increasing reporting transparency for large financial institutions and multinational corporations that are active in Europe. This has exposed major intra-EU distributional conflicts, such as that between 'tax havens' Luxembourg, Ireland and the Netherlands, and large EU markets such as Germany and France. While the momentum may simmer down, we should expect the battles between interests and ideas to continue in the years to come.

The financial crisis of 2008, which destabilised the US and Europe, has been accompanied by tectonic geopolitical shifts that have contributed to the profound transformation of the world order inherited from the post-World War II era. Against this backdrop, Jolyon Howorth investigates whether the EU CSDP is heading towards 'strategic autonomy', that is the capacity to engage autonomous conventional action vis-à-vis the US and/or NATO. Since 2016, there has been a concerted effort across the EU to reactivate and maximise the potential of CSDP with a flurry of initiatives and instruments such as the Military Planning and Conduct Capability, Battle Groups and a European Defence Fund. Yet at the same time a quasi-consensus emerged that strategic autonomy also demanded intensified cooperation between the EU and NATO. The post-2016 dynamics behind CSDP are helpful and creative, but they will not, in and of themselves, change anything fundamental. There are still many obstacles standing in the way of 'strategic autonomy' and the major challenge remains the parallel existence of NATO.

6

Cohesion and the EU Budget: Is Conditionality Undermining Solidarity?

JOHN BACHTLER AND CARLOS MENDEZ

6.1   Introduction

Cohesion and solidarity between member states are fundamental values of the EU, recognised in Article 3 of the Treaty on the Functioning of the EU (TFEU). The goal of cohesion is to reduce regional disparities across the EU. The main instruments of Cohesion Policy are the European Structural and Investment Funds (ESIF), comprising the European Regional Development Fund (ERDF), European Social Fund (ESF) and Cohesion Fund – as well as agriculture and fisheries funds. As the most direct expression of financial solidarity, Cohesion Policy accounts for around one-third of the total budget (around €370 billion) over the 2014–20 period and significant public investment in many less developed countries. Funding is highly concentrated on less developed EU countries and regions and invested in areas like transport infrastructure, business development, training and education to improve sustainable growth and quality of life.

Cohesion Policy is governed by a common regulatory framework with extensive obligations regarding the management of funding. The increasing use of conditionality is justified in changing member state behaviour to conform to agreed EU objectives. However, the effectiveness of conditionality is questionable, and its increasing use raises questions about the EU commitment to solidarity and the goal of reducing regional disparities at a time of increasing populism and Euroscepticism when effective and visible EU policy responses to economic recovery and inequality are needed.

This chapter charts the evolving relationship between the EU budget, Cohesion Policy and conditionality and assesses the implications for the effectiveness and legitimacy of Cohesion Policy. It reviews the history of EU budget and Cohesion Policy reform before describing the institutional decision-making framework. The rise of conditionality in Cohesion Policy is discussed, explaining why conditionality has gained an important role and the implications for policy effectiveness and legitimacy. A final section draws together the key conclusions.

6.2   Historical Overview

6.2.1   Reforms of the EU Budget

In the foundational years of the EU, the small Community budget was financed annually through national contributions. Following the creation of the CAP (see Chapter 7), steps were taken to create 'own financial resources' from agricultural levies and customs duties. However, the 1965 proposal from the Commission President Walter Hallstein for independent financial resources precipitated the 'empty chair crisis'. This was resolved by the 'Luxembourg Compromise' in 1966, but it was not until 1970 that the Community agreed on an own resources system – based on 'traditional' own resources (agricultural levies and customs duties) and a VAT-based resource – to finance the budget. A budgetary procedure to ensure more accountability granted the EP greater decision-making power over annual budgets. The next milestone was the Fontainebleau agreement of 1984, which increased the rate of VAT accruing to the Community and established the UK's rebate, and a commitment to budgetary discipline because of 'unsustainable' increases in spending under the CAP and inequalities in country receipts.

During the 1980s, important steps in European integration – the SEA and accession of new member states – created new demands for Community spending on the internal market, economic and social cohesion, social policy, R&D, environmental policy and foreign policy. Further reform of own resources came in 1988, notably the introduction of a GDP-based 'fourth resource' and capping the VAT base. From 1988, EU budgetary planning was also based on multi-annual 'financial perspectives', covering income and expenditure over five- to seven-year periods – 1988–92, 1993–9, 2000–6, 2007–13 and 2014–20. In each period, expenditure planning was accompanied by adjustments to the own resources ceiling and sources of revenue (mainly VAT).

The first two financial perspectives for 1988–92 (Delors I) and 1993–9 (Delors II) increased the EU budget significantly, rising to 1.2 per cent of Community gross national product (GNP) by 1992 and 1.27 per cent by 1999. These two expansionary budgets provided the financial underpinning to relaunch European integration through the single market programme and then EMU. By contrast, the financial perspective for 2000–6 (Agenda 2000) maintained the budget ceiling (at 1.27 per cent of GNP) despite the demands of enlargement and accession of mostly poorer EU12 member states, with resistance among richer countries to increased contributions. The next reform for 2007–13 maintained the same budget ceiling of 1.27 per cent of gross national income (GNI). However, the 2014–20 Multi-annual Financial Framework (MFF) (at a time of economic crisis) reduced the EU budget for the first time by around 3 per cent in real terms; the commitments limit was set at 1 per cent of EU GNI (€959 billion) compared to 1.12 per cent (€994 billion) in 2007–13. At time of writing, further cuts in Cohesion Policy spending are being debated as part of the negotiations on the MFF for 2021–27.

Budgetary decision-making in the EU has always been politically contentious, particularly because of is its redistributive function. For the two biggest areas of the EU budget (the CAP and Cohesion Policy), funding is largely pre-allocated. Since 1999, successive reforms have seen the Commission being pressured by member states to be more transparent about how its funding allocation model operates. Increasingly, member states have been able to estimate their receipts under reform proposals, and their negotiating positions are invariably directed to securing the best possible net balance. This limits the scope for making policy decisions that are in the best interests of the EU as a whole and is a cause of inertia in changing the structure of the budget (Begg, 2009).

6.2.2 Reforms of EU Cohesion Policy

The ERDF was established in 1975. The key drivers were the accession of Ireland and the UK, which supported the establishment of a Community regional policy to address development challenges and increase their receipts from the Community budget, as well as wider concerns about the impact of moves towards EMU on regional disparities. The ERDF was initially a small fund to support member state projects under their own regional policies. Reforms in 1979 and 1984, and the creation of a new regional policy instrument (Integrated Mediterranean Programmes), gradually increased the fund's budget, enhanced its Community orientation by granting the Commission more control, and provided a blueprint for the landmark reform of 1988.

In the context of treaty reform, enlargement and the single market, the 1988 reform marked the arrival of Cohesion Policy as a core EU policy. With a treaty commitment to cohesion and a substantial budget, the reform introduced a new governance framework bringing three structural funds (ERDF, ESF, European Agricultural Guarantee and Guidance Fund: Guidance Section) together with a common framework. The policy was based on the principles of concentration (on less developed regions), programming (through multi-annual strategies), partnership (involving subnational governments and other stakeholders) and additionality (to avoid substitution for national funding).

The political and economic integration under the Maastricht Treaty also established economic and social cohesion as a core treaty objective on a par with the internal market and EMU, and created a new Cohesion Fund to support infrastructure development and macroeconomic convergence in the poorest member states. A substantial financial boost to Cohesion Policy doubled the 1994–9 budget relative to 1989–93. By contrast, for 2000–6 the Cohesion Policy budget remained stable, reflecting the imperatives of fiscal consolidation in preparing for EMU and containing the costs of enlargement.

The key regulatory principles of the 1988 reform were retained in the 1993, 1999, 2006 and 2013 reforms but each time modifying the objectives, thematic focus, spatial coverage and governance of the policy (Manzella and Mendez, 2009; Bachtler et al., 2013). The main trends in the policy are threefold. First, Cohesion Policy was increasingly aligned with EU policy objectives, initially the Lisbon Agenda (in 2006) and later the Europe 2020 Strategy (in 2013). Second, progressively more emphasis was placed on financial management, control and audit following the resignation of the Jacques Santer Commission in 1999, and concerns about the probity of EU expenditure. Third, from the mid-2000s more attention was placed on policy effectiveness, with strengthened monitoring and evaluation requirements, incentives and sanctions on performance and spending – and, as discussed in Section 6.4, the controversial introduction of institutional and policy conditionalities.

6.3   Current Institutional Framework

The Treaty on the Functioning of the EU provides the legal basis for pursuing cohesion objectives and specifies the main funds along with their aims (see Box 6.1).

BOX 6.1 Legal basis

Title Xviii – Economic, Social and Territorial Cohesion

Article 174: The Union shall develop and pursue its actions leading to the strengthening of its economic, social and territorial cohesion. In particular, the Union shall aim at reducing disparities between the levels of development of the various regions and the backwardness of the least favoured regions.

Article 175: […] The Union shall also support the achievement of these objectives by the action it takes through the Structural Funds (European Agricultural Guidance and Guarantee Fund, Guidance Section; European Social Fund; European Regional Development Fund), the European Investment Bank and the other existing Financial Instruments.

Article 176: The European Regional Development Fund is intended to help to redress the main regional imbalances in the Union through participation in the development and structural adjustment of regions whose development is lagging behind and in the conversion of declining industrial regions.

Article 177: A Cohesion Fund set up in accordance with the same procedure shall provide a financial contribution to projects in the fields of environment and trans-European networks in the area of transport infrastructure.

Title Xi – European Social Fund

Article 162: ... a European Social Fund is hereby established in accordance with the provisions set out below; it shall aim to render the employment of workers easier and to increase their geographical and occupational mobility within the Union, and to facilitate their adaptation to industrial changes and to changes in production systems, in particular through vocational training and retraining.

The European Commission's power of initiative gives it sole responsibility for drafting legislative proposals for Cohesion Policy (see Box 6.2). The Commission begins the process by setting out proposals for reform as part of the EU budget negotiations for the period ahead (currently seven years) covering all EU budgetary headings, and accompanied by legislative proposals for the implementation of Cohesion Policy.

BOX 6.2 Key actors

Decision-making actors

European Commission
Council of Ministers
European Parliament
Council of the European Union

Consultative actors

Committee of the Regions
Economic and Social Committee

Negotiation and adoption of the budget and regulations is the responsibility of the Council of the EU and EP. The Council comprises government ministers from each member state with responsibility to negotiate laws and coordinate policies. Rotating Council presidencies have played a crucial role in negotiating the MFF and the reform of Cohesion Policy during the debate stages – when they influence the agenda and seek conclusions – and in the negotiation stages, when progress depends on the crafting of compromises (Bachtler and Mendez, 2016).

Much of the legislative work on Cohesion Policy reform is undertaken in the Council. The General Affairs Council of member state ministers is responsible for adopting the MFF and Cohesion Policy regulations. Preparatory work is done by the Committee of Permanent Representatives of Brussels-based missions of the member states and in Council working groups such as the Friends of the Presidency for financing issues and the Working Party on Structural Measures and the Coordination Committee for the ESIF.

As the co-legislator for Cohesion Policy regulations under the ordinary legislative procedure, the EP can amend the regulations and on contested issues have trilogue negotiations with the Commission and Council. By contrast, the Parliament's role in MFF negotiations is governed by the consent procedure allowing it to approve or reject proposals without amendments, and withhold consent unless its concerns are addressed.

The European Council defines the EU's overall political priorities. It plays a crucial role in the final stages of MFF negotiation when it is invariably left to heads of state and government to find agreement on the intractable issues: the size and allocation of the budget by heading and (for Cohesion Policy) by member state. Decisions require unanimity. The negotiations for the 2014–20 MFF were the first in which the president of the European Council was involved, and were notable for the important role played in facilitating agreement and in determining key Cohesion Policy reforms, notably in the area of macroeconomic conditionality.

6.4   Recent Policy Developments

Conditionalities are long-standing tools in multilevel governance systems where performance and accountability are difficult to manage. When authority is diffused vertically between levels of government and horizontally between state and non-state actors, the challenge is to ensure that actors at different levels (with different priorities, values, capacity and resources) deliver policy outcomes in line with policy objectives (Bauer, 2006; Bovens, 2007; Bachtler and Ferry, 2013; Viță, 2017). Conditionalities have been used to set preconditions, manage administrative processes or stipulate outcomes, often involving sanctions or rewards.

The increased use of conditionality in Cohesion Policy is particularly notable during the 2014–20 period (see Box 6.3), partly as a political spillover from the eurozone crisis, which saw opportunistic moves by the Council and parts of the Commission to promote greater fiscal and budgetary discipline in member state economic and monetary policies, using the leverage of funding allocated under Cohesion Policy (Tokarski and Verhelst, 2012; Mendez, 2013; Coman, 2018). While the Parliament could not prevent the introduction of macroeconomic conditionality, it moderated its influence in the implementation regulations. Similar institutional contestation is emerging over the conditionalities proposed by the Commission for 2021–7 relating to structural reforms (again associated with economic governance) and, controversially, a conditionality on the rule of law – related to post-accession 'backsliding' in compliance with core EU values in countries such as Poland and Hungary (Halmai, 2018).

BOX 6.3 Key concepts

Cohesion Policy is subject to a complex mix of conditionalities, in part related to the post-crisis evolution of EU economic governance, and partly to the objective of strengthening policy effectiveness. Regulatory innovations introduced for the 2014–20 period comprise four categories of conditionality:

BOX 6.3 (Cont.)

- *Macroeconomic conditionalities* to ensure stability as a basis for growth.
- *Structural conditionalities* to provide a supportive policy framework for interventions.
- *Institutional conditionalities* to provide appropriate regulatory, strategic and administrative conditions are in place.
- *Performance conditionalities*, linking funding to the achievement of policy objectives.

For the 2021–7 period, a further type of conditionality has been proposed:

- *Values conditionality* to ensure compliance with fundamental EU values such as the rule of law.

Other institutional and performance conditionalities have been introduced in response to evidence of ESIF spending being undermined by a lack of appropriate legal, institutional, administrative and policy preconditions at national or regional levels (Table 6.1; see also Bachtler and Ferry, 2013).

Table 6.1 Conditionality in Cohesion Policy: key dates

Category	Instrument	Programme period of introduction	Purpose
Macroeconomic	Macroeconomic conditionality	1994–9	Compliance with the SGP. Initially applied to the Cohesion Fund in 1994, it was strengthened and extended to all shared management funds in 2014–20 with more automatic enforcement and sanctions
Structural	Structural reform conditionality	2014–20	Implementation of structural and administrative reforms in policy areas subject to country-specific recommendations under the European Semester
Institutional	Ex ante conditionality	2014–20	Fulfilment of ex ante preconditions: (1) *regulatory*, mainly the transposition of EU legislation; (2) *strategic*, linked to overarching strategic frameworks for investments; (3) *institutional*, the effectiveness of institutional and administrative structures and systems
Performance	Performance reserve	2000–6	Achievement of EU/programme objectives and targets through a reward mechanism, i.e. a performance reserve (obligatory in 2000–6 and 2014–20, voluntary in 2007–13)
Values	Rule of law conditionality	2021–27	Protection of the EU budget from deficiencies in the rule of law in a member state

6.4.1   Ex ante Conditionality

Ex ante conditionalities were introduced for 2014–20 to ensure that the strategic, institutional and administrative conditions for effective Cohesion Policy investments are in place before funding is paid out. *Thematic conditionalities* are specific to policy objectives and require domestic strategies (e.g. on smart specialisation), the transposition and implementation of EU directives (e.g. on water or waste), addressing EU guidelines (e.g. employment and social policy) and capacity-building activities (e.g. sufficient project pipelines in the transport sector). *General conditionalities* require compliance with EU law (e.g. strategic environmental assessment, public procurement, state aid) and capacity building, as well as the strengthening of statistical systems and monitoring and evaluation data.

For 2021–7, the Commission proposes to reduce the number of ex ante conditionalities (labelled 'enabling conditions') and specify more precise conditions. Action plans would no longer be required in cases of non-fulfilment, but member states' payment claims would be conditional on fulfilment and more rigorous monitoring.

6.4.2   Macroeconomic Conditionality

Macroeconomic conditionality (see Table 6.1) in Cohesion Policy dates back to the Maastricht Treaty in 1992 and EMU. A Cohesion Fund was established to fund infrastructure projects in member states with a per capita GNP of less than 90 per cent of the Community average (i.e. Greece, Ireland, Portugal and Spain) and which had a programme to fulfil the EU's economic convergence conditions on government deficits. The conditionality mechanism entailed potential suspension of payments if conditions were not fulfilled, i.e. if the deficit ceiling of 3 per cent of national GDP (set under the EMU convergence criteria) was exceeded. Suspensions would be cancelled if the excessive deficit procedure was lifted within one year or any other period specified by the Council.

The 2013 reform of Cohesion Policy for the 2014–20 period widened the application of macroeconomic conditionality to all shared management funds, made the procedure more automatic and extended its scope beyond the Excessive Deficit Procedure to cover the Macroeconomic Imbalance Procedure as well as countries under an economic adjustment programme. Although opposed by the EP, the mechanism requires the Commission to propose the suspension of funding commitments (or payments in serious cases) when the Council decides that a member state has not taken effective action to address an excessive deficit (or other Council decisions/recommendations set out in the regulation). The Commission was also empowered to request reprogramming of national strategies and programmes to support the implementation of Commission recommendations under the Macroeconomic Imbalance Procedure where relevant to the ESIF, and to maximise growth and competitiveness in countries with assistance programmes. In the event of non-compliance by the member state, the Commission could propose financial suspensions to the Council.

6.4.3   Structural Reform Conditionality

The EU promotes structural reforms primarily through its annual economic and fiscal policy coordination cycle known as the European Semester, which issues Country Specific Recommendations (CSRs) in areas such as labour and product markets, the business environment, innovation, taxation and welfare systems.

To support the EU's evolving economic governance framework, structural reform conditionality (see Table 6.1) in Cohesion Policy was first mooted in the EU budget review debates during 2010 and proposed in the Fifth Cohesion Report (European Commission, 2010a). The aim was to provide incentives for reforms in areas linked to Cohesion Policy, such as flexicurity policies, education or innovation. More detailed discussion in the EU's conditionality task force in 2011 considered Commission proposals to make CSRs on structural reform mandatory with enforcement through ESIF suspensions for non-compliance. Positive incentives were proposed in the form of rewards for fulfilling recommendations such as higher EU co-financing rates and advance payments, and flexibility in the application of spending rules. However, member state representatives in the task force rejected the introduction of this form of structural reform conditionality principally because of subsidiarity concerns regarding member state competences for structural reform, lack of alignment between the scope and timing of the European Semester and Cohesion Policy processes and administrative burdens.

This opposition led to the 2013 reform of Cohesion Policy introducing structural reform conditionality through other mechanisms. Member states were required to address relevant CSRs in the programming of Partnership Agreements and programmes. As noted, the Commission was also empowered to request revisions of Partnership Agreements and programmes to support CSR implementation and to propose payment suspensions where a member state failed to respond effectively.

The creation of the Structural Reform Service Programme (SRSP) provides another conditionality mechanism for supporting structural reforms in member states through positive financial incentives funded by ESIF and the creation in late 2019 of a new Commission service, DG REFORM.[1] The SRSP was proposed in November 2015 and agreed in May 2017 with a budget of €142.8 million for 2017–20. For 2021–7, the Commission has proposed creating a Reform Support Programme and a European Investment Stabilisation Function, as part of the deepening of EMU. The Reform Support Programme would support priority reforms in all member states with a much larger budget of €25 billion and comprising a Reform Delivery Tool to provide financial support for reforms, a Technical Support Instrument to share technical expertise and a Convergence Facility to support member states to join the euro.

[1] DG REFORM is the commonly used short name of the Directorate-General for Structural Reform Support.

6.4.4   Values Conditionality (Rule of Law)

The latest addition to the Cohesion Policy conditionality toolbox is a rule of law conditionality linked to breaches of fundamental EU values. In response to EU criticism of the independence of judiciaries in Hungary and Poland, the Commission's 2021-7 MFF proposals introduced a rule of law conditionality in relation to EU budgetary procedures and policies (Bachtler et al., 2018) (see also Chapter 18). In the case of shared management funds, financial sanctions are envisaged to protect the EU budget where there is a risk of a generalised deficiency in the rule of law in a member state. These would take the form of a suspension, reduction or restriction of EU funding, applied where the deficiency risks sound financial management or EU financial interests. The decision-making procedure would involve the Commission proposing measures to the Council, which would make a decision based on a reversed qualified majority vote.

6.5   Current Political and Academic Controversies

The institutionalisation of conditionality can be explained by two factors. The first is internal to the policy and related to efforts to improve policy performance; the second relates to external spillover effects relating to EU economic governance and negotiations on the EU budget.

The case for stronger ex ante conditionality to improve policy performance was made forcefully in an influential independent review of Cohesion Policy known as the Barca Report (Barca, 2009). It concluded that the policy was not sufficiently results-oriented and proposed the introduction of contracts and conditionalities on strategic and institutional preconditions (Barca, 2009). The report had a significant influence on the reform debate (Mendez, 2013; Berkowitz et al., 2017), evident in the EU budget review and Fifth Cohesion Report, which proposed setting up Cohesion Policy contracts underpinned by conditionalities. The Commission was also influenced by successive European Court of Auditors reports and evaluations highlighting weaknesses in member state administrative capacity to implement Cohesion Policy (Berkowitz et al., 2017; Mendez and Bachtler, 2017).

External lessons were drawn from the World Bank and the IMF with consolidated experiences in applying conditionalities in development policies (Berkowitz et al., 2017). The Commission's Directorate-General for Regional and Urban Policy commissioned a study to identify lessons from conditionality in World Bank lending, European Bank for Reconstruction and Development (EBRD) operations and country regional policies (Ferry and Bachtler, 2011).

There is, however, a contested relationship between conditionality and performance (Bachtler and Ferry, 2013; Berkowitz et al., 2017). While conditionality may be a key element in the funder–recipient relationship, effectiveness is difficult to establish – changes in performance are rarely related to conditionality. Conditionalities are problematic to implement, due to conflicts over objectives and ownership, and they can have negative consequences in terms of perceived legitimacy and fairness (see Table 6.2). Much depends on whether they are designed in collaboration with actors affected and whether their operation is predictable and transparent. The fact that the effectiveness of conditionality is highly contested indicates that there are other factors at play in explaining the adoption of conditionality in Cohesion Policy.

The second factor explaining the rise of conditionality is the economic and financial crisis and resulting changes to European economic governance to

Table 6.2 Application of conditionalities in public policy

Category	Aim	Application	Strengths	Weaknesses
Macroeconomic	Macroeconomic stability as a basis for sustainable growth	Funding linked to indicators such as inflation rates, levels of government debt, ability to finance deficit	Clear and measurable conditions	Top down – controls are outside the control of funding recipients No link to performance
Structural	Supportive policy framework for interventions	Funding requires specified policy or institutional framework conditions (e.g. business environment)	Provides relevant framework to facilitate implementation	Controls may be outside control of recipients Frameworks may not be achievable in the short to medium term
Performance	Linkage of intervention to policy objectives	Funding is linked to achievement of specified outcomes	Focuses attention of implementers on progress and outcomes Promotes accountability among recipients	Difficulty of identifying measurable and relevant indicators and targets Requires effective monitoring Outcomes may be influenced by external factors Outcomes difficult to verify
Institutional	Appropriate governance and institutions for implementing interventions	Funding requires provision of specified level of governance systems, capacity, regulatory compliance	Addresses deficits in administrative capacity Relates directly to implementation of funding Potential for spillovers	Conditions complex to assess – require qualitative judgements Institutional and system changes take time

strengthen the resilience of EMU, with major spillover effects on Cohesion Policy policy-making (Mendez, 2013; Berkowitz et al., 2017; Coman, 2018). Bailout loans to Greece, Ireland and Portugal involved strict conditionality on the implementation of austerity and structural reforms, followed by Commission proposals to reinforce EU macro-fiscal governance (European Commission, 2010b). These proposals – which included the European Semester for coordination of structural reforms and macroeconomic conditionality for all Cohesion Policy funds and the CAP – were part of the reform of the 2014–20 MFF (European Commission, 2011). Net payer member states have strongly supported efforts to use EU funding to advance economic governance objectives and reduce the risk of contagion effects from macroeconomic and fiscal imbalances. A financially motivated subtext was also to reduce the EU budget and Cohesion Policy spending.

During 2015–18, the migration crisis also spilled over into Cohesion Policy conditionality debates. To encourage 'fair' burden sharing of refugee placements across member states, some proposed a migration conditionality in Cohesion Policy by making the disbursement of EU funding conditional on the acceptance of migration quotas (e.g. Austria, Finland, Germany, Sweden). This controversial proposal did not gain traction due to opposition from Central and Eastern European countries and the Commission.

Assessing the institutionalisation of conditionality from the perspective of European integration theories raises two key insights. First, EU budgetary and Cohesion Policy policy-making has taken an intergovernmental turn because of increased politicisation of the EU budget in the post-crisis era and the alignment between Cohesion Policy and economic governance (Bachtler and Mendez, 2016). Theories of integration stressing the role of supranational actors in decision-making remain relevant but incomplete. Clearly, the Commission continues to be a powerful actor by virtue of its power of initiative and agenda-setting role. The EP has acquired greater formal co-legislative power under the Lisbon Treaty, but remains the junior partner in budgetary matters.

However, intergovernmental dynamics and negotiations surrounding the EU budget and wider EU objectives – led by the most powerful member states – are increasingly determining the policy content and implementation of Cohesion Policy. The role of the European Council has acquired greater significance; its conclusions on the 2014–20 MFF impinged directly on the competence of the co-legislators (Council and Parliament) relating to Cohesion Policy regulations on macroeconomic conditionality, definitions and eligibility, the Connecting Europe Facility, the performance reserve and co-financing rates.

Second, Cohesion Policy decision-making has become more politicised, and public opinion is more influential in line with post-functional theories of European integration. The level of division in the negotiations among member states and across EU institutions has been compounded by linking EU funding to wider macroeconomic and political goals. Analysis of media stories on Cohesion Policy over time shows that news coverage of conditionality has increased and is largely negative in tone (Mendez et al., 2020). Further, there is evidence that public opinion is influencing decision-making. The Commission's decision not to suspend funding for Spain and Portugal in 2016 was partly motivated by concerns about negative political backlashes in a context of deteriorating trust in the EU (European Commission, 2016a).

6.6 Paradigmatic Case Study: Is Cohesion Policy Conditionality Effective and Legitimate?

Macroeconomic conditionality is a paradigmatic case of the application of conditionalities in Cohesion Policy, with some experiences also reflected in the implementation of ex ante, structural reform and values conditionalities.

6.6.1 Macroeconomic Conditionality: A Politicised and Blunt Tool?

The provisions for macroeconomic conditionality have been difficult to apply in practice and arguably have been a blunt tool. Greece, Portugal and Spain did not comply with the 3 per cent deficit target in the first few years of the Cohesion Fund's implementation but were not subject to suspensions. Greece and Portugal were also subject to excessive deficit procedures for a number of years in the 2000s, as were several member states that joined the EU in 2004. No member state was subject to a formal decision by the Commission or the Council to recommend Cohesion Fund suspensions (Begg et al., 2013).

The lack of enforcement can be explained by the discretion available to the Council and the weakened credibility and legitimacy of the SGP. SGP sanctions had been waived against Germany and France by the Council against recommendations by the Commission. The SGP was eventually watered down in 2005 by defining several situations that could justify a violation of the 3 per cent reference value for excessive deficits.

The implementation of macroeconomic conditionality in 2007–13 took place in a turbulent environment of economic and political crisis with intense pressure on public finances and the eurozone system, requiring bailouts of several troubled economies, and growing public mistrust in EU institutions. The first country subject to a financial suspension decision under the Cohesion Fund, in 2012, was Hungary – the only member state to have been permanently under the excessive deficit procedure since its accession in 2004. However, the suspension decision was lifted three months later (in June 2012) based on a Commission assessment that Hungary had taken effective action to reduce its deficit to 2.5 per cent in 2012 and to remain below the 3 per cent SGP reference value in 2013. As a result, no suspensions were made to Hungary's Cohesion Fund commitments in 2013 and the Council terminated the excessive deficit procedure for Hungary in mid-2013.

The strengthened macroconditionality provisions in 2014–20 were highly controversial from the outset. Several member states, the EP and the Committee of the Regions strongly opposed the introduction of macroconditionality. Support was mainly from the Commission (notably the ECOFIN Council), the ECB and Germany (later supported by France). Some member states explicitly rejected macroeconomic conditionality (Belgium, Greece, Italy, the UK), while others were concerned with the disproportionate impact on poorer countries/regions (Bulgaria, Hungary, Poland), the unfair penalisation of regions for non-compliance by national governments and negative fiscal consequences for troubled economies (Hungary) (Begg et al., 2013). In practice, the application of the new rules was problematic. As noted above, suspension procedures for Spain and Portugal due to excessive deficits in June 2016 were terminated less than six months later given new fiscal commitments by the two countries and negative political reactions, including strong EP opposition (European Commission, 2016a; Coman, 2018; Viță, 2018).

Similar tensions are evident regarding proposals for macroeconomic conditionality in 2021–7. Net payers such as Austria, Finland and Germany are in favour of strengthened macroeconomic conditionality, but others are opposed (Greece) or have called for it to either be abolished (France), reconsidered given the potential to endanger investments in areas with structural difficulties (Italy) or replaced with more positive incentives (Poland, Portugal, Romania) (Bachtler et al., 2018).

6.6.2   Ex Ante Conditionality: A Sound Rationale with Mixed Success

Turning briefly to the new ex ante conditionalities applied to Cohesion Policy in 2014–20, the Commission's assessment of their implementation, supported by independent evaluations, is largely positive (European Commission, 2017). They have contributed to improving the framework within which the EU budget operates, ensuring a direct link between the investments and EU-level policies, contributing to the transposition and implementation of EU legislation, helping to tackle investment barriers and supporting climate change. Moreover, strategic, regulatory, institutional and administrative changes in the member states were triggered that should lead to more effective and efficient spending. However, the European Court of Auditors has been less positive (European Court of Auditors, 2017), finding that some of the conditionalities are vague, open to misinterpretation and have a weak basis for enforcement. Other policy analysts have also noted that the rules lack the necessary cogency to ensure effective implementation (Heinen, 2013).

6.6.3   Structural Reform Conditionality: From Weak Conditionality to Positive Incentives

A first analysis by the Commission of the integration of CSRs into Cohesion Policy programming in 2014–20 found that recommendations were generally well reflected in the strategies but that few linked the expected results to the CSRs or provided detail on how the CSRs would be implemented through programmes

(European Commission, 2016b). Comparative analysis of a selection of national Partnership Agreements found significant variation in detail provided on CSRs across member states and that, in some countries, few if any CSRs were relevant to Cohesion Policy (Kah et al., 2015). Evaluation evidence showed that the CSRs were defined vaguely, rarely specified targets and milestones for implementation, and lacked systematic monitoring (ISMERI Europa and WIIW, 2018). Further, the Commission has not requested the reprogramming of Partnership Agreements or programmes to support the implementation of CSRs (European Commission, 2017).

The creation of the EU's SRSP provides a positive incentive for supporting structural reform with Cohesion Policy funding, financed through ESIF technical assistance. However, there are potential risks in the division of competences between the EU and member states, as the implementation of the reforms is the responsibility of the member states although the Commission would follow up the reform progress.

There are also questions about the relevance, accountability and political implications of the SRSP. First, it aims to link Cohesion Policy to all/any structural reforms, instead of CSRs that are relevant to ESIF programming. Second, it is based on bilateral relationships between an individual member state and the Commission, implying less transparency – unlike the European Semester approach, which is more transparent. Third, the structural reform programme only funds technical assistance at present, i.e. funding to design not implement reforms. Lastly, and fundamentally, it conflicts with Cohesion Policy's aim of reducing regional disparities across the EU (Huguenot-Noel et al., 2018) and could incentivise member states to transfer funds away from Cohesion Policy to the new instrument owing to its more favourable funding conditions, which do not require a national contribution.

6.6.4 Values Conditionality: A Political Time-bomb?

The Commission's rule of law conditionality proposals for the 2021–7 period are controversial and have elicited mixed reactions from member states and EU institutions. Poland and Hungary remain in highly politicised disputes with the EU about breaches in the rule of law with respect to judicial independence; they oppose the conditionality on the grounds that it would be implemented subjectively, lacks transparency, politicises the EU budget and does not support the objectives of cohesion. Net payers are supportive in principle, notably Germany, Finland, France, the Netherlands and Sweden. The EP has also provided support for rule of law conditionality as long as final beneficiaries of funds are not penalised for breaches of rules for which they are not responsible.

Procedural issues have been raised by the European Court of Auditors (2018), which considers that the proposals grant the Commission too much discretionary power and do not provide clear criteria and guidance for determining breaches in the rule of law. In line with the European Court of Auditors' views, a study for the

EP argues that significant revisions are needed for the instrument to be effective and workable including greater legal coherence/consistency, a focus on a limited number of key rule of law breaches linked to EU spending, credible guarantees that final beneficiaries would not be affected and involvement of the Council and Parliament in enforcement decisions to ensure legitimacy (Viţă, 2018).

6.7   Conclusions

EU Cohesion Policy is the most tangible expression of solidarity between member states in the EU through a redistributive programme of public investment to reduce economic, social and territorial disparities across member states and regions. In the post-crisis era, reforms to Cohesion Policy have introduced conditionality as a mechanism to ensure compliance with wider EU objectives linked to economic governance, structural reform and other institutional and policy preconditions. As a consequence, the underlying principles of solidarity and cohesion upon which Cohesion Policy is founded are being undermined. As argued by Viţă (2017), this new conception of 'conditional solidarity' departs from the foundational principles and ethical convictions underpinning a unified Europe based on solidarity.

The rise of conditionality can be explained by a functional imperative to improve Cohesion Policy performance, and external spillover effects relating to economic governance and negotiations on the EU budget. The latter raises important implications for theoretical perspectives on EU decision-making and integration theory in the post-crisis context. First, EU budget and Cohesion Policy policy-making has taken an intergovernmental turn as a consequence of the increased politicisation of the EU budget and alignment between Cohesion Policy and economic governance. This is manifested in a stronger role for the European Council in determining the regulatory framework than previously by issuing conclusions on the MFF that impinged directly on the competence of the co-legislators (Council and Parliament) in negotiating Cohesion Policy regulations, notably in the areas of macroeconomic conditionality. Second, the institutionalisation of conditionality provides support for post-functional theories of European integration stressing the increasing importance of public opinion and politicisation for the direction of EU institutional and policy outcomes. Cohesion Policy decision-making and debate has become more politicised, especially in relation to macroeconomic, rule of law and migration conditionality debates, and public opinion is playing a more important role in policy-making deliberations.

Looking forward to the 2021–7 period, the Commission has proposed expanding conditionality in two main areas. The most controversial is a conditionality on the rule of law. While this has a justifiable rationale, it risks politicising Cohesion Policy and could generate resentment and mistrust in member states in breach of the rule (Mendez *et al.* 2020). By contrast, structural reform conditionality is being strengthened through positive financial incentives and technical assistance support. The question is whether the experience with this new tool will lead to creeping pressures for the introduction of negative financial incentives for structural reform through Cohesion Policy or the transfer of Cohesion Policy funds to the new instrument in the future, thereby reducing the EU's commitment to economic, social and territorial cohesion.

GROUP DISCUSSION

- What was the impact of the crisis on EU Cohesion Policy implementation and reform?
- To what extent has the cohesion rationale of the ESIF been weakened over time?

TOPICS FOR INDIVIDUAL RESEARCH

- Multilevel governance. The influence of different actors at EU, national and subnational levels on the design and implementation of Cohesion Policy.
- Impact. The effectiveness of EU Cohesion Policy in reducing economic, social and territorial disparities.

FURTHER READINGS

Bachtler, J., Mendez, C. and Wishlade, F. (2013). *EU Cohesion Policy and European Integration: The Dynamics of EU Budget and Regional Policy Reform.* Aldershot, Ashgate.

Begg, I., Macchiarelli, C., Bachtler, J., Mendez, C. and Wishlade, F. (2013). *European Economic Governance and EU Cohesion Policy.* Report to the EP, European Policies Research Centre, University of Strathclyde, Glasgow.

Coman, R. (2018). 'How Have EU "Fire-fighters" Sought to Douse the Flames of the Eurozone's Fast- and Slow-burning Crises? The 2013 Structural Funds Reform', *The British Journal of Politics and International Relations* 20(3): 540–54.

European Commission (2017). *Seventh Cohesion Report on Economic, Social and Territorial Cohesion, Commission Communication*, COM(2017) 583, Brussels.

Viţă, V. (2017). 'Revisiting the Dominant Discourse on Conditionality in the EU: The Case of EU Spending Conditionality'. *Cambridge Yearbook of European Legal Studies*, 1–28.

REFERENCES

Bachtler, J. and Ferry, M. (2013). 'Conditionalities and the Performance of European Structural Funds: A Principal–Agent Analysis of Control Mechanisms in European Union Cohesion Policy'. *Regional Studies*, 49(8): 1258–73.

Bachtler, J. and Mendez, C. (2016). 'Cohesion Policy Reform and the Evolving Role of the Council'. In S. Piattoni and L. Polverari (eds), *Handbook on Cohesion Policy in the EU*. Cheltenham and Northampton: Edward Elgar,.

Bachtler, J., Mendez, C. and Wishlade, F. (2013). *EU Cohesion Policy and European Integration: The Dynamics of EU Budget and Regional Policy Reform*. Aldershot, Ashgate.

Bachtler, J., Mendez, C. and Wishlade, F. (2018). 'Reforming the MFF and Cohesion Policy 2021–27: Pragmatic Drift or Paradigmatic Shift?'. *European Policy Research Papers*, European Policies Research Centre, University of Strathclyde/TU Delft.

Barca, F. (2009). 'An Agenda for a Reformed Cohesion Policy: A Place-Based Approach to Meeting European Union Challenges and Expectations'. Report to European Commissioner for Regional Policy, Danuta Hübner, European Commission, Brussels.

Bauer, M. W. (2006). 'Co-managing Programme Implementation: Conceptualizing the European Commission's Role in Policy Execution'. *Journal of European Public Policy*, 13(5): 717–35.

Begg, I. (2009). *Fiscal Federalism, Subsidiarity and the EU Budget Review*. Swedish Institute for European Policy Studies, Stockholm, Sweden.

Begg, I., Macchiarelli, C., Bachtler, J., Mendez, C. and Wishlade, F. (2013). *European Economic Governance and EU Cohesion Policy*. Report to the European Parliament, European Policies Research Centre, University of Strathclyde, Glasgow.

Berkowitz, P., Rubianes, A. C. and Pieńkowski, J. (2017). *The European Union's Experiences with Policy Conditionalities, EC-OECD Seminar Series on Designing Better Economic Development Policies for Regions and Cities*. Paris: OECD.

Bovens, M. (2007). 'Analysing and Assessing Accountability: A Conceptual Framework'. *European Law Journal*, 13(4): 447–68.

Coman, R. (2018). 'How Have EU "Fire-fighters" Sought to Douse the Flames of the Eurozone's Fast- and Slow-burning Crises? The 2013 Structural Funds Reform'. *The British Journal of Politics and International Relations*, 20(3): 540–54.

European Court of Auditors (2018). *Opinion No 1/2018*. European Court of Auditors, Luxembourg.

European Commission (2010a). *Conclusions of the Fifth Report on Economic, Social and Territorial Cohesion: The Future of Cohesion Policy*. Brussels, COM(2010) 642 final.

European Commission (2010b). *Enhancing Economic Policy Coordination for Stability, Growth and Jobs: Tools for Stronger EU Economic Governance*. Commission Communication, COM(2010) 367/2, European Commission, Brussels.

European Commission (2011). *A Budget for Europe 2020*. SEC(2011)868, Brussels.

European Commission (2016a). *Structured Dialogue of Vice President Katainen and Commissioner Creţu with the European Parliament*. Draft Briefing, Structured Dialogue with the European Parliament, Brussels, 3 October 2016.

European Commission (2016b). *Effectiveness and Added Value of Cohesion Policy*. Non-paper assessing the implementation of the reform, European Commission, Brussels.

European Commission (2017). *Seventh Cohesion Report on Economic, Social and Territorial Cohesion, Commission Communication*. COM(2017) 583, Brussels.

European Court of Auditors (2017). *Ex Ante Conditionalities and Performance Reserve in Cohesion: Innovative but Not Yet Effective Instruments*. ECA Special Report no.15, European Court of Auditors, Luxembourg.

Ferry, M. and Bachtler, J. (2011). 'EU Cohesion Policy in a Global Context: Comparative Study on EU Cohesion and Third Country and International Economic Development Policies'. Report to DG REGIO, European Policies Research Centre, University of Strathclyde.

Halmai, G. (2018). 'The Possibility and Desirability of Rule of Law Conditionality'. *Hague Journal on the Rule of Law*, 11(1): 1–18.

Heinen, N. (2013). *Not Quite Fit for Purpose: Conditionality under the EU's Financial Framework for 2014–2020*. Research Briefing, 28 March 2013, Deutsche Bank AG, DB Research.

Huguenot-Noel, R., Hunter, H. and Zuleeg, F. (2018). *Future Links between Structural Reforms and EU Cohesion Policy*. DG for Internal Policies, September 2018, Brussels.

ISMERI Europa and WIIW (2018). *Support of ESI Funds to the Implementation of the Country Specific Recommendations and to Structural Reforms in Member States*. Report to the European Commission, Brussels.

Kah, S., Mendez, C., Bachtler, J. and Miller, S. (2015). *Strategic Coherence of Cohesion Policy: Comparison of the 2007–13 and the 2014–20 Programming Periods*. Report to the European Parliament, Brussels.

Manzella, G.-P. and Mendez, C. (2009). *The Turning Points of EU Cohesion Policy*. Working Paper Report to Barca Report.

Mendez, C. (2013). 'The Post-2013 Reform of EU Cohesion Policy and the Place-based Narrative'. *Journal of European Public Policy*, 20(5): 639–59.

Mendez, C. and Bachtler, J. (2017). 'Financial Compliance in the European Union: A Cross-National Assessment of Financial Correction Patterns and Causes in Cohesion Policy'. *Journal of Common Market Studies*, 55(3): 569–92.

Mendez, C., Mendez, F., Triga, V. and Carrascosa, J. M. (2020). 'EU Cohesion Policy in the Media Spotlight: Exploring Territorial and Temporal Patterns in News Coverage and Tone'. *Journal of Common Market Studies*. https://doi.org/10.1111/jcms.13016

Mendez, C., Triga, V., Bachtler, J., Djouvas, C., Mendez, F. and Stier, S. (2019). 'The Visibility and Communication of Cohesion Policy in Online Media'. Research for REGI Committee, Policy Department for Structural and Cohesion Policies, European Parliament.

Tokarski, P. and Verhelst, S. (2012). 'Macroeconomic Conditionality in Cohesion Policy: Added Value or Unnecessary Burden?'. *European Policy Brief*, 13, November 2012, Egmont Royal Institute for International Relations. www.cohesify.eu/downloads/Cohesify_Research_Paper_3.pdf#zoom=100.

Viţă, V. (2017). 'Revisiting the Dominant Discourse on Conditionality in the EU: The Case of EU Spending Conditionality'. In *Cambridge Yearbook of European Legal Studies*, Centre for European Legal Studies, Faculty of Law, University of Cambridge, 1–28.

Viţă, V. (2018). *Conditionalities in Cohesion Policy, Research for REGI Committee*. DG for Internal Policies, PE 617, 498, September 2018, Brussels.

7 Agriculture and Environment: Greening or Greenwashing?

GERRY ALONS

7.1 Introduction

Agriculture is one of the oldest and most developed policy domains in the EU. Approximately 40 per cent of the EU budget is spent on the CAP. Current EU farm policy is very encompassing, affecting all types of agricultural issues ranging from production quota to food safety and animal welfare. Due to agriculture's increasing multidimensional character – based on its interconnectedness with trade, environmental, development and social policies – a multitude of actors now mobilises and seeks access to decision makers when CAP reforms are negotiated. Despite the enhanced involvement of non-agricultural actors, an important point of critique on the CAP still focuses on the environmentally polluting effects of the intensive agriculture that it supports. Although the Commission has been trying to give the CAP a greener image for more than a decade, its efforts have only had mixed results.

This chapter will start with a historical overview of the commencement and development of the CAP, introducing the policy's objectives as well as the shifts in dominant policy instruments over time. It will subsequently discuss the institutional framework within which decisions on the CAP are made, focusing on how the policy network (see Chapter 4) appears to be in the process of a transition from a closed network favouring agricultural actors and interests, to a network more open to a wider range of interests (environmental, societal). The discussion of recent policy developments and current controversies shows how policy makers perform a continuous balancing act between different sectors and different interests: weighing the importance of supporting European agriculture against other issues on the EU agenda, and finding the right mix of environmental instruments that brings genuine environmental benefits while not confronting farmers with more costs and red tape than necessary. Finally, the chapter ends with a case study on the 2013 CAP reform in which the Commission sought to regain legitimacy for the CAP, in particular for direct income support for farmers, by introducing greening requirements. The results were very limited, as the Council and the EP succeeded in watering down the Commission's proposals. A disconnect, therefore, remains between the 'green' CAP discourse and the CAP's actual policies.

BOX 7.1 Key concepts

Multidimensionality. The interconnectedness of agricultural policy with other policy domains, such as trade, environmental and development policies.

Guaranteed prices. Fixed prices for a number of agricultural commodities – set by the Council of Agriculture Ministers once per year. This was the mainstay of agricultural support until the introduction of direct income payments.

Direct income payments. Income support payments for farmers, first based on production capacity (land and animal count), but later decoupled from production and subject to meeting a number of environmental criteria.

Modulation. Policy initiatives aimed at shifting funds from the market and income support in 'pillar I' of the CAP (including price support and direct payments), to the rural development policies of 'pillar II', such as agri-environment measures.

7.2   Historical Overview

A 'common' agricultural policy was part of the plans for the EEC from the start, both because the member states wished to continue existing national support for their farmers by means of European policy, and because they wished to be self-sufficient in the provision of food. The CAP's legal basis can be found in articles 38 to 44 of the Treaty on the EEC (1957). In order to facilitate the operation and development of an internal market for agricultural products, a CAP was to be established. Article 39 enshrines the official aims this policy should serve (see Box 7.2). These official objectives have remained unaltered ever since, although not all objectives have been translated in effective policies in equal measure.

BOX 7.2 Legal basis

Art. 39 TFEU, ex Art. 33 TEC

The objectives of the CAP shall be:

(a) to increase agricultural productivity by promoting technical progress and by ensuring the rational development of agricultural production and the optimum utilisation of the factors of production, in particular labour;

(b) thus ensure a fair standard of living for the agricultural community, in particular by increasing the individual earnings of persons engaged in agriculture;

BOX 7.2 (Cont.)

(c) to stabilise markets;
(d) to assure the availability of supplies;
(e) to ensure that supplies reach consumers at reasonable prices.

Establishing a 'common' agricultural policy involved coordination between the then six member states of the EEC – each of which had its own support system for farmers in place – and required strict regulation to prevent unfair competition and ensure a level playing field. To this end, three important principles underpinned the CAP: market unity, community preference and financial solidarity.

A *unified* or *common market* meant that agricultural products could flow freely within the EEC borders. In order to guarantee a sufficient level of income for farmers, a system of target prices and intervention prices was implemented (see Box 7.1 for definitions of key concepts). If market prices fell below the intervention price, intervention agencies would buy up surplus production to stabilise farm prices (see Figure 7.1). This policy instrument did not only aim to guarantee a stable income for farmers, it also acted as a production incentive (as there was no quantity limit for the price guarantee). This was a deliberate decision at the time in order to gain food security after the food shortages the countries had suffered during World War II.

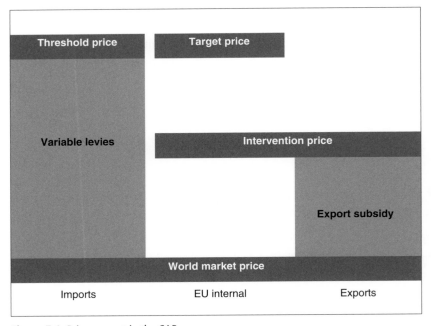

Figure 7.1 Price support in the CAP

In order to secure *community preference*, a system of variable levies was applied to imports from third countries. The rate of the import levies changed daily, covering the difference between what was called the 'threshold price' in the EEC and the price on the world market, which usually tended to be lower (see Figure 7.1). This policy ensured that no products could enter the market at a price below the internal price, thus securing competitiveness of European farmers in the EEC market. As many of their agricultural products were not competitive outside the EEC, export subsidies (covering the difference between the world market price and the EEC's 'intervention price') were further applied to export surplus production on the world market.

Finally, the principle of *financial solidarity* stipulated that the CAP was funded from the EEC budget and not from national budgets. This was meant to guarantee a level playing field for farmers in all member states – the EEC regulations equally applying to all of them – and inhibited preferential treatment through national member state policies.

While these policies successfully contributed to providing food security and increasing farm income, they also created problems. First, the guarantee prices soon led to production surpluses, because supply started to exceed demand by the late 1970s. This resulted in 'butter mountains', 'wine lakes' and 'milk lakes', which European intervention agencies bought and had to dispose of. Second, the export subsidies used to export these surpluses on the world market brought the EEC into conflict with important trade partners such as the US. Third, buying and stockpiling surpluses as well as the export subsidies used to dispose of them were costly and also instigated concerns for the EEC's budget.

By the late 1970s it became clear that the CAP had to be reformed to address these problems. The Commission first sought to do this by introducing production controls in the dairy sector (quota) in 1984 and 'stabilisers' in 1989 to balance supply and demand. When these new policy instruments did not prove sufficiently effective, Commissioner Ray MacSharry realised that more far-reaching reform was required. In the 1992 CAP reform, he introduced significant intervention price cuts compensated by direct income payments for farmers. This policy change initiated a shift from support through price and market intervention (paid by consumers through higher agricultural prices) to direct income support (paid by taxpayers through the EU budget). Fearing that this new type of support would be more easily dismantled come financially hard times, farmers, particularly those in France and Germany, initially opposed the policy change. Nevertheless, the policy shift was continued in the two subsequent CAP reforms through further price reductions and direct payment expansion (Agenda 2000 reform of 1999) and by decoupling the payments from production factors (Fischler reform of 2003). While these policy changes made the CAP more market-oriented, it did not actually make the policy more affordable. The savings on the variable expenses for market intervention and export subsidies did not cancel out the new structural expenses on direct income payments.

Meanwhile, the 'multidimensional' character of agriculture – the interconnectedness with trade, environmental and rural policies – became increasingly obvious with the integration of new themes in the CAP. The Agenda 2000 reform separated the CAP in to two pillars: the first included the existing market intervention and income support policies, while the second 'rural development' pillar contained structural policies, environmental policies and instruments aimed at supporting the rural economy. This is where much of the environmental policy integration in the CAP has taken place. The agri-environment measures, enabling member states to enhance environmentally friendly farming, are funded through this pillar. Commissioner Franz Fischler's reform of 2003 and the 2008 Health Check of the CAP augmented the rate of 'modulation' – shifting of funds from the market and income support pillar to the rural development pillar – increasing funding for environmental measures. Nevertheless, the budget for rural development remains rather small compared to the first pillar budget. The Commission, however, also sought to enhance the image of the first pillar by introducing compulsory cross compliance in 2003, making income support conditional on abiding by a number of environmental and animal husbandry rules. In the 2013 reform, cross compliance was partly replaced by three 'greening' criteria: not meeting these requirements would cost farmers 30 per cent of their direct payments.

Over the years, a combination of considerations and forces has resulted in a policy shift within the CAP from a focus on production support (market support and export subsidies) to producer support (direct income payments) – increasingly subject to environmental conditionality (see Box 7.3). It is, however, a matter of debate to what extent this has resulted in genuine and effective policy integration of environmental considerations in the CAP. Environmental actors and consumers remain critical and are exerting pressure to extend environmental measures in the ongoing negotiations on a new CAP reform. At the same time, the increasing complexity of the CAP with its different pillars and policy instruments has also caused member states, implementing agencies and farmers alike to complain about the surging administrative burden involved with implementing the policy.

BOX 7.3 Key dates

1957. Treaty of Rome or Treaty Establishing the European Economic Community. The development of the CAP was foreseen in this treaty.

1960s. The early years of the CAP, with a focus on price support and productivity improvement.

1970s and 1980s. The crisis years of the CAP: overproduction, trade frictions and budgetary problems.

> ## BOX 7.3 (Cont.)
>
> **1992.** The MacSharry reform: introduction of direct income payments in exchange for decreases in guarantee prices started a shift from price (production) support to income (producer) support. Agri-environment measures were introduced as an accompanying measure.
>
> **1999.** Agenda 2000 reform: continued the shift to producer support and introduced the two-pillar structure with market intervention and income support in the first pillar and rural development measures in the second pillar.
>
> **2003.** Fischler reform: decoupled direct payments from production capacity and introduced mandatory cross compliance.
>
> **2008.** The CAP Health Check: increased 'modulation' of funding from market and income support to rural development measures.
>
> **2013.** Post-2013 CAP reform: introduction of 'greening', making eligibility for 30 per cent of the direct payments dependent on meeting three greening requirements.

7.3   Main Features of the Current Institutional Framework

As in many developed countries, agricultural policy-making in the EU has long been characterised by a closed policy network with a limited number of participants and largely consensus about the proper objectives and instruments of agricultural policy. According to Alan Greer, it is particularly this high degree in which ideas about agricultural policies are shared that explains the durability of these closed policy communities (2005: 29). The idea of agricultural 'exceptionalism' – that agriculture is not like other economic sectors and hence deserves special treatment – has been dominant for a long time. The sector is not only considered special because it is subject to exceptional market and natural conditions, but also for its contribution to national food security. With the increasing multidimensionality of the agricultural policy agenda, however, a more diverse set of actors has started to mobilise and seek access to the decision-making process (see Box 7.4). Some claim that this has effectively made agriculture a more pluralist domain (Buller, 2002: 115), while others argue that the extent to which there has been a substantial reshaping of the configuration of institutions and actors, and the introduction of new values, can be questioned (Greer, 2017). Taking the middle ground, Daugbjerg and Feindt (2017) propose that agriculture has entered a phase of 'post-exceptionalism' characterised by a partial transformation of exceptionalist ideas, institutions and interest constellations, while at the same time maintaining important policy heritage.

The Commission's Directorate-General of Agriculture and Rural Development (DG Agriculture), together with the member states' ministers of agriculture (through the Council of Ministers and its Special Committee on Agriculture) and major farming unions are at the core of the original agricultural policy network (Lowe and Baldock, 2000: 31). The Commission plays a key role in proposing new legislation and usually takes the initiative for reform. CAP reform subsequently has to be agreed upon by the Council of Ministers (usually agriculture ministers), which tends to be less inclined to accept far-reaching reform, all ministers seeking to maintain their share of the CAP budget. Furthermore, considering the privileged access of European farm organisations (the major organisation being Comité des Organisations Professionnelles Agricoles) to DG Agriculture and of national farm organisations – such as the French Fédération Nationale des Syndicats d'Exploitants Agricoles and the Deutsche Bauernverband – to their agriculture ministries (Keeler, 1996), the odds for radical reform of the CAP are limited, and the changes introduced tend to be incremental.

Over the years, agricultural policy's increasing interconnectedness with trade relations and environmental policies has changed the policy dynamics, however. Environmental degradation caused by intensive agriculture entered the debate on the CAP in the 1980s. This had two important effects. First of all, within the Commission it resulted in a greater involvement of DGs other than DG Agriculture in the policy formulation stage. Apart from DG Health and DG Trade, DG Environment and Climate Action are argued to have played an important role in the 2013 CAP reform (Knops and Swinnen, 2014). Second, new actors, ranging from environmental groups to consumers and citizens favouring environmentally friendly production methods, began to seek access to the decision-making process. They have now gained formal access through DG Agriculture's Advisory Groups (Civil Dialogue Groups since 2014), improving the representation of environmental interests (Feindt, 2010), but they still tend to be overshadowed by the far larger number of agricultural representations in the Civil Dialogue Groups that bring together representatives of a range of farm organisations, agricultural cooperatives, the agriculture and food industry, agricultural trade associations and environmental organisations (Alons, 2017).

Finally, the role of the EP in the CAP was limited for a long time, because decision-making took place under the consultation procedure. As a result, it had to rely on informal means to influence policy outcomes (Garzon, 2006). This has changed since the Treaty of Lisbon, which extended the ordinary legislative procedure to the CAP, and to its budget. Interinstitutional power dynamics have thus developed to the relative advantage of the EP. While there were hopes that this would lead to a broader range of interest groups gaining influence through the EP, this effect was only limited in the 2013 reform. Since the EP's Committee on Agriculture and Rural Development (COMAGRI) – known for its conservative stance and defence of farm interests – took the lead and the plenary largely followed its position (Knops and Swinnen, 2014), the new involvement of the EP did not enhance the CAP reform agenda nor contribute to a more ambitious 'greening' of the CAP.

To conclude, EU agricultural policy-making is slowly transforming from a closed policy network to more open decision-making arrangements, increasingly including non-agricultural interests. At the same time, the interinstitutional power relations shifted to the advantage of the EP, which is now on an equal footing with the Council. While this has complicated decision-making and necessitated trilogue meetings – interinstitutional negotiations between Commission, Council and EP – to reach agreement on the 2013 reform, it also allowed the EP to exert genuine influence. The agricultural case does, therefore, not support the new intergovernmentalist claim assuming complete Council dominance, but shows both the importance of the Commission in the decision-making process, as well as the EP's increasing role (see Chapter 5). The discussion of the 'greening' case later in this chapter will show the EP's greater assertiveness. Nevertheless, despite these institutional developments, the degree of environmental policy integration in the CAP remains limited.

BOX 7.4 Key actors

Institutional actors

European Commission (DG Agriculture, DG Trade, DG Environment)
Council of Ministers
Council Special Committee on Agriculture
EP (COMAGRI, Committee on Environment)

Non-institutional actors

Agricultural organisations (Committee of Professional Agricultural
    Organisations-General Confederation of Agriculture Cooperatives)
Environmental organisations
Civil society organisations
Consumers

7.4   Recent Policy Developments

Two relatively recent developments are likely to affect CAP decision-making in the future: the changing issues in agricultural trade and the increasing room for manoeuvre for member states in policy implementation.

Trade concerns in the past entailed trade partners mobilising against the EU's extensive intervention in the agricultural sector – particularly the export subsidies and variable levies. Nowadays, agriculture-related trade issues are much broader and also include divergent food safety (think about growth hormones and genetically modified organisms) and environmental regulations that inhibit trade. This has led to increasing politicisation of agricultural policy in general and agricultural trade in particular, enhancing citizen, consumer and environmental actor mobilisation and turning agriculture into an issue of increasing public debate. The Commission, realising that the legitimacy and acceptability of the CAP in the eyes of citizens is at stake, has sought to involve the general public through consultation procedures before developing their proposals for the previous and the ongoing CAP reform. These relatively new procedures fit the Commission's objective of 'better regulation', aimed at increasing both the legitimacy and the effectiveness of EU regulation. At the same time, an enhanced role for public debate and contestation makes EU decision-making on the CAP more political, which may inadvertently make significant policy reform even more unlikely.

While the CAP is still a 'common' policy, member states are provided with increasing freedom to implement CAP policies (Greer, 2005). Since the 2013 CAP reform it has become easier for them to move (a limited amount of) money from the rural development pillar back to pillar 1. They are also allowed to implement their own 'greening' measures, as long as they apply methods that are equivalent to the Commission methods. Developments such as these have caused scholars to argue that flexibility is the hallmark of the 2013 CAP reform (e.g. Roederer-Rynning, 2015). Judging from the Commission's most recent plans for a new CAP reform, they will move forward on this trajectory, allowing member states to develop their own 'greening' measures, as long as they are clearly connected to the environmental objective to be obtained (Commission, 2017). While this prevents the problem of a 'one-size-fits-all' approach – an oft-cited critique of the existing greening measures – it also raises issues of the potential 'renationalisation' of the CAP and its adverse effects on a genuinely 'single' market.

7.5   Current Political and Academic Controversies

Over the years, the legitimacy of farm support, particularly direct payments to farmers, has increasingly been called into question for a number of reasons. First of all, the effectiveness of the policy as an instrument of income support is questionable, because larger farms receive most of the support, while smaller farmers arguably need it more. Second, direct payments are considered to be conducive to intensive farming practices with adverse environmental effects. Finally, if direct income payments are not payments for production, then what do farmers offer in return for receiving these payments? As the case study on greening will show, these considerations were at the heart of the Commission's rationale for adapting the direct payment system in the 2013 reform. The greening requirements were meant to relegitimate the direct payments, because a specific part of these payments (30 per cent) could now be considered payments for the delivery of environmental public goods (Zwaan and Alons, 2015). The problem, however, is that the greening measures were watered down to such an extent that most farmers arguably hardly needed to change their operations to meet the requirements. A disconnect, therefore, continued to exist between the green discourse and the actual policy action. Legitimacy concerns like these continue to be at stake in the CAP and it remains to be seen whether the new reform that is currently being negotiated will provide a solution.

Next to the issue of legitimacy, another recurring focus of debate is the CAP budget. The CAP is an expensive policy, and even though the percentage of its budget as a share of the total EU budget has decreased over time, from approximately 70 per cent in the 1980s to 40 per cent now, it remains the EU's main common policy in financial terms. In the context of the financial and economic crisis – coinciding with the debate on the 2013 CAP reform – there was intense pressure to reduce the CAP budget in order to free finances for other EU objectives. Member states favouring more liberal economic policies and member states that were net contributors to the EU budget were particularly supportive of an overhaul of existing budgetary distributions. With the plans for Brexit, this issue is likely to remain pressing. While the departure of the United Kingdom from the Union implies the loss of one of the most liberal member states inclined to more far-reaching CAP reform, it also has budgetary consequences, the United Kingdom being a net contributor to the CAP.

Apart from these political issues, an academic challenge for researchers is understanding the implementation of the CAP and how implementation experiences feed back into subsequent policy reforms. The increasing flexibility for member states that was mentioned earlier will make the implementation phase a much more important policy stage for the CAP. However, little research (with the exception of rural policy) has been conducted on the implementation of the CAP (Treib, 2014), while research on feedback mechanisms translating implementation experience in policy adaptation has only just started (Polman, 2018). The possible adverse effects on market unity and a level playing field for producers from all member states will make implementation a topic that deserves increasing attention.

7.6   Analysis of a Paradigmatic Case Study

7.6.1   The Context of the 2013 CAP Reform and its Greening Component

Negotiations about the 2013 CAP reform took place in the context of mounting criticism on the CAP, a financial and economic crisis, and rising concerns about food security. First of all, the CAP was arguably experiencing a legitimacy crisis (Bréhon, 2011). The direct payment scheme in particular was criticised for its polluting effects and unequal distribution of payments between member states and farm types, while citizens and consumers demanded more value for (public) money. Second, the existing critique that the CAP budget was too high was exacerbated by the economic and financial crisis that caused a large number of member states to strive for cutting the overall EU budget. Finally, food security concerns – securing a sufficient amount of food at reasonable prices for consumers – re-entered the debate after several agricultural price hikes. It was in this context that the Commission, member states and EP had to balance multiple and partly conflicting interests into a new CAP reform.

7.6.2   The Commission's Solution: Greening

Aware of the CAP's legitimacy crisis in the eyes of citizens, the Commission decided to conduct a consultation procedure, before developing specific reform proposals. At the launch of these consultations Agriculture Commissioner Dacian Cioloş stated that 'European agriculture must address the demands of the market and the expectations of society concerning public goods, the environment and climate change' (Cioloş, 2010), a claim he would repeat often during this phase of the reform process (Zwaan and Alons, 2015). This fits well with existing analyses arguing that the Commission evaluates the involvement of 'civil society' as a source of legitimacy (Kohler-Koch, 2010: 101) that will enhance 'the EU's image in the eyes of the citizens' (Fischer-Hotzel, 2010: 341). The way in which the Commission subsequently sought to relegitimate and justify the direct payment instrument, was by splitting direct payments in to a basic payment (70 per cent) and a greening payment (30 per cent), thus explicitly and directly linking direct payments to the provision of public environmental goods.

The greening plans were originally instigated by DG Environment and environmental groups such as Birdlife and the European Environment Bureau (Roederer-Rynning, 2015; interview with Birdlife official, 19 May 2016), but were quickly incorporated by DG Agriculture, because the measures could be applied universally in the different member states (Matthews, 2013). Enhancing funding for the second pillar – which environmental actors would have preferred – would not have had that benefit, nor would it have enabled a 'public goods' justification for spending on the direct payments in the first pillar. The Commission's legislative proposal therefore included compulsory greening: 30 per cent of national direct payments envelopes were to be linked to three agricultural practices providing environmental benefits: crop diversification, permanent pasture, and a 7 per cent so-called Ecological Focus Area (EFA). The Commission proposed that a farmer's entire direct payments should be conditional on meeting these requirements.

Greening was thus presented as the means to achieve the 'redistribution, redesign and better targeting' of direct income support needed to increase the legitimacy of the CAP in the eyes of citizens and taxpayers (Commission, 2010: 8). Commissioner Cioloş argued that the enhanced environmental conditionality would establish a closer link between the direct payments and public environmental services and would therefore make them more acceptable to society (2011; 2013). While civil society organisations (CSOs) welcomed the greening requirements and acknowledged that the focus on public money for public goods marked a significant shift in the CAP, they also argued that 'whether this is a major change or light greening depends on the detail' (IEEP, 2010). In that respect environmental groups argued that the Commission proposal lacked ambition and they feared that the Council and EP would water it down even further (EEB and others, 2010; EEB, 2012). Some even claimed that the Commission could well be using the citizen demand and public good argument in favour of greening simply to justify direct payments without genuinely seeking environmental advantages. As Baldock and Hart (2011) suggest: 'The proposal leaves doubt over how much really will be delivered. Bold ambitions to green the CAP become diluted by a focus on legitimacy for direct payments – at the expense of measures capable of maximizing the delivery of environmental public goods'.

7.6.3   From Greening to Greenwashing?

These fears were substantiated considering how both the EP and the Council contributed to watering down the greening requirements. The EP was the first institution to come up with a formal reaction to the Commission's legislative proposal. A report to this end was first prepared by the EP's COMAGRI – whose members tend to be biased in favour of farm interests and were subject to intense farm lobby pressure (Roederer-Rynning, 2015) – and subsequently debated and adopted in the EP's plenary session. COMAGRI proposed that non-compliance with the greening measures should only affect the 30 per cent greening payment and not the 70 per cent basic payment part of the direct payments. This would essentially make greening a voluntary measure for farmers, putting up to a third of their direct payments on the line. COMAGRI further suggested that farmers should be able to receive double funding for agri-environmental measures in the second pillar that were also included in the greening measures in the first pillar (Jambor, 2013). Both CSOs and Commissioner Cioloş immediately rejected these plans. Environmental organisations argued they would 'mark [...] a step backwards in terms of the environmental advances made in past reforms' (IEEP, 2013), while Cioloş (2013) emphasised that:

> [We] cannot fall to the temptations of green-washing or to artificial measures which would have a doubtful effect and which would be very complicated, leading to unacceptably high error rates. For taxpayers' money to be used efficiently [...] it is important that the greening measures be the baseline for the 2nd pillar agri-environment measures.

The EP plenary indeed decided to remove the double funding from their report, but it did vote in favour of watering down the greening measures, particularly by limiting the EFA to initially 3 per cent instead of the 7 per cent the Commission had proposed. In a similar way, the Council also wanted to limit the EFA (to 5 per cent), and they further proposed that member states should be able to use 'equivalent' practices to the greening measures proposed by the Commission, as long as these practices could be connected to similar environmental benefits. This would prevent a one-size-fits-all policy and allow member states to implement the policy in a fashion that would be most feasible and effective in their specific circumstances (Council of the European Union, 2013).

When it comes to the discourse with which the EP and Council defended their proposals, it is interesting to see that the EP – just like the Commission – also focused on a public goods discourse (COMAGRI, 2010): 'The multifunctional role of the European agricultural sector [...] delivers public goods of major importance to our societies, whose supply cannot be secured through the market: food security, safety and quality at an affordable price for EU citizens.' What is striking, however, is that EP and Commission are emphasising different public goods, the EP being focused on productivity-related aspects of farming – in line with the mounting food security concerns – while the Commission had accentuated environmental public goods. Based on an analysis of the discourse of the different EU institutions throughout the reform process, Rutz et al. (2013) conclude that, compared to previous reforms, there was a renewed emphasis on a 'productivist' discourse, which is most likely the consequence of the politicisation of the food security issue.

The different positions of Commission, Council and EP had to be reconciled through trilogue meetings. In the final agreement, a range of exemptions was agreed upon which made all three of the greening criteria easier to meet. The threshold for the crop rotation criterion to be applicable was set at ten hectares instead of three hectares from the Commission's original proposal, while a threshold of fifteen hectares was included for the EFA criterion (where the Commission had not wanted to apply a threshold at all). This effectively excluded approximately 35 per cent of all farmland from these two greening requirements, which were even further watered down by allowing them to be fulfilled by 'equivalent' measures. In addition, with respect to the amount of land to be set aside as EFA, the Council's proposal of 5 per cent was adopted, further limiting the effect of this measure. Finally, member states were allowed to apply the criterion of permanent grassland at regional or national level instead of at the individual farm level, making it easier for farmers to meet this demand collectively. Both the involvement of the Council and the EP resulted in significant watering down of the Commission's original greening proposals, but could not prevent its introduction. This is testament to the continued importance of the Commission's agenda-setting powers and newly enforced position of the EP – negating the new intergovernmentalist claim of complete Council dominance.

While the Commission tried to sell the new reform as a paradigmatic shift in the CAP, CSOs argued that 'the new CAP has ended up resembling a continuation of the status quo' (*European Voice*, 3 July 2013), and 'does not lead to a decisive paradigm shift in favour of a "public money for public goods" philosophy' (Matthews, 2013). The World Wide Fund claimed that 'the well of public support for a European subsidy system for farmers has just dried up' (World Wide Fund, 2013), while Birdlife – a supporter of the original greening measures – indicated it would now rather seek a complete overhaul of the CAP support system, including bringing an end to the direct payment system (interview with Birdlife official, 19 May 2016).

The subsequent implementation of the greening measures deteriorated matters further (Hart, 2015). Based on the agreement, it was already expected that most farmers would hardly have to change their production processes (Bureau and Mahé, 2015). On top of that, national implementation agencies mainly focused on maintaining existing practices and supporting farm income rather than designing the implementation in a way that would reap the greatest environmental benefits. In this vein they allowed non-productive land to be taken out of production instead of environmentally vulnerable land as a measure to comply with the EFA criterion. Even the Commission, which was more optimistic about the measures' effectiveness, found that farmers 'optimized their EFA choices on economic grounds rather than ameliorating environmentally damaging practices' (Commission, 2016: 19).

7.6.4 How Do We Explain What Happened?

This decision-making process on greening, and its outcome, raise a number of questions. First of all, what was the genuine intention of the Commission? Were they merely interested in maintaining direct income payments and did they decide to use environmental objectives discursively to enhance the chances of reaching this goal, as Daugbjerg and Swinbank (2016) argue? Or were they really motivated to achieve environmental effects? The answer is probably mixed. DG Environment was certainly aiming at environmental results, and while DG Agriculture undoubtedly also welcomed such effects, their key objective seems to have been to get the reform adopted, including direct payments. The Commission discourse that increasingly emphasised environmental concerns is clearly not followed by action, enhancing the persuasiveness of the argument that the discourse was applied strategically as a vehicle to legitimate existing practices (Alons, 2017). Far-reaching environmental objectives and instruments thus only appear to be feasible as long as there are no other important objectives that clash with the environmental concerns, such as the food security issue did in the perspective of the Council and the EP (Swinnen, 2015). Environmental concerns are thus a part of the agricultural policy-making equation, but one with a relatively small coefficient.

A second question is to what extent have the new interinstitutional power relations after implementation of the Lisbon Treaty resulted in changes in policy-making and policy outcomes? The changes had a significant effect on the policy-making process, in which the EP played a far greater role than before, a role that COMAGRI used to support existing farm practices and reduce the effect of greening on farmers. Also, the institutional changes resulted in a more complex decision-making process, now including trilogue meetings between Commission, Council and EP to bring together their divergent views in a final agreement. Since COMAGRI succeeded in gaining the lead on behalf of the EP, enhanced access of environmental groups through the Committee on Environment was hardly effective, limiting the institutional changes' effect on policy outcomes. The Council has now had to share the reputation of the conservative player in the CAP reform process with the EP, a situation that is unlikely to change as long as either the power relations between the EP committees, or the average position in the general plenary or within member states, do not shift.

Finally, to what extent did the role of civil society change because of the Commission's increasing responsiveness to the needs of civil society and the related focus on 'better regulation' and enhanced transparency? In the policy process, this resulted in a 'public consultation' taking place before the presentation of the Commission plans, a procedure the Commission decided to continue in the CAP reform that is currently on the negotiating table. Similar attempts were earlier disqualified as a strategic resource to improve the chances of gaining support for more far-reaching reform measures (Fouilleux, 2004), by creating a counterweight of reform-oriented CSOs against the actors in the original agricultural policy network. This raises another issue: whether the focus on environmental objectives was to appease the general public rather than out of genuine concern for the environment (Alons and Zwaan, 2016). Indeed, political considerations appear to have trumped other concerns. A combination of material interests, institutional power relations favouring conservative actors and the specific circumstance of the renewed politicisation of food security explain the reform outcome. The food security concerns further broadened political actors' discursive repertoire with a productivist discourse to legitimate continued agricultural intervention, favouring productivist considerations over environmental ones.

It should not come as a surprise that many CSOs were exceptionally critical of the 2013 reform outcome, as this outcome indicates a continuing disconnect between policy discourse and actual policies. In the Commission's proposals for a new CAP reform, the answer is to make the direct payments conditional on enhanced environmental and climate requirements, while member states have to develop eco-schemes to make farmers go beyond the mandatory requirements. By providing member states with increased flexibility – the appropriate level of subsidiarity according to the Commission – it hopes to increase policy effectiveness. Reactions to the Commission's proposal to date have been mixed, with many environmental organisations pointing out that giving more freedom to the member states is more likely to result in less environmental action rather than more, while others contend that given the right circumstances the plan may bring environmental benefits (Matthews, 2018). Only time will tell what the outcome will be.

GROUP DISCUSSION

- Why (rationale) and in what way (instruments) should the agricultural sector receive state support?
- Are environmental and climate change challenges so pressing that the integration of environmental concerns in the CAP should trump all other interests and considerations?

TOPICS FOR INDIVIDUAL RESEARCH

- Interstate comparison: While almost all developed states supported their agricultural sector after World War II, some countries have decreased state intervention far more significantly since then. Compare the EU with countries such as the US and Australia to find very different trajectories. How can we explain these differences?
- Environmental and food safety standards: Despite the limits to environmental policy integration in the CAP, many farmers already believe that the EU's relatively strict (in comparison to third countries) environmental and food safety standards harm their position as exporter on the world market. How does the EU try to translate their regulation to the international level to counterbalance such potential trade consequences? Are they successful?

FURTHER READINGS

Daugbjerg, C. and P. H. Feindt (2018). *Transforming Food and Agricultural Policy: Post-Exceptionalism in Public Policy*. Journal of Public Policy Series. Routledge.

Greer, A. (2005). *Agricultural Policy in Europe*. Manchester: Manchester University Press.

Hill, Berkeley (2012). *Understanding the Common Agricultural Policy*. Earthscan: London and New York.

Josling, T. E. and S. Tangermann (2015). *Transatlantic Food and Agricultural Trade Policy: Fifty Years of Conflict and Convergence*. Edward Elgar: Cheltenham.

Swinnen, J., (2015). *The Political Economy of the 2014–2020 CAP. An Imperfect Storm*. London: Rowman and Littlefield.

REFERENCES

Alons, G. C. (2017). 'Environmental Policy Integration in the EU's Common Agricultural Policy: Greening or Greenwashing?'. *Journal of European Public Policy*, 24(11): 1604–22.

Alons, G. C. and Zwaan, P. J. (2016). 'New Wine in Different Bottles: Negotiating and Selling the CAP post-2013 Reform'. *Sociologia Ruralis*, 56(3): 349–70.

Baldock, D. and Hart, K. (2011). 'The CAP Proposals: Green in More Than Name?'. CAP2020, 12 October 2011, www.cap2020.ieep.eu/2011/10/12/the-cap-proposals-green-in-more-than-name (accessed 8 October 2018).

Bréhon, N. J. (2011). 'The CAP on the Quest of Legitimacy'. *Fondation Robert Schuman, European Issue*, 209. Available online at: www.robert-schuman.eu/en/doc/questions-d-europe/qe-209-en.pdf (accessed 8 October 2018).

Buller, H. (2002). 'Integrating European Union Environmental and Agricultural Policy'. In A. Lenschow (ed.), *Environmental Policy Integration: Greening Sectoral Policies in Europe*. London: Earthscan.

Bureau, J. C. and Mahé, L. P. (2015). 'Was the CAP Reform a Success?'. In J. Swinnen (ed.), *The Political Economy of the 2014–2020 Common Agricultural Policy*. London: Rowman and Littlefield.

Cioloş, D. (2010). 'Speech to the European Parliament's Agriculture Committee'. SPEECH/10/150, 12 April 2010.

Cioloş, D. (2011). 'The CAP Beyond 2013: Challenges and Opportunities for European Agriculture'. *Speech at the Oxford Farming Conference*. SPEECH/11/3, 6 January 2011.

Cioloş, D. (2013). 'Six Key Points for a Consistent CAP Reform'. Speech at the European Parliament. SPEECH/13/215, 12 March 2013.

COMAGRI (2010). 'Draft Report on Agriculture and International Trade'. 2010/2110 (INI) PR/833565EN.doc, 12 October 2010.

Commission (2010). 'The CAP Towards 2020: Meeting the Food, Natural Resources and Territorial Challenges of the Future'. COM(2010)627 final, 18 November 2010.

Commission (2016). 'Commission Staff Working Document: Review of Greening after One Year'. SWD(2016)218 final, 22 June 2016.

Commission (2017). 'The Future of Food and Farming'. COM(2017)713 final, 29 November 2017.

Council of the European Union (2013). 'Reform of the Common Agricultural Policy (CAP): Main Elements of the Council Position'. www.consilium.europa.eu/uedocs/cms_data/docs/pressdata/en/agricult/136582.pdf (accessed 8 October 2014).

Daugbjerg, C. and Feindt, P. H. (2017). 'Post-exceptionalism in Public Policy: Transforming Food and Agricultural Policy'. *Journal of European Public Policy* 24(11): 1565–84.

Daugbjerg, C. and Swinbank, A. (2016). 'Three Decades of Policy Layering and Politically Sustainable Reform in the European Union's Agricultural Policy'. *Governance*, 29(2): 265–80.

EEB (2012). 'Briefing: Reform Proposals for the Common Agricultural Policy'. European Environmental Bureau, www.ifoam-eu.org/sites/default/files/page/files/ngo_policy_cap_reform_council_position_201206.pdf (accessed January 2020).

EEB and others (2010). 'Environmental and Farming NGO's Response to CAP Reform Communication: Rising to Environmental Challenges?'. European Environmental Bureau, 18 November 2010. www.pan-europe.info/old/Campaigns/documents/NGO%20 Communication%20response%20-%20EEB%20conference%2030-11-2010.pdf (accessed January 2020).

Feindt, P. H. (2010). 'Policy Learning and Environmental Policy Integration in the Common Agricultural Policy 1973–2003', *Public Administration*, 88(2): 296–314.

Fischer-Hotzel, A. (2010). 'Democratic Participation? The Involvement of Citizens in Policy-making at the European Commission'. *Journal of Contemporary European Research*, 6(3): 335–52.

Fouilleux, E. (2004). 'CAP Reforms and Multilateral Trade Negotiations: Another View on Discourse Efficiency'. *West European Politics*, 27(2): 235–55.

Garzon, I. (2006). *Reforming the Common Agricultural Policy*. Basingstoke: Palgrave Macmillan.

Greer, A. (2005). *Agricultural Policy in Europe*. Manchester University Press: Manchester.

Greer, A. (2017). 'Post-exceptional Politics in Agriculture: An Examination of the 2013 CAP Reform'. *Journal of European Public Policy*, 24(11): 1585–603.

Hart, K. (2015). 'Green Direct Payments: Implementation Choices of Nine Member States and their Environmental Implications'. IEEP, www.eeb.org/index.cfm?LinkServID=0D-FEF8B2-5056-B741-DB05EBEF517EDCCB (accessed June 2016).

IEEP (2010). 'Leaked CAP2020 Proposals: Reading the Runes'. CAP2020, Institute for European Environmental Policy, 10 November 2010. www.cap2020.ieep.eu/2010/11/10/ leaked-cap2020-proposals-reading-the-runes (accessed 8 October 2018).

IEEP (2013). 'Disappointing Outcome for the Environment from COMAGRI CAP Reform Vote'. CAP2020, Institute for European Environmental Policy, 29 January 2013. http://cap2020.ieep.eu/2013/1/29/disappointing-outcomefor- the-environment-from-comagri-cap-reform-vote (accessed 8 October 2018).

Jambor, A. (2013). 'Who is Happy with EP COMAGRI's Recent Vote?'. CAP Reform.eu, 29 January 2013. http://capreform.eu/who-is-happy-with-ep-comagris-recent-vote (accessed 8 October 2018).

Keeler, J. T. A. (1996). 'Agricultural Power in the European Communicty: Explaining the Fate of CAP and GATT Negotiations'. *Comparative Politics*, 28: 127–49.

Knops, L. and Swinnen, J. (2014). 'The First CAP Reform Under the Ordinary Legislative Procedure: A Political Economy Perspective'. Study for the European Parliament. www.europarl.europa.eu/RegData/etudes/STUD/2014/529067/IPOL_STU(2014)529067_ EN.pdf (accessed 8 October 2018).

Kohler-Koch, B. (2010). 'Civil Society and EU Democracy: "Astroturf" Representation?'. *Journal of European Public Policy*, 17(1): 100–16.

Lowe, P. and Baldock, D. (2000). 'Integration of Environmental Objectives into Agricultural Policy Making'. In F. Brouwer and P. Lowe (eds), *CAP Regimes and the European Countryside*. Wallingford: CAB International.

Matthews, A. (2013). 'A Triumph for the Irish Presidency – a Damp Squib for CAP Reform'. CAP Reform. http://capreform.eu/a-triumph-for-the-irish-presidency-a-damp-squib-for-cap-reform/ (accessed 8 October 2018).

Matthews, A. (2018). 'The Greening Architecture in the New CAP'. *CAP Reform*. http://ca-preform.eu/the-greening-architecture-in-the-new-cap/ (accessed 8 October 2018).

Polman, D. (2018). 'Learning from Practical Experience: Implementation Epistemic Communities in the European Union'. In C. A. Dunlop, C. M. Radaelli and P. Trein (eds), *Learning in Public Policy: Analysis, Modes, and Outcomes*. Cham: Palgrave Macmillan.

Roederer-Rynning, C. (2015). 'COMAGRI and the "CAP after 2013" Reform'. In J. Swinnen (ed.), *The Political Economy of the 2014–2020 Common Agricultural Policy*. London: Rowman and Littlefield.

Rutz, C., Dwyer, J. and Schramek, J. (2013). 'More New Wine in the Same Old Bottles? The Evolving Nature of the CAP Reform Debate in Europe, and Prospects for the Future'. *Sociologia Ruralis*, 54(3): 266–84.

Swinnen, J. (2015). *The Political Economy of the 2014–2020 Common Agricultural Policy: An Imperfect Storm*. London: Rowman and Littlefield.

Treib, O. (2014). 'Implementing and Complying with EU Governance Outputs'. *Living Reviews in European Governance*, 9. http://europeangovernance-livingreviews.org/Articles/lreg-2014–1 (accessed 8 October 2018).

World Wide Fund (2013). 'Environment in Danger Because of EU Agriculture Deal'. WWF European Policy Office, 26 June 2013. www.wwf.eu/?209195/Environment-in-danger-because-of-EU-agriculture-deal (accessed 8 October 2018).

Zwaan, P. and Alons, G. (2015). 'Legitimating the CAP: The European Commission's Discursive Strategies for Regaining Support for Direct Payments'. *Journal of Contemporary European Research*, 11(2): 162–78.

The Internal Market: Increasingly Differentiated?

MICHELLE EGAN

8.1 Introduction

Although the financial and economic crisis have ushered in a decade of lasting damage to the European economy, the political consequences have also been severe. Conflict among member states has threatened the progress of European integration, while polarisation and unrest have unsettled domestic politics in a host of European countries. The crisis has brought into question the ability of the single market to weather the pressures of the past decade as national governments have sought to address the slow economic growth and recovery by instituting a variety of protectionist measures to stimulate their economies. While such measures can shore up key industries, protect jobs and maintain a strategic international advantage in the wake of the financial crash, it puts the viability and effectiveness of the single market at risk.

BOX 8.1 Legal basis

Single market legislation is that considered to have an impact on the functioning of the single market, as defined in Articles 26 and 114(1) of the TFEU.

Many observers were concerned that government support for struggling car firms and public bailouts of crisis-ridden banks would undermine the uniform application of single market rules designed to ensure that no single country or company gain a competitive advantage by undercutting regulations or subsiding failing firms. In his report on 'The Future of the Single Market', former Commissioner Mario Monti stressed the need to 'safeguard' the single market against the surge of economic nationalism, while also suggesting that it provided an opportunity for improving Europe's overall macroeconomic performance (Monti, 2010). He saw three key challenges: sense of market 'fatigue', uneven policy attention to the various components of the single market and complacency that the single market was complete and hence of limited political salience (Monti, 2010).

To date, there has been substantial analysis of the causes as well as the policy responses undertaken in response to the crisis, focusing on the incomplete institutional architecture of the euro as well as measures to stabilise the economy through financial assistance and macroeconomic surveillance (see Chapter 9). However, less attention has focused on the single market (see Box 8.1), even though it is one of the core policies shaping the dynamics of European integration. Built around a tight set of rules and principles, many of the core characteristics of the single market have remained unchanged even after more than a decade of slow growth. The European Commission pushes for deep integration in the face of domestic resistance, framing the single market narrative as a key to European prosperity and growth. While varying institutional membership across member states exists in specific policy areas such as the eurozone or Schengen, for example, the institutional rules that underpin the single market are to be uniformly applicable to all member states, to ensure that market access is not distorted or discriminatory in effect. It appears that the single market has proved resistant to political demands for a more differentiated framework to deal with the increased heterogeneity of interests and preferences of member states in comparison to the management of the euro, where institutional reforms differentiate between the 'ins' and the 'outs'. There are, however, three areas suggesting increased differentiation in relation to the single market:

- Functional differentiation due to the different scope and depth of integration across the four freedoms (goods, capital, service and labour).
- Territorial differentiation due to the regulatory alignment of neighbouring states to single market rules, as well as the derogations and exemptions secured by member states in specific policy areas.
- Governance differentiation regarding different types of single market rules, implementation and compliance, litigation and wider liberalisation commitments; and contested adjudication over negotiated bargains and legislative outcomes.

8.2   Historical Overview: The Single Market as an 'Incomplete Contract'

How has the EU created a 'common market' out of diverse national markets? Although the single market is the core business of the EU, it has evolved considerably since its foundation when a 'common market' along the lines of the United States was the specified goal (Spaak, 1956). Considered one of the greatest achievements of European integration, its scope has repeatedly widened. What began as a customs union expanded to address non-tariff restrictions to trade, to ensure the free movement of goods, services, capital and labour, in order to create internal unification and external demarcation of economic borders. The construction of a single market rested on a dichotomy between negative and positive integration. The former refers to the removal of obstacles and restrictions for cross-border provision of goods and services through the direct application of treaty-derived economic rights, and the latter referrs to the adoption of common rules to ensure and guarantee access to the European market (Armstrong, n.d.). Over fifty years later, the single market as it is commonly known remains a work in progress. It advanced significantly with the '1992 program', which provided a blueprint for addressing the various physical, technical and fiscal barriers that hampered cross-border trade. This effort was successful, in part, due to changes in decision-making style, with institutional reforms to promote QMV in legislative decision-making related to the functioning of the single market to avoid gridlock, coupled with judicial activism that fostered the concept of mutual recognition (see Box 8.2) to advance a new approach to market liberalisation.

BOX 8.2 Key concepts

Mutual Recognition and Mutual Trust. The mutual recognition of rules, applicable initially to goods, was then extended to recognition of professions and financial services, in which all national rules were in principle equivalent. While this avoided the need for detailed regulatory harmonisation among states with differing national regulatory styles, it requires a high degree of mutual trust to accept their neighbour's standards without additional regulatory scrutiny before entering their own home market.

As such, the single market experienced the growth of cross-border trade beyond tariffs to include the streamlining of customs procedures, the rise of FDI and the emergence of cross-border supply chains that enhanced efficiency and increased competition. In reality, the single market was, and is, dependent on further policy actions in an ever-widening range of fields with a direct impact on the single market, including taxation, employment, industry, transport, social policy, education, culture, public health, consumer protection, energy and the environment (Barnard, 2016). At the same time, the incomplete nature of the single market has hampered its ability to keep pace with the surge of productivity in the United States, so it has fallen short of its potential as efforts to calculate its overall benefits have not met initial expectations due to incomplete liberalisation (Aussiloux et al., 2017).

This is, in part, the result of a number of factors. First, the single market has evolved in response to changes in the nature of production where integrated supply chains mean that products cross back and forth across borders (see Box 8.3). As the European economy has undergone profound structural changes, the legislative agenda has moved into sectors and areas where the cross-border barriers are different, due to changes in technology and commercial practices. The remaining barriers to cross-border integration, in particular in services, including the energy sector, rail transport, telecoms, consumer insurance markets, banking and professional services, are difficult to eliminate, as services require regulation that differs from goods. While goods are tangible, subject to cross-border checks, services are intangible, so that barriers in services can impede mobility to provide services, or establish a commercial presence in another member state. The global context in which the single market now operates has fundamentally changed, moving away from economies of scale and mass production towards a knowledge and service economy based on product differentiation and global value chains (Erixson, 2016).

Second, the single market faces increased political contestation, as it pushes member states to undertake domestic structural reforms to make their product and labour markets function more efficiently. The result is often piecemeal reforms, in part, as member states have wanted to slow down economic liberalisation in the face of domestic political resistance. This selective liberalisation means that governments were often reluctant to switch strategies, further exacerbating the problem by preventing institutional adaptation and delaying member state responses to global challenges of rapid technological development. For example, privileged professions such as French notaries, or German länder savings banks, have sought derogations, exceptions or restrictions on competition, while Italy has intentions to restrict free movement of Roma and Britain sought temporary restrictions on intra-European mobility through an emergency brake on claiming benefits (Egan, 2015; Ritzén and Sandström, 2017). Governments were often reluctant to switch strategies, further exacerbating the problem by preventing institutional adaptation and delaying member state responses to global challenges of rapid technological development. Yet as the economy shifts towards intellectual property and data, internet companies pose a similar challenge in maintaining unfair commercial advantages, exempted from many tax and regulatory laws that applied to traditional businesses. States have thus maintained restrictions that affect cross-border trade in services and goods, while placing limitations on labour mobility.

Third, the distributional effects of increased market liberalisation are uneven across member states. Central and Eastern European members have become increasingly hostile to the single market, passing restrictions on land ownership, opposing restrictions on posted workers and complaining about lower agricultural subsidies, as they face the end of transitional agreements that now requires them to bring their domestic practices in line with the single market. Yet manufacturing production is concentrated in Central and Eastern Europe as part of German-led supply chains, which tends to provide higher gains for these more competitive countries while accelerating deindustrialisation in other member states.

Fourth, there is variation in implementation and compliance across member states, so at times the benefits of an integrated market may not materialise because rules are either incorrectly implemented or the legal deadline for implementation is not met, leading to problems of credible commitments (Egan and Guimareas, 2017). At face value, the national scorecards and transposition records produced by the European Commission suggest high rates of compliance with European laws. By 2015, more than a thousand infringement proceedings were pending in relation to the single market, highlighting the failure of member states to put agreed-upon policies into practice (Egan and Guimareas, 2017).

Despite the ongoing reform process to liberalise the economy, the EU has achieved piecemeal, incomplete results, as services markets are still predominantly local, but the degree of integration in goods and capital markets has rather than had become much higher. Prior to the crisis, intra-EU trade had developed even faster than world trade, pointing towards the strong integration among European countries (European Commission, 2016). The trade slump in the wake of the crisis came to a standstill or decline in the wake of slow growth, though some countries including Austria, Germany and the Netherlands performed better in terms of intra- and extra-European trade, while others such as Britain and Italy lost overall shares in EU exports. Cross-border lending and cross-border banking had taken off, as the single currency did not impede the single market, but intensified financial integration within the euro area (see Chapter 9). As the eurozone periphery incurred large amounts of international debt, capital flows fuelled a peripheral boom, and wages and prices rose sharply in the eurozone periphery relative to the eurozone core. The crisis exposed how the effects of binding commitments required the imposition of painful and potentially unpopular policies. The crisis resulted in a 'core' of surplus countries and a 'periphery' of deficit countries, which in economic terms further widened the different growth models in the eurozone, reduced cross-border lending, and brought an abrupt end to fledging efforts at economic convergence (see Chapter 17).

At the same time, subsequent efforts to deal with the impact on financial markets had generated concerns that the effects of differentiated integration arising from efforts to complete both the EMU and Banking Union led to the proposed Capital Markets Union (CMU). Designed to strengthen the single market for all member states, not just those in the euro, the CMU included those 'outs' who had feared that increased financial integration would create 'a market within a market'. While this appears to overestimate the degree to which euro members collectively agreed upon single market financial measures, signalling that the CMU was a single market measure was meant to address the concerns of 'differentiated integration' (Quaglia et al., 2016). The Commission continued to be a 'purposeful opportunist' even though states were struggling to respond to the process of forced economic adjustment. Yet this masked the degree to which the single market had evolved at different speeds, as the scope and depth of market integration varies across the four freedoms, resulting in an 'incomplete contract'.

BOX 8.3 Key dates

1957. Treaty of Rome
1979. Court of Justice of the European Union *Cassis De Dijon* decision on mutual recognition.
1985. Launch of '1992 Single Market programme' in June 1985.
1994. The European Economic Area (EEA) agreement.
2010. A New Strategy for the Single Market (Monti Report).
2015. Digital Single Market.

8.3 Current Institutional Framework

When thinking about differentiated integration, one rarely thinks about the single market – and with good reason. The legal provisions expressly provide for approximation of policies, the indivisibility of the four freedoms and the constitutional space to enforce mutual obligations. Perhaps most importantly, the institutional context of the single market represents a key example of supranational decision-making as distinct from the intergovernmental nature of euro governance (see Box 8.4 and Chapters 3 and 5), with 'institutional differentiation' between the 'ins' and the 'outs' regarding new policy instruments towards crisis management in the eurozone.

Yet the single market is far more than just legal provisions as it has incorporated differentiated modes of governance into the single market, as well as allowing differentiation across the four freedoms even if it impedes cross-border exchange and mobility.

BOX 8.4 Decision-making

Regarding the regulatory policies of the single market, the Commission has the prerogative of monopolising legislative initiatives, the Council resolves interstate conflicts that could block the functioning of the market and the legislative co-decision-making role of the Council and EP through the ordinary legislative procedure is to foster dual approval for European laws (Fabbrini, 2016).

As Fabbrini notes, the supranational EU has moved towards the system of inter-institutional checks and balances, structured around reciprocally separate institutions as in a federal union like the US (Fabbrini, 2010). Supranational governance applies to almost all policies of the single market, with the governance structure providing for input legitimacy from all three institutions – Council, Parliament and Commission (see Box 8.5) – through coordination and bargaining, albeit with differing powers of the states in shaping regulatory policies of the single market.

BOX 8.5 Key actors

The European Commission plays a key role in promoting single market initiatives to increase competitiveness and innovation, while monitoring compliance and implementation of single market obligations.

Paul-Henry Spaak produced an original report promoting economic integration.
Mario Monti refocused on completing the internal market.
Michel Barnier focused on indivisibility of four freedoms of single market.
The ECJ (Court of Justice of the European Union) has jurisdiction over single market measures, to determine their appropriateness in terms of treaty base, as well as assessing complaints against restrictive trade practices of member states, by determining discriminatory intent, as well as balancing whether different public policy objectives may hinder cross-border trade for legitimate reasons.

Four specific institutional mechanisms shape the degree of differentiation in the single market. First, the legal basis of legislation to reduce barriers to cross-border economic transactions in the single market can determine whether there can be derogations, limitations and flexibility for intergovernmental bargaining and enforcement.[1] Second, the impact of enlargement has increased the heterogeneity of states, and changed the recipients of financial adjustment assistance previously alleviating the social costs of market integration from deficit countries in Southern Europe towards Central and Eastern Europe (see Chapter 17). Third, the political and institutional developments within the EU in response to the credit-induced boom and structural imbalances in trade and capital flows created tensions derived from different growth models within the single market (Caporaso, 2018). Fourth, judicial decisions will affect the balance between free movement obligations and national imperatives on the grounds of public interest objectives, which may reinforce market integration or justify national restrictions on specific issues.

---

[1] TFEU explicitly recognises that public policy, public security and public health can justify the adoption of discriminatory rules, and settled case law Access to Museums, case C-388/01, and Temp Work Agencies, case C-490/04.

In fact, the ECJ has advocated the right of free movement, even over other national fundamental rights (e.g. *Laval*, *Viking*[2]), which has consequences for economic convergence such as the decision to allow such market forces to work.[3]

In addition, there has been legislative innovation and statutory developments in which the expansion of policy initiatives extended the European regulatory state and created new modes of governance to deal with changes wrought by market integration. While the single market includes the classic EU method of harmonisation, and a 'new approach' based on mutual recognition and the use of standards, it has also opted for 'new modes of governance', which does not entail any formal delegation of powers to the EU and operates through self-regulation, soft law mechanisms and administrative cooperation (Barnard, 2017). The different modes of governance mean that there are varying institutional rules impacting single market policies, which have shifted from an emphasis on uniform implementation and compliance through regulatory enforcement towards more coordinated, soft law measures to resolve internal distortions to trade for both consumers and business. The effort at 'better governance for the single market' has led to closer consultation with member states, a stress on lighter, smarter regulation, along with guidelines to promote effective implementation, considered as a necessary response to the crisis to prevent unjustified barriers to trade. Such regulatory flexibility in goods and services is at odds with post-crisis institutional reforms in financial services, which have shifted from mutual recognition and home control towards a more centralised rule book, which changes the traditional legislative requirements to provide greater uniformity and harmonisation with a more elaborate regulatory framework.

Yet the new crisis management has generated increased demands for judicial oversight, as member states have challenged and actively litigated the political decisions taken during negotiations. Some national constitutional courts have reserved the right to review and, if necessary, nullify changes in European governance. Member states have also disputed decision-making procedures, as single market measures take place in the shadow of enhanced judicial review, shifting the role of the European Court from that of negative to positive integration (Armstrong, n.d.). Such litigation, to assess the validity of the rules to govern the market, has led to post-legislative litigation as member states have sought annulment of crisis measures, including the ESM and Fiscal Compact, in both German and Portuguese constitutional courts.

[2] Judgment of the Court of 18 December 2007 C-341/05 – Laval un Partneri; Judgment of the Court of Justice of 11 December 2007, C-438/05 – The International Transport Workers' Federation and The Finnish Seamen's Union.
[3] *Viking* (C-438/05) and *Laval* (C-341/05) judgments from 2007 and subject the right to strike under national law to certain potential limitations deriving from European law, putting market integration and freedom of establishment as primary obligations.

Difficulties of collective action have contributed to a multi-speed Europe. Differentiated integration has emerged in the single market, in areas of the financial transaction tax and the unitary patent, so that those who choose not to participate find themselves excluded from the legislative decision-making arena, so they have turned to the judicial arena based on the single market principles of market access and non-discrimination. As such, the crisis has strengthened supranational centralisation on the one hand, relating to issues of economic governance and fiscal policy, and on the other hand has created more complex institutional interactions, where different policy instruments and expansion of enforcement policies has made the single market appear more flexible and differentiated. In reality, this strategy has contributed to its politicisation (see Chapter 1), as European policymakers have used both law-based and market-based strategies that have deepened structural divisions, as inefficient public regimes and extractive private economies have led to current discontent with the single market.

Moreover, the EU uses regulation to shape markets beyond its borders, providing for territorial integration as well as differentiation of single market authority. The extra-territorial effects of single market governance apply to non-member states, who have sought market access and regulatory alignment with the EU. The resulting extension of single market rules without a customs union towards the EEA, of neighbouring Norway, Liechtenstein and Iceland, includes financial contributions to the European budget, along with the adoption of select institutional rules covering social policy, consumer protection, environmental policy and research policy (Schimmelfennig et al., 2015). Similarly, the bilateral relationship with Switzerland creates an institutionally different mode of horizontal integration into the internal market (Gstöhl, 2015).

8.4 Recent Policy Developments

The single market has deepened during the crisis, driven by functionalist pressures arising from the internal market logic, but in a highly splintered manner. Unlike the visibility and support for the '1992' single market programme, subsequent initiatives have lacked a long-term strategic vision. Though the EU moved 'decisively into services, beginning with transport, financial services and, more hesitantly, professional services, and then network industries' (Pelkmans, 2016: 1105), there was a sense of 'market fatigue' (Monti 2010: 6) as member states were continually presented with an endless series of action plans, declarations and reviews that provided a gradual and piecemeal strategy for single market reform. Yet high debt burdens and a low growth environment led to the single market project as an alternative source of growth. While the European Commission pushed for effective action from member states to create the conditions for a strong and sustained recovery, member states were still adjusting to the political turmoil created by controversial initiatives such as the posted workers directive, the new chemical regime (REACH – Registration, Evaluation, Authorisation and Restriction of Chemicals) and copyright laws (European Commission, 2008). Facing an erosion of political and social support, the European Commission proposed both a Single Market Act I and II detailing more than fifty proposals to reform the single market, which were later streamlined into twelve action areas, as the first foray in the crisis context to actually frame concrete actions and measures (Camisão and Guimareas, 2017). Though aimed at recapturing the dynamism of the 1992 single market project from twenty years earlier, the results were a series of incremental policy measures. Rather than alleviate the social costs of the crisis (see Chapter 10 and 11), the European Commission ultimately did not deviate from its traditional *modus operandi* of seeking to deepen integration.

With the prevailing rhetoric about a better-functioning single market, the Commission pushed forward in three areas: modernisation and upgrading of existing regulatory requirements, new initiatives in the service sector to increase market openness and integration and improvements in implementation and compliance. During the crisis, the single market for financial services went through an overhaul. The rules for financial services and capital were tightened, resulting in new rules on financial markets and banking supervision, along with measures for previously unregulated financial services, such as credit rating agencies and hedge funds. Requirements for regulatory alignment for foreign firms to continue access to the single market were to ensure that differentiation of market surveillance rules would not undermine European financial stability. Euro area member states agreed reluctantly to move towards a banking union. Those not in the euro area supported the project as a solution to the sovereign debt crisis, provided that there were safeguards in place for those outside the euro, given the myriad different governance institutions that emerged to supervise banking, insurance, and securities markets (Quaglia et al., 2016; Howarth and Quaglia, 2016). Beyond upgrades in the financial sector, concerns about inadequate levels of investment in product and service markets have centred on burdensome regulations that undermine innovation and competitiveness. The Commission sought to deflect criticism about its regulatory agenda, by framing all of the single market initiatives as part of the 'Better Regulation Agenda'. As part of a coordinated effort to move its work programme forwards during and after the crisis, the Commission has pushed for greater institutional coordination, encouraging increased awareness of the regulatory responsibility of member states.

In addition, the Commission has been striving to take account of the changes in business practices that are emerging in services, technology and assets where new market operators face increased regulatory fragmentation and market entry barriers, necessitating new regulatory initiatives. These include the Energy Union,

Capital Markets Action Plan, and Digital Single Market. The Digital Single Market Strategy emerged in 2015, amid concerns that there were no digital champions in Europe compared to the United States and China. With the expectation that the digital sector will encompass 1.4 million jobs and €415 billion in revenue (4 per cent of GDP) by 2020, Europe needed to address the regulatory fragmentation that led to only 4 per cent of cross-border online sales compared to 43 per cent within domestic markets. While constituting a quarter of single market legislative efforts, the Digital Single Market will not meet the scheduled 2020 deadline despite progress on geo-blocking, roaming charges, copyright, privacy and non-personal data flows.

By contrast, the collaborative economy[4] is still an emerging area, where the Commission is offering guidelines rather than establishing a distinctive European regulatory framework. Though the sector primarily covers transportation and accommodation services, the incompleteness of the single market in services has meant that these platforms face outdated market access designed for traditional sectors not new business models. The European context seems less conducive for new collaborative platforms to emerge as national and local authorities have adopted regulations that have resulted in outright bans or burdensome limits to market access. Airbnb has faced legal challenges in France and Spain, and Uber, the platform providing alternative urban transportation, has been banned in European cities such as Sofia and Budapest, while it is only partially available in Rome and Milan. If the current state of regulatory affairs remains unchanged, the €527 billion economic potential of this market will decrease to roughly €110 billion. Regulating this market is difficult given prevailing national competences of member states in areas such as labour (see Chapter 11) and taxation (see Chapter 15), causing the political responses to the sharing economy to be fragmented, reactive and narrow in scope, with different national priorities, such as taxation in Belgium, social protection in France and competition in Spain. That said, the single market has climbed back onto the political agenda, as European policymakers stress the need to 'deliver the single market' (Jean-Claude Juncker) in order 'to greatly benefit if dynamic and innovative players could operate in a truly EU-wide market' (Almunia, 2014).

8.5 Current Political and Academic Controversies

While the EU is widely believed to have one of the most developed and functioning internal markets, this claim has led to academic debates about the dynamics that create cross-jurisdictional markets in different federal systems (Egan, 2015;

---

[4] A decentralised digital networked economic system circumventing traditional business models.

Egan, forthcoming; Hoffman et al., 2017). We have limited comparative analysis about whether its ambitions and achievements are in fact distinctive in theoretical or empirical terms. Some scholars note that the degree of European market integration is high in comparison to other federal systems, due to formal institutional rules and judicial outcomes that have actively addressed market discriminatory practices (Hoffman et al., 2017; Egan and Guimarães, 2016). They argue that the EU has centralised authority with liberalised core rules that are essential in promoting the freedom of goods, services, capital and people. For others, there has been a functional widening and deepening of the single market in response to large-scale shifts in patterns of economic production, as structural changes in the global economy highlight the need for new innovative strategies (Pelkmans, 2016). Yet these initiatives have in practice proven modestly successful or even suffered setbacks. While the easy gains have been secured, as the single market provides reliable access for goods, services, capital and technology to some degree, it confronts the need to address increasing public doubts about the benefits of trade openness.

In recent discussions on comparative market integration, a consensus has emerged that internal barriers are a major concern in federations such as Canada or Australia, and have been an ongoing target of policy reforms in marked comparison to the United States (Egan, 2015; Elijah, forthcoming). While constitutions usually furnish the federal level with the authority to establish and maintain a domestic economic union, there needs to be more comparative analysis to evaluate the extent to which judicial activism or restraint influences the integration process. While patterns of acceptance of federal authority – and the supremacy of law – did encounter member state resistance in the early period of market integration, Europe is not unlike the United States where state defiance of federal legal authority meant that clashes over the market were endemic. This continues today where challenges to collective power within the EU have led to national confrontation about the conformity of single market measures to protecting fundamental rights, the exceptions and derogations from obligations regarding free movement of people and the indivisibility of single market rules in Brexit negotiations.

Studies of European integration have relied heavily on the role of law as a causal factor in propelling the single market forward, and serving as a legal catalyst for the extension of regulatory governance into new policy sectors. Studies highlight how federal courts are more likely to make expansive constitutional and statutory interpretations to facilitate the removal of trade barriers in the face of legislative gridlock, built on an acceptance of the legitimacy of the legal order (Egan and Guimarães, 2016; Keleman, 2011). Such judicial safeguards to avoid shirking and enforce legal obligations, including litigation to secure 'market' rights, have led some scholars to argue that social considerations permeate market-driven practices (Caporaso and Tarrow, 2009). Others have been more critical, arguing that the abandoning of the model of embedded liberalism and institutionalising economic rationality has undermined the social acceptance of the European project (Scharpf, 2002). Yet both perspectives recognise the crucial role of judicial authority in creating and regulating the market, although they disagree about the ability of European states to maintain their social models in the face of market integration.

While the literature has acknowledged judicial empowerment in addressing internal market barriers, the European literature has rarely considered the relevance of cross-national comparisons in constructing internal markets. While the Australian High Court, for example, has always been more inclined to strike down state law that created internal trade barriers, the Canadian Supreme Court has been more reluctant to encroach on subnational authority, preserving the ability of provinces to regulate interprovincial trade. Unlike the EU and Australia, Canada has consistently supported regional diversity and provincial sovereignty to regulate markets, rejecting constitutional provisions that would foster economic union, thus lacking the judicial impulse to address interprovincial barriers (Egan, 2018). While the United States also has myriad state regulations, as the relationship between markets and federal authority is complex, cross-border trade is stronger than in Europe, even after excluding language and distance (Egan, 2015; Aussilloux et al., 2017). In Europe, there is a 'home bias' in terms of high levels of national consumption and investment patterns that warrants more attention (Delgado, 2006). As a result, trade in goods and services between European countries is estimated to be about four times less than between US states, so there is a preference in Europe for greater investment in domestic 'home' country assets and products. This has increased during the financial crisis due to the heightening inclination of banks to hold greater sovereign local debt and reduce capital investment flows outside of their home state.

More recently, scholars have focused on the extent to which Europe externalises its market-related policies and practices, exporting its single market rules beyond its borders (Damro, 2012). For some, the EU exercises its power in international affairs, because pressures for regulatory alignment with single market rules foster compliance with European norms, as the threat of market closure can force recalcitrant states to switch their regulatory standards (Drezner, 2007: 32). Neighbouring European states have, to varying degrees, sought more integration into the internal market, but the institutionalisation of these relationships takes differing forms. These range from bilateral relations that revolve around reciprocal market access and regulatory equivalence as in the Swiss case, or membership in the EEA or full acceptance of market rules as a precondition of accession and membership in the case of Turkey, Macedonia, Montenegro and Serbia. While external 'differentiated' integration means that non-member states enjoy different levels of access to the internal market, the prevailing view is that leveraging of their single market strategies, such as mutual recognition or regulatory equivalence agreements, also provides an opportunity to shape markets. While several studies make it clear that the inherent uncertainty over the nature of mutual equivalence means that it may be inappropriate or problematic in building the European single market, there is an assumption that European market strategies can be easily replicated in other markets (Nicolaïdis and Egan, 1998; Sieglinde, 2015).

Case studies highlight how the EU has been successful in promoting its single market rules in product markets, such as chemicals or cosmetics, as well as a few areas where single market rules apply to service providers outside Europe, notably in data protection and financial services (Bradford, 2015; Newmann and Posner, 2015). Yet the notion that single market rules are 'exported' through trade negotiations fails to highlight the extent and limits of that influence, which can vary across goods, capital and service markets (Young, 2015). The predominant consensus that Europe 'exports' its laws and standards to other countries by offering improved access to its single market may not hold, as 'domestic political costs associated with harmonising to EU rules is difficult', suggesting that the EU does not 'export its single market regulations bilaterally much beyond its borders' (Young, 2015: 1270).

8.6   Paradigmatic Case Study: Brexit and Single Market – Increasingly Differentiated Markets

What happens if a member state wants to leave the single market and customs union?[5] The British government, having decided to trigger Article 50 of the Lisbon Treaty in March 2017, immediately faced a decision about the future relationship with the EU. Although the referendum did not provide an explicit mandate to leave the EU customs union or the single market, the negotiations have drawn attention to the key institutional arrangements that have anchored Britain's commitment to the European project for over four decades. Many economic assessments of British withdrawal have pointed to the potential effects within Britain across regions and industries, with varying scenarios depending on the degree of market access and future trade deal (Baldwin, 2016; Ries et al., 2017). Both domestic and foreign businesses have amplified their concerns about the disruptive effects of no deal, and the costs and uncertainty in terms of investment and production of reduced access to the single market (Baldwin, 2016; Ries et al., 2017). Yet the negotiations are also a process in which the subsequent outcome will establish some form of differentiation outside the scope of formal EU membership (Glencross, 2018). Losing such a key proponent of the single market will undoubtedly have a significant impact on the British economy, and on the ability

[5] This section is drawn extensively from Egan (forthcoming).

of member states to weather the pressure of the departure of a major economy, particularly for those member states with significant investment ties and exports to Britain.

Britain joined the European Community 'common market' deeply divided and in the throes of low productivity, dysfunctional industrial relations and growth rates that lagged behind those of both Germany and France (Crafts, 2016). Though membership reduced protectionism, encouraged FDI and increased trade, the improvement in Britain's growth performance after accession has not stopped debates about the 'costs' of membership, whether in terms of budget contributions, agricultural prices or excessive regulations, in spite of Britain's ability to maintain a regulatory 'style' that is much lighter than many advanced industrial economies. With eroding social protection and stagnant wages, Brexit generated a countermovement against this neoliberal mode of European integration. Britain had touted all the market access advantages while downplaying the European regulatory and protective regimes in its economic discourse. As a liberal market economy, Britain championed the single market (Egan, 2001; Egan and Guimarães, 2016) in which the interests of capital are predominant (Blyth, 2013). The British political economy emphasised flexible labour markets, light-touch regulation, privatisation, open capital flows and a competitive low-tax regime promoted as a model for EU-induced liberalisation, in an often-contested environment of diverse socio-economic models (Pettifor, 2017). Yet austerity, coupled with the financial crisis, highlighted the unbalanced nature of the British economy, as past policy choices reflected the differentiation between the British financial economy and the rest of the EU, with services playing a significant role in creating a trade surplus, as European member states served as the largest market for British service exports. This divergent growth model, dependent on financial services, net immigration and opt-out from the euro, emphasised how domestic politics in Britain sought to replicate this 'differentiation' within the EU to its current negotiations on future access to the single market (Thompson, 2017).

For Britain, the push to cushion the initial economic impact of Brexit has led to proposals for a more 'differentiated' arrangement that allows Britain to remain in a free trade area covering goods and agriculture. During the time-limited transition phase, Britain will be required to comply with all the rules of the single market, including freedom of movement, as these are legal obligations of membership. Member states have been resistant to British efforts to have a bespoke 'cherry-picking' deal. In response, European negotiators have insisted that participation in the single market requires acceptance of all four freedoms: movement of goods, capital, services and people. Any arrangement for selective rule compliance undermines the integrity of the single market, as the EU emphasises the concurrent application and indivisibility of single market rules and practices. This insistence is in part due to British efforts under Theresa May to treat incoming EU citizens differently from those that arrived while it was still a member state, and its dogged pursuit of mutual recognition and equivalence in financial services, given the loss of its single market 'passport'. Coupled with mixed messages on the 'frontstop' arrangement concerning Northern Ireland, and its persistent wavering over its financial settlement if no deal is agreed, there are expectations in the withdrawal agreement that post-Brexit obligations should be similar to those of a member state. This concern about credible commitments in Brussels is heightened not only by Boris Johnson's equivocations, but also by proposals from Corbyn's Labour Party to nationalise public utilities and promote a strategic industrial policy in ways that would be inimical to European competition policy.

Ironically, successive British governments have sought to promote the benefits of the single market and advance further liberalisation in services, while finding themselves increasingly isolated in regulating finance and stabilising the euro, as their interests have increasingly diverged from other member states (Thompson, 2017). With the devolution of power back to constituent units, Britain will lose access to political and judicial safeguards that sustain the single market, requiring domestic legal and political changes to the institutional status quo. British negotiating demands have focused on the 'integrity' of their own internal market, concerned that varying institutional rules may apply within their own polity, with contrasting logics of single market governance applicable to one territorial region (Northern Ireland) but not others (Scotland, Wales and England). As trade negotiations reach a critical point, European policymakers are engaged in contingency plans in the event of no deal. For them, the immediate effects of leaving the single market may lead to a host of 'differentiated' legal and regulatory outcomes. There may be limited provisions for cross-border financial services, implementation of ownership requirements for airlines to receive a European operating licence, possible reciprocal visa travel and security exemptions, limitations on access rights for road haulage and reinstatement of agricultural controls. The Commission expects 'a combination of substantive rules aligned with EU and international standards, adequate mechanisms to ensure effective implementation domestically, enforcement and dispute settlement mechanisms in the agreement as well as Union autonomous remedies that are all commensurate with the depth and breadth of the EU–UK economic connectedness' (European Council, 2018). What seems likely to emerge is a 'regulatory patchwork' with alignment in select goods, social and environmental rules, and institutional cooperation, albeit with sectoral variation, all of which is dependent on the long-term relationship that emerges with the customs union and single market.

What is evolving in British discourse are two different visions of its post-Brexit economy that are at odds with the European single market (Egan, 2018).

One approach, pushed by those seeking new trade deals beyond Europe, undercuts previous EU standards in areas such as product regulation, labour relations or service provisions to foster competitiveness by rejecting single market norms, and emphasising the competitive advantage of differentiation in market rules. The other approach seeks to strengthen the scope and intervention of government in the economy, through a fundamental reorganisation of political authority involving labour, financial and service markets. This inward-looking approach would in fact find some support among member states, who have less confidence in the ability of the single market to deliver growth and prosperity given the poor performance of their economies over the past decade (Bickerton, 2018).

While single market integration was initially a shared ideal, its shape and attributes were not always the source of consensus. Europe has continuously sought to enhance its institutional capacity in order to make markets work effectively, and to reconcile different ideas about the constitutive nature of markets. The process is an ongoing one that needs viable rules, structures and norms for the single market to operate effectively. While overshadowed by the eurozone crisis, the single market has proved durable, emerging largely unscathed from the financial and economic crisis despite the surge of protectionism and austerity measures. There has continued to be routine incremental expansion of the single market into new areas, such as digital and energy markets, as well as revision and refinement of existing areas, including financial services and transportation. Often touted as a model for regional integration, the single market is still a differentiated market that is much more developed for goods than it is for services and labour. The European single market is thus an 'incomplete' contract. Currently, it faces two challenges. First, the effective functioning of the single market, dependent on member state compliance and implementation of European norms and rules, along with judicial enforcement of breaches of treaty obligations. Second, the withdrawal of a key supporter of the single market, with efforts to ensure that such actions do not lead to the undermining of the single market, in light of the risk and uncertainty surrounding Brexit. Explaining the dynamics of market integration may gain further traction through a comparative perspective, and bring into sharper focus the variation that has emerged across federal systems, buttressed by the division of authority across jurisdictions, the allocation of competences, and responses to economic, social, political and technological pressures to address barriers to cross-border trade. Though the single market has gained increased political visibility as a response to the crisis, and as a member state negotiates leaving the economic bloc, the project has been one of piecemeal, incremental expansion into new core policy areas, rather than a *finalité économique*.

GROUP DISCUSSION

• Why is the single market an 'incomplete contract'?
• What does 'differentiated integration' mean in the context of the single market?

TOPICS FOR INDIVIDUAL RESEARCH

• How has the EU created a 'common market' out of diverse national markets?
• What does 'differentiated integration' mean in the context of the single market?

FURTHER READINGS

Camisão, I. and Guimarães, M. H. (2017). 'The Commission, the Single Market and the Crisis: The Limits of Purposeful Opportunism'. *Journal of Common Market Studies*, 55(2): 223–39.
Dougan, M. (2016). 'What is Single Market?'. www.youtube.com/watch?v=R6F0iny JPDc.
Egan, M. (2015). *Single Markets: Economic Integration in Europe and the United States.* Oxford: Oxford University Press.
Egan, M. and Guimarães, M. H. (2016). 'The Single Market: Trade Barriers and Trade Remedies'. *Journal of Common Market Studies*, 55(2): 294–311.
Pelkmans, J. (2016). 'Why the Single Market Remains the EU's Core Business'. *West European Politics*, 39(5): 1095–113.

REFERENCES

Almunia, J. (2014). 'Fighting for the Single Market'. Speech, Vice President of the European Commission responsible for Competition Policy, European Competition Forum, Brussels, 11/02/2014.
Armstrong, K. (n.d.). 'Negative and Positive Integration After 1992: Courts, Harmonisation and the (Economic) Constitution of EU'. Unpublished paper.
Aussilloux, V., Bénassy-Quéré, A., Fuest, C. and Wolff, G. (2017). 'Making the Most of the Single European Market'. Bruegel, Policy Issue No. 3, 1–18. http://bruegel.org/2017/02/making-the-best-of-the-european-single-market/.
Baldwin, R. (2016). 'The World Trade Organization and the Future of Multilateralism'. *Journal of Economic Perspectives*, 30(1): 95–116.
Barnard, C. (2017). 'Brexit and the EU Internal Market'. In F. Fabbrini (ed.), *The Law and Politics of Brexit.* Oxford: Oxford University Press.
Bickerton, C. (2018). 'Brexit and the British Growth Model'. *Policy Exchange.* https://policy-exchange.org.uk/publication/brexit-and-the-british-growth-model/.
Blyth, M. (2013). *Austerity: The History of a Dangerous Idea.* Oxford: Oxford University Press.
Bradford, A. (2015). 'Exporting Standards: The Externalization of the EU's Regulatory Power Via Markets'. *International Review of Law and Economics*, 42: 158–73.
Camisão, I. and Guimarães, M. H. (2017). 'The Commission, the Single Market and the Crisis: The Limits of Purposeful Opportunism'. *Journal of Common Market Studies*, 55(2): 223–39.

Caporaso, J. (2018). 'Europe's Triple Crisis and the Uneven Role of Institutions: The Euro, Refugees and Brexit'. *Journal of Common Market Studies*, 56(6): 1345–61.

Caporaso, J. and Tarrow, S. (2009). 'Polanyi in Brussels: Supranational Institutions and the Transnational Embedding of Markets'. *International Organization*, 63(4): 593–620.

Crafts, N. (2016). 'The Impact of EU Membership on UK Economic Performance'. *Political Quarterly*, 87(2): 262–8.

Damro, C. (2012). 'Market Power Europe'. *Journal of European Public Policy*, 19(5): 682–99.

Delgado, J. (2006). *Single Market Trails Home Bias*. Brussels: Bruegel.

Drezner, D. (2007). *All Politics in Global: Explaining International Regulatory Regimes*. Princeton: Princeton University Press.

Egan, M. P. (2001). *Constructing a European Market: Standards, Regulation, and Governance*. Oxford: Oxford University Press.

Egan, M. (2015). *Single Markets: Economic Integration in Europe and the United States*. Oxford: Oxford University Press.

Egan, M. (2018). 'Imperfect Markets: Federal Safeguards and Economic Integration in Canada'. Paper presented at the Symposium, November 9–10 University of Pittsburgh.

Egan, M. (forthcoming). 'Brexit and the Single Market'. In J. Laible and S. Greer (eds), *The EU After Brexit*. Manchester: Manchester University Press.

Egan, M. and Guimarães, M. H. (2016). 'The Single Market: Trade Barriers and Trade Remedies'. *Journal of Common Market Studies*, 55(2): 294–311.

Elijah, A. M. (forthcoming). 'Trade Politics and the Australian States and Territories'. In J. Broschek and P. Goff (eds), *The Multilevel Politics of Trade: Configurations, Patterns and Dynamics*. Toronto: Toronto University Press.

Erixson, F. (2016). *What is Wrong with the Single Market?* Brussels: ECIPE.

European Commission (2008). 'Green Paper. Copyright in the Knowledge Economy'. COM(2008)466final.

European Commission (2016). 'The Evolving Composition of EU Trade'. Commissioned Report for DG GROW.

European Council (2018). 'Guidelines'. 23 March 2018, EUCO XT 20001/18.

Fabbrini, S. (2010). *Compound Democracies: Why the United States and Europe are Becoming Similar*. Oxford: Oxford University Press.

Fabbrini, S. (2016). 'From Consensus to Domination: The Intergovernmental Union in a Crisis Situation'. *Journal of European Integration*, 38(5): 587–99.

Glencross, A. (2018). 'This Time it's Different: Legitimacy and the Limits of Differentiation after Brexit'. *The Political Quarterly*, 89(3): 490–96.

Gstöhl, S. (2015). 'Models of External Differentiation in the EU's Neighbourhood: An Expanding Economic Community?' *Journal of European Public Policy*, 22(6): 854–70.

Hoffman, L., et al. (2017). 'How Europe's Single Market Surpassed America's'. Paper presented at the EUSA Conference, Miami, May.

Howarth, D. and Quaglia, L. (2016). 'Brexit and the Single European Financial Market'. *Journal of Common Market Studies*, 55(51): 149–64.

Keleman, D. (2011). *Eurolegalism*. Cambridge, MA: Harvard University Press.

Monti, M. (2010). 'A New Strategy for the Single Market: At the Service of Europe's Economy and Society'. Report to the President of the European Commission, Brussels, 9 May. http://ec.europa.eu/internal_market/strategy/docs/monti_report_final_10_05_2010_en.pdf.

Newmann, A. and Posner, E. (2015). 'Putting the EU in Its Place: Policy Strategies and the Global Regulatory Context'. *Journal of European Public Policy*, 22(9): 1316–35.

Nicolaïdis, K. and Egan, M. (1998). 'Transnational Market Governance and Regional Policy Externality: Why Recognize Foreign Standards?'. *Journal of European Public Policy*, 8(3): 454–73.

Pelkmans, J. (2016). 'Why the Single Market Remains the EU's Core Business'. *West European Politics*, 39(5): 1095–113.

Pettifor, A. (2017). 'Brexit and its Consequences'. *Globalizations*, 14(1): 127–32.

Quaglia, L., Howarth, D. and Liebe, M. (2016). 'The Political Economy of European Capital Markets Union'. *Journal of Common Market Studies*, 54(S1): 185–203.

Ries, C. P. et al. (2017). *After Brexit Alternate Forms of Brexit and their Implications for the United Kingdom, the European Union and the United States*. Santa Monica and Cambridge: RAND Corporation.

Ritzén, S. and Sandström, G. Ö. (2017). 'Barriers to the Circular Economy: Integration of Perspectives and Domains'. *Procedia CIRP*, 64: 7–12.

Scharpf, F. (2002). 'The European Social Model'. *Journal of Common Market Studies*, 40(4): 645–70.

Schimmelfennig, F., Leuffen, D. and Rittberger, B. (2015). 'The European Union as a System of Differentiated Integration: Interdependence, Politicization and Differentiation'. *Journal of European Public Policy*, 22(6): 764–82.

Sieglinde, G. (2015). 'Models of External Differentiation in the EU's Neighbourhood: An Expanding Economic Community?'. *Journal of European Public Policy*, 22(6): 854–70.

Spaak, P.-H. (1956). *Intergovernmental Committee on European Integration: The Brussels Report on the General Common Market*. Archive of European Integration (AEI), April. http://aei.pitt.edu/995/.

Thompson, H. (2017). 'Inevitability and Contingency: The Political Economy of Brexit'. *British Journal of Politics and International Relations*, 19(3): 434–49.

Young, A. (2015). 'Liberalizing Trade, Not Exporting Rules: The Limits to Regulatory Co-ordination in the EU's "New Generation" Preferential Trade Agreements'. *Journal of European Public Policy*, 22(9): 1253–75.

9 The Economic and Monetary Union: How Did the Euro Area Get a Lender of Last Resort?

CORNEL BAN

9.1 Introduction

Having an LoLR to the financial system and the state is one of the essential preconditions of economic stability (see Box 9.1). Since the late nineteenth century the LoLR function was played by national central banks acting as custodians of both national currencies and domestic monetary systems. Since central banks do not have to make profits and since they cannot have liquidity problems with their own money, they can create as much money as they want within their mandates to keep prices stable. In other words, they issue the 'last' money and are therefore uniquely well-positioned to address systemic liquidity problems. Moreover, even under normal conditions, financial institutions may need to borrow overnight from the central bank at a low 'administered' rate (the so-called discount window) whenever they experience short-term liquidity shortfalls and are in need of a quick cash infusion.

> ### BOX 9.1 Key concepts
>
> *Lender of last resort.* In times of deep financial crises (financial panics, contagious bank runs and other unusual increases in demand for liquidity that cannot be met from the market), a bank or the financial system as a whole may find themselves unable to obtain sufficient financial liquidity to continue their operations. To deal with these challenges one needs a public provider of liquidity to the financial institutions that find themselves in such moments of distress. This provider is known as a 'lender of last resort' or LoLR, able to deliver liquidity 'to illiquid but most likely solvent counterparties on whatever terms' (Buiter and Rahbari, 2012: 8). To be credible, the LoLR needs to 'be able to issue unquestionably liquid instruments in any amount and on demand – that is, without delay; at a minimum, a credible LoLR should be able to cover the plausible liquidity needs of the agents that are potentially vulnerable to a funding strike by private investors' (Buiter and Rahbari, 2012: 21).

But LoLR interventions should be seen in a broader political economy context. Thus, in terms of their dependence on an LoLR, states are not all that different from banks. Like banks, most contemporary governments cannot control their central bank due to the latter's constitutionalised independence from both the political arena and the markets (De Haan et al., 2018). Under these conditions, central banks are essential in facilitating lending to the government when it faces problems with rolling over its debt. During the postwar period of shared prosperity, the central banks accommodated fiscal policies that addressed the fall in aggregate demand during recessions and made sure that full employment objectives were met and high employment targets were hit. But after the 1970s, as inflation became a key concern, central banks began to refrain from accommodating the state's demand for fiscal policy space (Ugolini, 2018).

The EMU is interesting as a case of how an LoLR emerges at the international level. It has been argued that sovereign debt markets in a currency union without a robust LoLR can be devastated by pessimistic investor sentiment that can trigger government default (De Grauwe, 2013; De Grauwe and Ji, 2015; Saka et al., 2015). However, during the crisis of 2008 many central banks took cues from the US Federal Reserve and the Bank of England to bring this accommodative regime back to life, with the ECB doing the same, albeit only after late 2012, and therefore with a very costly three-year lag. To do this, the ECB had to resort to some creative interventions while cajoling the EU political elite to provide it with complementary institutions (emergency liquidity funds) that had to be created from scratch. In effect, the EU got a full LoLR function after it announced unlimited purchases *and* the ESM, a permanent bailout fund, was established.

Moreover, faced with the demand destruction wrought by the financial crisis and austerity, the Commission and the bank of the EU jointly assumed a countercyclical lender role targeted at the real economy: firms and municipal governments in the EU. Indeed, in an illustration of the old dictum that EU integration advances one crisis at a time, the LoLR function within the confines of the EMU was accompanied by the boosting of the EU capacity to act as a countercyclical lender via the EIB and the so-called Juncker Plan.

9.2   Historical Overview

9.2.1   From the Snake to Maastricht (1969–91)

The ECB is the central bank of the nineteen-country euro currency, the central monetary thrust of the EMU. Broadly speaking, the EMU is a cluster of policies designed to ensure economic convergence among the member states having the euro as a common currency as well as of the non-euro EU member states. At the highest (and third) stage of this convergence, a member state joins the euro after having participated for at least two years in a policy experiment demonstrating that it can maintain the deviation of their currency within a tight 'band' of variation vis-à-vis the euro. That said, not all member states have actually committed to join. Famously, the UK did not and, together with Denmark (whose currency is 'pegged' to the euro), the UK obtained a legal opt-out from the convergence process, a decision that liberated the Brexit process from the difficult outcomes faced by Greece when Grexit was on the table.

BOX 9.2 Key dates

1972. Introduction of the 'snake in the tunnel' coordination mechanism.
1979. Creation of the European Monetary System (EMS).
1988. Publication of the Delors Report.
1991. Adoption of the Maastricht Treaty.
2002. Launch of the euro as legal tender.

The idea of a common European currency was broached by the European Commission in 1969. This happened in the aftermath of a wave of financial market turbulence that had forced some European currencies up and others down, leading to trade disruptions inside the European Community. As a response, a three-stage blueprint for the monetary union was drafted by a group of experts led by Luxemburgish finance minister Pierre Werner (hence the name Werner Plan), followed by the so-called 'snake in the tunnel', a mechanism adopted in 1972 by the EEC central bankers whereby they would buy and sell currencies within a small fluctuation margin (2.25 per cent) within the 'tunnel' provided by the dollar. But since the 'snake' was based on the assumption that the dollar would be stable and tied to gold, its life was cut short by the instability of the global monetary system unleashed by the US decision to unbuckle the dollar from gold in 1971. The main consequence of this decision was to devalue the dollar, a process that led to global monetary instability amplified by the manifold increases in the price of oil in late 1973 (McNamara, 1998).

Faced with this monetary turmoil, the EC member states began to focus on reducing fluctuation margins within the EC currencies, taking the German currency as a reference point rather than the US dollar. As a result of this policy shift at the EC level, in 1979 eight member states launched the EMS, a new currency stability arrangement that set national exchange rates relative to a common currency unit called ECU. In simple terms, the EMS 'allowed countries with their own currencies to go in and out of a target zone of cross-exchange rate stability, as called for by national economic circumstances' (Schelkle, 2017). As such, the EMS (rather flexibly) constrained the possibility of countries such as Italy to use currency devaluations to boost their exports, and was used by others (France) to strengthen their macroeconomic discipline by imitating the monetary policy of Germany, the only European economy unscathed by the slow growth and high inflation malaise of the 1970s popularly known as 'stagflation' (McNamara, 1998).

However, the boldest step towards using the EMS as a springboard for an actual common currency was taken by the European Council in 1988 in the form of the so-called Delors Report (named after the president of the European Commission, Jacques Delors) that advanced the targets of monetary union and of a newly funded Committee for the Study of Economic and Monetary Union that defined the objectives and stages of the monetary union (Ross and Jenson, 2017). However, it took three years, the end of the Soviet Union and a remarkable climate of euro enthusiasm for such initiatives to develop some 'bite' in the form of the 1991 TEU (La Malfa, 2017). Signed in Maastricht (the Netherlands), the TEU stipulated that member states were 'resolved to achieve the strengthening and the convergence of their economies and to establish an economic and monetary union including, in accordance with the provisions of this Treaty, a single and stable currency'. This meant specific treaty provisions that bound all member states to a common monetary policy, the establishment of ECB to run it and the specific convergence criteria for joining the EMU.

9.2.2   Forging the Euro and the Rise of the ECB (1991–2002)

The early years of the process leading up to the establishment of the euro were rocky. In 1991–2, following a Danish referendum rejecting the Maastricht Treaty and a French referendum coming close to doing the same, market speculation that the member states were weakly committed to the common currency objective forced a currency crisis in the EMS, leading the UK and Italy to leave it altogether and the EMS member states as a whole to temporarily widen the margins of currency devaluation (Ban, 2016). Despite these tensions, European leaders ploughed on and created a monetary policy and surveillance body (the European Monetary Institute) to ensure policy convergence.

The sceptics of the euro were dismayed to learn at a 1995 European Council meeting that the EMU would become a reality in 1999, with member states fixing their currencies against the euro. Things went rather smoothly from there onwards, and on 1 January 2002 the euro was launched as legal tender in eleven EU states as of January 2002. Since then, a wave of (mostly) Eastern European countries joined between 2007 and 2015 and brought the number of its member states to nineteen. Today, the euro covers more people (335.4 million) than the dollar does (316 million), and has led to a significant increase in trade and financial flows, lower costs in corporate bond markets, integrated interbank markets and low inflation across the euro area.

9.3   Main Features of the Current Institutional Framework

The fiscal architecture of the euro is the SGP, a set of rules based on a draft of the famously orthodox German Treasury that demanded public debt levels at 60 per cent of GDP, a level maintained by fiscal deficits no higher than 3 per cent (going above that limit entailed sanctions) and inflation below 2 per cent. To ward off 'moral hazard', a no bailout clause (i.e. no bailout of another member state unless there occurred 'exceptional occurrences beyond its control') was introduced in the SGP.

The logic underpinning all this was that if fiscal and monetary restraint prevailed and financial investors increased the risk premia on the undisciplined member states, convergence would be ensured through a mix of peer and market pressure (Blyth, 2013; Princen & Esch, 2016). Given that the ECB had a strong and minimalistic anti-inflationary mandate, in case of competitiveness or solvency crises the member states would be forced to 'internal devaluation', a set of policies aimed to reduce prices relative to others. The typical means to do this include wages cuts and easing hire and fire rules for workers (Armingeon and Baccaro, 2012). In effect, under these constraints austerity should have become automatic. In reality, however, both before and after the 2010 crisis, cyclical behind-the-scenes political negotiations frequently softened the supposedly hard numbers of the SGP (Schmidt, 2016). Indeed, Germany and France were among the first to break the deficit limit and to date no euro area member has been sanctioned under the so-called Excessive Deficit Procedure.

BOX 9.3 Legal basis

Articles 119–44, 219, and 282–4 of the Treaty on the Functioning of the European Union.

Protocols annexed to the TEU: Protocol (No 4) on the statute of the European System of Central Banks and the ECB, Protocol (No 14) on the Eurogroup.

The ECB sits at the centre of the EMU's institutional infrastructure. The financial crisis that started in 2008 tested this institutional infrastructure and initially found the ECB's LoLR function wanting. Indeed, neither the treaty nor the ECB Statute provided for ECB responsibilities in the area of lending of last resort to banks. By treaty, the ECB had 'to promote the smooth operation of the payments system' and 'contribute' to member states' conduct of prudential supervision (Art. 127 (2) of the Treaty of the Functioning of the European Union). Indeed, financial stability could not even have been in its mandate as the ECB models had no financial sector in them. If there were any risks to Europe's economy they were expected to come not from the instability of the financial sector but from fiscal indiscipline or lack of structural reforms in labour and especially product markets. Or, as it has been extensively demonstrated (Blyth, 2013; Tooze, 2018), Europe's crisis was predominantly a financial crisis ripping through a political-economic structure eroded by poor risk-sharing mechanisms.

Although its narrow price stability mandate and strong independence are suggestive of the strong influence of Germany, in its operations the ECB management is less German-dominated and inegalitarian than conventionally thought. Thus, the Bundesbank representatives were outvoted in crucial moments and although the largest five economies (Germany, France, Italy, Spain and the Netherlands) hold 57 per cent of ECB capital, they take turns to abstain in the ECB's Governing Council every five months while the countries holding barely 13 per cent of ECB capital abstain every three months (Schelkle, 2017; Tooze, 2018).

BOX 9.4 Key actors

The ECB. The central bank of the euro area.
The European Council. The heads of state of the member states that decide main priorities but do not pass laws.
The Eurogroup. Informal group of the ministers of finance from EMU countries.
ECOFIN. The Economic and Financial Affairs Council, composed of the economics and finance ministers of the EU member states (passes laws).
The Bundesbank. The central bank of Germany.
Financial markets. Markets used to raise long-term finance (capital markets) and short-term finance (money markets).
Shadow banking. Financial activities (e.g. securitisation, secured funding markets) and loosely regulated non-bank financial entities (e.g. private equity firms, structured investment vehicles, money market funds or hedge funds) that fund themselves with uninsured short-term funding not always backstopped by central banks.

However, it was not the failures of the SGP that posed a mortal danger to the euro area. Indeed, the causal generators of the crisis could be found at the intersection of a transnational crisis of financialised globalisation, the financialisation of government debt engineered by the EC and the ECB, and the ECB's own hesitation to act as a LoLR early and with massive firepower. Indeed, as the next sections show, the problems with the risk-sharing institutions of the euro area combined to bring the euro area into an unprecedented financial crisis that spilled over into a sovereign debt crisis. All this led to pressures on the euro area to develop the robust LoLR functions that had not been part of the original architecture of the monetary union. Unfortunately, it took nearly four years before a full-fledged LOLR response materialised itself.

9.4 Recent Policy Developments

9.4.1 Cooking the Crisis

The Great Financial Crisis of 2008 was a crisis of shadow banking that the ECB neither anticipated nor controlled. When most people talk about finance they mean the conventional banking sector that is subject to reserve requirements and other regulations by the central bank and bank supervisory agencies but enjoys the safety nets offered by the central bank. Yet banks were not at the epicentre of the crisis and this matters for LoLR. Instead, they were anchored largely in the non-bank part of the financial system, in so-called 'shadow banking', where looser regulations and thinner public safety nets for financial institutions were the norm. Critically, the shadow financial world includes not just non-bank financial institutions with obscure names such as 'off-balance sheet financial entities' (often set up by conventional banks), or the 'broker-dealers', 'structured investment vehicles', 'money market funds' or 'hedge funds', but also activities such as securitisation (or transformation of loans into securities that could be traded) (Ban and Gabor, 2016; Thiemann, 2018).

A solid consensus now connects various 'runs' on US shadow banking to the Lehman crisis (see Ban and Gabor, 2016, for an overview). The spread of securitisation and repo markets was not a phenomenon affecting just the United States, but Europe as well. As part of the growing transatlantic financial integration transforming Western capitalism in the 1990s and the 2000s, leading European banks such as Deutsche Bank dived into the US financial market and funded their portfolios of US mortgage- and asset-backed securities by borrowing in repo markets from US banks and shadow banks (Tooze, 2018).

This was also a moment when it became obvious that European finance had feet of clay, for in terms of the size of bank balance sheets relative to national GDP, the Lehman European economies were more 'financialised' than the US by a factor of three. But rather than bolster the ECB's LoLR function more directly with the creation of a European monetary fund proper while proceeding with large-scale public and private debt restructuring followed by the bailouts of the countries unable to refinance their public debt, the EU elites muddled through the crisis with inadequate responses.

Although no provisions had been made for the ECB to act as LoLR, the central bank of the euro began its series of mediated supports to the EMU member states between May 2010 and September 2012. The first LoLR programme was called the Securities Markets Programme (SMP) and was launched in May 2010. The SMP was a series of outright purchases of euro area periphery sovereign debt (Buiter and Rahbari, 2012; Schelkle, 2017) through which the ECB 'bought government bonds, not least Greek bonds, from banks keen to offload them' (Schelkle, 2017: 211). A total of €7.8 billion of net income interest was culled by the ECB from the SMP between 2012 and 2016, and then distributed among the national central banks in the euro area.

As the crisis deepened, the longer-term refinancing operations (LTROs) of December 2011 and February 2012 were the second indirect LoLR interventions for the Spanish and Italian governments. Stripped to their bare bones, LTROs offered cheap liquidity to private banks to incentivise them to purchase periphery debt at a higher price while addressing a liquidity crunch that plagued euro area banks as a whole.

The effect of these interventions was mixed. They initially reassured the sovereign debt markets that all EMU member states could pay their debts, but it was not long before the SMP and the LTROs proved unable to arrest the increase in the debt levels of Greece, the hotspot of the crisis. In part, this owed to the fact that, like the SMP, the LTROs had an announced cap and their impact would soon be read as limited by bond market investors worried about the EU institutions' proclivity to muddle through the Greek crisis rather than address it with bolder measures. To top it off, the ECB raised interest rates at the peak of the crisis. The result was waves of market panic not only about Greek debt, but about all 'peripheral' debt markets in the EU. The crisis reached a climax in late 2012, when sovereign bond investors' reactions raised the spectre of an Italian default, a risk that, given Italy's large size in the sovereign bond, was too much to take for anyone, especially the ECB (Matthijs and Blyth, 2018).

9.4.2   Unlimited LoLR Interventions (2012–)

Italy was the third largest issuer of debt in the world (after the US and Japan) so the major risk in the collapse of the Italian bond led the ECB into new LoLR territory in terms of scale. During a speech to financiers in London, the new ECB president, Mario Draghi, effectively saved the euro with an off-script sentence previously agreed with the main heads of state of the euro area. This sentence read that the ECB was ready '[w]ithin our mandate ... to do whatever it takes to preserve the euro', adding: 'And believe me, it will be enough'.[1] With that sentence the ECB left behind the principle that its bond market interventions should be capped. Now, the bond buying programme called Outright Monetary Transactions (OMT)

---

[1] 'Draghi sends strong signal that the ECB will act', *Reuters*, 26 July 2012, www.reuters.com/article/us-Euroarea-ecb-draghi-idUSBRE86P0HM20120726.

was unlimited and, to further reassure bondholders, the ECB did not declare the higher status (seniority) of its bonds in case of default relative to those of private investors.

In concrete terms, the OMT was a backdoor monetary relief to strapped member state governments: the ECB provided banks in the euro area with €1 trillion in credits at fixed 1 per cent interest rate for three years; since government bonds had yields that were higher than 1 per cent, the banks had an incentive to buy them, using the margin to raise the capital that they needed to cut the losses incurred by several years of financial distress; in so doing the banks recapitalised themselves and the more government debt the banks bought, the more the risk premium fell, a side effect that stopped the European sovereign debt crisis (Blyth, 2013; Schlekle, 2017).

The impact of the 'whatever it takes' moment and the deployment of OMT was spectacular: risk premia on 'periphery' bonds dropped and have not experienced worrying spikes since.

The politics of this bold intervention of the ECB was critical. The ECB management knew that OMT exceeded its tightly defined mandate (price stability) and its management ably negotiated tacit support from the country that could have used strong domestic opposition (including via a Constitutional Court case filed by tens of thousands of citizens): Germany (Jones and Kelemen, 2014).

OMT is a clear episode of (substantially delayed) policy learning, yet its positive record should be nuanced. While the ECB has used its liquidity assistance to coerce change in European economic governance and economic policy in the bailout countries in a market-oriented direction, it nevertheless employed monetary measures to save large euro area banks from correlated bankruptcies without controlling how these banks use their provided liquidity (Fontan, 2018).

9.4.3 Financial Assistance Funds: From Patchwork to the European Monetary Fund?

The first response to the conversion of the financial crisis into a full-blown sovereign debt crisis in Portugal, Greece and Ireland was not the establishment of a European monetary fund proper. Instead, they cautiously laid the foundations of the temporary EFSF and the European Financial Stability Mechanism (EFSM). The latter was administered by the Commission and could raise up to €60 billion. The larger EFSF financed itself by issuing debt in capital markets based on the guarantees offered on a bilateral basis by the member states of the euro area. Based on these guarantees, the EFSF could then lend countries in difficulty up to €440 billion at low rates.

The purpose of international liquidity assistance to governments is to calm down bond markets by reassuring creditors that the debtor will make good on her promises. At 5 per cent, EFSF loans to Greece were lower than market rates (7 per cent). But in the light of Greece's dramatic situation they were too high to deliver the required reassurance, particularly once private bondholders were forced to lose money on Greek national debt following a second bailout in 2012. Moreover, since the guarantees were added to the public debt of the guarantors, high-debt countries like Italy were extremely stressed by the negative repercussions this would have in the event of a run on Italian debt. All this did little to bolster the distressed country's creditworthiness and thus calm down markets. Consequently, investors quickly sent the EU institutions and the member states back to the drawing board.

Faced with the fecklessness of the temporary EFSF/EFSM, in June 2011 the EMU authorities agreed to establish a *permanent* financial assistance fund: the ESM. The ESM was a public company based in Luxembourg empowered to borrow in bond markets on its own account. Backed by the credibility of the surplus countries, this enabled the ESM to acquire the lending firepower commensurate to the challenge of pacifying bond markets that had not been convinced by the EFSF and the EFSM (Henning, 2019). Thus, the member states deposited €80 billion paid in capital which the ESM, using the underlying credibility of its shareholders (which translates into low borrowing costs), can mobilise to raise around €700 billion. Since this was a stake in the ESM, not a liability, the paid-in capital did not increase risk for the high-debt member states. Once the capital was paid, the member states could not opt out of the loan assistance programme. This is one aspect that made the ESM superior to the EFSF and EFSM. Most importantly perhaps, the ESM's maturity and interest rates compare extremely favourably with those of the IMF, the world's LoLR to governments facing debt refinancing problems (Corsetti et al., 2018).

Of all the regional liquidity assistance institutions created in the world (Chang Mai, Fondo Latinoamericano de Reservas), the ESM has the clearest *central bank-like* organisational identity regarding its mandate: it intervenes directly in the primary and secondary government bond markets (something the ECB cannot do) and in case of financial crisis provides banks with direct recapitalisation resources in exchange for the undertaking of financial sector reforms and, critically, for taking shares in those banks via the so-called bank recapitalisation facility. In contrast, the IMF and peer regional institutions are meant only to provide emergency liquidity support for government balances in distress. In short, through the SMP and the LTROs the ECB nudged the member states to provide more room for manoeuvring in fiscal policy.

9.5   Current Political and Academic Controversies

After 2010, all EU institutions involved in crisis management, including the ECB and the ESM, consistently framed the crisis as one of public debt rather than a financial crisis resolved by socialising private debt accumulated through reckless investment driven in part by the policies that had been adopted by the EU before 2008 (Blyth, 2013; Gabor and Ban, 2016; Carstensen and Schmidt, 2018). Specifically, they took the view that the euro area crisis was caused by excessive state spending and growing labour costs which in turn led to unsustainable public debts and loss of competitiveness (Lombardi and Moschella, 2015, 2016).

Some political economists uphold the competitiveness story. For Alison Johnston (2016), for example, the fragility of the EMU was rooted in the fact that the economies of Southern Europe lacked the labour–capital coordination that moderated costs in Northern EU member states, and with domestic levels of inflation no longer checked by national central banks after the establishment of the EMU the euro periphery gradually lost competitiveness and found itself with growing current account deficits. In these conditions they became sitting ducks for the bond vigilantes once their declining competitiveness was exposed by the Great Recession (Johnston, 2016).

A larger literature disputed the importance of both the sovereign debt build-up and competitiveness decline as critical mechanisms of the crisis. Some scholars showed that the sovereign debt increases paled next to the private sector debt build-up, which in turn facilitated unsustainable asset price booms (Blyth, 2013; Clift, 2018; Jones, 2016; Tooze, 2018). The medicine for this should not have been austerity but financial sector reform. Indeed, the mismanagement of the LoLR function meant that the Europeanisation of European capital had been entirely reversed, with intra-euro area bank-to-bank lending falling below the levels when the euro was introduced.

Had European elites narrated the crisis as one of cross-border private finance turbocharged by the ECB's own policy to accept Greek and German debt as collateral of comparable value, perhaps the LoLR function activated on a massive scale in 2012 would have been adopted three years earlier, at considerably lower costs in terms of lost output, employment and health affecting millions of people (Perez and Matsaganis, 2018; Kentikelenis et al., 2014). The counterfactual in this regard is the Federal Reserve and the Bank of England, both of whom used LoLR interventions earlier on to give fiscal breathing room to their governments, and in so doing they benefited from the explicit support of their countries' executive branches (Gabor, 2014; Tooze, 2018).

Yet the ECB's distinct profile needs to be fully appreciated here, for the ECB LoLR function required some creative tackling of the EU legal order. This forbids (direct) funding of the euro area sovereigns by the ECB and the national central banks of the euro area. It was only after Mario Draghi secured support from the German chancellor and finance minister, whose trust he had enjoyed, that the stabilisation of the European sovereign bond markets through OMT could be achieved.

9.6   Paradigmatic Case Study: Is There a Keynesian Europe?

To austerity as a condition for liquidity support for cash-strapped member states, in 2015 the EU also added a 'Keynesian' lending function to the 'real' economy. For the Eastern European member states this came in the form of loosening the rules for the so-called 'structural funds' (Coman, 2018), a form of development aid that provided around 5 per cent of demand-side stimulus in their GDP in the form of public works for the most part. As a result, these funds became more important for these states than FDI (Bohle, 2018).

For everyone else, the stimulus came later, via the establishment of the European Fund for Strategic Investments (EFSI) under the umbrella of the EIB. In this context the term Keynesian does not refer to countercyclical *fiscal* policy but to means of *financial* support for aggregate demand in recessions and credit crunch periods. In effect, when public financial institutions act in these ways they provide an economic stimulus, create new markets and fund innovation (Ban, 2013; Mazzucato and Penna, 2016).

Already before the crisis the EIB was the world's largest public multilateral bank. Following a slow recovery from a deep economic crisis, the EIB has received two capital increases, emerging as a central actor in delivering much-needed investment to the European economy, which remains below pre-crisis levels. As a pillar of EU crisis management, it has taken on ever more roles on behalf of the Union, leveraging limited EU budget funds on financial markets via investment vehicles such as the Project Bonds Initiative, a policy programme designed to promote investment in European infrastructure (Mertens and Thiemann, 2019).

What is more, in 2014 the EIB was chosen to deliver President Juncker's landmark investment initiative, the EFSI, which the Commission recently declared a success and doubled its lending capacity and lifespan. Set under the EIB umbrella, the EFSI went fully operational in 2015 as part of the Investment Plan for Europe (the so-called Juncker Plan). Its establishment reflected concerns with stagnant investment, a prolonged recession followed by a weak recovery, high unemployment (especially among the young) and legal-political constraints that ruled out the general stimulus favoured in 2008–9.

Specifically, the EFSI was intended to crowd in additional investment to the tune of €315 billion over the next three years. The funds to be leveraged stem from the EU budget (€8 billion) and the European Investment Fund (€5 billion for SME financing) and are meant primarily for three objectives: to boost job creation and economic growth, for long-term competitiveness and for strengthening Europe's productive capacity and infrastructure.[2] Given its critical importance and initial success in reaching the preset targets in terms of speedy take-up of investment

---

[2] Brochure of the Investment Plan for Europe, July 2017.

volumes, the Commission decided in September 2016 to double its duration and financial firepower, extending the EFSI until 2020 and mobilising €500 billion by 2020 with the help of EU budget and EIB guarantees amounting to €33.5 million.

It is of critical importance to emphasise, however, that when one looks at the details of the EFSI mandate and actual lending, this fund appears not as a traditional countercyclical fund but as a hybrid between such a fund and as a vehicle focused on promoting long-term investment, with key competitiveness-enhancing items as part of the portfolio. Of the projects approved by the end of 2017, only 43 per cent went to employment-rich sectors such as SMEs, transport and social infrastructure, with sectors targeting long-term growth (R&D, energy and digital) mopping up the rest. To illustrate, the EFSI funded health care research in Spain, the expansion of Croatian and Slovakian road and airport infrastructures and the technological updating of steel rolling in Italy. Merstens and Thiemann (2018: 2) also found that national development banks 'received positions in EFSI as both stakeholders and contributors' and were enabled to use EFSI to expand their activities and organisational capabilities, leading these authors to speak about the emergence of a 'European investment state' at the EU level.

But how Keynesian has EFSI been in reality? If the European Investment Fund operations through the SME window are subtracted, one finds that half of the EU's member states have five or less EIB-administered projects each (loans, guarantees and equity-type operations). A small number of member states received a much larger number of funded projects. Although some of the winners are countries that struggle with an extreme dearth of investment (Italy, Spain, Portugal), or are generally larger economies with far more projects eligible for EFSI financing (Germany, France), it is nevertheless an issue that the new member states are grouped towards the low end of the spectrum, with Romania and Lithuania getting a paltry €5 per capita GDP approximately, while France got €237 and Germany €154 respectively.

To get out of its many socio-economic vicious circles, the euro area's recessions will need more than the kind of massive capacity for the LoLR infrastructure developed between 2010 and 2014 that a serious crisis in Italy or Spain would demand. At a minimum, the EU needs two things. First, it needs a better designed institutional infrastructure for the euro that would include guarantees by the euro area member states via a form of joint liability (Eurobonds). This could have relieved pressure on the ECB to intervene in the sovereign bond markets. Unfortunately, the Eurobond idea went live in 2010 but it also went nowhere largely because of Franco-German dynamics. Indeed, the Eurobond was consistently rejected by Germany and after a period of passivity France adopted the German view (by 2010).

Second, the EU needs a countercyclical public investor framework, that is, a common EU-level fiscal infrastructure and investment state for delivering a coordinated demand stimulus, countercyclical credit to European firms and a pan-European income support scheme that could play the role of an automatic stabiliser of aggregate demand. This means coordinated demand stimulus programmes, a directing of credit towards productive investments and 'smart' innovation, a bailing out of cash-strapped and insolvent governments on countercyclical terms and 'mission-oriented' industrial policies to restructure and upgrade peripheral manufacturing (Mazzucato, 2015).

It is clear that the Keynesian arm of the EU needs a lot more strength. The EFSI should become a permanent institution rather than the temporary fund it is today. Furthermore, given the prospect of a socio-economic catastrophe brought on by climate change, Europe needs emergency investment towards the building of a new energy and transportation system whose price tab far exceeds the lending firepower of the EIB and EFSI combined. Without a massive expansion of development banking in the EU capital will continue to pour in to social inequality-maximising and Earth-warming activities. This developmental state shift in the EU requires not just an expansion of the network of public banks and funds linking the EIB, EFSI and national promotional banks but also constitutional reforms in the EU that link the ECB balance sheets to a much broader notion of the public interest than price stability. Moreover, it needs the emergence of a public banking elite with a 'developmental mindset' (Thurbon, 2016) in Luxembourg and national capitals, rather than the 'investment mindset' that characterises the current managerial status quo.

Where does all this leave us in times of economic recovery but with the prospect of automatic austerity in case of recession becoming a fixture of economic life in the EMU? The institutional frictions of the EU and the EMU in particular facilitate an emphasis on austerity and market-oriented structural reforms as the chief adjustment and competitiveness strategies (Matthijs and McNamara, 2015; Jones, 2016; Matthijs and Blyth, 2015; Crespy and Vanheuverzwijn, 2017). Thus, most European states seem caught between the Scylla of booming global demand for European goods and services and the Charybdis of unprecedented political turmoil unleashed by the downward mobility, inequality and labour precariousness generated by internal devaluation (Matthijs and Blyth, 2015; Hopkin and Rosamond, 2018; see Chapter 10). As the rise of extreme nationalist politics in many European democracies shows, the political costs of these socially disruptive economic measures for politics as usual at the EU and domestic level have reached unprecedented levels.

GROUP DISCUSSION

- What are the strengths and weaknesses of the EMU institutional infrastructure, and is it ready for a repeat of the 2010–12 sovereign debt crisis?
- How can the EIB and the EFSI stem the Eurosceptic tide?

TOPICS FOR INDIVIDUAL RESEARCH

- Should the ESM become a European Monetary Fund, obviating the need to resort to IMF bailouts in Europe?
- How can the 'Keynesian' arm of the EU mitigate the consequences of the current slide into catastrophic climate change?

FURTHER READINGS

Blyth, M. (2013). *Austerity: The History of a Dangerous Idea.* Oxford University Press.

Helgadóttir, O. (2016). 'Banking Upside Down: The Implicit Politics of Shadow Banking Expertise'. *Review of International Political Economy* 23(6): 915–40.

Mehrling, P. (2010). *The New Lombard Street: How the Fed Became the Dealer of Last Resort.* Princeton University Press.

Roos, J. E. (2019) *Why Not Default?: The Political Economy of Sovereign Debt.* Princeton University Press.

Sandbu, M. (2017). *Europe's Orphan: The Future of the Euro and the Politics of Debt – New Edition.* Princeton University Press.

REFERENCES

Armingeon, K. and Baccaro, L. (2012). 'Political Economy of the Sovereign Debt Crisis: The Limits of Internal Devaluation'. *Industrial Law Journal*, 41(3): 254–75.

Ban, C. (2013). 'Brazil's Liberal Neo-Developmentalism: New Paradigm or Edited Orthodoxy?'. *Review of International Political Economy*, 20(2): 298–331.

Ban, C. (2016). *Ruling Ideas: How Global Neoliberalism Goes Local.* Oxford: Oxford University Press.

Ban, C., and Gabor, D. (2016). 'The Political Economy of Shadow Banking'. *Review of International Political Economy*, 23(6): 901–14.

Blyth, M. (2013). *Austerity: The History of a Dangerous Idea.* Oxford: Oxford University Press.

Bohle, D. (2018). 'European Integration, Capitalist Diversity and Crises Trajectories on Europe's Eastern Periphery'. *New Political Economy*, 23(2): 239–53.

Buiter, W. and Rahbari, E. (2012). 'The European Central Bank as Lender of Last Resort for Sovereigns in the Euro Area. *JCMS: Journal of Common Market Studies*, 50: 6–35.

Carstensen, M. B. and Schmidt, V A. (2018). 'Power and Changing Modes of Governance in the Euro Crisis'. *Governance* 31(4): 609–24.

Clift, B. (2018). *The IMF and the Politics of Austerity in the Wake of the Global Financial Crisis.* Oxford: Oxford University Press.

Coman, R. (2018). 'How Have EU "Fire-fighters" Sought to Douse the Flames of the Euro Area's Fast- and Slow-burning Crises? The 2013 Structural Funds Reform'. *The British Journal of Politics and International Relations*, 20(3): 540–54.

Crespy, A. and Vanheuverzwijn, P. (2017). 'What "Brussels" Means by Structural Reforms: Empty Signifier or Constructive Ambiguity?'. *Comparative European Politics*, 17(1): 1–20.

De Grauwe, P. (2013). 'The European Central Bank as Lender of Last Resort in the Government Bond Markets'. *CESifo Economic Studies*, 59(3): 520–35.

De Grauwe, P. and Ji, Y. (2015). 'Correcting for the Euro area Design Failures: The Role of the ECB'. *Journal of European Integration*, 37(7): 739–54.

De Haan, J., Bodea, C., Hicks, R. et al. (2018). 'Central Bank Independence Before and After the Crisis'. *Comparative Economic Studies*, 60: 183–202.

Fontan, C. (2018). 'Frankfurt's Double Standard: The Politics of the European Central Bank during the Euro Area Crisis'. *Cambridge Review of International Affairs,* https://doi.org/10.1080/09557571.2018.1495692.

Gabor, D. (2014). 'Learning from Japan: The European Central Bank and the European Sovereign Debt Crisis'. *Review of Political Economy*, 26(2): 190–209.

Gabor, D. and Ban, C. (2016). 'Banking on Bonds: The New Links Between States and Markets'. *JCMS: Journal of Common Market Studies*, 54(3): 617–35.

Henning, C. R. (2019). 'Regime Complexity and the Institutions of Crisis and Development Finance'. *Development and Change*, 50(1): 24–45.

Hopkin, J. and Rosamond, B. (2018). 'Post-truth Politics, Bullshit and Bad Ideas: "Deficit Fetishism" in the UK'. *New Political Economy*, 23(6): 641–55.

Johnston, A. (2016). *From Convergence to Crisis: Labor Markets and the Instability of the Euro.* Cornell University Press.

Jones, E. (2016). 'Competitiveness and the European Financial Crisis'. In J. A. Caporaso and M. Rhodes (eds), *The Political and Economic Dynamics of the Euro Area Crisis*, 79–99.

Jones, E. and Kelemen, R. D. (2014). 'The EURO Goes to Court'. *Survival*, 56(2): 15–23.

Johnston, A. (2016). *From Convergence to Crisis: Labor Markets and the Instability of the Euro.* Ithaca, NY: Cornell University Press.

Kentikelenis, A., Karanikolos, M., Reeves, A., McKee, M. and Stuckler, D. (2014). 'Greece's Health Crisis: From Austerity to Denialism'. *The Lancet*, 383(9918): 748–53.

La Malfa, G. 'Architects of the Euro'. *The Journal of European Economic History* 46(3 (2017): 162–4.

Lombardi, D. and Moschella, M. (2015). 'The Institutional and Cultural Foundations of the Federal Reserve's and ECB's Non-Standard Policies'. *Stato e Mercato*, 35(1): 127–52.

Lombardi, D. and Moschella, M. (2016). 'The Government Bond Buying Programmes of the European Central Bank: An Analysis of Their Policy Settings'. *Journal of European Public Policy*, 23(6): 851–70.

McNamara, K. R. (1998). *The Currency of Ideas: Monetary Politics in the European Union.* Ithaca, NY: Cornell University Press.

Matthijs, M. and Blyth, M. (2015). *The Future of the Euro.* Oxford: Oxford University Press.

Matthijs, M. and Blyth, M. (2018). 'When Is it Rational to Learn the Wrong Lessons? Technocratic Authority, Social Learning, and Euro Fragility'. *Perspectives on Politics*, 16(1): 110–26.

Mazzucato, M. (2015). 'The Green Entrepreneurial State'. In I. Scoones, M. Leach and P. Newell (eds), *The Politics of Green Transformations.* London: Routledge.

Mazzucato, M. and Penna, C. C. R. (2016). 'Beyond Market Failures: The Market Creating and Shaping Roles of State Investment Banks'. *Journal of Economic Policy Reform*, 19(4): 305–26.

Mertens, D. and Thiemann, M. (2018). 'Market-based but State-led: The Role of Public Development Banks in Shaping Market-based Finance in the European Union'. *Competition & Change*, 22(2): 184–204.

Mertens, D. and Thiemann, M. (2019). 'Building a Hidden Investment State? The European Investment Bank, National Development Banks and European Economic Governance'. *Journal of European Public Policy*, 26(1): 23–43.

Perez, S. A., and Matsaganis, M. (2018). 'The Political Economy of Austerity in Southern Europe'. *New Political Economy*, 23(2): 192–207.

Princen, S. and Van Esch, F. (2016). 'Paradigm Formation and Paradigm Change in the EU's Stability and Growth Pact'. *European Political Science Review*, 8(3): 355–75.

Ross, G. and Jenson, J. (2017). 'Reconsidering Jacques Delors' Leadership of the European Union'. *Journal of European Integration*, 39(2): 113–27.

Saka, O., Fuertes, A.-M. and Kalotychou, E. (2015). 'ECB Policy and Euro Area Fragility: Was De Grauwe Right?'. *Journal of International Money and Finance*, 54: 168–85.

Schelkle, W. (2017). *The Political Economy of Monetary Solidarity: Understanding the Euro Experiment*. Oxford: Oxford University Press.

Schmidt, V. A. (2016). 'Reinterpreting the Rules "By Stealth" in Times of Crisis: A Discursive Institutionalist Analysis of the European Central Bank and the European Commission'. *West European Politics*, 39(5): 1032–52.

Thiemann, M. (2018). *The Growth of Shadow Banking: A Comparative Institutional Analysis*. Cambridge: Cambridge University Press.

Thurbon, E. (2016). *Developmental Mindset: The Revival of Financial Activism in South Korea*. Ithaca, NY: Cornell University Press.

Tooze, A. (2018). *Crashed: How a Decade of Financial Crises Changed the World*. London: Allen Lane.

Ugolini, S. (2018). 'The Historical Evolution of Central Banking'. In S. Battilossi, Y. Cassis and K. Yago (eds), *Handbook of the History of Money and Currency*. New York: Springer Nature.

10 Social Policy: Is the EU Doing Enough to Tackle Inequalities?

AMANDINE CRESPY

10.1 Introduction

The objective of social policy is to limit inequalities in resource distribution within societies. On the one hand, it consists in regulating markets and working conditions; on the other, it uses redistributive mechanisms (i.e. cash transfers and services) to offset contrast in income distribution and tackle poverty. The EU exhibits the lowest level of inequalities compared to countries around the globe, including the United States. However, recent studies also show that, in some respects, the EU falls short of its promise of welfare and social cohesion for all. While general levels of income have been rising continuously over the past decades, inequalities among individuals have only declined slowly. When looking at the Gini coefficient, the most common indicator for measuring inequalities, it appears that the decrease of inequalities has come to a stalemate in the EU-27, with the euro area even displaying an increase of the index since 2008 (while the US has known a sharper increase of inequalities, starting from a significantly higher level). Moreover, the catch-up process of the poorest regions in terms of living standards has not taken place to the expected extent. In some regions of Southern and Eastern Europe or the Baltic countries, the recession has meant a severe degradation of welfare for many people. Today, the EU still exhibits a clear contrast between a wealthy core of Continental and Northern countries versus the poorest peripheries in the south and east of the continent (see chapter 17).

It is argued in this chapter that the weak and fragmented governance applying to social policy at a European scale has done little to help tackle social inequalities. Today, the EU runs the risk of seeming too intrusive by prescribing welfare state reforms which, more often than not, lead to retrenchment while, at the same time, remaining powerless and ineffective in the face of persisting stark inequalities. The absence of political will to match the strong monetary and economic interdependence within the euro area with adequate social policy instruments is particularly problematic.

What is often called 'social Europe' takes the form of a patchwork made of various policy areas,[1] modes of governance[2] and diverse national welfare state

---

[1] Free circulation, labour law, employment and training, struggle against discrimination, healthcare, fight against poverty and social exclusion.

[2] Essentially the Community method and soft coordination. The intergovernmental method has been rather marginal in the field of social policy.

models. Historically, an implicit understanding among European decision makers has prevailed whereby the EU should promote the integration of markets, and upward social convergence would result automatically from economic growth. While Article 3 TFEU stipulates that the EU should have a 'highly competitive social market economy', the extent to which social justice should be a main policy goal of the EU remains controversial.

The continuous decline of social democracy and the rise of conservatism and far-right Euroscepticism have made political agreements over pan-European social policy increasingly difficult. At the same time, the enlargement to the Baltic states and Central and Eastern Europe in 2004–7 has resulted in a much wider spectrum of preferences and interests. Countries from the ex-communist bloc tend to display significantly lower levels of wealth and social protection, thus relying on low taxation of capital to attract foreign investment as well as on the export of cheap labour. Meanwhile, the reforms of national welfare states have been piecemeal and uneven, depending on national resources and politics.

Against this background, the financial crisis and the subsequent debt crisis in the EU (2008–10) have only exacerbated pre-existing trends. Public resources for social policy have shrunk at a time where unemployment and poverty levels were on the rise. This has been especially dramatic in countries such as Greece, Ireland, Italy, Portugal or Spain, which were hit by skyrocketing debt levels and have been submitted to conditionality mechanisms requiring social retrenchment in exchange for financial support. As of November 2014, the European Commission headed by Jean-Claude Juncker sought to go beyond 'austeritarianism' (Hyman, 2015). Yet, a truly pan-European agenda promoting social investment (see Box 10.4) remains elusive, while many citizens witness socially regressive policy-making at national level.

10.2 Historical Overview

From the point of view of social policy, three periods can roughly be distinguished in the history of EU integration (see Box 10.1).[3] From the origins and the original impetus for European integration up to the end of the 1980s, social policy remained residual as the emphasis lay on the economic imperative. The social provisions included in the Treaty of Rome from 1957 aimed to accompany the building of a common market through the liberalisation of trade within the EEC. Political elites trusted that postwar reconstruction and increased output and wealth would automatically lead to a rise in living standards and social welfare. The treaty therefore spelled out broad objectives such as the improvement of

[3] For a more in-depth historical overview see Geyer (2000).

living conditions and the preservation of wage levels against the background of intensified competition among workers. The ESF was created to implement compensation measures for workers laid off as a result of industrial restructuration and promote an economic catch-up process for the poorest regions. While very active on the European stage, trade unions voiced criticism of the liberal turn operated by the Treaty of Rome and concerns about possible social dumping (see Box 10.4).

In this period, the Court of Justice of the European Union (CJEU) asserted itself as the main driving force of social Europe, and its jurisprudence paved the way for social regulation. This is, for instance, the case with the coordination of national social security systems for mobile workers or the principle of equal pay for men and women, which the court famously anchored into EU law with three decisions on the case *Defrenne* in 1971, 1976 and 1978.

When EU integration was relaunched in the 1980s, the political climate was dominated by economic liberalism, notably under the influence of Margaret Thatcher in power in the United Kingdom, which had accessed the EEC in 1973. The SEA, signed in 1986, aimed mainly at advancing the single market by stimulating free trade. But it also introduced a key institutional innovation, namely the introduction of decision by qualified majority in the Council. This de facto element removed any veto possibility from one single country and had important implications for social policy-making.

The decade from the late 1980s to the late 1990s is considered by many as the golden age of social Europe, a period which was strongly marked by the Commission presidency of Jacques Delors, a French socialist from the liberal wing of the party, from 1985 until 1994. In that period, he endeavoured to flank the single market with effective social policy mechanisms, including a form of supranational corporatism for involving the social partners. The objective was to tackle the negative effects of competition on the weaker territories or social groups. Thus, the European Commission strategically used QMV in order to pass new regulations aimed at the improvement of workers' health and security at work, or strengthening the rights of mobile workers. Meanwhile, social democratic parties had rallied the EU integration project; but there was also an awareness that the creation of a monetary union would have detrimental social consequences and hence fuel resentment among their electorate (Geyer, 2000).

While launching the common currency, the Treaty of Maastricht opened new possibilities for social policy with a Social Protocol appended to the treaty (due to the objection of the UK, which did want to sign it). The Social Protocol included the Community Charter of Workers' Fundamental Rights signed in 1989, which proclaimed a number of social rights in the EEC such as decent remuneration and the improvement of living and working conditions. Moreover, it considerably strengthened the European social dialogue with a new procedure whereby the agreements negotiated by the social partners could be turned into binding legislation. Some specific institutional reforms included in the treaty were also favourable to social integration such as the extension of QMV on social matters and the strengthening of legislative powers of the EP, then more favourable to social regulation.

BOX 10.1 Key dates

1957. Treaty of Rome, creation of the ESF.

1971. Decision *Defrenne* of the CJEU, which anchors the principle of equal pay for men and women into EU law.

1992. Creation of the European social dialogue procedure for binding agreements between social partners in the Treaty of Maastricht (Social Protocol).

1997. A European Employment Strategy is included in the Treaty of Amsterdam.

2000–1. Adoption of the Lisbon strategy: extension of the method of open coordination to social protection, social inclusion and pensions.

2017. Proclamation of the European Pillar of Social Rights.

The Treaty of Amsterdam signed in 1997 did not introduce any major transfer of social competences to Brussels but confirmed the progressive climate of the 1990s. The role of the EU in the field of anti-discrimination was strengthened, and a new chapter for the coordination of employment policies was introduced at a time where many European countries were struggling with high unemployment levels. The extent of developments in social policy must nevertheless be put into perspective. While ten out of fifteen EU member states were governed by social democrats, this period did not witness any substantial modification of the rules, competences or resources dedicated to social policy. Rather, many decision makers embraced, under the influence of British Prime Minister Tony Blair, the 'third way', that is a neoliberal agenda for conducting socio-economic policies and reforming welfare states.

The 2000s witnessed a neoliberal turn, thus opening a third period characterised by the decline of social integration in Europe. Often seen as an institutional innovation, new mechanisms for coordinating domestic social policies without legal constraint have reflected the absence of political agreement on what should be done at the EU level. Both social regulation in the internal market and the European social dialogue have lost momentum. At the same time, social democracy saw the beginning of a long electoral decline, while conservative and far-right forces were gaining ground in all EU institutions. The Lisbon Strategy adopted in 2000, which should have put Europe on the path towards modern knowledge economies and progressive welfare state reforms, has meanwhile been widely seen as a failure. The 2008–10 financial and debt crises have exacerbated the subordination of social policy to economic imperatives. The dominant conception of competitiveness relies heavily on the containment of labour costs, and austerity policies have even led to a deterioration of working and living conditions for millions of Europeans. While the necessity to approach welfare state reforms through social investment (see Box 10.4) has gained ground, the EU has so far not developed a coherent discourse or tangible policy instruments for promoting its implementation (De la Porte and Palier, forthcoming).

10.3   Main Features of the Current Institutional Framework

The EU was given both *shared* and *supporting* social policy competences in the treaty. This means that in the first case, the EU can legislate to complement national policies; in the second, it can only foster a soft coordination of national policies via the Open Method of Coordination (OMC). Far from being a European welfare state, the EU has weak redistributive capacities (through transfers or services), relying heavily on regulatory policies. It is possible to distinguish four constitutive areas of EU social policy-making: social regulation, redistribution via cohesion policy, neo-corporatism via the European social dialogue and the soft coordination of national welfare states (see Box 10.4).

10.3.1   Social Regulation in the Internal Market

Social regulation is adopted through the ordinary legislative procedure via the *Community method* (see Box 10.2 and Chapter 3). The main area relates to *workers' rights* either in the context of mobility (portability of social security entitlements) or at their workplace (security, safety, information, etc.) (Article 153 TFEU). According to the European Trade Union Institute, the corpus of EU law on *workers' mobility and labour law* as of 1957 consists of 135 acts (Pochet and Degryse, 2017). In addition to labour law, the EU is also entitled to regulate over *discriminations* in order to ensure the principle of equal pay for men and women (Article 157 TFEU) and to fight all discriminations based on sex, racial or ethnic origin, religion or belief, disability, age or sexual orientation (Article 19 TFEU). A third field of EU action is *public health* (Article 168 TFEU). Here, the EU has adopted common quality and safety norms relating to organs and substances of human origin (blood), veterinary and phytosanitary standards, as well as medicinal products and devices for medical use. Most importantly, there is a common

> ### BOX 10.2 Legal basis
>
> ***Article 153 TFEU.*** The EU can adopt regulation in the following areas:
>
> (a) Improvement in particular of the working environment to protect workers' health and safety.
> (b) Working conditions.
> (c) Social security and social protection of workers.
> (d) Protection of workers where their employment contract is terminated.
> (e) Information and consultation of workers.
> (f) Representation and collective defence of the interests of workers and employers, including co-determination, subject to paragraph 5.
> (g) Conditions of employment for third-country nationals legally residing in Union territory.
> (h) Integration of persons excluded from the labour market.
> (i) Equality between men and women with regard to labour market opportunities and treatment at work.

EU procedure for authorising the marketing of medicines. The EU competences also include the fight against drugs and abuse (including tobacco and alcohol).

Liberalisation policies have also had an important impact on regulation and deregulation in the social realm (Crespy, 2016). In EU law, most public services have been redefined as economic *services of general interest*, which are submitted to the rules of EU competition law. In many sectors (including energy distribution, postal services, transport, social services and healthcare) liberalisation directives were adopted through the 1990s and 2000s which have abolished former public monopolies. In some sectors, the emergence of (semi-)competitive markets has created issues regarding the accessibility and/or affordability of services. The rampant marketisation of healthcare, for instance, raises acute issues regarding social cohesion. A new Article 19 has been introduced into the Treaty of Lisbon, which allows the EU to adopt legislation on services of general interest. However, there is no political will to adopt pan-European rules for the functioning and funding of such services.

The Court of Justice of the EU has had a tremendous impact on the development of EU social law. Its jurisprudence has often been aggressive and contributed to the extension of social rights, e.g. for mobile citizens or discriminated groups. However, a linear, continuously progressive trend should not be taken for granted. Over the past ten years, it has proved more cautious in making certain social rights included in the EU Charter of Fundamental Rights effective.

10.3.2   Neo-corporatism and the European Social Dialogue

The *European social dialogue* tries to replicate neo-corporatism at the EU level (see Box 10.4), that is the adoption by workers' and employers' unions of rules on working conditions (bipartite concertation), often under the auspices of political authorities (tripartite concertation). Like industrial relations at the national level, the European social dialogue takes place both at the sectoral level and at the interprofessional level (across sectors). The key institutional innovation was introduced by the Social Protocol appended to the Treaty of Maastricht, which can lead to delegation of the legislative/regulatory competence to the social partners. According to Article 154 TFEU, the European Commission has the obligation to consult social partners on most social policy proposals (see Box 10.3); if the latter want, they can negotiate an agreement among themselves, which can then be turned into a legally binding text (directive) through a Council decision. If the social partners do not succeed in finding an agreement, the Commission can take over and launch the ordinary legislative procedure. So far, three of these so-called statutory agreements have been adopted at the interprofessional level, namely framework agreements on parental leave in 1996, on part-time work in 1997 and on fixed-term contracts in 1999. Seven have been adopted in various sectors, most of them dealing with working time (in the fishery industry, civil aviation or fluvial transportation). Most observers have noted that the political impulse of the Commission was key in securing effective negotiations.

In addition to statutory, legally binding agreements, the social partners have the possibility to adopt so-called autonomous agreements negotiated independently of the legislative procedure and without Commission involvement. Instead of being integrated into the EU social legal *acquis*, they can be implemented according to the practices and procedures existing in the various national realms. Thus, the nine autonomous agreements[4] adopted since 2002 have led to very uneven levels of implementation, ranging from constraining collective agreements to a total absence of information on the matter at stake.

BOX 10.3 Key actors

The Council
The Council for Employment, Social Policy, Health and Consumer Affairs.
At the committee level, the Employment Committee and the Social Policy Committee prepare the work of the Council.

---

[4] At an interprofessional scale, agreements were concluded on distance work in 2002, on stress at work in 2004, on harassment and violence at work in 2007 and on inclusive labour markets in 2010.

BOX 10.3 (Cont.)

The Commission
Especially the Directorate-General for Employment, Social Affairs and Inclusion (EMPL), the Directorate-General for the Internal Market, Industry, Entrepreneurship and SMEs (GROW), the Directorate-General for Economic and Financial Affairs (ECFIN), and the Secretariat-General as far as the European Semester is concerned.

The Court of Justice of the European Union
Rules over conflicts in the implementation of social regulation.

The social partners
The European Trade Union Confederation (ETUC).
Confederation of European Business (BusinessEurope).
European Centre of Employers and Enterprises Providing Public Services (CEEP).
European Association of Craft, Small and Medium Sized Enterprises (UEAPME).
The social partners take part in formal and informal consultation, and can agree on legally binding or non-binding agreements.

10.3.3   Redistribution via the ESF

The main EU instrument for redistribution in the EU is the ESF, (which is now part of all ESIF) accounts for approximately 10 per cent of the total EU budget. Unlike in national welfare states, the EU does not operate redistribution among individuals, but across regions according to their level of socio-economic development (measured against the mean GDP per capita in the EU). Historically, it was conceived as a tool for compensating the detrimental effects of economic competition in the internal market on weaker territories and groups. Nowadays, it is rather used as an investment tool. Funding aims at enhancing workers' adaptability through the acquisition of new skills, vocational training and lifelong learning. The purpose is to increase employment levels especially among young people and women. The ESF also funds social inclusion programmes to help disadvantaged groups (such as ex-offenders, recovering drug abusers, ethnic minorities such as the Roma and recent immigrants with poor language skills) to access the labour market.

The implementation of the ESF relies on multilevel governance. Policy objectives, as well as the global budget of the ESF, are decided together for each financing period (e.g. 2014–20). Subsequently, operational programmes are negotiated between national authorities and the Commission to set more specific policy objectives for each region. Funding rests on the co-financing principle, whereby the ESF funding stands for 50 to 85 per cent of a programme's budget and has to be complemented by national or regional money. Implementation on the ground is managed by regional agencies and is project based. Thus, a variety of public, semi-public or private organisations are in competition as they have to submit project proposals, which are then selected by regional authorities to receive funding. Although 'partnership' among all levels of government is the key principle, the capacity for regional authorities, private stakeholders and local operators to shape the policy objectives and operational workings of the ESF remains fairly limited. In turn, they have had to adapt to the increasingly heavy and bureaucratic functioning of EU cohesion policy. Evaluating the capacity of EU funds to improve territorial and social cohesion remains challenging and is hotly debated among experts (see Chapters 6 and 17).

10.3.4   The Soft Coordination of National Welfare States

In 2000, European decision makers decided at the Lisbon Council to apply the OMC to social matters where the EU does not have hard law competences such as employment, the fight against poverty and social exclusion or the reform of social security (especially pensions). This new mode of governance relied on what had already been used within the context of European Employment Strategy since 1997, namely a voluntary coordination of national policies according to common guidelines decided at EU level and a set of indicators and benchmarks allowing for regular reporting and comparison of national performance. Around 2005, various OMC processes in different areas were integrated into one single 'social OMC'. While often considered as a form of innovative 'experimentalist governance' (Sabel and Zeitlin, 2010), the OMC has brought about changes in ways of thinking about social policies and in some practices at the national level (Zeitlin et al., 2014), but has mostly fallen short in terms of implementation and tangible policy change (Radaelli and Borras, 2010).

Since 2011, the coordination of national social policies takes place in the framework of the European Semester. The European Semester is a broad, hybrid governance framework which coordinates budget and fiscal policy based on hard law, macroeconomic policies and social policy. The adoption of country-specific recommendations for socio-economic reforms represents the climax of the coordination process. The European Commission first formulates these recommendations on the basis of a pan-European study of the economic situation (the Annual Growth Survey), on the one hand, and on the other hand after months of exchanges with national authorities on the country report drafted for every member state which identifies country-specific problems to tackle. The recommendations formulated by the Commission are also discussed in the committees of the Council preparing the ministerial meetings; namely, the Economic Policy Committee, the Employment Committee and the Social Protection Committee. This serves to foster an exchange on practices among national governments and multilateral surveillance. Country-specific recommendations can be amended by the Council through the so-called 'reverse qualified majority procedure'. This means that the recommendations are adopted as proposed by the Commission, unless a qualified majority can be gathered to adopt modifications. Therefore, the recommendations suggested by the Commission are not often modified – and if so, only on the margins.

The European Semester is at the centre of critical discussions, notably from the point of view of governance and democracy. Recent research shows that it remains a top-down bureaucratic exercise of surveillance which offers no framework for democratic debate over the nature of reforms advocated and possible policy alternatives (Vanheuverzwijn and Crespy, 2018). National administrations have the opportunity to provide expertise and input through a continuous dialogue with the European Commission (mainly the Secretariat-General, DG ECFIN and DG EMPL). Social partners are asked to provide input, too, but they cannot contest the underpinning logic of flexicurity nor alternative paradigms for policy change (see Box 10.4). National parliaments are the least involved actors. National MPs are often not aware of what the European Semester is, and there are very few incentives for them to invest time in following a non-binding process. They do not necessarily perceive the indirect and diffuse constraint exerted by the EU through policy coordination.

10.4 Recent Policy Developments

Developments on the front of social regulation in EU law show that progress towards establishing pan-European social rights has somewhat stalled. The ability of member states to agree on social regulation has clearly declined over the past decade. While regulation has not necessarily decreased in quantitative terms, it has often been limited to revisions and technical adaptations. In contrast, there have been few new initiatives (Graziano and Hartlapp, 2018; Pochet and Degryse, 2017). Between 2007 and 2012, both the social partners (via the social dialogue) and the co-legislators failed to revise the contentious 2003 Working Time Directive as employers as well as several member states (including France, Italy and the UK) refused to suppress the *opt-out* from the forty-eight-hour weekly time limit. As for the revision of the 1992 Maternity Leave Directive, after seven years of disagreement between the Council and the Parliament it was withdrawn by the Commission. Thus, the revision of the Posted Workers Directive following highly contentious debate stands out as an exceptional success in passing social legislation (see Chapter 11). Similarly, the European social dialogue has lost momentum and, overall, borne relatively meagre fruit with only twelve binding agreements adopted since 1995.

> ## BOX 10.4 Key concepts
>
> *Social investment* emerged in the early 1990s as a paradigm prescribing reforms to adapt welfare states to new social risks such as ageing, single-parent families, flexible work contracts or rapid skill depletion due to technological progress. In order to ensure an adequate level of social protection for all, the emphasis is put on the need to invest ex ante in individuals' capabilities through services which foster inclusion (childcare, education and lifelong learning, targeted support for disadvantaged groups including women, etc.) rather than using cash transfers to compensate *ex post* for social exclusion.
>
> *Social dumping* happens when firms exploit the comparatively low cost of labour in one place as an advantage to win markets over competitors. It also describes the practice consisting in weakening or not complying with social regulations (including fiscal and environmental norms) to use such an advantage.
>
> *Neo-corporatism* refers to all forms of concertation and negotiations between employers and workers at local, sectoral or cross-sectoral levels. Often taking place under the auspices of the state (or political authorities), these discussions lead to agreements regulating industrial relations and the functioning of the economy (working conditions, pay, governance, etc.).
>
> *Flexicurity* is a model for reforming labour markets which aims to combine a greater flexibility for employers (through the deregulation of working hours and contracts), on the one hand, with a performant system of social protection and training to prevent unemployment and social exclusion among workers, on the other hand.

The financial and debt crisis has brought about political tensions between various parts of the continent which have eroded the inclination to solidarity. Redistributive tools such as the ESF have been increasingly put under pressure for more control, surveillance and evaluation. Multiple modalities for conditionality have been made more systematic in order to condition the distribution of EU funds to certain objectives, principles and practices. When decision makers were discussing the next financial period in the heat of the crisis in 2012, creditor countries (led by Germany) sought to make the distribution of all structural funds conditional upon national governments abiding by the deficit and debt rules enshrined in the SGP and the European Semester. The proposal to use the suspension of funds as an automatic sanction against member states in excessive deficit has been watered down by the EP and debtor countries. Yet, the conditionality principle remains enshrined in the latest regulation defining the functioning of the funds, thus opening the possibility to exert political pressure for the enforcement of fiscal discipline using the EU's distributive policies (Coman and Sbaraglia, 2018; see Chapter 6).

Due to its complex and diffuse nature, the soft coordination of national policies and welfare state reforms is difficult to assess. Some scholars note a progressive 'socialisation' of EU socio-economic governance. Whereas social issues were not taken into account in the first cycles of the European Semester, social policy actors within the Council and the Commission have strengthened their position and imposed notably the inclusion of a social scoreboard for monitoring domestic policies (Zeitlin and Vanhercke, 2017). Other scholars argue that, when looking at the broader picture, it appears that the absorption of the social OMC into the European Semester has only accentuated the subordination of social policy to the imperatives of competitiveness and fiscal discipline (De la Porte and Heins, 2016; Crespy and Menz, 2015; Copeland and Daly, 2018). Objectives such as the EU poverty target, which aimed at reducing the number of poor people in Europe by 20 million by 2020, have been largely marginalised and thus remain wishful thinking (Copeland and Daly, 2014).

From the outset, the recommendations made by the Commission and the Council for implementing so-called 'structural reforms' displayed an ambivalence by advocating the decrease of public expenditure through social retrenchment, while at the same time urging governments to modernise their welfare states through social investment (Crespy and Vanheuverzwijn, 2017). As a matter of fact, many reforms have been conducted which were necessary to decrease public expenditure, especially pension reforms (De la Porte and Natali, 2014), reforms of unemployment benefits and labour markets, and cost-containment measures in healthcare systems.

In an attempt to rebalance its approach to socio-economic issues, since 2013 the Commission has sought to promote social investment through its Social Investment Package (see Box 10.4). The Communication contained recommendations urging member states to simplify their social systems by targeting specific groups, pursue activation and social inclusion policies (including closing the gender pay gap) and to invest especially in children, school leavers and young people. The Commission pointed to a number of available EU resources, notably the redirection of ESF budget lines and other more specific resources to investment policy issues. The bulk of funding required for implementing social investment remains with national budgets (see Box 10.4). In this regard, a recent study shows that EU countries can roughly be clustered in three groups. Those which traditionally have a robust welfare state and still have sufficient resources to carry out social investment (nine countries from Continental and Northern Europe), those where the awareness towards social investment is increasing but reforms remain piecemeal (a group of nine countries where the UK sides with countries such as Poland, Spain, Hungary and Cyprus) and those where no tangible social investment approach could be detected (the remaining ten countries from the southern, eastern and Baltic peripheries) (Bouget et al., 2015). Thus, EU recommendations advocating more social investment have more often than not remained either poorly implemented or not implemented at all, especially in countries with less budgetary room for manoeuvre.

In contrast, a consensus has emerged among European and national decision makers alike on the need to make labour markets more flexible through deregulation measures such as allowing shorter contracts and easier conditions of hiring and firing, more adaptability of working hours, less taxation on labour and the decentralisation of collective bargaining making it easier to introduce ad hoc arrangements over pay and working time at the enterprise level. While the UK and Germany introduced such reforms as early as the 1990s and 2000s, the Italian Job Act of 2014 and the French *Loi Travail* adopted in 2017 are examples of more recent reforms. The European Semester focuses very strongly on labour market reforms: they account for the largest share (18–30 per cent) of all country-specific recommendations adopted through the European Semester since 2011 (Crespy and Vanheuverzwijn, 2017).

Such reforms had been depicted, in the debates from the mid-2000s, as a move towards the model of flexicurity in place in Scandinavia or the Netherlands (see Box 10.4). However, their implementation across the continent shows that, while resulting in a breakthrough in increasing labour market flexibility, progress in terms of new rights or security is meagre. Moreover, in these countries there is no evidence that (vocational) education and training systems, or unemployment services, have been significantly improved. As inequality is on the rise in most EU countries, it appears that (1) in-work poverty is becoming more prevalent as a result of part-time and temporary jobs (European Parliament Research Service, 2016: 11–12) and (2) the reforms of the welfare states through the prism of so-called active labour market policies 'operate mainly through the reduction of security for insiders, not by increasing job security for outsiders' (Arpe et al., 2015: 50). As a result, the target set by the Europe 2020 strategy, especially with regard to having 20 million fewer poor people at risk of poverty or social exclusion by 2020, barely has a chance of being met.

The latest initiative is the launch of the European Pillar of Social Rights, a catalogue of objectives and principles for fostering social progress which was adopted, proclaimed and endorsed by the EU Heads of States and Governments at the Social Summit in Gotenburg in October 2017. Enjoying strong support from Commission President Juncker, it was thought to materialise the plea made when he took office in 2014 that the EU should achieve a 'Social Triple A'. The pillar was presented as a set of twenty principles falling into three chapters on equal opportunities in accessing the labour market, working conditions and social protection and inclusion. It encompasses both existing law (the so-called social *acquis*) and broader principles which can only be attained through member state policy-making and voluntary coordination thereof, such as the right to 'quality and inclusive education' or the right to 'fair wages that provide for a decent standard of living'.

As evidence of the will to 'deliver' through constraining instruments, in 2017 the Commission put forward a proposal for a directive on the work–life balance of parents and carers, thus picking up again, among other things, on maternity leave. In the face of resistance from several member states (including Denmark and France) against improving paternity leave rights, the proposal was watered down by the Council in 2018, leaving the current situation little changed. In 2017, the EP adopted a resolution on the pillar, demanding new instruments such as a guarantee to support children at risk of poverty. As far as the soft coordination of national policy is concerned, many have called for implementing the pillar through the recommendations of the European Semester. While the Commission has started to take into account the principles of the pillar in its Annual Growth Survey, there is still a lack of consistency between the logic of rights of the pillar, the logic of soft coordination of the European Semester and the logic of investment of the ESF (Sabato and Corti, 2018). As a result, there is wide scepticism across the board as to whether, in the current political context, the European Pillar of Social Rights is not doomed to fall short of expectations.

10.5 Current Political and Academic Controversies

10.5.1 What Are the Main Institutional Features of Today's EU Socio-economic Governance?

In 2005, Stefan Leibfried argued that EU social policy was 'left to courts and markets', thus pointing to the prominent role of the CJEU and the building of the single market. While the former still matter, the 2008–10 crisis has arguably placed the member states and domestic politics at the centre of the game. In several respects, as argued above, the CJEU has given way to a contentious politicisation of social matters and pressure from member states. This is powerfully exemplified by the way in which, with a series of decisions from 2013 to 2016, the court reversed its previous jurisprudence to grant the member states considerable leeway to refuse access of non-nationals to welfare benefits (such as unemployment or child-based benefits), in particular for non-working individuals. The most recent decision, which involved the British government and was taken one week before the referendum on Brexit, is a case in point.

But more significantly, the developments of the past two decades seem to reflect the type of institutional dynamics described by the neo-intergovernmentalists (Bickerton et al., 2015). Instead of delegating more regulatory competences to the EU institutions, governments have strengthened the European constraints through voluntary coordination and multilateral surveillance on the part of the Council with the Commission playing a key steering role. In fact, the European Semester has advanced integration in the realm of social policy by making it more hybrid since it combines elements of intergovernmentalism (member states remain central), supranationalism (strengthened surveillance powers of the Commission) and voluntary coordination (non-binding recommendations) (see Chapter 5). As a result, EU governance is no longer confined to regulating the social aspects of the single market, but seeks to reach further into domestic welfare state reforms, though with poor results in terms of progressive modernisation.

10.5.2   Are We Going Towards More Social EU Integration?

Social policy offers a telling illustration of the paradox of today's EU politics. On the one hand, common problems and interdependence, e.g. youth unemployment, call for more integration and new instruments to tackle common problems Europe wide. The neo-functionalist logic of a spillover of economic integration towards social integration has set actors in motion and brought about initiatives such as the Youth Guarantee and the tighter coordination of labour market or pension reforms. On the other hand, the feeling is widespread that the EU and the way in which it works is a cause of today's acute social problems. Especially widespread is the feeling that the integration process has mainly favoured market building and actors (banks and large corporations) while ignoring workers' everyday problems, especially those who are less highly educated and not very mobile individuals who identify less with Europe. Following a postfunctionalist logic (Hooghe and Marks, 2009) emphasising the primacy of domestic politics, these feelings have fuelled support for nationalist parties which vigorously oppose any further involvement of the EU into the social realm. This being said, the idea that most citizens are against more Europe in the realm of social policy should not be taken for granted. Recent surveys show that social issues such as unemployment and poverty rate among the most important concerns of people across the EU, and that majorities can be found to support more EU action in these domains (Ferrera and Pellegata, 2017; Vandenbroucke et al., 2018).

From a normative point of view, requirements for the EU to generate social justice depend on how one conceives of the social relations binding European citizens. Many share the diagnosis that, depending on the country and type of socio-economic model which they belong to, not all citizens have benefited equally from European integration. Some authors claim that democracy and social justice can only truly be realised within the framework of the nation states and that, therefore, member states need to regain more autonomy vis-à-vis the EU.[5] In contrast, others

---

[5] Claus Offe, Fritz Scharpf or Wolfgang Streeck.

have argued that the EU needs to equip itself with tools to compensate for the inequalities stemming from competition and monetary integration.[6]

10.5.3   Which Instruments Could Serve to Advance Social Integration and Tackle Inequalities?

The recent recession has fuelled debates about the possible creation of new social policy instruments at the EU level which would help tackle social inequalities within as well as between member states. A group of scholars has called for a 'European social union', in which the role of the EU should be to create a 'holding' environment for national welfare states through, for instance, automatic stabilisers (in the form of an unemployment insurance fund), common standards for upward convergence, or wage coordination (Vandenbroucke et al., 2016).

The idea of a European unemployment benefits scheme was much discussed among researchers and policymakers. The most realistic options do not involve direct transfers from the EU to unemployed individuals. Rather, the prevailing design being promoted is a sort of insurance fund which would flow into national schemes. The funds could be activated by those countries most affected by external shocks, thus tackling the problems of collective coordination and reduced national budgets in times of crisis. Although the idea has been much discussed and has been on the European agenda at least since 2013, the time does not yet seem ripe for the European Commission to make such a bold proposal, as it cannot yet rely on the support of a strong enough majority of member states. Especially among the richer, creditor countries, there are concerns that such a European unemployment insurance fund would act as a de facto mechanism for organising permanent financial transfers towards the more vulnerable EU countries with high unemployment figures and thus reduce their willingness to adopt efficient policies.

The creation of a European minimum wage has been discussed since the mid-2000s onwards as a means to tackle social dumping and promote convergence in living standards (see Box 10.4). Supported by some trade unions, it has remained contentious within the workers' movement with notable resistance from the powerful Deutscher Gewerkschaftsbund as well as other confederations in countries where various minimum wages are being negotiated autonomously and in a decentralised manner by the unions as opposed to a legal minimum wage (Dufresne, 2015). In 2012, however, an agreement was found on the idea of a 'wage floor' inspired by the international benchmark for fair wages from the Council of Europe set at 50–60 per cent of the national median wage. With median wages in the EU ranging from €2 per hour in Bulgaria to €14.1 per hour in Luxembourg, setting a minimum floor could lead to an increase in several countries. Yet, a non-regression

---

[6] Andea Sangiovanni, Franck Vandenbroucke, Jürgen Habermas or Philippe Van Parijs.

clause would have to be adopted to avoid a possible downward pressure in countries with higher minimum wage levels.

Both the unemployment insurance fund and a common standard for minimum wages were mentioned in the French-German roadmap for reforming the euro area issued in June 2018. However, there has been a blatant lack of political will to move forwards on these matters, as the European Council meeting of December 2018 only agreed on rather technical measures relating to the banking union and the ESM. Both a framework for minimum wages and a European Unemployment Re-insurance Scheme have been included in the work programme of the European Commission chaired by Ursula von der Leyen since October 2019. As the Commission launched a consultation of the social partners on minimum wages in January 2020, the initiative met strong resistance from decision makers and unions, particularly from Denmark and Sweden, who claim that wages is not an EU competence under the TFEU and that such an EU framework could damage wage setting systems which work well.

Finally, a number of academics have argued that a European basic income, in the form of an amount of money distributed unconditionally to all Europeans and funded through taxation, would be an efficient tool for tackling poverty, imbalances within the euro area and the changing structures of labour markets with the rise of part-time and independent work (e.g. Van Parijs and Vanderborght, 2017).

10.6   Analysis of a Paradigmatic Case Study

The implementation of the Youth Guarantee is a good example of the issues currently facing the EU when trying to develop new policy instruments for tackling social problems.

Adopted in 2013 upon a proposal of the European Commission, the aim of the Youth Guarantee is to tackle the high level of unemployment among young people in Europe, which on average in the EU increased from 15.9 per cent in 2007 to 22.2 per cent in 2014. While it had been significantly high in many countries in the past, it skyrocketed in those countries most hit by the debt explosion and economic recession.

The aim of the guarantee is to ensure that all young people under twenty-five receive a quality job, internship or education offer within four months of finishing school or becoming unemployed. The initiative was adopted in 2013 as a Council recommendation. This means that, while it has been negotiated and adopted through the ordinary legislative procedure, unlike directives or regulations it is without legal force. This reflects the fact that the funding of the policies needed to achieve these goals relies mainly on national resources complemented by EU funds.

In December 2016, the European Commission presented a report on the implementation of the Youth Guarantee showing that implementation has been slow and uneven across the EU. Alongside funding from the ESF, a further €6.4 billion was earmarked for the Youth Employment Initiative, bringing total funding up to €12.7 billion for the period 2014–20. A substantial part of the money was used to advance funds and help member states speed up implementation. Three years on, the Commission pointed to some encouraging results, notably a three-point drop in youth unemployment,[7] and reported that the guarantee benefited some fourteen million young Europeans. However, fifteen EU countries still have youth unemployment rates above 15 per cent, with peaks of around 45 per cent for Spain and Greece (OECD data). Moreover, 12 per cent of young Europeans are still 'not in employment, education or training'.

The Youth Guarantee scheme has been criticised by MEPs and the European Trade Union Confederation for failing to tackle the full scale of the problem and often leading young people into precarious jobs. One main problem detected is that young people exiting a youth guarantee scheme may take up a job offer, but often only on a temporary basis, thus returning them to a youth guarantee scheme soon afterwards. Both the EP and the International Labour Organization reckoned that approximately €20 billion was needed to properly address youth unemployment (ILO, 2012). Furthermore, the Commission and the EP assessed that the actual implementation was still at an early stage as of 2016 and that only one in five member states had achieved full implementation of the various measures planned within the framework of the Youth Guarantee (European Parliament, 2017).

Thus, the Youth Guarantee seems to be paradigmatic of the weaknesses of the EU's social policy for tacking severe and urgent social issues. The first main issue is the non-binding nature of the policy, which leaves the EU with little means to oblige national governments to act for implementation. The second issue relates to the weakness of the available resources to fund such policies. On the one hand, the budget of the EU represents around 1 per cent of the EU's GDP. Its means to conduct redistributive policies are therefore nowhere near what can be done at the national level through the welfare state. On the other hand, member states' resources have been reduced as a result of the debt crisis, the bail out of banks in crisis and the economic recession since 2009. The fiscal orthodoxy of the EU, which limits deficit and debt levels under the SGP, exerts considerable constraints for those member states which have slow economic growth and therefore lower fiscal resources, high debt and thus almost no room for manoeuvre in their budget for modern and progressive social policies such as the Youth Guarantee or social investment more generally.

---

[7] It must be underlined, though, that there is no way to prove that the improvement in the situation was causally due to the implementation of the Youth Guarantee rather than simply an improvement in the overall economy.

GROUP DISCUSSION

- Is there something like a European social model?
- Should the competences of the EU in the social realm be strengthened? Why and how?

TOPICS FOR INDIVIDUAL RESEARCH

- Is there a convergence of European social models with regard to labour market regulation?
- How can the dynamics of social regulation in the internal market since 2000 be explained?

FURTHER READINGS

Barcevicius, E., Weishaupt, T. and Zeitlin, J. (eds) (2014). *Assessing the Open Method of Coordination*. Basingstoke: Palgrave.

Crespy, A. and Menz, G. (2015). *Social Policy and the Euro Crisis. Quo Vadis Social Europe?* Basingstoke: Palgrave Macmillan.

De la Porte, C. and Heins, E. (eds) (2016). *The Sovereign Debt Crisis, the EU and Welfare State Reform*. Basingstoke: Palgrave.

Vanhercke, B., Sabato, S. and Bouget, D. (eds) (2017). *Social Policy in the European Union: State of Play 2017*. Brussels: ETUI.

Vandenbroucke, F., Barnard, C. and De Baere, G. (2016). *A European Social Union after the Crisis*. Cambridge: Cambridge University Press.

REFERENCES

Arpe, J., Milio, S. and Stuchlik, A. (2015). 'Social Policy Reforms in the EU: A Cross-national Comparison'. Social Inclusion Monitor Europe, Reform Barometer, www.bertelsmannstiftung.de (accessed 7 February 2019).

Bickerton, C., Hodson, D. and Puetter, U. (eds) (2015). *The New Intergovernmentalism*. Oxford: Oxford University Press.

Bouget, D., Frazer, H., Marlier, E., Sabato, S. and Vanhercke, B. (2015). *Social Investment in Europe: A Study of National Policies*. European Social Policy Network, European Commission, Brussels.

Copeland, P. and Daly, M. (2014). 'Poverty and Social Policy in Europe 2020: Ungovernable and Ungoverned'. *Policy & Politics*, 42(3): 341–65.

Coman, R. and Sbaraglia, F. (2018). 'Gouverner par la conditionnalité ou la flexibilité? La réforme de la politique de cohésion de l'Union européenne (2014–2020)'. *Gouvernement et action publique*, 3 : 35–55.

Copeland, P. and Daly, M. (2018). 'The European Semester and EU Social Policy'. *Journal of Common Market Studies*, 56(5): 1001–18.

Crespy, A. (2016). *Welfare Markets in Europe: The Democratic Challenge of European Integration*. Basingstoke, Palgrave.

Crespy, A. and Menz, G. (2015). *Social Policy and the Euro Crisis. Quo Vadis Social Europe?* Basingstoke: Palgrave Macmillan.

Crespy, A. and Vanheuverzwijn, P. (2017). 'What "Brussels" Means by Structural Reforms: Empty Signifier or Constructive Ambiguity?'. *Comparative European Politics*, 17(1): 92–111.

De la Porte, C. and Heins, E. (eds) (2016). *The Sovereign Debt Crisis, the EU and Welfare State Reform*. Basingstoke: Palgrave.

De la Porte, C. and Natali, D. (2014). 'Altered Europeanisation of Pension Reform in the Context of the Great Recession: Denmark and Italy Compared'. *West European Politics*, 37(4): 732–49.

De la Porte, C. and Palier, B. (forthcoming). 'The Politics and Policies of Social Investment at the EU Level: A Longitudinal Analysis'. In J. Garritzmann, S. Hausermann and B. Palier (eds), *The World Politics of Social Investment*. Oxford: Oxford University Press.

Dufresne, A. (2015). 'Euro-Unionism and Wage Policy: The German Paradox: A Driving Force, but Also a Brake?'. In A. Crespy and G. Menz (eds), *Social Policy and the Euro-crisis: Quo Vadis Social Europe*? Basingstoke: Palgrave.

European Parliament (2017). 'Youth Guarantee: Lessons from Implementation, Briefing'. *Employment and Social Affairs PE* 602.024.

European Parliament Research Service (2016). 'Poverty in the European Union: The Crisis and its Aftermath'. March 2016 – PE 579.099. www.europarl.europa.eu/RegData/etudes/IDAN/2016/579099/EPRS_IDA(2016)579099_EN.pdf.

Ferrera, M. and Pellegata, A. (2017). 'Can Economic and Social Europe Be Reconciled? Citizen Views on Integration and Solidarity'. Research report, RESCUE. https://air.unimi.it/retrieve/handle/2434/608892/1125069/REScEU_mass_survey_report.pdf (accessed 7 February 2019).

Geyer, R. (2000). *Exploring European Social Policy*. Oxford: Polity Press.

Graziano, P. and Hartlapp, M. (2018). 'The End of Social Europe? Understanding EU Social Policy Change'. *Journal of European Public Policy*, 26(6): 1484–501.

Hooghe, L. and Marks, G. (2009). 'A Postfunctionalist Theory of European Integration: From Permissive Consensus to Constraining Dissensus'. *British Journal of Political Science*, 39(1): 1–24.

Hyman, R. (2015). 'Austeritarianism in Europe: What Options for Resistance?'. In D. Natali and B. Vanhercke (eds), *Social Policy in the European Union: State of Play*. Brussels: ETEUI/OSE.

ILO (International Labour Organization) (2012). 'Eurozone Job Crisis: Trends and Policy responses'. Studies on Growth with Equity, Geneva. www.ilo.org/wcmsp5/groups/public/---dgreports/---inst/documents/publication/wcms_393024.pdf.

Leibfried, S. (2005). 'Social Policy: Left to the Judges and the Markets?'. In H. Wallace, W. Wallace and M. Pollack (eds), *Policy Making in the European Union*. Oxford: Oxford University Press.

Pochet, P. and Degryse, C. (2017). 'La dynamique sociale européenne au prisme d'une approche quantitative'. *Politique européenne*, 58(4): 72–108.

Radaelli, C. and Borras, S. (2010). *Recalibrating the Open Method of Coordination: Towards Diverse and More Effective Usages*. Stockholm: Swedish Institute for European Policy Studies.

Sabato, S. and Corti, F. (2018). '"The Times They Are A-changin"? the European Pillar of Social Rights from Debate to Reality Check'. In B. Vanhercke et al. (eds), *Social Policy in the European Union: State of Play 2018*. Brussels: ETUI.

Sabel, C. and Zeitlin, J. (eds) (2010). *Experimentalist Governance in the European Union*. Oxford: Oxford University Press.

Vandenbroucke, F., Kuhn, T., Nicoli, F., Sacchi, S., Van der Duine, D. and Hegewald, S. (2018). 'Risk Sharing When Unemployment Hits: How Policy Design Influences Citizen Support For European Unemployment Risk Sharing (EURS)'. Research Report, Amsterdam Institute for Social Science Research. https://dare.uva.nl/search?identifier=4fc41934-5fc9-45d1-a0f3-5b2694661874 (accessed 7 February 2019).

Van Parijs, P. and Vanderborght, Y. (2017). *Basic Income: A Radical Proposal for a Free Society and a Sane Economy*. Cambridge, MA: Harvard University Press.

Vandenbroucke, F., Barnard, C. and De Baere, G. (eds) (2016). *A European Social Union After the Crisis*. Cambridge: Cambridge University Press.

Vanheuverzwijn, P. and Crespy, A. (2018). 'Macro-economic Coordination and Elusive Ownership in the European Union'. *Public Administration*, 96(3): 578–93.

Zeitlin, J., Barcevicius, E. and Weishaupt, T. (2014). 'Institutional Design and National Influence of EU Social Policy Coordination: Advancing a Contradictory Debate'. In T. Weishaupt, E. Barcevicius and J. Zeitlin (eds), *Assessing the Open Method of Coordination*. Basingstoke: Palgrave, 1–15.

Zeitlin, J. and Vanhercke, B. (2017). 'Socializing the European Semester: EU Social and Economic Policy Co-ordination in Crisis and Beyond'. *Journal of European Public Policy*, 25(2): 149–74.

11 Labour Markets and Mobility: How to Reconcile Competitiveness and Social Justice?

LÁSZLÓ ANDOR

11.1 Introduction

Free movement of labour, migration and immigration have been hotly debated recently, notably during election campaigns, often with a particular focus on the migration of poorer people.[1] What is free may not necessarily be fair, and this concern applies to trade as well as labour mobility. The freedom to move in the EU single market should help member states to higher economic performance and citizens to higher standards of living, but the legitimacy of open labour markets depends on the distribution of advantages and gains but also risks between various countries and other stakeholders.

Labour mobility should be a win-win game for all involved. Workers have more job opportunities than what they would have in a restricted geographical space. Companies can recruit from a wider circle than just from within their national boundaries. Receiving countries enjoy higher competitiveness and economic growth, and countries of origin benefit from remittances – and a more experienced workforce once some of the migrants return.

While the economic case for labour mobility is fairly strong, the related risks and concerns are often overlooked at the level of governance. In the real world, the well-known advantages materialise in an imbalanced way and they are also associated with various costs, tensions and controversies. The migration of people has transaction costs: families might be disrupted, workers become vulnerable in a less well-known environment, people may end up in jobs for which they are overqualified and the risk of undeclared employment may also increase.

It is, of course, not a good thing if economic stagnation, high unemployment and rising poverty force people to move to other countries in large numbers. Growth prospects and job creation dynamics have to be restored in all countries and regions of the EU, and this should be a priority. However, it is very unfair when some people want EU migrants to pay twice for a recession and lack of opportunities that prevails in their countries.

[1] Research for this chapter has been supported by the European Union and Hungary and co-financed by the European Social Fund through the project EFOP-3.6.2–16–2017–00017, titled Sustainable, Intelligent and Inclusive Regional and City Models.

This chapter argues that labour mobility in the EU is an opportunity rather than a threat. Since European countries have regulated labour markets and this particularly applies to cross-country mobility, the benefits of free movement far exceed the costs and risks. Nevertheless, EU level as well as national level government action is always needed to ensure fairness and uphold the principle of non-discrimination in the labour market. This requires legislative activity but also appropriate budgetary decisions and institution building in order to address the controversies of the time. We will show through practical examples that a lot can be done without EU treaty change to manage migration better, and reconcile mobility with the broader social objectives of the EU.

11.2   Historical Overview

11.2.1   Early Mobility and Enlargement Effect

European integration had created a space for cross-border mobility before the EU was established by the Maastricht Treaty. Italian working-class families moved to Belgium, French professionals migrated to the City of London and Portuguese employees appeared on the construction sites of Luxembourg. Labour migration continued between Ireland and the United Kingdom, and such opportunities were increasingly exploited in a macro-region formed by Luxembourg, Wallonia in Belgium, Alsace-Lorraine in France and Rhineland-Palatinate and Saarland in Germany.

While community law and policy coordination established the rights and opportunity for intra-EU migration, the actual numbers of mobile workforce remained relatively low, due to relatively even patterns of economic development. Important barriers also remained, linguistic diversity being the most important among them.

The enlargements of the EU towards the east[2] brought about a significant increase in intra-EU labour mobility (Kahanec, 2012; Galgóczi et al., 2013). The volume of labour mobility has practically doubled following the enlargements to the east of 2004 and 2007 (although leading only up to about 3 per cent of the total EU labour force working in a member state outside their country of origin). In most cases, it was not the date of entry to the EU which was the starting point of greater flows: abolishing visa requirements already triggers larger numbers, although at that stage there is a greater risk of newly mobile workers ending up in a grey zone of employment.

The fact that Poland entered the EU with a recent history of excessively high unemployment, and Romania was among the poorest countries on the continent, meant that the most populous eastern member states represented a high migration potential. Some typical channels developed quickly. Poles tended to move to the

[2] See among others Galgóczi et al. (2013).

UK in large numbers, while Romanians (and Bulgarians) sought employment in Spain and Italy.

In the 2004–7 period the EU economy experienced strong growth as measured in GDP, and mobile Poles, Romanians and others from the east found jobs in high numbers. Nevertheless, the new trends of mobility were also accompanied by concerns or suspicion, which developed into full-blown controversies after a few years.

11.2.2   East to West, South to North

Disparities in wages have been assumed to be and also observed as a main factor driving labour mobility, especially what concerns the east–west axis. However, other shorter-term factors such as the level of unemployment, the availability of vacancies, political developments, social cohesion and the overall expectations concerning all of these also play a role.

Labour mobility from east to west gave rise to concerns of brain drain, though measuring brain drain is not an easy task. In the first decade of EU membership, highly skilled people were not overrepresented among migrating Eastern Europeans, while from some countries, notably Romania, low-skilled and poorer people have been overrepresented.

The post-2007 financial crisis[3] (and especially the 2009 recession) reduced mobility temporarily but affected the directions of population movements in Europe. South–north migration has markedly increased while remaining far below east–west mobility in absolute numbers. People do not only migrate from the eurozone periphery to the northern EU countries but also to non-EU countries where language connections make it easier to start a business or get a job. Some circular mobility, e.g. from Germany to Poland, has also been observed. With increased migration from south to north, the profile of migrants has also changed. The new migrants tend to have higher levels of education and they are less likely to be overqualified for the job they get than their Eastern European peers.

While it is not common to consider overall mobility excessive, debates have concentrated on two issues: the question of social dumping and the rights of poorer migrants. These topics became frequently discussed in countries receiving significant flows, where specific groups were also concerned about migrants from other EU countries crowding out local workers from old and new jobs.

In depopulating regions of the east, but at the time of the crisis also in the south, concerns about a brain drain were increasingly discussed as well. However, it was the first two which developed into full-blown controversies at EU level, making a strong impact on whether Europeans consider mobility fair or not. Such EU-level debates were followed by various steps in developing and upgrading EU law (as seen in Box 11.1).

---

[3] On the early crisis effects on labour mobility see Koehler et al. (2010).

BOX 11.1 Key dates

Year	Legislative initiative/decision	Significance
1996	Posted Workers Directive	Tackling risk of social dumping, defining core rights
2004	Free Movement Directive	Updating framework for right to work and reside
2014	Enforcement directives	Help with interpretation and implementation
2017	Proposal for Labour Authority	Ensuring uniformity of implementation
2018	Revised Posted Workers Directive	Equalising remuneration and confirming temporary nature

The first major debate around east–west labour mobility took place around workers sent from one country to another by their companies. They represent a modest share of the total workforce, amounting to about 1.2–1.5 million workers, mainly in labour-intensive sectors like construction. The debate on social dumping is a typical product of a context in which economic competition is seen as legitimate but social competition[4] is not. However, separating the two has become increasingly difficult since enlargements towards the east.

The second major debate developed around the access of EU migrants to the social benefits of host countries. In the EU, one cannot defend the right of workers to free movement without ensuring that mobile workers don't lose social security coverage and don't end up in inferior or outright discriminatory jobs. This, however, does not mean that there should or would be free movement between different welfare systems. EU law does not oblige member states to support citizens of other countries if they have not worked there, unless they are a family member of a worker or 'habitually resident' in the host country – a status gained only by meeting strict criteria.[5]

In certain periods, and in the crisis years in particular, the general discourse in Western and Northern European countries towards poorer EU migrants has been less than welcoming. In the UK, the widespread use of the expression 'benefit tourism' was observed, while in Germany the word 'poverty migration' (*Armutszuwanderung*) was coined. Such expressions actually shifted the blame

---

[4] On the myth and reality of social competition see Maslauskaite (2013).

[5] For those who had doubts before, the so-called Dano case at the ECJ (C-333/13) clarified that the host country has no obligation to provide social benefits to a family with no genuine connections with the host country (in this particular case, Romanian citizen in Germany), even if there is no uniform practice in the application of this principle.

onto the migrating poor people themselves for the anomalies and controversies around them. Leaders like David Cameron (UK) and Sebastian Kurz (Austria) championed proposals aiming at cuts in the benefits of workers who came from other EU countries.

11.3 Main Features of the Current Institutional Framework

11.3.1 Institutional Framework of Policy-making

In EU governance, the questions of labour mobility belong to employment policy.

All related issues fall under the responsibility of the Directorate-General Employment, Social Affairs and Inclusion (or DG EMPL), which is one of the directorates-general in the European Commission. The commissioner[6] in charge also supervises agencies[7] that support the development and implementation of EU policies in the given area.

To make law, to take budgetary decisions or to discuss any aspect of the policy portfolio, the Commission works with the Employment and Social Affairs Committee of the European Parliament and the Employment, Social Policy, Health and Consumer Affairs Council configuration of the Council, in which the ministers representing the member states sit. The Employment portfolio is also responsible for social dialogue, which takes place between the Commission and representatives of employers and employees at EU level. This is more formalised than dialogue with civil society, given some treaty-based meeting formats like the semi-annual Tripartite Social Summit and Macroeconomic Dialogue. In the area of employment and social policy, regular exchange of views with the European Economic and Social Committee also has high importance.

The emphasis on free movement of workers since the beginning of the EEC distinguished labour regulation in the Community from national labour laws of the member states, where free movement was not of concern, as well as from international labour standards. Labour standards focused on employment protection and industrial relations were not a primary concern of an EC aiming at free movement of workers, certainly in the earlier stages of the Community, but even later in the EU. The primary objective of establishing free movement of workers in a labour market was for a long time the dominant feature of EU regulation of employment and industrial relations.

---

[6] At the time of writing, the Commissioner in charge is Marianne Thyssen (Belgium), whose portfolio is defined as employment, social affairs, skills and labour mobility.

[7] The agencies under the employment portfolio are: Cedefop (Thessaloniki), European Training Foundation (Turin), Eurofund (Dublin) and EU-OSHA (Bilbao).

BOX 11.2 Legal basis

The legal framework for labour mobility is primarily based on the free movement of persons, which is one of the fundamental freedoms guaranteed by Community law. It is perhaps the most important right under Community law for individuals, and an essential element of European citizenship. For workers, this freedom has existed since the foundation of the European Community (then EEC) in 1957.

It is laid down in Article 45 TFEU and it entails:

- The right to look for a job in another member state.
- The right to work in another member state.
- The right to reside there for that purpose.
- The right to remain there.
- The right to equal treatment in respect of access to employment, working conditions and all other advantages which could help to facilitate the worker's integration in the host member state.

The provisions[8] of the treaty entitle any EU national to take up and engage in gainful employment on the territory of another member state (see Box 11.2), and to equal treatment to national workers as regards working and employment conditions, social and tax benefits; his or her family members are also entitled to establish themselves, together with the worker, whatever their nationality. It is important to note that employment in public services is excluded from this provision (Article 45(4) TFEU), and there are permissible limitations when justified on grounds of public policy, public security or public health (Article 45(3) TFEU).

An important piece of legislation is the EP and Council Directive 2004/38/EC of 29 April 2004 about the right of citizens of the Union and their family members to move and reside freely within the territory of the EU and EEA member states. This new directive brought together most of the piecemeal measures previously found in European law. The new measures are designed, among other things, to encourage Union citizens to exercise their right to move and reside freely within member states, to cut back administrative formalities to the bare essentials, to provide a better definition of the status of family members[9] and to limit the scope for refusing entry or terminating the right of residence.

---

[8] The provisions of Article 45 TFEU are further developed in Council Regulation 1612/68 of 15 October 1968 on freedom of movement for workers within the Community (as amended up to Regulation 2434/92) and Council Directive 68/360/EECof 15 October 1969 on the abolition of restrictions on movement and residence within the Community for workers of member states and their families. Further provisions include Regulation (EEC) No. 1251/70 of the Commission of 29 June 1970 on a worker's right to remain in the territory of a member state, after having been employed in that state.

[9] Very importantly, the directive broadens the definition of family to also include non-married partners.

The subsequent enlargements of the EU resulted in an adaptation of the principles as well as practice of free movement. States seeking membership of the EU have often had specific provisions in the Accession Treaty subjecting free movement to conditions. Following enlargement of the EU to twenty-five members by the accession of ten countries on 1 May 2004, there were transitional periods[10] that limited the free movement of workers from these member states, except Malta and Cyprus. From 2011, complete freedom of movement for workers from the member states which joined in May 2004 is guaranteed. Similar transitional periods were agreed with regard to the 2007 enlargement by Bulgaria and Romania.

11.3.2 Posted Workers as a Specific Category in EU Law

Under the EU single market, a service provider may win a contract in another country and send his employees there to carry out the contract. This is an important feature of an integrated market, and the free movement of services more specifically (see Box 11.3). However, in an unevenly developed and regulated system (from the point of view of wage levels, industrial relations and welfare systems), cross-border provision of services may give rise to controversies regarding the fairness of such forms of activity.

BOX 11.3 Key concepts

Posted workers are different from EU *mobile workers* because they remain in the host member state only temporarily and do not integrate its labour market. More precisely, a posted worker is an employee who is sent by his employer to carry out a service in another EU member state on a temporary basis, in the context of a contract of services, an intragroup posting or a hiring out through a temporary agency.

The 1996 directive made an exception to the general requirement according to which all workers are protected by the law of the member state in which they work. But it did not acknowledge the authority of the home country of the posting company and the posted worker either. Instead, it created an in-between category which has to reflect a balance between competitiveness in the single market and the protection of the social rights of workers involved. The rules as set out in

---

[10] Until 2006, the access to the labour markets of the fifteen former member states exclusively depended on national policies. After mid-2006, these fifteen member states had to notify the Commission regarding whether they would continue with national restrictions or allow free movement of workers. After 2009, any of these fifteen member states had to ask the Commission for authorisation to continue to apply national measures for a further two years, but only if it was experiencing serious disturbances in its labour market. This requirement had to be 'objectively justified'.

1996 establish that, even though workers posted to another member state are still employed by the sending company and subject to the law of that member state, they are entitled to a set of core rights in force in the host member state.

This set of rights consists of:

- Minimum rates of pay.
- Maximum work periods and minimum rest periods.
- Minimum paid annual leave.
- The conditions of hiring out workers through temporary work agencies.
- Health, safety and hygiene at work.
- Equal treatment between men and women.

Whether the 1996 directive is sufficient or not became a heated political dispute in EU institutions after the eastward enlargements of 2004 and 2007, and in particular after some controversial rulings by the ECJ. Box 11.4 sums up the nature of polarisation of various stakeholders in the debates and negotiations around the experience and future of posting. This polarisation set the scene for the legislative and policy activities of the past decade.

BOX 11.4 Key actors in the social dumping debate

Position	For more regulation/restrictions	Against more regulation/restrictions
Social partner	Trade unions (European Trade Union Confederation)	Business (Europe) SMEs (supporting)
Political group	Socialists, social democrats Most Christian democrats Greens (mostly supportive)	Most liberals Conservatives
Regional actor	West and north (excluding UK/Ireland) South (supporting)	East UK/Ireland

---

11.4   Recent Policy Developments

11.4.1   Crisis Response and the Promotion of Mobility

At the time of the long financial and economic crisis, experts and politicians were thinking about ways to manage intra-European migration better and exploit job opportunities better than before. This primarily depended on improvements that can increase the level of satisfaction with mobility among host and home countries, employers and employees alike.

Despite occasional controversy, scepticism, animosity and even welfare chauvinism, the EU has maintained an overall positive attitude towards labour mobility, beyond simply insisting on the right to free movement. The Commission's 2012 April 'Employment Package' outlined the vision of a genuine pan-European labour market; and in a supplementary Youth Employment Package (December 2012) it repeatedly highlighted the potential benefits of cross-border mobility.

By ascribing a strategic importance to labour mobility, the Commission confronted two common fallacies. One is that immigration might be a cause of unemployment, and the other that labour mobility can play a dominant role in addressing imbalances within the EU and especially inside the eurozone. In the wake of the employment package, several initiatives were launched to tackle problems arising from closer labour market integration in the EU. Proposals were made to create a cross-border network of Public Employment Services (EURES), to reinforce the European Employment Service and its website, and to establish an EU platform against undeclared work (hinting towards potential development towards an EU-level labour inspectorate).

Historically, intra-EU labour mobility was promoted in the context of deepening the single market of the EU. However, EU policy in recent years has not only aimed at 'removing barriers' but also at creating greater transparency in the labour market and improving the legal framework for the benefit of all participants. A prime goal has been to protect better the employability and the social rights of workers outside their home countries, and to help member states, regions and municipalities deal with the aftermath of tensions related to mobility either on the sending or the receiving side. On the latter issue, the allocation and absorption of EU funds also had to play a role.

11.4.2   Enforcing and Adapting EU Law on Mobility

In 2014, three important legislative proposals were adopted to facilitate a better-functioning European labour market. First, a directive about the exercise of the rights of mobile workers (adopted April 2014), then a directive about the portability of occupational pensions (adopted April 2014) and, finally, an enforcement directive about the posting of workers (adopted May 2014). Needless to say, it was the last of these which received most political attention at the time.

In order to tackle abuse and improve the implementation and interpretation of the 1996 directive (also in view of the notorious court cases on this matter), in 2012 the European Commission put forward an enforcement directive, which was adopted two years later. This introduced, for example, joint and several liability in the construction sector, clarified the list of possible control measures and eliminated the so-called letter-box companies. While some concerns continued to be voiced, the new legislation offered major improvement to practice on the ground.

While some were calling for a more general overhaul of EU legislation regarding free movement, the Commission was driven by the belief that there was clearly scope for steps that can be made within the strictly national context without questioning the right to free movement and without opening the door to discrimination. Better enforcement of existing rules can help eliminate abuse and prevent controversies in other fields. If, for example, companies use their power to prevent EU migrants from organising, there should be intervention to stop such abuse. If some employers abuse the Temporary Agency Workers Directive and make workers 'redundant' after three months in order to avoid equal treatment requirements, there should be ways to sort this out.

The point is that it is equal treatment, including ensuring equal social rights, that creates fairness, and not the opposite. However, it is one thing to defend the right to free movement (together with associated social rights) as something that belongs to all citizens, and another one to manage migration better. Working on the second should be possible without calling the first into question. It is indeed the role of EU institutions, and the Commission in particular, to clarify that enlargements of the EU imply not only an expansion of markets, but also the accession of people with equal rights, including equal social rights. The EU also needs to be an honest broker when dispute emerges among various member states in the context of free movement.

Beyond better enforcement of the rights of posted workers (provided by the 2014 Enforcement Directive), the discussion on equal remuneration was reopened in 2016, also in connection with more general conflicts between old member states and some of the eastern ones. In this round, more attention was paid to the fact that wage levels and working conditions in the east were not converging on the EU average as dynamically as they should have. On this basis, the new Posted Workers Directive was adopted in 2018.

The revised rules bring changes in three main areas: the remuneration of posted workers, long-term postings and temporary agency workers. Under the new rules, posted workers are entitled to the same remuneration as local workers for the same work at the same place. Collective agreements that are declared universally applicable apply to posted workers as well in all sectors. After twelve months, posted workers are entitled to all terms and conditions of employment of the host state that are mandatorily applicable with very few exceptions. Finally, member states must ensure that the principle of equal treatment as provided for in the Temporary Agency Work Directive also applies to posted temporary agency workers.

11.4.3   Portability of Unemployment Benefit

In the name of fairness,[11] the Commission presented a revision of the EU legislation on social security coordination at the end of 2016. The proposal aimed at creating a

---

[11] When presenting the package on labour mobility, Commissioner for Employment, Social Affairs, Skills and Labour Mobility Marianne **Thyssen** emphasised the need to reconcile competitiveness and fairness in the following way: 'Free movement is a fundamental right of our Union cherished by its citizens. It brings benefits to workers, employers and the economy at large, helping

uniform framework for cross-border portability of unemployment benefits, and also dealt with the social security coordination for frontier workers and posted workers.

Regarding the portability of unemployment benefit, it was understood that EU law could provide greater clarity in the coordination of social security regimes to help both jobseekers and the receiving countries at the same time. For instance, since May 2013 the EC has been floating the idea of creating a rule that migrant jobseekers are covered by unemployment insurance for a standard period of, say, six[12] months after losing a job. Currently, member states can choose anything between three and six months, and most migrant jobseekers turn to their host state for support.

A more uniform rule about portability – receipt of benefit from the member state where the person lost their job even if he/she lives or seeks work in another – would be better understood by jobseekers as well as by the member states. Of course, one would not rely on Slovak unemployment benefit when looking for a job in Germany, and not even on Danish benefits when making similar efforts in Croatia. Nor does this imply that benefit levels need to converge.

11.4.4 Establishing a European Labour Authority

In September 2017, Commission President Jean-Claude Juncker somewhat unexpectedly announced the creation of a European Labour Authority (ELA), as part of a broader Commission effort aimed at ensuring fairer worker mobility within the EU (Fernandes, 2018). The following coordination and legislative process clarified the likely functions and competences of this new agency.

According to the Commission, the ELA would need to facilitate access for individuals and employers to information on their rights and obligations as well as to relevant services. The ELA will provide information on employment, learning, mobility, recruitment and training opportunities, as well as guidance on the rights and obligations of those who live, work or are engaged in cross-border activities in another EU member state. The ELA would also support cooperation between member states in the cross-border enforcement of relevant Union law, including facilitating joint inspections. For example, the ELA will help to improve the exchange of information, support capacity building in national administrations and assist them in carrying out joint inspections. The objectives are to enhance mutual trust between the actors, to improve day-to-day cooperation and to prevent possible fraud and abuse. Finally, the ELA would mediate and facilitate a solution in cases

---

tackling labour shortages and skills gaps. We need labour mobility to help restore economic growth and competitiveness. But mobility needs to be based on clear, fair and enforceable rules. This is what our proposal to update the EU rules on social security is about: it safeguards free movement and protects citizens' rights, while strengthening the tools to address possible abuse' (European Commission, 2016).

[12] A six-month stay is allowed in a country by free movement rules, but having just three months' income leaves a hole in the system. This hole could be eliminated without treaty change.

of cross-border disputes between national authorities or labour market disruptions such as restructuring of companies affecting several member states. In order to deliver its mission effectively, the creation of the ELA would allow for significant institutional consolidation.[13]

Rule enforcement and labour inspection are currently national competences and it is not obvious for many why this new agency is necessary. In some countries, trade unions play a major role in this area and this must also be respected when an EU-level authority is established. According to the Commission, the creation of the ELA will not result in a transfer of competences from the member states to the EU and must be implemented, at least initially, in compliance with the current treaty provisions.

The political push for such a new agency was also enhanced by the argument that the initial crisis response after 2009 resulted in the creation of a European Banking Authority. While delivering on its duties, ELA would match the developments on the side of banking supervision by enhancing a similar capacity on the side of integrated labour markets. The legislative work in the Council and Parliament made significant headway in the course of 2018.

11.5   Current Political and Academic Controversies

11.5.1   Analysing Mobility in the Context of Imbalances

As we have seen in previous chapters, the EU has regularly addressed frictions and controversies around mobility in order to improve its legislative framework as well as public perception. But this does not mean that all issues could be or would be settled by now. Political and academic debates continue and they face the challenge of combining economic, sociological and cultural aspects of the same phenomenon, and take into account a multitude of stakeholder perspectives when forming a judgement about labour markets and cross-border mobility.

The strong preference, and perhaps even bias for mobility and freedom of movement in the EU is embedded in the concept of the single market, and it feeds on some general economic assumptions. These suggest that on both sides – sending and receiving – mobility actually improves the economic opportunities, while the associated costs are either minimal or can be minimised or remedied without great difficulties (see Barslund and Busse, 2016). However, it is also recognised that there

---

[13] It is foreseen that the ELA will take over management of the EURES European Coordination Office, as well as replace the Technical Committee on the Free Movement of Workers, the Committee of Experts on Posting of Workers, the Technical Commission, the Audit Board, the Conciliation Board of the Administrative Commission for the Coordination of Social Security Systems and the European Platform on tackling undeclared work. ELA will also cooperate and build synergies with other EU agencies, including Eurofound, Cedefop, EU-OSHA, ETF, Europol and Eurojust.

is always scope to manage migration and mobility better at the EU level. For that, mobility has to be analysed in a broader context of imbalances and convergences.

Original assumptions about the circular nature of mobility (see Zimmermann, 2014) were dominant when integration was more homogeneous and such great disparities were not observed. Since eastward enlargement we have to appreciate that the EU has become more imbalanced, and from the point of view of mobility its member states have to be categorised as typical home (or source) countries and host (or destination) countries. A separate assessment is required about costs and risks of mobility from the perspectives of both. It is the first decade or so, together with the crisis years, that allows experts to develop a more complex balance on the basis of findings. And on the basis of the evidence, a matrix of benefits and risks (see Table 11.1) can be developed in order to take into account all risks and benefits for a comprehensive assessment.

11.5.2 Benefit–Risk Balance for Host Countries

For the receiving 'host countries' of mobility, it is assumed that countries receiving EU migrants experience an overall positive economic impact, i.e. GDP would be smaller without it. The positive impact on the economy is linked to the potential in mobility to fill labour shortages. Controversies around labour mobility are often linked to the assumption that it puts downward pressure on wages in the host country, which is particularly strong in the low-wage categories. However, it has been very hard to prove such assumptions through statistics. If such pressures exist, they are moderate, and depend on broader macroeconomic conditions. The more general trend is that the incoming workforce makes the domestic economy more competitive, which results in greater demand for labour, including among the low skilled.

Of course, these general trends may not fully work out in major destination countries or in specific periods. Possible negative impacts can be observed occasionally in the short run and in the case of groups more likely to be substituted

Table 11.1 The benefit–risk matrix of mobility

Perspective	Individuals	Countries/economies
Origin	More job opportunities, better income prospects and working conditions Risk factors: lack of local knowledge, overqualification, abuse, informal employment	Falling unemployment, more experienced workforce (after return), remittances (boosting demand) Risk factors: social security deficit, sectoral shortages
Destination	Cheaper services, more reliable services (e.g. health and care) Risk factors: crowding out less skilled workers, pressure on local welfare budgets	Greater labour supply, filling skills shortages, boosting competitiveness Risk factors: less incentives for innovation, training and social investment

(past immigrants, low-skilled natives). The assessment of the fiscal impact is similar to the labour market impact: it tends to be positive (i.e. the mobile workforce makes a greater contribution to the public budgets of host countries than it receives), as mobile EU citizens tend to be economically active and also younger on average.

11.5.3   Benefit–Risk Balance for Home Countries

For a typical country of origin, the effects of mobility on GDP growth have been assumed to be negative, even if it is understood that this is not a zero-sum game. It is only recently that quantitative analysis is possible. And, even if it is proved that there is a GDP loss out of large-scale outward migration if sustained for a long time, we are speaking about countries where economic growth has been exceptionally robust in the last two decades. This particularly applies to Poland, which even managed to avoid recession in 2009.

Even if one may demonstrate a negative effect on GDP, the impact on GDP *per capita* is even more limited. The likelihood of that increases when the share of tertiary educated increases, which tends to be the case at a time of crisis (e.g. the eurozone crisis). A source country can be, and is normally, compensated by remittances for weaker GDP growth. However, a major difference is that domestic tax policy can connect with GDP, but not with remittances.

Brain drain is a general risk for source countries, although the definitions of brain drain may differ. If one defines brain drain as highly skilled people being overrepresented among migrants who leave, there is very little evidence of brain drain in the EU except for specific periods in specific countries. If we use a wider definition and consider practically all outward mobility as brain drain (see e.g. Hasselbalch, 2017), then it becomes a major issue for contemporary Europe.

The way to measure risks is not so much through focusing on GDP per head but by looking at the sustainability of social security systems, since young people are usually overrepresented among the leavers, which affects the dependency ratio of the country. A weakening of the welfare state is also risked by the fact that health care belongs to the sectors where outward migration, even with small numbers, creates a big effect and can result in serious shortages.

Whether circularity works out at some point for typical source countries in the EU is something to be analysed and discussed. Strongly growing Poland has seen some return migration, proving that mobility is not necessarily a permanent phenomenon, and mobile workers come back with additional experience.

11.5.4   An EU Migrant Fund to Boost Integration

Reflections on EU mobility often arrive at new proposals. They can be of a legal or of a financial nature, and they have to take into account legislative developments of the recent years. As the past decade saw a high level of activity in the legislative field, more attention is paid today to the possibilities of budgetary instruments playing a role in intra-EU migration management. A widely discussed idea is that there should be a European fund to support migration (see e.g. Andor, 2015). This seems all the more relevant since, as results of recent research by Eurofound (Fóti, 2015) on the impact of mobility on public services revealed, integration costs and other problems arise mainly at a subnational level within local communities.

Municipalities may need more support to integrate the children of migrants or to prevent/deal with various social problems. Poorer migrants are not free riders in the welfare systems of the receiving countries. The point is not simply to spend more on poor migrants but to invest in ensuring that all working-age EU migrants can participate in economic activity. While, for example, homelessness did not emerge with EU enlargement in richer member states, it is true that migrants are overrepresented among the homeless and this is a common concern for EU member states. Some additional fiscal and institutional capacity would certainly improve the prospects for many of these migrants to remain in (or return to) decent employment.

In reality, there is an EU fund to support EU migration – the ESF (worth about 8 per cent of the EU budget) and the Commission have been actively encouraging member states to use the ESF for the purpose of easing integration into the labour market and society. When the current (2014–20) EU budget was drafted in 2011, the Commission did not propose a separate fund for managing migration, but such needs were not voiced at all (by the UK or any other country). It was also the case because the general philosophy has always been to keep the ESF as a universal fund whose main spending priorities can be defined by beneficiary countries and regions themselves.

On the other hand, there are examples of compartmentalisation within the ESF such as the Youth Employment Initiative, a €6 billion envelope created to support the introduction of the EU-wide Youth Guarantee. If member states want to have a migration fund, as many have advocated, then one could be created to support those communities that take in higher numbers of migrants. Interestingly, the MFF proposal submitted by the Juncker Commission did propose an increase in EU funding for migration, but it was primarily about a fund supporting migrants from non-EU countries. This reflected the fact that following the 2015 refugee crisis, the arrival of non-EU migrants, and refugees in particular, created a lot more anxiety and raised demands for adequate EU response, including through funding. For a variety of reasons, including robust GDP growth in the east, the momentum for the creation of an intra-EU migrant fund may have passed.

11.5.5   Fighting Poverty in Countries of Origin

Push factors like higher poverty rates, fewer jobs and inferior working conditions are often discussed when people contemplate ways to bring more fairness into mobility inside the EU. And this is not wrong, since these factors prevailing in countries of origin and affecting potential migration are not entirely exogenous in Europe. The EU should not restrict free movement, but should strive to reduce the number of people who want to migrate out of despair. The stronger the role professional ambition plays in migration (as opposed to economic and political ones), the greater the chance we have to improve both the quality of and satisfaction with mobility.

Indeed, more can be done to ensure that the EU financial instruments available for creating prosperity and opportunities in less developed regions are used better and more efficiently and thus reduce migration push factors. It is not only new member states where there are problems with the absorption of EU funds, though there are cases like Romania where neither the speed nor the quality of absorption have been encouraging. Hungary since 2010 displayed a masterclass of EU funds abuse. Better absorption of EU funds on the EU (and eurozone) periphery would certainly help create prosperity locally and reduce incentives for mobility, but that clearly requires different types of management and conditionalities within Cohesion Policy.

Those who make a close connection between the use of EU funds and migration often ask the whether the unused funds could be diverted to the countries of migrants' destination in order to help their integration there. However, it is better to avoid this by ensuring there is a more effective method for managing funds than under conventional shared management. Introducing elements of direct management to supplement, or even replace, shared management when needed, without taking away funds completely, is a possibility that has to be explored. And in order to tackle brain drain and depopulation risks, a stronger focus on social investment is needed in both programming and implementation.

11.6   Analysis of a Paradigmatic Case Study

11.6.1   Smoke and Mirrors around EU Mobility

A major debate around labour mobility took place in the UK which also contributed to the outcome of the June 2016 referendum about continued membership in the EU. There are, of course, many debates in Europe about free movement and various aspects of migration, but the UK debate has been by far the most vivid and politically most consequential. It has been a debate in which facts and feelings have been mixed, and economic, cultural and legal issues can combine in a most confusing way (Tilford, 2015).

A very important fact is that in the 1990s and 2000s the UK experienced an unprecedented growth of immigration. But another fact is that in practically every year immigration from non-EU countries exceeded immigration from EU member states. A third key fact is that, unlike the majority of EU member states, in 2004 the UK government decided against 'transitional arrangements' and opened up the UK labour market to employees from the ten new member states.

It did not matter much in domestic UK debates that the contribution of EU migrants to the British economy, and the welfare of British people in general, has been very significant. Various surveys showed (see e.g. Dustmann et al., 2008) that EU migrants were more likely to be in employment than the domestic population, and also significantly more so than non-EU migrants. While the adjective 'hard working' was often preserved for the indigenous population and EU migrants were called 'lazy' or 'scrounging' by various politicians and tabloid newspapers, this had very little evidence base.

The rise of an overly politicised and increasingly hostile discourse in the UK put a wedge between the government in London and the EU institutions, and the European Commission in particular, which challenged the UK over an infringement against the free movement of workers. Overcoming the widening divide was made harder by language, since in the UK the employment of workers from other EU countries is regularly discussed in the context of 'immigration'. This differs from the Brussels terminology, since it ignores the different legal base for entry and employment of EU and non-EU workers and conceals the incontrovertible evidence that the UK has consistently received more 'immigrants' from non-EU countries than from the EU.

In the first decade after the 2004 EU enlargement, many British people saw the number of Polish 'immigrants' living around them increasing. However, in the crisis years and the period preceding the referendum, the focus shifted to Romanian and Bulgarian citizens who tend to be poorer than the Poles. The government missed many opportunities to clarify that Romanian and Bulgarian citizens cannot be expected to arrive on a comparable scale to that of Poles. Discussing poor Romanian and Bulgarian migrants, often as alleged benefit tourists, became a kind of obsession, overlooking the fact that a rise in migration at the time of crisis was due to 'push factors' in the southern region of the eurozone.

11.6.2   Complaining about Free Movement, Fiddling with Benefits

The UK's new experience of high levels of immigration produced a government commitment to reduce the overall numbers coming in. Sharp but unrealistic reductions were promised by the new Prime Minister David Cameron in 2010. Such targets, however, would not have emerged without the increasing popularity of the UK Independence Party (UKIP), which created a link between anti-EU and anti-immigration sentiments and politics.

Given the unexpectedly high levels of (mainly Polish) immigration from Eastern Europe, and the importance of the free movement principle for the EU in general, UKIP managed to instrumentalise migration in order to serve their overall anti-EU campaign. On the other hand, instrumentalisation was not alien from the

Conservative Party either. By connecting Eastern European workers with economic or fiscal hardships, they also shifted attention to the fact that it was the government of Tony Blair (Labour Party) that opted against transitional arrangements (restrictions of up to seven years) in 2004, and also gave a wrong forecast about the expected inflows. This pressure has forced some recent or earlier leaders of the Labour Party to apologise for what in reality was more a forecasting error than a policy mistake.

While UKIP demanded direct controls, or a ceiling, over how many other EU citizens can work in the UK, Cameron's proposals (28 November 2014) focused instead on the conditions and circumstances of residence and employment. This more practical (rather than ideological) approach recognised the business case for labour immigration, but also that Germany and other countries would be highly unlikely to agree with arbitrary limits on EU labour mobility. Instead, new limitations on the benefits of EU workers were presented as a possible pragmatic way forward.

In fact, migrant workers already had fewer entitlements than UK citizens, but were now expected to accept further discrimination, for example that they would not get child benefit if their children did not live with them, despite paying the same taxes and social security contributions as indigenous workers. David Cameron's written demands[14] in November 2015 broadened the scope of renegotiation of British EU membership, but confirmed earlier discriminatory ideas like cancellation of in-work benefits for (non-UK) EU workers in the first four years of their employment in the UK.

11.6.3   Renegotiation and Referendum

The new UK effort at legalising discrimination was consistent with the government's official position on the posting of workers. The UK was reluctant to agree with a new directive put forward to improve enforcement of the existing EU safeguards against social dumping. However, it is easy to conclude that if workers from poorer regions are not treated equally – even if employed side by side with native employees – it is even harder to address concerns about either social cohesion or the so-called push factors that encourage many to leave their home region.

Though the philosophy of the 'Cameron package' was mainly about weakening the *pull* factors for migration, the UK could have done more to weaken the *push* factors. Unfortunately, the coalition was doing the opposite. Up to 2011, the UK government rightly spoke about the 'remorseless logic' of the eurozone's need to move towards fiscal union in order to exit the current crisis. Since then it has sided with a different argument in the European Council, focusing on 'competitiveness'

---

[14] After his re-election in 2015, David Cameron demanded concessions from the EU in order to campaign for continued EU membership.

and pushing for internal devaluation in deficit countries, thus contributing to recession and high unemployment – that, in turn, result in the recent rise of migration from south to north.

Together with three other countries (Germany, the Netherlands and Sweden), the UK was also behind the successful effort to cut the EU budget and, crucially, funding for a Cohesion Policy, which is the key instrument for creating economic activity and employment in the less developed EU countries and regions. That's an own goal in the migration debate and a factor that cannot be expected to soften the stance of eastern member states in the negotiations on UK membership.

The pre-referendum period in EU–UK relations was also overshadowed by an infringement procedure concerning the social rights of EU migrants in the UK. The Commission challenged the UK for applying a 'right to reside test' instead of the standard 'habitual residence test' to determine whether EU mobile workers are entitled to particular forms of social assistance and benefits. In its judgment[15] of 14 June 2016, the Court of Justice backed the United Kingdom all the way and rejected the Commission's appeal. The social rights of mobile workers were contradicted with the need to protect the finances of the host member state, and the second was given priority over the first. Consequently, the right to reside test can be applied for all social benefits, not only for social assistance.

According to Verschueren (2017),

> this judgment must be considered in the political context in which economically inactive Union citizens claiming solidarity in a host member state are often regarded as 'benefit tourists' who should not have access to the solidarity circle of this member state. It is probably not a coincidence that this judgement, in which the United Kingdom was a party, was passed in the week before the Brexit referendum of 23 June 2016. We now know that this referendum did not produce the result that the judges in Luxembourg probably had in mind.

GROUP DISCUSSION

- What are the benefits and risks associated with intra-EU labour mobility?
- How did the financial and economic crisis affect volumes and directions of mobility?

TOPICS FOR INDIVIDUAL RESEARCH

- Social dumping in the single market and the evolution of EU legislation.
- The contribution of migration controversies to the UK decision to leave the EU.

---

[15] The ECJ judgment, as in most cases, followed the spirit and argumentation of an earlier Opinion of the Advocate General, in this case Pedro Cruz Villalón from Spain.

FURTHER READINGS

Batsaikhan, U., Darvas, Z. and Raposo, I. C. (2018). 'People on the Move: Migration and Mobility in the European Union'. *Bruegel Blueprint Series*, 28. http://bruegel .org/2018/01/people-on-the-move-migration-and-mobility-in-the-european-union/.

Castles, S. and Miller, M. J. (2009). *The Age of Migration: International Population Movements in the Modern World*. Basingstoke: Palgrave Macmillan.

Dale, G. and Cole, M. (eds) (1999). *The European Union and Migrant Labour*. Oxford: Berg.

Eurofound (2014). *Labour Mobility in the EU: Recent Trends and Policies*. www .eurofound.europa.eu/publications/report/2014/eu-member-states/labour-market-social-policies/labour-mobility-in-the-eu-recent-trends-and-policies.

Portes, J. (2015). 'Labour Mobility in the European Union'. *Palgrave Dictionary of Economics*. Basingstoke: Palgrave Macmillan.

REFERENCES

Andor, L. (2015). 'A Fairer Deal on Free Movement'. Policy Network. www.policy-network.net/pno_detail.aspx?ID=4855&title=A+fairer+deal+on+free+movement.

Barslund, M. and Busse, M. (2016). 'Labour Mobility in the EU Addressing Challenges and Ensuring "Fair Mobility"'. CEPS Special Report, No. 139. www.ceps.eu/system/files/SR139%20MB%20and%20MB%20LabourMobility.pdf.

Dustmann, C., Glitz, A. and Frattini, T. (2008). 'The Labour Market Impact of Immigration'. *CReAM Discussion Paper Series*, CDP No 11/08. www.ucl.ac.uk/~uctpb21/doc/CDP_11_08.pdf.

European Commission (2016). 'Fairness at the Heart of Commission's Proposal to Update EU Rules on Social Security Coordination'. Press release, 13 December 2016, https://ec.europa.eu/commission/presscorner/detail/en/IP_16_4301 (accessed 3 February 2020).

Fernandes, S. (2018). 'What Is Our Ambition for the European Labour Authority?' Jacques Delors Institute, Policy Paper No 219. www.delorsinstitut.de/en/all-publications/what-ambition-for-the-european-labour-authority/.

Fóti, K. (2015). '"Welfare Tourism": An Unproven Case'. *Social Europe Journal*. www .socialeurope.eu/2015/12/welfare-tourism-unproven-case/.

Galgóczi, B., Watt, A. and Leschke, J. (2013). *EU Labour Migration since Enlargement*. Aldershot: Ashgate.

Hasselbalch, J. A. (2017). 'The European Politics of Brain Drain: A Fast-or Slow-Burning Crisis?'. CSGR Working Paper 285/17. https://warwick.ac.uk/fac/soc/pais/research/researchcentres/csgr/papers/285–17.pdf.

Kahanec, M. (2012). 'Labour Mobility in an Enlarged European Union'. IZA DP No. 6485. www.iza.org/MigrationHandbook/07_Kahanec_Labor%20Mobility%20in%20an%20Enlarged%20European%20Union.pdf.

Koehler, J., Laczko, F., Aghazarm, C. and Schad , J. (2010). *Migration and the Economic Crisis*. IOM. http://publications.iom.int/bookstore/free/Migration_and_the_Economic_Crisis.pdf.

Maslauskaite, K. (2013). *Social Competition in the EU: Myth and Realities*. Paris: Notre Europe.

Tilford, S. (2015). *Britain, Immigration and Brexit.* Centre for European Reform. www
.cer.org.uk/publications/archive/bulletin-article/2015/britain-immigration-and-brexit.

Verschueren, H. (2017). 'Recent Case Before the Court of Justice of the European Union'.
European Journal of Social Security, 19(1): 71–82.

Zimmermann, K. F. (2014). 'Circular Migration: Why Restricting Labor Mobility Can Be
Counterproductive'. IZA World of Labour series. http://wol.iza.org/articles/circular-
migration.pdf.

12 Managing the Refugee Crisis: A Divided and Restrictive Europe?

SARAH WOLFF

12.1 Introduction

Adopted by 152 countries on 19 December 2018, the Global Compact for Safe, Orderly and Regular Migration is the first meaningful attempt to organise global migration governance and to diminish the negative consequences of restrictive migration policies by calling explicitly for the creation of humanitarian visas and improved migration statistics and encouraging stakeholders and in particular states to respect migrants' rights. It also makes international cooperation between countries of origin, transit and destination a central pillar of a global strategy.

Surprisingly, while the compact stipulates that states are sovereign in determining their migration policies, several EU member states – under the leadership of conservative governments like Poland, populist governments like Italy, the authoritarian Viktor Orbán or Austrian chancellor Sebastian Kurz – have decided to abstain or to withdraw from the agreement. They argue that this new international non-binding agreement is creating a right to migration, in breach of their national sovereignty. Populism has managed to hijack an important instrument of multilateral cooperation, and through an active social media campaign online even led to the resignation of the then liberal Belgian Prime Minister Charles Michel, under pressure from the nationalist Flemish party in coalition.

Although the then Commission President Jean-Claude Juncker has criticised EU countries who withdraw from the pact, it is a major blow for European unity over migration and asylum policy, showing once more the deep lines of rupture among EU member states. It is within this context that this chapter reflects upon the policy context and institutional level playing field of the so-called 'migration crisis'. Starting in Section 12.2 with a historical overview, I argue that post-World War II Europe was a place of refuge and resettlement which until the 1970s had put in place generous migration regimes to rebuild its economy. Then, since the 1970s, power, national interests, sovereignty and economic benefits became key factors in explaining the current institutional setup (Section 12.3). This explains why, during and after the migration 'crisis', the EU has mostly resorted to strengthening agencies, while leaving a strong leadership to JHA bureaucrats who favour the status quo and letting divergences between EU member states become more acute (Section 12.4). Academically and politically controversies have focused on the issues of trust, politicisation and liberalisation of migration and asylum policies (Section 12.5). Our case study on the European Border and Coast Guard Agency (EBCG) exemplifies how the revision of the mandate of Frontex confirms the 'liberal paradox' with a quest by EU security actors for renewed legitimacy through a new humanitarian function of rescue at sea.

12.2   Historical Overview

Although Europe has been a continent of migration and mobility for centuries, the development of a migration and asylum policy at EU level is a relatively recent endeavour (see Box 12.1). Immediately after World War II, Europe was a place of refuge, mobility and resettlement. Devastated by the war, many European nationals such as Greeks or Italians emigrated outside Europe. The global refugee regime, which is based around the 1951 Geneva Convention, is also tightly linked to the end of the war in Europe, which led to the expulsion of 11.5 million Germans from Eastern Europe (Wasserstein, 2011). Many surviving Jews also left for Palestine. The predecessor of the International Organization for Migration (IOM) was created to help resettle migrants back in their countries.

Generous migration regimes were put in place to facilitate intra-European migration and attract third-country nationals through 'guest workers' systems. Rules were put in place to facilitate the freedom of movement of European workers and residents (see Chapter 11). Accordingly, Belgium, France, Italy, Luxembourg, the Netherlands and West Germany issued eight million working permits between 1958 and 1972 (Koikkalainen, 2011). While at first, guest workers wanted to go back to their home countries, many of them became permanent residents. The oil price crisis in the seventies put a halt to economic migration and guest workers programmes (Wolff and Hadj-Abdou, 2017). European immigration policies became more restrictive and family reunification is today one of the main legal channels of migration to Europe, representing two-fifths of all permanent flows in Europe (OECD, 2013). The development of an EU migration and asylum policy has thus been marked by this legacy with a commitment to international refugee law and the facilitation of intra-European workers' mobility, while restricting legal migration channels for third-country nationals.

BOX 12.1 Key dates

1951. The Treaty on the ECSC establishes a right to freedom of movement for workers in the industries of coal and steel.

1957. The Treaty of Rome extends that freedom of movement to all workers of the six founding fathers.

BOX 12.1 (Cont.)

1985. The Schengen Agreement is signed between Belgium, France, the then Federal Republic of Germany, Luxembourg and the Netherlands.

1990. The Schengen Convention implementing the agreement is signed among the same signatories in the village of Schengen in Luxembourg. Also the Dublin Convention is signed on 15 June 1990.

1992. The Treaty of Maastricht establishes the freedom of movement and residence for EU citizens.

1995. The Schengen Convention enters into force and is incorporated into EU law with the Treaty of Amsterdam in 1997.

1997. The Dublin Convention enters into force for Austria, Belgium, Denmark, France, Germany, Greece, Ireland, Italy, Luxembourg, the Netherlands, Portugal, Spain, Sweden and the UK.

2003. Adoption of the Dublin II regulation, Denmark has an opt-out.

2005. Frontex, the European Agency for the Management of Operational Cooperation at the External Borders, starts to work.

2008. Adoption of the Dublin III regulation.

The acceleration of the single market (see Chapter 8) and the 1992 programme was one of the main reasons for the creation of the JHA policy, which includes migration and asylum. The lifting of internal borders to facilitate freedom of movement in order to improve trade, business and people's mobility led to the conclusion of the Schengen Agreement in 1985,[1] seen as a 'compensatory measure' by ministers of the interior to fight jointly against cross-border crime (see Chapter 13). A common visa policy was decided as well as common rules on police and judicial cooperation. The strengthening of what is known as EU internal security and the Area of Freedom, Security and Justice (AFSJ) thus emerged out of a necessity to deepen economic cooperation. The Dublin Convention was adopted in 1991 to stop asylum shopping, a practice that enabled asylum seekers to apply in other European countries once their application had be rejected in one member state. The Convention endorsed the principle of the first country of entry, which stipulates that asylum seekers need to apply in the EU country where they entered first and where their fingerprints are stored in the Eurodac database, established in 2003.

---

[1] Initially signed amongst six countries, the Schengen Agreement has expanded to twenty-six countries. The UK, Ireland, Bulgaria and Romania are not part of it, while Norway, Iceland and Switzerland are signatory parties.

BOX 12.2 Key actors

The European Commission has the right of initiative on JHA. Directorate-General Home takes the lead on most of the dossiers, but DG European Neighbourhood Policy and Enlargement is also involved in negotiations with third countries.

The EEAS also deals with migration and asylum through EEAS delegations, but DG Home is in the lead in terms of agenda setting and in the conduct of negotiations with third countries.

The Council. Various Council working groups are involved such as the Strategic Committee on Immigration, Frontiers and Asylum, one of the key committees for examining issues of harmonisation of legal and illegal migration policy, visa and asylum before it goes for discussion at the level of Council of ministers. The Justice Affaires Intérieures-Relations Extérieures Working Party ensures the coordination between EU's external relations and JHA matters. Other relevant working party and groups involve the High-Level Working Group on Asylum Migration, the Asylum Working Party, the Visa Working Party and the Working Party on Schengen Matters.

The European Parliament and its Civil Liberties, Justice and Home Affairs European Parliament Committee play a key role in legislation on asylum, migration and border policies. Its Foreign Affairs Committee may also look into the external dimension of the policy. Next to co-deciding, the EP also has an important role in the assent procedure where the EP needs to give its green light on international agreements with JHA implications such as readmission agreements with third countries.

The EBCG agency, also known as Frontex, is in charge of coordinating joint operational cooperation of the European border guards and to assist member states at external borders. It can deploy rapid intervention teams, and it helps member states with the screening, debriefing, identification and fingerprinting of migrants. It also provides risk analysis on migratory flows.

Yet, since the mid-1980s, and in spite of progress in European integration, most of the regulation concerning migration and asylum has focused on strengthening border management with the creation of a European border agency (Frontex), also known as the EBCG. Rules to sanction irregular immigration with the Return Directive and the Carrier Sanctions Directive were adopted. Progress towards a common asylum policy have been cumbersome but have managed to lay the ground for minimum common conditions for reception, qualification directives, asylum procedures and temporary protection.

12.3   Main Features of the Current Institutional Framework

In spite of the establishment of a Common European Migration System and the expansion of supranational competences with the Lisbon Treaty, EU member states' governments, ministries, migration and border services have been very aptly adapting to the devolution of decision-making in the field of migration. This devolution involves 'decision making in monitoring and executive powers upward to intergovernmental fora, downward to elected local authorities, and outward to private actors such as airline carriers, shipping companies, employers, and private security agencies' (Guiraudon and Lahav, 2000: 164). EU member states have been able to devolve authority in a way that it 'meets their national policy goals' (Guiraudon and Lahav, 2000: 165). This is reflected in the institutional framework and the frequent turf wars opposing the European Council and the Council of the EU, the European Commission and the EP. Over the years and following a new intergovernmentalist reading of the migration crisis (Wolff, 2015), European heads of state have gained, under the presidency of Donald Tusk, a central role on crisis governance, and in particular on migration.

Between December 2014 and January 2017, migration has been the most discussed topic at the European Council (Drachenberg, 2018: 6), an institution that plays an increasingly central role. In 2018, clashes occurred between the newly elected populist Italian government and the rest of the member states. The Italian minister of the interior, Matteo Salvini, refused to disembark migrants from NGO boats, such as the *Aquarius* from SOS Méditerranée, and threated to stop paying Italy's contribution to the EU budget if his European counterparts would not share the 'burden' of hosting and processing asylum applications. President Tusk, in a letter of June 2018, made migration a central priority of his presidency, asking the European Council to set up regional disembarkation outside of Europe, and to increase EU funding to combat irregular migration (Council of the EU, 2018). Rotating presidencies have also paid a lot of attention to EU migration policy. Delivering results on migration has been a priority for leaders eager to show their efficiency in controlling migratory flows. Although with different objectives, migration and asylum remained a constant concern for older member states such as the 2016 Dutch presidency (Schout, 2017) and newer member states such as Slovakia or Malta. The 2018 Austrian presidency, headed by an extreme-right interior minister, also added migration to the core of its agenda but with the slogan a 'Europe that protects'.

Another key institutional player is the European Commission. Although the European Council and the Council have increasingly taken a strategic lead on migration and asylum, the presidency of Jean-Claude Juncker has attempted to put forward a common agenda. The 2015 Common Agenda on Migration led to the transformation of Frontex created in 2004, which became the EBCG (see Section 12.5), but also to the revision of the Schengen agreement and the Dublin Convention, and of the Community Code on Visas. In fact, in a context of debated decline of the European Commission (Bickerton et al., 2015), migration was one of the areas strategically used by President Juncker to place the Commission back on the political stage through agenda setting (Dinan, 2016: 103). In his 2018 State of the Union address, he announced the need to transform the European Asylum Support Office (EASO) into an EU Asylum Agency. He also proposed to substantially increase the means of the agency, offering to increase the budget from €321 million for the period 2019–20 to €1.25 billion for the period 2021–27 (European Commission, 2018b). Similarly, the EBCG was promised subsequent financial means and human resources. The reinforcement of these two non-executive agencies has been presented by the Commission for Migration, Home Affairs and Citizenship as the way to 'ensure EU solidarity on the ground at all times, in all situations, while fully respecting Member states' competences' (European Commission, 2018a). This renewed political activism of the Commission was, however, only made possible through the support of Germany and its willingness to have other EU member states 'sharing' refugees, after it welcomed more than a million refugees in 2015 (Dinan, 2016: 108).

BOX 12.3 Key concepts

Relocation. Under the leadership of the European Commission, the Council decided on 14 December 2015 to relocate 40,000 refugees from Greece and Italy to other EU member states. Relocation is defined as 'a distribution among member states of persons in clear need of international protection' (European Commission, 2015). A decision of 22 December 2015 added 120,000 people. In total, 160,000 refugees were supposed to be relocated, 39,600 from Italy and 66,400 from Greece. As of 7 March 2018, only 29,314 refugees had been resettled. Surprisingly some associated countries like Norway have welcomed 3,500 refugees (European Commission, 2018a). Bulgaria, Cyprus, Hungary, Slovakia, Slovenia or Poland instead refused this mechanism, revealing a deep rupture over the concept of 'burden sharing'. Sweden and Austria asked for a temporary suspension of their obligations invoking a high influx.

Resettlement. Resettlement programmes are an old instrument, pioneered by Sweden originally in 1950 and popularised in the 1970s. Since 2005, it has been introduced with the Regional Protection Programs established in Eastern Europe, the African Great Lake Region and currently implemented in the Horn of Africa and North Africa (Egypt, Libya and Tunisia) (European Resettlement Network, nd). The Commission announced its ambition to create an 'EU resettlement'

BOX 12.3 (Cont.)

framework 'with a unified procedure and common criteria' and has also encouraged EU member states to resettle refugees under private schemes. Resettlement is defined as 'the transfer of individual displaced persons in clear need of international protection, on submission of the United Nations High Commissioner for Refugees and in agreement with the country of resettlement, from a third country to a member state, where they will be admitted and granted the right to stay and any other rights comparable to those granted to a beneficiary of international protection' (European Commission, 2015). Yet civil society has raised concerns regarding the potential use of this EU instrument to increase migration control and deter irregular arrival. According to the European Council for Refugees in Europe, 'this runs counter to the long-standing function of resettlement as a life-saving and protection tool for the world's most vulnerable' (ECRE, 2016). Other concerns of the proposal are that it could exclude 'many categories of refugees in need of resettlement, including vulnerable cases and those with no other solution in sight' (ECRE, 2016).

The EP has become an important player in the area of migration, asylum and border policies. The extension of the ordinary legislative procedure to most of these areas, including legal migration after the Treaty of Lisbon, has extended its competences. Overall, the EP is perceived as playing an increasingly 'pivotal leadership role in transforming the character of representative democracy at EU level' (Shackleton, 2017: 191). Analysis of the roll call votes has shown that 2014 was a critical juncture in terms of how MEPs voted on legislation with a change of the 'policy space'. Yet 'attitudes towards migration are [still] strongly [defined] along the left–right dimension' (Hix et al., 2018: 16). Policy developments seem to have remained isolated from the growing politicisation by anti-immigrants and populist movements of the crisis (see Box 12.4). At the same time, the EP has not necessarily played the role of 'liberalising' agent in defence of migrants' rights that it claims to play. MEPs have been eager to show their electorates they are efficient legislators and to respond to the concerns of controlling migration.

These institutional actors all play an important role in EU migration and asylum policy as a level playing field. Since 2015 the institutional framework has become quite different from the 1999 Tampere Council that strategically set out the objective to create an AFSJ, where common policies were still understood in supranational undertakings (Council of the EU, 1999). Between the 1999 Tampere programme and the 2009 adoption of the Lisbon Treaty – which put an end to the pillar structure and extended the ordinary legislative procedure to a significant number of migration and asylum policies, as well as QMV in the Council – the legislative pace went rather fast in the area of migration and asylum. The 2004 The Hague and the 2009 Stockholm Programs led to multiple policy initiatives. In the field of asylum the first phase of the Common European Asylum System 1999–2004 saw the adoption of the Qualification Directive, the Reception Conditions Directive and the Asylum Procedures Directive. All these directives were recast after the Lisbon Treaty and most of them entered into force just two years before the crisis, including the Eurodac regulation and the Dublin III regulation. This meant that when the crisis erupted in mid-July 2015, some of that legislation had just been transposed into national law. Yet, in spite of common directives, the leeway granted to EU member states is still important. A study of the EP thus concluded that 'the CEAS [Common European Asylum System] is not "common", in the sense of one EU-wide asylum system, nor has it developed into a single "system" used in each EU MS. On the contrary, the Common European Asylum System still consists of twenty-seven different asylum systems, with different actors responsible, different procedures and different results (e.g. recognition rates)' (Wagner et al., 2016: 8). Thus, there is ample evidence that the Temporary Protection Directive 2005/55/EC adopted in the aftermath of the 1999 Kosovo refugee crisis is 'commonly ignored' by EU member states.

BOX 12.4 Legal basis

The Dublin Convention. Enforced originally on 1 September 1997, the latest recast of the Dublin III Regulation 604/2013 applies to all EU member states, including the UK but not Denmark. Norway, Switzerland, Liechtenstein and Iceland also apply Dublin III.

According to the principle of the country of first entry, asylum seekers apply for asylum in the EU member state where they entered first. During the 2015 crisis, it put a disproportionate burden on Italy and Greece, who found the system unfair as they did not have the capacity to face the surge of applications. The system is also unfair as asylum seekers cannot choose freely in which country they can apply for asylum. The ECJ and the European Court of Human Rights have issued case law asking EU member states to suspend their transfers to the country of first entry. In the 2011 *M.S.S. vs. Belgium and Greece*, the European Court of Human Rights condemned Greece following problematic conditions of detention for asylum seekers. Belgium suspended transferring asylum seekers to Greece. Similar jurisprudence from national courts happened in Austria, France, Hungary, Italy and Romania (European Parliament, 2012).

> **BOX 12.4 (Cont.)**
>
> A 2016 Commission 'Communication towards a reform of the CEAS and enhancing legal avenues to Europe' proposes an 'automatic fairness mechanism' which could be triggered once an EU member state has an excess by 150 per cent of its asylum applications. A reference key will help to identify if a member state is under pressure, and is likely to be implemented by the European Asylum Agency.

Legal migration only became an area for the ordinary legislative procedure and QMV in the Council after the Lisbon Treaty. Article 79 (5) of the Treaty on the Functioning of the EU stipulates that EU member states have the right 'to determine volumes of admission of third-country nationals coming from third countries to their territory in order to seek work, whether employed or self-employed'. In the 2015 European Agenda on Migration most of the measures concentrate on irregular migration, border control and asylum, relegating legal migration to the bottom of the list of EU priorities. The main policy development is the revision of the Blue Card Directive (Directive 2009/50/EC), which was adopted before the Lisbon Treaty but under unanimity, and only in consultation with the EP, leading to a directive that only focuses on the minimal common denominator. Modelled on the US Green Card to attract high-skilled migrants, it is deemed 'insufficiently attractive and underused' by EU member states. Thus, in 2013 Germany delivered 93 per cent of the Blue Card directives in the EU (European Commission, 2014a), confirming the wide disparities among EU member states. Future employees also need to have a contract signed and that his/her salary threshold should nominally be 1.5 times higher than the average of the gross annual salary (Article 5.3 of the directive). The Blue Card also competes with national systems such as the Dutch High Skilled Migrant Program, which has been much better promoted over the Blue Card (Prpic, 2017: 3). Other key legal migration directives include the Single Permit Directive (2011/98/EU), which harmonises residence and work permit application procedures for third-country nationals, and Directive 2014/36/EU regarding seasonal workers, Directive 2014/66/EU for intra-corporate transfers, and Directive 2016/801 on the conditions of entry and residence of third-country nationals for the purposes of research, studies, training, voluntary service, pupil exchange schemes or educational projects and au pairing.

Given the salience of migration in the EU, integration of third-country nationals (TCNs) is an area that should be prioritised but again meets severe constraints. EU institutions highlighted this challenge in the 2014 Common Basic Principles for

Immigrant Integration Policy and the 2016 Integration Action Plan (Council of the EU, 2014; European Commission, 2016). In spite of these efforts and the implementation of the European Integration Fund, today most TCNs have difficulties in accessing decent employment, while children are at particularly high risk of poverty. The Commission unequivocally states that 'there is a clear risk that the cost of non-integration will turn out to be higher than the costs of investment in integration policies' (European Commission, 2016: 4). In 2015, 37 per cent of them had low education, 49 per cent of them were at risk of poverty or social exclusion and their employment rate was only around 56.5 per cent, partly due to the financial and economic crisis (MIPEX, 2015).

Finally, since the beginning of the 2000s the EU has developed an external dimension to its asylum and migration policies, which involves cooperation with third countries. This policy expansion beyond EU borders is seen as the development of an external governance of EU policies (Lavenex and Wichmann, 2009), as well as further securitisation. Overall this has led to the strengthening of the EU's internal security with the inclusion of JHA cooperation in all the European Neighborhood Policy action plans, and of clauses regarding issues such as counter-terrorism in association agreements with Mediterranean countries for instance (Wolff, 2009). The 2005 Global Approach to Migration and Mobility, revised in 2011, is the main policy framework for the external dimension. It is interesting to note that until 2011 asylum was not an external priority. In the field of asylum, Regional Protection Programmes enhance the capacity of third countries to protect refugees through repatriation, local integration or resettlement.

The Global Approach to Migration and Mobility sets the framework for a wide range of dialogues over visa liberalisation action plans, mobility partnerships and readmission agreements. Next to bilateral dialogue with third countries, regional dialogues are also prominent. The Prague Process, for instance, focuses on cooperation between the EU and nineteen eastern partners including Russia. The Eastern Partnership Panel on migration and asylum focuses on cooperation with Armenia, Azerbaijan, Belarus, Georgia, Moldova and Ukraine while the Budapest Process, initiated in 1991, involves more than fifty countries including Eastern Partnership countries, Western Balkans, Central Asia, Afghanistan, Iraq, Russia, Pakistan and Turkey. The EU has also been involved in the Africa-EU Migration, Mobility and Employment Partnership since 2007. The Rabat Process, under the leadership of Morocco, was launched in 2006 at the occasion of the first Euro-African Ministerial Conference on Migration and Development. There is also a dialogue with Latin America and the Caribbean via a Structured and Comprehensive Dialogue and Migration launched in 2009. Although these regional dialogues enable high-level policy dialogue, 'operational results are more mixed' and EU member states are not necessarily sufficiently engaged (European Commission, 2014b: 13–14).

12.4   Recent Policy Developments

This section analyses the policy developments prompted by the so-called 2015 crisis. From an outsider perspective, the EU has appeared as a weak actor in the crisis, unable to stop migration for some, unable to rescue and provide decent conditions to migrants and refugees for others. In spite of years of European integration, it has failed to bring more 'successful problem-solving' (Börzel, 2018: 477). Overall the 'crisis' policy development story is one of continuity with past patterns of policy-making. Three policy trends can be identified: agencification, a leadership of JHA bureaucrats who favour the status quo and strong divergences between EU member states.

First, the EU has decided to continue with the same good old recipe of delegating expertise to (new) agencies. One of the most prominent pieces of legislation that was adopted very swiftly was the transformation of Frontex into the EBCG agency (Section 12.6). Similarly, the EASO, created in 2010 and based in Malta to support member states with asylum applications in particular in Greece and Italy, should become a European Asylum Agency. Faced with constraints in deploying experts, in hotspots for instance, and its inability for the moment to grant international protection status to applicants directly, EASO has been considered too weak and requiring more extensive powers. The draft regulation proposes to extend its competences with third countries and that EU member states would have a duty to cooperate and to exchange information (European Commission, 2016). EASO could deploy an asylum intervention pool of at least 500 experts which member states would be obliged to put at the disposal of the agency. The budget and the staff resources would also increase considerably. One of the main problems with the extensive delegation to agencies is that they are non-majoritarian agencies whose legitimacy is under question (Wolff and Schout, 2013). The choice of agencies as policy instruments over other options (i.e. a network) is not neutral. Although they are framed as credible actors and experts, better able to solve the tensions around Dublin, as preconised by the principal–agent theory, their ability to coerce member states to ask for their intervention might in fact be detrimental to building trust in the Dublin and Schengen systems. These agencies are perceived by weaker member states, which are more exposed to migratory flows but with low capacities, to act as proxies of stronger member states (Ripoll Servent, 2018). In addition, the agencification of EU migration and asylum policies also participates to a process of depoliticisation of highly salient issues (Wolff, 2015) which with the crisis has undergone a strong backlash.

Second, the policy trend is that of a reinforced JHA monopoly over the definition and direction of EU migration and asylum policy. While I do not find securitisation theories particularly helpful, it is difficult to see how migration during the crisis has been addressed outside of a security lens. Arguments about the social and economic added value of refugees and migrants, and demographic and skills' labour challenges, have been almost nonexistent among EU policy makers. Too rarely, scholars show that European migration policies are socially classed with discourses on the selection of migrants and their skills, but also their integration and ethnicity (Bonjour and Chauvin, 2018). Instead, the crisis has strengthened the bureaucratic monopoly of JHA practitioners. This idea is not new since intensive transgovernmentalism (Lavenex and Wallace, 2005) has led law enforcement agents and interior and justice ministries' bureaucrats to bypass national constraints through the EU as a new venue for influence. During the crisis, street-level bureaucrats have continued with 'business as usual' and the status quo in favour of restrictive policies and border control has prevailed. The crisis is more an example of policy 'inertia' with little if 'any reorientation of policy goals or means' (Guiraudon, 2017: 150). Far from agreeing with those who see strong supranational trends (Niemann and Speyer, 2018), I concur that the 'transnational field of EU border security' is definitely one where its 'stakeholders resist change' (Guiraudon, 2017: 151). Even where new actors have joined the 'circle', the monopoly of JHA actors is not contested. These include diplomatic actors (foreign affairs ministries and the EEAS), but also private actors in charge of border security, including biometrics, or managing detention centres.

Finally, strong divergences between EU member states, in particular between eastern and western states, have worsened. Distrust among EU member states, and vis-à-vis existing instruments, has increased. Internal border controls were reintroduced in Autumn 2015 at the German-Austrian border, but also by Slovenia, Sweden and Norway (see Chapter 13). Hungary, which saw the arrival of 350,000 refugees in the summer of 2015, developed strategies to stop migrants and to return them. A fence was constructed along the border with Serbia and Croatia, and the border with Croatia was closed down (Kallius et al., 2016: 27). The Dublin Convention, as explained in Box 12.4, rapidly got into in trouble. Italy and Greece decided to renounce to their legal responsibilities under the Convention and to let through migrants to other EU member states. The main initiatives tabled during the crisis by the European Commission, such as the relocation system (see Box 12.3), were never as far reaching as the ones made during the eurozone crisis (Biermann et al., 2017). The measures proposed by the Commission were a drop in an ocean and therefore one may even question the political leadership in the first place regarding the measures tabled during the migration crisis. In spite of President Juncker's initiatives, the Commission is not hard wired anymore for more integration, giving some credit to the new liberal intergovernmentalist thesis (Wolff, 2015).

12.5   Current Political and Academic Controversies

Controversies in political and academic circles have centred on three main issues: trust, politicisation and liberalisation. First, while some had already identified 'little evidence for inter-state solidarity in the EU' (Thielemann, 2003: 253) and that a norm-based understanding of burden sharing provided a more compelling explanation, the Dublin system has mainly served interstate cooperation and instead shifted 'responsibility for the examination of asylum claims to member states situated at the EU external border' (Mitsilegas, 2014: 184). Because the system organises the transfer of individual asylum seekers between EU member states, this requires a 'high level of mutual trust' between European asylum systems that should entail similar conditions and the respect of fundamental rights (Mitsilegas, 2014: 190).

Another aspect of the crisis is that after years of depoliticising integration of asylum and migration policies by devolving its management to JHA experts and agencies, EU migration and asylum policies have become highly politicised. Politicisation is defined holistically as 'contestation within the political system; within society; and within a media that communicated between views in society and between society and the political system' (De Wilde and Lord, 2016: 149). This politicisation is taking place between the political forces that denounce the European policy of migration and has taken different forms across Europe. In Central and Eastern Europe, for instance, the refugee crisis has been fuelling 'defensive nationalism', which Kriesi defines as 'asserting itself against internal enemies (such as ethnic minorities, including Roma and Jews) and external ones (such as foreign corporations colonizing the national economy)' (Kriesi, 2018: 38). In Western Europe, this would rather be associated with a process of 'denationalisation' particularly felt as a result of globalisation and those who are losing out from global economic integration (Kriesi, 2018: 37). Combined the east/west divisions, and to some extent north/south too, political leaders have adopted reactive or status quo policies.

Anti-immigrant narratives that are central to Eurosceptical and populist parties have contributed to this politicisation. Europe and the migration crisis have provided these parties with transnational venues to join up forces beyond national borders. Thus, we have seen anti-immigrant movements mobilising transnationally although not always successfully. This is, for instance, the case with Patriotic Europeans Against the Islamisation of the Occident, the extreme-right movement that originated in Germany and has been active in Austria, Norway, Sweden and Switzerland. On the other hand, pro-immigrant movements have also shown transnational solidarity across borders to provide assistance to refugees such as across the UK/French border (Help Refugees/Auberge des migrants) or in the Alps between France and Italy. SOS Méditerranée is saving lives with multinational teams. The refugee crisis, in a way, has enabled a certain politicisation of the EU that has impacted 'Europeanised national public spheres' (De Wilde and Lord, 2016: 148).

In political circles, compliance with EU law is also contested by an increasing number of actors at national level (Börzel, 2018: 481): 'non-compliance then becomes a way for member states to dodge adjustment costs, which regulatory policy, such as [the relocation system] shifts to the implementation at the domestic level rather than addressing them at the decision-making stage at EU level (Majone, 1997)' (Börzel, 2018: 481). Instead, we observe tendencies among member states to circumvent and suspend existing rules, such as in the relocation scheme, the Dublin Convention or the reinstatement of border controls within the Schengen area (Biermann et al., 2017: 2).

Last but not least, an important controversy that defines the academic debate is whether the refugee crisis is symptomatic of a restrictive migration policy trend. Many scholars agree that the 'European migration regime' is mostly targeting the control of irregular migration (Hampshire, 2016: 539), and that like at state level, a lot of attention is devoted to controlling borders and externalising migration control to the EU's external partners. The Determinants of International Migration Database found that even though it is possible to identify an overall historical trend towards the liberalisation of rights of migrants and refugees once they are in the country of destination, the trend is towards increasingly restrictive border controls (De Haas et al., 2018). Based on a database of 6,500 policy changes in forty-five countries, the DEMIG Policy team has shown that overall liberalisation of policy outnumbers restrictions. However, it varies across policy areas and migrant categories: 'entry and integration policies are less restrictive' but 'border control and exit policies have become more restrictive' (De Haas et al., 2018). They conclude that border controls and laws have become more restrictive, even if other policies regarding family migrants, high-skilled and low-skilled migrants as well as refugees and asylum seekers have become more liberal. This is a global paradox of increased border controls in a mobile world.

12.6   Analysis of a Paradigmatic Case Study: The EBCG

One of the most paradigmatic case studies of the migration crisis is the way in which EU actors have developed a new discourse regarding rescue at sea and the rapid adoption of the regulation on the new mandate of Frontex, the EBCG (European Commission, 2016). This case study evidences several paradoxes discussed earlier in the chapter: the choice of depoliticised instruments to respond to the crisis while framing their functions from a humanitarian perspective that brings a renewed legitimacy, based on more liberal commitment of EU migration and asylum policies.

The picture of Danish police officers playing a game with a young Syrian refugee girl at the German-Danish border[2] has been diffused worldwide and illustrates how European border guards are being framed as new humanitarian actors: they save lives. The new humanitarian discourse is being 'used for framing and giving meaning to institutional and operational practices' (Pallister-Wilkins, 2015: 53). This stands in stark contrast to reports of police and border guards' violence denounced by NGOs. In 2015, in Macedonia, a candidate country to EU accession, Human Rights Watch reported abuse by Macedonian officials, which involved physical beatings and the systematic detention until July 2015 of asylum seekers and migrants 'including children and pregnant women' in the Gazi Baba detention facility (Human Rights Watch, 2015).

In the light of the rising number of deaths in the Mediterranean Sea, which peaked at 3,771 during 2015 (IOM, 2015), and the criticisms addressed by UN Special Rapporteur on Human Rights François Crépeau, or even Pope Francis, Jean-Claude Juncker proposed to transform Frontex into the EBCG. The new mandate of the agency was adopted in less than nine months by the EP and the Council, which wanted to adopt this symbolic piece of legislation quickly. The main concern was to provide the agency with the ability to rescue people at sea, which was not initially in its mandate. In addition, the agency was highly dependent on EU member states, and had difficulties buying its own equipment for instance (although allowed since 2011) (Wolff and Schout, 2013). Existing mechanisms to cope with a sudden influx of migrants such as the Rapid Border Intervention Teams (RABITs) could have been used. These teams can be deployed on the request of a member state within five days upon receiving the request, which leads to an operational plan drafted by Frontex. But RABITs have in fact only been deployed once on the Greek-Turkish border in 2010, demonstrating the limitation of deploying common teams acting under a single command (European Parliament and Council, 2007).

The new mandate (Regulation 2016/1624) has expanded the agency competences with a sort of RABIT-plus and the possibility that a 'member state may request that the Agency launches joint operations to face upcoming challenges, including illegal immigration, present or future threats at its external borders or cross-border crime, or to provide increased technical and operational assistance when implementing its obligations with regard to the control of the external border' (Article

---

[2] www.huffingtonpost.com/entry/danish-police-officer-syrian-refugee_us_55f8d9d3e4b0b48f67013caf.

15), which has somehow given rise to the hotspots approach. The agency can also process personal data (Article 46), which is balanced by more safeguards regarding fundamental rights. The agency has expanded slightly its 'right to intervene' as it can 'carry out a vulnerability assessment including the assessment of the capacity and readiness of member states to face threats and challenges at the external borders' (Article 8). Many have deplored the fact that this reform is in fact limited and 'falls short of establishing a [Union] professional culture in border control cooperation', that it focuses mostly on return and that it does not for instance establish an independent complaint mechanism, outside of the fundamental rights officer which sits in the agency (Carrera and Den Hertog, 2016).

Paradoxically, the saving lives narratives contrast with the practice of the hotspot approach developed since 2015 at the southern peripheries of the EU. In Lampedusa, Pozzallo, Taranto and Trapani in Italy, but also on the islands of Chios, Kos, Lesvos, Leros and Samos in Greece, the EU has organised a reinforced and concerted effort of EU agencies to identify, select and standardise the selection of refugees (Tazzioli, 2017: 2). This policy development is contested by asylum seekers who 'refuse to comply with the restrictive conditions established by EU asylum and migration policies, enacting and claiming freedom of choice' (Tazzioli, 2017: 3).

The 'paradox of the liberal state' has become a true reality for the EU. Although the EU would, through a traditional neo-functionalist logic, encourage free trade and the mobility of people, as well as respond to its normative commitments such as the commitment not to send refugees back to countries where their lives are at risk (principle of non-refoulement of the 1951 Geneva Convention), the EU also sees migration as a political risk (Hollifield, 2004: 886). The EU, at supranational level, prioritises its own internal security and the economic well-being of its citizenry (Hollified, 2004: 886). Although EU member states remain the main gatekeepers, we see that EU institutions are not necessarily upholding this liberal paradox against restrictive member states, and that EU migration and asylum policies present both liberal and restrictive features. The rise of populist movements, however, is a real danger for the direction that migration and asylum policies may take in the future.

GROUP DISCUSSION

- Are EU migration and asylum policies liberal or restrictive?
- Who leads the agenda on EU migration and asylum policies?

TOPICS FOR INDIVIDUAL RESEARCH

- Research the EU position during the negotiations on the Global Compact for Migration and explain why the EU did not manage to maintain a united front.

- Research to what extent the Mediterranean Sea has become a contested humanitarian space for NGOs and European border guards.

FURTHER READINGS

Bauböck, R. (2018). 'Refugee Protection and Burden-Sharing in the European Union'. *Journal of Common Market Studies*, 56(1): 141–56.

Lavenex, S. (2018). '"Failing Forward" Towards Which Europe? Organized Hypocrisy in the Common European Asylum System'. *Journal of Common Market Studies*, (56)5: 1195–212.

Natter, K. (2018). 'Rethinking Immigration Policy Theory Beyond "Western Liberal Democracies"'. *Comparative Migration Studies*, 6(1): 4.

Tazzioli, M. (2014). *Spaces of Governmentality*. London: Rowman & Littlefield International.

Van Ballegooij, W. and Navarra, C. (2018). *The Cost of Non Europe in Asylum Policy*. European Parliamentary Research Service. www.europarl.europa.eu/RegData/etudes/STUD/2018/627117/EPRS_STU(2018)627117_EN.pdf.

REFERENCES

Bickerton, C., Hodson, D. and Puetter, U. (2015). *The New Intergovernmentalism: States and Supranational Actors in the Post-Maastricht Era*. Oxford: Oxford University Press.

Biermann, F., Guérin, N., Jagdhuber, S., Rittberger, B. and Weiss, M. (2017). 'Political (Non)-reform in the Euro Crisis and the Refugee Crisis: A Liberal Intergovernmentalist Explanation'. *Journal of European Public Policy*, 26(2): 246–66.

Bonjour, S. and Chauvin, S. (2018). 'Social Class, Migration Policy and Migrant Strategies: An Introduction'. *International Migration*, 56(4): 5–18.

Börzel, T. A. (2018). 'Researching the EU (Studies) into Demise?'. *Journal of European Public Policy*, 25(3): 475–85.

Carrera, S. and Den Hertog, L. (2016). 'A European Border and Coast Guard: What's in a Name?'. CEPS Paper in Liberty and Security in Europe No. 88, CEPS, Brussels.

Council of the EU (1999). 'Tampere European Council 15 and 16 October 1999 Presidency Conclusion'. www.europarl.europa.eu/summits/tam_en.htm (accessed on October 2018).

Council of the EU (2014). *Council Conclusions of the Council and the Representatives of the Governments of the Member States on the Integration of Third-country Nationals Legally Residing in the EU*. JHA Council meeting Luxembourg, 5 and 6 June 2014.

Council of the EU (2018). *Invitation Letter by President Donald Tusk to the Members of the European Council Ahead of Their Meetings on 28 and 29 June 2018*. Press Release 409/18.

De Haas, H., Natter, K. and Vezzoli, S. (2018). 'Growing Restrictiveness or Changing Selection? The Nature and Evolution of Migration Policies'. *The International Migration Review*, 52(2): 324–67.

De Wilde, P. and Lord, C. (2016). 'Assessing Actually Existing Trajectories of EU Politicisation'. *West European Politics*, 39(1): 145–63.

Dinan, D. (2016). 'Governance and Institutions: A More Political Commission'. *Journal of Common Market Studies*, 54, Annual Review: 101–16.

Drachenberg, R. (2018). *European Council: Facts and Figures*. European Parliament, July 2018. www.europarl.europa.eu/RegData/etudes/BRIE/2018/625119/EPRS_BRI(2018)625119_EN.pdf (accessed 3 September 2018).

ECRE (2016). 'Untying the EU Resettlement Framework: ECRE's Recommendations on Breaking the Link with Migration Control and Preserving the Humanitarian Focus of Resettlement'. www.ecre.org/wp-content/uploads/2017/07/Policy-Note-06.pdf. (accessed 1 November 2018).

European Commission (2014a). *Communication from the Commission to the European Parliament and the Council on the Implementation of Directive 2009/50/EC on the Conditions of Entry and Residence of Third-country Nationals for the Purpose of Highly Qualified Employment ('EU Blue Card')*. Brussels, 22 May 2014, COM(2014) 287.

European Commission (2014b). 'Report on the Implementation of the Global Approach to Migration and Mobility 2012–2013'. Brussels, 21 February 2014, COM(2014) 96.

European Commission (2015). 'European Agenda for Migration. Annex. European Schemes for Relocation and Resettlement'. https://ec.europa.eu/home-affairs/sites/homeaffairs/files/what-we-do/policies/european-agenda-migration/background-information/docs/communication_on_the_european_agenda_on_migration_annex_en.pdf (accessed 1 November 2018).

European Commission (2016). 'Proposal for a Regulation of the European Parliament and of the Council on the European Union Agency for Asylum and Repealing Regulation (EU) No 439/2010'. COM/2016/0271 final – 2016/0131 (COD).

European Commission (2018a). 'Annex to the Communication from the Commission'. Progress report on the implementation of the European Agenda on Migration, Brussels, 14 March 2018. COM(2018) 250.

European Commission (2018b). 'State of the Union 2018: Commission Proposes Last Elements Needed for Compromise on Migration and Border Reform'. Press Release, Strasbourg, 12 September 2018.

European Court of Human Rights (2011). *M.S.S. vs. Belgium and Greece*, 21 January 2011.

European Parliament (2012). *Transfer of Asylum-seekers and Fundamental Rights*. Brussels: Library Briefing, 30 November 2012.

European Parliament and Council (2016). *Regulation 2016/1624 of 14 September \2016 on the European Border and Coast Guard and Amending Regulation (EU) 2016/399 of the European Parliament and of the Council and Repealing Regulation (EC) No 863/2007 of the European Parliament and of the Council, Council Regulation (EC) No 2007/2004 and Council Decision 2005/267/EC*. OJ L 251, 16 September 2016.

European Parliament and Council (2007). *Regulation (EC) No 863/2007 of 11 July 2007 Establishing a Mechanism for the Creation of Rapid Border Intervention Teams and Amending Council Regulation (EC) No 2007/2004 as Regards that Mechanism and Regulating the Tasks and Powers of Guest Officers*. OJ L 199, 31 July 2007: 30–9.

European Resettlement Network (nd). 'Resetlement in Europe'. www.resettlement.eu/page/resettlement-in-europe (accessed 3 February 2020).

Guiraudon, V. (2017). 'The 2015 Refugee Crisis Was Not a Turning Point: Explaining Policy Inertia in EU Border Control'. *European Political Science*, 17(1): 151–60.

Guiraudon, V. and Lahav, G. (2000). 'A Reappraisal of the State Sovereignty Debate: The Case of Migration Control'. *Comparative Political Studies*, 33(2), 163–95.

Hampshire, J. (2016). 'European Migration Governance Since the Lisbon Treaty: Introduction to the Special Issue'. *Journal of Ethnic and Migration Studies*, 42(4): 537–53.

Hix, S., Noury, A. and Roland, G. (2018). 'Changing Political Cleavages in Advanced Democracies: Evidence from the European Parliament'. IPSA. https://wc2018.ipsa.org/sites/default/files/ipsa-events/wc2018/papers/paper-103050-2018-07-05t060414-0400.pdf.

Hollifield, J. F. (2004). 'The Emerging Migration State'. *International Migration Review*, 38(3): 885–912.

Human Rights Watch (2015). 'As Though We Are Not Human Beings: Police Brutality against Migrants and Asylum Seekers in Macedonia'. www.hrw.org/report/2015/09/21/though-we-are-not-human-beings/police-brutality-against-migrants-and-asylum (accessed 3 February 2020).

IOM (2015). 'IOM Counts 3,771 Migrant Fatalities in Mediterranean in 2015'. www.iom.int/news/iom-counts-3771-migrant-fatalities-mediterranean-2015 (Accessed 2 November 2018).

Kallius, A., Monterescu, D. and Rajaram, P. K. (2016). 'Immobilizing Mobility: Border Ethnography, Illiberal Democracy, and the Politics of the "Refugee Crisis" in Hungary'. *American Ethnologist*, 43(1): 25–37.

Koikkalainen, S. (2011). 'Free Movement in Europe: Past and Present'. Migration Policy Institute. www.migrationpolicy.org/article/free-movement-europe-past-and-present/ (accessed 29 August 2018)

Kriesi, H. (2018). 'The Politicization of European Integration'. *Journal of Common Market Studies*, 54: 32–47.

Lavenex, S. and Wallace, W. (2005). 'Justice and Home Affairs'. In H. Wallace and W. Wallace (eds), *Policy-making in the European Union*. Oxford: Oxford University Press.

Lavenex, S. and Wichmann, N. (2009). 'The External Governance of EU Internal Security'. *European Integration*, 31(1): 83-102.

Majone, G. (1997). 'From the Positive to the Regulatory State: Causes and Consequences of Changes in the Mode of Governance'. *Journal of Public Policy*, 17(2): 139–67.

MIPEX. (2015). 'Migrant Integration Policy Index 2015'. http://mipex.eu/what-is-mipex (accessed 1 August 2017).

Mitsilegas, V. (2014). 'Solidarity and Trust in the Common European Asylum System'. *Comparative Migration Studies*, 2(2): 181–202.

Niemann, A. and Speyer, J. (2018). 'A Neofunctionalist Perspective on the "European Refugee Crisis": The Case of the European Border and Coast Guard'. *Journal of Common Market Studies*, 56(1): 23–43.

OECD (2013). 'Global Trends in Family Migration in the OECD'. Presentation by Johan Chaloff. www.oecd.org/els/mig/Chaloff.pdf (accessed 31 August 2018).

Pallister-Wilkins, P. (2015). 'The Humanitarian Politics of European Border Policing: Frontex and Border Police in Evros'. *International Political Sociology*, 9(1): 53–69.

Prpic, M. (2017). *Revision of the Blue Card Directive*. European Parliament Research Service, Briefing, EU Legislation in Progress.

Ripoll Servent, A. (2018). 'A New Form of Delegation in EU Asylum: Agencies as Proxies of Strong Regulators'. *Journal of Common Market Studies*, 56(1): 83–100.

Shackleton, M. (2017). 'Transforming Representative Democracy in the EU? The Role of the European Parliament'. *Journal of European Integration*, 39(2): 191–205.

Schout, A. (2017). 'The Dutch EU Presidency: The Continuing Relevance of the Rotating Presidency in a Political Union'. *Journal of Common Market Studies*, 55: 54–63.

Tazzioli, M. (2017). 'Containment Through Mobility: Migrants' Spatial Disobediences and the Reshaping of Control Through the Hotspot System'. *Journal of Ethnic and Migration Studies*, DOI:10.1080/1369183X.201.1401514.

Thielemann, E. R. (2003). 'Between Interests and Norms: Explaining Burden-Sharing in the European Union'. *Journal of Refugee Studies*, 16(3): 253–73.

Wagner, M. et al. (2016). *The Implementation of the Common European Asylum System*. Brussels: European Parliament.

Wasserstein, D. (2011). 'Europe Refugee Movements after World War Two'. BBC. www.bbc.co.uk/history/worldwars/wwtwo/refugees_01.shtml (accessed 10 January 2019).

Wolff, S. (2015). 'Integrating in Justice and Home Affairs: A Case of New Intergovernmentalism Par Excellence?' In C. Bickerton, D. Hodson and U. Puetter (eds), *The New Intergovernmentalism: States and Supranational Actors in the Post-Maastricht Era*. Oxford: Oxford University Press.

Wolff, S. (2009). 'The Mediterranean Dimension of EU Counter-terrorism'. *Journal of European Integration*, 31(1): 137–56.

Wolff, S. and Hadj-Abdou, L. (2017). 'Mediterranean Migration and Refugee Politics: Between Continuities and Discontinuities', In F. Volpi and R. Gillespie (eds), *Routledge Handbook on Mediterranean Politics*. London: Routledge.

Wolff, S. and Schout, A. (2013). 'Frontex as Agency: More of the Same?' *Perspectives on European Politics and Society*, 14(3): 305–24.

13 Security in the Schengen Area: Limiting Rights and Freedoms?

JULIEN JEANDESBOZ

13.1 Introduction

'Schengen' refers to an agreement signed between five member states of the EC – the Benelux countries, France and Germany – in June 1985 in the Luxembourgish town of the same name. The 1985 Schengen agreement and its implementing convention signed in June 1990 (the Convention Implementing the Schengen Agreement, hearafter CISA) are best known for establishing the Schengen area, where systematic, internal border controls between participating countries have been removed. For the best part of the 1990s, Schengen operated as an intergovernmental framework that involved EU member state representatives, but outside of the Community legal order and Union institutions. This situation came to an end with the entry into force of the Treaty of Amsterdam on 1 May 1999, which incorporated the Schengen framework in EU law and policy.

For most EU citizens, Schengen primarily involves the possibility of travelling between two member states without having their identity or travel documents controlled. This experience is not systematic, though, because some member states are not part of the Schengen area. This is the result of choices made by governments to 'opt out' of Schengen provisions related to the lifting of controls at internal borders (Ireland, the United Kingdom) or because these member states are yet to be admitted to the Schengen area (Bulgaria, Croatia, Cyprus and Romania). Yet persons holding the passport of one of these EU member states do not have to apply for permission to enter the Schengen area, and the period during which they can circulate within the area is not limited as long they do not establish residence in another member state.

Persons who are not EU citizens – TCNs in the nomenclature of EU law – have an altogether different experience. They can be divided into three broad categories. The first category consists of TCNs who are required to hold a Schengen visa in order to travel to the EU for short stays (less than ninety days over six months). In 2017, more than sixteen million persons fell under this category, who first experienced Schengen in their country of departure by applying for a Schengen visa at an EU member state consulate. This is a procedure that requires them to demonstrate in particular that they do not pose a 'threat' to public security and order or an irregular immigration 'risk'. These persons are also citizens from some of the poorest, most conflict-ridden countries in the world. The second category of TCN travellers consists of persons hailing from the wealthiest and most peaceful parts of the world, who do not have to hold a Schengen visa to travel to the EU. For the time being, these persons only experience Schengen when they go through passport control at the external borders of the Union. The third category of TCN travellers includes those persons who attempt to cross the external borders of the EU outside of regular channels and official border crossing points. For these persons, who also predominantly come from some of the poorest and most conflict-ridden countries in the world, Schengen is experienced primarily and in an arguably much more tragic way as 'detention, deportation, [and/or] drowning' (Jansen et al., 2014).[1]

These widely different circumstances underscore the ambivalence of Schengen, which depending on where one is seen to belong to or where one stands ('inside' or 'outside' the Schengen area, 'inside' or 'outside' of the EU, 'inside' or 'outside' the Western and wealthiest parts of the world) can either mean freer cross-border travel or extensive scrutiny as well as psychological and physical harm in the name of security and migration control. Schengen therefore holds different meanings and has different implications depending on the circumstances, the actors involved and the persons affected. The ambivalence of Schengen is, accordingly, at the heart of this chapter. This ambivalence requires, it is argued, that we examine not just Schengen's institutional and legal location and decision-making procedures, but also how Schengen organises the relation between freedom, rights and security, and specifically how, in the context of Schengen, security concerns have come to be regarded as a limit to the freedoms and rights of persons. This examination is further warranted by the fact that since 2013 at least, the question of whether Schengen should be preserved, reformed or otherwise abandoned has become entangled with broader controversies about the values and future of European integration (e.g. Coman, 2017), and the shape, priorities and directions of post-crisis governance in the EU.

The chapter looks in turn at the history of Schengen, and at the evolution of the Schengen institutional framework since its integration within the EU's institutional and legal order since May 1999 and the entry into force of the Amsterdam Treaty. It then considers recent policy developments and ongoing controversies in the context of what has been called, among other things, the 'Schengen crisis'. Throughout, the chapter demonstrates the persistent element of ambivalence in the Schengen framework, whereby the assumption that freer cross-border travel is

---

[1] The EU's external border agency, Frontex, reported in 2018 that most detected irregular crossings of the EU external borders in 2014–17 happened at sea and predominantly in the Mediterranean (Frontex, 2018: 43). The largest group of persons involved are identified as Syrian nationals, followed by Nigerian nationals and Iraqi nationals (except for 2017 for the latter, see Frontex, 2018: 45). The Missing Migrants project of the IOM finds that over the same period, the Mediterranean is also the area of the world where most reported migrant deaths occur, peaking at 5,143 deaths in 2016 (2,160 in 2018, 1,866 in 2019).

a security concern (see Box 13.1) leads to considering non-EU foreigners as particularly suspicious, and to a range of fundamental rights being curtailed in the process. It further outlines how this framing of freedom of movement correlates with concerns stemming from home affairs and law enforcement officials to retain a modicum of discretion over the conduct of policies related to borders, visas and policing. The chapter wraps up with a case study focused on the Entry-Exit System (EES), a recently adopted EU measure related to one of the core Schengen matters, namely the control of EU external borders. The case study demonstrates that the association between crime, cross-border movements of persons, migration and now terrorism has been strengthened rather than weakened in the context of the measures adopted purportedly to deal with the Schengen crisis unravelling since 2015.

BOX 13.1 Key concepts

Security. Security is commonly understood as the provision of protection from threat. This particular understanding, and the very status of security as a concept, is, however, intensely discussed and contested. For post-positivist and post-structuralist scholars within critical approaches to security (c.a.s.e. collective, 2006), in particular, security is better understood as (in)security, that is as a process rather than a concept through which, by means of various practices, threats, referent objects (what is to be secured) and means of protection are defined.

Crimmigration. A notion developed in particular by criminologists and migration scholars to identify and study the process through which crime and immigration are associated with one another through administrative, legal, policing and representational practices, among others.

13.2   Historical Overview

The Schengen area was established by the Schengen Agreement in June 1985 and the CISA, signed in June 1990. CISA entered into force on 1 September 1993, and the abolition of internal border controls unfolded progressively between 1997 and 2000 (Guiraudon, 2011: 776). For more than a decade, Schengen operated in parallel to the Community and EU institutional structure and legal order, particularly the EU's 'third pillar' on JHA established with the Maastricht Treaty in 1993, until its incorporation as from 1 May 1999 with the entry into force of the Amsterdam Treaty. What became known as the Schengen 'acquis', that is the body of agreements, decisions, recommendations and rules adopted in the Schengen framework, was brought under the EU 'roof' on 20 May 1999 and made public for the first time in its (quasi) entirety in September 2000 (Council of the EU, 1999; OJEC, 2000).

Why did such a seemingly important development as the establishment of control-free travel for persons among EC member states, stated as the long-term objective of the 1985 agreement, initially unfold outside the EC framework? The question is legitimate insofar as the common or single market's four freedoms and the abolition of internal border checks would be expected to complement each other. Academics offer several contrasting explanations for this outcome. For some scholars, Schengen is the outcome of intergovernmental bargaining among EC member states aimed at removing 'customs formalities and non-tariff barriers' in a context where French and German economic preferences were converging towards market liberalisation, effectively reflecting a 'common economic programme' in the months following the 1984 Fontainebleau summit (Moravcsik, 1998: 337, 346). In this regard, it is certainly relevant to highlight that, prior to the 1985 agreement, France had experienced a series of strikes by customs officials and truckers who were protesting the delays and long queues they faced at the border with Germany. The strikes led to the conclusion of the Franco-German Saarbrücken Agreement of 13 July 1984, which foresaw the gradual abolition of border controls between the two countries for nationals of EEC member states. Under pressure from transport companies, the Dutch government rapidly opened negotiations with the German government on these issues, which led to an agreement on discussions with France and Germany among the Benelux countries in December 1984, and eventually to multilateral talks that resulted in the Schengen Agreement (Brouwer, 2008: 21–2).

For other scholars, the focus on the economic interests of powerful member states does not provide a satisfactory account of the other components of the Schengen framework, on external border cooperation, visa cooperation and police cooperation, which are harder to relate to economic policy concerns with customs and non-tariff barriers. Jörg Monar (2001) considers that the establishment of Schengen, its subsequent evolution and the parallel development of the EU's third pillar on JHA is in fact the outcome of a combination of four 'driving forces'. Economic aspects factor in as a 'spillover effect', which led to a 'change in mentality' among officials from national Interior ministries and law enforcement agencies and services who came to be aware of the functional necessity to handle issues such as immigration and organised crime in common (Monar, 2001: 754–5). This 'internal' driving force combined with what Monar considers to be an 'external' driving force, namely the emergence of new 'transnational challenges' such as international terrorism, organised crime and drugs trafficking, as well as asylum and irregular migration (Monar, 2001: 752–4). Unlike Moravcsik, finally, he considers that non-economic national interests in home affairs issues drove member state governments to 'Europeanise' the handling of the above-mentioned issues (Monar, 2001: 756–8). Ultimately, Monar argues that Schengen was one among several 'laboratories' where these driving forces initially unfolded, leading to intergovernmental European cooperation that then prepared the grounds for the establishment of the AFSJ in the Amsterdam Treaty.

> ## BOX 13.2 Key actors
>
> ***Club de Berne***. Established around 1969 at the initiative of the Swiss authorities, initially composed of domestic intelligence officers from Western Europe, North America and Israel, with a focus on counter-terrorism, still in existence as of 2018.
>
>   ***TREVI***. Established in 1976 to organise political cooperation among home affairs and security services of the member states of the EC. After the entry into force of the Maastricht Treaty, TREVI is brought under the EU's third pillar. Initially established with a focus on counter-terrorism, the TREVI framework developed activities in relation to drugs trafficking, organised crime, borders and immigration.
>
>   ***PWGOT***. The Police Working Group on Terrorism was established in 1979 at the initiative of the British authorities, bringing together specialised counter-terrorism police services of the UK, the Netherlands, the Federal Republic of Germany and Belgium (initially) as a reaction to the perceived lack of operational police cooperation within TREVI. Still in existence as of 2018.
>
>   ***Ad Hoc Group on Immigration***. Intergovernmental group established in October 1986 to bring together officials from asylum, borders and immigration services of the EC member states, initially foreseen as a TREVI group, eventually placed under the responsibility of the EC Commission. The group served as the framework for the negotiation of the 1990 Dublin Convention, and was brought in under the EU third pillar after Maastricht.

Such an account usefully stresses the role played by specific national actors, rather than assuming, as Moravcsik tends to do, that member state representatives bring a single, unified national position to the bargaining table. Schengen was indeed one of several arenas where officials of interior and justice ministries and law enforcement services from European countries started discussing home affairs matters prior to the 1985 agreement, such as the TREVI framework of ministerial and high-level official meetings that ran from 1975 to 1993, and existed alongside 'over 20 new intergovernmental bodies' established between 1986 and 1991 for this purpose (Monar, 2001: 754; see Box 13.2 for a few examples). These bodies served as mobilisation frameworks for home affairs actors to discuss and develop the 1990 CISA, which helps us explain two key differences between this document and the original Schengen agreement. On the one hand CISA is seven times longer and mostly focused on asylum, border and migration control and police coopera- tion rather than the removal of internal border controls. On the other hand, while the wording of the 1985 agreement refers to such measures as a 'complement' to the abolition of internal border controls, the 1990 CISA refers to 'compensatory' measures, related to drugs trafficking and organised crime, counter-terrorism and external border control, which tend to focus on non-EC/EU citizens by associating concerns with crime and violence with questions of visa-issuance, detention and expulsion (e.g. Lavenex, 1999: 36).

Over the course of just five years, the focus of the Schengen framework moved from establishing and complementing control-free cross-border movements between Schengen states to the *compensation* of control-free movements. What CISA does is inscribe at the heart of the Schengen framework the notion that freer cross-border movements of persons is *in tension* with law enforcement and security concerns – that *freedom should be compensated by security*. To account for this tendency, Virginie Guiraudon has shown that discussions on border controls, immigration and asylum in the context of CISA negotiations and other European fora for interior, justice and law enforcement officials happened in relation to 'the concomitant *future* planning of the single market' (Guiraudon, 2000: 255, italics in original) and not as a reaction or consequence ('spillover' in Monar's terminology) to the completion of the single market envisaged in the European Commission's 1992 agenda. Schengen and the development of the EU's 'third pillar' were the outcome of the 'venue shopping' practices of these officials, socialised to European interactions since the establishment of TREVI, the Club of Bern and other informal settings, and who looked to European cooperation as a way to escape domestic and European judicial constraints (including from the ECJ, which had no jurisdiction over Schengen and EU third-pillar measures until Amsterdam). By 'moving to Europe', these officials also sought to exclude rivals from other services such as employment, social and economic affairs ministries, avoid scrutiny from parliaments and NGOs and to enrol new allies from counterpart EU bureaucracies and beyond (Guiraudon, 2000: 257–67).

Explained in such a way, the Schengen framework appears less as a laboratory of control-free travel among EC/EU member states and more as a competing initiative. In the words of a former practitioner, Schengen could be conceived as a 'parallel track' to EU-related developments (Elsen, 2011: 78). The purpose of this 'parallel track' was to ensure that restrictive and control-oriented policies on movements of persons to and within Europe would remain pre-eminent and under the control of interior and law enforcement bureaucracies. As a result, for instance, most of the work in the areas of asylum and migration happened outside of the EU third-pillar framework (Guiraudon, 2000: 256–7).

One could argue, of course, that this focus is logical given concerns with evolutions in patterns of cross-border crime, political violence and migration (Monar's 'external' driving force). Studies have, however, demonstrated that the association of migration with security concerns such as crime or terrorism is the result of a political and professional construction that unfolded from the 1970s onwards rather than a reflection of facts (Huysmans, 2000). Didier Bigo (1996) has shown how the various informal and formal groups listed in Box 13.2 played a role not only in putting national actors in relation, but also in having these actors come up with common definitions, beyond national specificities and differences, of security concerns under headings such as serious organised crime or illegal migration – and in particular how these definitions contributed to a transfer of illegitimacy whereby irregular migration, despite not being a crime, has come to be narrowly associated with criminal activities (Bigo, 1992).

In sum, while the Schengen area is remembered, celebrated and occasionally mourned for the abolition of internal border controls between EC/EU member states, recalling its genesis reminds us of its other features. Because it allowed for the mobilisation of officials from interior and law enforcement bureaucracies over the negotiation of CISA, the Schengen framework became the staging ground for far-reaching cooperation over visas, external border control and policing, justified in terms of a purported need to 'compensate' control-free travel between Schengen states. In the words of another former practitioner who witnessed the incorporation of Schengen into the EU framework, the compensatory measures became 'an overriding self-standing objective' (De Capitani, 2014: 106). For interior and law enforcement actors, setting up Schengen was seen as a way to preserve the integrity of the home affairs and internal security domain and prevent border control from being reframed as a market- or labour-related issue. In the process, the Schengen framework has anchored in European discussions about migration the notion that migration is a risk or a threat, by including it into a 'continuum' (Bigo, 2002) of security concerns together with drugs trafficking, organised crime or terrorism.

BOX 13.3 Key dates

1984. The Saarbrücken Agreement is signed.

1985. The Schengen Agreement is signed.

1990. The CISA is signed.

1991. Italy, Spain and Portugal sign up to the CISA.

1992. Greece signs up to the CISA.

1993. The CISA enters into force for the initial five signatories.

1993. The Maastricht Treaty enters into force, establishing the EU's third pillar and incorporating the TREVI framework.

1995. The CISA is fully implemented by all nine parties.

1999. The Amsterdam Treaty enters into force, bringing the Schengen framework in the EU's legal order and establishing the AFSJ.

2009. The Treaty of Lisbon enters into force and puts an end to the pillar system.

13.3   Main Features of the Current Institutional Framework

Keeping these historical explanations in mind, we now move on to the main features of the current institutional framework concerning the Schengen area. Until the entry into force of the Amsterdam Treaty, the Schengen area was governed through a separate institutional arrangement centred around the intergovernmental Schengen Executive Committee (SEC) assisted by a small cadre of officials, the Schengen Secretariat, based in Brussels. Composed of the relevant (Interior) Ministries of the Parties to the Schengen Agreement supported by a preparatory body of high-ranking national civil servants (the 'Central Group'), the SEC was granted by Title VIII CISA the power to adopt binding decisions that had to be implemented by all Schengen states, acting unanimously (Curtin and Meijers, 1997: 20–1). Due to the Schengen framework's setup as a 'parallel track' to EU-related developments, SEC decisions fell outside the jurisdiction of the ECJ and the oversight of the EP, and it proved difficult to arrange oversight from national parliaments. According to Cruz (1993: 5) for instance, no domestic parliamentary debate on Schengen took place among the signatories of the 1985 agreement save for the Netherlands between 1985 and 1989. The SEC Rules of Procedure further made the publication of its decisions conditional upon their confidential character, which was determined on the basis of unanimity. In this sense, the Schengen framework was in fact more than an intergovernmental framework set up in parallel to and in competition with EU arrangements for the single market and the third pillar. It was also a discretionary space for national interior and law enforcement characterised by 'secret law, secret law-making and secrecy of documents' (Curtin and Meijers, 1997: 28) and 'secret diplomacy' (Thym, 2002: 221), where binding measures could be adopted by actors from national executive branches without being necessarily submitted to the usual checks and balances from their respective legislative and judiciary branches.

As indicated above, the Amsterdam Treaty folded the Schengen framework into the EU institutional and legal order, by way of the annexed 'Schengen Protocol'. Measures adopted by the SEC were redefined as 'Schengen acquis' by the Council in its Decisions 1999/435/EC and 1999/436/EC. It was therefore only after the entry into force of the Amsterdam Treaty, incidentally, that the full extent and substance of 'Schengen law' became known when it was published in 2000 in the *Official Journal* of the EC. This was a process that proved controversial and fraught with tensions due to the confidential nature of SEC proceedings and the reluctance of national authorities to do away with the discretion they had enjoyed under the Schengen regime (for a full analysis see Den Boer and Corrado, 1999; Peers, 2000). Even at that point, the SEC acted until the last minute before it was dissolved (in this case three days before the entry into force of the Amsterdam Treaty) to ensure that some decisions and documents would remain confidential for as long as possible (Thym, 2002: 221–2).

It is sometimes stated that Amsterdam 'communautarised' Schengen, which is not entirely accurate. What Amsterdam did is put an end to the coexistence of 'two parallel regimes for the same political objectives' (De Capitani, 2014: 107), the Schengen framework on the one hand and the EU's 'third pillar' on JHA on the other, which were brought together under the heading of the AFSJ. Matters related to asylum, borders, migration and visas were brought under the first, 'Community' pillar, although the treaty foresaw a transitional period of five years before the Community method of law making could apply. JHA and Schengen matters related to police and judicial cooperation, on the other hand, remained within the third pillar until the entry into force of the Lisbon Treaty. In the intervening years between Amsterdam and Lisbon, most measures adopted in the Schengen framework were replaced and/or 'built upon' by EU measures. However, this process, of which Box 13.4 provides some outstanding examples, can hardly be described only as 'communautarisation', because the incorporation, replacement or further development of Schengen law has actively contributed to transforming policies in the area of home affairs and security. For instance, the question of whether or not all EU member states should join the Schengen area (of control-free movement) and participate in measures based on or stemming from the Schengen framework has led to a complex body of provisions regulating the territorial scope of Schengen and the AFSJ. This concerns in particular Denmark, Ireland and the UK.[2] After the Amsterdam Treaty, the last two countries 'opted out' of the Schengen provisions related to border control, but have been granted partial 'opt-ins' in other areas, such as police cooperation.[3] Following the Amsterdam Treaty, Denmark has been granted an 'opt-out' for all measures concerning asylum and migration, but with the possibility to 'opt-in' measures related to other matters related to Schengen and the AFSJ.

The entry into force of the Lisbon Treaty formally put an end to the pillar system in force since Maastricht. Most Schengen matters are now dealt with under the ordinary legislative procedure.

---

[2] These complexities further concern EU member states that intend to join the Schengen area but have not been allowed in yet, and third countries that are considered as 'associated states'. These will not be dealt with here for the sake of concision.

[3] Such 'opt-ins' are, however, not systematically granted. For instance, the UK has been denied participation in the Visa Information System and the EU external border agency (Frontex). For the latter, a UK representative sits on the management board of the agency but as an observer with no voting rights.

BOX 13.4 Legal basis

The question of the current legal basis for Schengen measures is complex due to (1) the convoluted territorial scope of Schengen, (2) the combination of Schengen and third-pillar legal bases and measures within the AFSJ and (3) the accretion over time of measures 'building on', 'relevant for' or otherwise 'related to' Schengen law. The scope and applicable Schengen law in the EU's legal order have been described in an eponymous Council document shortly after the entry into force of Amsterdam (Council of the EU, 2000). As De Capitani (2014: 108) remarks, the most recent formal list of Schengen-related measures is found in Annex II of the accession treaty between the EU and Croatia.

Treaty basis. The objectives of Schengen cooperation are found in Article 3(2) TEU (on the AFSJ) and Article 77 TFEU

Key Schengen dispositions replaced by EU measures (see also De Capitani, 2014: 108–9):

Articles 2–8 CISA have been replaced in 2006 with the *Schengen Borders Code* (Regulation (EC) No. 562/2006), recently repealed and replaced by Regulation (EU) 2016/399 (still known as the Schengen Borders Code or otherwise the Union Code on the rules governing the movement of persons across borders).

Articles 9–17 CISA on visas have been replaced with the *Community Code on Visas* (Regulation (EC) No. 810/2009, Visa Code), which also includes procedural elements (on how Schengen short-stay visas are delivered) from the former Schengen Common Consular Instructions. On March 2018 the European Commission proposed a revision of the Visa Code, which is ongoing at the time of writing.

On police cooperation and judicial cooperation, *Articles 39(1) through (3) CISA* on exchanges of information and intelligence for criminal investigation and intelligence operations between member state law enforcement and security authorities have been replaced by the so-called 'Swedish Initiative' (Council Framework Decision 2006/960/JHA); while the *European Arrest Warrant* was modelled upon *Article 59–66 CISA*.

The Lisbon Treaty, in particular, has opened up areas related to police cooperation, which had remained in the third pillar after Amsterdam, to scrutiny from the Court and the involvement of the EP as co-legislator. The complexities related to the territorial scope of Schengen and the AFSJ remain, however. Denmark, for instance, has a general opt-out for all measures relating to the AFSJ, but retains an opt-in for measures considered to build upon Schengen law, with the notable difference that said measures are treated as international law rather than EU law in the Danish legal order.

How do these subsequent evolutions of the legal and institutional framework of Schengen relate to the original concerns and preoccupations underpinning the establishment of Schengen, surveyed in Section 13.2? Did the incorporation of Schengen in the EU institutional and legal order entail a loss of autonomy of home affairs and law enforcement officials over issues such as border control, visas and policing, and a correlated revision of the view that control-free movement of persons is a security concern? What transpires from the above is that the Amsterdam and Lisbon treaties have put an end to the existence of 'parallel' and arguably competing institutional and legal frameworks, to the extent that some contributors foresee that the CISA as the cornerstone of the Schengen framework 'will probably completely disappear' as a legal basis for EU measures (Huybreghts, 2015: 403). While this may be the case insofar as legislative decision-making is concerned, measures based on, building upon or related to Schengen law, particularly in the field of security, still leave considerable room for manoeuvre for national authorities, particularly at the operational level. This is the case for instance with the European external borders agency, Frontex, established in 2004 as a measure building upon the Schengen 'acquis', which remains a coordinating body for operations requested and steered by member state authorities rather than a corps of European border guards (see Chapter 12). In the same way, the evolution of the institutional and legal framework of Schengen did not put an end to the linking of cross-border movements of persons with security concerns. While some (former Schengen) practitioners readily acknowledge – after the fact – that the lifting of internal border controls 'did not have as a consequence a massive increase in crime or illegal migration' that constituted the working assumption of CISA negotiations (Elsen, 2011: 77, my translation), the notion that security, defined in terms of 'crimmigration' (Aas, 2011; see Box 13.1), that is the association between crime and migration, should constitute a limit to freedom of movement remained central to the Schengen/AFSJ mindset. In this respect, some scholars consider that it is less accurate to speak of a 'communautarisation' of Schengen than of how the EU institutional and legal framework has been 'Schengenised' (e.g. Zaiotti, 2011).

BOX 13.5 Key actors

COSI. Standing Committee on Operational Cooperation on Internal Security, Council working group staffed by member state officials from ministries of the interior and justice, the Commission and External Action Service, tasked with ensuring operational cooperation among national authorities in the areas of law enforcement, border control and judicial cooperation in criminal matters.

> ## BOX 13.5 (Cont.)
>
> ***DG HOME.*** Directorate-General for Migration and Home Affairs of the European Commission, whose services are in charge of policy-making in the areas related to Schengen.
>
> ***Europol.*** European Union Agency for Law Enforcement Cooperation, in charge of coordinating operational cooperation and intelligence sharing between EU member state law enforcement services in the areas of counter-terrorism and serious and organised cross-border crime.
>
> ***eu-LISA.*** EU agency for the operational management of large-scale IT systems in the AFSJ, manages all information systems related to this particular policy area, including the Schengen Information System, and the development and deployment of new systems such as the EES (see Section 13.6).
>
> ***Frontex.*** EBCG agency, in charge of coordinating operational cooperation in the field of border control (see Chapter 12).

13.4   Recent Policy Developments

The chapter has so far traced and demonstrated the ambivalence of 'Schengen' by looking at its history as well as at its evolving and current institutional framework since the entry into force of the Amsterdam and Lisbon Treaties. It now turns to some of the most recent Schengen-related policy developments, which involve the notion that the Schengen area has of late been going through a crisis.

Such 'crisis talk' emerged in 2011. A decision by the Italian authorities to issue a six-month temporary residence permit, mostly to Tunisian nationals who had arrived in the wake of the uprisings against the Ben Ali regime, led the French authorities to reinstate controls at the Ventimiglia land border between the two countries, and to threats from the Dutch government that they would deport all Tunisian nationals arriving from Italy (Carrera et al., 2011). The Franco-Italian row was eventually (and temporarily) worked out in a bilateral summit in Rome, leading to an agreement between the two governments that they would push for a reform of Schengen allowing member states to temporarily reinstate internal border checks for migration-related concerns (Zaiotti, 2013: 340), a resolution that took the form of a letter to then-Commission President José Manuel Barroso, signed by Italian Prime Minister Silvio Berlusconi and French President Nicolas Sarkozy in April 2011. In the meantime, further tensions flared up in Denmark. In April 2011, the far-right Danish People's Party made its support for a package of economic reforms introduced by the conservative-liberal coalition government conditional upon the reintroduction of (permanent) controls at internal borders (Wind, 2012: 132). The request and subsequent agreement to reintroduce controls (alternatively dubbed 'stronger' border controls or 'customs' rather than border controls per se, Wind, 2012) elicited strong critical reactions from both the European Commission and EU member state governments. Due to the political sensitivity of border and migration questions at the time, however, the European Commission ultimately did not, as it could have, take the Danish government to court over the breach of its Schengen commitments, and the matter was resolved following the September 2011 national elections in Denmark, when the newly elected centre-left government withdrew the plan (Wind, 2012: 149).

The Franco-Italian and Danish rows spurred the European Commission into considering a series of reforms of Schengen governance, the broad outline of which was presented in a September 2011 communication and legislative package foreseeing on the one hand the establishment of a new evaluation and monitoring mechanism to verify how the Schengen acquis is applied by member states, and on the other introducing changes to the Schengen Borders Code to clarify and specify the rules applying to the temporary reintroduction of internal border controls. The former initially empowered the European Commission, should an evaluation reveal deficiencies in the way a member state implements Schengen rules, to request the implementation of specific measures including the closing of border crossing points or the deployment of emergency European Border Guard Teams under the aegis of the Frontex agency (Carrera, 2012: 6–8; see also Chapter 12). The latter authorised the temporary reintroduction of internal border controls in cases of serious threats to public policy or internal security, including the unexpected arrival of significant numbers of TCNs at the external borders, or should a member state not address deficiencies in the way it implements Schengen rules, but on the basis of a decision taken by the European Commission (Carrera, 2012: 8–9).

In an illustration of the trends in the governing of the Schengen area outlined above, the initial version of the Schengen governance package elicited strong pushbacks from member states against the empowerment of the European Commission, supported by the Frontex agency in particular, to interfere with operational matters. The legislative proposal was subsequently revised to limit its role and ultimately adopted in November 2013. On the one hand, it establishes a system whereby the Commission and the member states are jointly responsible for evaluating and monitoring the implementation of Schengen rules at the national level, with reports submitted by the European Commission to both the Council and the EP . On the other, it permits national authorities to unilaterally reintroduce border controls at internal borders while providing for more detailed rules and outlining that this should be a measure of last resort, and allows for the Commission or member states to file a complaint with the ECJ should such reintroductions be considered as unjustified.

13.5   Current Political and Academic Controversies

Claims of a Schengen crisis re-emerged less than two years after the adoption of the Schengen governance package. Due to concerns over a sharp increase in the number of persons entering the EU and the Schengen area to seek refuge from the war in Syria in 2014–15, Schengen states started reintroducing internal border controls, making use of the possibilities afforded to them by the revised Schengen borders code. Most prominently, German authorities were the first to formally take that decision on 13 September 2015, closely followed by the Austrian and Slovenian governments. By February 2016, seven other Schengen states, including Belgium, Denmark, France, Hungary, Malta, Norway and Sweden, had taken similar steps. Those decisions were justified on grounds of the 'security situation in Europe and threats resulting from [...] continuous significant secondary movements' of persons who have entered the Schengen area irregularly, except in the French case where authorities referred to 'terrorist threats' in addition to the situation at the external borders. In some cases, these measures were short-lived, but what has been quite striking with this turn of events is that six Schengen states have officially maintained internal border controls for close to four years now, and at the time of writing will continue to do so until at least May 2020.

How can we make sense of Schengen today, given these circumstances? The latest (and still ongoing) episode in what has been called the 'Schengen crisis' underscores how the reforms adopted in 2013 have given a more prominent role to EU bodies but did not significantly curb the discretionary powers of member states. It is worth noting, in this respect, that most of the national measures reintroducing internal border controls have been communicated to the European Commission services and justified in relation to the rules laid down in the Schengen Borders Code. There are strong hints that these justifications were at times received with scepticism, but no member state has been brought in front of the ECJ as a result.

Given this situation, some scholars have suggested that the current institutional, legal and political configuration of the Schengen area should be analysed through the lens of new intergovernmentalism (Coman, 2017), i.e. as a case where integration unfolds without (or with limited) supranationalisation, through the deployment of 'de novo bodies' and mechanisms to which authority and competences are transferred without this amounting to a strengthening of the EU's supranational institutions per se (Bickerton et al., 2015). Such a diagnosis is useful insofar as it highlights the persistent institutional, legal and political ambivalence of Schengen and its subsequent development as an area of both EU and national policy, but it is also a label that by virtue of applying to a broad category of phenomena may well be less helpful than it might seem. Rather than looking at Schengen as a 'case of' new intergovernmentalism, it might be useful to examine it as an instance – of which there are multiple other occurrences either outside the EU or involving the

EU in a transatlantic or global context – of the transnationalisation of internal security policies and practices that became over time associated with European integration, starting in the 1970s as outlined in Section 13.2.

In the meantime, this latest episode of the Schengen crisis also underscores the entrenched character of the association between freedom of movement and security concerns and with security as a limit to freedoms and rights. By re-introducing internal border controls in the name of concerns with irregular border crossings, combined in some cases (especially France) with preoccupations with counter-terrorism, member states have effectively limited the freedoms of individuals in the name of security, over an extended period of time. The spectacular acts of violence involving individuals associated with Islamic State in Europe from early 2015 onwards, linked without any particularly convincing factual basis[4] with the increase in irregular crossings at the southern borders of the Union, have spurred EU institutions into considering and adopting a raft of Schengen-related measures that have given priority to security over all other considerations. There were attempts after 2014 to frame the issue of control-free movements of persons within the Schengen area as a matter of economic prosperity and a condition for the good functioning of the single market. The framing of Schengen in terms of security, however, returned to the foreground with the measures outlined in the Commission's 'European Agenda on Security' and the establishment of the so-called 'Security Union'. Section 13.6 will provide a case study of one such measure, the EES, as a specific illustration of this general trend.

13.6   Analysis of a Paradigmatic Case Study: The EES

In November 2017, the EP and the Council adopted legislation establishing the EU EES. The EES will be a computerised information system that registers the personal data, including biometric data (facial image and fingerprints), of all non-EU travellers admitted to the Schengen area for short stays – whether they are required to hold a Schengen visa or not – upon both entry and exit, for a duration of five years. The EES is part of a train of measures adopted in the wake of the European Agenda on Migration and European Agenda on Security. In an April 2016 communication on 'Stronger and Smarter Information Systems for Borders and Security', tabled the same day as a revised legislative proposal to establish the EES, the European Commission argued that further developments in one of the core Schengen areas, borders and internal security, are required due to 'conflict in Syria and crises elsewhere [that] triggered 1.8 million irregular border crossings' and '[t]he terrorist

---

[4] It is worth stressing that most of the persons involved in these attacks, particularly the most violent ones, were either EU citizens or individuals who were regularly residing in the EU (see e.g. Lucassen, 2018: 395).

attacks in Paris in 2015 and in Brussels in March 2016 [that] bitterly demonstrated the ongoing threat to Europe's internal borders' (European Commission, 2016b: 2). The EES is part of the measures deemed necessary in view of what the Commission services frame as a convergence of concerns, 'which should be adopted as a matter of urgency' (European Commission, 2016b: 18).

The underlying idea for the EES is that the system should allow national authorities to keep track, while they are within the Schengen area, of the authorised duration of stay of non-EU travellers and have the possibility to take action should a person exceed this duration. The exact steps to be taken, however, are left to the national authorities in charge. Because it stores biometrics in addition to biographic and travel document personal data, the EES is also expected to enable national authorities to identify, within their territory, persons who might be in an irregular situation or (under certain conditions) who are suspected of a serious criminal or terrorist offence, even if these persons do not carry identity or travel documents. This would be possible regardless of where the person has entered the Schengen area in the first place, since data collected at one entry or exit point will be shared across all of Schengen.

The adoption of legislation to establish the EES (the launch of which is expected in 2020) highlights several points that have been discussed throughout this chapter. To start with, it is in line with the original 'spirit' of Schengen in that it affords national authorities the possibility to exchange information and personal data and coordinate without encroaching upon their discretionary authority – in this case to admit a person in the Schengen area or deny them entry, or to take necessary measures in case that person is found to be in an irregular situation or involved in serious criminal or terrorist acts. In fact, the EES continues a trend initiated by a measure sometimes described as the 'crown jewel' (De Capitani, 2014: 104) of the original Schengen framework, namely the Schengen Information System (SIS), a computerised network allowing national authorities to exchange information and personal data for border and migration control as well as police cooperation. The SIS, which remains in existence today, is still considered the cornerstone of the measures initially adopted to 'compensate' for the lifting of internal border controls, and the EES has actually been presented as a 'complement' to this system (European Commission, 2016a: 3). The EES, in this sense, illustrates the ambivalence of the institutional, legal and political coordinates of Schengen in the processes of European integration.

The second point that the case of EES illustrates is the ambivalent relationship between freedom, rights and security embedded within the Schengen framework. The adoption of the EES Regulation in November 2017 was the outcome of a process that started fifteen years ago. As described elsewhere (Jeandesboz, 2016), the EES had originally been considered as a policy option in 2004, at the time when the European Commission was considering the possibility of establishing an information system collecting and storing the personal data of all Schengen visa applicants (Visa Information System, eventually adopted in 2008). The EES was discarded at the time, but was reintroduced in 2008 in discussions on measures to be adopted to strengthen border controls after the 2007 Schengen enlargement. In 2012, it subsequently became part of a legislative initiative known as the 'smart borders package', which proposed in 2012 to adopt the EES alongside another measure that aimed to make it easier for selected TCNs to enter the Schengen area, the Registered Traveller Programme (RTP). The package was rejected by the co-legislators due to concerns with costs and technical feasibility, as well as fundamental rights implications, especially with regard to the right to privacy and the right to data protection of foreign travellers.

The package was somewhat revised in its 2016 version, by abandoning the establishment of an EU-wide RTP system, by providing for law enforcement access to EES for criminal and counter-terrorism purposes and by addressing some of the concerns related to fundamental rights, chiefly data protection. In its opinion on the EES proposal, the European Data Protection Supervisor (EDPS) takes note of the latter, yet expresses concerns about the necessity and proportionality of a measure that would systematically collect personal data, including biometrics, on all non-EU foreigners (totalling 167 million records created after one year, and 269 million records after five years by official estimates – European Commission, 2013), outlining that it constitutes a 'wide-ranging interference with fundamental rights to privacy and data protection of third-country nationals' (EDPS, 2016: 22). The opinion further expresses concern that access to EES data would be granted to law enforcement 'even though these travelers are in principle not suspected of unlawful conduct or otherwise under investigation' (EDPS, 2016: 19). The adoption, despite these concerns, of the EES regulation goes some way to demonstrate that concerns with security have overridden concerns with rights.

One needs to highlight, in this regard, that EES is also typical of a trend that has considerably accelerated since 2015. Over the span of a few years and in the name either of counter-terrorism or migration control, the co-legislators have passed legislation or are currently considering a range of measures that had for years been mired in controversy due to their fundamental rights implications: the controversial EU Passenger Name Record initiative in 2016, which foresees that personal data from all passengers on inbound and outbound international flights in the EU is processed for criminal and counter-terrorism purposes; the EES, which as stated will process the personal data of all non-EU travellers; the European Travel Information and Authorisation System (ETIAS), adopted in 2018, which for migration, criminal and counter-terrorism purposes will also process the personal data of non-EU travellers who are not required to hold a Schengen visa to enter the EU.

What all of these measures have in common is that they focus on TCNs despite the fact that (to paraphrase the EDPS opinion on EES) they should not in principle be particularly suspected of wrongdoings, either actual or potential. To clarify this point, it may be sufficient to point out that UK citizens will, upon completion of Britain's exit from the EU and if no specific alternative measures are adopted, have their personal data processed in both EES and ETIAS for no particular reason other than having become TCNs. The other commonality between these measures is that although they constitute a serious interference with fundamental rights, they have all been adopted in the name of strengthening the security of the Schengen area. Yet, as a recent report from the EU's Fundamental Rights Agency underscores, the scope of said interference is serious and significant, beyond the right to data protection and the right to privacy, and includes among others the right to dignity, to the integrity of the person, to the prohibition of torture and inhuman or degrading treatment, to liberty and security of a person and to an effective remedy, and is also impactful for specific groups such as children.

Whether these measures actually provide a reasoned response to the crisis, or whether they are adopted as the result of inertia and unquestioned assumptions about freedom of movement and security, is an issue that the case of EES further illuminates. In this regard, and although this avenue has not been explored in much detail in the present contribution, one may ask whether studying and thinking about European integration in a 'post-crisis' context should be focused on the effects of the crisis, or on its political uses.

GROUP DISCUSSION

- Is the Schengen framework only about freedom of movement?
- To what extent have the recent Schengen 'crises' enabled continuity rather than discontinuity in the governing of the Schengen area?

TOPICS FOR INDIVIDUAL RESEARCH

- Law enforcement and security cooperation in Europe in the 1960s and 1970s.
- Large-scale information systems in the EU and the relation between fundamental freedoms and rights and surveillance.

FURTHER READINGS

Anderson, M. and Den Boer, M. (eds) (1994). *Policing Across National Boundaries*. London: Pinter.

Bigo, D. and Guild, E. (eds) (2005). *Controlling Frontiers: Free Movement Into and Within Europe*. London: Ashgate.

Guiraudon, V. (2003). 'The Constitution of a European Immigration Policy Domain: A Political Sociology Approach'. *Journal of European Public Policy*, 10(2): 263–82.

Mitsilegas, V., Monar, J. and Rees W. (2003). *The European Union and Internal Security*. Basingstoke: Palgrave Macmillan.

Zaiotti, R. (2011). *Cultures of Border Control: Schengen and the Evolution of European Frontiers*. Chicago: The University of Chicago Press.

REFERENCES

Aas, K. F. (2011). '"Crimmigrant" Bodies and Bona Fide Travelers: Surveillance, Citizenship and Global Governance'. *Theoretical Criminology*, 15(3): 331–46.

Bickerton, C. J., Hodson, D. and Puetter, U. (2015). 'The New Intergovernmentalism: European Integration in the Post-Maastricht Era'. *Journal of Common Market Studies*, 53(4): 703–22.

Bigo, D. (ed.) (1992). *L'Europe des polices et de la sécurité intérieure*. Brussels: Editions Complexe.

Bigo, D. (1996). *Polices en réseaux : l'expérience européenne*. Paris: Presses de Science Po.

Bigo, D. (2002). 'Security and Immigration: Toward a Critique of the Governmentality of Unease'. *Alternatives*, 27, Special Issue, 63–92.

Brouwer, E. (2008). *Digital Borders and Real Rights*. Leiden: Martinus Nijhoff.

Carrera, S. (2012). *An Assessment of the Commission's 2011 Schengen Governance Package: Preventing Abuse by EU Member States of Freedom of Movement?* Brussels: CEPS.

Carrera, S., Guild, E., Merlino, M. and Parkin, J. (2011). *A Race against Solidarity: The Schengen Regime and the Franco-Italian Affair*. Brussels: Centre for European Policy Studies.

c.a.s.e. collective (2006). 'Critical Approaches to Security in Europe: A Networked Manifesto'. *Security Dialogue*, 37(4): 443–87.

Coman, R. (2017). 'Values and Power Conflicts in Framing Borders and Borderlands: The 2013 Reform of EU Schengen Governance'. *Journal of Borderland Studies*, DOI:10.1080/08865655.2017.1402201.

Council of the EU (1999). *Council Decision of 20 May 1999 Concerning the Definition of the Schengen Acquis for the Purpose of Determining, in Conformity with the Relevant Provisions of the Treaty Establishing the European Community and the Treaty on European Union, the Legal Basis for Each of the Provisions or Decisions Which Constitute the Acquis*. OJ 1999 L176/1.

Council of the EU (2000). *The Schengen Acquis as Referred to in Article 1(2) of Council Decision 1999/435/EC of 20 May 1999*. OJ 2000 L239/1.

Cruz, A. (1993). 'Schengen, Ad Hoc Immigration Group, and Other European Intergovernmental Bodies'. *The Churches' Commission for Migrants in Europe Briefing Papers*, 13: 1–31.

Curtin, D. and Meijers, H. (1997). 'The Principle of Open Government in Schengen and the European Union: Democratic Retrogression?'. In H. Meijers (ed.), *Democracy, Migrants, and Police in the European Union: The 1996 IGC and Beyond*. Utrecht: FORUM.

De Capitani, E. (2014). 'The Schengen System After Lisbon: From Cooperation to Integration'. *ERA Forum*, 15(1): 101–18.

Den Boer, M. and Corrado, L. (1999). 'For the Record or Off the Record: Comments about the Incorporation of Schengen into the EU'. *European Journal of Migration and Law*, 1: 397–418.

Elsen, C. (2011). 'The Role of the Schengen Agreements in the European Construction'. *ERA Forum*, 12(1), Supplement: 69–85.

European Commission (2013). *Impact Assessment on Establishing an Entry/Exit System (EES)*. Brussels, SWD(2013) 47.

European Commission (2016a). *Proposal for a Regulation Establishing an Entry/Exit System (EES)*. Brussels, COM(2016) 194 final.

European Commission (2016b). *Stronger and Smarter Information Systems for Borders and Security*. Brussels, COM(2016) 205 final.

EDPS (2016). *Opinion on the Second EU Smart Borders Package*. Brussels, Opinion 06/2016.

Frontex (2018). 'Risk Analysis for 2018'. Warsaw, 2671/2018.

Guiraudon, V. (2000). 'European Integration and Migration Policy: Vertical Policy-making as Venue Shopping'. *Journal of Common Market Studies*, 38(2): 251–71.

Guiraudon, V. (2011). 'Schengen: une crise en trompe l'oeil'. *Politique étrangère*, 4: 773–84.

Huybreghts, G. (2015). 'The Schengen Convention and the Schengen *Acquis*: 25 Years of Evolution'. *ERA Forum*, 16(4): 379–426.

Huysmans, J. (2000). 'The European Union and the Securitization of Migration'. *Journal of Common Market Studies*, 38(5): 751–77.

Jansen, Y., Celikates, R. and de Bloois, J. (eds) (2014). *The Irregularization of Migration in Contemporary Europe: Death, Deportation, Drowning*. London: Rowman & Littlefield.

Jeandesboz, J. (2016). 'Smartening Border Security in the European Union: An Associational Inquiry'. *Security Dialogue*, 47(4): 292–309.

Lavenex, S. (1999). *Safe Third Countries: Extending the EU Asylum and Immigration Policies to Central and Eastern Europe*. Budapest: Central European University Press.

Lucassen, L. (2018). 'Peeling an Onion: the "Refugee Crisis" from a Historical Perspective'. *Ethnic and Racial Studies*, 41(3): 383–410.

Monar, J. (2001). 'The Dynamics of Justice and Home Affairs: Laboratories, Driving Factors and Costs'. *Journal of Common Market Studies*, 39(4): 747–64.

Moravcsik, A. (1998). *The Choice for Europe: Social Purpose and State Power from Messina to Maastricht*. London: Routledge.

OJEC (2000). *The Schengen Acquis as Referred to in Article 1(2) of Council Decision 1999/435/EC of 20 May 1999*. OJ 2000 L239/1.

Peers, S. (2000). 'Caveat Emptor: Integrating the Schengen Acquis into the European Union Legal Order'. *Cambridge Yearbook of European Legal Studies*, 2: 87–123.

Thym, D. (2002). 'The Schengen Law: A Challenge for Legal Accountability in the European Union'. *European Law Journal*, 8(2): 218–45.

Wind, M. (2012). 'The Blind, the Deaf and the Dumb! How Domestic Politics Turned the Danish Schengen Controversy into a Foreign Policy Crisis'. *Danish Foreign Policy Yearbook*, 14: 131–56.

Zaiotti, R. (2011). *Cultures of Border Control: Schengen and the Evolution of European Frontiers*. Chicago: The University of Chicago Press.

Zaiotti, R. (2013). 'The Italo-French Row over Schengen, Critical Junctures, and the Future of Europe's Border Regime'. *Journal of Borderland Studies*, 28(3): 337–54.

14 Trade Policy: Which Gains for Which Losses?

FERDI DE VILLE

14.1 Introduction

Since the very start, trade policy has been the showpiece of European integration. Together with agriculture and competition policy, it was one of the few policy domains that were transferred immediately to the supranational level by the Rome Treaties launching European integration. Thanks to the extraordinary European growth rates during the *trentes glorieuses* in the following decades and the consecutive enlargement rounds starting with the UK, Ireland and Denmark in 1973, the EU became the largest economy in the world by the beginning of the twenty-first century. Lacking 'hard' foreign policy and security competences, the 'Common Commercial Policy' allowed the EU to play a principal role on the world stage in, but also beyond, the trade sphere. The Union became not only a major power *in* trade, but also a power *through* trade (Meunier and Nicolaïdis, 2006), being capable of influencing the policies of third countries by asking them to make domestic reforms as a condition for access to the EU's formidable single market.

The centrality of trade policy to the EU's power and pride explains why the abrupt recent politicisation of the domain came as a shock to policy makers. Suddenly, tens of thousands of people took to the streets in European cities to protest against transatlantic trade negotiations, more than three million citizens signed a petition against these agreements and an already concluded deal with Canada was almost scuppered by a regional government in Belgium. This contestation shook one of the foundations of European integration.

This chapter shows how the EU's external trade policy has evolved in a way that is analogous to how European integration in general has developed. In that way, it should not come as a surprise that EU trade policy has recently become politicised, similar to what happened with European integration in general (see Chapter 1). As in other policy domains, the EU's trade policy response to the financial-economic and later euro crisis has been to double down on its traditional approach of more liberalisation. This has led to the unprecedented levels of contestation witnessed in recent years. While the European Commission, the key institution in trade policy (see Box 14.4), has tried to respond to this contestation through institutional and substantial reforms, it remains to be seen if these incremental changes will succeed in boosting legitimacy while maintaining the effectiveness of the policy domain.

The eternal question in trade policy – 'which gains for which losses?' – has taken on a more normative meaning, making it a more complex and more fascinating policy domain.

14.2   Historical Overview

When the founding fathers of European integration decided to establish a customs union (which would later be upgraded to a single market), the logical consequence of this step was to also develop a Common Commercial Policy. The transfer of the competence for trade policy to the supranational level was a 'logical corollary' of the raison d'être of the EU (Devuyst, 1992). Without a common external tariff, after the abolition of internal borders, exporters from outside the Union would simply be able to import their products via the member state with the lowest tariff, making independent national trade policies obsolete. Besides agreeing on common tariffs, a supranational machinery to negotiate trade agreements and to defend European firms against unfair foreign trade practices also had to be set up.

The establishment of the EU was preceded by the launch of the GATT in 1947, which regulated trade on a global level and provided a negotiating forum for states to reciprocally liberalise their markets. While the United States had actively supported European integration, it would quickly use the GATT to try to limit the discriminatory effects of European integration for American firms. They feared that liberalising trade between the Union's member states would provoke trade diversion, whereby imports from American firms are replaced by sales from European firms that no longer faced a tariff. Hence, the EU's trade machinery had to be put quickly to work to respond to American demands in the first GATT negotiating rounds.

Below, it is explained how the EU's institutional setup for and the substance of its trade policy has developed over the past sixty years (see Box 14.1).

14.2.1   Institutional Development

Similar to dynamics of internal economic integration in the EU, after industrial tariffs had been significantly reduced in consecutive GATT rounds, the international trade agenda would begin to focus on *behind-the-border barriers*. Because the Rome Treaties had not provided a clear definition of what 'commercial policy' entails, the broadening of the agenda would incite conflict between (and sometimes among) the member states and the European Commission about the scope of the EU's trade policy competence (Young, 2000). Eventually, this authority would be incrementally extended through treaty revisions and rulings by the CJEU. While the first two treaty revisions, the SEA (1987) and the Maastricht Treaty (1993), did not modify the article on the Common Commercial Policy itself, by contributing to the completion of the single market, the EU's trade competence was broadened through the doctrine of implied powers. The Treaties of Amsterdam (1999) and Nice (2003) made piecemeal changes to the article on the Common Commercial Policy. Only with the Lisbon Treaty (2009) was the EU's trade policy competence fully extended to services, intellectual property rights and investment, and hence considered 'complete'. The Lisbon Treaty also brought the policy domain in line with the ordinary legislative procedure. In a recent ruling on the EU-Singapore Agreement, the CJEU decided in its Opinion 2/15 that the EU is now fully competent for concluding a comprehensive 'twenty-first century trade agreement', except for the provisions on non-direct investment and for investor-state dispute settlement (ISDS).

BOX 14.1 Key dates

1957. Trade policy becomes a supranational competence from the very beginning (Art. 113 EEC).

1994. The EU is instrumental in the conclusion of the GATT Uruguay Round establishing the World Trade Organization (WTO).

2001. The Union is the main advocate behind the opening of the first round of WTO negotiations ('Doha Development Round') illustrating its leading role in the world trade system.

2006. The 'Global Europe' communication puts the EU on the path towards bilateral trade agreements with large economies.

2013. The EU launches trade negotiations with the US, resulting in unprecedented politicisation of the policy domain.

14.2.2   Substantial Development

The EU's substantial positions in trade have evolved significantly over the past six decades. From a reactive and defensive player focused on the multilateral level, the EU has become a proactive and offensive trade actor engaged in numerous bilateral negotiations (cf. Young and Peterson, 2014; Woolcock, 2014).

For a number of decades, the EU was preoccupied with defending its CAP against demands for liberalisation by other members of the GATT (Paarlberg, 1997; Daugbjerg and Swinbank, 2007). Increasing internal criticism against the financial cost of the CAP and the food surpluses it generated (see Chapter 7) made the EU able to compromise on agriculture in the 1990s and to, in return, ask for concessions from other GATT members in other areas. It allowed the EU to become the co-leader of the world trading system together with the US (Young and Peterson, 2014). While the EU was still hesitant at the beginning of the Uruguay Round negotiations (1986–94), it would become a big supporter of the new agreements on services (the General Agreement on Trade in Services, or GATS) and intellectual property rights (the Trade-Related Intellectual Property Rights Agreement) towards the end of the round, as it realised that the European economy had a comparative advantage in services and innovation (Paemen and Bensch, 1995). After the conclusion of the Uruguay Round and the establishment of the WTO that resulted from it, the EU further developed from a co-leader to the main champion of multilateral trade negotiations (see Box 14.2). In the late 1990s, the EU advocated a new 'Millennium Round' of trade negotiations (Van den Hoven, 2004). Not only was the lofty goal of effective multilateralism at the basis of the EU's leadership, but also blunt self-interest. To overcome outstanding divergence at the end of the Uruguay Round, the outcome included a 'rendezvous clause': the signatories agreed to reopen negotiations on agriculture and services by the year 2000. As the EU was still on the defensive in agriculture, it was in favour of a comprehensive negotiating agenda to increase the opportunity for trade-offs, in order to secure sufficient support for a new round at home. Moreover, the completion of the single market in the 1990s rendered the EU automatically more open to the rest of the world (Hanson, 1998), and hence interested in pursuing market access concessions by third countries in return.

The launch of a new multilateral trade round would fail at first in 'the battle of Seattle' in 1999. Unprecedented protest by CSOs on the streets of Seattle against what was depicted as a corporate power grab would spill over into the conference halls and result in the failure to start negotiations. The EU then reframed the proposal for a new round as geared particularly towards the interests of developing countries. Two years later, and in the spirit of global cooperation after the 9/11 attacks, a new round was launched in the Qatari capital of Doha, and became dubbed the 'Doha Development Round'. While successful in launching the talks, already in the first years of this round the EU had to give up on most of its 'deep trade' ambitions when the issues of rules on investment, government procurement and competition were taken off the agenda because of opposition by the US and developing countries. The EU's impact on the Doha Round would progressively wane as emerging economies became more vocal (Young, 2011). Eventually, the EU ended up in the inconvenient position where it was once more conceding on agricultural liberalisation to show goodwill without getting significant industrial or services market access to other countries in return. The Doha Round would eventually stall in 2008, when the July Package presented by then director-general of the WTO Pascal Lamy was rejected because of disagreement between the US and India and China over a special safeguard mechanism in agriculture, with the EU being unable to mediate. In response, the EU would turn towards bilateral agreements as an alternative for a multilateral deal within the WTO.

BOX 14.2 Key concepts

Multilateralism. EU trade policy is governed at three levels: the unilateral, bilateral and multilateral. At the unilateral level, the Union adopts trade policies autonomously, without engaging in negotiations with third countries. In this way, it imposes trade defence instruments like anti-dumping duties against imports from third countries when it argues that these are the result of unfair trading practices. The EU also autonomously gives more *preferential access* to its market to developing countries, more so if they respect a number of international sustainable development agreements, through its *Generalised System of Preferences* (GSP). On the bilateral level, the EU negotiates trade agreements with one other country (like Canada) or region (such as Mercosur). On the multilateral level, trade agreements are concluded between the full membership of the WTO. At the time of writing, the WTO has 164 members. Rules and concessions agreed here govern trade policies at the bilateral and unilateral level.

The key principle of the multilateral trading system is '**non-discrimination**'. States are supposed to treat third countries equally when their imports arrive at the border (*most-favoured nation*) and to treat imports equally to domestic goods and services once they have crossed the border ('national treatment'). The WTO has been in trouble for a number of years. Its rule book is seen as outdated, members are unable to agree to a new comprehensive agreement and the functioning of its dispute settlement mechanism is under threat as the US refuses to reappoint judges. Together with like-minded countries, the EU tries to safeguard the WTO by making reform proposals.

14.3   Current Institutional Framework

As explained in the Section 14.2, while EU trade policy was a supranational competence from the very beginning, the institutional framework has evolved over time. In the most recent Lisbon Treaty reforms (see Box 14.3), the scope of trade policy has been further broadened to fully include trade in services and investment (but not portfolio investment and ISDS). Moreover, trade policy has been brought under the umbrella of EU external action to better pursue coherence between commercial and other foreign policy goals. But the most important Lisbon Treaty change to trade policy has been the strengthening of the role of the EP (Devuyst, 2010; Woolcock, 2010). Since Lisbon, the ordinary legislative procedure applies to trade policy, including the conclusion of trade agreements.

Since the Lisbon Treaty, EU trade agreements come into being as follows. On its own initiative, or that of another institution or trading partner, the European Commission proposes to start trade negotiations to the Council of the EU. When asking for permission to start talks, it will present negotiating directives to the Council. The member states then discuss among themselves how to amend these guidelines (also known as the 'mandate'). This is an important and often tense stage. Formally, the EP does not have to give its permission to the Commission to start negotiations, but it has adopted the habit of drafting negotiating guidelines on its own initiative, which the Commission is expected to follow if it wants to secure the EP's consent to the agreement after the negotiations (Van den Putte et al., 2015). Once the Council has authorised the opening of talks, the Commission is the sole negotiator (or 'single voice') for the EU. However, it engages in constant interaction with the member states through weekly meetings of the Trade Policy Committee, a formal committee of the Council. The Commission also has to brief the International Trade Committee of the EP before and after each negotiating round. Once negotiations have been concluded (these often take several years), the Council and the EP have to give their consent to the agreement, by qualified and absolute majority respectively.

However, even after the Lisbon Treaty expansion of the scope of the Common Commercial Policy, discussions have remained about the qualification of trade agreements as exclusive EU or mixed agreements. Because EU trade agreements have become ever more comprehensive in substance, member states have argued that these still have to be considered as mixed agreements, hence requiring national ratification. In response to political pressure by member states, the CETA between the EU and Canada has been qualified as mixed and as a consequence the complicated ratification procedure in member states is still ongoing at the time of writing. Since opinion 2/15 of the CJEU, the EU has decided to negotiate trade agreements excluding portfolio investment and ISDS (these issues might be the subject of a separate agreement) in order to guarantee that trade agreements can be qualified as being of exclusive EU competence.

BOX 14.3 Legal basis

Article 207 of the TFEU (ex Article 133 TEC) establishes trade policy as an exclusive competence of the EU. It prescribes that the policy domain shall be conducted with regard to the principles and objectives of the Union's external action. The article explains how trade negotiations should be conducted and adopted, and defines the responsibilities of the different EU institutions.

14.4   Recent Policy Developments

Over the past ten years EU trade policy has undergone a significant transformation. The turn towards bilateral trade agreements that have become ever more comprehensive in scope and have been pursued with ever more important trading partners has led to an unprecedented politicisation of EU trade policy. The euro crisis has also been a significant critical juncture in that respect. It increased the expectations of what trade policy was supposed to achieve and at the same time increased scepticism in civil society vis-à-vis the European establishment, and their attempts at international economic integration in particular.

In its 2006 Communication 'Global Europe', the European Commission announced its ambition to pursue bilateral trade agreements with countries of significant commercial interest. As it had already become obvious that the Doha Development Round was going nowhere, the Commission felt the need to pursue better access to fast-growing markets to ensure economic growth in the future. In Global Europe, the European Commission announced that it would henceforth use economic criteria to identify interesting partner countries for bilateral trade negotiations, based on their economic size, growth and level of protection against EU export interests. On the basis of these criteria, the Association of Southeast Asian Nations (ASEAN), Korea, Mercosur, India, Russia and the Gulf Co-operation Council were selected. The Commission also announced that the scope of these agreements was to be broadened to include issues such as investment, public procurement, competition, regulatory issues and intellectual property rights protection. The EU now tried to pursue its 'deep trade agenda', which had been torpedoed at the WTO, through bilateral agreements. Negotiations with Korea were successfully concluded in 2009. Since this agreement, the EU also aims to include a 'sustainable development' chapter in every free trade agreement, which encourages the parties not to lower their domestic environmental and social regulations for trade purposes and to ratify and implement a number of international environmental and social agreements. Beyond Korea, negotiations on such broad free trade agreements with the other partners mentioned in Global Europe have proven more difficult to conclude. The EU abandoned region-to-region talks with ASEAN and has managed to conclude agreements with individual countries such as Singapore and Vietnam. With some larger emerging countries such as India, the sustainable development provisions that the EU wants to include in trade agreements have proven to be contentious.

The perceived need to conclude bilateral trade agreements to stimulate growth and jobs would become even stronger after the financial-economic crisis broke out, depressing demand within the EU. In trade policy, as in other EU policies, the period since the outbreak of the financial-economic crisis can be seen as a critical juncture (cf. Bollen et al., 2016). The European Commission responded to the financial-economic and euro crises by 'doubling down' on its traditional approach of increasing liberalisation. In the foreword of the second Barroso Commission's trade strategy, 'Trade, Growth and World Affairs', then trade commissioner Karel De Gucht wrote: '[t]he challenge in a changing world is for us to maintain and improve our position and to trade our way out of the current economic crisis' (European Commission, 2010). Increasing exports through concluding trade agreements was presented as the only way for the EU to grow again: while consumers were deleveraging, business was unwilling to invest and governments were applying austerity (De Ville and Orbie, 2014). De Gucht would continuously promote trade agreements as 'a stimulus that hardly costs a eurocent to the Treasury, and where the EU can deliver on thanks to our exclusive competence' (De Gucht, 2011).

Boosting economic growth and jobs and increasingly also maintaining the EU's global influence in the context of the rapid rise of emerging economies (China in particular) eventually led the EU to launch trade negotiations with the United States. However, these TTIP negotiations unleashed extraordinary debate and protest (De Ville and Siles-Brügge, 2015), as explained in more detail in Section 14.6. This contestation of TTIP spilled over to other negotiations such as CETA. This made the European Commission realise that it had to respond in order to ensure sufficient support for one of its key policy domains. In its latest trade strategy, 'Trade for All', current Trade Commissioner Cecilia Malmström wrote in the foreword:

> [i]n recent years, we have seen an intense debate about trade across the European Union, which has some important lessons for EU trade policy [...] In this new strategy, 'Trade for All', the Commission is adapting its approach to trade policy to take all of these lessons on board. As a result, trade policy will become more responsible, meaning it will be more effective, more transparent and will not only project our interests, but also our values. (European Commission, 2015: 5)

Indeed, the European Commission has made a number of substantial and institutional changes in response to the TTIP debate (see De Ville and Gheyle, 2019). It has replaced ISDS by a new 'Investment Court System', with the ultimate aim to establish a multilateral investment court, and has reiterated that trade agreements can neither lower levels of protection in the EU nor erode governments' right to regulate. Procedurally, the Commission has increased the transparency of trade negotiations through a number of transparency initiatives, including the publication of EU negotiating documents, the establishment of a trade advisory group and giving more European and national parliamentarians access to consolidated texts (see Gheyle and De Ville, 2017).

BOX 14.4 Key actors

Institutional actors

European Commission. The European Commission is the key institutional actor in EU trade policy with the sole authority to negotiate EU trade agreements. It also proposes regulations in the trade domain such as on GSP or anti-dumping.

Council of the European Union. The Council authorises the Commission to open trade negotiations, scrutinises these and has to authorise the signing of the agreement, its provisional application and ratification. It is the co-legislator for trade legislation.

EP. Since the Lisbon Treaty, the EP has to give its consent to every EU trade agreement. The EP is also, together with the Council, co-legislator for EU trade legislation.

Non-institutional actors

Business organisations. European firms, mainly through their umbrella organisation Business Europe, have been the main societal actors in trade policy. Dominated by big firms with an international orientation, Business Europe has always supported trade liberalisation.

Trade unions. Trade unions, represented through the European Trade Union Confederation, tend to support trade agreements while warning that these should not undermine social protection in the EU.

CSOs. Organisations that promote public causes are relatively new to EU trade policy. Since the 1990s, they have contested the broadening of EU trade agreements towards 'behind-the-border barriers', warning that this might lower levels of protection in the EU and limit policy space for governments.

14.5   Current Political and Academic Controversies

The political and academic debate on EU trade policy has largely followed the evolution of the policy domain as discussed above. First, there has been discussion about the desirability and consequences of transferring authority over trade to the national level. Subsequently, controversy moved to the relationship between the national and supranational level in conducting trade policy, and its effect. Then, political and academic debates became about the winners and losers of EU trade policy in economic terms. Finally, the trade debate today is broadened to include the balance between supposed economic gains from trade liberalisation and the possible losses in terms of policy space for governments and the levels of protection they can offer to their citizens.

Academic analyses of EU trade policy have long almost exclusively focused on institutional conflicts between the European Commission and the member states. Scholars came up with a concept that explains the decision in the Treaty of Rome to delegate trade policy to the supranational level to insulate it from protectionist capture: 'collusive delegation' (e.g. Dür and Zimmermann, 2007). Through the 'principal–agent approach', political scientists analysed how much autonomy the European Commission has, how the member states exert control and how this affects EU trade policy positions (e.g. Kerremans, 2004; Dür and Elsig, 2011). Through the 'two-level game' perspective, they bring in the international level (e.g. Da Conceição-Heldt, 2013). Those that take into account member states' domestic ratification competence extend this to a 'three-level game', with the international negotiations, the EU level and the national ratification arena as separate but interlinked spheres (e.g. Leal-Arcas, 2002).

Such debates about the consequences of the scope of the exclusive supranational trade competence and the roles of the European Commission and the member states that come with it have been held in terms of a 'legitimacy–efficiency trade-off' (Meunier, 2003). Those who favour a broad definition of the Common Commercial Policy and a strong supranational representation of the EU in trade argue that this brings two efficiency gains. Delegating the competence for trade to the supranational level would result in more liberal (and, according to neoclassical economics, more efficient) policies, as the European Commission is supposed to be more insulated from protectionist interest groups than national politicians. A single representation of the member states by the European Commission would, moreover, increase their influence in the international trading system. Others that favour a stronger role for the member states argue that the costs that come with liberalisation can only be legitimately accepted by involving national politicians. Also participants in the debate about strengthening the EP's role in EU trade policy have used these arguments (see Van den Putte et al., 2015). Advocates of a stronger role for the EP have argued that in this supranational policy domain that produces winners and losers and contains trade-offs between competing objectives, the institution that directly represents EU citizens has to be strongly involved. Opponents feared that giving the EP veto power on trade agreements would make the EU a less credible negotiating partner. These debates came to the fore in two recent contested agreements. First, the Anti-Counterfeiting Trade Agreement (ACTA) was rejected by the EP in 2012. Some saw their fears confirmed that the EU would become an unreliable partner in international trade negotiations. Others applauded that the EP had defended civil liberties over economic interests. Second, the CETA, as mentioned above, was almost scuppered when the Belgian regional government of Wallonia threatened to veto the deal because of concerns over agriculture and the effects of investor protection provisions on the right to regulate of governments (cf. Tatham, 2018: 680–3). The Walloon Minister-President Paul Magnette justified his stubborn position as a signal to the supranational level that modern trade agreements that go far beyond eliminating tariffs cannot be passed without sufficient democratic debate at several levels of government. Some saw this 'CETA saga' as proof that mixed agreements, necessitating approval by national (and in some member states even subnational) governments and parliaments, jeopardise the EU's ability to conclude trade agreements. Others perceived it as desirable that prominent national politicians take a position on these important agreements.

More recently, political and academic controversies have shifted from the institutional to the substantial (although the two cannot be neatly separated). Again, similar to what we have seen for European integration in general, debates have evolved from 'more or less EU competence (in trade policy)?' to 'what kind of EU (trade) policies?'. For a long time it was argued that EU trade policy was about achieving Pareto optimum outcomes: liberalisation would bring economic gains to society as a whole and this would be more than sufficient to compensate losers. Trade policy could hence rely on output legitimacy. This has changed, however. In recent trade agreements, debates about gains and losses go beyond economic consequences, but are rather about competing objectives. This has modified political as well as academic controversies. In the past, trade politics involved mainly a conflict between exporting firms with an interest in reciprocal liberalisation and import-competing firms with an interest in protection. There was a consensus in academia and politics that liberalisation is welfare optimal. Scholars saw it as their task to study and model how trade agreements allow governments to pursue liberalisation with sufficient domestic support (see Gstöhl and De Bièvre, 2017, for a discussion of this model).

Since modern trade agreements are mostly about removing behind-the-border barriers, the view that they increase aggregate welfare and that losing groups can be compensated has been challenged. When the focus is on 'regulatory barriers to trade', the question becomes how much protection or regulatory autonomy a society wants to give up to attain economic gains. Some even go as far as arguing that 'new trade issues' such as investment or intellectual property rights protection mainly serve multinationals (that have only become more important in the world economy because of liberalisation in the past) to advance their own self-interests rather than promoting aggregate welfare (e.g. Rodrik, 2017). Again, academic analyses are adapting to the changing nature of globalisation, EU trade agreements and the consequent societal conflict. They allow for new actors, new concerns and a changing international context (see Young, 2017, for a recent application). CSOs are given more prominence in analyses and the same goes for public actors from outside the trade sphere. Naturally, the increased power of the EP has also led to more studies on its role. In recognition of the shift from distributive towards normative conflict, ideas and norm entrepreneurs have received more attention in analyses, often of a more constructivist nature.

14.6   Analysis of a Paradigmatic Case Study

The TTIP is the perfect case to illustrate the shift that has taken place in political and academic controversies in EU trade policy. TTIP was supposed to become the EU's most comprehensive trade agreement ever, and with the most significant partner country so far. However, this resulted in unprecedented contestation of the negotiations, which were eventually 'put in the freezer' in the autumn of 2016.

In terms of scope, the TTIP negotiations were unparalleled in their ambition to tackle non-tariff barriers between the EU and the US. Because tariffs on transatlantic trade were already very low (below 3 per cent on average on a trade-weighted basis), the TTIP negotiations aimed to eliminate regulatory differences that drive up costs for firms that do business at both sides of the Atlantic. However, provisions to eliminate current regulatory differences and to avoid future divergence could reach deep behind the border. They were supposed to also bind governments below the federal or supranational level. This alarmed CSOs, which feared that this would undermine hard-fought-for protective regulations, and that they would be less able to influence regulatory decision-making at a higher level. The most controversial provision in TTIP was ISDS, which allows international investors to sue governments (again also those below the supranational level) before an international tribunal if they argue that a policy decision has illegitimately hurt their expected revenue. TTIP was different in one other respect: the US being the counterpart in the negotiations also made it unlike earlier negotiations. In the past, when the EU was negotiating bilateral trade agreements with developing, middle-income countries or smaller industrialised countries, the expansion of the scope of negotiations was not perceived as a threat to the EU. Rather, it was the EU that would try to export its rules to third countries by using its market power. Trade policy was seen as an important fundament of the EU's normative power (Manners, 2002). With the US, however, the EU was negotiating with an equal power and could not be expected to be able to impose its own regulations.

In this context, CSOs have successfully framed TTIP as a threat to European levels of protection and democratic decision-making (De Ville and Siles-Brügge, 2017). They argued that by pursuing transatlantic regulatory convergence, environmental, social and consumer protection would be sacrificed on the altar of economic gains. CSOs claimed that especially ISDS would further empower multinational companies and weaken public authority over them. Besides criticising the substance of TTIP, CSOs also lamented the process of the negotiations, depicting them as happening 'behind closed doors'. Because of this public contestation, EU negotiators had to take uncompromising positions at the negotiating table and the talks advanced at a very low speed. In April 2016, shortly before the negotiations were put on hold, only four out of twenty-six envisaged chapters had been concluded successfully (European Commission, 2016).

The fate of the TTIP negotiations helps to understand the current, post-crisis politics of EU trade. The launch of the talks demonstrates how trade policy is often used in the EU to compensate for the lack of strong supranational fiscal and traditional foreign policy tools. The negotiations also confirm the complexity of internal decision-making in EU trade policy and the usefulness of traditional principal–agent and two/three-level game approaches. As is often the case, difficulties already erupted before negotiations even started, when the member states had to agree on negotiating guidelines. A number of member states led by France wanted to explicitly preclude the European Commission from negotiating on 'audio-visual services' because they feared European music and film producers would be overrun by American productions. Other member states were concerned that if the EU took an issue off the table before even starting to talk, the US might respond in kind for one of their defensive interests. In general, the presence of different veto players at several levels of government at both sides of the Atlantic and the strict negotiating directives (in the US called the 'Trade Promotion Authority') they issued indicated early on that the agents (the European Commission and the United States Trade Representative) had little autonomy, and that finding a compromise that is acceptable domestically was always going to be difficult.

But TTIP also showed how a 'new politics of trade' (Young, 2017) has arrived due to changes in the nature of economic exchange and of trade agreements. In contrast with earlier trade negotiations, business interests were almost perfectly aligned within and between the EU and the US. But this has not resulted in easy negotiations that could be concluded on 'one tank of gas' as the negotiators had hoped. Instead, the focus on eliminating regulatory barriers to trade led to unprecedented contestation by CSOs and politicisation with the general public, although in different ways and to different extents in the US and the EU, and between European member states. CSOs were concerned that TTIP would lead to a lowering of levels of social, environmental, consumer and health protection in the EU and that it would further increase the power of multinationals over governments and societies, hollowing out democratic decision-making. Some 'rejectionist' CSOs therefore argued that TTIP had to be abandoned altogether, and that trade agreements in general need to be overhauled. Other more 'reformist' organisations argued that some provisions (such as ISDS) needed to be taken out of TTIP or had to be drastically reformed, and that the deal (and trade agreements in general) needed to focus on reregulation rather than deregulation.

This has also led students of EU trade policy to adapt their analyses. In the past, scholars focused mainly on how import-competing and exporting firms lobby governments in favour of or against trade liberalisation, and how these interests translate into EU trade policies as governments give authority to the European

Commission to negotiate while controlling the process such that it secures a deal in which expected economic benefits outweigh economic costs. Now, students of EU trade policy not only take into account new economic actors (such as retailers and importers) that have become more important in an economy characterised by 'global value chains', but also integrate CSOs into their analyses. Studies note how these new actors have changed the terms of the debate on trade policy, away from an exclusively economic discourse towards a more normative discussion. This allows for more constructivist analyses, where the salience of trade agreements, or specific provisions within them, and how these are framed become more important explanatory factors to account for EU trade policy.

The unexpected victory of Donald J. Trump in the US presidential elections led to a halt in the TTIP negotiations, which were already in bad shape before this shock. Trump has affected EU trade policy beyond these talks. His aggressive unilateral trade policies led the EU to present itself as the champion of an open trading system. It has allied with other countries to safeguard the WTO, and several partners approached the EU to demand upgrades in their trade relationship, because they wanted to differentiate their exports away from the American market assuming it would become less accessible. This implies a strengthening of the EU's traditional trade agenda. However, for critics of traditional EU trade policy, including CSOs, it has become more difficult to contest the EU's positions, as they can now be portrayed as 'objective allies' of Trump. In the spring of 2018, Trump also targeted the EU with increased tariffs on the import of steel and aluminium, and threatened the even more significant car sector with similar measures. In the hope of avoiding an escalation, the EU responded with offering Trump negotiations about reciprocal market opening. In that way, the TTIP talks have reappeared through the backdoor. However, it seems unlikely that negotiations have a higher chance of success in the current environment, and with Mr Trump in the White House.

GROUP DISCUSSION

- Is the increased politicisation of EU trade policy a good or a bad thing?
- Have (EU) trade agreements gone too far ? Should their scope be reduced to focus on eliminating tariffs, should they rather proceed in tackling new, behind- the-border barriers to trade or should they instead focus primarily on reregulating trade?

TOPICS FOR INDIVIDUAL RESEARCH

- How has the election of Donald J. Trump affected EU trade policies?
- How can we expect Brexit to influence EU trade politics?

FURTHER READINGS

De Ville, F. and Siles-Brügge, G. (2015). *TTIP: The Truth about the Transatlantic Trade and Investment Partnership*. Cambridge: Polity.

Dür, A. (2010). *Protection for Exporters: Power and Discrimination in Transatlantic Trade Relations, 1930–2010*. Ithaca, NY: Cornell University Press.

Gstöhl, S. and De Bièvre, D. (2017). *The Trade Policy of the European Union*. London: Palgrave.

Young, A. R. and Peterson, J. (2014). *Parochial Global Europe: 21st Century Trade Politics*. Oxford: Oxford University Press.

Young, A. R. (2017). *The New Politics of Trade: Lessons from TTIP*. Newcastle upon Tyne: Agenda Publishing.

REFERENCES

Bollen, Y., De Ville, F. and Orbie, J. (2016). 'EU Trade Policy: Persistent Liberalisation, Contentious Protectionism'. *Journal of European Integration*, 38(3): 279–94.

Da Conceição-Heldt, E. (2013). 'Two-level Games and Trade Cooperation: What Do We Now Know?'. *International Politics*, 50(4): 579–99.

Daugbjerg, C. and Swinbank, A. (2007). 'The Politics of CAP Reform: Trade Negotiations, Institutional Settings and Blame Avoidance'. *JCMS: Journal of Common Market Studies* 45(1): 1–22.

De Gucht, K. (2011). *Trade: A Growth Engine in the Crisis*. Speech /11/718, Rome, 28 October 2011.

De Ville, F. and Gheyle, N. (2019). 'The Unintended Consequences of the Transatlantic Trade and Investment Partnership'. *International Spectator*, 54(1): 16–30.

De Ville, F. and Orbie, J. (2014). 'The European Commission's Neoliberal Trade Discourse Since the Crisis: Legitimizing Continuity Through Subtle Discursive Change'. *The British Journal of Politics and International Relations*, 16(1): 149–67.

De Ville, F. and Siles-Brügge, G. (2015). *TTIP: The Truth about the Transatlantic Trade and Investment Partnership*. Cambridge: Polity Press.

De Ville, F. and Siles-Brügge, G. (2017). 'Why TTIP is a Game-changer and its Critics Have a Point'. *Journal of European Public Policy*, 24(10): 1491–505.

Devuyst, Y. (1992). 'EC's Common Commercial Policy and the Treaty on European Union – An Overview of the Negotiations'. *World Competition*, 16: 67.

Devuyst, Y. (2010). 'The European Union's Competence in International Trade After the Treaty of Lisbon'. *Georgia Journal of International and Comparative Law*, 39: 639.

Dür, A. and Elsig, M. (2011). 'Principals, Agents, and the European Union's Foreign Economic Policies'. *Journal of European Public Policy*, 18(3): 323–38.

Dür, A. and Zimmermann, H. (2007). 'Introduction: The EU in International Trade Negotiations'. *JCMS: Journal of Common Market Studies*, 45(4): 771–87.

European Commission (2010). 'Communication from the Commission to the Council, the European Parliament, the European Economic and Social Committee and the Committee of the Regions: Trade, Growth and World Affairs'. Brussels, 9 November, COM(2010) 612 final.

European Commission (2015). *Trade for All: Towards a More Responsible Trade and Investment Policy*. Brussels: European Commission.

Gheyle, N. and De Ville, F. (2017). 'How Much is Enough? Explaining the Continuous Transparency Conflict in TTIP'. *Politics and Governance*, 5(3): 16.

Gstöhl, S. and De Bièvre, D. (2017). *The Trade Policy of the European Union*. London: Palgrave.

Hanson, B. (1998). 'What Happened to Fortress Europe? External Trade Policy Liberalization in the EU?'. *International Organization*, 52(1): 55–85.

Kerremans, B. (2004). 'What Went Wrong in Cancun? A Principal–Agent View on the EU's Rationale towards the Doha Development Round'. *European Foreign Affairs Review*, 9: 363.

Leal-Arcas, R. (2002). 'The EC in the WTO: The Three-level Game of Decision-making. What Multilateralism Can Learn from Regionalism'. *European Integration Online Papers*, 8(14): 1–39.

Manners, I. (2002). 'Normative Power Europe: A Contradiction in Terms?'. *Journal of Common Market Studies*, 40(2): 235–58.

Meunier, S. (2003). 'Trade Policy and Political Legitimacy in the European Union'. *Comparative European Politics*, 1(1): 67–90.

Meunier, S. and Nicolaïdis, K. (2006). 'The European Union as a Conflicted Trade Power'. *Journal of European Public Policy*, 13(6): 906–25.

Paarlberg, R. (1997). 'Agricultural Policy Reform and the Uruguay Round: Synergistic Linkage in a Two-level Game?'. *International Organization*, 51(3): 413–44.

Paemen, H. and Bensch, A. (1995). *From the GATT to the WTO: The European Community in the Uruguay Round*. Leuven: Leuven University Press.

Rodrik, D. (2017). *Straight Talk on Trade: Ideas for a Sane World Economy*. Princeton: Princeton University Press.

Tatham, M. (2018). 'The Rise of Regional Influence in the EU: From Soft Policy Lobbying to Hard Vetoing'. *Journal of Common Market Studies*, 56(3): 672–86.

Van den Hoven, A. (2004). 'Assuming Leadership in Multilateral Economic Institutions: the EU's "Development Round" Discourse and Strategy'. *West European Politics*, 27(2): 256–83.

Van den Putte, L., De Ville, F. and Orbie, J. (2015). 'The European Parliament as an International Actor in Trade: From Power to Impact'. In S. Stavridis and D. Irrera (eds), *The European Parliament and its International Relations*. London: Routledge.

Woolcock, S. (2010). 'EU Trade and Investment Policymaking after the Lisbon Treaty'. *Intereconomics*, 45(1): 22–5.

Woolcock, S. (2014). 'EU Policy on Preferential Trade Agreements in the 2000s: A Reorientation Towards Commercial Aims'. *European Law Journal*, 20(6): 718–32.

Young, A. R. (2000). 'The Adaptation of European Foreign Economic Policy: From Rome to Seattle'. *JCMS: Journal of Common Market Studies*, 38(1): 93–116.

Young, A. R. (2011). 'The Rise (and Fall?) of the EU's Performance in the Multilateral Trading System'. *Journal of European Integration*, 33(6): 715–29.

Young, A. R. (2017). *The New Politics of Trade: Lessons from TTIP*. Newcastle upon Tyne: Agenda Publishing.

Young, A. R. and Peterson, J. (2014). *Parochial Global Europe: 21st Century Trade Politics*. Oxford: Oxford University Press.

15 Global Tax Governance: Is the EU Promoting Tax Justice?

RASMUS CORLIN CHRISTENSEN AND LEONARD SEABROOKE

15.1 Introduction

Continuing European integration, and more broadly global economic integration, has exposed the increasing discrepancy between nationally grounded tax policy and transnational economic affairs. Economic, political and cultural integration creates competitive pressures that challenge the fiscal and political sustainability of national policies, creating winners and losers (Genschel and Schwarz, 2011). National tax policy, in a transnational context, has significant distributional implications, both intranationally and internationally. Inside the EU, the highly uneven fiscal and political effects of integration in areas such as budget policy (see Chapter 6), monetary policy (see Chapter 9) and trade policy (see Chapter 14) are clearly visible.

Tax and fiscal policy is a particularly prominent arena for these problems, forming 'the skeleton of the state stripped of all misleading ideologies', as the Austrian sociologist Rudolph Goldscheid asserted (Goldscheid, 1919). As a supranational polity, the EU was founded primarily on ideology but has a particular institutional and regulatory basis that permits it to provide state-like tax and fiscal functions, such as its authority in the areas of the customs union, infrastructure development and cross-national programmes to boost skills and employment, among a range of others, as key levers for the EU to defend the 'four freedoms' for the movement of goods, services, capital and persons. However, the EU's tax basis is highly politically contentious (Hallerberg, 2004; see also Chapter 6). This is the case because taxation is always redistributive, taking revenue more from some than others. Moreover, taxation has historically been a policy area close to the heart of national governments, who have been unwilling to expand the EU's competences on tax and fiscal issues. Given this, the EU has operated on the basis of 'fiscal contracts' that permit multiple parties to get along by distributing the costs and benefits of tax policies and tax policy-making. A key component of the European tax policy context is thus the mutual recognition of sovereign national authority over tax policy, and the acknowledgement of domestic institutions governing fiscal policy (Holzinger, 2005; Hallerberg, 2011).

The rise of 'tax justice' as a key EU issue area over the past decade has exacerbated these distributional battles and tensions of EU tax policy. Since the global financial crisis of 2007–8, the EU has evolved into a highly contested arena of controversial tax justice discussions. Actors in and around the EU have played crucial roles in transforming the conversation on global tax governance, moving narratives and setting agendas in alignment with key EU goals in the area of taxation, such as enhanced harmonisation and the combating of tax evasion, tax avoidance and tax havens.

This transformation must be viewed against the backdrop of a series of political and institutional crises that have profoundly reshaped the context of tax policy-making in the EU (Christensen and Hearson, 2019). The global financial crisis provided an obvious break with established practice, bringing with it a need for shoring up fiscal systems in the Union, but equally important is the extensive politicisation of tax policy under the headings of 'tax justice' and 'fair taxation', promoted in large part by global media exposures such as LuxLeaks, the Panama Papers and the Paradise Papers. Moreover, the institutional crisis of legitimacy suffered by the EU, following successive sovereign debt crises and a perceived slowness of crisis responses in key policy areas (Coman, 2018; Seabrooke and Tsingou, 2018), has fostered a need for institutional rethinking and repositioning, which have manifested themselves in the area of tax policy in new strategies and identities for the EU's institutions.

The effect has been a newly contentious political context of EU tax policy. Expert activists have found unparalleled success in pushing radical new regulations in the name of 'tax justice', and the European Commission has played a crucial and entrepreneurial role in moving discussions of unprecedented tax harmonisation forwards, seemingly against the expressed interests of member states. However, member states have continued to reassert their historical dominance and exclusive policy-making right, resisting progress deemed harmful to 'the national interest and thus exposing intra-EU distributional conflicts, such as that between 'tax havens' Luxembourg, Ireland and the Netherlands, and large EU markets such as Germany and France. These conflicts over 'tax justice', in turn, have limited the Union's ability to promote radical tax reforms both inside and beyond Europe. In this chapter, we discuss these developments and conflicts, focusing specifically on two policy examples that illustrate the changing context of EU tax policy under the banner of 'tax justice': corporate tax transparency in the form of country-by-country reporting (CBCR) and tax harmonisation through the Common Consolidated Corporate Tax Base (CCCTB) (see Box 15.1).

BOX 15.1 Key concepts

Tax justice. Highly contested term meaning 'fair' or 'just' taxation – in terms of policies and political processes – for the distribution of tax burdens on persons and corporations.

> ## BOX 15.1 (Cont.)
>
> *Global tax governance*. The global political order governing the taxation of international economic activity.
>
> *CBCR*. Country-by-country reporting, a radical proposal for disclosure by multinational companies of nationally segmented information on tax payments and economic activity indicators.
>
> *CCCTB*. Common Consolidated Corporate Tax Base, a long-standing EU policy proposal to harmonise the national rules for the calculating of corporate taxable income, as well as the intra-EU distribution of such taxable income.

15.2   Historical Overview

Tax policy-making has a notably constrained history in the EU. While taxation was incorporated as a key policy area already at the founding of the Union, enshrined in the Treaty of Rome, it also explicitly restricted EU competences by requiring unanimity in the Council to any tax harmonisation efforts (Article 112 TFEU). And that direction, laid out early on, has critically shaped EU tax policy. Although every subsequent treaty has addressed tax policy, with harmonisation often articulated as central for the 'ever closer union', national sovereignty concerns have historically restricted EU cooperation on tax policy largely to indirect taxes, in particular VAT and excise duties. For a long time, harmonisation of policies on direct taxes, including personal income taxes and corporate taxation, remained limited.

However, towards the end of the twentieth century, an increased awareness of the impacts of globalisation, combined with the legal and institutional evolution of the Union itself, fostered significant change in the area of tax policy. Sketching out some cursory milestones for this change (see Box 15.2), the establishment of the European single market, in particular, expanded attention to tax issues and set a path for further cooperation. Arthur Cockfield, the British 'Father of the Single Market', wrote a 1985 White Paper for the Commission, which eventually laid the groundwork for the 1993 establishment of the single market, discussed tax policy extensively, identifying 'fiscal barriers' as one of three key batches of measures that needed to be removed (Commission of the EC, 1985). The updated Article 26 TFEU provided EU institutions with new powers (see Box 15.3).

A number of political and institutional innovations have followed, of which we shall highlight a few that are specifically relevant in the context of this chapter. First, in light of continuing economic integration, most developed countries – including

EU member states – undertook large-scale reforms of their tax systems in the late 1980s and early 1990s, although with uneven configurations (Hallerberg and Basinger, 1998). Second, EU leaders and institutions responded proactively to increasing international attention to the issue of 'harmful tax competition' and the threat of 'tax havens' to domestic fiscal systems (OECD, 1998; Sharman, 2006). In one stream of action, they began engaging more expansively with other international actors, most notably the OECD, which led to the international campaign against tax havens. In another, the EU established its own streams of action. In 1998, after several high-level meetings, the Council agreed to set up a Code of Conduct Group on Business Taxation, explicitly mandating the denouncement of harmful tax competition, and further to enact new directives on the taxation of savings and cross-border interest and royalty payments (Council of the European Union, 1997).

Alongside these political and institutional innovations, a cognitive revolution was in the works. Radaelli (1997, 1999a) details the late 1990s 'narrative campaign' by the European Commission to broaden the European tax agenda and expand the coalition of actors interested in it from the 'embryonic epistemic community', involving only experts at the Commission and a few friendly corporate interests. 'Harmful tax competition' would become a banner not just for specific political action but also a more general strategy for the EU to enhance its stake and place in direct tax policy. The result, Radaelli finds, was increased political attention, expansion of the EU's tasks on direct taxation and, critically, 'the shift of tax policy into the core of EU public policy' (1999a: 675). In contrast to Puchala's (1984) analysis of EU tax harmonisation in the 1960s and 1970s, which emphasised the 'mutual understandings' among a small group of like-minded policy makers as the key enabler of EU tax cooperation, the late 1990s campaign illustrated the power of politicisation (Radaelli, 1999b).

Since the 1990s, EU tax policy and cooperation has expanded significantly, including direct tax policy, although formally the competencies of EU institutions have not changed radically. Genschel and Jachtenfuchs (2011) show how, despite the EU's lack of a distinct tax resource, EU institutions have developed significant power over member states' tax policies: 'National governments still levy taxes, but often the EU determines the shape and occasionally even the level of taxation' (2011: 294).

These powers are applied through both secondary legislation, most notably directives and decisions, and the jurisprudence of the Court of Justice of the EU, but also through informal discussion fora such as the EU Joint Transfer Pricing Forum (set up in 2002). Prominent recent examples include the Anti Tax Avoidance Directive (2016/1164), which mandates member states to implement a range of specific rules to combat tax avoidance, and the ECJ's landmark *Cadbury Schweppes* ruling (C-196/04, 2006), which found that a specific anti-tax avoidance policy of the UK restricted the four freedoms, forcing the UK to change its legislation.

BOX 15.2 Key dates

1993. The single market takes effect, providing further momentum for the removal of 'fiscal barriers' in the Union.

1998. The OECD publishes the report 'Harmful Tax Competition: An Emerging Global Issue', prompting unprecedented attention on international corporate tax policy in the EU and beyond.

2011. The European Commission presents a proposal for a CCCTB, a controversial idea to harmonise corporate tax policy in the EU.

2014. The International Consortium of Investigative Journalists release the first of a series of blockbuster 'tax haven leaks', LuxLeaks, implicating newly elected European Commission President Jean-Claude Juncker.

2016. The European Commission proposes a radical new directive on corporate tax transparency, public CBCR.

15.3 Current Institutional Framework

Over the last decade, the EU has experienced another wave of transformation of institutions, policies and actors in tax policy. This is in the context of the global financial crisis, successive media leaks underscoring the problems of the European and global tax system, and the institutional crises faced by the EU itself. These crises exposed contradictory and hypocritical arrangements among institutions responsible for global economic governance, allowing the erosion of national fiscal sovereignty ostensibly in the name of global free markets and unrestrained capital (Eskelinen and Ylönen, 2017).

In this context, the EU has adopted notable *institutional* reforms in the area of taxation. The pre-crisis institutional landscape of EU tax policy mirrored its 'constrained' history, largely limited to technical discussions among a small group of core insiders from the Commission, government representatives in the Council of ministers and occasionally business interests. Broader stakeholder involvement was frequently absent, with neither European 'tax justice' specifically nor EU tax politics more generally high on the agendas of groups in the EP or civil society activists such as the Tax Justice Network (see Box 15.1). Even those with an organised and institutionalised interest in international tax policy cooperation, such as government tax policy experts, favoured the OECD as the focal point for coordination and discussion, it being the established de facto 'World Tax Organisation' since the 1960s (Sharman, 2012).

> **BOX 15.3 Legal basis**
>
> *Articles 110–13 TFEU.* Tax provisions, providing for non-discrimination and the exclusive policy-making power of the Council.
> *Article 26 TFEU.* Provisions concerning measures to ensure the functioning of the internal market.
> *Articles 107–9 TFEU.* State aid provisions prohibiting the distortion of the internal market through, among other things, fiscal state aid.
> *Article 115 TFEU.* Approximation of law provisions, providing for the issuing of directives, the main mechanism available for tax harmonisation.

Post-crisis, however, the EU context looks different. In addition to substantive policy initiatives, the Union has established new fora such as the Platform for Tax Good Governance (2013) to fight tax fraud and tax evasion. Established institutions have also pursued novel strategies, such as the European Commission engaging in a new campaign of politicisation (discussed below regarding the CCCTB), and the EP exploiting its growing influence and repertoire to impact legislation (cf. Hix and Høyland, 2013). Moreover, civil society activists such as the Tax Justice Network – traditional outsiders to EU tax policy – have successfully mobilised to shape policy agendas and decisions, as we discuss further below (Seabrooke and Wigan, 2015; Baden and Wigan, 2017). This reconfiguration of intra-EU institutional tax politics has also raised (anew) the question of the EU's 'place in the world', specifically its ambitions in global tax governance, a consistent theme across many EU policy areas (Bretherton and Vogler, 2005; Zielonka, 2008). While challengers of the policy status quo advocate for EU activism beyond the established 'OECD consensus', historical insiders, including member state tax experts, continue to question the prospect of such EU activism.

15.4   Recent Policy Developments

In terms of political substance, too, today's agenda is very different from that of a few years ago. Over the last decade, the EU has led the way in promoting new policies and political discussions under the banners of 'tax justice', 'fair taxation' and fiscal sustainability more generally.

In the immediate aftermath of the global financial crisis, the Financial Transactions Tax was a central item on the EU tax agenda. The idea was to place a small tax on financial transactions in order to 'make the financial sector pay its fair share for economic recovery' (Kastner, 2017: 1). Despite significant popular political momentum in the initial policy stage, the concerted lobbying of key financial actors has contributed to a significant cool down of the Financial Transactions Tax, which is now, ten years after the crisis, largely relegated from the EU agenda (Kastner, 2017; Kalaitzake, 2017; Braun, 2018).

The post-crisis years have also been marked by the exposure of large-scale fiscal leakages by whistleblowers in global media projects such as LuxLeaks, the Panama Papers and the Paradise Papers (Oei and Ring, 2018). While each of these leaks have revealed different kinds of activities – from outright fraud to legitimate tax planning – EU actors have been particularly aggressive in pursuing political responses to the scandals. Political groups in the EP have used its powers to establish issue-specific investigative committees, calling in high-profile actors such as Commission President Jean-Claude Juncker and Apple CEO Tim Cook for cross-examinations, building salience around political initiatives. In this context, the Commission has also been proactive in enhancing protections for whistleblowers (see e.g. COM/2018/218), proposing the extension of protections available to those who report on breaches of EU law.

In terms of political substance, the EU has also been at the forefront of implementing global policy initiatives, in particular the comprehensive OECD/G20-led Base Erosion and Profit Shifting (BEPS) initiative (Dover, 2016). With formal political support from the world's largest economies through the G20, and the tax-technical power of the OECD forum, the BEPS project has resulted in new international standards to address fiscal loopholes and mismatches through revisions of bilateral tax treaties, administrative cooperation, templates for domestic regulation and corporate tax transparency, as we discuss further below. The EU's implementation of these standards, in particular through the Anti Tax Avoidance Directive (2016/1164) and successive Directives on Administrative Cooperation, has ensured the speedy and consistent adoption of key political initiatives across Europe.

Moreover, in recent years, as the issue of international taxation has gained prominence, it has become closely entangled with other policy areas where the EU has been active. Most recently, this includes anti-money laundering, where the EU has taken on an active role, especially through the Money Laundering Directive and the Europol cooperation, in developing and implementing political initiatives to combat corruption, terrorism and fiscal sustainability (Unger, 2009; Tsingou, 2010).

Perhaps most prominently, however, in the EU policy area of 'tax justice' there are ongoing discussions about corporate tax transparency and harmonisation, specifically CBCR and the CCCTB proposal. In Sections 15.5 and 15.6, we discuss the ongoing controversies surrounding EU tax policy and 'tax justice' in these two cases.

15.5 Political and Academic Controversies

In the wake of the crisis and in light of ensuing fiscal weakness, concerns about inequality and calls for tax reform in EU countries, corporate tax transparency was identified as a key policy lever to 'fix things', and specifically the idea of CBCR, a radical new standard for disclosure by multinational corporations (MNCs) of information regarding their tax affairs.

The CBCR concept is simple: to require multinational groups to report information on their tax affairs and economic activity on a country-by-country basis, rather than aggregated to regional/global geographical scales and/or business lines, as conventionally done. The policy had first been under consideration in the United Nations in the mid-twentieth century, but it was after a revival and reformulation by expert activists in the Tax Justice Network (TJN) and others that it really took off, becoming a key policy goal and campaign flagship for Europe's civil society sector (Seabrooke and Wigan, 2015, 2016; Baden and Wigan, 2017). While these expert activists had historically been largely uninterested and uninfluential in the international tax space in Europe, the post-crisis years witnessed a substantial reversal of that situation, with expert activists notably successful in powering forward CBCR and other policy proposals using a variety of expertise-based and discursive strategies.

CBCR, TJN argued, would help outside stakeholders hold firms to account 'for paying the tax that those in civil society believe they should pay' (Murphy, 2010). However, CBCR was championed by TJN not just as a transparency tool but also as an important stepping stone in revolutionising the OECD-led international corporate tax system, which TJN argued had broken down in light of twenty-first-century business models, allowing companies to unduly escape national tax burdens (see e.g. Tax Justice Network, 2013; Murphy, 2013). CBCR had been one of the very earliest proposals from those associated with TJN, taking shape in the early 2000s, but really started to take centre stage as a policy ask for a broader coalition around the time of the global financial crisis. Here, TJN was able to enlist a number of other civil society partners in promoting the idea, linking the issue to other areas of post-crisis concern such as inequality, human rights, 'financing for development' and, centrally of course, 'tax justice' (Forstater and Christensen, 2017). The Publish What You Pay (PWYP) coalition, Global Witness, Global Financial Integrity, Oxfam, ActionAid, ChristianAid and others all took on CBCR as a key policy ask, often working closely with TJN in common cause (Lesage and Kacar, 2013).

Initially, these expert activists did not target the EU as a site for promoting CBCR; formal jurisdiction on tax and financial reporting rested with the OECD and the International Accounting Standards Board. However, a lack of broad political interest meant efforts at both organisations failed (Oranje and Parham, 2009; Baden and Wigan, 2017). Then, the coalition took up the idea in the EU, where expert activists familiarised allies in the European Commission and the EP with the CBCR standard. In November 2007, activist lobbying found early success as the EP adopted a resolution in support of the idea of CBCR, including its full publication, though limited to the extractives industry (a focus of PWYP in particular), and a minimalist version entailing a small number of data points. With additional traction from the US enactment of Dodd–Frank, which required a similarly minimalist CBCR regime for US extractive companies, and emerging support from critical European politicians including David Cameron and Nicholas Sarkozy, the case for CBCR was becoming stronger (Lesage and Kacar, 2013; Berg and Davidson, 2017). This effort ultimately led to the enactment of three new directives in the EU in 2013, requiring a minimalist, public CBCR for extractive industries companies (the Accounting and Transparency Directives) and financial institutions (the Capital Requirements Directive) (Wojcik, 2012).

However, not content with a minimalist, sector-specific CBCR, expert activists have continued to push for expansive, maximalist, publicly available CBCR (containing more data points), for all sectors of the economy. At the time of the implementation of the new EU directives, TJN and other expert activists had already succeeded in pushing CBCR onto the OECD/G20 tax agenda under the BEPS project (Christensen, 2020a). When that resulted in a recommendation, now taken up by more than a hundred countries, for national regulation requiring CBCR for all sectors, but limited to the very largest companies (revenues of over €750 million per year) and not available to the public (only tax authorities), campaigners reacted, again targeting the EU. In response to ongoing expert activism, and boosted by the April 2016 Panama Papers leak, the European Commission thus launched proposals for maximalist *public* CBCR for all sectors, explicitly inspired by activists (European Commission, 2016a).

It is worth noting that progress so far on CBCR has specifically come in a policy area where EU member states have relatively few formal veto powers, as the 2013 implementation of new CBCR demands for extractives and banks was classified as an accounting (financial reporting) measure, requiring only a qualified majority vote in the Council. In contrast, the policy area of direct taxation provides member states with an individual veto right in the Council, due to the unanimity requirement stipulated in the TFEU. Further progress (at least the kind of progress envisioned by civil society activists) has been challenged by state interests, with some member states unwilling to support further expansions of corporate tax transparency, and asserting their formal authority. As the discussions continue on public CBCR and the expansion of reporting requirements, a major fighting ground on the 2016 public CBCR proposal has become exactly the classification of the proposal: is it an accounting measure (proposed by the Commission) and thus subject to QMV, or a direct tax measure (asserted by the Council) and thus subject to unanimity (EY, 2017; European Parliamentary Research Service, 2017a). The specifics of the public CBCR proposal have also fostered substantial business opposition, framing publication of the data as a threat to commercial sensitivity, competitiveness and international investment (Christensen, 2020b). Thus, despite significant advances of the 'tax justice' agenda and the previous adoption of minimalist CBCR policies in Europe, alongside continued popular momentum for action on issues of 'tax justice' and 'fair taxation' and a proactive agenda setting by non-state coalitions, public CBCR has not yet materialised in the face of member state and business resistance, and for now the outlook remains murky.

15.6 Analysis of a Paradigmatic Case Study: Bureaucratic and State Politics on the CCCTB

The CCCTB has emerged as the flagship EC initiative to advance the harmonisation of member states' corporate tax systems. First formally proposed in 2011 with the aim to 'significantly reduce the administrative burden, compliance costs and legal uncertainties' of businesses (European Commission, 2011), and relaunched in 2016 with the added objectives to ensure 'fairness' and combat tax avoidance (European Commission, 2016b), the proposal would harmonise rules for the calculation and treatment of the taxable income of corporate entities across member states. Moreover, and controversially, the proposal would also harmonise the *apportionment* of taxable income between member states, so that each country's share of the total Union-wide corporate tax take would be determined by a commonly agreed factor of assets, sales and labour. That is in stark contrast to the established OECD-led regime, where such apportionment would take place based on the calculation of country-specific profits and losses earned by each multinational subsidiary. If, for instance, a large German multinational group – altogether – had half of its European assets, sales and labour in Germany (and the other half in other EU countries), Germany would be entitled to tax half of the group's profits under the CCCTB.

Given the benefits highlighted by the Commission from the adoption of a CCCTB system – dealing with the extraordinary complexity and diversity of countries' individual corporate tax systems, the associated administrative costs borne by businesses and authorities and cracking down on tax avoidance, as well as the perceived intuitiveness of a single corporate tax systems to go with a single market – one might have expected a smooth path forwards for the CCCTB proposal, driven by member states interested in shoring up national fiscal systems and strengthen the legitimacy of tax policy-making. However, similar to the case of CBCR discussed above, this has not been the case. Rather, the proposal has been almost universally met with indifference and opposition by member states, and instead it has been the European Commission that has been the main advocate behind the

CCCTB. The European Commission has broadly played an active role in post-crisis European tax policy-making, but the case of the CCCTB is its key policy proposal par excellence.

The Commission, the bureaucratic and administrative machinery of the EU, has often been cast as an apolitical and neutral force in European tax policy. However, EU scholarship has also occasionally highlighted the highly proactive role played by the Commission's leaders and bureaucrats in exercising regulatory power, shaping policy discussions and mobilising public attention towards issues of concern (Genschel and Jachtenfuchs, 2011; Radaelli, 1999b). By issuing binding legislative acts, mobilising issue salience through coalitions and guiding policy discussions, the Commission is a critical actor in its own right in the institutional environment of EU tax policy-making. The post-crisis years have underscored this trend, showing how the EC's leadership on key tax policy discussions have moved certain political issues forward (Wigan, 2012; Morgan, 2017).

The European Commission has become the key advocate behind the ambitious CCCTB proposal to (re-)engineer a new European corporate tax system, even in the face of unclear member state support or outright opposition. As Morgan (2017: 549) notes, 'The EC remains the main driving force behind the CCCTB. There is no consensus among EU members via the Council or Parliament regarding the CCCTB.' Leading up to and following its 2016 relaunch of the CCCTB proposal, the EC has employed a variety of strategies to manage and influence member state positions, as well as the positions of other stakeholders. We highlight three such strategies: leveraging politicisation, tactical framing and building alliances. Together, there are parallels to Radaelli's (1997, 1999b) foresightful analysis of the Commission's influential work on tax in the late 1990s, which describes a shift in the area of (direct) tax policy from a technocratic logic – characterised by high technical complexity and low political salience – towards politicisation: seeking to foster and exploit political salience, while avoiding technical language. Like then, the Commission has managed to push forwards a conversation that would otherwise not have progressed given the nature of the issue and member state authority.

First, the Commission has sought to leverage the increased politicisation of the issues of tax havens and corporate tax avoidance in the post-crisis years. From a situation of absent popular public interest in the pre-crisis years, popular and political interest has exploded in light of global whistleblower exposures, such as the Panama Papers and the Paradise Papers, as well as ongoing media coverage of the tax affairs of large multinationals (Dallyn, 2017; Berg and Davidson, 2017). The Commission has deliberately sought to utilise the momentum generated by these stories to push for the CCCTB (and other flagship proposals). To that end, it relaunched the CCCTB proposal in the aftermath of the Panama Papers coverage, and Commissioner Pierre Moscovici has repeatedly stressed the connection to salient issues, such as when he told the *International Tax Review* (2017):

We will be keeping up the pressure on EU countries to adopt the CCCTB. True reform of how corporate tax works in the EU is needed to solve the problem of cross-border tax avoidance once and for all, to the benefit of all Europeans. The Panama and Paradise Papers and tales of large-scale tax avoidance by big companies have brought much greater public attention to the ways in which tax avoidance have been able to infiltrate our tax systems on such a grand scale.

Second, and related, the Commission has tactically sought to shift the framing of the CCCTB away from technically complex and politically non-salient matters of compliance (as in the 2011 framing) towards the more popularly attractive and politically salient 'fairness', 'tax justice' and 'combating tax avoidance' (European Commission, 2016b). And third, the Commission has proactively set out to build alliances with like-minded stakeholders, enlisting business groups and CSOs to push for the CCCTB. While technical concerns remain, discussions have revealed strong support among these stakeholders for the general CCCTB idea, and so the Commission has strategically pushed positive respondents into the spotlight. For instance, in a promotion push headlined 'CCCTB – It's Good for Europe', the Commission had a Eurodad representative, an SME executive, a Lufthansa official and a European academic all speaking up for the proposal (European Commission, 2016c). Importantly, the strategy is less about creating an insulated epistemic community of vested interests in the policy issue at hand, as the Commission's approach had been in the mid-1990s on harmful tax competition and around 2011 on CCCTB, but rather to involve these stakeholders in the general politicisation of the issue.

Like the case of CBCR discussed above, however, these strategies pursued by the Commission have notably been checked by state interests. Given the decision-making structures in the EU and the scarcity of EU powers on tax issues, member states have significant leeway in imposing formal national interests in the area of direct tax policy by means of procedural blocking, as discussed above. CCCTB, in contrast to CBCR, remains firmly a direct tax measure and as such is subject to unanimity, although the Enhanced Cooperation procedure remains an option should at least ten member states want to proceed independently.

In asserting state preferences to constrain the implementation of CCCTB, the main national interests referred to by states have been twofold: (1) national tax sovereignty, and (2) distributional implications. First, states have appealed to national tax sovereignty, (re)asserting that direct tax affairs are the exclusive competence of national legislatures and a key area over which the EU has deliberately not been handed powers, and arguing that the introduction of the CCCTB would infringe upon this basic principle. Indeed, after a 'promotion tour' on the CCCTB and subsequent criticism of the proposal by Ireland, commissioner Moscovici had to concede, 'Ireland can be reassured that there won't be a CCCTB if Ireland doesn't want it' (Taylor, 2017).

Second, states have expressed concerns about the distributional implications of proposals, specifically the potential for reallocation of the corporate tax base and corporate investments. The struggles here are most clear in the case of the CCCTB, which visibly redistributes the total EU corporate tax base by changing the apportionment criteria and eliminates certain tax advantages offered by countries to foreign investors. On the former, while heavily caveated, the Commission's own impact assessment estimated the negative impacts of CCCTB on corporate tax revenue in nine EU countries, led by Luxembourg (−0.95 per cent of GDP), the UK (−0.37 per cent) and Spain (−0.20 per cent), while the 'winners' would especially be Croatia (+0.29 per cent), the Netherlands (+0.22 per cent) and Bulgaria (+0.14 per cent) (European Commission, 2016c). Despite the appeals of the Commission to the broader positive impacts of the CCCTB, member states standing to lose absolutely as well as relatively from the CCCTB are likely to continue asserting their veto powers. In that respect, resistance has in particular been met from member states that currently profit disproportionately from the economic affairs of non-domestic multinational groups or the foreign economic affairs of domestic multinational groups, i.e. what we might refer to as 'tax hubs' (e.g. Luxembourg, Ireland and the Netherlands) and small, internationally based economies (e.g. Denmark) (European Commission, 2016d; European Parliamentary Research Service, 2017b).

Taxation is about redistribution and therefore always a political act of placing burdens on some actors while relieving others. Debates over forms of taxation centre on how burdens fall onto particular actors – onto the rich, the working classes, corporations, richer states in the EU, or the poorer ones. As a political actor the EU has to maintain its own balancing act. Jean-Baptiste Colbert, the French minister of finance to King Louis XIV in the mid-seventeenth century, famously characterised the art of taxation as 'plucking the goose as to procure the largest quantity of feathers with the least possible amount of hissing' (McKechnie, 1896: 77).

The EU's long-stance stance on taxation is to permit its geese autonomy within the fences of the community, while plucking feathers in a manner that minimises complaint. Advanced plucking techniques have primarily come through technocratic extensions developed primarily by the European Commission. The EU's asserted stance on tackling 'tax justice' issues has permitted more aggressive actions on policies that not all member states can agree to, especially those that directly benefit from providing financial secrecy and tax optimisation services to corporations and economic and political elites. As such, the EU's position on tax matters has become more and more a compromise position due to battles between European agencies, member state governments, corporate interests and activist groups.

All of these actors are pursuing their own ideas and interests. The debates over CBCR and the CCCTB are reflective of these struggles. The global financial crisis of 2007–8 and the tax avoidance and evasion leaks of 2013 onwards have made these debates all the more salient. They have permitted activists and EU agencies to point to hypocrisies on taxation issues among core EU member states – those who claim that their actions are for economic competitiveness rather than undermining the fiscal stability of their neighbours. We should expect the battles between interests to continue, including the pursuit of tax justice ideals. While the momentum may simmer down, even with more scandals, the politics will continue through the EP and European Council, and in technocratic debates managed through the European Commission.

GROUP DISCUSSION

- How are the interests and strategies of different actors reflected in EU battles on tax justice?
- What are the prospects for systematic change to the EU tax policy substance and process in the coming years?

TOPICS FOR INDIVIDUAL RESEARCH

- Compare and contrast the policy positions and discussions in the EU on the CCCTB and public CBCR proposals.
- How do different stakeholders perceive and react to the strategic pushing by the European Commission of the CCCTB?

FURTHER READINGS

Christensen, R. C. and Hearson, M. (2019). 'The New Politics of Global Tax Governance: Taking Stock a Decade After the Financial Crisis'. *Review of International Political Economy*, 26(5), 1068–88.

Dietsch, P. and Rixen, T. (eds) (2016). *Global Tax Governance: What Is Wrong With It and How to Fix It.* Colchester: ECPR Press.

Genschel, P. and Jachtenfuchs, M. (2011). 'How the European Union Constrains the State: Multilevel Governance of Taxation'. *European Journal of Political Research*, 50(3): 293–314.

Puchala, D. J. (1984). *Fiscal Harmonization in the EC: National Politics and International Cooperation.* London: Bloomsbury.

Radaelli, C. (1997). *The Politics of Corporate Taxation in the European Union: Knowledge and International Policy Agendas.* London and New York: Routledge.

REFERENCES

Baden, A. and Wigan, D. (2017). 'Professional Activists on Tax Transparency'. In L. Seabrooke and L. F. Henriksen (eds), *Professional Networks in Transnational Governance.* Cambridge: Cambridge University Press.

Berg, C. and Davidson, S. (2017). '"Stop This Greed": The Tax-avoidance Political Campaign in the OECD and Australia'. *Economics Journal Watch*, 14(1): 77–102.

Braun, B. (2018). 'Central Banking and the Infrastructural Power of Finance: The Case of ECB Support for Repo and Securitization Markets'. *Socio-Economic Review*, published online February 20, doi:10.1093/ser/mwy008.

Bretherton, C. and Vogler, J. (2005). *The European Union as a Global Actor*. London: Routledge.

Christensen, R. C. (2020a). 'Elite Professionals in Transnational Tax Governance'. *Global Networks*. https://doi.org/10.1111/glob.12269.

Christensen, R. C. (2020b). 'Transparency'. In L. Seabrooke and D. Wigan (eds), *Global Wealth Chains: Asset Strategies in the World Economy*. Oxford: Oxford University Press.

Christensen, R. C. and Hearson, M. (2019). 'The New Politics of Global Tax Governance: Taking Stock a Decade After the Financial Crisis'. *Review of International Political Economy*, 26(5), 1068–88.

Coman, R. (2018). 'How Have EU "Fire-Fighters" Sought to Douse the Flames of the Eurozone's Fast and Slow-burning Crises? The 2013 Structural Funds Reform'. *The British Journal of Politics and International Relations*, 20(3): 540–54.

Commission of the EC (1985). 'Completing the Internal Market'. White Paper from the Commission to the European Council, Milan, 28–9 June 1985. http://europa.eu/documents/comm/white_papers/pdf/com1985_0310_f_en.pdf.

Council of the European Union (1997). 'Conclusions of the ECOFIN Council Meeting on 1 December 1997 Concerning Taxation Policy'. https://eur-lex.europa.eu/legal-content/EN/TXT/?uri=CELEX%3A31998Y0106%2801%29.

Dallyn, S. (2017). 'An Examination of the Political Salience of Corporate Tax Avoidance: A Case Study of the Tax Justice Network'. *Accounting Forum*, 41(4): 336–52.

Dover, R. (2016). 'Fixing Financial Plumbing: Tax, Leaks and Base Erosion and Profit Shifting in Europe'. *The International Spectator*, 51(4): 40–50.

Eskelinen, T. and Ylönen, M. (2017). 'Panama and the WTO: New Constitutionalism of Trade Policy and Global Tax Governance'. *Review of International Political Economy*, 24(4): 629–56.

European Commission (2011). 'Press Release – European Corporate Tax Base: Making Business Easier and Cheaper'. 16 March. http://europa.eu/rapid/press-release_IP-11-319_en.htm?locale=en.

European Commission (2016a). 'Press Release – European Commission Proposes Public Tax Transparency Rules for Multinationals'. 12 April. http://europa.eu/rapid/press-release_IP-16-1349_en.htm?locale=en.

European Commission (2016b). 'Press Release – Commission Proposes Major Corporate Tax Reform for the EU'. 25 October. http://europa.eu/rapid/press-release_IP-16-3471_en.htm.

European Commission (2016c). 'Common Consolidated Corporate Tax Base (CCCTB)'. 25 October. https://ec.europa.eu/taxation_customs/business/company-tax/common-consolidated-corporate-tax-base-ccctb_en.

European Commission (2016d). 'Impact Assessment Accompanying the Document Proposals for a Council Directive on a Common Corporate Tax Base and a Common Consolidated Corporate Tax Base (CCCTB)'. 25 October.

European Parliamentary Research Service (2017a). 'Public Country-by-Country Reporting by Multinational Enterprises'. Briefing.

European Parliamentary Research Service (2017b). 'Common Corporate Tax Base (CCTB)'. Briefing.

EY (2017). 'European Parliament Issues Opinion Concluding that Public Country-by-country Reporting Proposal Would Require Qualified Majority Rather Than Unanimity (Global Tax Alert)'. www.ey.com/Publication/vwLUAssets/European_Parliament_issues_ opinion_concluding_that_public_Country-by Country_reporting_proposal_would_ require_qualified_majority_rather_than_unanimity/$FILE/2017G_00576-171Gbl_ EU%20Parliament%20issues%20opinion%20on%20public%20CbCR%20review.pdf.

Forstater, M. and Christensen, R. C. (2017). *New Players, New Game: The Role of the Public and Political Debate in the Development of Action on International Tax Issues*. European Tax Policy Forum Research Paper. http://etpf.org/files/ETPF_Paper__ Forstater_and_Christensen_Final.pdf.

Genschel, P. and Jachtenfuchs, M. (2011). 'How the European Union Constrains the State: Multilevel Governance of Taxation'. *European Journal of Political Research*, 50(3): 293–314.

Genschel, P. and Schwarz, P. (2011). 'Tax Competition: A Literature Review'. *Socio-Economic Review*, 9(2): 339–70.

Goldscheid, R. (1919). 'Staatssozialismus oder Staatskapitalismus: ein finanzsoziologischer Beitrag zur Lösung des Staatsschuldenproblem'. In R. Hickel (ed.), *Rudolf Goldscheid, Joseph Schumpeter: Die Finanzkrise des Steuerstaats. Beiträge zur politischen Ökonomie der Staatsfinanzen*. Frankfurt: Suhrkamp.

Hallerberg, M. (2004). *Domestic Budgets in a United Europe: Fiscal Governance from the End of Bretton Woods to EMU*. Ithaca, NY: Cornell University Press.

Hallerberg, M. (2011). 'Fiscal Federalism Reforms in the European Union and the Greek Crisis'. *European Union Politics*, 12(1): 127–42.

Hallerberg, M. and Basinger, S. (1998). 'Internationalization and Changes in Tax Policy in OECD Countries: The Importance of Domestic Veto Players'. *Comparative Political Studies*, 31(3): 321–52.

Hix, S. and Høyland, B. (2013). 'Empowerment of the European Parliament'. *Annual Review of Political Science*, 16(1): 171–89.

Holzinger, K. (2005). 'Tax Competition and Tax Co-operation in the EU: The Case of Savings Taxation'. *Rationality and Society*, 17(4): 475–510.

International Tax Review. (2017, December 13). Global Tax 50 2017: Pierre Moscovici. www .internationaltaxreview.com/Article/3775152/Global-Tax-50-2017-Pierre-Moscovici. html.

Kalaitzake, M. (2017). 'Death by a Thousand Cuts? Financial Political Power and the Case of the European Financial Transaction Tax', *New Political Economy*, 22(6): 709–26

Kastner, L. (2017). 'Business Lobbying Under Salience: Financial Industry Mobilization Against the European Financial Transaction Tax'. *Journal of European Public Policy*, 1–19, 10.1080/13501763.2017.1330357.

Lesage, D. and Kacar, Y. (2013). 'Tax Justice through Country-by-Country Reporting: An Analysis of the Ideas' Political Journey'. In J. Leaman and A. Waris (eds.), *Tax Justice and the Political Economy of Global Capitalism, 1945 to the Present*. New York: Berghahn Books.

McKechnie, W. S. (1896). *The State and the Individual: An Introduction to Political Science, with Special Reference to Socialistic and Individualistic Theories*. Glasgow: J. MacLehose and Sons.

Morgan, J. (2017). 'Taxing the Powerful, the Rise of Populism and the Crisis in Europe: The Case for the EU Common Consolidated Corporate Tax Base'. *International Politics*, 54(5): 533–51.

Murphy, R. (2010). 'Time to Act on Tax Transparency'. *The Guardian*, 30 June. www.theguardian.com/commentisfree/2010/jun/30/tax-transparency-country-by-country-reporting.

Murphy, R. (2013). 'Lough Erne and Country-by-Country Reporting'. *Tax Notes International*, 71(3): 249–53.

OECD (1998). *Harmful Tax Competition: An Emerging Global Issue*. Paris: OECD.

Oei, S.-Y. and Ring, D. (2018). 'Leak-Driven Law'. *UCLA Law Review*, 65(3): 532–618.

Puchala, D. J. (1984). *Fiscal Harmonization in the European Communities: National Politics and International Cooperation*. London: Bloomsbury.

Radaelli, C. M. (1997). 'How Does Europeanization Produce Domestic Policy Change? Corporate Tax Policy in Italy and the United Kingdom'. *Comparative Political Studies*, 30(5): 553–75.

Radaelli, C. (1999a). 'The Public Policy of the European Union: Whither Politics of Expertise?'. *Journal of European Public Policy*, 6(5): 757–74.

Radaelli, C. (1999b). 'Harmful Tax Competition in the EU: Policy Narratives and Advocacy Coalitions'. *Journal of Common Market Studies*, 37(4): 661–82.

Seabrooke, L. and Tsingou, E. (2018). 'Europe's Fast- and Slow-burning Crises'. *Journal of European Public Policy*, 26(3): 468–81.

Seabrooke, L. and Wigan, D. (2015). 'How Activists Use Benchmarks: Reformist and Revolutionary Benchmarks for Global Economic Justice'. *Review of International Studies*, 41(5): 887–904.

Seabrooke, L. and Wigan, D. (2016). 'Powering Ideas Through Expertise: Professionals in Global Tax Battles'. *Journal of European Public Policy*, 23(3): 357–74.

Sharman, J. C. (2006). *Havens in a Storm: The Struggle for Global Tax Regulation*. Ithaca, NY: Cornell University Press.

Sharman, J. C. (2012). 'Seeing Like the OECD on Tax'. *New Political Economy*, 17(1): 17–33.

Tax Justice Network (2013). *Confronting Transfer Mispricing by the Use of Country by Country Reporting*. www.taxjustice.net/cms/upload/pdf/CbC_100319_reporting_-_TJN_summary.pdf.

Taylor, C. (2017). 'No Harmonised Taxes Without Irish Backing – Moscovici'. *The Irish Times*, 24 January. www.irishtimes.com/business/commercial-property/no-harmonised-taxes-without-irish-backing-moscovici-1.2949225.

Tsingou, E. (2010). 'Global Financial Governance and the Developing Anti-money Laundering Regime: What Lessons for International Political Economy?'. *International Politics*, 47(6): 617–37.

Unger, B. (2009). 'Money Laundering: A Newly Emerging Topic on the International Agenda'. *Review of Law & Economics*, 5(2): 807–19.

Van Oranje, M. and Parham, H. (2009). *Publishing What We Learned: An Assessment of the 'Publish What You Pay' Coalition.* www.publishwhatyoupay.org/wp-content/uploads/2015/06/Publishing-What-We-Learned.pdf.

Wigan, D. (2012). 'Tackling Tax Havens in the US and EU: A Strategy of Not In My Backyard (NIMBY)'. Policy Brief, Norwegian Institute of International Affairs.

Wojcik, D. (2012). 'Shining Light on Globalization: The Political Economy of Country-by-Country Reporting'. Employment, Work and Finance Working Paper, No. 12–07. https://papers.ssrn.com/sol3/papers.cfm?abstract_id=2163449.

Zielonka, J. (2008). 'Europe as a Global Actor: Empire by Example?'. *International Affairs*, 84(3): 471–84.

16 The CSDP in Transition: Towards 'Strategic Autonomy'?

JOLYON HOWORTH

16.1 Introduction

Prior to the end of the Cold War, Europe's security and defence depended critically on the United States' commitment to NATO. The EU, under its successive guises, had no role whatsoever in this policy area. This was in part because most EU member states preferred the Union – as a self-styled 'civilian actor' – not to dabble in matters of war and peace; and in part because 'Atlanticist' countries like the UK refused to allow it. All this changed in 1989 with the fall of the Berlin Wall (see Box 16.4), for three main reasons. First, Europe ceased, in the 1990s, to be at the centre of the US radar screen. Washington had new and more important demons to chase in the Middle East and Asia. Second, the EU was gradually emerging as a global player and was eager to emerge as a foreign and security policy actor in its own right. Third, eruptions were occurring all around the EU's periphery, from the Balkans to the Black Sea and from the Bosporus to the Atlantic. The need to engage in 'crisis management' in the neighbourhood became compelling. The US saw no reason why such a task should be assumed by Americans. A *European* agent was required to step up to the plate.

The only European agent available in the early 1990s was a semi-moribund organisation, the Western European Union (WEU), which embraced EU member states that were also members of NATO (Box 16.1).

BOX 16.1 Key concepts

The **WEU** arose from the Treaty of Brussels in 1948 as a body designed to coordinate the defence policies of the five signatory countries (the UK, France, Belgium, the Netherlands and Luxembourg). It was effectively superseded by NATO in 1949 as a significant defence organisation, but was relaunched in 1955, when Germany and Italy joined NATO, as an oversight organisation to monitor compliance (especially German) with the terms of the treaty. It remained relatively dormant until it was 'reactivated' in the 1980s (Deighton, 1997). Most of its activities were effectively phased out in 1999 and transferred to the EU. It passed into history in June 2011.

Throughout the early 1990s, the WEU attempted to identify a military role for EU member states from *within* NATO, an initiative labelled the European Security and Defence Identity (ESDI). However, the WEU proved inadequate to the task. In 1999, with the blessing of the UK, the EU itself, launching the CSDP, proclaimed its ambition to create a viable European military capacity *autonomously from* NATO. It pursued that goal for fifteen years, but with only limited success. Whenever a genuine crisis arose on Europe's borders, the CSDP was ignored and the challenge was taken up either by NATO (Libya in 2011; Ukraine/Crimea in 2014) or by France acting alone (Mali in 2013). As the world embarked on a period of power transition, it became clear to many Europeans that, although the United States is their closest partner in a multipolar system, the pursuit of autonomy is nevertheless wise. Hence, when in June 2016 the EU published its Global Strategy document (EEAS, 2016), the key takeaway was the ambition of 'strategic autonomy' (see Box 16.2). Since 2016, there has been a concerted effort across the EU to reactivate and maximise the potential of the CSDP. Yet, at the same time a quasi-consensus emerged that strategic autonomy also demanded intensified cooperation between the EU and NATO. This chapter will explore the seemingly contradictory dimensions of a quest for autonomy through closer cooperation with the very organisation from which the EU is seeking to become autonomous.

BOX 16.2 Key concepts

The concept of **strategic autonomy** was first formally used in the French *White Book* on defence in 1994. It set out why France, in order to remain master of its own destiny, required operationally capable *conventional* troops in addition to the nuclear deterrent. The notion that France should aspire to avoid dependency on the United States lies at the heart of Gaullism. In the European context, the notion was first posited in the Franco-British *Saint-Malo Declaration* of December 1998: 'The Union must have the capacity for autonomous action'. It was not until the EU's *Global Strategy* document of 2016 that the objective of 'strategic autonomy' appeared. However, unlike in the French case, nowhere does the EU attempt to define the concept, either politically, institutionally or militarily.

16.2 Historical Overview

The Intermediate Nuclear Forces crisis of the early 1980s provided the spark that eventually led to an attempt, in the 1990s and 2000s, to associate European security and defence policy with European integration (Nuti et al., 2015). NATO's plan to deploy a new generation of highly accurate – potentially first-strike – nuclear missiles across Europe was formally supported by European governments but massively opposed by the peoples of Europe. In 1987, a major WEU document stated that: 'the construction of an integrated Europe will remain incomplete as long as it does not include security and defence' (WEU, 1988: 37). Thus, even before the fall of the Berlin Wall, the need for a redefined relationship between Europe and America had forced itself onto the European agenda.

With the end of the Cold War, the US focus on Europe as the centrepiece of its global strategy shifted rapidly. Europe appeared to be increasingly 'whole and at peace'. US strategic priorities switched to the Middle East and Asia. After the collapse of the Soviet Union, many experts forecast the 'death of NATO', conscious that alliances have generally not outlived the demise of the adversary against which they were originally constructed (Walt, 1998). NATO nevertheless struggled on, constantly searching for a new role through a series of 'new strategic concepts' (Yost, 2014). In June 1991, hostilities wracked the former Yugoslavia, geographically situated within the borders of the EU. The Americans steadfastly averted their gaze, and Europeans were forced to confront the unpalatable reality that their military capacity was grossly inadequate to face up to the new challenges of the post-Cold War era. In June 1992, the WEU, scrambling to find a purpose, defined the so-called 'Petersberg Tasks'[1] (Ortega, 2005). These 'tasks' covered the entire spectrum of military operations from humanitarian and rescue tasks to warfighting. This proved to be a statement of the problem rather than of the solution. The physical capacity of the EU member states to engage even in small-scale military operations was extremely limited. Their capacity for power projection was virtually nonexistent, their conscript armies unqualified for overseas missions and their institutional and political capacity for making operational decisions uncatered for. This uncomfortable reality gave rise, in the early 1990s, to the project for an ESDI (Howorth and Keeler, 2003).

The ESDI was an attempt to create, *from inside NATO*, a non-US force structure and command chain for operations like those in the Balkans in which the US had little interest. It involved the Europeans borrowing military assets from NATO – in other words from the Americans. This project eventually gave rise to the 'Berlin Plus' process (see Box 16.3), which sought to nail down specifics as to which military assets might be borrowed – and how. These discussions dragged on for six years (1996–2002), mainly because Turkey (a NATO member) objected to Cyprus (an EU member) receiving NATO classified information. The basics of Berlin Plus were finally agreed in December 2002 but, just as with the Petersberg Tasks, this 'agreement' didn't actually resolve anything. It said nothing about the overall trajectory of the EU–NATO relationship. It said nothing about the circumstances under which a mission would become EU rather than NATO, nor which type of

---

[1] So-called because the WEU meeting was held in the Petersberg Castle Hotel outside of Bonn.

mission might be appropriate for this division of labour. Berlin Plus fails to address the long-term conundrum of a hypothetical EU–NATO partnership or a recasting of responsibilities.

BOX 16.3 Key concepts

The **'Berlin Plus'** arrangements refer to the agreed framework for EU–NATO cooperation in crisis management operations. Under these arrangements, the EU enjoys assured access to NATO planning, presumed access to NATO assets and capabilities and a pre-designated Europeans-only chain of command under the Deputy Supreme Commander Europe (DSACEUR), a European general. The initial arrangements were discussed between NATO and the WEU at a ministerial meeting in Berlin in June 1996 (hence Berlin Plus). The devil proved to be in the detail and it took six years of hard bargaining to nail down the specifics. At NATO's Washington Summit in April 1999, negotiations on the Berlin Plus mechanisms were stepped up, but the existence of CSDP called for a shift in negotiating partner away from the WEU and in favour of the EU. In January 2001, the talks entered a new phase involving the EU and NATO directly. After two years of hard bargaining, this led, in December 2002, to the *NATO-EU Declaration on ESDP* (16 December 2002) and the *Berlin Plus Arrangements* (17 March 2003).

ESDI reaffirmed a division of responsibilities within the alliance whereby collective defence remained firmly in the US camp and minor operations were subcontracted to the EU without any concomitant transfer of real authority, leadership or responsibility. US leadership remained unquestioned. EU followership was explicit. ESDI was really an insurance policy against American concerns that the Europeans might bite off more than they could chew and render a fraught international situation worse. However, ESDI didn't work, for at least three reasons. First, because the European interlocutor with NATO was – as mentioned – the WEU, which lacked the administrative wherewithal, the military clout and above all the political authority to assume such a role. Second, because the American military brass were not at all happy about handing over prized – and, after 9/11, increasingly scarce – US military assets to the Europeans. And third, because European military officers were uncomfortable with the 'double-hatting' procedures that were ESDI's concomitant. Soldiers like clarity of command and ESDI was extremely opaque. The WEU as an agency proved a non-starter. Something had to give.

The December 1998 Franco-British summit in Saint-Malo sidelined the WEU and conferred agency on the EU itself, asserting the objective of European autonomy, leading throughout 1999 to the launch of the European Security and Defence Policy (ESDP), later renamed CSDP as a direct EU policy instrument (Shearer, 2000).

In essence, the thinking was that *only an EU agency* would allow the Europeans to become mature security and defence actors. That could not happen through NATO and ESDI, for the reasons outlined above. The quest for European defence autonomy, promoted at Saint-Malo by France, suggested three spheres of ambition. At the political level, the EU was to decide for itself (without instructions from Washington) how to define its own strategic interests. At the level of capacity, the EU would generate the instruments, both military and civilian, that would allow it to pursue that strategy. The thinking here was that, within the NATO framework, Europeans would simply continue to free ride; whereas within a European framework, they would stump up the necessary resources (Kashmeri, 2011). And at the level of operations, the EU would gradually acquire the confidence, experience and ability to conduct significant overseas operations in the interests of and in the pursuit of the strategy.

From the start, an autonomous CSDP was highly controversial. Eurosceptics of all stripes hated it, denouncing and ridiculing what they claimed were plans for a 'European army'. American officials were initially aghast. Secretary of State Madeleine Albright warned that Washington would only support the European project if there were no *decoupling* (of the Atlantic alliance), no *duplication* (of key NATO assets) and no *discrimination* (by the EU against non-EU NATO allies in the European theatre like Norway and Turkey) (Albright, 1998). US academics convinced themselves that the EU was 'balancing' against America (Art, 2005/6; Posen, 2006). Europhiles, on the other hand, were exuberant, several predicting that the EU was becoming an embryonic superpower. The project was given dynamism by a deluge of external events over the following years: the war in Kosovo, the election of George W. Bush, 9/11, the Afghan and Iraq wars. In many ways, America's diversion to the Greater Middle East made it even more compelling for the EU to take care of its neighbourhood – essentially meaning everywhere from the Caucasus to the Balkans to Africa. A spate of 'autonomous' EU 'crisis management' operations was launched – no fewer than twenty-six missions between 2003 and 2008 – in seventeen countries and on three continents (Grévi et al., 2009; Howorth, 2014: 144–89). The Americans, increasingly bogged down in their Greater Middle East quagmire, gradually became enthusiastic. In 2008, the US ambassador to NATO, Victoria Nuland, expressed fulsome support for CSDP: 'Europe needs, the United States needs, NATO needs, the democratic world needs – a stronger, more capable European defense capacity' (Nuland, 2008). CSDP seemed, for one brief moment, to be on an irreversible roll.

However, instead the project began to fizzle out. Between 2008 and 2011, only one further CSDP mission was launched (a small training mission in Somalia). In 2009 the high-profile position of high representative for foreign affairs and security policy was launched, whose incumbent doubled as vice president of the European Commission.[2] The first post-holder, the UK's Catherine Ashton, cared little for CSDP and did nothing to promote it (Müller-Brandeck-Boquet and Rüger, 2011). Token CSDP missions in far-off destinations, such as the police mission in Afghanistan and the rule of law mission in Iraq, were, at best, failures, at worst serious embarrassments. The Arab Spring in general and the 2011 Libyan crisis in particular showed CSDP to be virtually irrelevant (Koenig, 2011). The Libyan crisis was precisely the scenario for which CSDP had been devised: a crisis of medium intensity, on the EU's immediate periphery, in which key European interests were directly at stake, a crisis of no real interest to the US, and one which, after twenty years of preparation, the EU should have been able to manage on its own. And yet CSDP as an instrument of response was not even invoked. NATO remained the only game in town. Eighteen months later, in 2013, when Mali began to descend into jihadist chaos, it was France alone that responded (Heisbourg, 2013). The same was true the following year in the Central African Republic. In parallel, the EU was making a terrible hash of the emerging Ukraine crisis,[3] so much so that the Americans' worst fears were confirmed, and when in 2014 Russia annexed Crimea and fuelled separatism in Eastern Ukraine, it was Washington – and eventually NATO – that had to step in to try to stabilise the Eastern neighbourhood. CSDP, far from becoming the autonomous, consequential actor foreseen at Saint-Malo, became a mere sideshow. By 2015, many commentators were writing its obituary.

BOX 16.4 Key dates

1994. Launch of ESDI via the WEU.
1998. Saint-Malo Declaration leads to launch of 'autonomous' CSDP.
2003. Launch of first EU military operation (Concordia in Macedonia).
2009. Treaty of Lisbon codifies arrangements for CSDP.
2016. European Union Global Strategy document published.

An abundance of evidence suggests that the CSDP project failed in all three of the spheres of ambition outlined above. It never developed a common, agreed *strategy*. There are few indications that the European framework generated any

---

[2] The inside joke in Brussels was the that title was too long to fit on a business card.
[3] It is my own view that the EU's policy towards Ukraine was seriously counter-productive. A special issue of the *Journal of Common Market Studies* (55(1), 2017) offers a range of perspectives on this controversial issue. Some authors share my negative analysis; others argue that the EU emerged from the crisis empowered.

more *resources* than would have been the case had it been done via NATO. Indeed, defence budgets declined throughout the 2000s and only began to rise again after the Ukraine crisis – ironically, under pressure from the US. As for *missions*, the EU's level of ambition was constantly redefined downwards. CSDP essentially became a project for offering training, policing, advice and assistance, rather than crisis management per se. There was a constant retreat from Saint-Malo. Although there had never been a clear blueprint for the CSDP project in terms of the eventual mix of military and civilian instruments, one thing seemed clear: what CSDP had morphed into was not what had been intended at the outset.

BOX 16.5 Legal basis

Article 28 (1) TFEU. The CSDP shall be an integral part of the CFSP. It shall provide the Union with an operational capacity drawing on civilian and military assets. The Union may use them on missions outside the Union for peace-keeping, conflict prevention and strengthening international security in accordance with the principles of the United Nations Charter. The performance of these tasks shall be undertaken using capabilities provided by the member states.

16.3   Current Institutional Framework

The institutional underpinnings of CSDP have been subjected to intense analysis (Smith, 2003; Dijkstra, 2013). Beginning in 1999, the EU conferred upon itself an institutional framework that replicated in almost every respect that of NATO. Political direction of the policy area was conferred upon a Political and Security Committee, comprising one ambassador from each member state. This was modelled on NATO's North Atlantic Council. It operated on the basis of consensus and unanimity. In addition, a European Union Military Committee brought together the twenty-seven Chiefs of the Defence Staff or their representatives. This body was served by a European Union Military Staff, bringing together senior officers from the member states. Again, these institutions replicated those of NATO. An innovation which distinguishes CSDP from NATO was the development of a Committee for Civilian Crisis Management that oversees those CSDP missions that are clearly non-military in nature. Theoretically, the most significant institutional innovation was the position of high representative for foreign affairs and security policy – vice president of the Commission. As noted above, the first incumbent, Catherine Ashton (2009–14), made virtually no real impression on the defence and security portfolio. The second incumbent, Federica Mogherini (2015–20), was more proactive and pursued the cause of CSDP with energy and political intelligence (Novotna, 2017). She drove the process leading to the publication of the European Union Global Strategy. She promoted EU diplomacy tirelessly around the world, contributing to a positive outcome in the Iran nuclear crisis (Alcaro, 2018), to a more comprehensive EU approach to the eastern neighbourhood and to a way forward both in Libya and in the migrant crisis. However, her margin of manoeuvre (like that of her predecessors) was constrained by the reality that EU foreign and defence policy depends primarily on unanimity among the twenty-seven member states. The tensions between the EU per se and its member states have constantly acted as a brake on the development of a genuine EU common policy (Pomorska and Noutcheva, 2017).

In terms of European integration theory, these tensions manifested themselves as a clash between two different perceptions of where power really lies in Europe: intergovernmentalism and supranationalism. The former approach sees control remaining in the hands of the member states who deploy bargaining power in the European Council to protect their national interest. The latter approach suggests power has shifted to the EU institutions in Brussels which drive integration via the institutional dynamics of spillover and entrepreneurship (see discussion in Chapter 5). Almost twenty years ago, I suggested, with respect to CSDP, that there were indications that we might be in the presence of a phenomenon I called 'supra-national inter-governmentalism' (Howorth, 2000). The basic argument was that the many intergovernmental agencies of the European Council working in the field of CSDP, through processes of socialisation and institutional learning, gradually adopt an approach that emphasises consensus-seeking over the narrow defence of national interest and, in effect, comes close to what a supranational position might be (Howorth, 2012). Since then, a huge number of studies have focused on decision-shaping and decision-making in foreign and security policy. Scholars have increasingly wondered whether we are witnessing the disappearance of any meaningful dichotomy between intergovernmentalism and supranationalism (Howorth, 2012).

However, the basic institutional reality is that the EU's member states remain firmly in the driving seat on all issues of significance (Box 16.5). It is relatively easy within the cosy confines of the Political and Security Committee to reach a consensus on sending a small police mission to Kinshasa, or on training Malian troops. It is virtually impossible to reach agreement on sending an EU division to Latvia. During the protracted process of drafting the European Union Global Strategy, the challenge was that of finding a form of words that would meet with the approval of all twenty-eight member states (Tocci, 2017).

BOX 16.6 Key actors

European Council. Comprises the heads of state and government of all member states. The ultimate authority for decision-making on all matters relating to security and defence policy.

    Political and Security Committee. Comprises one permanent representative (ambassador) from each member state. Operates on the basis of consensus/unanimity. Exercises political control and strategic direction of crisis management missions agreed by the European Council.

    European Union Military Committee. The highest EU military body. Delivers to the Council, via the Political and Security Committee, the unanimous advice of the Chiefs of the Defence Staff of all member states on all matters military.

    European Union Military Staff. Comprises 150 senior officers from across all member states and provides military expertise and capacity, including during the conduct of overseas military operations.

    High Representative for Foreign Affairs and Security Policy. Contributes to the development of CSDP and conducts that policy. Ensures implementation of the decisions made by the Political and Security Committee and the European Council. Represents the EU in international fora for all matters relating to foreign and security policy.

16.4 Recent Policy Developments

Beginning in 2016, the demand for a consolidated and effective European defence capacity, which some began to call the European Defence Union (EDU), rose rapidly to the top of the EU agenda. After the publication of the European Union Global Strategy in June 2016, a host of new initiatives revitalised CSDP. In what ways were matters different from the first phase of CSDP (2000–15)? The first and biggest difference was geostrategic. For the first time in decades, the EU seemed threatened in its very existence from without (Russian destabilisation of Central and Eastern Europe; relentless migratory pressure from Africa and the Middle East; Donald Trump's ambivalence about NATO). The second major difference in the EDU dynamic was the emergence of a strong European framework. National leaders finally began to be honest with their populations and to state relatively unambiguously that 'national sovereignty' in this policy area is largely mythical. European citizens, according to leaders such as Emmanuel Macron, Angela Merkel and Jean-Claude Juncker, are actively seeking 'protection' at the European level. This recognition still has a long way to go, but the more Europe's leaders continue to frame their objectives within an EU-wide context, the more real progress becomes possible. Third, and in parallel with this second development, the EU itself, particularly after the trauma of Brexit, was vitally concerned to forge and to demonstrate a sense of unity. Over 2016–17, all of the major EU institutions – including, significantly, the European Commission, hitherto held by the member states at arm's length from CSDP – came forward with strong statements of support and concrete proposals for the advancement of the EDU. A fourth new dimension was the relative convergence of previously diverging security cultures. Germany, under the impulsion of defence minister Ursula von der Leyen, made significant steps towards assuming an active expeditionary role for its military. While Germany and France still have quite different approaches to the deployment of military force, the gap closed in the late 2010s.

These new developments facilitated four apparent 'breakthroughs' in the post-2016 dynamic behind the EDU: the decision to go ahead with a Military Planning and Conduct Capability (MPCC – the new acronym for what used to be called the Operational Headquarters – OHQ); new financial arrangements for Battle Groups (BGs); the launch of the EDF; and the agreement, reached at the European Council in June 2017, to operationalise for the first time the process enshrined in the Lisbon Treaty (but never previously acted upon) known as Permanent Structured Cooperation (PESCO). How significant were these developments?

It was the UK (tacitly supported by a handful of other member states) that had always brandished its veto against the notion of the EU developing a genuine OHQ. After the Brexit referendum, many in Europe believed that plans for an OHQ could be revived. But the UK still sat as a full member on all EU agencies and London's defence minister continued to hold out strongly against the project. That is why the new facility was downgraded to an MPCC, with a brief limited to 'non-executive' CSDP missions (essentially military training operations). This effectively changed nothing significant. Only when the EU fields its own fully fledged OHQ can it begin to approach the status of 'strategic autonomy'.

The original idea behind BGs was that proximate groups of EU member states could cooperate (often in regional clusters) to stand up a 2,000-troop formation prepared to intervene at short notice if a security crisis emerged in the EU periphery (Lindstrom, 2007). Yet, a major problem with the concept was the funding basis, which called on the member states involved in a BG operation to assume the entire costs of the operation. This largely explains why no BG was ever deployed, although lack of political will was also a major factor (Jacoby and Jones, 2008). In June 2017, the Council decided that the deployment of BGs should be borne as a common cost by the EU. This removed one administrative hurdle but, as with the MPCC, did not change anything fundamental.

In June 2017, the European Defence Fund was also launched to much media acclaim. The involvement of the European Commission in offering funding for both research in innovative defence products and technologies, and the development and acquisition of key defence capabilities, was widely perceived as another EDU breakthrough. Yet the sums involved (€25 million for research and technology in 2017, compared with the €8.8 billion the EU-28 spent on this activity in 2014; and €500 million for development and acquisition, compared with a 2014 spend of €38 billion) while not insignificant, nevertheless seemed modest – especially in the context of the overall annual EU defence expenditure of around €230 billion. Most of the Commission's seed money is conditional on the member states raising 80 per cent of matching funds from their own resources. Those who perceive this new development as revolutionising European defence funding might be advised to reserve judgement.

Many commentators have latched on to PESCO as the great white EU hope of the future (Biscop, 2018). Participants in PESCO were intended to be restricted to those 'whose military capabilities fulfil higher criteria and which have made more binding commitments to one another, with a view to the most demanding missions' (Lisbon Treaty 42/6). PESCO was intended to be an advance guard. However, Paris and Berlin disagreed over the details. France wanted the list of participants to stop at about ten. Germany fought to prioritise the inclusion of as many states as possible. Germany won. When PESCO was officially launched in December 2017, it included twenty-five member states. The advance guard had become a convoy – with Poland in particular trying hard to slow the whole process down (Witney, 2017).

Moreover, PESCO is only one coordinated European defence initiative. There are three other initiatives that emerged in some ways as rivals. Germany's Framework Nation Concept (FNC), devised inside NATO, created a grouping, under German leadership, of seventeen states from Central, Eastern and Northern Europe to focus on building up a significant military force to deter Russia. The UK initiative, the Joint Expeditionary Force, embraces the UK and the Scandinavian and Baltic states. It is intended to demonstrate that certain nations in the northern region take Russian aggression seriously. The French alternative, announced by President Macron in September 2017, proposes a European Intervention Initiative designed to lead to European strategic autonomy. Macron foresees, by 2020, 'a common intervention force, a common defence budget and a common doctrine for action', as well as a European Intelligence Academy. This initiative lies outside both NATO and the EU. France has been very selective in its partners. Only nine countries were invited to join (Belgium, Denmark, Estonia, Germany, Italy, the Netherlands, Portugal, Spain and the UK). The European Intervention Initiative has been interpreted as a French counter to the German FNC and a sign that Paris has grown weary of in-fighting over the direction of PESCO. The very fact that the Europeans have managed to generate no fewer than four security and defence 'initiatives' (in addition to NATO) speaks volumes about the ongoing state of divisiveness on this most sensitive of policy areas.

The post-2016 initiatives and dynamics behind CSDP are helpful and creative, but they will not, in and of themselves, change anything fundamental. There are still many obstacles standing in the way of 'strategic autonomy': persistent nationalist member state reflexes; ongoing divergences in European strategic cultures; lack of consensus about the level of ambition in this policy area; challenges to defence budgets in a time of austerity; the fetish of sovereignty; the problem of trust; the sheer scale of the challenges facing Europe in its eastern and southern neighbourhoods; the absence of public awareness of and/or support for a more muscular or assertive Europe. The role of the UK remains problematic (though not necessarily fatal to the enterprise) and, at the time of writing, difficult to predict with any accuracy (Taylor, 2018). The major challenge facing the hypothetical EDU is the parallel existence of NATO.

16.5 Current Political and Academic Controversies

By the end of 2018, NATO and the EU had identified no fewer than seventy-four 'concrete actions' for closer cooperation. An entire scholarly industry has arisen devoted to exploring the details of that 'cooperation' (Smith et al., 2018). But how does the practice of ever closer cooperation with NATO square with that of 'strategic autonomy'? The Trump administration is aberrant in many ways, but in terms of the North Atlantic alliance it is more a picture of continuity with previous administrations than one of profound rupture. Trump's provocations about NATO being 'obsolete' are merely the most extreme formulations of a message that has been constant since the end of the Cold War: the allies (both European and Asian) must take more responsibility for their own security (Walt, 2018). What are the implications of that message? Many take the view that Europe is structurally and politically condemned, for at least as far ahead as it is possible to foresee, to remain existentially dependent on the United States for its ultimate security (which most people would assume to mean for 'protection' against a threat from Russia – as it did from 1949 to 1989). In such a scenario, the very notion of 'strategic autonomy' makes little sense. A literal or serious interpretation of 'strategic autonomy' would suggest that there is no ontological reason why Europe should eternally seek shelter behind a US shield or 'umbrella'. The EU is as wealthy as the US, it has a much greater population and it has equivalent scientific, technological and industrial resources and potential. It has as broad a range of policy instruments in its tool chest – including soft power – as the US. It is much closer geographically than the US to the sources of its own regional instability. It currently spends over

€230 billion on 'defence'. In comparison with Russia, the EU is massively superior in virtually every domain. The proposition that Europe is incapable of defending itself without a US protector is perplexing (Lucas, 2018).

Leading voices across Europe in the era of Donald Trump appear to concur (Box 16.7). Many intimated, in 2017 or 2018, that the EU can no longer afford to leave itself in a situation where its existential security is dependent on the United States. But what does that imply? The key variable is the level of political ambition. How far are Europeans prepared to go? On the other side of the Atlantic, American neorealists have been arguing for decades in favour of a radical reconfiguration of the Atlantic Alliance – one in which the Europeans will progressively become responsible for their own collective defence. In recent years, there have been several significant proposals on the US side for a progressive transfer of responsibility, of authority and even of leadership within NATO from the Americans to the Europeans (Bacevich, 2016; Kashmeri, 2011; Posen, 2015; Mearsheimer and Walt, 2016). During the Libyan crisis of 2011, Barack Obama coined the notion of US 'leadership from behind'.

BOX 16.7 Key actors

EU leaders call for 'strategic autonomy'

Emmanuel Macron (French president): 'Europe can no longer entrust its security to the United States alone. It is up to us to assume our responsibilities and to guarantee European security and thereby sovereignty' (28 August 2018).

Jean-Yves Le Drian (French foreign minister): 'Our agility on the international scene stems directly from our ability to act freely, to preserve our strategic autonomy [and] to make our independence the main objective of our diplomacy. Europe must embrace a culture of balance of power' (29 August 2018).

Angela Merkel (German chancellor): 'The era in which we could fully rely on others is over to some extent. We Europeans truly have to take our fate into our own hands. We Europeans must fight for our own future and destiny' (27 May 2017); 'A great many global conflicts are taking place on Europe's doorstep. And it is not the case that the United States of America will simply protect us. Instead, Europe must take its destiny in its own hands' (10 May 2018).

Jean-Claude Juncker (president of the European Commission): 'At this point, we have to replace the US, which as an international actor has lost vigor and, because of it, in the long term, influence' (18 May 2018).

Donald Tusk (EU Council president): 'Looking at the latest decisions of Donald Trump someone could even think: with friends like these, who needs enemies?' (16 May 2018).

16.6   Analysis of a Paradigmatic Case Study: EU–NATO Relations

The founding fathers never intended that NATO should be totally dominated by one hegemon with twenty-eight retainers following behind. The North Atlantic Treaty was designed as a stopgap that would allow the Europeans to catch their breath after World War II and organise their own collective security and eventually collective defence (Acheson, 1967). On assuming the NATO supreme command in December 1950, Eisenhower remarked: 'If NATO is still needed in ten years, it will have failed in its mission'. Twelve years later, President Kennedy invoked an alliance based on two equal pillars reflecting a 'Declaration of Interdependence' between the old continent and the new. How might that long-standing goal finally be achieved?

As presently conceived, CSDP's raison d'être is its distinctiveness from NATO. It exists in contradistinction to the alliance. It is complementary to NATO, but it aims to carry out different – less strategically significant – functions. NATO, in this configuration (meaning, essentially, the United States) will remain indefinitely charged with the ultimate responsibility for Europe's existential defence. That being the case, it is hard to see how – whether boosted or not by PESCO, the EDF, the MPCC and all the other post-2016 initiatives – CSDP can succeed in turning the EU into a consequential security actor, capable, eventually, of assuming responsibility for its own collective defence. If words have any meaning, that is what 'strategic autonomy' means. As long as the US remains prepared to act as 'defender of last resort' – via NATO – the European project, as separate and distinct from NATO, is unlikely to go much beyond what it currently is: a mechanism for delivering low-level crisis management facilities, policing, training, security sector reform, etc., mainly in the southern neighbourhood. Such a perspective reveals seriously limited ambition.

Despite much cheerleading from EU officials about the EU's move towards strategic autonomy, a barrage of recent scholarship casts doubt on the EU's ability, on its own, to define a clear strategy. Anne-Marie Le Gloannec (2018: 201–2) argued that EU enlargement (often presented as a major policy success) was done in a reactive, technocratic way rather than as a proactive strategy: 'it just happened [...] in a fit of absent-mindedness'. Frédéric Mauro (2018) demonstrated comprehensively that there is no clear understanding within the EU as to what the concept of 'strategic autonomy' implies, at the political, operational or even industrial levels. He concluded by quoting Seneca: 'There is no favourable wind for the sailor who knows not where he's heading' (Mauro, 2018). Sven Biscop (2019) maintains that the EU has never really known how to come to terms with power and therefore tends to avoid talking about it, preferring to behave like a glorified NGO. Scholars have coined the expression 'a-strategic' to designate the EU's ill-defined defence aspirations (Cottey, forthcoming).

The transatlantic relationship is entering uncharted waters, just as the world is undergoing a process of power transition (Posen, 2015; Brooks and Wohlforth, 2018; Walt, 2018). Nowhere does the EU attempt to state, in any detail, what the much-vaunted 'strategic autonomy' showcased in the EU Global Strategy might actually amount to. I shall therefore conclude with my own analysis. The key to the future lies in the transformation of the EU–NATO relationship. If Europeans truly believe that they and the Americans, despite their differences, share overall values and are closer to one another than either is to any other global actor, then the evolving transatlantic relationship will rise above short-term problems of adaptation. If Europeans fear abandonment because of a clash of transatlantic values and/or interests, then to accept a state of permanent dependency makes no sense. The solution, I argue, lies in a return to something akin to ESDI, but with a different objective. Instead of a plan designed to enrol EU follower-ship behind US leadership, the two sides should aim to foster EU empowerment through a shift in responsibilities and leadership. It was right and proper that the EU should have experimented with the autonomous implications of CSDP. It is to be hoped that the experience gained over the past twenty years has been fully absorbed both in Brussels and in European national capitals. The objective of strategic autonomy is appropriate, and the EU should interpret this as demanding the highest possible level of ambition. It is time to take EU–NATO cooperation to an entirely new and different level. It means, in effect, a European return to NATO. But this time, unlike in the mid-1990s – the EU would be working through NATO for the right reasons: to gain the necessary experience to transcend the limitations of CSDP and to create a genuinely two-pillar alliance. The EU should take up the challenge from the US and progressively assume leadership in meet-ing its own regional challenges, both south and east. This must be done in full transparency with the American partners. Both sides should embrace the overall game plan. The US, via NATO, can continue to backstop EU security initiatives with critical enablers such as intelligence, logistics, heavy lift, command and control – but only as a temporary measure while Europe acquires the experience, the capacity and the confidence needed to meet future challenges on its own. The best way of reaching that stage is gradually to merge CSDP into NATO, for Europeans to progressively take over command of the major agencies in NATO and to allow the US to focus on the areas of the world that are of the most stra-tegic importance to Washington. At that point, the EU, featuring a Europeanised NATO, might sign a bilateral, co-equal and different type of alliance with the US. Any other course of action will amount to the same 'muddling through' that we have witnessed since the end of the Cold War. There are many problems with this plan. It depends on the EU transcending its three current crises of sover-eignty (money, borders and defence). It assumes the EU will not only continue in business, but will solve the challenge of central political authority. The plan has to be aggressively sold in Washington, London and perhaps above all Warsaw, Prague and Vilnius. It will take time, lots of time. But it is the only serious route to 'strategic autonomy'.

GROUP DISCUSSION

- How can we assess the EU's first phase of attempts to put together a CSDP (2000–15)?
- What were the obstacles to a successful policy outcome?

TOPICS FOR INDIVIDUAL RESEARCH

- What might 'strategic autonomy' for the EU amount to in practice?
- What developments would be essential for the success of 'strategic autonomy'?

FURTHER READINGS

Davis Cross, M. K. (2011). *Security Integration in Europe.* Ann Arbor: University of Michigan Press.
Howorth, J. (2014). *Security and Defence Policy in the European Union.* London: Palgrave.
Kurowska, X. and Breuer, F. (eds) (2012). *Explaining the EU's Common Security and Defence Policy: Theory in Action.* London: Palgrave.
Mérand, F. (2008). *European Defence Policy: Beyond the Nation State.* Oxford: Oxford University Press.
Tocci, N. (2017). *Framing the European Union Global Strategy: A Stronger Europe in a Fragile World.* London: Palgrave, 2017.

REFERENCES

Acheson, D. (1969). *Present at the Creation.* London: Hamish Hamilton.
Albright, M. (1998). 'The Right Balance Will Secure NATO's Future'. *Financial Times*, 7 December.
Alcaro, R. (2018). *Europe and Iran's Nuclear Crisis: Lead Groups and EU Foreign Policy Making.* London: Palgrave.
Art, R. (2005/6). 'Striking the Balance'. *International Security*, 30(3): 177–85.
Bacevich, A. (2016). 'Ending Endless War: A Pragmatic Military Strategy'. *Foreign Affairs*, September/October.
Biscop, S. (2018). 'European Defence: Give PESCO a Chance'. *Survival*, 60(3): 161–80.
Biscop, S. (2019). *European Strategy in the 21st Century: New Future for Old Power.* London: Routledge.
Brooks, S. and Wohlforth, W. (2018). *America Abroad: Why the Sole Superpower Should not Pull Back from the World.* Oxford: Oxford University Press.
Cottey, A. (forthcoming), 'Astrategic Europe'. *Journal of Common Market Studies.*
Deighton, A. (ed.) (1997). *Western European Union 1954–1997: Defence, Security, Integration.* Oxford: European Interdependence Research Unit.

Dijkstra, H. (2013). *Policy-Making in EU Security and Defense: An Institutional Perspective.* London: Palgrave.

EEAS (2016). *Shared Vision, Common Action: A Stronger Europe.* Brussels, European External Action Service, 26 June.

Grévi, G. et al. (eds) (2009). *European Security and Defence Policy: The First Ten Years.* Paris: EU-ISS.

Heisbourg, F. (2013). 'A Surprising Little War: First Lessons of Mali'. *Survival*, 55(2): 7–18.

Howorth, J. (2000). *European Integration and Defence: The Ultimate Challenge?* Paris, WEU-ISS, Chaillot Paper No.43.

Howorth, J. (2012). 'Decision-making in Security and Defense Policy: Towards Supranational Inter-governmentalism?' *Cooperation and Conflict*, 47(4): 433–53.

Howorth, J. (2014). *Security and Defence Policy in the European Union.* London: Palgrave.

Howorth, J. and Keeler, J. (eds) (2003). *Defending Europe: NATO and the Quest for European Autonomy.* London and New York: Palgrave.

Jacoby, W. and Jones, C. (2008). 'The EU Battle Groups in Sweden and the Czech Republic: What National Defence Reforms Tell Us about European Rapid Reaction Capabilities'. *European Security*, 17(2–3): 315–38.

Kashmeri, S. A. (2011). *NATO 2.0: Reboot or Delete?* Washington, DC: Potomac.

Koenig, N. (2011). 'The EU and the Libyan Crisis: In Quest of Coherence'. Rome, IAI Working Paper 11/19, July.

Le Gloannec, A.-M. (2018). *Continent by Default: The European Union and the Demise of Regional Order.* Ithaca, NY: Cornell University Press.

Lindstrom, G. (2007). *Enter the EU Battle Groups.* Paris: EU-ISS.

Lucas, E. (2018). 'Europe Must Plan for Defence Without NATO'. *The Times* (London), 13 July.

Mauro, F. (2018). *Autonomie Stratégique: le nouveau Graal de la defense européenne.* Bruxelles, Les Rapports du GRIP, 2018/1.

Mearsheimer, J. and Walt, S. (2016). 'The Case for Offshore Balancing: A Superior US Grand Strategy'. *Foreign Affairs*, July–August.

Müller-Brandeck-Boquet, G. and Rüger, C. (2011). *The High Representative for the EU Foreign and Security Policy: Review and Prospects.* Baden-Baden: Nomos.

Novotna, T. (2017). 'The EU as a Global Actor: United We Stand, Divided We Fall'. *Journal of Common Market Studies*, 55, Annual Review: 177–91.

Nuland, V. (2008). 'U.S. Ambassador to NATO, Victoria Nuland, Speech in Paris: Ambassador Discusses Strengthening Global Security for Europe'. www.feelingeurope.eu/Pages/Victoria%20Nuland%20feb%202008%20AmCham.html (accessed 10 March 2010).

Nuti, L. et al. (2015). *The Euromissiles Crisis and the End of the Cold War.* Stanford: Stanford University Press.

Ortega, M. (2005). *Petersberg Tasks and Missions for the EU Military Forces.* Paris: European Union Institute for Security Studies.

Pomorska, K. and Noutcheva, G. (2017). 'Europe as a Regional Actor: Waning Influence in an Unstable and Authoritarian Neighbourhood'. *Journal of Common Market Studies*, 55(S1): 165–76.

Posen, B. (2006). 'European Union Security and Defense Policy: Response to Unipolarity?'. *Security Studies*, 15/2: 149–86.

Posen, B. (2015). *Restraint: A New Foundation for US Grand Strategy*. Ithaca, NY: Cornell University Press.

Shearer, A. (2000). 'Britain, France and the Saint-Malo Declaration: Tactical Rapprochement or Strategic Entente?'. *Cambridge Review of International Affairs*, 13(2): 183–298.

Smith, M. E. (2003). *Europe's Foreign and Security Policy: The Institutionalization of Cooperation*. Cambridge: Cambridge University Press.

Smith, S. et al. (2018). *EU–NATO Relations*. London: Routledge.

Taylor, P. (2018). 'Safer Together: The United Kingdom and the Future of European Security and Defence'. *Friends of Europe*, Summer 2018. www.friendsofeurope.org/events/safer-together-the-united-kingdom-and-the-future-of-european-security-and-defence/.

Tocci, N. (2017). *Framing the European Union Global Strategy: A Stronger Europe in a Fragile World*, London: Palgrave.

Walt, S. M. (1998). 'The Ties that Fray: Why Europe and America Are Drifting Apart'. *The National Interest*, 54, 1 December. https://nationalinterest.org/article/the-ties-that-fray-why-europe-and-america-are-drifting-apart-900 (accessed 3 February 2020).

Walt, S. M. (2018). *The Hell of Good Intentions: America's Foreign Policy Elite and the Decline of US Primacy*. New York: Farrar, Strauss & Giroux.

WEU (1988), *The Revitalisation of the Western European Union*. London: WEU.

Witney, N. (2017). 'EU Defence Efforts Miss the Open Goal Again'. London, European Council on Foreign Relations, Commentary, 15 November.

Yost, D. S. (2014). *NATO's Balancing Act. Washington, DC:* United States Institute of Peace Press.

PART III
Existential Debates

This part of the volume deals with the existential debates over the future of the Union as a community of states and citizens. The multiple crises of the past decade have only aggravated the ongoing crisis of legitimacy which has fed controversies about the democratic deficit of the Union since the 1990s. Neither the strengthening of the parliamentary character of the EU political system, nor efforts to generate 'good governance' or procedures to prompt citizen participation and deliberation provided an effective answer to the growing popular discontent towards Europe. The crises fuelled two types of centrifugal forces which today tear the EU apart. The first is the lack of sufficient socio-economic convergence across the continent. The gap between a wealthy northern and continental core, on the one hand, and struggling peripheries in the southern, eastern and Baltic fringes of the continent has persisted, and some disequilibria have even become more acute, tapping into contrasted ideas over the appropriate economic growth models and needs for social solidarity. Second, conflicts of values over societal issues (religion, multiculturalism, family and gender, etc.) or over liberal democracy and the rule of law have dramatically exacerbated over the past few years. Ultimately, the Brexit meltdown raises the question of whether and how differentiated integration can be institutionalised as a means out of a dangerous status quo.

Against this background, the following chapters explain:

- Why there is a core–periphery cleavage in the EU.
  - How EU integration has shaped socio-economic realities in different ways.
  - How effective EU instruments used to foster convergence have been.
  - What the impact of the financial and debt crisis has been.

- Why and how democracy has become an object of political contention in the EU.
  - How the EU has constitutionalised democratic values.
  - How the EU deals with breaches of the rule of law and the associated political contestation of liberal democracy.
- How the EU has become increasingly politicised and what the consequences of increased politicisation are.
  - How the EU's democratic deficit is understood.
  - Whether further democratisation of the EU is desirable.
  - How Article 50 came about and what the challenges of Brexit are.
  - Whether the EU is finally becoming a mature political system that is developing its own contestatory political theatre, or whether we are witnessing the development of forces that are fundamentally dangerous to EU integrity.

Back in the 1950s, the signatories of the Treaties of Rome were 'anxious to strengthen the unity of their economies and to ensure their harmonious development by reducing the differences existing between the various regions and the backwardness of the less favoured regions'. In this regard, some EU policies proved successful (at least temporarily), others have had mitigated results. Kristin Makszin, Gergő Medve-Bálint and Dorothee Bohle demonstrate that the gap between the core and periphery is multidimensional and persistent. Is it possible to bridge this gap? Can the periphery catch up with the core? With each enlargement, the EU has designed new strategies to bridge the gaps between poorer newcomers and the richer core and the austerity measures adopted to tackle the eurozone crisis have dramatically affected the EU's peripheries, which were already lagging behind the core. The chapter discusses the Irish success story and Hungary's decline. In a comparative perspective, the authors observe the convergence of the southern and eastern peripheries to a level of economic activity that is lower than 40 per cent of the level of the core countries. This persistent gap should be a matter of concern in the redefinition of EU policies in the future.

Democracy has been another existential and perennial debate in the EU polity. Historically, European decision makers have put forward a set of principles and values which have been enshrined in the treaties. They were meant not only to contribute to the legitimation of the integration process but also to strengthen the bonds between the peoples of Europe. Yet, Ramona Coman shows that democracy and the rule of law have been increasingly politicised in recent years in Western Europe as well as in Central and Eastern Europe. The chapter examines new tools designed at the EU level to prevent situations where domestic executives alter the democratic features of their political regimes by weakening the balance of power between institutions, by reducing the power of independent judicial institutions and by introducing limits to pluralism and freedom. While the rule of law conditionality (under discussion since 2018) seems to be a possible way forward, the chapter concludes that any attempt from the EU to uphold its values requires legal, political and social support.

In recent years, Brexit contributed to a resurgence of political and academic controversies over fundamental questions on the future of Europe, being among the most significant constitutional developments when it comes to the question of EU legitimacy. Joseph Lacey and Kalypso Nicolaïdis seek to understand the extent to which the issue of democratic legitimacy has become politically salient within the EU. The chapter explores the relationship between integrity (territorial, functional, procedural and existential) and legitimacy in the integration process. It provides a historical overview of the quest for legitimacy in the EU and outlines some of the main normative approaches (supranationalism, sovereigntism and democracy) to understanding how the EU ought to develop in order to become a more legitimate political system. The chapter discusses the causes of politicisation in the EU as well as the EU's attempts to democratisation, with a focus on Brexit and Article 50.

17 | North and South, East and West: Is it Possible to Bridge the Gap?

KRISTIN MAKSZIN, GERGŐ MEDVE-BÁLINT AND DOROTHEE BOHLE

17.1 Introduction

Since its foundation in 1951, the EC (and later EU) has grown from six to currently twenty-eight member states.[1] The six founding members were all advanced capitalist democracies, which had well-developed and competitive industries, generous welfare states and comparatively high living standards. This changed with the successive enlargement rounds. With almost every enlargement, the EU also admitted economically less developed countries (see Box 17.1).

BOX 17.1 Key dates

Year	Number of members	Member states that joined
1951	6	Belgium, France, Germany, Italy, Luxembourg, the Netherlands
1973	9	Denmark, Ireland, United Kingdom
1981	10	Greece
1986	12	Portugal, Spain
1995	15	Austria, Finland and Sweden
2004	25	Czech Republic, Estonia, Cyprus, Latvia, Lithuania, Hungary, Malta, Poland, Slovakia, Slovenia
2007	27	Bulgaria, Romania
2013	28	Croatia

Source: European Commission, 2018b

In 1973, two developed economies, Denmark and the UK, joined, but also Ireland. Ireland's economy was still based on agriculture, and the country suffered from poverty and mass emigration. Until the 1960s, it had also been a closed economy, which tried to protect domestic industry against foreign competition. In the 1980s, three Southern European countries joined the EC. Many of their enterprises were

[1] This became twenty-seven after the United Kingdom exited the EU in 2020.

owned by the state and mostly served domestic markets. These countries had a bigger public sector than most EU member states, which was also often inundated with clientelism and corruption, meaning public resources were allocated with the aim of creating loyal voter bases for political parties. Clientelism was very important to stabilise the new democracies, but economically inefficient (Mouzelis, 1986; Trantidis, 2016). Since 2004, eleven Eastern European countries (and two Mediterranean islands) joined. In contrast to Ireland and Southern Europe, the Eastern European countries were overindustrialised, but in outdated industries. This was a legacy of the communist system, which emphasised investment into heavy industry, such as mining or chemicals. In these countries, most of the economy was only recently privatised, and corruption was rampant.

As a result, with the successive enlargement rounds, significant gaps between Europe's economic core – the founding member states – and its multiple peripheries in the west (Ireland), south and east have emerged. Have these less developed countries been able to close the economic gap to the founding countries? The balance seems mixed. One country, Ireland, has indeed successfully caught up with and surpassed the richest EU countries. The Southern and Eastern European countries have also been able to catch up somewhat, but the economic gap compared to the richer EU countries has remained significant. Further, after the global financial crisis of 2008 and the eurocrisis of 2010–12, Southern European countries have fallen behind again and, according to some indicators, converged rather with the Eastern European countries than the core member states. How can we explain these different trajectories? Why has it been so difficult for most countries in Europe's periphery to close the economic gap? What has the EU done to manage the economic diversity? These are the questions this chapter seeks to address.

17.2   Historical Overview

Ireland, which joined the EC in 1973, has experienced a remarkable economic catch-up since the early 1990s and, overall, its EU membership is widely regarded as a success story. This is in stark contrast to the Greek case. Greece, the first Southern European country to join the EU, has struggled with deep economic problems and failed to follow a sustained path of catching up with the core member states. Since 2010 the country has plunged into an economic and social abyss, from which it is only slowly recovering. Hungary, which joined the EU in 2004, is located in between these two extremes. While the country has undergone a successful transformation from a planned to a market economy, and from a dictatorship to a democracy, the global financial crisis of 2008 and its dire economic consequences have triggered a major political backlash there. These three cases show remarkably different trajectories of peripheral European countries in the EU.

Economically, the rapid Irish convergence with the core EU countries contrasts with the increasing divergence of Greece, and the much more lacklustre growth in Hungary. Box 17.2 explains the concepts of core and periphery, as well as the concepts of convergence and divergence. Another major difference between the three cases is the role of the state. In Ireland, after a series of crises, a capable state has managed to nurture economic development. While in Greece, the state has partially hindered development through clientelistic practices. Finally, in political terms, the EU is being increasingly contested in Hungary, but not so in Ireland. Greece seems to be the intermediate case. Interestingly, political contestation in Hungary also goes hand in hand with a deterioration of the overall quality of democracy and the rule of law.

BOX 17.2 Key concepts

Periphery. A periphery is a region or country that is geographically located at the margins of an area. Peripheral regions or countries are usually less developed than the centre, where economic activities are concentrated. Periphery is thus a relational concept that highlights inequality and dependency between different regions or countries. In the EU, multiple peripheries exist. Typically, we distinguish between the southern periphery (the Mediterranean EU countries), the western periphery (Ireland) and the eastern periphery (the Eastern European EU countries).

Catching up and convergence. In economics, there is an assumption that poorer countries grow faster than their richer counterparts. This allows them to close the developmental gap and eventually achieve the same developmental level as richer countries (convergence). However, this catch-up effect is not automatic. A number of factors can limit catching up. For instance, the lack of technology, skilled labour force or a capable state might hinder fast growth.

Overall, these cases help us think about the gaps that exist between the founding countries[2] of the EU and its peripheral members, and the question of whether the periphery manages to catch up with the core. First, and probably most important, is the economic gap. We look at the value of goods and services produced in a peripheral country in comparison to that of the core countries. This measure – called GDP – is one important component of economic development and enables the identification of developmental gaps. Figure 17.1 shows the average GDP per

---

[2] Italy is a partial exception, given the country also faced a gap in development with the southern part of the country lagging behind the north.

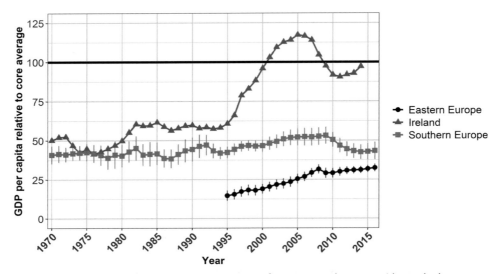

Figure 17.1 Average GDP per capita as a percentage of core average by group with standard errors
Source: Calculated based on World Bank Data, 2018

capita for each periphery group as a percentage of the core average, where core is defined as the six original members.[3] The eastern periphery includes the eight Eastern European countries that joined the EU in 2004 (excluding Cyprus and Malta), and south refers to Greece, Portugal and Spain. Ireland converged on the level of development of the core member states by 2000 and, although it has had a worse experience in the crisis than the core average, its level of economic activity recovered by 2015. For the southern periphery, there is no notable convergence, but rather a persistent gap where the level of economic activity hovers around 50 per cent of the core average with a clear deterioration after the crisis. Eastern Europe even lagged behind the south when most of it joined the EU. However, there was a clear convergence trend from the beginning of the post-communist transition until the 2008 crisis. The crisis has led to a setback, but the east has started to grow again earlier than the south. The result is actually a convergence of the southern and eastern peripheries to a level of economic activity that is less than 40 per cent of the level of the core. This suggests that the economic development gaps between the EU's core and peripheries are persistent.

The second type of gap concerns the state and administrative capacity to foster development. States play an important role in bringing about development: they have to guarantee property rights, regulate markets, ensure fair competition

---

[3] Fully 'catching up' would be defined as reaching 100 per cent in the figure. The standard errors are shown to display any changes of dispersion within each group.

and invest in infrastructure. Europe's core countries typically have capable states, while peripheral countries are often much more prone to clientelism and corruption, which imposes a restriction on development. Figure 17.2 shows the differences in state capacities between Europe's core and the three peripheries. The state capacity indicator is the average of measures of government effectiveness, regulatory quality, rule of law and control of corruption. Ireland, again, caught up to the core. The eastern member states showed some meaningful improvements in the time leading up to the accession and more meagre improvements since then, but a significant gap remains. For the southern periphery, we detect a widening gap. This suggests that the capability of states to address development in the peripheries lags far behind that of the core member states.

In order to visualise the gaps in both economic development and state capacity, we present a snapshot of the level of economic development (measured via GDP per capita) and state capacity in 2017 in Figure 17.3. This shows that the gaps between the core member states and the peripheries, both southern and eastern, are multidimensional and persistent.

This section clearly demonstrates that there are persistent gaps between the core and the peripheries on both economic and political dimensions. In many indicators, the eastern and southern peripheries converged with each other, which suggests a two-tiered EU.

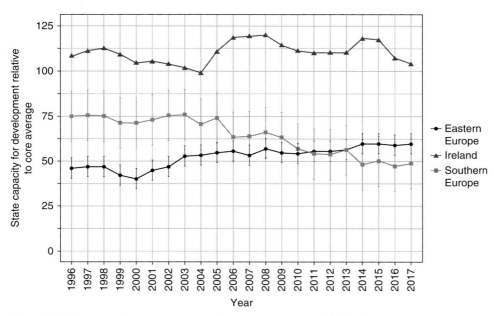

Figure 17.2 State capacity as a percentage of core group average, 1996–2017
Source: Calculated based on World Bank Governance Indicators

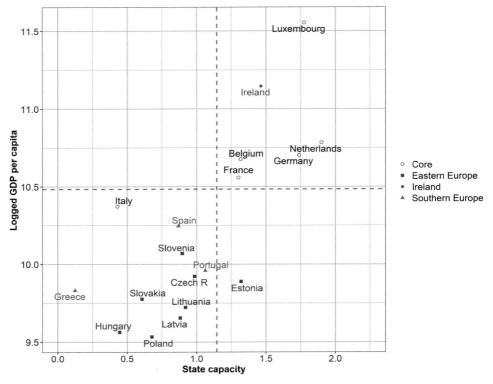

Figure 17.3 Logged GDP per capita by state capacity, 2017

17.3   Main Institutional Issues at Stake

This section introduces how EU actors and institutions thought about the gaps and the instruments devised in order to reduce them, which were developed in a piece-meal fashion from the early days of the EC. The focus of EU policies was mostly on economic and social inequality (Chapter 6), but with the eastern enlargement, the EU also devised instruments to counter the gaps in state capacity, rule of law and democracy (Chapter 18). Overall, the effects of EU funding for convergence have proved insufficient, as we detect sustained gaps without hopeful trends. Partly the goal of 'catching up' was just too arduous, as the gaps represented structural differences in the new member states' economies and states that could not be easily overcome, even with significant EU support. Furthermore, the tension between the goals of promoting competitiveness of the single market (Chapter 8) and redistribution within the EU is an ongoing struggle that implies variation in the prioritisation of convergence as a goal over time. Finally, redistributive EU instruments and policies require sustained commitment from member states that are net contributors, which is politically challenging (Coman, 2018). Nevertheless, substantial effort and resources have been devoted to addressing inequalities in the EU, which we summarise below.

17.3.1 The First Enlargement: Oil Crisis and Increasing Economic and Social Heterogeneity

The Treaty of Rome in 1957 already established some of the instruments that would eventually become important for bridging the gaps in the successive enlargement rounds. The treaty declared the aim of a 'harmonious development' in the Communities, laid out the plans for a social fund (ESF) to address the costs to labour resulting from economic restructuring, and established the EIB (Bussière et al., 2008). The EIB supports integration and development in the new members through loans with lower interest rates than the market offers. Until the 1970s, Italy was the main beneficiary of support from the Social Fund (European Commission, 1998: 14). This changed in the 1970s, when the first enlargement round coincided with the oil crisis, which both resulted in more supportive economic institutions and policies. The ERDF, with the purpose to invest in less developed subnational regions of the EU, was established in 1975. It was a demand by the UK and Ireland as part of the western enlargement deal in 1973, as these countries included regions suffering from industrial decline that would not have been net beneficiaries of agricultural funding schemes (Wishlade, 1996: 29). Ireland benefited substantially from EIB and ERDF funding (Clifton et al., 2018: 40). Box 17.3 summarises these instruments.

BOX 17.3 Legal basis

Treaty	Year	Purpose
Treaty of Rome Article 123 and 130	1957	To support balanced growth and employment-related struggles in response to economic integration Established the ESF and the EIB
Treaty of Accession European Council Regulation (EEC) No. 2895/77	1973	Established the ERDF in 1975 to address inequalities between regions
Single European Act	1987	Established the single market
Delors I	1988	Introduction of a fixed budgetary period and the doubling of the budgetary allocation for structural funds in response to the expected rising disparities with the creation of the single market

BOX 17.3 (Cont.)

Treaty	Year	Purpose
TFEU Article 174–8	2007	Integrated the legal basis for European cohesion policy stipulating that the EU 'shall develop and pursue its actions leading to the strengthening of its economic, social and territorial cohesion' (Art. 174)
		Specifies the main instruments and objectives of the structural funds
Rule of law framework established by European Commission	2014	Monitors case of deterioration of rule of law within member states and attempts resolution through dialogue

17.3.2 The Southern Enlargement: The Issue of Cohesion

The southern enlargement of the EU in the 1980s coincided with the neoliberal turn of the EU, which manifested itself in the completion of the European single market and the EMU (Chapter 8 and 9). Policy makers in the EU were well aware that these projects needed to be counterbalanced by policies that would increase the social and economic cohesion of the EU, especially with the presence of less developed member states, namely Greece, Spain and Portugal. This was demonstrated clearly in the Delors Report on the EMU, which states: 'If sufficient consideration were not given to regional imbalances, the economic union would be faced with grave economic and political risks' (Delors, 1989: 18). Under this double pressure of marketisation and enlargement, the EU devised a coherent strategy of fostering cohesion (Chapter 6). The introduction of cohesion policy in 1988 substantially transformed the framework for addressing regional disparities by incorporating multiple policy instruments under one umbrella, the so-called 'structural funds', establishing common standards across the EU, and involving subnational actors in the process of allocating the funds. European funding for development has increased significantly over time (European Commission, 1998). Throughout the 1990s, Greece, Portugal and Ireland received around 3 per cent of GDP from EU funds (Rodríguez-Pose and Fratesi, 2004: 99). These funds also played an important role in infrastructural development in the east from 2004 on.

Figure 17.4 shows the structural fund payments as a percentage of GDP since 2004. It is clearly visible that Eastern and Southern Europe benefited from these payments in the period between 2005 and 2017 much more than Ireland. The graph also shows that there is a steep rise and subsequent drop in the percentage values in the south and in the east between 2009 and 2014. This has to do with a number of factors, such as spending patterns in structural funds and shrinking

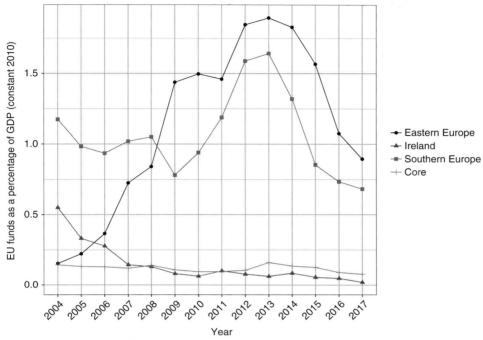

Figure 17.4 EU structural fund payments as a percentage of GDP
Source: European Commission, 2018a

GDP during the crisis. The drop towards the end of the period also is explained by the fact that the funds for the years 2007–13 had to be used by 2015, while the start of the new financing period (2014–20) was delayed until 2016.

How much have these funds helped to bridge the gap between Europe's poorer and more developed regions? Research shows that while structural funds have overall contributed to growth, they have not reached their objective of reducing the gap between poorer and richer regions (Le Gallo et al., 2011). This is in part because the funds are not targeted at the least developed regions in the peripheries. Rather, all regions with GDP per capita below the 75 per cent threshold of the EU average are eligible. Almost all regions in the peripheries meet this requirement, which qualifies them for the highest level of funding. While emphasis on physical infrastructure instead of prioritising education and human capital projects restricted the effectiveness of funds in the south (Rodríguez-Pose and Fratesi, 2004); within the east the funds mostly benefited the relatively richer regions, at the detriment of poorer ones (Medve-Bálint, 2018).[4] Moreover, the distribution of funds within the peripheral member states seem to be exposed to political manipulation (Bloom and Petrova, 2013; Medve-Bálint, 2017; Veiga, 2012). Recently, there

[4] This is because applicants in richer regions often have greater human capital and resources required to devise stronger project applications.

has been a creep in structural funds to support competition over redistribution, including enabling funding for more developed regions if it promoted economic productivity (Bachtler and Mendez, 2016; Cohesion Policy, 2018). After the eurozone crisis this trend was exacerbated, suggesting that funds may not contribute to greater convergence in the future (see Chapters 6 and 10).

17.3.3   Eastern Enlargement: Strengthening the East's Markets and States

Compared to the northern and southern enlargement, eastern enlargement was considered a much bigger challenge. The EU had to integrate a greater number of countries, which were much less prepared as they had just emerged from an authoritarian regime with a command economy. To master these challenges, the EU developed criteria for membership and devised new policy instruments to assist countries in the process.

The membership criteria were formulated at the European Council of June 1993 in Copenhagen (see Chapter 18), which required the 'stability of institutions guaranteeing democracy, the rule of law, human rights, respect for and protection of minorities, the existence of a functioning market economy, as well as the capacity to cope with competitive pressure and market forces within the Union'.[5] To ensure that the new member states comply with these criteria, the EU introduced a new instrument, the Accession Partnerships (Grabbe, 1999), which united all demands of the EU and the financial assistance granted to the applicant states within a single framework that defined priorities for reforms, covering a broad range of economic, political and administrative areas, and set a timetable for meeting them. The applicant's progress was reviewed regularly and membership was made conditional on meeting the Commission's requirements. The encompassing and detailed reform agenda was more thorough than previous rounds of accession.

Overall, the Accession Partnerships can be considered successful. Their conditionality, regular monitoring and targeted financial support enabled the Eastern European countries to implement far-reaching reforms, and strengthen their competitiveness and administrative capacities (Bruszt and Vukov, 2017; Vachudova, 2005). This also produced greater state capacity for utilising EU funds for effective development, but as Figure 17.3 shows, a massive gap persists relative to the core. For those countries, whose progress was not yet deemed entirely satisfactory, new measures were introduced. Thus, in the Bulgarian and Romanian cases, the Commission set up the so-called Cooperation and Verification Mechanism (CVM) to further monitor and

---

[5] Presidency Conclusions, Copenhagen European Council 1993, 7. www.europarl.europa.eu/ enlargement/ec/pdf/cop_en.pdf.

assist reform progress in the fields of judicial reform and corruption, where progress prior to accession was insufficient (European Commission, 2019).

The influence of the EU on political developments weakened dramatically after accession. When member states faced deteriorating quality of democracy or rule of law, mechanisms to enforce the expectations defined in the membership criteria were lacking (Bohle and Greskovits, 2009; Kelemen, 2017). As a reaction the EU developed new instruments, such as the Rule of Law Framework introduced in 2014, which formalised the social pressure of EU actors in cases of deteriorating rule of law (see Chapter 18). While in some cases EU-level actors had a decisive influence, such as in Romania in 2012 (Perju, 2015; Sedelmeier, 2017), in other cases, such as Poland and Hungary, this framework proved insufficient (Halmai, 2019; Pech and Scheppele, 2017).

In sum, with each new enlargement round, the EU has also devised new strategies to bridge the gaps between poorer newcomers and the richer core. Whereas initially the focus was on the economic dimension, with eastern enlargement catching up was defined more broadly as economic, administrative and political. Box 17.4 summarises the main actors that had an influence on the developmental path in Europe's peripheries.

BOX 17.4 Key actors

Multinational corporations (MNCs). These are enterprises that have their headquarters in one country but establish fully or partially owned subsidiaries in other countries to perform economic activity there. MNCs are the primary sources bringing FDI into the host economies.

National governments. They are responsible for implementing the EU funds allocated to them through the cohesion policy. National governments set up their own institutional system for designing, managing and implementing those programmes funded by EU support.

EBRD. An international financial institution that was established in 1991 with the initial objective of assisting the post-communist countries in transforming to market economies. Through various credit programmes, EBRD has supported the development of the private sector in the target countries

EIB. This is the EU's bank, which provides loans to finance investment projects that are expected to contribute to the EU's broad developmental objectives.

IMF. An international financial institution headquartered in Washington, DC. Its main objective is to ensure the stability of exchange rates and international payments. It provides financial support with specific conditions to crisis-ridden countries to restore their economic growth.

17.4   Main Policy Developments at Stake: Market Integration and its Effects on the Developmental Gap

While structural funds have specifically targeted disadvantaged areas, they were not key to the EU's economic development strategy. Especially since the EU's 'neoliberal turn' in the 1980s, the completion of the internal market with its four freedoms – movement of goods, capital, services and persons – as well as the introduction of the common currency have been the focal points of EU socio-economic governance. Full participation in these projects was seen as the best way to foster economic and social development. The capacity to participate in these projects was also set as a precondition for accession, as detailed in the Copenhagen criteria (Chapter 18). In terms of economic catching up, the most consequential effects have resulted from FDI, eurozone entry and the free movement of labour.

FDI occurs when a firm or an individual from one country invests into a business of another country, such as for instance when the German car company Volkswagen invested into the Spanish car manufacturer SEAT or the Czech company ŠKODA. FDI became a major vehicle of development, especially in Eastern Europe. While the EU had no specific legal instruments to foster FDI, it relied on membership conditionality and the Accession Partnerships to promote foreign capital inflows. FDI is also a critical part of Ireland's development (see below and Section 17.6). Further, it should be noted that in some countries, FDI has also poured into domestic services such as banking, retail or energy sectors (Pula, 2018).

Eurozone membership was not devised as a developmental tool, and initially nobody expected Europe's peripheral countries to join (Eichengreen, 2014: 93). However, all Southern European countries – including Malta and Cyprus – and five Eastern European countries by now have joined the exclusive club. Eurozone membership required reining in public debt and deficit, and making their economies more competitive. Many peripheral countries adopted institutions such as a social pact to deliver these outcomes prior to joining (e.g. Hancké and Rhodes, 2005). However, once in the eurozone, abundant credit was channelled into the European peripheries. This led to higher growth, but it also fuelled construction and housing booms and public debt. This made the periphery very vulnerable when the financial crisis of 2008 broke out (see e.g. Dellepiane et al., 2013).

Finally, the impact of free movement of labour on the development in Europe's periphery is a double-edged sword (Chapter 11). Most importantly, it leaves the home country bereft of its most educated and motivated workforce. At the same time, migration does bring benefits to home countries – partly through return migration and partly in the form of remittances.

Europe's diverse peripheries have developed very different capacities to deal with the pressures and opportunities of market integration. The 'growth model' or 'varieties of capitalism' literature distinguishes two main types of growth that have resulted from the interaction of domestic institutions and international factors in Europe's periphery: the FDI-led growth model in Ireland and the Visegrád countries (i.e. the Czech Republic, Hungary, Poland and Slovakia), and consumption-led growth in Southern Europe and the Baltic states (Baccaro and Pontusson, 2016; Bohle and Regan, 2018; Hope and Soskice, 2016; Johnston and Regan, 2016).

In FDI-led growth models, the export sector is dominated by MNCs, who set up production sites in the host countries because of comparatively cheap and skilled workforces, generous investment incentives and low taxes. These MNCs do not seek to service the domestic markets of the home countries, but to strengthen their companies' overall export competitiveness.

While in all FDI-led growth models, MNCs play a major role in shaping the export sectors, the export sector itself can differ. Thus, Ireland has concentrated on attracting high-tech firms in the information and computer sector. Already in the 1980s, the country managed to convince companies such as Apple, Microsoft, Dell and IBM to invest. Since the 2000s, companies such as Google, Amazon and Facebook followed. As a result, Ireland increasingly exports services related to the computer and information technology sector (Bohle and Regan, 2018). In contrast, building on their industrial legacy and proximity to Germany, the four Visegrád countries have focused much more on attracting segments of the automobile industry. They privatised their industries to foreign investors, hoping that this would lead to a modernisation and upgrading of their outdated industry. For German and other continental European companies, outsourcing to the Visegrád countries allowed them to increase their own competitiveness (Greskovits, 2014; Pula, 2018). All major German car makers such as Volkswagen, Audi, BMW and Daimler Benz have set up assembly lines and engine companies in the Visegrád countries.

Attracting FDI to strengthen the export sector was not a developmental strategy in all peripheral countries. In Southern Europe and the Baltic states, growth is based much more on domestic consumption by households and/or the state. Consumption-led growth was particularly vigorous during the 1990s and 2000s, when liberalisation of financial markets and the eurozone made access to credit very cheap. As a consequence, in the Baltic States and most Southern European countries, increasing private or public debt fuelled growth. In the Baltic states, credit was channelled into the economies via foreign-owned banks, mostly from Sweden and Denmark, which developed mortgage and credit markets (Bohle and Greskovits, 2012). Some authors therefore call the Baltic states' growth model 'dependent financialisation' (e.g. Becker and Jäger, 2010). In addition to credit, rising wages were also a source of growth in Southern Europe and the Baltic states. Because of rising wages, these countries lost their competitiveness, and their credit dependency made them very vulnerable to and impacted by the global financial crisis and the eurozone crisis.

17.5   Current Political and Academic Controversies: Peripheries in Crisis

Figures 17.1 and 17.2 show the limited extent to which Europe's diverse peripheries have caught up with the core. They also show that a sharp reversal of fortunes has occurred since the outbreak of the 2008 crisis. Europe's south has been particularly hard and lastingly hit by the euro crisis, and in Europe's east the crisis has smashed the hopes of reaching Western European social and economic standards in the foreseeable future. Not surprisingly, in the wake of the crisis and the EU's crisis management, the EU's recipes for catching up have come under increased scrutiny. Two issues have become particularly controversial: the enforcement of austerity, which was already enshrined in the Treaty on Stability, Coordination and Governance in the EMU (2012), but has become particularly damaging since the crisis; and the high dependency on FDI.

17.5.1   Austerity versus Solidarity in the Wake of the Debt Crisis

In the wake of the global financial crisis, many peripheral European countries suffered deep economic crises and had to turn to the IMF and EU for financial assistance. Figure 17.5 shows the timeline of financial assistance. It reveals that before the eurozone crisis broke out, three Eastern European countries already received financial assistance: Hungary, Latvia and Romania. In terms of the amount of assistance, the programmes for the eurozone members were much more expensive than for those outside of the eurozone (Mabbett and Schelkle, 2015; Schelkle, 2017). It is also interesting to note that the FDI-led economies recovered much faster from the crisis than the consumption-led economies. There is one exception: Latvia also recovered relatively quickly despite pursuing a strategy of internal

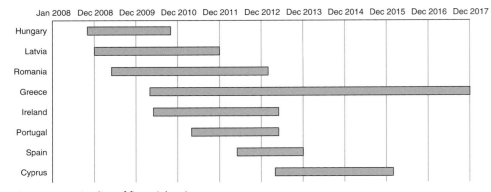

Figure 17.5 Timeline of financial assistance
Sources: European Court of Auditors, 2015: 12; Schelkle, 2017: 169, https://ec.europa.eu/info/business-economy-euro/economic-and-fiscal-policy-coordination/eu-financial-assistance_en

adjustment. This means that although Latvia was not yet a member of the euro-zone when the crisis hit, it did not devalue its currency, which would have made its exports more competitive. Rather, it adopted the euro in 2014.

As usual with financial assistance, it was tied to strict conditions. The programme countries had to commit themselves to far-reaching structural reforms and harsh austerity (Blyth, 2013; Cafruny, 2015; Crespy and Vanheuverzwijn, 2017). However, the merits of austerity amid a deep recession are hotly debated (Blyth, 2013; see also Chapter 17). Among northern creditor countries, and especially Germany, there is a deep conviction that budgets have to be balanced. Economists here follow ordoliberal reasoning that 'governments should focus on strengthening contract enforcement and fostering competition' (Eichengreen, 2014: 10). On the other hand, mostly Anglo-Saxon economists sharply criticised the austerity drive in the EU, claiming that it made the recession even worse and that the government needs to step in when private actors cannot spend (Blyth, 2013; Sandbu, 2015). Interestingly, economists in the IMF also acknowledged that they underestimated the impact of austerity, and the resulting recession was much stronger than they had forecast (Blanchard and Leigh, 2013).

This closely relates to the question of whether the richer member states have really shown solidarity towards the periphery in the crisis or whether they mostly pursued their own interests and pushed the costs of the crisis on to Europe's poorer regions. Here, the governments and populations of Northern European countries often point to the costs associated with the financial assistance. While this approach has fuelled a sense of impatience, for instance among German taxpayers with the Greek population, others point to the fact that some of the financial support was actually used to bail out German and French banks rather than the Greek state (Galbraith, 2016). Moreover, in 2017 it turned out that Germany was a major beneficiary of the Greek debt crisis, because it received interests on the loans to Greece (Stam, 2018). More broadly, the crisis has shown that there is an increasing need for European solidarity, while it has at the same time undermined the willingness for solidarity in creditor countries.

17.5.2   The Drawbacks of FDI Dependency

Another topic that has been hotly debated since the crisis is the drawbacks of FDI dependency, especially in the Eastern European economies. Here the crisis brought long-simmering discontent with foreign ownership of national economic assets to the fore. There is a growing sense that foreigners have exploited the resources of the Eastern European economies for their own private gains. At the same time, they have not invested enough in innovation and upgrading. Moreover, domestic entrepreneurs can often not compete successfully with their foreign counterparts. FDI inflows have also become more scarce since the crisis broke out, which is partly due to the global restructuring of value chains (Hunya, 2017).

The debate is perhaps best presented with the example of a recent controversial blogpost by Thomas Piketty. Here, the French economist argues that the profits and income from foreign-owned property flowing out of the countries was nearly double the net transfers from the EU flowing in (Piketty, 2018). For Piketty, net outflows that far exceed net inflows form the background for the increasingly nationalist rhetoric on European integration in the east.

Piketty's interpretation of Eastern Europe's 'exploitation' by Western Europe has generated significant interest in Eastern Europe. While nationalist forces have embraced this view, more liberal political forces have refuted his argument. For instance, Oblath (2018) argues that Piketty incorrectly classifies debt service, reinvested profits and export earnings that stem from FDI as outflows. He also ignores the income from remittances. Taken together, net inflows from Western to Eastern Europe are much higher than net outflows (see also Ghodsi et al., 2018, for a debate on the topic).

17.6   Case Studies: Ireland in the West, Hungary in the East

17.6.1   The Irish Success Story

When Ireland joined the EC in 1973, its GDP per capita was far below the average level of the founding countries and it was industrially less developed than Europe's core. Ireland's GDP per capita hovered around 50 per cent of the core average for the 1970s and 1980s (see Figure 17.1). Therefore, the early years of EU membership did not bring convergence with the core member states. The country faced high unemployment, peaking at 16.3 per cent in 1988 (Central Statistics Office, 2004). Catching up with the core took place in the 1990s and 2000s when the country experienced sudden growth resulting from an intersection of factors, including increased structural funds, significant economic reforms in response to an economic slowdown in the 1980s and an influx of high-tech FDI from the United States.

From the time of joining the EU, Ireland was a recipient of ERDF and ESF, but these were insufficient to facilitate convergence. The level of these funds increased dramatically after the Delors reform of 1988 and more than tripled their value by 1991, which led to a 3 to 4 per cent increase in economic output as estimated by a model-based macroeconomic assessment (Honohan, 1997: 29). The funding was divided relatively evenly between infrastructure projects, human resources and investment aid to the private sector (Honohan, 1997: 34). This upsurge in funds was particularly well timed for Ireland as it compensated for the fiscal consolidation reforms in 1987 associated with the 'Tallaght strategy' which ushered in other major restructuring, including tax cuts, welfare reforms and wage moderation (Ó Riain, 2013). This marked the beginning of the 'Celtic Tiger', a period of sustained high growth that catapulted the country from 'the sick man of Europe' to one of the richest in the EU. The remarkable growth, over 7 per cent per year from 1994 to 2000, was based on the FDI of high-tech enterprises from the United States, attracted by a highly skilled, young, English-speaking population and low corporate taxes. Ireland also represented a point of access to the EU single market. As a result of FDI, Ireland's exports to the EU, USA and beyond surged from 36.1 per cent of GDP in 1973 to 98 per cent in 2000 (Barry, 2003: 902). Unemployment fell more gradually, but remained reliably below 5 per cent in the 2000s, which was a remarkable success compared to earlier experiences of high unemployment and resulting emigration.

In 2001, the so-called dot-com bubble in the United States burst, with many high-tech firms experiencing hard times. This also affected FDI inflows to Ireland. It is partly because of this that, during the 2000s, debt-fuelled private consumption and domestic demand – based on a housing boom – became the most important source of growth (Kirby, 2010: 35). Private debt was also fuelled by Ireland's entry to the eurozone. The housing bubble burst in the global financial crisis, and when the Irish state tried to save its troubled banks it got so indebted that it had to ask for financial assistance (see Section 17.4). What is remarkable, however, is that the Irish economy recovered very fast from the shock. Many European policy actors argue that this is because of successful austerity. However, the real reason for Ireland's recovery is that it could rely once again on export-oriented FDI from the US (Brazys and Regan, 2017). All in all, the story of Ireland's exemplary development was primarily based on a major influx of US FDI, but three well-timed factors were also vital to attracting this investment and facilitating successful development: the fundamental domestic reform in the late 1980s creating an investment-friendly climate, an expansion in EU funds at the same time utilised for improvements in human capital and infrastructure, and the establishment of the EU single market in 1993. Ireland's EU membership therefore played a critical role in its economic boom, but its path also depended upon a state that prioritised investment in promising industries and good timing. This implies that it would be difficult to reproduce in other peripheries which lack state capacity, have different sectoral profiles and experience less luck in timing.

17.6.2 Hungary's Declining Trajectory

Hungary was once considered a success story of post-communist transformation. Following the first democratic elections in 1990, the EU actively shaped democratic consolidation and the shift from command to market economy with pre-accession funding and technical expertise (Bruszt and Vukov, 2017; Jacoby, 2010). The country's changing economy has relied on the inflow of FDI, which was strongly encouraged by the EU as a way to speed up economic reforms and facilitate integration into global markets, but increasing its dependency (Medve-Bálint,

2014). However, the golden age was soon over. In 2000–9, Hungary's annual real GDP growth rate (3.4 per cent) remained well below the Eastern European average (5.6 per cent) and the global economic crisis also hit the country particularly hard. As recovery proved slow, Hungary, which in 2000 had the third highest GDP per capita in Eastern Europe, is currently the poorest among those countries that joined the EU in 2004. Why did a former Eastern European front runner become a laggard?

The answer to this puzzle lies in the structural weaknesses of the country's dependent market economy. First, excessive export and FDI dependence have made the economy particularly vulnerable to external economic shocks. Second, both the state and households accumulated considerable debt before the crisis, which was exacerbated by repayment of debt inherited from the past regime (Mihályi, 2001). In the 2000s, households tended to cover real estate purchases with cheap but risky foreign currency-denominated mortgages that were exposed to exchange rate risks (Bohle, 2014). Moreover, the relatively generous welfare system required far more resources than the state could afford, thus it also was increasingly financed from foreign credit (Bohle and Greskovits, 2012). The high material expectations of the population, rooted in the strong legacy of 'goulash communism', caused the failure of every major attempt at cutting back welfare expenses (Benczes, 2016). The burden of debt financing and the costs of the 'paternalist welfare state' (Kornai, 1996) led to loose fiscal policies and prevented sufficient investments into education, health care, R&D and innovation.

As a consequence of the 2008 crisis, the ruling socialist government was unable to raise revenue from credit markets and had to turn to the IMF for help. The value of the Hungarian currency plummeted, generating a mortgage crisis as households became unable to pay back loans. Export decline and the drying up of FDI gave further blows to the already sluggish economy. Corruption scandals eroded the popularity of the socialist government and at the 2010 elections the right-wing Fidesz party earned a two-thirds majority in parliament. The new government, led by Viktor Orbán, began to change Hungary's institutional landscape by adopting a new constitution and a new electoral law benefiting Fidesz, and politically loyal figures occupied every key position in public administration. Tight central control over the media, superior financial resources relative to the fragmented opposition and an unprecedented anti-immigration campaign drawing on the European migration crisis brought supermajorities to Fidesz at the 2014 and 2018 elections. This has reinforced clientelistic and authoritarian tendencies and strengthened democratic backsliding (Jenne and Mudde, 2012). The government launched an attack on CSOs and academic freedom and further restricted the media and the judiciary. The EP condemned these developments in September 2018 with the approval of the Sargentini Report.

Although Orbán's government has managed to balance the state budget, it failed to resolve the roots of the economic problems. The government renationalised utility companies and private pension funds; introduced a flat tax regime benefiting high-income households; reshuffled the welfare system to support middle-class families; levied special taxes on the banking sector and telecom operators; and has discouraged FDI into retail, banking and energy while promoting foreign investments into manufacturing. Although the country's economic growth is largely driven by the inflow of EU funds, the government's rhetoric is increasingly hostile to the EU. Nevertheless, it tends to channel EU grants to loyal firms, thereby creating politically dependent entrepreneurs (Fazekas and King, 2019). Yet, heavy reliance on FDI still prevails, making the economy vulnerable to external shocks. Failure to increase spending on education, health care, innovation and R&D challenges future growth prospects. Hungary may risk falling into a middle-income trap, where further upgrading of the economy remains nearly impossible because it would require a substantial increase in wages and a shift to more knowledge-intensive economic activities.

GROUP DISCUSSION

- What type of inequalities can market integration trigger and why?
- What are the strengths of and limitations to the EU's influence on domestic economic and political developments in the member states?

TOPICS FOR INDIVIDUAL RESEARCH

- Why are some peripheral EU countries and regions more successful at economic catch-up than others?
- Why did similar crisis management policies deliver different results in different EU member states?

FURTHER READINGS

Baumeister, M. and Sala, R. (eds) (2016). *Southern Europe? Italy, Spain, Portugal and Greece from the 1950s until the Present Day*. Frankfurt and New York: University of Chicago Press/Campus Verlag.

Bohle, D. and Greskovits, B. (2012). *Capitalist Diversity on Europe's Periphery*. Ithaca, NY: Cornell University Press.

Lux, G. and Horváth, G. (eds) (2018). *The Routledge Handbook to Regional Development in Central and Eastern Europe*. Abingdon and New York: Routledge.

Molle, W. (2015). *Cohesion and Growth: The Theory and Practice of European Policy Making*. Abingdon and New York: Routledge.

O'Riain, S. (2014). *The Rise and Fall of Ireland's Celtic Tiger: Liberalism, Boom and Bust*. Cambridge: Cambridge University Press.

REFERENCES

Baccaro, L. and Pontusson, J. (2016). 'Rethinking Comparative Political Economy: The Growth Model Perspective'. *Politics & Society* 44(2): 175–207.

Bachtler, J. and Mendez, C. (2016). *EU Cohesion Policy and European Integration: The Dynamics of EU Budget and Regional Policy Reform*. London: Routledge.

Barry, F. (2003). 'Economic Integration and Convergence Processes in the EU Cohesion Countries'. *JCMS: Journal of Common Market Studies* 41(5): 897–921.

Becker, J. and Jäger, J. (2010). 'Development Trajectories in the Crisis in Europe'. *Debatte: Journal of Contemporary Central and Eastern Europe* 18(1): 5–27.

Benczes, I. (2016). 'From Goulash Communism to Goulash Populism: The Unwanted Legacy of Hungarian Reform Socialism'. *Post-Communist Economies* 28(2):146–66.

Blanchard, O. and Leigh, D. (2013). *Growth Forecast Errors and Fiscal Multipliers. IMF Working Paper WP/13/1*. www.imf.org/en/Publications/WP/Issues/2016/12/31/Growth-Forecast-Errors-and-Fiscal-Multipliers-40200 (accessed 24 March 2018).

Bloom, S. and Petrova, V. (2013). 'National Subversion of Supranational Goals: "Pork-Barrel" Politics and EU Regional Aid'. *Europe-Asia Studies* 65(8): 1599–620.

Blyth, M. (2013). *Austerity: The History of a Dangerous Idea*. Oxford and New York: Oxford University Press.

Bohle, D. (2014). 'Post-socialist Housing Meets Transnational Finance: Foreign Banks, Mortgage Lending, and the Privatization of Welfare in Hungary and Estonia'. *Review of International Political Economy*, 21(4): 913–48.

Bohle, D. and Greskovits, B. (2009). 'East-Central Europe's Quandry'. *Journal of Democracy*, 20(4): 50–63.

Bohle, D. and Greskovits, B. (2012). *Capitalist Diversity on Europe's Periphery*. Ithaca, NY: Cornell University Press.

Bohle, D. and Regan, A. (2018). *Business Power, Growth Models, and Politics of Comparative Capitalism: Explaining the Continuity of FDI-led Growth in Ireland and Hungary*. Unpublished manuscript.

Brazys, S. and Regan, A. (2017). 'The Politics of Capitalist Diversity in Europe: Explaining Ireland's Divergent Recovery from the Euro Crisis'. *Perspectives on Politics*, 15(2): 411–27.

Bruszt, L. and Vukov, V. (2017). 'Making States for the Single Market: European Integration and the Reshaping of Economic States in the Southern and Eastern Peripheries of Europe'. *West European Politics*, 40(4): 663–87.

Bussière, É., Dumoulin, M. and Willaert, É. (2008). *The Bank of the European Union: The EIB, 1958–2008*. European Investment Bank. www.eib.org/infocentre/publications/all/the-bank-of-the-european-union-1958-2008.htm (accessed 1 December 2018).

Cafruny, A. W. (2015). 'European Integration Studies, European Monetary Union, and Resilience of Austerity in Europe: Post-mortem on a Crisis Foretold'. *Competition & Change*, 19(2): 161–77.

Central Statistics Office (2004). *Statistical Yearbook of Ireland*. www.cso.ie/en/statistics/statisticalyearbookofireland/statisticalyearbookofireland2004edition/ (accessed 29 November 2018).

Clifton, J., Díaz-Fuentes, D. and Gómez, A. L. (2018). 'The European Investment Bank: Development, Integration, Investment?'. *JCMS: Journal of Common Market Studies*, 56(4): 733–50.

Cohesion Policy (2018). http://ec.europa.eu/regional_policy/en/faq/#3 (accessed 23 March 2018).

Coman, R. (2018). 'How have EU "Fire-fighters" Sought to Douse the Flames of the Eurozone's Fast- and Slow-burning Crises? The 2013 Structural Funds Reform'. *The British Journal of Politics and International Relations*, 20(3): 540–54.

Crespy, A. and Vanheuverzwijn, P. (2017). 'What "Brussels" Means by Structural Reforms: Empty Signifier or Constructive Ambiguity?'. *Comparative European Politics*, 17(1): 92–111.

Dellepiane, S., Hardiman, N. and Las Heras, J. (2013). *Building on Easy Money: The Political Economy of Housing Bubbles in Ireland and Spain*. Working Paper, October. University College Dublin. Geary Institute. http://researchrepository.ucd.ie/handle/10197/4929 (accessed 17 December 2017).

Delors, J. (1989). *Report on Economic and Monetary Union in the European Community. Presented 17 April 1989 (Commonly Called the Delors Plan or Report) By Committee for the Study of Economic and Monetary Union*. EU Commission, Working Document. http://aei.pitt.edu/1007/ (accessed 24 March 2018).

Eichengreen, B. (2014). *Hall of Mirrors: The Great Depression, the Great Recession, and the Uses and Misuses of History*. New York: Oxford University Press.

European Commission (1998). *The European Social Fund: An Overview of the Programming Period 1994–1999*. Luxembourg : Lanham, MD: European Commission.

European Commission (2018a). 'EU Expenditure and Revenue Data'. http://ec.europa.eu/budget/figures/interactive/index_en.cfm (accessed 2 December 2018).

European Commission (2018b). 'From 6 to 28 members – European Neighbourhood Policy and Enlargement Negotiations'. https://ec.europa.eu/neighbourhood-enlargement/policy/from-6-to-28-members_en (accessed 18 March 2018).

European Commission (2019). 'Cooperation and Verification Mechanism for Bulgaria and Romania'. https://ec.europa.eu/info/policies/justice-and-fundamental-rights/effective-justice/rule-law/assistance-bulgaria-and-romania-under-cvm/cooperation-and-verification-mechanism-bulgaria-and-romania_en (accessed 24 January 2019).

European Court of Auditors (2015). 'Special Report No 18/2015: Financial Assistance Provided to Countries in Difficulties'. 18/2015. Luxembourg. www.eca.europa.eu/en/Pages/DocItem.aspx?did=35016.

Fazekas, M. and King, L. P. (2017). 'Perils of Development Funding? The Tale of EU Funds and Grand Corruption in Central and Eastern Europe'. *Regulation & Governance*, 13(3):405–30.

Galbraith, J. K. (2016). *Welcome to the Poisoned Chalice: The Destruction of Greece and the Future of Europe*. New Haven: Yale University Press.

Ghodsi, M., Gligorov, V., Havlik, P. et al. (2018). *WIIW Report, March 2018*. Vienna Institute for International Economic Studies. https://wiiw.ac.at/monthly-report-no-3-2018-p-4454.html (accessed 2 December 2018).

Grabbe, H. (1999). *A Partnership for Accession?: The Implications of EU Conditionality for the Central and East European Applicants*. European University Institute, Robert Schuman Centre.

Greskovits, B. (2014). 'Legacies of Industrialization and Paths of Transnational Integration After Socialism'. In M. R. Beissinger and S. Kotkin (eds), *Historical Legacies of Communism in Russia and Eastern Europe*. New York: Cambridge University Press.

Halmai, G. (2019). 'The Possibility and Desirability of Rule of Law Conditionality'. *Hague Journal on the Rule of Law*, 11(1): 171–88.

Hancké, B. and Rhodes, M. (2005). 'EMU and Labor Market Institutions in Europe: The Rise and Fall of National Social Pacts'. *Work and Occupations*, 32(2): 196–228.

Honohan, P. (1997). *EU Structural Funds in Ireland: A Mid-Term Evaluation of the CSF 1994–99*. Research Series. Economic and Social Research Institute (ESRI). https://econpapers.repec.org/bookchap/esrresser/prs31.htm (accessed 29 November 2018).

Hope, D. and Soskice, D. (2016). 'Growth Models, Varieties of Capitalism, and Macroeconomics'. *Politics & Society*, 44(2): 209–26.

Hunya, G. (2017). 'Conditions for an Investment Revival in Central and Eastern Europe'. In B. Galgóczi and J. Drahokoupil (eds), *Condemned to Be Left behind? Can Central and Eastern Europe Emerge from Its Low Wage Model?* Brussels: ETUI.

Jacoby, W. (2010). 'Managing Globalization by Managing Central and Eastern Europe: The EU's Backyard as Threat and Opportunity'. *Journal of European Public Policy*, 17(3): 416–32.

Jenne, E. K. and Mudde, C. (2012). 'Can Outsiders Help?'. *Journal of Democracy*, 23(3): 147–55.

Johnston, A. and Regan, A. (2016). 'European Monetary Integration and the Incompatibility of National Varieties of Capitalism'. *JCMS: Journal of Common Market Studies*, 54(2): 318–36.

Kelemen, R. D. (2017). 'Europe's Other Democratic Deficit: National Authoritarianism in Europe's Democratic Union'. *Government and Opposition*, 52(2): 211–38.

Kirby, P. (2010). *Celtic Tiger in Collapse: Explaining the Weaknesses of the Irish Model*. Basingstoke and New York: Palgrave Macmillan, 2nd edition.

Kornai, J. (1996). 'Paying the Bill for Goulash Communism: Hungarian Development and Macro Stabilization in a Political-Economy Perspective'. *Social Research*, 63(4): 943–1040.

Le Gallo, J., Dall'erba, S. and Guillain, R. (2011). 'The Local versus Global Dilemma of the Effects of Structural Funds'. *Growth and Change*, 42(4): 466–90.

Mabbett, D. and Schelkle, W. (2015). 'What Difference Does Euro Membership Make to Stabilization? The Political Economy of International Monetary Systems Revisited'. *Review of International Political Economy*, 22(3): 508–34.

Medve-Bálint, G. (2014). 'The Role of the EU in Shaping FDI Flows to East Central Europe'. *JCMS: Journal of Common Market Studies*, 52(1): 35–51.

Medve-Bálint, G. (2017). 'Funds for the Wealthy and the Politically Loyal? How EU Funds May Contribute to Increasing Regional Disparities in East Central Europe'. In J. Bachtler, P. Berkowitz and S. Hardy et al. (eds), *EU Cohesion Policy*. London and New York: Routledge.

Medve-Bálint, G. (2018). 'Implementing EU Cohesion Policy in the Eastern Member States: Quality of Government Balancing Between Equity and Efficiency'. In M. Matlak, F. Schimmelfennig and P. Wozniakowski (eds), *Europeanization Revisited: Central and Eastern Europe in the European Union*. Florence: European University Institute, Robert Schuman Centre for Advanced Studies.

Mihályi, P. (2001). 'The Evolution of Hungary's Approach to FDI in Post-Communist Privatization'. *Transnational Corporations*, 10(3): 61–74.

Mouzelis, N. (1986). 'On the Rise of Postwar Military Dictatorships: Argentina, Chile, Greece'. *Comparative Studies in Society and History*, 28(1): 55–80.

Ó Riain, S. (2013). 'The Crisis of Financialisation in Ireland'. *The Economic and Social Review*, 43(4): 497–533.

Oblath, G. (2018). 'Nem fosztogatnak, hanem osztogatnak – Magyarország kizsákmányolásáról' (They don't rob us, they give us). Portfolio.hu, 31 January. www.portfolio.hu/gazdasag/nem-fosztogatnak-hanem-osztogatnak-magyarorszag-kizsakmanyolasarol.274917.html (accessed 24 March 2018).

Pech, L. and Scheppele, K. L. (2017). 'Illiberalism Within: Rule of Law Backsliding in the EU'. *Cambridge Yearbook of European Legal Studies*, 19: 3–47.

Perju, V. (2015). 'The Romanian Double Executive and the 2012 Constitutional Crisis'. *International Journal of Constitutional Law*, 13(1): 246–78.

Piketty, T. (2018). '2018, the Year of Europe'. In *Le Blog De Thomas Piketty*. http://piketty.blog.lemonde.fr/2018/01/16/2018-the-year-of-europe/ (accessed 24 March 2018).

Pula, B. (2018). *Globalization Under and After Socialism: The Evolution of Transnational Capital in Central and Eastern Europe*. Stanford: Stanford University Press.

Rodríguez-Pose, A. and Fratesi, U. (2004). 'Between Development and Social Policies: The Impact of European Structural Funds in Objective 1 Regions'. *Regional Studies*, 38(1): 97–113.

Sandbu, M. E. (2015). *Europe's Orphan the Future of the Euro and the Politics of Debt*. Princeton: Princeton University Press.

Schelkle, W. (2017). *The Political Economy of Monetary Solidarity: Understanding the Euro Experiment*. Oxford: Oxford University Press.

Sedelmeier, U. (2017). 'Political Safeguards Against Democratic Backsliding in the EU: The Limits of Material Sanctions and the Scope of Social Pressure'. *Journal of European Public Policy*, 24(3): 337–51.

Stam, C. (2018). 'Germany Earned €2.9 Billion from Greece's Debt Crisis'. Euractiv.com. www.euractiv.com/section/economy-jobs/news/germany-earned-2–9-billion-euros-from-greeces-debt-crisis/ (accessed 24 January 2019).

Trantidis, A. (2016). *Clientelism and Economic Policy: Greece and the Crisis*. London: Routledge.

Vachudova, M. A. (2005). *Europe Undivided: Democracy, Leverage, and Integration After Communism*. Oxford: Oxford University Press.

Veiga, L. G. (2012). 'Determinants of the Assignment of EU Funds to Portuguese Municipalities'. *Public Choice*, 153(1): 215–33.

Wishlade, F. (1996). 'EU Cohesion Policy: Facts, Figures, and Issues'. In L. Hooghe (ed.), *Cohesion Policy and European Integration: Building Multi-Level Governance*. Oxford and New York: Oxford University Press.

World Bank Data (2018). https://data.worldbank.org/indicator/NY.GDP.PCAP.CD (accessed 24 March 2018).

18 Democracy and the Rule of Law: How Can the EU Uphold its Common Values?

RAMONA COMAN

18.1 Introduction

The nature of the EU has always been uncertain. Depending on the contexts, it has oscillated between a form of intergovernmental economic cooperation and a sui generis political supranational construction. While proponents of intergovernmentalism see the EU as an organisation that brings together nation states with the aim of increased economic cooperation, promoters of the EU as a polity conceive it as a union where the bonds between the peoples of Europe beyond the nation states are strengthened. These contrasting visions have shaped the integration process over time. This satisfied both federalists and intergovernmentalists as the outcomes of integration 'proved to be compatible with analyses from each of these perspectives' (Bellamy and Castiglione, 2000: 67). However, the issue of what the EU is and what can be expected from it remains a matter of heightened political debate and academic controversies. Today we know that the EU is more than an intergovernmental form of economic cooperation. However, despite the development of the political Union over time, the EU is not either a state as it lacks a demos and a shared identity.

The nature of the EU matters. Indeed, the extent of how democratic it should be depends on how it is apprehended: for those who see it as a form of intergovernmental cooperation the EU is democratic enough (Moravcsik, 2002), while a wide majority of scholars consider that it suffers from an acute democratic deficit (Vauchez, 2016). Not only has the integration process challenged European democracies in many ways, but it has also given rise to questions about whether democracy can emerge beyond the nation state or whether a supranational construction without a demos such as the EU can be a democracy (Lacroix, 2008: 7).

The democratisation of the EU is ongoing. Its pace has increased since the 1990s as a reaction to mounting resistances to the integration process. For decades, EU integration has been driven by elites *for* the people but *without* the people (Schmidt, 2006). The signature of the Maastricht Treaty – meant to democratise the EU – revealed that 'the era in which relatively insulated elites bargained grand treaties in the shadow of an uninterested and generally approving public has come to an end' (Saurugger, 2016: 935). To legitimise its raison d'être, the EU draped itself 'in the rhetoric of democracy' (Bellamy and Castiglione, 2000: 65), seeking not only to democratise its internal decision-making structures but also to promote democracy abroad in its relationship with the wider world. The perspective of the eastern enlargement strengthened the idea that the EU had an obligation to promote democracy and the rule of law on the continent (Whitman, 2011).

If democracy defines a form of government characterised by institutions, rights and practices designed to give people a say in the decision-making process, the treaties sought to strengthen the powers of the EP and to put it on an equal footing with the Council (see Chapter 3). If democracy refers to its underlying values, the treaties sought to legitimise the integration process by putting forward citizens' rights (Fossum, 2000: 112). Democracy and the rule of law were meant to guide the EU's action both internally and externally. By constitutionalising values common to all member states, political elites sought to unify the people of Europe, to generate a feeling of belonging and, ultimately, to legitimise the EU's raison d'être both internally and in its relationship with the wider world.

Paradoxically, in recent years, democracy and the rule of law have been increasingly politicised. The salience of these two values has spectacularly increased both at the EU and the domestic level, thus intensifying the polarisation of visions of Europe. This phenomenon is happening in a specific context: on the one hand, in Western Europe, traditional political parties face electoral defeat at the hands of Eurosceptic, nationalist, xenophobic parties who contest not only the integration process per se but also the very idea of democracy itself as well as the values enshrined in the treaties. On the other hand, in Central and Eastern Europe – where the democratisation process that followed the collapse of communism was supposed to be irreversible – new forms of authoritarian politics have emerged as nationalist and xenophobic parties win elections and large majorities in national parliaments with a discourse that rejects liberal democracy and its values. If democracy's main virtue is its tendency to promote pluralism, freedom and equality (Bellamy and Castiglione, 2000), recent developments within EU member states reveal that these values are under considerable strain.

This chapter will show that values are increasingly politicised and that there is increased disagreement as to how to address instances of non-compliance. The finalité of the EU and its nature are under strain. Examining the cases of Austria in the 2000s as well as recent attempts to dismantle the rule of law in Hungary and Poland since 2010 onwards, this chapter will demonstrate how the EU seeks to uphold its values by creating new tools and mechanisms of compliance.

18.2   Historical Overview

Peace and liberty were the main aspirations of those who survived World War II. By creating the EC in the 1950s, the founding fathers sought to prevent the rise of new waves of nationalism through the reconciliation of the states and of the peoples of Europe (see Chapters 2 and 13). References to democracy were relatively rare in the political declarations then (Weiler, 2012: 835). The aim of the six founding member states was to restore 'a sense of legitimate order and normalcy' (Conway and Depkat, 2010: 134), to find a 'shared destiny' by 'creating a genuine solidarity'. Democracy and human rights were not mentioned in the ECSC Treaty. The founding fathers sought to promote peace and economic cooperation, instead of relying on supranational guarantees of democracy and human rights which had been stipulated as strict criteria for membership by the Council of Europe in 1949 (Thomas, 2006: 1194).

Over time, law shaped the integration process. The political elites of the founding member states designed an institutional framework (see Chapter 3) in which the Court of Justice of the EU was set up to prevent the misuse of powers by the newly created supranational institutions (in particular the High Authority) and to ensure that member states respect the obligations enshrined in the treaties (Saurugger and Terpan, 2017).

While initially democracy was not in the DNA of the Communities, it soon emerged as an important issue between member states and the newly created supranational institutions. In 1962, Spain under the rule of Franco requested to negotiate an association agreement aimed towards enlargement (Thomas, 2006: 1195). The executives of Germany, France and Belgium (although divided) were in favour, only conditioning Spain's accession to economic criteria such as the adjustment of the common external tariffs and the absence of internal tariffs (Thomas, 2006: 1196). However, the members of the Parliamentary Assembly were opposed to the association of a non-democratic member state. In the Assembly the social democrats argued that opening the market to an authoritarian political regime contradicted the objectives of the Communities and the principles enshrined in the preamble of the treaty (Thomas, 2006: 1200). Although the Assembly's powers were limited to deliberation, its members played an active role of oversight, questioning the actions of the Council and the High Authority. The Assembly upheld democracy and human rights as sine qua non conditions for the integration of new member states. In contrast, within the Council, member states were hard to convince of the need for any criteria for membership. According to Article 237 of the Treaty of Rome (see Table 18.1) accession was open to 'any European state' and the conditions of admission were to be determined by 'an agreement between the member states and the applicant State'. Nevertheless, the members of the Parliamentary Assembly kept on arguing that Europe 'was not only about oranges and tomatoes, coal and steel, cars and furniture [...] it is also and above all to strive to create a political community' (Thomas, 2006: 1200).

Overall, as Saurugger puts it, the integration process has in fact happened through law, not through a transfer of loyalty or the creation of a common identity (2016: 936). The integration through law has been seen as a form of constitutionalisation

Table 18.1 Chronology and legal basis

Treaty	Preamble	Accession conditions	External action	Common values	Sanctions
Rome	–	Article 237	–	–	–
SEA	Promote democracy and compliance with the law				
Maastricht	Attachment to the principles of liberty, democracy and respect for the fundamental rights and freedoms, and the rule of law		Art. J.1 Objectives of the CFSP Develop democracy and consolidate the rule of law and respect for human rights and fundamental freedoms		
Amsterdam		Article 0 Any European state which respects the principles set out in article F(1) may apply to become a member of the Union		Article F The Union is founded on the principles of liberty, democracy, respect for human rights and the rule of law, principles which are common to the member states.	Article F.1 The Council [...] may determine the existence of a serious and persistent breach of values
Lisbon	Attachment to the principles of liberty, democracy, respect for human rights and fundamental freedoms, and of the rule of law	Article 49: Any European State which respects the values referred to in Article 2 and is committed to promoting them may apply to become a member of the Union	Article 21	Article F becomes Article 2 Article 10 The functioning of the EU shall be founded on representative democracy.	Article F.1 becomes Article 7

Democracy and the rule of law in the EU treaties

of the EU (Saurugger, 2016: 936) in which economic considerations took precedence over political considerations.

In the 1970s, heads of state and government of the nine member states issued a Declaration on European Identity at the European Council meeting in Copenhagen (1973). The principles of representative democracy, rule of law, social justice and respect for human rights were put forward as 'the deepest aspiration of their people' and 'fundamental elements of the European identity'. In the 1980s, the accession of Spain, Portugal and Greece represented a new opportunity for the members of the EP to restate that the Community's duty was 'to welcome all European States which apply the principles of a pluralist democracy and observe human rights and civil liberties and support the ideal of a strong and united Europe' (Resolution on the enlargement of the Community to include Spain and Portugal, 17 November 1982).

The SEA – signed on 17 February 1986 and entering into force on 1 July 1987 – was the first major revision of the treaties. It aimed to speed up the establishment of the single market and to reform the Communities' institutions in preparation for the accession of new countries. In the Preamble, the signatories expressed their will to 'promote democracy on the basis of the fundamental rights recognised in the constitutions and laws of the member states, in the Convention for the Protection of Human Rights and Fundamental Freedoms and the European Social Charter, notably freedom, equality and social justice' (see also Chapter 10). While this new step in the integration process was driven by the elites, the references to these values were presented as 'the wishes of the democratic people of Europe' (see Table 18.1).

From the 1990s, governing *for* the people but *without* the people of Europe was no longer possible. The democratic deficit of the Communities was a matter of concern both in political and academic circles. A new revision of the treaty was envisaged which was meant to allow the 'refoundation' of the communities (Magnette, 2000). The Maastricht Treaty – signed on 7 February 1992 and entering into force on 1 November 1993 – was an attempt to democratise the integration process and strengthen the identity of the EU's political regime (Magnette and Nicolaïdis, 2004). Seeking to establish an 'ever closer Union among the people of Europe', the signatories of the treaty confirmed their attachment to 'the principles of liberty, democracy and respects for human rights and fundamental freedoms and of the rule of law' (see Box 18.2). But the rejection of the Maastricht Treaty by referendum in France and Denmark marked the end of the 'permissive consensus'.

While the EU was seeking to democratise its structures by increasing the role of the EP in the decision-making process, in the eastern part of the continent citizens were celebrating and chanting the triumph of democracy and their 'return to Europe' after the collapse of communism in 1989. New states introduced requests to join the EU. In 1993, the European Council in Copenhagen noted progress in enlargement negotiations with Austria, Finland and Sweden and held a 'thorough discussion on the relations between the Community and the countries of Central and Eastern Europe'. Two decades after the adoption of the Declaration on European Identity, the European Council laid down the conditions that every European state willing to join the EU should meet in terms of democracy, market economy and administrative capacity (Copenhagen criteria).

The Amsterdam Treaty signed on 2 October 1997 and entering into force on 1 May 1999 marked a step forward with a new Article F stipulating that 'the Union is founded on the principles of liberty, democracy, respect for human rights and fundamental freedoms and the rule of law, principles which are common to the member states'. This treaty was also a move towards constitutionalisation as Article F enumerates the values common to all EU member states and Article F.1 details the action that EU institutions can take when one of the member states fails to uphold the values referred to in Article F (now Article 2) (see Box 18.1).

In the 2000s, the process of drafting a Constitution for Europe led to long debates on the EU's common principles and referred to them in terms of values. Despite the rejection of the Constitutional Treaty by referendums in the Netherlands and in France, the signatories of the Lisbon Treaty restated their commitment to 'the principles of liberty, democracy and respect for human rights and fundamental freedoms and of the rule of law' and reiterated in Article 2 the values enshrined in the Amsterdam Treaty.

BOX 18.1 Key actors

Which institution(s) can trigger Article 7?	One-third of the member states The EP The European Commission
Which institution(s) may determine that there is a clear risk of a serious breach of the values referred to in Article 2?	The Council acting by a *majority of four-fifths of its members* The EP gives its consent
Which institution(s) may determine the existence of a serious and persistent breach by a member state of the values referred to in Article 2?	The European Council acting by *unanimity* on a proposal by one-third of the member states or by the Commission and after obtaining the consent of the EP
Which institution(s) may decide to suspend certain rights deriving from the application of the treaties to the member state in question?	The Council acting by a *qualified majority*, may decide to suspend certain of the rights, including the voting rights of the representative of the government of that member state in the Council
Which institution(s) may decide to modify or revoke these measures?	The Council acting by a qualified majority

18.3   Main Institutional Issues at Stake

The progressive constitutionalisation of values was meant to strengthen the EU's identity and normative power, that is its ability to define what is normal in its relationship with the wider world (Manners, 2002: 252). However, while the constitutionalisation of values received considerable support among the signatories of the treaties, it appears that within EU member states said consensus over values was more a myth than a reality. An illustration of this is the case of Austria in the early 2000s.

Four years after Austria's accession to the EU, in 1999, the Freedom Party of Austria (FPÖ), an openly racist and xenophobic party, won 26.9 per cent of the vote in the elections held on 3 October. It was the first time in the history of the integration process that several European leaders made alarming declarations on the political situation in another EU state (Coman, 2018: 148). The French President Jacques Chirac, the Spanish Prime Minister José-Maria Aznar and the Belgian Foreign Secretary Louis Michel were eager to take action at the EU level owing to the growth of national right-wing parties in their countries (Cramér and Wrange, 2000: 30; Merlingen et al., 2001). In contrast, the British Foreign Secretary Robin Cook favoured a 'wait-and-see approach' (Coman, 2018: 148). For their part, the governments of Sweden and Denmark expressed reservations on the idea of adopting sanctions at the EU level. In Germany, the main political parties were divided (Merlingen et al., 2001: 66).

The accession to power of the FPÖ raised a wide range of questions about the ability of the EU to uphold the values recently enshrined in the treaties. Though Article 7 clearly detailed the roles and attributions of EU institutions in suspending the rights of a member state that fails to observe the EU's common values (see Box 18.1), the following issues remained unclear:

- What does 'a clear risk of a serious breach by a member state' mean?
- Who has the authority to assess the existence of a serious breach?
- How should 'the existence of a serious and persistent breach by a member state of the values' be determined?
- When can Article 7 be triggered?

In other words, while the legitimacy of Article 7 was strong in terms of input (who can take decisions) and output (sanctions or not), the stages in between remained in a grey zone (Coman, 2018).

Under the Portuguese presidency of the Council, the fourteen EU member states issued a declaration stating that if the Austrian government was formed with the FPÖ, 'they would freeze bilateral relations, that is no longer conduct state visits or receive Austrian diplomats at the ministerial level'. At the end of January 2000, the Portuguese prime minister informed the president and the chancellor of

Austria that 'there would be no business as usual' in the bilateral relations with the Austrian government and that:

1. Governments of the fourteen member states would not promote or accept any bilateral official visit at political level with an Austrian government integrating the FPÖ.
2. There would be no support in favour of Austrian candidates seeking positions in international organisations.
3. Austrian Ambassadors in EU capitals would only be received at a technical level.

The fourteen did not act under the procedure of Article 7 to adopt diplomatic sanctions against Austria. These measures emerged from their consensus rather than from any official EU action. The Commission, under the leadership of Romano Prodi, disapproved of coordinating decisions outside the treaties (Merlingen et al., 2001). The Commission's exclusion from the debates by member states weakened its role and reduced its visibility, although the treaties granted it powers of its own as a *gardienne des traités* (Coman, 2018: 150). Romano Prodi declared that the sanctions imposed on Austria were 'an error of judgment and should be swiftly lifted'. The president of the Commission contented that it was 'the duty of a strong supranational institution not to isolate one of its members' because 'when one of its members is in difficulty, the whole Union is in difficulty' (Merlingen et al., 2001: 66). In contrast, after a two-day debate in Strasbourg, MEPs demanded that EU member states withdraw Austria's voting rights if the coalition with the FPÖ was created.

The Austrian government contended that the EU's action itself violated 'fundamental legal principles and the spirit of the European Treaties', including 'the recognition of a democratic government committed to the rule of law' (Duxbury, 2000: 3). Jörg Haider, the FPÖ leader, lamented that it was 'unacceptable for other countries to determine what is happening in Austria' (see also Leconte, 2005). In a joint declaration with Wolfgang Schussel, he expressed Austria's attachment to the 'spiritual and moral values which are the common heritage of the peoples of Europe and the true source of individual freedom, political liberty and the rule of law, principles which form the basis of all genuine democracy' (Coman, 2018).

These debates revealed new lines of division between old and new member states, between Western Europe and the accession countries from Central and Eastern Europe. When sanctions against Austria were adopted, the Slovenian Prime Minister Jan Drnovsek argued that the EU action was 'exaggerated'. In Prague, the former Czech prime minister, Vaclav Klaus, said that 'Brussels' arrogance was far more dangerous than Haider's rhetoric' (Höbelt, 2003: 194). Only Bulgaria stood apart, with Nadezhda Mihailova saying the government 'would not support an Austrian government which would close Europe's door and would stand against EU eastward enlargement' (Coman, 2018: 150).

Thus, although political actors deplored the violation of the EU's common values in Austria, Article 7 was silent on how to determine the existence of a clear risk of a serious breach of the values referred to in Article 2. To sum up, the debates over the Austrian situation revealed the limitations of the existing legal framework to suspend the rights of member states that are found to be in 'serious and persistent breach' of these common values (Berit Freeman, 2002: 110; Coman, 2018: 152).

18.4   Main Policy Developments

The saga around democracy and common values did not end with the Austrian case. While EU institutions were discussing how to deal with Austria, the European Council in Copenhagen set the conditions for the enlargement towards the former communist countries. The Commission – mandated to conduct the accession process – was seeking to support the transition to democracy of the former communist countries by developing tools and instruments to strengthen their democratic institutions and the rule of law.

18.4.1   The Rule of Law as a Sine Qua Non Condition for Accession

Back in the 1990s, many argued that the conditions set by the European Council in Copenhagen were vague and did not define what a 'stable democracy' was (Grabbe, 2002: 253; Sadurski 2010). For instance, the rule of law (see Box 18.2) was a sine qua non condition for accession. However, its implementation remained an open question. The Commission played an important role in explaining why the rule of law was important for the EU's economic integration without promoting. A specific model of judicial organisation. Through its regular reports on the progress made by candidate countries, the Commission recommended consolidating the independence of the judiciary and reducing political interference in any field related to the appointment or promotion of magistrates, as well as in any disciplinary proceedings. After accession, national judges would become judges of EU law. The Commission therefore pointed out that the judiciary should be independent and well-staffed, and that judges must be well trained, well paid, efficient, respected and accessible to people (Coman, 2009).

Each candidate country sought to reform its judicial institutions to ensure their independence vis-à-vis political power (Coman, 2009). In 2004, the Commission was satisfied with the progress in ten candidate countries and postponed the accession of Romania and Bulgaria to 2007 because of their lack of progress in the fight against corruption and in the independence of the juiciary.

BOX 18.2 Key concepts

The **_rule of law_** is about:
(1) Legality, including a transparent, accountable and democratic process for enacting laws.
(2) Legal certainty.
(3) Prohibition of arbitrariness.
(4) Access to justice before independent and impartial courts, including judicial review of administrative acts.
(5) Respect for human rights.
(6) Non-discrimination and equality before the law.

Source: Venice Commission – Rule of Law – Report – CDL – AD (2011)003 rev.

18.4.2 New Challenges to Democracy and the Rule of Law

After their accession, the governments of the new member states modified the provisions on the independence of the judiciary that had been adopted to meet the accession criteria.

In 2005, the Law and Justice (PiS) Government in Poland had planned to change the attribution of the Constitutional Tribunal. In 2010, Hungary made the headlines with Fidesz's attempts to adopt a new Constitution and thus cement controversial institutional, cultural, religious, moral and socio-economic policies into law. Critics saw these measures as a dangerous deviation from democratic norms and EU treaties. The Hungarian decisions imposing governmental control over institutions whose independence is protected by the EU treaties have been considered a threat to democracy. Beside the revision of the Constitution, the Fidesz government also retired 274 judges. The mandate of the former president of the Supreme Court, elected for six years in June 2009, was prematurely terminated at the end of 2011. Applying the general retirement age to judges was questionable in light of the core principles and rules pertaining to the independence and immovability of judges (Council of Europe, Opinion no.621/2011, p. 10). The retirement of a large number of judges could affect the operational capacity of the judicial institutions (Council of Europe, Opinion no.621/2011, p. 10). Also controversial was the nomination by the government of the president of the National Judicial Office for a nine-year term, considered to be excessively long by the Council of Europe.

In January 2012, the president of the European Commission, José Manuel Barroso, initiated legal action against Hungary. Members of the EP called for a triggering of Article 7. However, the EU's requirements regarding its values remain vague (Kochenov, 2008; Coman, 2009). Therefore, they did not provide sufficient basis for the legal action against Hungary (Blauberger and Kelemen, 2016: 5). Thus, when the Hungarian government decided to retire a large number of judges, the infringement procedure (see Box 18.3) of the Commission was based on a breach of the EU legislation on equal treatment and the Hungarian decision to lower the pension age, not on Article 2. The Commission won, and the Hungarian government complied with the ruling of the Court on the retirement age of judges (Batory, 2016). However, the case brought in front of the Court did not prevent Viktor Orbán from adopting new measures which threatened constitutional checks and balances (Batory, 2016), undermined the rule of law and weakened human rights protections (Halmai, 2018). Scholars have argued that infringement proceedings were ill-suited to such cases. Infringements seemed to be 'too narrow to address the structural problem which persistently non-compliant member states pose' (Halmai, 2018: 7).

BOX 18.3 Key concepts

Infringement procedure. Article 258 (TFEU) grants the European Commission the right to initiate infringement proceedings against member states that have failed to fulfil a treaty or secondary legislation obligation.

In this context, the Commission and representatives of some member states indicated that new tools and mechanisms were needed to enhance the capacity for action in upholding the EU's values prior to triggering Article 7. The EP and the Council have proposed different solutions.

The EP and a series of academics suggested creating a Copenhagen Commission, inspired by the Venice Commission of the Council of Europe, to ensure the continuity of the Copenhagen criteria in all member states (Muller, 2013) and to monitor, assess and enforce the rule of law.

In contrast, the Council, wary of this EU Commission's power, favoured 'an increased cooperation with the Council of Europe (European Council, May 2013; June 2013; the JHA Council, June 2013) and its bodies, including the Venice Commission.

18.4.3   New Tools

Against this backdrop, the European Commission set up two new tools: The first was the EU Justice Scoreboard (see Box 18.4) created in 2013. This information tool aims at assisting the EU and its member states to reach a more effective justice system by providing objective, reliable and comparable data on the quality, independence and efficiency of justice systems in all member states.

The second was designed by the Commission in 2014 and is the Rule of Law Framework (Figure 18.1), a complementary tool to infringement procedures and to Article 7. This framework seeks to address 'threats to the Rule of Law which are of

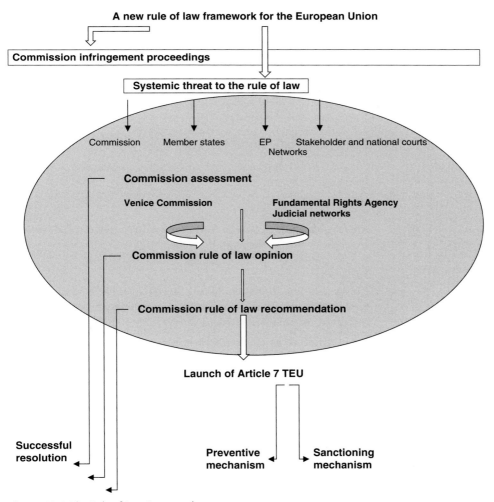

Figure 18.1 The Rule of Law Framework

a systemic nature' (COM 2014). Its purpose is a dialogue that helps the Commission find a solution with the member state in question in order to prevent a systemic threat to the rule of law that could develop into a 'clear risk of a serious breach' which would then potentially trigger the use of the 'Article 7 TEU Procedure'.

However, neither the EU Justice Scoreboard nor the Rule of Law Framework prevented changes in the organisation of the judiciary in some EU member states. Since 2015, the Polish executive led by the Party Law and Justice (PiS) has followed a similar path to the Hungarian government, reducing the independence of the Constitutional Tribunal and of the Judicial Council (see Table 18.2). The Commission initiated the Rule of Law Framework. Over twenty-five letters were exchanged with the Law and Justice members of the government. Since November 2015, the Commission has issued one rule of law opinion and four rule of law recommendations. The vice president of the European Commission, Frans Timmermans, stated that the Polish authorities did not provide reasons for optimism. 'The situation is getting worse', he declared at the end of the dialogue (*EUObserver*, 23 March 2017). 'More than one year of bilateral dialogue has so far not been sufficient to convince the Polish government to address the situation', he said (*EUObserver*, 23 March 2017). As a result, in December 2017, the Commission called for triggering Article 7.

Table 18.2 Chronology: legal changes in Poland and EU action (non exhaustive list)

Legislation adopted by the Polish government	The *law on the Supreme Court* approved by the Senate on 15 December 2017 The *law amending the law on the Ordinary Courts' Organization* in force since 12 August 2017 The *law amending the law on the National Council for the Judiciary* approved by the Senate on 15 December 2017 The *law amending the law on the National School of Judiciary and Public Prosecution* in force since 20 June 2017 The law allowing to subject ordinary court judges to disciplinary investigations, procedures and ultimately sanctions, on account of the content of their judicial decisions since December 2019.
January 2016 Rule of Law Framework	The EU launched an inquiry into whether Poland's government had breached the EU's democratic standards by taking greater control of the judiciary
2017 and 2019 Infringement proceedings	*July 2017*. The Commission launched an infringement procedure on the Polish Law on Ordinary Courts, on the grounds of its retirement provisions for male and female judges and their impact on the independence of the judiciary • This was contrary to Article 157 (TFEU) and Directive 2006/54 on gender equality in employment • The Commission referred this case to the Court of Justice on 20 December 2017

Table 18.2 (cont.)	
	September 2018. The Commission decided to refer Poland to the Court of Justice due to the violations of the principle of judicial independence created by the new Polish Law on the Supreme Court, and to ask the Court of Justice to order interim measures until it issued a judgement on the case *April 2019*. The Commission launched an infringement procedure on the grounds that the new disciplinary regime established by the Polish government undermines the judicial independence of Polish judges and does not ensure the necessary guarantees to protect judges from political control, as required by the Court of Justice of the EU.
2018 Article 7	The Commission adopted a *reasoned proposal in accordance with Article 7.1 TUE* for a Council decision on the determination of a clear risk of a serious breach of the rule of law by the Republic of Poland

The Commission did not activate the Rule of Law Framework in the case for Hungary. Many have argued that this was a political decision by the Juncker Commission, strongly influenced by members of the European People's Party, the political group to which the Fidesz is affiliated (Blauberger and Kelemen, 2016). In Hungary, the government continued to make decisions that have led the EP to adopt resolutions and reports expressing its belief that the situation in the country represents 'a clear risk of a serious breach of the values referred to in Article 2' and warrants the launch of the Article 7(1) (Resolution adopted on 17 May 2017). In 2018, the EP adopted a report drafted by MEP Judith Sargentini with 448 votes in favour, 197 against and 48 abstentions calling on the Council to determine the existence of a clear risk of a serious breach by Hungary of the values on which the EU is founded (2017/2131(INL)).

Poland and Hungary are not the only cases raising concerns at the EU level. In 2017, the Social Democratic government in Romania sought to change the legislation related to the organisation of the judiciary, the criminal code and the provisions concerning the fight against corruption. These actions disregarded the recommendations the European Commission had formulated in the CVM. This tool was created in 2007 to address the shortcomings in judicial reforms and the fight against corruption, and to ensure that Romania and Bulgaria would continue to improve their judiciaries after accession. On 3 October 2018, in the EP, Prime Minister Viorica Dăncilă questioned the CVM's raison d'être and the methodology of the Commission. It is a fact that the leverage of the tools that were set up prior to accession is decreasing.

18.5 Current Political and Academic Controversies

The changes in their legal systems introduced by the Hungarian, Polish and Romanian governments have raised a wide range of questions both in academic and political circles. These controversies can be summarised around the following points.

Liberal democracy vs. authoritarian politics. At a very general level, there is a debate around the electoral success of political parties who challenge the EU's liberal democratic foundations and put forward an alternative model of so-called 'illiberal democracy' (which is an oxymoron). Within academia, this has been analysed as the rise of authoritarian politics and autocratic legalism (Scheppele, 2018; Sadurski, 2018). Scholars have argued that from the 2010s onwards, in Central and Eastern Europe, political parties such as the Fidesz and PiS have undermined the rule of law, steering politics in 'a dangerous authoritarian direction' (Bugaric and Kuhelj, 2018: 21). This phenomenon is not limited to the new democracies that emerged after the collapse of communism. In Austria, the FPÖ presents itself as an alternative to the mainstream political parties, which are criticised for their inability to deal with complex economic and global problems such as immigration (Bugaric and Kuhelj, 2018: 29). What scholars have shown is that leaders like Orbán or Kaczynski seek to alter the nature of their political regime, reducing political pluralism and the independence of judicial institutions. In other words, they introduce reforms that remove the checks on executive power by dismantling constitutional constraints (Scheppele, 2018). These are not isolated examples of democratic regression. They reveal a deep tension between democracy and constitutionalism in Europe. Said tensions occur when elected politicians seek to 'give what the people want' by overriding constitutional principles and by putting liberalism on the line (Scheppele, 2018).

A multicultural Europe vs. a Christian Europe? The rule of law is not the only value enshrined in the EU treaties that has been challenged by the governments of Poland and Hungary, as well as the Czech Republic, Slovakia and Romania. These countries' refusal to welcome Muslim refugees (see Chapter 12) is a case in point. In Hungary and Poland, the Fidesz and PiS portray multiculturalism as a threat to their values. They promote conservative political agendas founded on 'moral values' as a reaction to the decadence of Western Europe. Moreover, they reject not only refugee protection but also Roma and LGBT rights (Bugaric and Kuhelj, 2018: 26), adopting measures which are incompatible with EU law. The Hungarian and Polish governments are seeking a profound political and social transformation which is in stark contradiction with EU law and principles.

A polity based on values or an intergovernmental cooperation between member states? Supranational sovereignty vs. parliamentary sovereignty. These countries' governments oppose national sovereignty and supranational sovereignty, criticising any Commission attempt to uphold the values enshrined in Article 2. The legitimacy of the Commission is called into question as well as that of the EP. In 2016, Jaroslaw Kaczynski proposed reducing the powers of the Commission after Brexit (*Politico*, 15 March 2017). When the EP in 2017 decided by 438 votes to 152 with 71 abstentions to prepare a formal request that the Council activate the preventive mechanism provided for in Article 7.1, the Polish prime minister declared that the discussions in the EP were 'scandalous'.

The existing tools upholding the rule of law have significant shortcomings and therefore the EU is facing problems of compliance. Ultimately, part of the academic and political debates focuses on the tools recently adopted at the EU level to prevent systemic threats to the rule of law and to combat democratic backsliding. Despite the activation of the Rule of Law Framework in the case of Poland in January 2016, scholars have concluded that the EU responses to the measures taken by the Hungarian and the Polish governments have been 'ineffective' (Sedelmeier, 2016; Kochenov and Pech, 2016; Pech and Scheppele, 2018; Kochenov and Bard, 2018; Van Bogdandy and Ioannidis, 2014). They argue that preventing the consolidation of an autocratic regime within the EU requires a quick reaction. The Rule of Law Framework is, however, conceived to encourage dialogue. It is designed for 'normal times' and therefore it gives domestic leaders sufficient time to pursue their plans. Scholars have maintained that the Commission should use the instruments at its disposal, in particular infringement proceedings, arguing also that judicial safeguards alone will not be sufficient 'to stop democratic backsliding by a determined national government: if the Union is to rein in such attacks on its core values, heads of government and other EU leaders will have to intervene politically as well' (Blauberger and Kelemen, 2016: 2). Ultimately, academics have pointed out that the EU is confronted with a problem of compliance, as member states 'engage in symbolic/and or creative compliance, designed to create the appearance of norm-conforming behaviour without giving up their original objectives' (Batory, 2016: 685). Such instances of non-compliance put the credibility of the EU at risk.

18.6 Analysis of a Paradigmatic Case Study: Towards a New Rule of Law Conditionality?

Against this backdrop, when the Commission presented a broad overview of its budget proposal for the post-Brexit era (2021-7) on 2 May 2018, it included a proposal for a rule of law conditionality for EU funding. This came about as a consequence of the fruitless years-long political dialogue that it had been engaged in with the Polish government. It is designed to complement the series of tools developed as preliminary or complementary stages prior to triggering Article 7. This proposed rule of law conditionality stipulates that payments and EU-funded programmes would be suspended when breaches to the rule of law are observed in member states. If adopted, the Commission would be allowed 'to suspend, reduce and restrict access to EU funding in a manner proportionate to the nature, gravity and scope of the rule of law deficiencies' (Halmai, 2018: 14).

Conditionality is not a new principle of governance. Several international organisations have used it to foster compliance, to encourage reforms, and to implement policies. It is often associated with the idea of sanctions or rewards for the implementation of specific measures.

The Commission wishes to integrate within the 2021–7 Multiannual Financial Framework rules that would be applied in cases of generalised breaches in the rule of law in member states (COM(2018) 324 final 2018/0136 (COD)). The rule of law would be therefore linked to EU spending policies (see Chapter 6).

In 2018, the Commission's proposal enjoyed significant political support from the governments of Germany, Italy, France and the Netherlands. Unsurprisingly, the proposal was disapproved by the parties in power in the Czech Republic, Hungary, Poland and Romania.

The idea of new forms of conditionality has given rise to contrasting views in both the academic and political fields. How can a misuse of the EU budget where the rule of law is under strain be avoided? How can member states be convinced to contribute more to the EU budget when the number of irregularities in the use of EU money increases? How can mutual trust and financial solidarity be ensured when corruption relates to EU funds and when domestic institutions are reluctant or unable to investigate corruption cases or to cooperate with the European Anti-Fraud Office? Stories about corruption and the misuse of EU funds undermine solidarity among member states and pushes the EU to govern by conditionality.

Arguments in favour of conditionality abounded. Several think tanks published detailed reports weighting the pros and cons and concluded that, at least from a political standpoint, putting funds under political conditionality was justifiable. EU funds are important leverage for the Commission and effective spending cannot be guaranteed without the rule of law. The expected effect of this new form of conditionality is to provide incentives to the governments in question to enter into a constructive dialogue with the Commission and to seriously take into account its recommendations. The measure, it has been argued, is not meant to target specific member states, but to prevent the erosion of democratic values in any EU member state. A member state that does not meet the requirements related to the respect of the rule of law 'does not fulfil the legal conditions of the funds and consequently cannot get them' (Halmai, 2018: 15).

On the one other hand, scholars and experts alike argued that such conditionality would be counterproductive for three reasons. Sanctions have the hypothetical potential of increasing nationalist and anti-EU sentiments, with the risk of increased polarisation between east and west. They would also be a penalty for citizens in poorer regions, not for the governments undermining the checks and balances of their political regimes. Last but not least, sanctions would damage the process of economic convergence as well (Heinemann, 2018: 300). In this context, some scholars have argued that social pressure is also a way to exert influence without material leverage. Sedelmeier contends that the Romanian case demonstrates the possibility for the EU to induce member states' governments to reverse breaches of liberal democracy without threatening material sanctions (2016: 8). Recent events, however, show that social pressure alone – meaning massive protests in Bucharest against the attempts of the government to change legislation related to the fight against corruption – is not sufficient (Coman, 2018), as governments can act against the pressure of the street and even repress said protests with violence. Ultimately, to sort out the current impasses it has been argued that a reform of the EU as such is needed so that 'the EU law embraces the rule of law as an institutional ideal'. 'The result would be an emergence of a supranational constitutional system at the EU level [...] which would play a significantly more productive role in solving the backsliding challenges' (Kochenov and Bard, 2018: 26).

How to deal with violations of the rule of law in member states depends on the political identity of the Union, which requires political, legal and social support.

GROUP DISCUSSION

- What are the reasons for the increased politicisation of values in the EU?
- Does the EU need new tools to uphold its values? Is the rule of law conditionality a suitable tool? In your opinion, what are the weaknesses of the tools presented in this chapter? Provide arguments for your position.

TOPICS FOR INDIVIDUAL RESEARCH

- Is supranational sovereignty in tension with national sovereignty when democracy is challenged by authoritarian politics at the domestic level?
- Analyse the politicisation of the rule of law in a case study (EU member state) or in several contexts (in a comparative design). Examine the arguments of national governments seeking to legitimise the limitation of power of judicial institutions.

FURTHER READINGS

Blauberger, M. and Kelemen, D. R. (2016). 'Can Courts Rescue National Democracy? Judicial Safeguards Against Democratic Backsliding in the EU'. *Journal of European Public Policy*, 1–28, https://doi.org/10.1080/13501763.2016.1229357.

Kochenov, D. and Bard, P. (2018). 'Rule of Law Crisis in the New Member States of the EU: The Pitfalls of Overemphasising Enforcement', *RECONECT*, Working Paper No. 1.

Kochenov, D. and Pech, L. (2016). 'Better Late than Never? On the European Commission's Rule of Law Framework and its First Activation'. *Journal of Common Market Studies*, 54(5): 1062–74.

Leconte, C. (2005). 'The Fragility of the EU as a "Community of Values": Lessons from the Haider Affair'. *West European Politics*, 28(3): 620–49.

Von Bogdandy, A. and Ioannidis, M. (2014). 'Systemic Deficiency in the Rule of Law: What It Is, What Has Been Done, What Can Be Done'. *Common Market Law Review*, 51(1): 59–96.

REFERENCES

Batory, A. (2016). 'Defying the Commission: Creative Compliance and Respect for the Rule of Law in the EU'. *Public Administration*, 94(3): 685–99.

Bellamy, R. and Castiglione, D. (2000). 'The Uses of Democracy: Reflections on the European Democratic Deficit'. In E. O. Eriksen and J. E. Fossum (eds), *Democracy in the EU: Integration through Deliberation?* London and New York: Routledge.

Berit Freeman, H. (2002). 'Austria: The 1999 Parliamentary Elections and the European Union Members' Sanctions'. *Boston College International and Comparative Law*, 25: 109–24.

Blauberger, M. and Kelemen, D. R. (2016). 'Can Courts Rescue National Democracy? Judicial Safeguards Against Democratic Backsliding in the EU'. *Journal of European Public Policy*, 24(3): 321–36.

Bugaric, B. and Kuhelj, A. (2018). 'Varieties of Populism in Europe: Is the Rule of Law in Danger?'. *Hague Journal on the Rule of Law*, 10: 21–33.

Coman, R. (2009). *Reformer la justice dans un pays post-communiste. Le cas de la Roumanie.* Bruxelles: Editions de l'Université.

Coman, R. (2018). 'Protecting the Rule of Law and the State of Democracy at the Supranational level: Political Dilemmas and Institutional Struggles in Strengthening EU's Input, Output and Throughput Legitimacy'. In L. Tomini and G. Sandri (eds), *Challenges of Democracy in the 21st Century*. London: Routledge.

Conway, M. and Depkat, V. (2010). 'Towards a European History of the Discourse of Democracy: Discussing Democracy in Western Europe, 1945–60.' In M. Conway and K. K. Patel (eds), *Europeanization in the Twentieth Century*. London: Palgrave Macmillan.

Cramér, P. and Wrange, P. (2000). 'The Haider Affairs, Law and European Integration'. *Europarättslig tidskrift*, 28.

Duxbury, A. (2000). 'Austria and the European Union: The Report of the Three Wise Men'. *Melbourne Journal of International Law*, 1(1): 1–6.

Fossum, J. E. (2000). 'Constitution-making in the European Union'. In E. O. Eriksen and J. E. Fossum (eds), *Democracy in the EU: Integration through Deliberation?* London and New York: Routledge.

Grabbe, H. (2002). 'European Union Conditionality and the Acquis Communautaire'. *International Political Science Review*, 23(3): 249–68.

Halmai, G. (2018). 'The Possibility and Desirability of Rule of Law Conditionality'. *Hague Journal on the Rule of Law*. https://doi.org/10.1007/s40803-018-0077-2.

Heinemann, F. (2018). 'Going for the Wallet? Rule-of-Law Conditionality in the Next EU Multiannual Financial Framework'. *Intereconomics*, 6: 297–301.

Höbelt, L. (2003). *Defiant Populist: Jörg Haider and the Politics of Austria*. West Lafayette, IN: Perdue University Press.

Kochenov, D. (2008). *EU Enlargement and the Failure of Conditionality: Preaccessionn Conditionality in the Fields of Democracy and the Rule of Law*. The Hague: Kluwer Law International.

Kochenov, D. and Bard, P. (2018). 'Rule of Law Crisis in the New Member States of the EU: The Pitfalls of Overemphasising Enforcement', *RECONNECT*, Working Paper No. 1.

Kochenov, D. and Pech, L. (2016) 'Better Late than Never? On the European Commission's Rule of Law Framework and its First Activation'. *Journal of Common Market Studies*, 54(5): 1062–74.

Lacroix, J. (2008). 'Théorie politique'. In C. Belot, P. Magnette and S. Saurugger (eds), *Science politique de l'UE*. Paris: Économica.

Leconte, C. (2005). 'The Fragility of the EU as a "Community of Values": Lessons from the Haider Affair'. *West European Politics*, 28(3): 620–49.

Magnette, P. (2000). *L'Europe, l'état et la démocratie*. Brussels: Editions Complexe.

Magnette, P. and Nicolaïdis, K. (2004). 'The European Convention: Bargaining in the Shadow of Rhetoric'. *West European Politics*, 27(3): 381–404.

Manners, I. (2002). 'Normative Power Europe: A Contradiction in Terms?'. *Journal of Common Market Studies*, 40(2): 235–58.

Merlingen, M. et al. (2001). 'The Right and the Righteous? European Norms, Domestic Politics and Sanctions Against Austria'. *Journal of Common Market Studies*, 39(1): 59–77.

Moravcsik, A. (2002). 'In Defence of the "Democratic Deficit": Reassessing the Legitimacy of the European Union'. *Journal of Common Market Studies*, 40(4): 603–34.

Müller, J.-W. (2013). 'Safeguarding Democracy Inside the EU: Brussels and the Future of Liberal Order'. Paper Series 2012–2013, No 3, Transatlantic Academy.

Sadurski, W. (2010). 'Adding a Bite to a Bark? A Story of Article 7, the EU Enlargement, and Jörg Haider'. *Sydney Law School, Legal Studies Research Paper*, 10(1): 1–37.

Sadurski, W. (2018). 'How Democracy Dies (In Poland): A Case Study of Anti-constitutional Populist Backsliding in Poland'. *Sydney Law School Research Paper* no. 18/1.

Saurugger, S. (2016). 'Politicisation and Integration Through Law: Whither Integration Theory?'. *West European Politics*, 39(5): 933–52.

Saurugger, S. and Terpan, F. (2017). *The Court of Justice of the European Union and the Politics of Law*. London, Palgrave.

Scheppele, K. L. (2018). 'Autocratic Legalism'. *The University of Chicago Law Review*, 85(2): 545–84.

Schmidt, V. A. (2006). *Democracy in Europe*: *The EU and National Polities*. Oxford and New York: Oxford University Press.

Sedelmeier, U. (2016). 'Political Safeguard against Democratic Backsliding in the EU: The Limits of Material Sanctions and the Scope of Social Pressure'. *Journal of European Public Policy*, 24(3): 337–51.

Thomas, D. C. (2006). 'Constitutionalization through Enlargement: The Contested Origins of the EU's Democratic Identity'. *Journal of European Public Policy*, 13(8): 1190–210.

Van Bogdandy, A. and Ioannidis, M. (2014). 'Systemic Deficiency in the Rule of Law: What it is, What Has Been Done, What Can Be Done'. *Common Market Law Review*, 51: 59–96.

Vauchez, A. (2016). *Democratizing Europe*. New York: Palgrave.

Weiler, J. H. H. (2012). 'In the Face of Crisis: Input Legitimacy, Output Legitimacy and the Political Messianism of European Integration'. *Journal of European Integration*, 34(7): 825–41.

Whitman, R. G. (ed.) (2011). *Normative Power Europe*: *Empirical and Theoretical Perspectives*. New York: Palgrave Macmillan.

19 Democracy and Disintegration: Does the State of Democracy in the EU Put the Integrity of the Union at Risk?

JOSEPH LACEY AND KALYPSO NICOLAÏDIS

19.1 Introduction

'Take back control': in the lead up to a June 2016 plebiscite on whether to remain in or leave the EU, this was the rallying cry that framed the predominant narrative on the pro-Brexit side. Whatever might explain the determinants of individual voter choice in the eventual decision of the British electorate to leave by a majority of 52 per cent to 48 per cent, public debate during the campaign crystallised around the proposition that the UK should reclaim its sovereignty. The content of this cry for sovereignty was not empty. It was understood to mean the return of powers to the UK government for unilateral decision-making – powers that had been previously ceded to the EU, even though UK representatives are integral to EU decision-making processes. While the supposed material advantages of greater sovereignty outside the EU were emphasised, including the ability for the UK to adopt a more sustainable migration regime and to strike its own trade deals, a more principled case for national self-government undergirded the case to leave the EU. Reviewing the final pre-plebiscite statements of prominent publications and political figures who advocated a vote to leave the EU is telling in this regard. The editorial of a weekly conservative magazine, *The Spectator*, referred to 'the EU's fundamental lack of democracy', an EP that 'represents many nations, but with no democratic legitimacy' and 'the unelected President of the European Commission' for whom 'even the notion of democratic consent' seems a distant concern. The article concludes: 'To pass up the chance to stop our laws being overridden by Luxembourg and our democracy eroded by Brussels would be a derogation of duty ... democracy matters. Let's vote to defend it' (*The Spectator*, 2016). Boris Johnson, a prominent Conservative politician who was a leading voice in the leave campaign, wrote in his broadsheet op-ed: 'If Britain votes to Remain in the EU, then we continue to be subject to an increasingly anti-democratic system'; 'we believe in democracy ... and we are mad to throw it away' (Johnson, 2016).

This account should alert us to two things about the EU. First, the democratic credentials of the EU have the capacity to become politically salient. Second, there may be a connection between the democratic credentials of the EU and the risk of disintegration, whether that disintegration takes the form of returning competences to the member states or the withdrawal of member states altogether. In this chapter, we seek to understand the extent to which the issue of democratic legitimacy has become politically salient within the EU, and whether or not this higher salience puts the 'integrity' of the EU in a more vulnerable position.

To complete this task, we should first be clear on what we mean by the ideas of integrity and legitimacy. The integrity of a political system may be defined as *the ability to persist through time*, while the legitimacy of a political system may be defined as *the rightful claim to do so*. In other words, integrity is a way to characterise the EU itself, while legitimacy relates to a set of standards (however they may be defined) that the EU must embody and uphold if it is to have a justifiable claim to the support of its citizens. Four main types of integrity may be distinguished (Lacey, 2017a), each of which has its own relationship to the idea of legitimacy (see Box 19.1).

First, *territorial integrity* refers to the ability of a political system to maintain (or expand) an established geographic scope. Territorial legitimacy is the claim that the political system should be supported because it provides a framework for cooperation across distinct regions that in some way belong together (Lacey and Bauböck, 2017).

Second, *functional integrity* relates to the capacity of the political system to carry out the tasks with which it is charged. When a political system has a high degree of functional integrity, it may be expected to generate what is known as output legitimacy. This kind of legitimacy is defined by the claim that the political system should be supported because of its capacity to deliver upon good policies for its members (Crespy, 2016). Here 'good' policies may be defined in terms of a range of values, such as effectiveness or efficiency, but also in terms of more demanding values like justice (Kochenov et al., 2015).

Third, *procedural integrity* pertains to the principles upon which the political system is based, as well as its ability to live up to these standards in practice. What these principles are or should be is of course widely contested, but it is fair to say that they rest first and foremost on the norms attached to democratic legitimacy (Piattoni, 2015). Accordingly, scholars tend to distinguish between two kinds of legitimacy: input legitimacy, reflecting whether those who are affected by decisions believe that they are given an appropriate role in shaping those decisions; and throughput legitimacy, when political institutions are perceived to be accountable and transparent in their decision-making and implementation processes (Schmidt, 2013).

A final and overarching type of integrity is *existential integrity* or the extent to which citizens identify with and generally support the existence and overall trajectory of the political system. In other words, it is a product of what is sometimes referred to as social legitimacy, which itself combines the other three in complex and variable ways. The less citizens approve of the territorial scope, policy outputs and procedural values of their political system, the less likely they are to view its authority as legitimate tout court. Such low levels of existential integrity will inevitably translate into calls for radical reform of the political system, dissent from its authority or even withdrawal from the political system where possible.

In this chapter, we explore the relationship between integrity and legitimacy in the following steps. First, we present a historical overview of the quest for legitimacy in the EU. Second, we outline some of the main normative approaches to understanding how the EU ought to develop in order to become a more legitimate political system. Third, we identify Article 50 of the TEU (one of the EU's core constitutional documents), which provides the outline of procedures for a state to leave the EU, as among the most significant constitutional developments in recent years when it comes to the question of EU legitimacy. In the penultimate section, we reflect on how the Brexit process has contributed to a resurgence of political and academic controversies over fundamental questions on the future of Europe. Finally, we conclude with some reflections on what the example of Brexit may have to teach us about the relationship between political legitimacy and integrity in the EU.

BOX 19.1 Key concepts

Existential integrity. The extent to which citizens identify with and generally support the existence and overall trajectory of the political system.
Functional integrity. The capacity of the political system to carry out the tasks with which it is charged.
Procedural integrity. The principles upon which the political system is based and its ability to live up to these principles in practice.
Territorial integrity. The ability of a political system to maintain (or expand) an established geographic scope.

19.2   Historical Overview: The Quest for EU Legitimacy

As early as 1979, British political scientist David Marquand was among the first to root the idea that the then European Community suffered from what he referred to as a 'democratic deficit'. Resolving this deficit, he believed, was essential to the progress and sustainability of European integration. He summed up the situation as follows:

> the Community is caught at an *impasse*. If it does not move forward, it is almost certain to slide back. But it cannot move forward – should not, indeed, be allowed to move forward – so long as the motive force has to come from an unrepresentative technocracy with no popular mandate or popular base, and so long as there is no machinery to make the Community's decision-makers accountable at Community level to the elected representatives of the people. (Marquand, 1979: 65–6)

Marquand was critical of how European integration had been progressing through the Monnet method – later referred to by Giandomenico Majone (2005) as 'integration by stealth' – which prescribed that integration should move incrementally and involve as little politicisation as possible (see Chapter 1). Should European integration become a political issue – subject to the electoral whims of ever-changing party governments among the member states – proponents of the Monnet method believed that the integration project would become vulnerable to obstacles caused by the short-term thinking often attributed to electoral politics. Instead, a relatively stable consensus was reached among successive governments and European officials that integration should be pursued on a purely technical or rationalistic basis, where sovereignty would be gradually pooled at the European level.

Let us take a step back to understand how the problem evolved. Like any political system, ever since its inception as the EC in the 1940s and 1950s, the European project has had two primary sources of legitimacy available to shore up its existential integrity: its ability to achieve the purposes with which it is tasked (output legitimacy) and its ability to embody the procedural standards held by member states and their citizens (input and throughput legitimacy).

Initially, the major motivation behind the integration project was to secure peace in Europe following World War II by creating mutual dependency among European nations and, crucially, to do so while safeguarding smaller states from the hegemony of larger one. And to the extent that the EC functionally achieved the goal of peace, while procedurally satisfying the ideal of equality between states, it was widely viewed positively among the citizens of its member states.

Meanwhile, as the EU's novel institutional framework developed in step with its increasing competences, it adopted a similarly unique combination of normative principles to guide its operation: a combination of principles suited to an organisation that was neither a state nor an international organisation, and therefore representing a normative political order with which ordinary citizens were unfamiliar. Liesbet Hooghe and Gary Marks (2009) have famously characterised the first decades of the integration project as involving a 'permissive consensus' among the citizens of Europe. In other words, for much of integration history, citizens were largely content to give their representatives free rein in integration decisions, large and small. This relaxed attitude may be at least partly attributed to the lack of politicisation by political parties on the national stage, but also by widespread impressions that European integration was a positive, or at least benign, development that didn't impact on the most salient issues that tend to define national political debate (e.g. tax, social welfare, healthcare, etc.). So long as the EU was achieving the purposes for which it was assigned, it could free ride on the more or less free pass given to it on the basis of its functional legitimacy. The obvious problem with such fair weather schemes is that when endogenous or exogenous shocks hit – and they always will – (major) policy failures are inevitable. In such times, functional legitimacy runs thin. Unless a political system can draw on its procedural legitimacy to maintain the support of citizens, the sustainability of the system comes into doubt (Eriksen and Fossum, 2004; Føllesdal, 2004).

A key source of procedural legitimacy is that the process for making decisions is fair, and is seen to be fair, by those who have a stake in the political system. In modern times, democratic procedures are widely viewed as the only kind of procedures that can meet these standards. There has been much debate over the extent to which the EU is a democratic political system. And, this debate has evolved as the EU has attempted to incrementally address its purported democratic deficit. This has included the transformation of the EP from an assembly of nominated national parliamentarians into a directly elected institution in 1979 and the subsequent increase in the EP's powers so that it is now a co-legislator with the Council, with a range of other important powers, such as the ability to accept or reject the proposed Commission president and individual commissioners.

The democratisation of the EU, however, has not taken place simply through the EP. From the late 1990s onwards, the debate about the adequacy of Europe's democratic credentials intensified as major integration decisions had been taken in the previous decade, most notably by way of the SEA in 1986 and the Maastricht Treaty in 1992, both of which involved the integration of core state powers under the EU (Genschel and Jachtenfuchs, 2015). Any efforts to democratise the Union were criticised as inadequate on a variety of grounds, with primary targets being the accountability of the Commission to citizens; the disempowerment of citizens and national parliaments vis-à-vis governments, given the latter's seat at the table in European institutions; and the lack of opportunities for meaningful citizen engagement. In response, the Lisbon Treaty of 2009 introduced a litany of reforms. These included (1) making Council meetings public and thereby decision-making by national governments at the EU level more transparent to citizens and national parliaments alike; (2) introducing the Early Warning Mechanism for national parliaments, which gave them the collective power to object to a legislative proposal of the Commission on the basis that it violated the principle of subsidiarity; and (3) introducing the European Citizens' Initiative, which gives one million citizens from at least seven countries the right to petition the Commission with a view to making a legislative proposal. Despite initial optimism about these reforms, none has quite managed fulfil the hopes of their promoters in the last decade, in large part due to the significant transaction costs involved in tracking Council meetings and triggering the Early Warning Mechanism or the European Citizens' Initiative.

On one view, the EU is already sufficiently democratic since all decisions must pass through the hands of directly elected representatives (whether heads of state and government in the European Council or government ministers in the Council, and very often the EP) (Moravcsik, 2008). However, there remains a litany of critics who believe that the EU's democratic credentials are not yet commensurate with the power that it wields. One type of critique focuses on the supranational level and another on the national level. In the first instance, the Commission remains a central target. As the only institution with the capacity to initiate legislation, and thereby substantially control the legislative agenda of the Union, it has been argued that the appointment of the Commission must be tied to the outcome of European elections.

Other critics insist upon the need to combat the second-order nature of European elections, by incentivising the creation of stronger pan-European political parties. In the ideal scenario, these parties would coordinate transnational electoral campaigns that focus on European issues, in contrast to the current norm where national parties run European elections on idiosyncratic national issues (Bardi et al., 2010). Meanwhile, a further set of critics advocate the need for referendums as a means to shore up the participation deficit in the EU. This includes referendums on treaty ratification within each nation state (Cheneval, 2007) and European-wide referendums that may be called by citizens either to propose legislation (Papadopoulos, 2006) or to block legislation that has already passed through the European institutions (Lacey, 2017b).

Those who focus their critique on the national level remain primarily concerned about the limited role of national parliaments in (1) holding governments to account for their actions at EU level and (2) participating in the EU legislative process. On the first point, the deficit is not so much attributed to the EU, but to the inadequate approach that many national parliaments have taken to monitoring and engaging with the government's European agenda (Piris, 2012). On the second point, and in addition to the negative power granted by the Early Warning Mechanism mentioned above, some critics maintain that national parliaments require formal empowerment by the EU to impact the legislative process. One such proposal would be to allow a minimum number of national parliaments, acting in concert, to initiate legislation in their own right (Bellamy and Kröger, 2014).

As the debate concerning Europe's democratic credentials has intensified over the years, and as member states and European institutions have attempted to respond to criticism, two positions have crystallised about the potential impacts of democratising the EU. On the one hand, those who advocate for its greater democratisation believe that the increased politicisation that this would bring will hold out positive long-term prospects for the integrity of the Union. According to this view, when citizens and their representatives feel that they are tangibly involved in shaping the direction of their political community, this will confer a greater sense of legitimacy upon and corresponding support for that community. Crucially, this involves accepting the turbulence and spates of sclerosis that can come from contestatory forces. As Peter Mair (2007) famously explained, political systems that do not allow for adequate means of opposition to policy concerning the future development of their community will eventually find that opposition against the political system itself will gain momentum. An EU that offers the conditions for greater politicisation through competitive democratic processes is expected to provide a framework within which competing visions can be publicly and visibly pursued in a way that is fair, and perceived to be fair by all. In essence, by bringing its institutional structure into greater line with democratic norms familiar to and valued by citizens, democratisation is expected to deepen the EU's procedural integrity in a way that will also strengthen its existential integrity.

On the other hand, there are those who echo the presuppositions of the Monnet method, insisting that politicisation could put European integration at serious risk. Stefano Bartolini (2006) expresses this view with unique insight. Unlike the standard kind of democratic contestation we tend to associate with EU member states, where the territorial boundaries and constitutional basis of the states are largely taken as given, Bartolini maintains that the EU has no such territorial or constitutional settlement. For this reason, he believes that the politicisation of policy through greater democratisation will quickly run into questioning the very bases of the EU. In tension with Mair's position, where avenues of contestation should prevent deeper forms of opposition, Bartolini expects that democratisation would merely serve as a platform to amplify the voice of those who would seek to undermine the EU or radically alter its nature and purpose. This position dovetails nicely with those who argue that the EU is already sufficiently democratic, such that further politicisation would add no value.

Since the turn of the century, the EU has in fact become increasingly politicised. Institutional developments to democratise the EU, such as those mentioned above, would appear to have weakly contributed to this trend. Two other causes stand out as far more influential in this politicisation trend. One is the greatly expanded competences of the EU, and its increased ability to deliver on its policies, at least since the process of treaty reform beginning with the SEA. According to Hooghe and Marks (2009), the gradual realisation of the power and significance of the EU among the population ended the period of permissive consensus and heralded a period of 'constraining dissensus', where citizens are no longer willing to give their representatives free rein in deciding upon the future of the Union. The major event supporting this characterisation was the rejection of the Constitutional Treaty in 2005 by France and the Netherlands by popular vote, with similar rejections expected in countries where popular votes were also lined up before the treaty was abandoned in light of the French and Dutch results. These two events in turn reflected a broader and increasingly identity-based hostility towards European integration (Coman and Lacroix, 2007).

The second major cause of politicisation has been the euro crisis beginning in 2009, and the migrant crisis peaking in 2015 (see Box 19.2). Arguably, these events have contributed to setting in motion a process that has moved things beyond a constraining consensus to the point where political conflict has been restructured along a 'transnational cleavage' (as opposed to just or primarily a left–right cleavage) (Hooghe and Marks, 2018). This transnational cleavage may be characterised as a tension between Euroscepticism, demanding a reassertion of the nation state on the international stage, and Europeanism, insisting upon the importance of a strong EU for the prosperity of member states. The policy failures associated with the aforementioned crises have made the EU a ripe target for the emergence of right-wing nationalist parties who identify the EU as a threat to both (economic) sovereignty and national identity (Lacey, 2018), while some left-wing parties have also denounced the hollowing out of national democracy (Crum, 2013). As a result, political parties are now forced to shape their own identity, at least partly, in terms of their stance on major issues of European integration. As we shall see in discussing the case of Brexit below, the potential impacts that the continued democratising of the EU would have on its integrity remain unclear.

BOX 19.2 Key dates

1979. EP becomes directly elected assembly.
1986. SEA (significant integration treaty).
1992. Maastricht Treaty (significant integration treaty).
2005. Rejection of the European Constitutional Treaty.
2009. Lisbon Treaty (treaty involving significant democratic reforms).
2009. European debt crisis.
2015. Migrant crisis.

19.3   Main Institutional Issues at Stake: A Third Way?

Here is the good news for the integrity of the EU. What we referred to in the introduction as its *existential integrity* – citizens' identification with and support for its very existence or raison d'être – does not seem to be overly threatened. There is actually a decreasing proportion of what we may call existential Eurosceptics, who simply advocate leaving the EU as parties or want to vote for this as citizens. Moreover, we observe that broad majorities of EU citizens support greater cooperation across a wide array of issues, from stimulating investments and jobs to securing energy supply to protecting the environment or the equality of men and women. They see these as functions or missions that it makes sense to pursue through cooperation among states (Eurobarometer, 2018) But this then suggests two threats to EU legitimacy. Its *functional integrity*, or the perceptions that it has not demonstrated its actual capacity to carry out these tasks; and second and relatedly its *procedural integrity*, above all its democratic credentials in the ways it does so. In other words, publics seem to worry much less about *what* the EU is doing and more about *how* it is doing it. As a result, there may be less existential Eurosceptics, but policy and institutional Euroscepticism is on the rise (De Vries, 2018). Are there ways then of adapting, reforming or even transforming the EU to respond to these developments?

Generally speaking, there have been two primary approaches to answering this question (for a longer summary see Nicolaïdis, 2004, and Bellamy and Lacey, 2018). On the first approach, variously referred to as federalism or supranationalism, an EU demos or people must be gradually brought into existence to legitimate collective decisions. According to this somewhat mimetic view (reproducing the state at the EU level), the EU should tend to look more and more like a federal state such as Germany or the US. This means, for instance, more powers for the EP including that of nominating the Commission through the *Spitzenkandidat* procedure, more voting in the Council through majoritarian procedures, a greater weight for bigger member states, increased EU competences and an enhanced capacity for EU institutions to issue binding decisions. At the extreme, those adopting a supranationalist perspective may even regret the constitutionalisation of the right for a member state to withdraw from the Union since the Lisbon Treaty came into force in 2009.

On the second approach, generally referred to as sovereigntism, there are inherent limits to legitimate European integration, which the EU has already breached in some respects. According to this account, the 'we-feeling' or existential integrity characterising the national demos – supported by a common political culture, language and history – cannot be substantively replicated at the supranational level in a way that would be robust enough to allow for a democratically legitimate supranational state. As a result, proponents of this view support the strengthening of the EU's intergovernmental institutions (like the European Council) and the possible return of competences to the national level. At the extreme, there are those who advocate the withdrawal of their state from the EU, unless the latter's competences are reduced while member states take greater control through their veto rights over collective decision-making.

A third view, variously referred to as demoicracy (Nicolaïdis, 2004; Cheneval and Schimmelfennig, 2013) or multilateral democracy (Cheneval, 2011), has recently emerged that offers an alternative approach. Whereby demoicracy is defined as 'a union of peoples, defined as states and citizens, who govern together but not as one' (Nicolaïdis, 2013). This is the view that, we believe (Nicolaïdis, 2013; Lacey, 2017b), best describes the EU as it is, while providing a normative ideal which it should seek to embody much more fully (see Box 19.3). On the demoicratic account, the EU cannot be based simply on the idea of a supranational demos or a national demoi. Instead, for demoicrats, the EU is best understood as an association with two normative subjects: states and citizens. This view is more than one in between supranationalism and sovereigntism, since these two alternatives are fundamentally alike in equating democracy with the rule of a single people, either at the national or European level. While demoicratic theory is often described as based on the 'no-demos' thesis, this need not be the case. A weaker 'many demoi' thesis recognises elements of transnational political practice in Europe while still arguing that national demoi remain the dominant political units where compulsory solidarities are institutionalised and disparate interests aggregated. Therefore, the need to demoicratise the EU starts from the increased disconnect between the (pooled) locus of managerial authority and the (national) locus of political life. In short, demoicratic theory can be thought of as a theory of correspondence between transfers of powers and 'people power'. Normatively, this gap needs to be accommodated rather than denied.

Crucially, this can happen not primarily through vertical delegation to the centre but through greater attention paid to the horizontal dimension of democracy-across-borders. A demoicratic approach seeks to lay out the ways to sustain the tension between two concurrent requirements: the legitimacy of separate self-determined demoi on the one hand and their mutual openness and other-regarding impulses and institutions, as implied by the notion of liberal democratic demoi, on the other. As a result, the EU can be a single polity, but not a state (at least not in the Weberian sense of an administrative apparatus endowed with the kind of authority over its citizenry which can justify the monopoly of violence). Instead, the 'state functions' which the EU does exercise (its functional integrity) derive from the resources and authority of its member states (Genschel and Jachtenfuchs, 2015). Demoicratic gaps appear over time as the EU concurrently centralises more powers and fails to ground them in *both* national and supranational democratic authorisation and monitoring.

When it comes to the architecture of the EU, such a demoicratic approach means that the current setup represents a fragile but desirable equilibrium. Perhaps the most paradigmatic expressions of demoicracy in the EU, where the normative subjectivities of states and citizens are well-balanced, is the co-legislative relationship between the EP (representing European citizens) and the Council (representing member states); the QMV formula in the Council (requiring 55 per cent of member states representing 65 per cent of European citizens) and the principle of digressive proportionality in the EP (which allocates seats in such a way that citizens in the most populous member states are not overrepresented and citizens in the least populous member states are not underrepresented) (Lacey, 2017b). Typical reforms advocated by demoicrats include an enhanced role for national parliaments as both an expression of respect for and a contribution to the health of national democracies, as well as greater horizontal cooperation between them; greater weight for smaller member states in voting procedures and institutions including through the rotating presidency; ensuring collective authorisation by each demos for primary law (i.e. the ratification of treaties); more recourse to sunset clauses to ensure that unanimity does not only support the status quo; and the multiplication of democratic channels between citizens and European institutions.

Proponents of all three perspectives – supranationalism, sovereigntism and demoicracy – are concerned with the integrity of the EU. While supranationalists tend to believe that the sustainability of the EU is dependent upon it growing to replicate the structures of some of the most successful federal states, sovereigntists worry that the EU has become overstretched such that its growing powers and lack of corresponding democratic legitimation put its very existence in jeopardy. Although critical of the EU's failings, demoicrats, by contrast, are typically more optimistic about the EU's constitutional equilibrium in terms of its ability to generate the conditions required for its long-term integrity.

BOX 19.3 Legal basis

Articles 10, 11 and 12 of the TEU. These articles lay out some of the primary democratic credentials of European institutions.

19.4   Main Policy Developments

From a procedural perspective, in addition to the democratic reforms previously mentioned, the introduction of a right to withdraw from the EU through Article 50 of the Lisbon Treaty was one of the most significant constitutional developments in the last decades. But how did Article 50 come about? And has this development enhanced the procedural legitimacy – and thus perhaps the existential integrity – of the EU in the eyes of its citizens?

Let us take you back to the beginning. The need to introduce a clause in the EU treaties that would spell out the right for a member state to withdraw was introduced in 2002, during a European Convention busy writing a new Constitutional Treaty for the EU (Nicolaïdis, 2019). At the time what 'leaving the EU' could actually mean was up for grabs. In truth, Convention delegates were primarily concerned with how to deal with a rogue state which might have had its voting rights suspended for bad behaviour incompatible with EU rules and values but could not stay indefinitely in purgatory. It would either have to return to the fold chastened or leave voluntarily. Article 50 was to be the polite invitation: please leave voluntarily if you persist. But many Euro-federalists saw the draft exit clause as a sovereigntist ploy and opposed it vehemently, for in their minds stable polities do not have in-built clauses for secession. Introducing an exit clause in European treaties meant that the EU would never cross the Rubicon to become a state as did the United States in 1865, the crucial moment when 'secession' was redefined as 'civil war', and ceased to be an option for the discontented. If those delegates were to support an exit clause it would only be as an expulsion clause for misbehaving countries. Otherwise, the clause was not meant to be used.

Not everyone on the Convention floor agreed. If you believed in a demoicratic third way, as discussed in the Section 19.3, the idea of exit meant that the EU would not become a federal state, but would remain a union of peoples who remain together by choice and whose acceptance of common rules must be repeatedly offered. The idea is that the essence of a union is defined by the way one may or may not leave it. Indeed, in this view, the right of exit is the demonstration of the EU's essence as a freely chosen association between like-minded and geographically proximate peoples, the ultimate proof of the idea of auto-limitation applied to the EU: if a state agrees to subordinate its sovereign powers to a higher authority, it retains the final say on its membership (Nicolaïdis, 2019).

The sovereign decision of the British people to leave the EU, made by referendum on 23 June 2016, resulted in the first use of Article 50. This article requires that a withdrawal agreement and a declaration of intent on the future relationship between the EU and the departing state be negotiated. It also requires that negotiations take place between the withdrawing state and an appointed negotiator to represent the EU. The negotiating process itself demonstrated what each of these stipulations meant in practice. First, a withdrawal agreement with a departing state would have a threefold structure: (1) a financial settlement concerning the withdrawing state's budget commitments, (2) the guarantee of European citizens' rights who are residents in the withdrawing state prior to withdrawal and (3) reasonable accommodations to any member state whose core state interests may be at significant risk due to the withdrawing state's decision to leave. Second, there would be no grand bargaining between the withdrawing state and the EU's most powerful member states. The UK's attempt to negotiate terms directly with Germany and France was rebuffed as it was made clear that the UK must negotiate directly with the EU's appointed negotiator, Michel Barnier, himself accountable to the European Council represented by its president, Donald Tusk (see Box 19.4).

However fair Article 50 may be in principle, its legitimacy in large part depends on how fair it is seen to be. Although the EU has been accused of too much inflexibility in its negotiating strategy, all things considered the execution of the Article 50 process appears to have generated substantial procedural legitimacy for the EU. First, the fact that the UK was able to trigger Article 50 after a self-organised referendum based on a simple majority sent out a powerful signal: the EU is not too sacred or state-like to be left and it is not too precious to be based on anything other than the freely affirmed will to govern together.

Second, the insistence that the rights of European citizens residing in the UK be protected sent a powerful signal to all European citizens that the guarantee of their rights was a priority and more important than securing a good trade agreement.

Third, the foregrounding of Michel Barnier as the EU's negotiator visibly demonstrated that major decisions in the EU followed procedures respecting the equality of states. Fourth, the insistence that reasonable accommodations were made to Ireland as a condition of any withdrawal agreement demonstrated that the EU prioritises the core state interests of even its smaller member states over the value of any future lucrative trade deal with a major world economy like the UK. In this particular case, the EU insisted that the Good Friday Agreement underwriting peace in Northern Ireland must be respected through stipulations that would obviate the need for a customs border dividing Ireland and Northern Ireland.

As we shall see in Section 19.5, the procedural legitimacy generated by the Article 50 process may be at least partly to explain for a recent shoring up of the EU's existential integrity. However, it would be naïve to think that Brexit will be costless to the EU's existential integrity. At least two potential negative effects are worth highlighting. First, the EU's territorial integrity will be breached when the UK finally leaves. The EU's zone of freedom, security and justice will therefore shrink and the opportunities and privileges associated with European citizenship will diminish (Lacey, 2017a). Second, with the departure of the UK, the EU is losing one of the world's most well-established and respected democracies. Meanwhile, the EU has proven largely unable to stem democratic backsliding among some of its member states, most notably Hungary and Poland (see Chapter 18). Article 50, therefore, has not been used by states who have decided to depart from the EU's fundamental values, but by a state whose constitutional order remains entirely compatible with European values. As a result, the idea that the legitimacy of European decisions are underwritten by representatives of liberal democratic states is further compromised by the loss of a stolid democratic state in the context of democratic backsliding among other states.

BOX 19.4 Key actors

Convention on the Future of Europe (European Convention). An extraordinary conference of diverse actors called to make concrete proposals in preparation for treaty reform between 2001 and 2004.

MICHEL BARNIER. Lead Brexit negotiator for the EU, reporting to the European Council.

DONALD TUSK. President of European Council, in close liaison with lead Brexit negotiator Michel Barnier.

EUROPEAN COUNCIL. Heads of state and government must provide mandate to lead negotiator and approve the withdrawal agreement.

_EP._ Must approve the withdrawal agreement.

19.5   Current Political and Academic Controversies

The UK's decision to leave the EU emerged in a wider context of crises and disquiet. In particular, the European debt crisis strained relations among European states. These shocks jeopardised both the functional and procedural integrity of the EU. Functionally, the EU found it difficult to manage its banking system and wider economy in the euro crisis, while it faced difficulty in managing its external borders and the movement of people during the refugee and migrant crisis (see Chapter 1). Procedurally, standard cooperative practices between member states frayed as the EU's strategies for dealing with these crises were challenged by those states who had the most to lose from decisions taken collectively. One powerful example is resistance by the Greek government and the Greek people in 2015 to austerity measures imposed on the country by the EU and the IMF as a condition of sovereign debt bailout packages. Another example is the explicit resistance by some countries, most visibly Hungary in 2016, to accept an agreed quota of refugees (see Chapter 13). As a result of such developments, the picture of the EU as an emerging supranational Leviathan that could dictate terms to its member states gained currency and found its political expression throughout Europe in a major spurt in Euroscepticsm among new and some older political parties. Those seeking to bring the UK out of the EU capitalised on the negative existential sentiments emerging from such perceived deficits in the EU's functional and procedural legitimacy. To this extent, Brexit served as a canary in the mine, calling for some sort of reckoning on the part of the rest of the EU (Nicolaïdis, 2019).

The challenges posed to European integration by Brexit and events relating to the euro crisis and migrant crisis have induced reflective stances within European institutions themselves, among scholars and in the wider public sphere. Within academia, the call has been made for developing theories of European integration so that they can also provide an explanatory framework for the processes involved in disintegration (Schmitter and Lefkofridi, 2016). Meanwhile, in 2017, on the sixtieth anniversary of the signing of the Treaty of Rome, the European Commission published a *White Paper on the Future of Europe.* In it, several very different scenarios were outlined on the possible future direction of Europe (European Commission, 2017). Should the EU remain as it is, functionally and procedurally? Should it do less and under different institutional arrangements? Should some member states with the will to do so forge ahead with deeper integration, while others may opt out of deeper integration projects? Or should integration only move as quickly as the most reluctant member state? These basic questions concerning what we want the EU to do, and how we want it to do it, have never really gone away. However, in light of the last ten turbulent years, they are resurgent in both political and academic contexts (e.g. Lacey, 2017b; Bellamy, 2019; Hennette et al., 2019; Nicolaïdis, 2019).

The increasing politicisation of the EU, in large part as a result of these turbulent times, has itself raised a number of pressing questions. Perhaps most importantly, how should we understand the dramatic increase of Euroscepticism? Is the EU now just finally becoming a mature political system that is developing its own contestatory political theatre? Or are we witnessing the development of forces that are fundamentally dangerous to EU integrity? Furthermore, should the EU attempt to meet the challenge of Euroscepticism with its traditional approach of trying to insulate EU decision-making as much as possible from electoral cycles – remaining as much as possible a polity of 'policy without politics' (Schmidt, 2006)? Or should the EU embrace politicisation, engage in democratic reforms and attempt to visibly undermine the populist Eurosceptical claim that it is run by unaccountable elite technocrats? A further look at the Brexit case can help to give some indications as to how these questions might be answered.

19.6 Analysis of a Paradigmatic Case Study: Brexit and the Integrity of the Union

Let us first return to Bartolini's thesis that the politicisation of the European issue will quickly spill over into fundamental questions of European integration. The Brexit case lends substantial support to this thesis. The EP, the most public and paradigmatically democratic institution of the Union, has served as the main platform from which British Eurosceptics in the form of Nigel Farage and UKIP were able to exert pressure on the British Conservative Party to call a referendum on British membership. In one sense, Bartolini could not have dreamed up a better case for demonstrating how opening up the door for the politicisation of the EU could lead to an institution like the EP (mainly designed for debating day-to-day policy) becoming a battle platform on the territorial and even existential integrity of the Union. Indeed, the astonishing success of Farage and his party in the EP has been instructive to other Eurosceptical parties, some of which have played with the idea of pursuing a policy to leave either the EU or the euro (e.g. Le Pen in France, La Lega in Italy), notwithstanding the caveats discussed in Section 19.4. Relatedly, the EU's negotiating stance in the Brexit negotiations is a double-edged sword. While it has demonstrated the EU's unity in the face of an existential challenge, such unity has also been viewed by some as shoring up an overly inflexible and unfriendly attitude to the UK – leading some to call for a more self-reflexive sacrifice of Britain on the altar of EU unity (Nicolaïdis, 2019).

On the other hand, despite the evident dangers of politicisation to the EU, we should not discount the possibility that such politicisation may serve to strengthen support for the Union. Rather than producing a domino effect, whereby the Brexit example encourages citizens to question the EU and detach themselves from it existentially, indicators suggest that the reverse has been the case. Compared with a first survey in 2010, where 62 per cent of Europeans claim that they 'feel like they are a citizen of the EU', 68 per cent were willing to make the same claim in 2017 (Eurobarometer, 2018). Furthermore, in a 2019 continent-wide survey asking how citizens would vote in a hypothetical referendum on EU membership within their own country, the Czech Republic comes in as the country with the highest support for leaving the Union at 24 per cent (when the UK is excluded). While some countries, like Hungary, had a high number of citizens who were undecided on the question (32 per cent), twenty-three countries registered definite support for EU membership above 60 per cent (often well above this figure) (Eurobarometer, 2019).

None of this is to say, however, that there is as widespread satisfaction with the current setup or general direction of the EU. Witness the increased support for Eurosceptical parties in national elections over the last decade, as well as the 2014 and 2019 European elections. What these polling data do indicate, however, is that the EU's constitutional settlement may be stronger than some believe, but that its social foundations may need to be strengthened (Nicolaïdis, 2018). While constitutional questions are by no means off the table, and the restructuring of political conflict along transnational lines will ensure that these questions are asked, it would appear that the EU has achieved a degree of existential integrity that is mature enough to allow for these political conflicts to play out without imminently jeopardising its territorial integrity or radically undermining the procedural legitimacy it has achieved. There is, however, little room for complacency.

Whether further democratisation of the EU is desirable in light of recent developments is a matter for further normative and empirical analysis. However, the case of the UK offers us some clues. We have already seen that the EP was an instrumental democratic venue in generating political leverage for Brexit. But we may wonder if there is anything that could have been done to weaken the claims of those advocating exit on the basis of a democratic deficit? Would it have made a difference to British citizens' support for the EU, and thereby the Union's existential integrity, had the Commission been better democratised beyond issues of nomination, for example? Or would it have made a difference if the British Parliament, along with other national parliaments, were seen to have greater sway in the running of Europe? Or if EU institutions had been more receptive to people empowerment though such instruments as citizens' initiatives, deliberative assemblies or better participatory use of social media?

Clearly, those who advocate for the democratisation of the EU believe that such developments do have an impact on legitimacy and citizens' support for the Union. But unsurprisingly from a demoicratic viewpoint, evidence from the British case suggests that more democracy in the UK, rather than simply reforming the

EU, could have made a difference. Simon Hix (2014: 193) analyses public opinion towards membership in the EU among Danish and British citizens. While public opinion on this score has followed similar patterns since both countries joined the EC in 1973, these patterns began to diverge in the 1990s. Over time, Danish public opinion has become much more favourable towards the EU, with British public attitudes becoming substantially less so. A variety of factors may help to explain the difference. However, in an ironic twist, Hix speculates that the absence of referendums on major EU questions in the UK was a missed opportunity. In contrast to the UK's insistence on parliamentary sovereignty for making important integration decisions, Denmark has weighed in with a referendum on every major EU reform, with some being successful and others not. These referendums, Hix argues, have generated regular public debates about the EU in Denmark, giving the Danish people a sense of ownership over their relationship with the EU and an understanding of their place within the Union. From this perspective, the Brexit vote over *whether* to leave gives credence to the demoicratic motto that the EU's democratic health rests in large part on the democratic empowerment in its member states. And the Brexit saga over *how* to leave the EU further demonstrates that the contract in the UK over the balance between popular, executive and parliamentary authority over the 'European question' is far from being settled.

GROUP DISCUSSION

- What factors do you believe will determine whether or not Brexit has a positive or negative impact on the EU's existential integrity?
- If the EU has a democratic deficit, is it located at the European or national level?

TOPICS FOR INDIVIDUAL RESEARCH

- Is politicisation of EU institutions a threat to integration?
- Is Article 50 fair to withdrawing states?

FURTHER READINGS

Bellamy, R. (2019). *A Republican Europe of States: Cosmopolitanism, Intergovernmentalism and Democracy in the EU*. Cambridge: Cambridge University Press.

Hennette, S., Piketty, T., Sacriste, G. and Vauchez, A. (2019). *How to Democratize Europe*. Cambridge, MA: Harvard University Press.

Lacey, J. (2017). *Centripetal Democracy: Democratic Legitimacy and Political Identity in Belgium, Switzerland, and the European Union*. Oxford: Oxford University Press.

Nicolaïdis, K. (2013). 'European Demoicracy and Its Crisis'. *JCMS: Journal of Common Market Studies*, 51(2): 351–69.

Schmidt, V. A. (2013). 'Democracy and Legitimacy in the European Union Revisited: Input, Output and "Throughput"'. *Political Studies*, 61(1): 2–22.

REFERENCES

Bardi, L., Bressanelli, E., Calossi, E., Gagatek, W., Mair, P. and Pizzimenti, E. (2010). *How to Create a Transnational Party System*. European Parliament Directorate-General for Internal Policies. www.eui.eu/Projects/EUDO-OPPR/Documents/StudyOPPR-PE.pdf (accessed 18 March 2012).

Bartolini, S. (2006). 'Should the Union be "Politicized"? Prospects and Risks. Politics: The Right or the Wrong Sort of Medicine for the EU?' *Notre Europe, Policy Paper No. 19.*

Bellamy, R. (2019). *A Republican Europe of States: Cosmopolitanism, Intergovernmentalism and Democracy in the EU*. Cambridge: Cambridge University Press.

Bellamy, R. and Lacey, J. (2018). 'Balancing the Rights and Duties of European and National Citizens: A Demoicratic Approach'. *Journal of European Public Policy*, 25(10): 1403–21.

Bellamy, R. and Kröger, S. (2014). 'Domesticating the Democratic Deficit? The Role of National Parliaments and Parties in the EU's System of Governance'. *Parliamentary Affairs*, 67(2): 437–57.

Cheneval, F. (2007). 'Caminante, No Hay Camino, Se Hace Camino Al Andar: EU Citizenship, Direct Democracy and Treaty Ratification'. *European Law Journal*, 13(5): 647–63.

Cheneval, F. (2011). *The Government of the Peoples: On the Idea and Principles of Multilateral Democracy*. New York: Palgrave Macmillan.

Cheneval, F. and Schimmelfennig, F. (2013). 'The Case for Demoi-cracy in the European Union'. *Journal of Common Market Studies*, 51(2): 334–50.

Coman, R. and Lacroix, J. (2007). *Les résistances à l'Europe: cultures nationales, idéologies et stratégies d'acteurs*. Brussels: Editions de l'Université libre de Bruxelles.

Crespy, A. (2016). *Welfare Markets in Europe: The Democratic Challenge of European Integration*. Heidelberg: Springer.

Crum, B. (2013). 'Saving the Euro at the Cost of Democracy?' *JCMS: Journal of Common Market Studies*, 51(4): 614–30.

De Vries, C. E. (2018). *Eurosepticism and the Future of European Integration*. Oxford: Oxford University Press.

Eriksen, E. O. and Fossum, J. E. (2004). 'Europe in Search of Legitimacy: Strategies of Legitimation Assessed'. *International Political Science Review*, 25(4): 435–459.

Føllesdal, A. (2004). 'Legitimacy Theories of the European Union (No. 15)'. Arena Working Paper 04/15. www.sv.uio.no/arena/english/research/publications/arena-working-papers/2001-2010/2004/wp04_15.pdf Accessed 03/02/2020.

Eurobarometer (2018). *Standard Eurobarometer 89*. https://data.europa.eu/euodp/en/data/dataset/S2180_89_1_STD89_ENG (accessed 2 February 2020).

Eurobarometer (2019). *Closer to the Citizens, Closer to the Ballot: Complete Survey Results*. www.europarl.europa.eu/at-your-service/files/be-heard/eurobarometer/2019/parlemeter-2019/results-annex/en-parlemeter-2019-results-annex.pdf (accessed 28 October 2019).

European Commission (2017). *White Paper on the Future of Europe*. https://ec.europa.eu/commission/sites/beta-political/files/white_paper_on_the_future_of_europe_en.pdf (accessed 2 February 2020).

Genschel, P. and Jachtenfuchs, M. (2015). 'More Integration, Less Federation: The European Integration of Core State Powers'. *Journal of European Public Policy*, 23(1): 42–59.

Hennette, S., Piketty, T., Sacriste, G. and Vauchez, A. (2019). *How to Democratize Europe.* Cambridge, MA: Harvard University Press.

Hix, S. (2014). 'Democratizing a Macroeconomic Union in Europe'. In O. Cramme and S. B. Hobolt (eds), *Democratic Politics in a European Union Under Stress.* Oxford: Oxford University Press.

Hooghe, L. and Marks, G. (2009). 'A Postfunctionalist Theory of European Integration: From Permissive Consensus to Constraining Dissensus'. *British Journal of Political Science*, 39(1): 1–23.

Hooghe, L. and Marks, G. (2018). 'Cleavage Theory Meets European Crises: Lipset, Rokkan and the Transnational Cleavage'. *Journal of European Public Policy*, 25(1): 109–35.

Johnson, B. (2016). 'Please Vote Leave on Thursday, Because We'll Never Get This Chance Again'. *The Telegraph*, 19t June. www.telegraph.co.uk/news/2016/06/19/please-vote-leave-on-thursday-because-well-never-get-this-chance/ Accessed 02/02/2020.

Kochenov, D., De Búrca, G. and Williams, A. (eds) (2015). *Europe's Justice Deficit?* London: Bloomsbury Publishing.

Lacey, J. (2017a). 'National Autonomy and Democratic Standardization: Should Popular Votes on European Integration be Regulated by the European Union?'. *European Law Journal*, 23(6): 523–35.

Lacey, J. (2017b). *Centripetal Democracy: Democratic Legitimacy and Political Identity in Belgium, Switzerland and the European Union.* Oxford: Oxford University Press.

Lacey, J. and Bauböck, R. (2017). 'Enlargement, Association, Accession: A Normative Account of Membership in a Union of States'. *Journal of European Integration*, 39(5): 592–43.

Lacey, J. (2018). 'Populist Nationalism and Ontological Security: On the Construction of Moral Antagonisms in the UK, Switzerland and Belgium'. In L. Herman and J. Muldoon (eds), *Trumping the Mainstream: The Conquest of Mainstream Democratic Politics by Far-Right Populism.* London: Routledge.

Mair, P. (2007). 'Political Opposition and the European Union'. *Government and Opposition*, 42(1): 1–17.

Majone, G. (2005). *Dilemmas of European Integration: The Ambiguities and Pitfalls of Integration by Stealth.* Oxford: Oxford University Press.

Marquand, D. (1979). *Parliament for Europe.* London: Jonathan Cape.

Moravcsik, A. (2008). 'The Myth of Europe's Democratic Deficit'. *Intereconomics*, 43(6): 331–40.

Nicolaïdis, K. (2004). 'We, the Peoples'. *Foreign Affairs*, 83(6): 97–110.

Nicolaïdis, K. (2013). 'European Demoi-cracy and its Crisis'. *Journal of Common Market Studies*, 51(2): 351–69.

Nicolaïdis, K. (2018). 'Braving the Waves? Europe's Constitutional Settlement at 20'. *Journal of Common Market Studies*, 56(7): 1614–30.

Nicolaïdis, K. (2019). *Exodus, Reckoning, Sacrifice: Three Meanings of Brexit.* London: Unbound.

Papadopoulos, Y. (2006). 'Implementing (And Radicalizing) Art. I-47.4 of the Constitution: is the Addition of Some (Semi-)direct Democracy to the Nascent Consociational European Federation Just Swiss Folklore?'. *Journal of European Public Policy*, 12(3): 448–67.

Piattoni, S. (ed.) (2015). *The European Union: Democratic Principles and Institutional Architectures in Times of Crisis.* Oxford: Oxford University Press.

Piris, J.-C. (2012). *The Future of Europe: Towards a Two-speed EU?* Cambridge: Cambridge University Press.

Schmidt, V. A. (2006). *Democracy in Europe: The EU and National Polities.* Oxford: Oxford University Press.

Schmidt, V. A. (2013). 'Democracy and Legitimacy in the European Union Revisited: Input, Output and Throughput'. *Political Studies*, 61: 2–22.

Schmitter, P. and Lefkofridi, Z. (2016). 'Neo-Functionalism as Theory of Disintegration'. *Chinese Political Science Review*, 1(1): 1–29.

Spectator, The (2016). 'Out and into the World: Why the Spectator is for Leave'. 18 June. www.spectator.co.uk/2016/06/out-and-into-the-world-why-the-spectator-is-for-leave/ Accessed 02/02/2020.

APPENDIX 1
EU Institutions and Organs

European Parliament

Composed of 705 (after Brexit) directly elected MEPs from twenty-seven countries, the EP represents EU citizens. It acts as a co-legislator with the Council on nearly all EU law and holds the other EU institutions to account. It is one of the seven EU institutions.[1]

European Commission

The European Commission is the EU's executive body and represents the interests of the EU as a whole. It proposes new EU legislation and ensures its correct application. It is one of the seven EU institutions.[2]

Council of the European Union

The Council of the European Union, generally known as the Council (previously the Council of Ministers), represents EU member state governments.[3] Together with the EP, the Council adopts legislation proposed by the European Commission. It is one of the seven EU institutions.

The Council of the European Union is a single legal entity, but it meets in ten different 'configurations', depending on the subject being discussed:

- Agriculture and fisheries.
- Competitiveness.
- Economic and financial affairs.
- Education, youth, culture and sport.
- Employment, social policy, health and consumer affairs.
- Environment.

[1] www.europarl.europa.eu/portal/en.
[2] https://ec.europa.eu/.
[3] www.consilium.europa.eu/en/council-eu/.

- Foreign affairs.
- General affairs.
- Justice and home affairs.
- Transport, telecommunication and energy.

The Council of the European Union takes its decisions by:

Simple majority (fourteen member states vote in favour).
Qualified majority (55 per cent of member states, representing at least 65 per cent of the EU population, vote in favour).
Unanimous vote (all votes are in favour).

The Eurogroup

The Eurogroup is an informal body where the ministers of the *eurozone member states* discuss matters relating to their shared responsibilities related to the euro.

European Council

The European Council is one of the seven EU institutions.[4] However, it is not one of the EU's legislating bodies, so does not negotiate or adopt EU laws. Instead its main role is to *determine the EU's general political direction and priorities* – essentially setting the policy agenda for the EU.

Traditionally, this is done by *adopting conclusions* during each European Council meeting. These conclusions *identify specific issues of concern* for the EU and outline *particular actions to take* or goals to reach. European Council conclusions can also set a deadline for reaching agreement on a particular item or for the presentation of legislative proposal. In this way, the European Council is able to influence and guide the EU's policy agenda.

Euro Summit

The Euro Summit brings together the heads of state or government of the eurozone countries, the Euro Summit president and the president of the European Commission. Euro Summit meetings provide strategic guidelines on euro area economic policy.

[4] www.consilium.europa.eu/en/.

European Central Bank (ECB)

The ECB manages the EU's single currency – the euro – and tries to ensure price stability in the EU. It is responsible for framing and implementing the EU's economic and monetary policy. It is one of the seven EU institutions.[5]

Court of Justice of the European Union (CJEU)

The CJEU (also known as the European Court of Justice or ECJ) interprets EU law and makes sure it is applied uniformly in all member states. It also settles legal disputes between EU governments, individuals, companies or organisations and EU institutions. It is one of the seven EU institutions.[6]

European Court of Auditors

The European Court of Auditors audits EU finances. Its role is to improve EU financial management and report on the use of public funds. It is one of the seven EU institutions.[7]

European Investment Bank (EIB)

The EIB supports projects in EU countries, and invests in future member and partner countries.[8] It borrows money on capital markets rather than drawing on the EU budget and lends it on favourable terms to projects in line with EU policy objectives. It is owned by the twenty-seven EU countries.

European Economic and Social Committee (EESC)

The EESC is an EU consultative body with 326 members (after Brexit, March 2020) representing civil society, employers and workers.[9] It must be consulted about EU decision-making on the economy and social policy.

---

[5] www.ecb.europa.eu.
[6] https://curia.europa.eu.
[7] www.eca.europa.eu/en/Pages/ecadefault.aspx.
[8] www.eib.org/fr/index.htm.
[9] www.eesc.europa.eu/en.

Committee of the Regions

The Committee of the Regions is an EU consultative body with 329 members (after Brexit, March 2020), representing local and regional authorities.[10] It must be consulted during EU decision-making in the fields of: economic and social cohesion, trans-European infrastructure networks, health, education and culture, employment policy, social policy, the environment, vocational training and transport.

European Ombudsman

The European Ombudsman investigates complaints about maladministration in the institutions and bodies of the EU.[11]

European Anti-Fraud Office (OLAF)

OLAF investigates fraud in connection with the EU budget, corruption and serious misconduct within the European institutions. It also supports the EU institutions in the development and implementation of anti-fraud legislation and policies.[12]

[10] https://cor.europa.eu/en.
[11] www.ombudsman.europa.eu/en/home.
[12] https://ec.europa.eu/anti-fraud/home_en.

APPENDIX 2

Decision-Making in the EU: The Ordinary Legislative Procedure

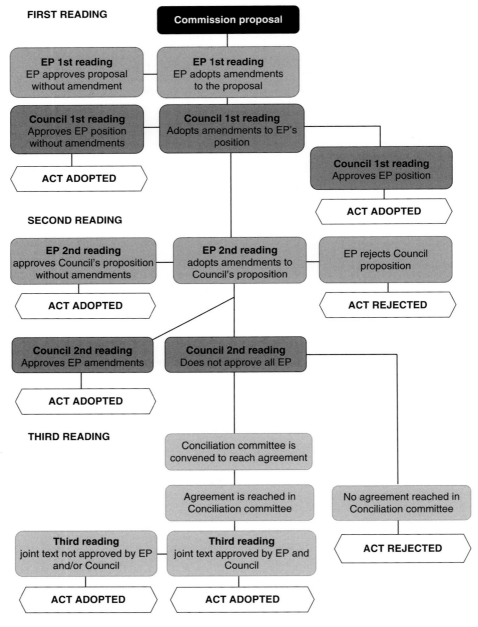

FIRST READING

Commission proposal

EP 1st reading
EP approves proposal without amendment

EP 1st reading
EP adopts amendments to the proposal

Council 1st reading
Approves EP position without amendments

Council 1st reading
Adopts amendments to EP's position

Council 1st reading
Approves EP position

ACT ADOPTED

ACT ADOPTED

SECOND READING

EP 2nd reading
approves Council's proposition without amendments

EP 2nd reading
adopts amendments to Council's proposition

EP rejects Council proposition

ACT ADOPTED

ACT REJECTED

Council 2nd reading
Approves EP amendments

Council 2nd reading
Does not approve all EP

ACT ADOPTED

THIRD READING

Conciliation committee is convened to reach agreement

Agreement is reached in Conciliation committee

No agreement reached in Conciliation committee

ACT REJECTED

Third reading
joint text not approved by EP and/or Council

Third reading
joint text approved by EP and Council

ACT ADOPTED

ACT ADOPTED

Figure A2.1 Functioning of the ordinary legislative procedure

APPENDIX 3
Distribution of Competences between the EU and the Member States

The EU has only the competences conferred on it by the Treaties (principle of conferral).[1] Under this principle, the EU may only act within the limits of the competences conferred upon it by the EU countries in the Treaties to attain the objectives provided therein. Competences not conferred upon the EU in the Treaties remain with the EU countries. The Treaty of Lisbon clarifies the division of competences between the EU and EU countries. These competences are divided into three main categories: exclusive competences, shared competences and supporting competences.

Table A3.1 Distribution of competences between the EU and the member states

Type of competence	Legal base and definition	Policy areas concerned
Exclusive competences	*Article 3 TFEU* Areas in which the EU alone is able to legislate and adopt binding acts. EU countries are able to do so themselves only if empowered by the EU to implement these acts	Customs union The establishing of competition rules necessary for the functioning of the internal market Monetary policy for euro area countries Conservation of marine biological resources under the common fisheries policy Common commercial policy Conclusion of international agreements under certain conditions
Shared competences	*Article 4 TFEU* The EU and EU countries are able to legislate and adopt legally binding acts; EU countries exercise their own competence where the EU does not exercise, or has decided not to exercise, its own competence	Internal market Social policy, but only for aspects specifically defined in the treaty Economic, social and territorial cohesion (regional policy) Agriculture and fisheries (except conservation of marine biological resources) Energy AFSJ Shared safety concerns in public health matters, limited to the aspects defined in the TFEU

Type of competence	Legal base and definition	Policy areas concerned
	Table A3.1 (Cont.)	
Supporting competences	Article 6 of the TFEU The EU can only intervene to support, coordinate or complement the action of EU countries; legally binding EU acts must not require the harmonisation of EU countries' laws or regulations	Research, technological development, space Development cooperation and humanitarian aid Protection and improvement of human health Industry Culture Tourism Education, vocational training, youth and sport Civil protection Administrative cooperation

[1] All the information in Appendix 3 is from: https://eur-lex.europa.eu.

APPENDIX 4
Differentiated Integration and Varying Membership

Differentiated integration means that not all member states participate in all policies of the EU. This makes the EU a complex system of intertwined policy communities.

Differentiated integration can be analysed along three lines:

- *Time:* some member states launch an initiative and others join later.
- *Space:* a group of countries form a coherent space (although perhaps geographically fragmented) in which a policy is applied.
- *Sectors:* some policies of the EU will apply in a limited number of member states.

Figure A4.1 shows the differentiated and embedded memberships in the EU, the eurozone and the Schengen area.

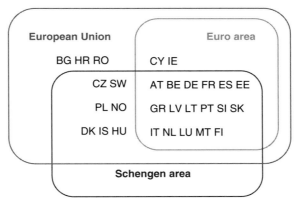

Figure A4.1 Differentiated and embedded memberships in the EU, the eurozone and the Schengen area

Members of the EU cover much of the European continent.[1] The EU is home to over 446 million people. This corresponds to 6 per cent of the world's population. The EU is currently made up of twenty-seven countries. Look at the list of country names below. They are all European but they are not all members of the EU. Identify which are members and then locate them on the map. If you need help, look at this website: www.europa.eu/!cW78Hk.

- Albania
- Austria
- Belgium
- Bosnia and Herzegovina
- Bulgaria
- Croatia
- Cyprus
- Czech Republic
- Denmark
- Estonia
- Finland
- Former Yugoslav Republic of Macedonia
- France
- Germany
- Greece
- Hungary
- Iceland
- Ireland
- Italy
- Latvia
- Lithuania
- Luxembourg
- Malta
- Moldova
- Montenegro
- Netherlands
- Norway
- Poland
- Portugal
- Romania
- Serbia
- Slovakia
- Slovenia
- Spain
- Sweden
- Switzerland
- Turkey
- Ukraine
- United Kingdom

[1] All the information in Appendix 5 is adapted from: http://publications.europa.eu/webpub/com/eu-and-me/en/.

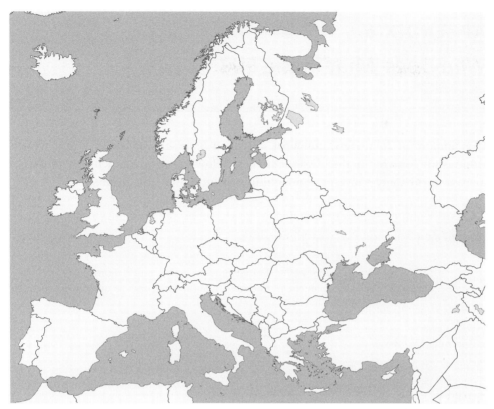

Figure A5.1 Map of the European Union

APPENDIX 6

Who Does What in the EU?

It is important to understand what so-called 'Brussels' actually is and who is responsible for what in the EU. Take the test below to see how much you know. Put a cross in the table against the matching institution (or institutions).

Table A6.1 Who does what in the EU?

Who?	European Parliament	European Council	Council of the European Union	European Commission	ECJ
Makes proposals for EU laws					
Approves EU laws					
Consists of only one member per member country					
Is elected by EU citizens					
Executes the budget					
Represents the interests of EU countries/their governments					
Decides on the interpretation of EU laws					
Defines the general political direction of the EU					
Represents the interests of citizens					

Index